LIBERTY

*The French-American Statue
in Art and History*

LIBERTY

The French-American Statue
in Art and History

The New York Public Library and the
Comité Officiel Franco-Américain
pour la Célébration du Centenaire
de la Statue de la Liberté with
Pierre Provoyeur and June Hargrove

A Stonesong Press/
Roundtable Press Production

PERENNIAL LIBRARY
Harper & Row, Publishers
Cambridge, Philadelphia, San Francisco, Washington
London, Mexico City, São Paulo, Singapore, Sydney

Published for the exhibition
*Liberty: The French-American
Statue in Art and History*
The New York Public Library
D. Samuel and Jeane H.
Gottesman Exhibition Hall
June 21–August 30, 1986

Musée des Arts Décoratifs, Paris
October 28, 1986–February 1, 1987

National Touring Exhibition
June 1986–December 1987

References in the text to
"cat. __" refer to the
Catalogue list, which
begins on p. 289. Not all
Catalogue items are
illustrated, nor are all
Catalogue items included in
the exhibitions. The items
illustrated out of sequence
on pp. 13 and 17 are
referred to in Chapter 4.

Frontispiece:
*Commerce of Nations
Rendering Homage to
Liberty*
Edward Moran
1876
(cat. 347)

The Library and the Comité wish to express their appreciation to *Forbes* and *American Heritage*, to The Florence J. Gould Foundation, Inc., and to the National Endowment for the Humanities, Washington, D.C., a Federal agency, for their generous support of this publication. Additional assistance has been provided by Louis Vuitton, Air France, Christian Dior, Comité Français pour le Rayonnement International de Paris La Defénse, Galeries Lafayette, and Lazard Frères & Co.

Library of Congress Cataloging-in-Publication Data

Liberty : the French-American statue in art and history.

1. Statue of Liberty (New York, N.Y.)—History.
2. Statue of Liberty National Monument (New York, N.Y.)—History.
3. Bartholdi, Frédéric Auguste, 1834–1904.
4. New York (N.Y.)—Buildings, structures, etc.—History. I. Provoyeur, Pierre. II. Hargrove, June Ellen. III. New York Public Library. IV. Comité officiel franco-américain pour la célébration du centenaire de la Statue de la Liberté.
F128.64.L6L53 1986
974.7′1   86-45569
ISBN 0-06-096122-8 (pbk.)

For information address Harper & Row, Publishers, Inc. 10 East 53rd Street New York, New York 10022

Published simultaneously in Canada by Fitzhenry & Whiteside Limited, Toronto.

A Stonesong Press/ Roundtable Press Production

86 87 88 89 90 10 9 8 7 6 5 4 3 2 1

Contents

Acknowledgments

The Trustees of The New York Public Library and the members of the Comité Officiel Franco-Américain pour la Célébration du Centenaire de la Statue de la Liberté express their gratitude to the sponsors of *Liberty: The French-American Statue in Art and History*, without whom the exhibitions and the publication would not have been possible. In particular, the Library and the Comité acknowledge the exceptional combination of French and American public support and private sponsorship, a combination that in spirit and in actuality reflects in 1986 the very same transatlantic cooperation that made the statue itself a reality.

To the following French officials we offer our special thanks:

M. le Ministre de l'Education Nationale

M. le Président du Conseil Régional d'Alsace

M. le Maire de Tours

M. le Maire de Vesoul

S.E. M. l'Ambassadeur de France aux États-Unis

M. le Consul Général de France à New York

M. le Conseiller Culturel près l'Ambassade de France aux États-Unis

M. le Conseiller, Directeur du Service de Presse et d'Information de l'Ambassade de France aux États-Unis

M. le Conseiller Commerciel auprès de l'Ambassade de France aux États-Unis

MM. les Consuls Généraux de France à Boston, Chicago, Houston, Los Angeles, Miami, New Orleans, et San Francisco

MM. les Consuls de France Honoraires à Austin, Denver, Atlanta

M. le Conseiller Culturel adjoint près l'Ambassade de France aux États-Unis

MM. les Attachés Culturels à Boston, Chicago, Houston, Los Angeles, Miami, New Orleans, New York, San Francisco, et Washington

M. le Directeur Général des Relations Culturelles, Scientifiques et Techniques au Ministère des Affaires Etrangères

M. le Directeur du Cabinet du Ministre de la Culture et de la Communication

M. le Président de l'Association Française d'Action Artistique

Mme. la Directrice de l'Association Française d'Action Artistique

Mlle. le Commissaire Administratif, Association Française d'Action Artistique, Bureau des Arts Plastiques Secteur Amérique

M. le Chef du Bureau des Arts Plastiques de l'Association Française d'Action Artistique

M. le Directeur des Musées de France

M. le Delégué aux Arts Plastiques

M. le Directeur de l'Académie de France à Rome

M. l'Administrateur de la Bibliothèque Nationale

M. le Directeur du Conservatoire National des Arts et Métiers

M. le Directeur de l'École Nationale Supérieure des Beaux-Arts

M. le Recteur de l'Académie de Versailles

M. le Directeur des Affaires Culturelles de la Ville de Paris

M. le Président de l'Association du Musée d'Unterlinden

M. le Président de l'Association du Souvenir de Ferdinand de Lesseps

M. le Président de la Société Nouvelle d'Exploitation de la Tour Eiffel

M. le Président du Conseil d'Administration de l'Académie d'Architecture

The New York Public Library
June 21–August 30, 1986

Musée des Arts Décoratifs, Paris
October 28, 1986–February 1, 1987

Exhibition made possible by generous grants
from

Louis Vuitton

and the

National Endowment for the Humanities

Washington, D.C., a Federal agency

Additional assistance for both exhibition
venues provided by
Etude Gide, Loirette, Nouel
Air France

National Touring Exhibition
June 1986–December 1987

Chicago
Museum of Science and Industry
June 24–September 1, 1986

Boston
Boston Public Library
September 10–October 18, 1986

Austin
Texas State Capitol
October 28–November 15, 1986

Denver
State Historical Society of Colorado
November 22–December 28, 1986

Miami
Miami-Dade Public Library
January 9–February 27, 1987

Houston
Houston Public Library
March 5–April 7, 1987

San Francisco
Chevron Gallery
April 15–May 5, 1987

Los Angeles
Natural History Museum of L.A. County
May 12–June 25, 1987

New Orleans
Louisiana State Museum
July 10–August 30, 1987

Atlanta
Atlanta-Fulton Public Library
September 9–October 29, 1987

Washington, D.C.
National Building Museum
November 10–December 31, 1987

Exhibition made possible by grants from

Air France

Christian Dior

Comité Français pour le
Rayonnement International
de Paris La Défense

Galeries Lafayette

Lazard Frères & Co.

Preface

François de Laboulaye

Ambassador of France,
Co-President of the Comité Officiel
Franco-Américain pour la Célébration
du Centenaire de la Statue de la Liberté

All honor to The New York Public Library, which at the initiative of its distinguished President, Dr. Vartan Gregorian, is hosting a special exhibition on the Statue of Liberty in her Centennial Year, an exhibition which has been organized by the Musée des Arts Décoratifs of Paris. There could be no gesture more meaningful, nor more moving, for a Frenchman well read in the history of his own country. The Library, itself founded a century ago for the dissemination of learning in a vast new land, is testifying that we have forgotten neither the convictions nor the intentions of those who inspired the people of France to offer this gift to the people of America.

The breath of History, blowing across the Atlantic now from east to west, now from west to east, carries with it always the special air of Liberty. Two centuries ago, from Newport to Williamsburg, the fleets and armies of the French Crown under the command of Rochambeau, de Grasse, and Lafayette played their part in the epic victories of Washington that culminated in the achievement of independence. Five generations later the territorial integrity of France could not have been reestablished, nor freedom restored throughout her territories, had not the armies of the star-spangled banner landed on her shores in 1917 under Gen. John J. Pershing. Not one more full generation had passed before young men again crossed the Atlantic, again joined battle, again put their lives at hazard, to redeem France from the bondage into which she had fallen.

The Statue of Liberty stands at the portal of the New World, bearing witness to this bond of mutual trust, and to these sacrifices offered in a common cause. That is why she is still, as she was always intended to be, the symbol of all the aspirations of mankind. Over the years she has become the token not simply of French-American friendship, but of Freedom as well, and at last of the United States themselves.

This, then, is the message that this exhibition will proclaim to its visitors. Especially for those of the younger generation, who will live most of their lives in the coming century, it will serve as a reminder of all that is best and finest in our common inheritance. And it is for this reason that I offer to The New York Public Library, its President, and all those who have helped to make this exhibition possible, our warm and heartfelt thanks.

Preface

Vartan Gregorian
President and Chief Executive Officer
The New York Public Library

For Americans the Statue of Liberty is an American symbol. It stands for immigration and is inseparable from the moving lines by Emma Lazarus carved on its pedestal. It is a symbol of welcome to a free and open America.

The French and Americans of the 1870s and 1880s thought of the statue as a symbol of the French-American friendship born of the alliance that enabled the United States to win its independence. In the words of the nineteenth-century orator Chauncey M. Depew at the inauguration ceremony in 1886, the statue encouraged «the people of the two countries to celebrate their unity in Republican institutions, in government founded upon the American idea, and in their devotion to liberty. Together they rejoice that its spirit had penetrated all lands and is the hopeful future of all peoples.» The statue above all else was for Bartholdi, its creator, the symbol of Freedom, hence the official title of the sculpture: *Liberty Enlightening the World.*

The statue embodied for Bartholdi the history of mankind's struggle for freedom, a struggle that extends back until it is lost in the dim past. It reminds us of some luminous chapters of that struggle, exemplified in the English tradition of the Magna Carta (1215), the Petition of Rights (1628), and the Bill of Rights (1689); and in the United States in the Declaration of Independence (1776), the Bill of Rights of the Federal Constitution (1789), and the Constitution itself (1787). The statue symbolizes the ideals of the French Revolution and Declaration of the Rights of Man and of the Citizen, which promulgated the universal concepts of Liberty, Equality, and Fraternity.

The Statue of Liberty thus became a universal symbol not confined to American ideals or to French-American friendship. It is a witness to mankind's past struggle and a reminder to the present generation that the concept of Liberty subsumes four kinds of freedom: freedom of choice, or moral freedom; freedom from external restraint, or physical freedom; civil liberty, or political liberty, freedom of speech, thought, conscience, press, assembly or organization, and a share in the control and conditions of our lives; and social and economic freedom, namely the delicate relationship or balance between individualism and collectivism.

But the Statue of Liberty not only symbolizes the past and embodies the present. It is a symbol also of hope for the future: a hope for enlightenment, hence a hope for freedom as a continuing quest and a continuing goal. It was this aspect of the significance of the Statue of Liberty to which President Grover Cleveland addressed himself in his inauguration speech on October 28, 1886: «We will not forget that Liberty has here made her home; nor shall her chosen altar be neglected. Willing votaries will constantly keep alive its fires, and these shall gleam upon the shores of our sister Republic in the East. Reflected thence, and joined with answering rays a stream of light shall pierce the darkness of ignorance and man's oppression, until liberty enlightens the world.»

On the occasion of the Centennial of the Statue of Liberty, we at The New York Public Library are proud to host the official French-American exhibition examining the history of the origins and construction of the statue as well as its changing meanings for Americans since its dedication in October 1886. Our exhibition is the most comprehensive of its kind in tracing the history, art, and technology of the statue. It is interdisciplinary in its character and international in content. We are particularly gratified that Ambassador François de Laboulaye, the great-grandson of Edouard de Laboulaye—the inspiration for the idea of the statue and a great exponent of French-American friendship and the ideals of Liberty—has given his patronage to the official French-American exhibition. His leadership and inspiration have made this entire project a reality.

We are grateful to Louis Vuitton for their generous support of the installation of the exhibition here at the Library.

The Idea Behind the Symbol: The Changing Meaning of Liberty in American History

Henry Steele Commager

For over twenty-five hundred years the major political problem confronting all the states or nations of the Western world has been the reconciliation of Liberty and Order. That problem still confronts us, and still eludes solutions. Over the centuries, perhaps never more eagerly than today, the vast majority of peoples have preferred order to liberty, especially if that order is associated with equality. But at the beginning of our history—and this whether we take our stand in early Jamestown or Plymouth, or at the time of the Revolution—Americans assumed that there was no incompatibility between the two. How inevitable, too, that these terms—domestic tranquility (i.e., Order) and Liberty—are forever linked in the Preamble to the Federal Constitution, and with them that third member of the trinity, Justice.

Since Plato and Aristotle, philosophers have agreed that all three of these ingredients are indispensable to «welfare» and «happiness»—words almost interchangeable in the American political vocabulary—but circumstances, rather than logic or philosophy, have determined which of these—shall we call them principles—was accorded priority.

Over the long arch of years, from Magna Carta to our own time, it is the English-speaking peoples who have made the most affluent contributions to the interpretation and application of these concepts. While the English have relied on freedom «broadening down,» Americans have relied rather on legal and constitutional precepts, and have been the more resourceful in formulating them.

The explanation is pretty much what the remarkable Hector St. John de Crevecoeur suggested in his *Letters of an American Farmer* as early as the 1780s, and what, fifty years later, another Frenchman, Alexis de Tocqueville, endorsed in his *Democracy in America*. It resided in that happy combination of habits and laws inherited from the Old World with an environment so lavish that it permitted Americans to frame their own habits and laws, and their history, on a clean slate. At the same time history conspired to induce in Americans a greater sensitivity to threats to liberty than to threats to justice—history as they themselves had experienced it in the Old World, and as they read it in the sacred literature of the Scriptures, of Greece, and of Rome. After all, their own history encompassed over a century of flight from religious and political persecution, from poverty and the class system, from military proscriptions and incessant wars—flight from a life that held little hope of improving their own lot or that of their posterity. No wonder that, to generations of newcomers and down to our own day, the essence of America was that it was not Europe. It was the experience of almost all newcomers with their Old World governments that led them, as Edmund Burke put it in his «Speech on Conciliation,» to «augur misgovernment at a distance, and snuff the approach of tyranny on every tainted breeze.» On the eve of the Revolution, John Dickinson of Pennsylvania said much the same thing: with Americans «the question was not what evil has actually attended particular measures, but what evil, in the nature of things, is likely to attend them.» Nations in general, he added, «are not apt to *think* until they *feel*; therefore nations in general have lost their liberties.» Surely no other people have known so little tyranny and have been so obsessed with it as Americans.

Thus, when Americans came to draw up their own Constitutions (something no other people had ever done), they were more concerned with limiting governmental authority than with enlarging it, and they embraced readily enough Tom Paine's aphorism that «government, like dress, is the badge of lost innocence.» They had, so many of them asserted, long suffered unbearable tyranny. They were, so the North Carolina «Regulators» claimed, «crouch'd beneath their sufferings and slaves to remorseless oppression.» The Continental Congress—made up for the most part of sensible men—alleged of Parliament that «stimulated by inordinate passion for power, they attempted to effect their cruel purpose of enslaving these colonies.» Even Jefferson was able to conjure no fewer than thirty examples of «absolute tyranny over these States» to vindicate a declaration of independence.

Much of the Americans' passion for freedom and obsession with tyranny was a product of good fortune: the vast oceans that separated them from the iniquitous Old World; «land enough,» as Jefferson put it, «for our descendants to the thousandth and thousandth generation»; a heterogeneous people who had to learn to live and let live and who, in any event, achieved homogeneity with unprecedented rapidity; a more widespread enlightenment than was to be found elsewhere in the Western world; an «individualism» (the word had not yet been coined) that encouraged every man to interpret freedom in personal terms, and to exercise it in those terms, often regardless of larger social consequences.

But love of freedom was not merely a product of the American experiment; it had deeper and nobler antecedents in theology, classical literature, philosophy, and history. What is more, in the new United States it could boast a galaxy of political spokesmen who were themselves philosophers. The brief era of the American Founding Fathers is probably the only chapter in history when the Platonic ideal of Philosophers as Kings was truly realized. For to John Adams and Thomas Jefferson, James Otis and George Mason, James Wilson and John Dickinson, George Wythe and John Marshall, James Madison and Alexander Hamilton and John Jay, and Benjamin Franklin and George Washington, statesmanship was a religion, History their Bible, Athens and Rome their models. Even those without a classical education or, for that matter, any formal education at all (such as Dr. Franklin and Washington) remained faithful to these scriptures. They were familiar with Antigone's defiance of the tyrant Creon—«Nor did I think that thou, a mortal man, would'st by a breath annul and override the immutable laws of Heaven: they were not born today or yesterday, they die not!»— and they knew, too, those lines from the greatest of Funeral Orations, Pericles' tribute to those who had fallen in defense of Athens: «To you it remains to rival what they have done, and, knowing the secret of happiness to be freedom and the secret of freedom a brave heart, not to stand aside from the onset of the enemy.» They were as versed in the history of the English Commonwealthmen of the seventeenth and eighteenth centuries as in that of Athens and Rome, and welcomed not only the regicides who sought asylum with them, but took to heart the reasoning of the famous Army Debates of the English Civil War. As the crisis of independence approached, they named one of their new cities after those champions of English liberty, John Wilkes and Lord Barre, and when the war came they conferred honorary citizenship on that friend of American independence and indefatigable heretic, Dr. Richard Price.

205

Niagara Falls
Frédéric-Auguste Bartholdi
1871

207

A Chicago Street
Frédéric-Auguste Bartholdi
n.d.

But no need, really, to go to the ancient world, or to the Mother Country, for inspiration to vindicate liberty. Roger Williams had provided that, and Thomas Hooker of Connecticut, and the sagacious John Wise of Ipswich who had chosen jail rather than pay an illegal tax to the hated Governor Andros. «The great immunity of Man,» so Wise wrote in his *Vindication of the New England Churches*, «is an original liberty stampt upon his rational nature. He that intrudes on this liberty violates the Law of Nature. Man's original Liberty ought to be cherished in all wise Governments, or otherwise Man, in making himself a subject, alters himself from a freeman to a slave, which to do is repugnant to the Law of Nature.» All this—a hundred pamphlets, a thousand sermons—was the pith and substance of the arguments of that galaxy of spokesmen for American independence: not only the distinguished leaders like Franklin and Jefferson and Dickinson, but preachers and editors and village philosophers as well, who sprang up in the town meetings that discussed the State Constitutions with an eloquence comparable to that which adorned the Army Debates of the Puritan Revolution. It was the Sons of *Liberty* who led the challenge against the Stamp Act; Patrick Henry, himself a village Demosthenes, who declaimed «give me *Liberty* or give me Death»; Tom Paine who proclaimed the New World «an asylum for the lovers of civil and religious *liberty* from every part of Europe»; and his associate John Dickinson who concluded that «our *liberties* were not annexed to us by parchments and seals. They were born with us, exist with us, and cannot be taken from us by human power.» None was more eloquent than Thomas Jefferson, who chose as his own motto «Rebellion to tyrants is obedience to God,» and dedicated his University of Virginia to «the illimitable Freedom of the human mind.»

With independence Americans could do what had never been done before in recorded history: they could, in the words of John Adams, «realize the theories of the wisest writers.» This is what they did in both State and Federal Constitutions. From Massachusetts to Georgia they dedicated their new governments to liberty and (with tragic exceptions in the South) to equality, and provided them with what they thought to be insurmountable barriers against tyranny. In this they had the guidance of the «Pennsylvania Farmer,» John Dickinson:

«Who are a free people? not those over whom a government is reasonably and equitably exercised, but those who live under a government so constitutionally checked and controuled that proper provision is made against its being otherwise exercised.» With a creativity unprecedented in history they contrived, in a single generation, a body of political institutions adequate to sustain free government for centuries to come.

Contemplate not the whole immense body of their contrivance but just those provisions designed to secure liberty by constitutionally checking and controlling every authority and transaction of government:

First: written Constitutions which were «fundamental» law, and not subject to change except by the authority that made them—the people.

Second: Bills of Rights—eloquent Bills such as that drafted by George Mason of Virginia, elaborate Bills like that drafted by John Adams of Massachusetts, and the historic Bill of Rights added to the Federal Constitution, largely drafted by James Madison, the first Bill of Rights in history to embrace not merely procedural, but also substantive rights.

Third: a Federal system which, by distinguishing between powers of the National and State governments, confined most authorities within careful limits.

Fourth: «separation of powers,» executive, legislative, and judicial, both in Federal and State Constitutions, with each authority having some check upon the others.

Fifth (an outgrowth of the fourth): independence of the Judiciary, and with it the assumption that the Judiciary had the authority to pass on the constitutionality of acts of other branches of the government, and of all subordinate agencies as well, and to disallow those deemed contrary to the Constitution—what we call simply «judicial review.»

Sixth: the repudiation of «colonialism» and the establishment, for the first time in history, of the principle that every new State entering the Union came in on terms of full equality with the original States.

Seventh (in the eyes of contemporaries the most astonishing of all): the separation of Church and State, with complete religious freedom for all, something unknown in the Old World, and still not fully recognized there.

Eighth: the subordination of the military to the civilian authority, explicit in State Constitutions such as that of Massachusetts, which provided for «an exact subordination,» or that of Pennsylvania, which recognized the rights of conscientious objectors; implicit in the Federal Constitution's simple declaration that the President was the Commander-in-Chief of the armed forces and its assignment (at the same time) to Congress of the powers to declare war, raise the armed forces, and control the purse.

Ninth (again for the first time in history): specific and deliberate provision for a popularly—though indirectly—elected Head of State, and elected representatives, both for short terms of office, and thus for a «frequent recourse to the will of the people.»

Tenth (and not the least astonishing): legalizing and institutionalizing «revolution» by making provision for amending or revising Constitutions, both National and State. Some States went so far as to guarantee the right of revolution; witness John Adams' contribution on this point to the Massachusetts Constitution of 1780:

> Government is instituted for the common good, for the protection, safety, prosperity and happiness of the people, and not for the profit, honor, or private interest of any one man, family, or class of men: therefore, the people alone have an incontestable, unalienable and indefeasible right to institute government, and to reform, alter and totally change the same when their protection, safety, prosperity, and happiness require it.

Old World critics, unfamiliar with written Constitutions, might well conclude that a constitutional system so checked and balanced simply could not work. How did Americans manage to make their new constitutional system function? How did they manage to achieve, over the long run, both Liberty and Order?

Not by imposing unity upon a nation vaster even at birth than any nation of the Old World except Russia, but by exploiting that vastness (and with it a heterogeneous population and a diversity of interests analogous to that of the whole of western Europe), by working *with* Nature, as it were, not against it. Montesquieu, whose authority could scarcely be questioned, had made clear that while Empire could boast extensive territory and Monarchies maintain those of a middling size, Republics must of necessity be small for, as he put it, «in a Republic the public good is sacrificed to a thousand private views.» Americans stood this theory on its head, for it was precisely spaciousness, and a heterogeneity of ethnic, religious, and interest groups that James Madison made the basis for this theory of triumphant republicanism. «Extend the sphere,» he wrote in *Federalist* No. 10, «and you take in a greater variety of practice and interests and make it less probable that a majority of the whole will have a common motive to invade the rights of other citizens, or, if such a common motive exists, it will be more difficult for all who feel it to discover their own strength and to act in unison with each other.» And later, in *Federalist* No. 51, «If a majority be united by a common interest, the rights of the minority will be insecure. There are but two methods of providing against this evil: the one by creating a will in the community independent of the majority—that is, of society itself, the other by comprehending in the society as many separate descriptions of citizens as will render an unjust combination of the majority very improbable.»

There spoke the man who just two years earlier had pushed Jefferson's Statute of Religious Freedom through the Virginia General Assembly and who, in another two years, was to draw up and sponsor the Federal Bill of Rights. He was able to achieve what had not heretofore been achieved, because long experience with sectarianism had taught most Americans the practical necessity of toleration. How illuminating that when that stout Congregationalist, Ezra Stiles of Yale, was induced to draft a charter for the College of Rhode Island, a Baptist stronghold, he provided for representation on its Board of Trustees of Congregationalists, Friends, and Anglicans. Imagine anything like that at either Oxford or Cambridge where, as late as the 1860s, all students and dons were required to be members of the Church of England!

In all this, too, fortune favored the Americans. Thus «interests» were not ancient, fixed, and formal, and therefore formidable, as in the Old World, but constantly fluctuating. Americans were always on the move—from State to State, from frontier to frontier, from farms to towns and cities, from church to church, from job to job, from profession to profession. What, we may well ask, was Joel Barlow's interest? He was a poet, to be sure—the eight thousand lines of his *Vision of Columbus* proclaim that: but he was also

a clergyman, something of a doctor, something of a lawyer, a soldier, a diplomat, a land speculator, and a politician whom Mr. Jefferson admired at a distance! What interest did the Rev. Manasseh Cutler have? He too had an interest in the western lands and was largely responsible for the Northwest Ordinance, but he was at the same time a clergyman, a teacher, a storekeeper, an attorney, an astronomer and botanist who made important contributions to both sciences, a member of philosophical, historical, scientific, and medical societies, leader of the first major migration to the new Ohio Territory and Founding Father of the first Ohio University. . . .

Clearly the American rejection of fixed Orders, formal Interests, professional Commitments, even local Loyalties encouraged enterprise in conduct, thought, and expression. Liberty and independence were not so much guaranteed by constitutions and bills of rights as by opportunity and necessity. Listen to Colonel Richard Henderson addressing a small band of pioneers he had induced to follow him to the new «state» of Transylvania as early as 1774, and admonishing them to draw up a Constitution for that State:

> You are called and assembled for a noble and an honorable purpose. You are fixing the palladium of an edifice, the height and magnificence of whose superstructure is now in the womb of futurity and can only become great and glorious in proportion to the excellence of its foundation. . . . If any doubt remain amongst you with respect to the force and efficacy of whatever laws you now or hereafter make, be pleased to consider that all power is originally in the people. Therefore, make it their interest by impartial and beneficial laws and you may be sure of their inclination to see them enforced. We have a right to make such laws without disturbing the repose of any society or community under Heaven, certain that the laws may derive force and efficacy from mutual consent, arising from our own virtue, interest, and convenience.

What the pioneers of the short-lived State of Transylvania dared to do anticipated what pioneers on scores of frontiers were to take for granted all through the nineteenth century: that rights do not derive exclusively from Governments, or even from Constitutions, but from Nature and Human Nature.

To philosophers from Socrates to Abelard, from John Stuart Mill to Hannah Arendt, Liberty has had many meanings. It is the

most complex of political ideas and the most elusive, and this because it is a moral, a religious, a social, an economic, even an artistic, as well as a political concept. To the philosophers of the American Revolution, Liberty was almost wholly political: it meant (sometimes metaphorically) freedom from the «tyranny» of George III. To an independent America, Liberty meant freedom to worship at whatever altar one chose—a freedom achieved with surprising ease under the auspices of both State and Federal governments. To slaves, and all those who saw slavery as reprehensible, freedom was brought about, again, by intervention of the National government and by constitutional decision. Thus, in a single century Government appeared as the enemy of Liberty, the protector of Liberty, and finally the instrument that decreed Liberty for all (at least in theory). The Americans' ambivalent view of the relationship between Liberty and Government continues with us.

To the «common man» Liberty meant pretty much the right to be let alone. Few of them were involved in the great issues of slavery or freedom of worship, or freedom of speech and of the press: these issues concerned them only remotely. What Liberty meant to the ordinary American man—and as yet women had little voice in these matters—was that he could live where he pleased and move on when he pleased; build his own house and farm his own land; choose whatever work or career caught his fancy, and change these at will; marry for love, regardless of religion, wealth, or social standing—considerations essential in the Old World even down to our own day (contrast *Abie's Irish Rose* with *My Fair Lady*); and raise his children without sending them out to work at the age of seven or eight because he could send them to free public schools. It meant that he could join any organization he wished—the militia, a labor union, a farmer's Grange, a fraternal Order, a club or a team, the Army, Navy, or Marine Corps—and that he could be part of the political party of his choice and vote for any candidate who caught his fancy—and that he might even be a candidate himself. To millions of newcomers to the American scene Liberty meant that they did not have to pull their forelock or stand, hat in hand, in the presence of their Betters, for they had no call to recognize any Betters. It meant, too, that as Nature was bountiful there would always be enough food on the table, and—for the most part—enough to drink as well. Here, to be sure, government did intrude; but it is not wholly fortuitous that the only part of the Constitution ever formally repealed was that outlawing intoxicating beverages, and the attack on the Eighteenth Amendment was accorded the misguided respectability of a crusade for personal «liberty»!

Liberty meant, too, that there were no legal classes. We now take this for granted, but it was not taken for granted in any of the Old World countries during the eighteenth or the nineteenth centuries. It was said, then, of Denmark that the population was divided into nine classes, the first three of which never spoke to the lower six, and England had paid dearly for insisting that even the lowest-ranking officer of the British Army outranked the highest-ranking officer in the Colonies.

In short, the burden of the past and the burden of government both rested lightly on America.

How interesting, then, that a people who agreed with Thomas Jefferson that only «a wise and frugal Government which shall restrain men from injuring one another and leave them otherwise free to regulate their own pursuits of industry and improvement» was «necessary to make us a happy and a prosperous people» should expect so much and demand so much from their governments! For we delude ourselves if we suppose that laissez faire dominated the political and economic scene from the beginning of nationhood. Quite the contrary. The people demanded, and obtained, far more from their State and National governments than did any people in the Old World. What they demanded was indeed something close to a «welfare State»—welfare in the simple sense in which the word was used in the age of the Enlightenment (and we should not forget that it was used twice in the Constitution), but embracing far more than in any Old World nation. Americans expected that governments would do no end of things that no Old World government took on: provide schools for all and even—as early as the 1780s—State universities for all who were qualified; build roads and bridges and canals (the Erie Canal, built by the State of New York, was probably the greatest engineering project since the Pyramids); clear the Indians out of their ancestral hunting grounds and give (or sell at less than a dollar an acre) millions of acres of public lands both to speculators and to settlers;

finance large-scale explorations into the trans-Allegheny West and even into foreign territory (Jefferson himself sent out not only the great Lewis and Clark Expedition but five others as well); authorize State and National Banks and create corporations with advantages greater even than those which the British Joint-Stock Companies enjoyed; provide public protection by law for inventions and for works of literature and of art; organize new territories in the West and supervise their transformation into States; protect native manufactures; supervise immigration; provide protection for seamen and, before too many decades, play an active role in the protection of public health, in the traffic in spirits, and in providing an enlightened American (rather than inherited) prison and penal system— one which, mirabile dictu, excited the admiration of the Old World. (Indeed, Tocqueville's original purpose in journeying to the United States was to study American prisons for a report that he and his friend Beaumont were to prepare for the French government.)

In the generation after Appomattox the pattern of modern American society and economy took shape. Growth—in territory, population, wealth, power, social complexity, and economic if not cultural maturity— was the most interesting fact. Population increased from thirty-one to seventy-six million. Fifteen million immigrants, ever more of them from southern and eastern Europe, poured into the Promised Land, and great cities like New York, Chicago, and Pittsburgh doubled their size. The Indians were harried out of their ancient hunting grounds; the mining and cattle kingdoms rose and fell; the West was peopled and farmed, and by the end of the century the «frontier» was no more. Small businesses grew into giant corporations that became masters of the economy, while great banking houses like that of Morgan rivaled government itself in influence and power. Americans completed the world's most elaborate railroad network, increasing track mileage from thirty thousand to two hundred thousand miles. Labor unions, few and feeble before the war, increased in membership and reached out for both political and economic power, though with limited success to be sure. The fledgling Republic became a World Power, expanding into the Caribbean and the Pacific and adapting itself as readily to political as to economic imperialism. No other generation in American history has witnessed change as swift or as revolutionary—except perhaps our own.

Enriched by the profits of war, by the construction of the railroad network, by the opening of overseas markets, and by a flood of new scientific and engineering developments, business flourished as never before. «The truth is,» wrote John Sherman to his brother the General, «that the close of the war with our resources unimpaired gives an elevation, a scope to the ideas of leading capitalists far higher than anything ever undertaken before. They talk of millions as confidently as formerly of thousands.» In the decade after Appomattox almost every industrial record was shattered. More coal and iron ore and silver and gold were mined, more steel forged, more rails laid, more houses built, more oil refined, than in any previous decade in American history. Bankers and investors shared in the new prosperity. Within a generation, wanting heroes of the stature of Lincoln and Lee, Americans turned to a new brand of hero: railroad builders like Vanderbilt and Harriman, meat packers like Armour and Swift, iron masters like Carnegie and Abram Hewitt, and oil princes like John D. Rockefeller. Even piratical speculators like Jay Gould attracted grudging admirers. Money greased the way not only to social favor but to political favor as well, and with it to political influence and even power.

Much of this prosperity could be traced to government policies adopted in response to the necessities of war and of the social and economic revolutions that the war brought on. Much of it could be traced to individual enterprise, too—to that enterprise displayed by the new generation of Titans of Industry and Captains of Finance who dominated the scene. Americans had been long accustomed to honor that private enterprise which Nature all but dictated, and to believe that those who exploited the boundless riches of the soil, who founded new settlements, who built roads and railroads, and who gave work to the thousands pouring into the new nation almost every day, were social benefactors, and had taken for granted that such rewards as they achieved were honorably earned. They had dismissed with contempt the accusation of antebellum apologists for slavery that the Industrial Revolution brought with it a slavery just as oppressive as, and an exploitation of its hapless workers (women and children among them) even more ruthless than, that of slavery.

Yet the ruthlessness was there, and the exploitation too—exploitation of natural and of human resources—and they raised awkward questions about the boast of «liberty» in the New World. Was the acquisition and control of the natural resources of the nation which belong properly to future generations a legitimate exercise of liberty? Was the exploitation of men, women, and children consistent with principles of liberty and equality? And yet was intervention by governments, State or National, in such exploitations not itself a dangerous limitation on that very freedom of private enterprise that accounted for the triumph of Democracy over all its rivals?

Inevitably the new economy acquired a new philosophy to justify itself. This new philosophy had been formulated by none other than Herbert Spencer, the English philosopher-scientist whom contemporaries thought the greatest intellect of all time, a Master whose genius, it was said, «surpassed that of Aristotle and Newton as the telegraph surpassed the carrier pigeon.» Spencer's formula—if we may use that term—was called «Social Darwinism» (though Darwin himself entered a quiet but firm dissent from applications to human society of his theory of evolution by means of natural selection). He taught that if man would only refrain from interfering with the great processes of Nature, and allow the law of the survival of the fittest to operate, Progress was inevitable. «Progress,» Spencer wrote, «is not an accident but a necessity. It is certain that man must become perfect.»

Spencer worked all this out in a score of learned scientific and philosophical studies. What caught the Americans' fancy was Spencer's summary of his own argument in his well-named book *The Man versus the State*, an argument which went so far as to deplore any State participation in the education of the young as an intrusion on the rights and duties of parents.

210
Great Plains
Frédéric-Auguste Bartholdi
n.d.

211
Rocky Mountains
Frédéric-Auguste Bartholdi
n.d.

217
Sequoias and Riders
Frédéric-Auguste Bartholdi
1872

The Spencerian litany was taken up with enthusiasm by his leading disciples—John Fiske, William Graham Sumner of Yale University, and Edward Youmans of the *Popular Science Monthly*. Sumner put the matter most appropriately for the American scene and argued most persuasively that laissez faire must apply to politics and economics as well as to the world of Natural evolution if Americans were to preserve Liberty and achieve Progress:

> Whatever we gain will be by growth, never in the world by any reconstruction of society on the plan of some enthusiastic social architect. The latter is only repeating the old error over again, and postponing all our chances of real improvement. Society needs first of all to be free of these meddlers—that is, to be let alone—the old doctrine, laissez-faire. Let us translate it into blunt English—Mind your own business. It is nothing but the doctrine of *Liberty*.

And he added, with triumphant irony: «Projects to abolish poverty are worthy of an age which has undertaken to abolish disease. Why not abolish death, and be as gods, once and for all.»

This was the basic issue: the role of government in the preservation and the enlargement of liberty. The Captains of Industry saw this clearly enough and welcomed the new gospel and even elaborated upon it. Admiration for Social Darwinism spurred Andrew Carnegie to come to Spencer's financial rescue by buying his splendid library—and leaving it where it was originally shelved! And this new secular gospel moved John D. Rockefeller to one of his rare flights of imagery: «The American Beauty rose can be produced in all the splendor and fragrance which bring cheer to its beholder only by sacrificing the early buds which grow up around it.» In the end, this philosophy persuaded economic and political conservatives to wrestle themselves into the rhetorical clothes of that radical Tom Paine and intone once again the litany «government, like dress, is the badge of lost innocence.»

The most elementary difficulty with Social Darwinism was that exposed by the Single-Taxer Henry George when he asked its ardent champion Edward Youmans how long it would take to achieve its objective of universal harmony and progress: «Perhaps in four or five thousand years evolution may have carried men beyond this stage of society,» was Youmans' not-so-heartening response. A far more fundamental difficulty, proclaimed by the great sociologist-philosopher Lester Ward, was that all progress comes not through letting Nature take her course, but through human control over and exploitation of Nature.

Ward, who possessed scientific credentials far more respectable than those of either Spencer or Youmans, resolutely rejected the claims they made for Darwinism in the realm of human Nature. Here Man is the master, and transforms Nature. What is more, he does this not by a blind struggle, but by cooperation and applied intelligence:

> We are told to let things alone and allow nature to take its course. But is not civilization itself . . . the result of man's *not* letting things alone, and of his not letting nature take its course. Every implement or utensil, every mechanical device is a triumph of mind over the physical forces of nature in ceaseless and aimless competition. All human institutions—religion, government, law, marriage, innumerable other modes of regulating industrial and commercial life, are only so many ways of checkmating the principle of competition as it manifests itself in society.

Ward therefore called for a philosophy that would accept the elementary fact that progress had been and would be achieved only through education and government. Neither politics nor economy was created by Nature, nor did Nature impose such concepts as liberty or equality or justice: these, too, were the products of civilization.

No other nation on the globe in the nineteenth century could boast a longer experience with liberty than the United States—liberty not as an abstraction to be celebrated on the Fourth of July, but as taken for granted by all but blacks, and eventually by them. It is at the same time a conservative experience, for it embraces the whole people, and posterity as well. Posterity is one of those concepts ever in the minds of the Founding Fathers, but now largely ignored: imagine any modern President celebrating, as did Jefferson, «our descendants to the thousandth and thousandth generation»! It is at once liberal—because dedicated, in Jefferson's words, «to the illimitable freedom of the human mind»—and conservative too, for freedom is the only bulwark against losing the heritage of the past. And it is radical, finally, insofar as it proclaims (again we turn to Jefferson) that «the earth is made for the living, not the dead,» and therefore requires a reexamination of Constitutions by every new generation. It was not chance that made Jefferson the unrivaled champion of liberty: he had made «liberty» the connective tissue of «life» and «happiness» in the Declaration; he fought, for most of his life, for an end to slavery; he dedicated his University of Virginia to «illimitable liberty.» How characteristic that letter to Mayor Weightman of Washington, celebrating the fiftieth anniversary of the Declaration, and written just a few days before the pen fell from his lifeless hands: «All eyes are open or opening to the rights of man. The general spread of the light of science has already laid open to every view the palpable truth that the mass of mankind has not been born with saddles on their backs, nor a favored few booted and spurred, ready to ride them legitimately by the grace of God.»

It took time for that practical, commonsense view of liberty as equality and justice to sink in—that view which addressed itself to the actual social and economic conditions of the millions of men, women, and children who made up American society rather than those who had somehow fought their way to the top. The average Americans of the nineteenth, as of the twentieth, century valued liberty not so much because it gave them access to the ballot box (to this day only half of our people bother to vote) or because they were free to worship as they pleased, or to speak up when and where they pleased: Americans took all this pretty much for granted. No: the threats to liberty which they felt, and still feel, are for the most part economic. The «Roosevelt Revolution,» after all, was fought largely on behalf of that «one-third of the people who are ill-housed, ill-clad, ill-nourished,» and, we might add, ill.

That was Lincoln's view of liberty too, one he proclaimed appropriately enough on the Fourth of July in his first year in office: «The struggle for the Union is a struggle for maintaining in the world that form and substance of government whose leading object is to elevate the condition of men—to lift artificial weights from all shoulders, to afford to all an unfettered start and a fair chance in the race of life.» It was a theme to which he returned in his Annual Message that same year: «Labor is prior to and independent of Capital. Capital is only the fruit of labor, and could never have existed if labor had not existed. Labor is the superior of Capital and deserves much higher consideration.»

Who can doubt that during the first century of our history Jefferson and Lincoln (they did, after all, overlap) represented the mainstream of American democracy. Indeed, when Sumner and Youmans and their cohorts were trying to recruit Darwin and Spencer into the galaxy of the Founding Fathers, the Supreme Court went back to more legitimate spokesmen. In *Munn v. Illinois*, they established what is still the authoritative interpretation of the relation of the State to property in our constitutional law: «Property does become clothed with a public interest when used in a manner to make it of public consequence, and affect the community at large. When, therefore, one devotes his property to a use in which the public has an interest, he, in effect, grants to the public an interest in that use, and must submit to being controlled by the public for the common good.»

It was to be another generation before Woodrow Wilson gave political blessing to that principle, and it is from Wilson's first Inaugural Address that we can date the philosophical, though not as yet the legislative beginnings of the welfare state:

We have built up a great system of government which has stood through a long age as a model for those who seek to set liberty upon foundations that will endure against fortuitous change, against storm and accident. Our life contains every great thing and contains it in rich abundance.

But the evil has come with the good. . . . With riches has come inexcusable waste. We have squandered a great part of what we might have used and have not stopped to conserve the exceeding bounty of nature. We have been proud of our industrial achievements but we have not hitherto stopped thoughtfully enough to count the human cost, the cost of lives snuffed out, of energies overtaxed and broken, the fearful physical and spiritual

cost to the men and women and children upon whom the dead weight and burden of it all has fallen pitilessly the years through. The groans and agony of it all had not yet reached our ears, the solemn, moving undertone of our life, coming up out of the mines and factories of every home where the struggle had its intimate and familiar seat. With the great Government went many deep secret things which we too long delayed to look into and scrutinize with candid, fearless eyes. The great Government we loved has too often been made use of for private and selfish purposes, and those who used it had forgotten the people.

At last a vision has been vouchsafed us of our life as a whole. We see the bad with the good, the debased and decadent with the sound and vital. With this vision we approach new affairs. Our duty is to cleanse, to reconsider, to restore, to correct the evil without impairing the good, to purify and humanize every process of our common life. There has been something crude and heartless and unfeeling in our haste to succeed and be great. Our thought has been, «let every man look out for himself, let every generation look out for itself» while we reared giant machinery which made it impossible that any but those who stood at the levers of control should have a chance to look out for themselves. We had not forgotten our morals. We remembered well enough that we had set up a policy which was meant to serve the humblest as well as the most powerful, with an eye single to the standards of justice and fair play. But we were very heedless and in a hurry to be great.

Now the scales of heedlessness have fallen from our eyes. We have made up our minds to square every process of our national life again with the standards we so proudly set up at the beginning. Our work is a work of restoration.

Alas, World War I intervened, and then fate, by striking down the leader of the New Freedom, and it was to be more than a decade before a new leader could raise up once again the fallen banner. That came during the presidential campaign of 1932, when Franklin D. Roosevelt inaugurated what he called a New Deal. In his historic address to the Commonwealth Club of San Francisco, he called for an «economic declaration of rights» and «an economic

constitutional order» which would distribute wealth more equitably. «Government, political and economic,» he asserted, «owes to everyone an avenue to possess himself of a portion of that plenty sufficient for his needs. Everyone has a right to own property, which means a right to be assured in the fullest extent in the safety of his savings. By no other means can men carry the burdens of those parts of life which in the nature of things afford no chance for aid to labor, childhood, sickness, old age.» And here, as Roosevelt said,

is where Government comes in. Whenever in the pursuit of this objective the Ishmael whose hand is against every man declines to join in achieving an end recognized as being for the public welfare, the Government may be asked to apply restraint. Should the group ever use its collective power contrary to the public welfare, the Government must be swift to protect the public interest.

We have learned a great deal in the past century. We know that individual liberty and individual happiness mean nothing unless both are ordered in the sense that one man's meat is not another man's poison, and that the old rights to read, to think, to speak, to choose a mode of life must be respected at all hazards. We know that Government is the maintenance of a balance within which every individual may have a place and may find safety; in which every individual may attain such power as his ability permits.

Thus, tardily, Americans conceded that obligation to «general welfare» unequivocally stated in both the Preamble and the body of the Constitution. Tardily, too, the Courts, in a long array of decisions, incorporated into the Constitution the principle that «equal protection of the laws» requires affirmative action by government in the realms of access to education, work, medical care, and comfort in misfortune and old age. Thus, at last, liberty took its place beside equality and justice as a positive obligation of every branch of the government and of the whole of society.

Edouard-René Lefebvre de Laboulaye (cat. 1) is generally regarded as the father of the Statue of Liberty. At a dinner party at his chateau in 1865 he initially suggested such a statue to his assembled guests, who included many prominent French republicans. That, at least, is the story related by one of the guests, the sculptor Frédéric-Auguste Bartholdi, twenty years after the event. Whatever the truth of the story, it is certain that in a far more profound manner Laboulaye was a major figure in the remarkable series of events that brought the statue idea to fruition. Through a lifetime of speaking, teaching, writing, and acting on behalf of republican government, Laboulaye helped create the intellectual and political atmosphere in which it was possible for a Statue of Liberty to be conceived of and built. Laboulaye was one of the most important political thinkers of his day, and his ideas must be understood if we are to appreciate the initial meaning of the statue idea and the manner in which it attained completion. Central to his thinking was the concept of a «common law of free peoples,» which spanned oceans and language in its expression of true liberty.

Born in 1811, the grandson of a secretary to Louis XVI, Laboulaye belonged to a family from Auvergne that owed its nobility to public office. After a classical education at the Lycée Louis-le-Grand he unenthusiastically undertook the study of law. In fact, he cared more for history, and after being admitted to the Paris bar published several studies that won him scholarly esteem. In 1838 his essay *L'Histoire du droit des propriétés foncières en Occident* received a prize from the Académie des Inscriptions et Belles-Lettres; four years later, his *Recherches sur la condition civile et politique des femmes* was honored by the Académie des Sciences Morales et Politiques. In 1845 he became a member of the Académie des Inscriptions et Belles-Lettres, which had honored him again for his *Essai sur les lois criminelles des Romains*.

In the 1872 foreword to his *Questions constitutionnelles* he explained that the Revolution of 1848 had compelled him to become a political writer. He witnessed a rebirth of the ideas of the Convention, which, mingling with socialist dreams, had brutally cut into the liberal tradition. He understood, further, that the errors of the new Constitution (of 1848)—notably the single Assembly—were a serious threat to liberty. An informed historian of institutions, he could not help seeing clearly what was at stake and, feeling obliged to take a stand in the constitutional debate, he pub-

lished, in 1848, *Considérations sur la Constitution*, which he dedicated to General Cavaignac in the hope that he would play the role of George Washington in the new Republic.

In 1849 Laboulaye was appointed professor of Comparative Legislation at the Collège de France and began to concentrate his research on free institutions. In February 1851 he made a pressing appeal to the public in a work entitled *La Revision de la Constitution*. Under the Second Empire (1856–70) his courses on the Constitution of the United States and on the French Revolution allowed him to enter more deeply into the political theory of the republican opposition; they also created a meeting place for passionately involved young liberal students, in a period when free assembly had been suppressed. At the same time he contributed frequently to the *Journal des Débats* and made use of every possible means to reach the public. He did not disdain to write fiction, some of which was very successful, notably *Paris en Amérique*, in which he humorously compared French and American political practices, and, above all, *Le Prince-Caniche*, in which he satirized the French government. His fame as a historian of institutions and his talent for political philosophy led him to become a spokesman for the Union Libérale, which came into being with the election of 1863. During that year he published his two major political works: *L'État et ses limites* and *Le Parti libéral*. In the first of these we find a statement of his basic principles or political philosophy, in the second his practical teaching, the action he recommended in the coming struggle. In this second work he applied to the contemporary situation conclusions based on his study of what he called constitutional government and expressed his admiration for American institutions. Two years later, in 1865, when he was one of the most conspicuous leaders of the moderate republicans, he conceived the idea of giving the Statue of Liberty to the United States for the centenary of its independence.

In 1872 Laboulaye again participated in constitutional discussions by publishing his *Esquisse d'une Constitution républicaine*. Elected a deputy in 1871, he played an essential role in discussions on the constitutional laws of 1875; today we can see him as one of the founding fathers of the Third Republic. Having reflected throughout his life on the precariousness of French political institutions, he had the satisfaction of working to achieve their stability.

Laboulaye and the Common Law of Free Peoples

Jean-Claude Lamberti

Laboulaye's political action was in no way improvised; rather, it was the faithful and logical expression of the political doctrine he had built up beginning with his scholarly study of the common law of free peoples. He has often been portrayed as a follower of Benjamin Constant (cat. 2) and Alexis de Tocqueville (cat. 3),[1] and while this description is not inaccurate, we must correct the image of a line of direct descent, in which influence passes from one man to the next. In reading *L'État et ses limites* we see that the memory of Constant is much closer and deeper than that of Tocqueville. Laboulaye gathered together and published Constant's writings on constitutional policy in 1861, stressing in a long introduction their acute and up-to-date quality.[2] Precise references to Constant abound in Laboulaye's works whereas he rarely quotes Tocqueville, even, paradoxically, in his *Histoire des États-Unis*. In the chapter of the former work devoted to Tocqueville he went so far as to say: «Already some of M. de Tocqueville's ideas have become so familiar to us that we have forgotten their originator.»[3] Laboulaye also showed a certain lack of understanding of Tocqueville's role at the Commission for the Constitution of 1848 and in the debate of 1851 on the Constitution's revision.[4]

In his optimism and enthusiasm Laboulaye was closer to Constant than to Tocqueville, and he found the principles of his political philosophy in the former's famous discourse on «the liberty of the ancients as compared to that of the moderns.» Under the same banner of liberty, the moderns pursued aims different from those of their predecessors. «The aim of the ancients,» Constant had said, «was the division of social power among all the citizens of a given country. This is what they called liberty. The aim of the moderns is security in the enjoyment of their privileges, and they call liberty the guarantees that institutions accord to such enjoyment.»[5] The error of Rousseau and, after him, of Robespierre, was their attempt to return to the ancient conception by putting political liberty, or their idea of it, above the rights of the individual. For Laboulaye, on the contrary, and for Constant, the sovereignty of the State could only be relative and restricted, and individual rights set limits to collective action. Following Constant, Laboulaye catalogued the various stages of the historic affirmation of modern liberty: the Bill of Rights of 1789; the return to modern ideas in the Constitution of the Year III after the period of the Convention during which, he believed, France reverted to ancient sovereignty; the usurpation of Napoleonic Caesarism; and, finally, the Restoration.

In his genealogy of modern liberty Laboulaye went farther back than Constant and reasoned quite differently. Constant explained the transformations of liberty from ancient times to his own by comparing the taxes imposed by various States, the leisures enjoyed by their citizens, and, above all, the growth of civilization and trade. «We should be more attached than we are to our personal independence,» he concluded. «When the ancients sacrificed this independence to political rights they gave up less in order to gain more. If we were to make the same sacrifice we should give up more and obtain less.»[6] Constant does not name Christianity as a basis for the individual's liberation from the State whereas for Laboulaye the individual's autonomous existence was one of Christianity's major consequences:

> When Christ said: «Render unto God the things that are God's» he set forth a new principle in contradiction to ancient ideas. Among the ancients the gods were attached to the city walls; they existed only by permission of Caesar and the Senate. To assert the claim of God was to break the unity of despotism. Here is the seed of the revolution which separates the ancient and the modern world. . . . It was the sovereignty of God that shattered the tyranny of the Caesars. Indeed, from the day when this sovereignty was recognized, there were duties, and hence rights pertaining to the immortal soul, over which no prince had authority. Conscience was set free, the individual existed.[7]

Thus Laboulaye explicitly gave a Christian foundation to the political individualism he had inherited from Benjamin Constant.

A member of the opposition under the Second Empire, Laboulaye was irritated by the French clergy's subservience to Napoléon III. In *La Liberté religieuse* (1858), one of his best works, he pleaded for separation of Church and State, denounced the disastrous effects of the alliance between them forged by the Emperor Constantine, and praised the Reformation for freeing men's conscience. Although an enemy of all dogmatism, Laboulaye, like Tocqueville, sought to reconcile the «spirit of religion» with the «spirit of liberty.»[8] Through this concept Tocqueville sought to be «a new kind of liberal,»[9] and when Laboulaye took up this theme it still had a certain originality.[10] But in most cases the meeting of the two philosophers' minds was around themes popularized to the point of banality by

Tocqueville, such as the search for de-centralization and for a link between liberty and equality, which Laboulaye found in all Tocqueville's works from *La Démocratie en Amérique* to *L'Ancien Régime et la Révolution*. «M. de Tocqueville's political symbol,» he rightly noted, «is that of the Constituent Assembly: liberty, equality.»[11] But after 1848, the eruption of universal suffrage, and the new Napoleonic despotism, these ideas did not have the same value as in 1835 when Tocqueville prophetically declared that from then on men's only choice was between liberal democracy and democratic despotism. On one point Laboulaye was a follower of Tocqueville: he showed a persistent interest in American institutions, which stemmed neither from Constant nor from the prevailing ideas of the time.[12] During the Empire, as during the Restoration and the July Monarchy, the «American school» was a minority while most French liberals—notably the brilliant Prévost-Paradol, who shared with Laboulaye the leadership of the moderate opposition—were faithful to an English model.

His receptiveness to the flow of European and American ideas exposed Laboulaye to the criticisms of men more narrow-minded than himself. Schérer called his Americanism an intellectual quirk, while Ledru-Rollin attacked him for being pro-German. Actually, by virtue of the breadth of his culture, he was, more than any of his contemporaries, an heir to the intellectual cosmopolitanism of Madame de Staël. Readers of *L'État et ses limites* could easily discover the foreign sources of his ideas: the Germans Savigny and Humboldt, the Englishman John Stuart Mill, and the American William Ellery Channing.[13]

In his *Essai sur les doctrines de F. de Savigny* (1842), Laboulaye credited the founder of the German historical school with revealing to him a way to combat certain eighteenth-century errors, notably the illusion, too readily accepted in France, of the supreme power of the lawmaker. Law, Laboulaye believed, is not and cannot be the product of legislation; one of the forces that affect society according to the well-defined character of a peculiar people, law gradually and organically develops from an inner necessity, ensuring a link between past and present. Since it expresses the spirit of a particular society, it can be understood only through history; it can be studied and recognized, but it cannot be created or lastingly imposed by legislative force. Laboulaye's originality lies in his coming to liberalism through the study of history and through criticism of the eighteenth-century abstractions that led

most of his contemporaries to espouse the theories of Joseph de Maistre and to join the ranks of the counterrevolution. Laboulaye's logic has a solid base,[14] for although law spontaneously expresses the spirit of a people, government should intervene as little as possible. The same conclusion was reached by Humboldt, while Savigny affirmed the total power of the State as the highest organic expression of the people. From Savigny's work Laboulaye took only the idea of a history of law and institutions and the principles of a criticism of what he called «legislative violence.»

Quite soon the influence of Channing succeeded that of Savigny. By his practical Christianity, his exaltation of the will to individual perfection, and his reconciliation of philosophy and the Christian religion, the Unitarian preacher deeply moved his American audiences.[15] The enthusiastic Laboulaye described him as an American Fénelon, a Christian rationalist, inspired by love of his fellowmen and a religious respect for their freedom. Thanks to Channing the American idea of individual liberty and perfectibility supplanted, in Laboulaye's mind, the German theory of civic progress and collective conscience. His attachment to the slow maturation of the past gave way to a taste for movement and free, life-inspired creativity.[16] From this time on his political philosophy rested on a conception of man composed of religious idealism and confidence in the powers of the individual. «The purpose of humanity,» he wrote, «can only be the purpose of the individual, that is, a divine purpose.»[17] In this metaphysical dimension of his view of the individual, Laboulaye went beyond both Savigny and Constant.

For Laboulaye, as for Humboldt and Mill, the final goal of politics was to ensure the full development of the individual's abilities. The liberal program could no longer be, as at the time of the Restoration, to diminish the power of the State in order to protect the individual sphere. He proposed to educate and strengthen the individual; he put his trust in schooling and in the liberty of communities and associations. He sought to favor the development of the individual without weakening the authority of the State, which was entirely legitimate when exercised in its specific domain: «the army, the navy, diplomacy, finance, lawmaking, administration and police.»[18] In its proper activities the State should be strong and enjoy respect; that it has the last word guarantees independence and liberty. But outside this realm it should give free play to individual, social, and municipal liberties.

In the doctrinal or teaching portion of Laboulaye's works, primarily in *Le Parti libéral*, his political philosophy expresses itself in two ways, one stemming from reason, the other from history and the comparative method. The justification of civil liberties, which, Laboulaye tells us, are natural rights,[19] cannot be found by the same method as the search for political liberties, which, in order to provide effective guarantees to the former, must adapt themselves to the time, place, and condition of a society. In the first type of exposition we easily discover traces of Constant and Channing; in the second type Constant is rarely lost from view but Tocqueville and Savigny also figure prominently. What distinguished Laboulaye from other writers and journalists of his time is that he revealed to his compatriots what he called «the common law of free peoples» and also the difficulties that obstructed the permanent adoption of free institutions.

Three kinds of civil liberties are analyzed in *Le Parti libéral*: individual, social, and municipal. In the domain of individual liberties—liberty of the person, of work, and of property—Laboulaye did not depart from classical models, with some significant exceptions: he strongly condemned all monopolies and the crime of conspiracy, this one year before it was brought to an end by Émile Ollivier's famous report to the Chamber of Deputies.[20] Of the four social liberties the one most important to him was religion; he explained that State and Church would gain equally from their separation. He also urged freedom of the press, of education—excluding any monopoly—and, above all, of justice. Like Tocqueville before him and Prévost-Paradol in his *France nouvelle* several years after, Laboulaye condemned centralization and called for the independence of municipalities. This demand was that of almost the liberal school, Dupont-White and Thiers (cat. 4) excepted. Laboulaye showed more courage and more originality, in view of the relative indifference of the general public, when, following the example of Tocqueville, he demanded a broad scope for voluntary associations.[21] His intention was to strengthen the individual with State encouragement, to educate him to tasks of common interest and bypass the dangerous and overly schematic opposition between State and citizen characteristic of the liberalism of the Restoration and negative in nature, even when supported by Constant.

Unlike Sieyes, whom he detested, Laboulaye never claimed to be expert in the construction of new Constitutions. He wanted only to draw on the lessons of experience, those that he had learned in the comparative study of institutions. In the preface to *Le Parti libéral* he warned readers: «Here there is no ingenious theory, no seductive utopia; I do not aspire to make over the human race. I have simply put together the lessons of experience, telling how the English, American, Dutch, Belgian, and Swiss peoples understand and practice liberty.»[22] This statement is not merely a clue to his method; it expresses the conviction, reasonably established at the end of his inquiry, that «there is a common heritage of free peoples» and that comparative history evidences «the common law of constitutional States, the common heritage of civilization.»[23] Like Montesquieu and Tocqueville, Laboulaye used the comparative method, but, as he learned from Savigny, he systematically brought history into the study of institutions. Thus, at the beginning of his 1850 course, he declared that he could not be content to retrace the history of the most striking events of the French Revolution or to submit French Constitutions from 1789 on to a strictly juridical analysis. He intended to adopt a new approach, defined in the title of his course: «La Révolution française étudiée dans ses institutions.» In 1855, when he devoted his course to the history of the United States, he began by stressing the usefulness for Frenchmen of studying the American Constitution: «It is not a man-made government, a counterproof modeled on an ancient pattern by scholarly revolutionaries, pupils of Montesquieu and Mably; it is the natural endproduct of two centuries of work and freedom.» The American example was closer to the French then, in 1855, than it was in 1789, he noted, pointing out not the whole body of American institutions but the spirit that produced and the idea that inspired them.[24] This was the true object of his course, which marked one of the great moments of the liberal opposition under the Second Empire.

In all his works, Laboulaye attempted to demonstrate how widely fundamental political ideas could differ from one side of the Atlantic to the other. Thus, for instance, in America the word «Constitution» had a much narrower meaning than in France:[25] in France a constitutional text was «the body of provisions and laws embracing the entire public life of the nation» whereas in America it concerned only «the organization and distribution of public powers.»[26] On this point he defended the «American» idea, recalling that it had been that of Constant.[27]

Moreover, he noted, Americans had never been trapped by the illusion of the French «philosophes,» who imagined that France—and all mankind—could be regenerated only if *they* were allowed to write a good Constitution, thereby reducing a people's Constitution to a written text. Having learned from Savigny that a Constitution has infinitely deeper roots than the will of lawmakers, Laboulaye opposed all such chimeras, even quoting the counterrevolutionary de Maistre but, at the same time, very cleverly quoting an equivalent text of the irreproachable republican Sismondi:

> The Constitution embraces all the customs of a nation, its affections, memories and the demands of its imagination as well as its laws. . . . Thus nothing is more indicative of a superficial and misguided mind than the attempt to transplant one country's Constitution to another or to impose a new Constitution on a people, not in accord with its own history and spirit but on the basis of general rules glorified under the name of principles.[28]

While many countries had found a constitutional government suited to them, France seemed unable to make a lasting choice of free institutions. This singularity led Laboulaye, the student of comparative history, to the heart of nineteenth-century France's political problem: why had the country had so much trouble, since 1789, in establishing a government based on liberty? Laboulaye found the cause of this misfortune in a twist of the public mind born of the Revolution: too often, he argued, the people confounded everyday liberties with the revolution whose purpose was to establish them. The constant object of his studies, he wrote in the 1872 *Questions constitutionnelles*, was to show that liberty and revolution have two very distinct and often contrary meanings.[29]

Laboulaye identified two main errors, which he denounced from the *Considérations sur la Constitution* of 1849 to the *Esquisse d'une Constitution républicaine* of 1872.[30] Born under the July Monarchy and brought up on the liberal beliefs of the Restoration, he thought that the errors of the Revolution were largely to be explained by the single Assembly. In this respect he went along with the teachings of Boissy d'Anglas and Daunou, writers of the Constitution of the Year III, which he always quoted favorably. In his understanding of the necessary balance of powers he echoed the ideas of Montesquieu and Delolme, but he knew that the hereditary paymaster's office, dear to Benjamin Constant,[31] was outdated, and looked to the American example of a second democratic chamber.

The second capital error, which Laboulaye attacked with as much perseverance and more originality, was excessive legislative power and its tendency to take over the constituent process. Thus the Constitution of 1848 created a politically dangerous situation by making constitutional revision almost impossible. In February 1851 he proposed that the people be consulted on this revision,[32] a solution that might have forestalled the coup d'état of December 2 and, above all, one which he argued was legally mandatory for any constitutional change.[33] In treating the tendency of the Assemblies to acquire constituent powers, he was both classical and at the same time close to us: classical, because he reflected Rousseau's idea that sovereignty cannot be delegated, although he applied it only to constitutional matters; close to us, because as one of the founders of the Third Republic, he was aware of the danger of the Assemblies' takeover.

4
Maquette for a Monument to Thiers
Frédéric-Auguste Bartholdi
n.d.

The purpose of Laboulaye's constitutional studies was to endow Frenchmen with «the experience of free peoples . . . in order to help them to found a lasting government and to do away with the revolutionary spirit.»[34] What he meant by revolutionary spirit was not that of 1789 but that of 1793, «the cult of revolution in its falsest guise . . . the scorn of political liberty,» and the ideas of that political faction in which he included «the leaders of the Commune, the veteran Jacobins and all the socialist schools.»[35] At the opposite pole he placed the constitutional governments exemplified in England, Holland, Belgium, Switzerland, and, above all, the United States, whose representative republic seemed to him the model nearest to perfection.[36]

In his generation Laboulaye was the uncontested leader of the «American school,» in the line of Tocqueville and Lafayette; he marked the climax of the evolution of liberalism into democracy. In this regard his progressive allegiance to the cause of universal suffrage is characteristic. In his *Considérations sur la Constitution* (1849) he was still in favor of a property qualification, but at a low level, for he had always considered the electoral base of the July Monarchy to be too narrow.[37] In *Le Parti libéral* he totally accepted universal suffrage while insisting on the urgency of popular education, once more holding up the United States as an example. «Many people are afraid of this rising tide of democracy,» he wrote; «they accept it in a spirit of resignation. But, as for me, I like it. In it I see the triumph of equality and justice; nothing seems to me more beautiful than a society where everyone is master of his rights and takes part in the government.»[38]

In general, and especially at the beginning, there was great consistency between Laboulaye's ideas and his political action. There was a slight but logical discrepancy in his approval of the Senate Consultation of 1870, but a return to normal in the discussion of the constitutional laws of 1875, in which he played a fundamental but insufficiently recognized role. Although in his courses at the Collège de France he never expressed dissent, he contributed to the *Journal des Débats*, along with Renan, Rigault, Saint-Marc-Girardin, and Prévost-Paradol, perhaps the most brilliant journalist of the opposition.[39] Over his signature we find all the theses characteristic of the opponents of the Second Empire, particularly rejection of centralization, a policy linked to the discredit of the Napoleonic government. His opposition took a variety of forms, but we may particularly note his defense of Lincoln and the Union, at a time when business circles, legitimists, and the French government itself were favorable to the Confederacy.[40] Many Catholics were also in the Confederate camp and this fact, along with the 1864 publication of the papal Syllabus, fueled the anticlericalism of republican circles, often atheistic in character but sometimes linked to liberal Protestantism or to a Christian spirituality devoid of dogma, such as that professed by Laboulaye in *La Liberté religieuse*.[41] By now universal suffrage was an irreversible trend, and as it gradually won the support of the new liberal generation, Laboulaye was among the first to espouse it and to investigate the counterweights necessary for its integration with future liberal institutions.

At the end of the 1850s and the beginning of the 1860s intellectual developments made Laboulaye, as author of *Le Parti libéral*, the outstanding spokesman of the Union Libérale, which came into being just before the 1863 election.[42] From the works of Jules Simon and Vacherot it appeared that moderate republicans had become genuine liberals;[43] as liberalism ceased to be the trademark of monarchists, many former Orleanists drew closer to the republicans. Laboulaye's political philosophy combined features borrowed from Orleanism—such as the second Chamber—with his own ideas as a moderate republican, interested in forward-looking democratic projects, such as universal compulsory education. His amiable and conciliatory nature made him, for some years, the symbol of the liberal ecumenism he set forth in the Preface to *Le Parti libéral*: «This party, which is in process of formation and growing every day, is not a small sect closely bound to a literal symbol; it is a universal Church for all those who believe in liberty and wish to enjoy it.»[44] He defined this party, to which he rallied 1863 voters, as «a return to the principles of 1789,» summing it up in the triple slogan: «liberty, individual, social, and political.»[45] However, the union of liberals for which the writer appealed would not restrict itself to an oppositional role. «The new liberalism,» he wrote, «formed of the most diverse elements, does stem from the principles of 1789, but, as a political party, it has no past. It was not defeated in 1839 and 1848; it has no regrets, memories, or after-thoughts. Nothing prevents the government from taking over its leadership; indeed, public opinion today demands nothing better.»[46] The plea for unity of 1870, for which Laboulaye has often been taken to task, arose from the attempt to reconcile the government and liberty[47] for which Laboulaye was praised at the beginning of the 1860s. Actually, he was always true to himself and to the liberal tradition, which, ever since Mme. de Staël and Constant, had displayed a certain indifference toward the nature of the political regime, as long as it was free. Fidelity to the monarchy or to the republic could not be the criterion, since any moderate regime could be free or not free. This was why the liberals made it a point of honor to fight for freedom under any regime rather than to demand a monarchical or republican form of government. Prévost-Paradol, like Laboulaye, «refused to choose a regime because he had opted for liberty under any regime.»[48] For both the decisive borderline was between an authoritarian Empire and a parliamentary one, whereas doctrinaire republicans, in their hardened opposition, left the Union Libérale during the 1869 election, refusing to trust and go along with the Empire's evolution in the direction of a parliamentary government. In his *Esquisse d'une Constitution républicaine* Laboulaye evoked Constant: «Between a constitutional monarchy and a republic there is a difference only of form. Between a constitutional monarchy and an absolute monarchy the difference is one of substance.» It may be said that this plea comes after the event, but this is not so. The same comment appears in *Le Parti libéral*, proving thereby how faithful Laboulaye was to his own teachings.[49]

In the plebiscite of 1870, to vote *Yes* meant to accept and consolidate the Empire; to vote *No* was to reject the ministerial responsibility before the Chamber that the opposition had so long demanded.[50] The left-wing republicans voted *No*; Rémusat advised a *No* or abstention; Thiers and Dufaure abstained. But Odilon Barrot, Guizot, and Prévost-Paradol voted *Yes*, as did Laboulaye. «I had combatted personal government,» Laboulaye explained, «but I had always spoken up for the constitutional transformation of the Empire. . . . In the new Constitution I saw only one thing, the return of parliamentary freedom.» He was accused of having betrayed his convictions and faced a protest from his students, many of whom were left-wing republicans, and several stormy public meetings. He answered his accusers with clarity and dignity, as a man who had always hewn to his principles.[51]

In October 1871, some three months after his election to the National Assembly, Laboulaye clearly indicated his choice in the Preface to the eighth edition of *Le Parti libéral*: «The Constitutionalists made the greatness of the Restoration and raised up a France that had been crushed by invasion. . . . Let us rally under the healing banner and, under the name of the Republic, may we set up that constitutional government which alone can assure the reign of justice and liberty!» We know what a constitutional government meant to him: guaranteed liberties, two legislative chambers, and a balanced organization of public powers. In the *Esquisse d'une Constitution républicaine*, he once more set forth his constitutional teachings and affirmed his commitment to the center-left in support of Thiers' conservative Republic. But one question remained: was the executive branch to be organized on a parliamentary or a presidential basis? Laboulaye expressly noted that the problem presented itself in different terms in the United States and in such a highly centralized country as France. «The ultimate decision,» he concluded, «is up to France.»[52] He might have preferred a presidential system, American-style, but the Assembly's growing intolerance of Thiers,

the obvious parliamentary trend, and, above all, the need to reconcile the various parties inclined him to favor a parliamentary government. During the debates of 1875 he concluded an address to the Assembly with: «Our republic is parliamentary; thus everything depends on the responsibility of the ministers and that is the guarantee of its endurance.»[53]

By virtue of his constitutional studies and the principles he had drawn from them, Laboulaye was generally expected to play a major role in the establishment of the constitutional laws of the Republic. And so he did. In 1873, when a Committee of Thirty was chosen to examine these laws, he and Waddington were called upon to present a study of both European and American constitutions.[54] After the failure of an attempted restoration of the monarchy, passage of the constitutional laws could be effected only by a coalition of the centrist parties. Albert de Broglie, on the center-right, and Thiers, on the center-left, were both liberals, Thiers a conservative liberal of bourgeois and Voltairean tradition, Broglie one of aristocratic and Catholic stamp. On January 29, 1875, when discussion of the first constitutional law began, Laboulaye recalled liberal doctrine to the Orleanists, who were still hanging back. Between a constitutional Monarchy and a moderate Republic he saw a difference only of form. He pointed out that the Third Republic did not necessarily have the faults of its two predecessors and voiced doubt that a monarch could bring stability to a country where for the past century no kingly ruler had been able to hand down the throne to his son. «The general discussion,» Rémusat noted in his *Mémoires*, «was incredibly shallow and mediocre. . . . Only Laboulaye did himself honor, as in all our difficult debates.»[55] In the name of the Committee's minority Laboulaye presented the following amendment: «that the government of the Republic consist of two Chambers and a President»; the amendment failed, receiving 336 votes against 356. «It was set aside,» writes Marcel Prelot, «in spite of a remarkable speech by its author, the only one in the whole discussion which is worth re-reading today.»[56] But Laboulaye's arguments did break down the last resistance, and the next day Henri Wallon's amendment, reading: «The President of the Republic is elected by a plurality of votes

from the Senate and the Chamber of Deputies, gathered together as a National Assembly,» succeeded. The passage of this apparently mild text by 353 votes over 352 marked the true birth of the Third Republic.

Laboulaye was one of the first to guess what compromises were necessary. Although he himself was close to Thiers, he understood certain Orleanist positions, notably the demand for a second chamber. Gambetta effected the final agreement by rallying the republicans to a Senate presented as the Grand Council of the communes of France. Senators were to be chosen by electoral colleges made up of Deputies, local (*arrondissement*) and general councillors, and a delegate from every commune. An irremovable fourth of the Senate was to be chosen by the Assembly and then by the Senators themselves. Laboulaye was among the first Senators elected for life. As for the law on the organization of public powers, presented by him, it passed on July 16 by a vote of 502 to 102.

Contrary to Laboulaye's hopes, the constitutional laws of 1875 were not submitted to nationwide ratification, and revisional procedure on the part of the National Assembly could not satisfy him. Otherwise, however, these laws fulfilled all his wishes: they introduced into France a parliamentary government in harmony with what he called the common law of free peoples. And he was among those who had striven the hardest to translate liberal principles into constitutional practices. Was his task completed? Perhaps, in his last years, he thought back to a sentence from *Le Parti libéral*: «It was for liberty that our fathers, in 1789, made a revolution that still endures; only liberty will complete it.»[57]

Translated, from the French, by Frances Frenaye

The centennial of the Statue of Liberty provides the occasion for an exhibition devoted to the full spectrum of the statue's history: from its conception as a casual suggestion at a legendary dinner party in France to its current status as the symbol of America. The exhibition has required an examination of the statue itself and of its creators, and also of the artistic, political, technological, and other worlds that provided the circumstances out of which the great monument came into being. Perhaps more than any other project of the nineteenth century, the Statue of Liberty characterized the ideals and hopes of its era. To study the statue, and to attempt to «explain» it to others, inevitably require a comprehensive approach, which the curators have sought to follow in the exhibition and the catalogue. This approach seeks to place the statue in a broad context while detailing its specific development through an in-depth examination of the visual and factual data, including material previously unavailable or untapped. The statue is considered as both object and icon; its existence as a physical entity—its design, realization, and restorations—is balanced by an analysis of its meanings—from its initial signification of French-American friendship to its present, multifaceted symbolism.

LIBERTY
The French-American Statue in Art and History
An Introduction

Pierre Provoyeur,
June Hargrove, and
Catherine Hodeir

For the casual observer the fascination of the statue lies perhaps in its sheer size; or in its magnificent setting in the center of a great natural harbor, adjacent to the largest city in the United States. Views of New York (cat. 5) around 1850 show how impressive must have been the entrance into the harbor through the Narrows, an effect that would have been even more striking after a long sea voyage. Bartholdi's letters to Laboulaye (cat. 6) and his mother contain cries of delight that he had found what he had before only imagined in his dreams: a breathtaking backdrop for his heroic statue. Rather surprisingly, but very logically from his point of view, Bartholdi changed the original orientation of the statue as he developed the idea, in numerous watercolors painted before 1886 (cat. 7, 8) and engravings for the press (cat. 10). Linked both to the ocean and the city, the statue, in his mind, was intended to welcome travelers from the Old World to the New (cat. 9), thus giving a conclusion and culmination to the adventurous discoveries of Christopher Columbus (cat. 11).

For the scholar, as for anyone who seeks to go beneath the obvious, the statue's interest lies in the driving forces of its creation: not only the motives of those individuals directly involved, but also the fundamental forces that crystalized in the nineteenth century—nationalism, technological progress, mass communication, entrepreneurial vigor, the public monument as a vehicle of moral instruction. The statue's transcendence of its origins to acquire independent vitality in the twentieth century renews its appeal for us, which in turn is the real impetus for this exhibition.

Three broad themes seem appropriate as a prelude to the more specific story of the statue told in the exhibition: first, French-American friendship; second, the role of Auguste Bartholdi as master entrepreneur and publicist; and third, the position of Bartholdi as one of the nineteenth century's great visionaries, whose career embodied aspects relating not only to the statue itself but also to broader themes of literature in his day.

Until the statue's centennial, probably few citizens of the United States or France were aware that the statue came into being as a

9

gift from France to the United States. In a remarkable transformation, over the past century the statue has become identified with immigration and appropriated by Americans as something totally their own. When the monument was unveiled in 1886, however, the theme of French-American friendship was inseparable from its meaning.

When the Franco-American Union began its fund-raising effort for the statue in 1875, diplomatic relations between France and the United States were not yet a century old. For the next hundred years relations between the two countries were secondary to their respective political ambitions. Nevertheless, over the decades a myth arose based on France's importance in recognizing the new nation in its struggle against England. A second myth arose when France underwent its own revolution and began a new page in its history. French-American friendship boasts a rich inheritance of political and cultural interchange, which has grown up around the point where the two myths intersect. Above all, it is a fabric of memories held in common.

The Golden Age of French-American friendship began with the birth of the Third Republic, and lasted until World War I. Its beginning was marked by a change in the tone of diplomatic relations. The sympathies of the United States, which blamed Napoléon III for the war of 1870, were originally aligned with Prussia, but when the new French Republic was declared in 1875, the United States was the first power to recognize it. For her part, France, standing alone amid Europe's monarchies, eagerly grasped at the legitimacy thus conferred by her sister Republic. The young French Republic also saw in America a constitutional model to be imitated, if not in every particular, at least in its durability. The circumstances favored a flowering of French-American friendship. Indeed, France's reaffirmation of a republican form of government in the great tradition of 1789 occurred just as the United States was preparing to celebrate the centennial of its independence.

The romantic history of the Statue of Liberty, the monument presented by the people of France to the people of America on the occasion of the U.S. Centennial, was thus contemporaneous with the beginning of

11

10

"LIBERTY ENLIGHTENING THE WORLD" BARTHOLDI'S COLOSSAL STATUE ON BEDLOW'S ISLAND, NEW YORK HARBOR.—DRAWN BY HARRY FENN.

French-American friendship, and became a cardinal episode of its development. Throughout the fund-raising effort in France one theme was enunciated again and again by the Franco-American Union: that of the part played by France in the founding of the United States. With epic consistency one orator after another put the heroes of the two countries through their paces: Lafayette and Rochambeau disembarked again and again with enthusiasm undimmed by repetition; again and again Washington welcomed the young Marquis with undiminished warmth. In the words of Edouard de Laboulaye, «such a friendship must needs be embodied; every great idea should have its visible symbol.» Liberty, for which Frenchmen had fought side by side with Americans, was to have her statue.

Two other works by Bartholdi, *Lafayette* in New York's Union Square (cat. 342) and a monument to Lafayette and Washington in Paris's Place des États-Unis (cat. 12), were the first in a series of variations on the sustained theme of the two heroes of French-American friendship. For example, in 1900 the schoolchildren of America offered France a new statue of Lafayette. Congress took the project under its wing, negotiating with the French government through its Ambassador in Washington, Jules Cambon. The site finally chosen is considered one of the finest in Paris: opposite the main gate of the Louvre, and at the head of the perspective which links the Tuileries and the Arc de Triomphe.

For Paris, 1900 was the year of the Universal Exposition, and in France and America alike the celebrations attendant on this international undertaking imparted new life to French-American friendship. On July 4, at noon Paris time, the President of the United States pressed a button in the White House and caused a gigantic American flag to unfurl at the top of the Eiffel Tower. The Spirit of Electricity, which played a leading role in the Exposition, had joined France and the United States in a simultaneous moment of commemoration. Four years later, at the St. Louis Exposition, one hall in the French pavilion was given over to Lafayette.

Such stereotypes were to figure more and more prominently in French-American friendship. Perhaps the only instance of renewed spontaneous enthusiasm occurred during World War I when Gen. John J. Pershing, Commander of the U.S. Expeditionary Forces, exclaimed as he set foot on the soil of France: «Lafayette, nous voilà!» At last America could discharge its debt of friendship.

This was an isolated moment, however; thereafter, French-American relations rapidly worsened, and regained their earlier splendor only with the coming of the Bicentennial. Edouard de Laboulaye had foreseen it all: «In a hundred years America will celebrate another centennial of her independence. By then she will have forgotten our names—but this statue [the Statue of Liberty], will still stand. . . . She will bear witness, to generations yet unborn, that the countrymen of Lafayette are still friends and brothers of the countrymen of Washington. To the friendship, the everlasting friendship, which joins France and America!»[1]

If the dual myths of French-American friendship provide the background for understanding how the idea for a Statue of Liberty might have come into being, the personality of Frédéric-Auguste Bartholdi is the key to explaining how so grand a vision was brought to completion.

Auguste Bartholdi possessed the talents of a great entrepreneur, whose vision and pragmatism made him the artistic equivalent of a Rothschild or a Pulitzer. He was an artist of his generation, embracing both the classical tradition and new themes of inspiration that arrived with the industrial revolution. His strange painting, *Faunes et nymphes effrayées par un train* (cat. 13), also called in the archival records *Goodbye to Mythology*, is itself an expression of this uncomfortable straddling of two worlds. But Bartholdi did not take refuge in a self-created world of pure symbolism—like Boecklin, from whom the left side of the painting is derived, or his contemporary Richard Wagner. Bartholdi's willingness to embrace the most up-to-date technology, his global political manoeuvres,

12
Washington and Lafayette
Frédéric-Auguste Bartholdi
1895

13
Faunes et nymphes effrayées par un train
Frédéric-Auguste Bartholdi
n.d.
reproduced in color
on p. 35

his strategic manipulation of publicity, and his perception of the creation of art as a total process indicate his true genius. His fervent involvement in every aspect of the statue's realization was a step toward expanding the artistic mentality to see process as integral to creation. In treating each phase of the statue's creation as a public performance, he anticipated the «happenings» of the 1960s. Radically different though his end result was, Bartholdi could be described as a forerunner to Christo (cat. 14), who likewise perceives the entire process as the work of art, and legal negotiations as no less integral to the creation than sketches envisioning the fruits of his imagination. And for both Bartholdi and Christo, site and scale are indispensable to the definition of form.

Bartholdi's penchant for the colossal reveals more than a question of taste: it characterizes a mode of thinking. The artist thought in vast and long-range terms, in which his every work of art, colossal or not, was a component in the building of a great career. The energies that he focused on achieving the statue had a dual motive. Without minimizing the sincerity of his commitment to the Franco-American Union, it can also be noted that the occasion offered him an opportunity to establish a reputation as the definitive maker of great monuments. Bartholdi lost no opportunity to present himself in this light. The «dollhouse» maquettes of the construction of the statue (cat. 251, 252) were the miniature stage by which he could educate potential patrons about the fabrication of his grand ideas, to enthral them with the dynamics of production that justified the heavy expenditures. The Gontrand *Album* (cat. 15) recorded for posterity the making of a historic art work, but Bartholdi used it as a pretext for currying patronage from great princes and heads of state. It was certainly to this end that he asked Richard Butler for a copy of the *Inauguration* book bound in the «chic américain» to offer the president of the Republic.[2] Bartholdi may even have dictated history to support his objectives, as there is no mention prior to his 1885 publication (cat. 379) of that famous 1865 dinner party at Laboulaye's chateau.

Because the persona of the artist was so thoroughly entwined with the implementation of his vision, the two became synonymous. *Liberty* was more often than not referred to as his, and even official events used the artist's name to identify their purpose, such as the Brooklyn Art Association's exhibition «in aid of the Bartholdi Pedestal Fund» (cat. 369). Bartholdi knew well that too much attention was deflected from the Franco-American Union to him. Gratified as he might feel by the recognition of his role, this emphasis ultimately detracted from the fundamental premise of international reciprocity that was the statue's «raison d'être.» And he sensed the damage that might result from the impression that he was an opportunist who exploited his benefactors for self-glorification. He voiced his concerns to William Maxwell Evarts, who he hoped could make the press aware of the inappropriateness of labelling the monument «Bartholdi's Statue.»[3] The circumstances were beyond anyone's control, however, and the next two years saw an acceleration of the association

of Bartholdi's name with his figure. The sculptor found himself the hero of a veritable cult, generating a Bartholdi Club, which the sculptor vaguely remembered authorizing, and a Bartholdi Day.[4] His name was appended, presumably at no profit to him, to a hotel and an inn in New York City; later, the main street of Butler, New Jersey (named after Richard Butler) was to be called Bartholdi Avenue.

Bartholdi brought to his project another immeasurable strength: he was driven by the commitment to an idea whose time had come. The decade of the statue's realization witnessed the widespread acceptance of the public monument as an expression of collective values. Since the late eighteenth century, the commemorative monument had gained a new dimension with the evolution of egalitarian attitudes that were reshaping the social and political structure of Western civilization. Enlightened thinkers espoused monuments in the service of their ideals, and the monument's destiny was bound to the democratization and secularization of so-

14
Wrapped Coast—Little Bay Australia 1969 (One Million Square Feet) Christo; co-ordinator John Kaldor 1969

15
Dedication page of *Album des Travaux de Construction de la Statue Colossale de la Liberté destinée au Port de New-York*
Paris: Gontrand, Reinhard et Cie., 1883

ciety that characterized the nineteenth century. The more tolerant liberalism of the 1880s ushered in a new era for the public monument, which by the turn of the century had become so popular it warranted the appellation of «statuomania.»

An ardent republican and patriot, Bartholdi aspired to create a monument that, as he put it, would possess «great moral value,» a celebration of the virtues of freedom. His wish to encircle *Liberty* with the portraits of American worthies was an extension of the pedagogical idealism of the Enlightenment (cat. 16). He wrote to Butler in 1890: «My idea has always been that it would be in the future a kind of Pantheon for the glories of American Independence. That you would build around the monument of Liberty the statues of your great men, and collect there all the noble memories.»[5] Faith in the instructive mission of public art in fact provided the rationale for honorific monuments into the twentieth century.

In addition to its symbolic value, the statue was originally intended to function also as a lighthouse, which made the torch a dual metaphor, alluding to its role as both a spiritual and a practical beacon. Even aside from the statue, torch imagery was becoming synonymous with the progress so dear to Bartholdi's contemporaries, as indicated by Antonio Rosetti's frivolous *Genius of Electricity* (cat. 17) at the Philadelphia Centennial. That *Liberty*'s torch was to be illuminated by electricity at the 1876 fair further asserted its modernity in the context of an international display calculated to glorify the latest achievements of science and art. *Liberty* not only celebrated technical prowess, the statue embodied it literally.[6] It combined the aesthetic, didactic, and functional in a form that used the most up-to-date techniques of structural and electrical engineering. Whereas twentieth-century critics tend to deprecate Bartholdi's figure as too conventional, his contemporaries praised it as innovative. The statue itself became a frequent symbol for progress in industrial wares (cat. 18). *Liberty*'s proximity to the recently completed Brooklyn

Bridge augmented its claim to be an icon of the achievements of civilization. As the bridge became an emblem of America's «Manifest Destiny» (cat. 19), so *Liberty* was to radiate that vision to distant shores.[7] That role made *Liberty* the appropriate inspiration for the colossal plaster *America*, which ornamented the inaugural ball of James Garfield on March 4, 1881, «grasping a large electric light in her uplifted hand, «indicative of the skill, genius, progress and civilization of the nineteenth century.»[8]

On the heels of progress came a man-made access to heights, the audacity of which took the viewer's breath away. Even before the statue's completion, the torch (cat. 20) was hailed as a viewing platform, a quaint prototype of such twentieth-century towers as London's and Seattle's.[9] *Puck* seized upon the humor of the nineteenth century's craze for views from these technological wonders when it suggested a composite—the Brooklyn Bridge, the Eiffel Tower, and *Liberty* (cat. 21).

16
Bartholdi's Design for the Statue
From *The Daily Graphic*
October 27, 1886

17
Genius of Electricity
Antonio Rosetti
1876

Bartholdi understood the demands of colossal sculpture. *Liberty*'s greatness resides in Bartholdi's ability to synthesize the specifics of his image into broad planes and sweeping lines. Not an «object» intended for intimate scrutiny, the statue must be considered in its entirety from a distance, preferably on a moving craft—as Bartholdi intended (cat. 7). What seems bland when confronted in close detail becomes from afar part of the serene grandeur that enables *Liberty* to dominate the harbor, even against today's dramatically more pronounced cityscape.

Given Bartholdi's self-glorification and showmanship, it is not surprising that his life and work bear overtones of fantasy, or at least of the fictive creations of literature. His was an age appropriate for grand ideas. During the nineteenth century the rapid development of industry and technology opened up undreamt-of possibilities in the arts, sciences, and applied disciplines. Engineers like Roebling and Eiffel designed stunning bridges and other large-scale structures. Naval architects experimented with

18
Announcement Card
American Institute. 51st
Grand National Industrial
Exposition
1882

19
*American Progress
(Manifest Destiny)*
John Gast
1872

20
*The Torch of the Statue of
«Liberty,» as It Will Appear
When Completed, on
Bedloe's Island*
From *Frank Leslie's
Illustrated Newspaper*
June 20, 1885

21
*Puck's Patent Plan for a
Tremendous Tower at the
Great Fair*
From *Puck*
ca. 1889

Puck's Patent Plan for a Tremendous Tower at the
Great Fair.

Combine the Present Famous Features of the Harbor in
One Stupendous Pile.
Balloon Communication Every Fifteen Minutes.

steam propulsion and the use of iron and steel to replace wood; and in the case of Isambard Kingdom Brunel designed and built the ship of the future—the *Great Eastern* (cat. 22)—for the astonishment of a world not yet jaded by sheer size or scale. With the *Great Eastern* and the Statue of Liberty, not to mention the Brooklyn Bridge, the previous generation's fantasies or imaginings became real. Only in the realms of art and literature, perhaps, was it still possible to find visionaries whose minds could stay ahead of the onrushing technological surge. The name that comes readily to mind here is of course that of Jules Verne, who was not only Bartholdi's contemporary but also his compatriot.

Was it mere coincidence that two men should appear in France at the same time to create marvels of copper or words that test the bounds of reality? What did they share in their outlook, and how did they differ, these two manipulators of the fantastic? These are not idle questions in the context of the Statue of Liberty, for if we are to appreciate fully how that monument came to be, and what it meant for its age, we must begin with a consideration of the phenomenon of creative fantasy.

The first (and to our knowledge the only) observer to remark on the affinities between *Liberty* and Jules Verne's *Extraordinary Journeys* is Marvin Trachtenberg, who has unearthed in the novel *Robur the Conqueror* (publication of which began, by coincidence, in 1886 but was not completed until 1891) not merely an allusion but an explicit reference to the Statue of Liberty.

The novel opens with a mystery: the same flag, black and bearing a golden sun surrounded by stars, has been discovered simultaneously at the very top of each of mankind's tallest structures.

In the course of a single week the burghers of Hamburg at the top of St. Michael's tower; the Turks, on the tallest minaret of Agia Sophia; the Rouennais, on the metal spire of their cathedral; the Strasbourgeois, at the highest point of the Münster; the Americans, on the head of their Statue of Liberty at the mouth of the Hudson and at the summit of the Washington Monument in Boston [sic]; the Chinese, on the pinnacle of the Temple of Five Hundred Genii at Canton; the Hindus, at the seventh level of the pagoda of Tanjore; the Romans, atop the cross of St. Peter's; the English, on the cross of St. Paul's in London; the Egyptians, at the point of the Pyramid of Gizeh; the Parisians, on the lightning-conductor of the three-hundred-meter iron tower erected for the Exposition of 1889—all beheld the self-same flag streaming from each of these almost-inaccessible elevations.[10]

This catalog of the world's highest monuments bears witness to Verne's preoccupation with the colossal, the gigantic, the superhuman. The author's taste for great scale is his most obvious characteristic, and it often provides the mainspring of his plots. The *Nautilus*, for example, travels *Twenty Thousand Leagues Under the Sea* (1870); Phileas Fogg needs only eighty days to go around the world (1874). *A Floating City*

22
Great Eastern
Pannemeker and P. Ferat
From Jules Verne's *Une Ville flottante*, 1926 ed.

23
Albatros
L. Benett and G. Roux
From Jules Verne's *Robur le Conquérant*, 1886 ed.

1
Edouard de Laboulaye
ca. 1865

3
Alexis de Tocqueville
Théodore Chasseriau
1850

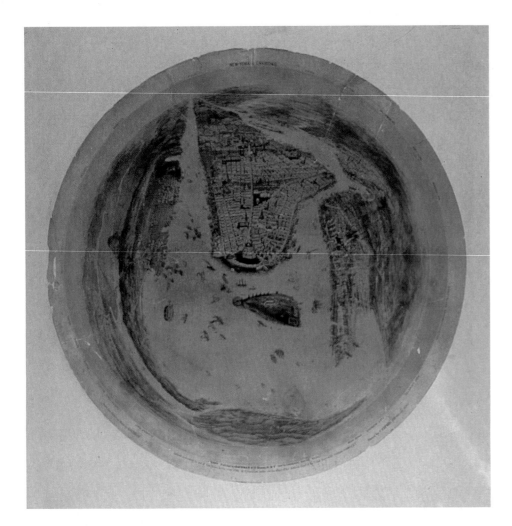

5
New-York & Environs
Bachman
1850

7
La Statue de la Liberté
en place
Frédéric-Auguste Bartholdi
n.d.

13
Faunes et nymphes effrayées
par un train
Frédéric-Auguste Bartholdi
n.d.

37

31

98

97

37
Jeanne Bartholdi
Jean Benner
1884

31
Charlotte Bartholdi
Ary Scheffer
1855

98
*Frédéric-Auguste Bartholdi
with the Legion of Honor*
Joseph Frappe
n.d.

97
Frédéric-Auguste Bartholdi
Jean Benner
1886

(1872) introduces the *Great Eastern* (cat. 22), a real vessel which at that time was the largest ever constructed, and of which Victor Hugo writes in *Le Légende des Siècles*:

> Her anchor weighed like a tower; her
> bulwarks
> Sought the sea, for no landward
> portal was wide enough
> to let them pass.[11]

There were other bonds as well between the two men: both were fascinated by the sea. In Bartholdi's case this resulted not only in two projects (the Suez lighthouse and the Statue of Liberty) whose pedestals are washed by its waves, but in ten crossings of the Atlantic (in 1871, 1876, 1877, 1885, 1886, and 1893) and four of the Mediterranean (1856 and 1869). The lighthouse theme was often treated by Verne also; it crops up not only in *The Lighthouse at the End of the World* (1905) but also earlier, in *Twenty Thousand Leagues Under the Sea*, *The Mysterious Island* (1895), and *Robur the Conqueror*, and finally in *Master of the World* (1904), as the *Albatros* (cat. 23).

Of all the devices born of the engineer's fertile imagination, it is the train that figures prominently in more than twenty of Verne's novels: it is no less prominent in Bartholdi's early photographs of America. Trains have an affinity with the concept of gigantic scale: they allow great distances to be covered quickly, and in particular they open up to the traveler the whole immense extent of the United States. A train carried Phileas Fogg from San Francisco to New York at the end of 1872; the completion of the transcontinental line in May 1869 enabled Bartholdi, in 1871, to take it in fact, though in the opposite direction. His photographs betray a lively interest in railroad bridges (cat. 24) and in strange machines such as the snowplow train (cat. 25), as impressive as the *Epouvante* (cat. 26) which figures in Verne's *Master of the World*. Elevators, airships, and even balloons (Bartholdi's *Monument aux Aéronautes du siège de Paris* [1904; cat. 27]; Jules Verne's *The Question of Balloons* [cat. 28], illustration for *Robur the Conqueror*) are so many devices for counteracting the force of gravity, for annihilating distance, for dominating the countries of the world. No Universal Exposition was complete without some spectacular ascent for its visitors. Bartholdi had in his possession a series of views of the Chicago Exposition of 1893, where the Balloon Ascent challenged the Great Wheel for preeminence (cat. 29). By elevator or stairway visitors could reach a «panoramic viewpoint»—a concept to which Bartholdi

24
*Transcontinental
Train on
Bridge*
Frédéric-Auguste Bartholdi
n.d.

25
*Snowplow
Train*
Frédéric-Auguste Bartholdi
n.d.

26
Epouvante
F. Duplessis and G. Roux
From Jules Verne's *Maître
du monde*, 1904 ed.

pledged allegiance no fewer than five times: in 1876 in Philadelphia, where visitors could climb to the gallery of the Statue of Liberty's torch; in 1878 in Paris where he similarly permitted access to her crown; in 1879 when he constructed a diorama at the Tuileries; in 1886 in New York, when he retained in the finished statue the openings in the diadem and the stairway within the arm that holds the torch; and in 1900 when he placed a diorama in the pedestal of his reduced-scale statue in plaster (cat. 283).

The last and best reason for comparing the two men is that Bartholdi *was* a character out of Jules Verne. In *Robur the Conqueror* there is a portrait of him, touched up a little but in most respects quite accurate:

> My name is Robur; I am a citizen of the United States. . . . I am forty years old, though I look no more than thirty; my constitution is of iron, my health excellent, my physique muscular, my digestion one that an ostrich might envy. . . . You see before you an engineer whose spirit is in no way inferior to his person. I fear nothing and nobody. The strength of my will has never yet yielded to another's. When my purpose is once fixed it would be vain for all America—for the whole world—to attempt to stand between me and it. When I have a notion, I intend that all should concur in it, and I will brook no contradiction. . . .[12]

Like all French popular writers before World War II, Verne was a nationalist. His character Michel Ardan (an anagram of the name of his close friend the photographer Nadar) is the indispensable craftsman who contributes the most to the success of the journeys *From the Earth to the Moon* and *Around the Moon* (1872). He might well be an idealized Bartholdi: «A Frenchman, a Parisian, a whimsical man, an artist both witty and daring, was seeking to shut himself inside a projectile so that he could be shot to the Moon and reconnoiter Earth's satellite. The name of this fearless explorer was Michel Ardan. He went to America, was greeted with enthusiasm, held public meetings, was carried shoulder-high in triumph. . . .»[13] Ardan is the engineer-hero of a scientific fantasy; it was the real, historical achievements of men such as de Lesseps and Eiffel which alone could make Robur or Captain Nemo plausible. By 1886 Verne was figuring as the prophet of things to come, declaring: «We know today that Robur is the science of the future, perhaps even of tomorrow; quite certainly this is in store for us. . . . As to the future of aerial locomotion, it lies with the dirigible rather than with the balloon.»[14]

Both Bartholdi and Verne were eager to add to the legendary list of Wonders of the World, but they approached the task in different ways. It is true that for the writer the Mysterious Island was «the Ninth Wonder of the World, since the Eiffel Tower must surely be esteemed the Eighth»; nevertheless «to create an artificial island which moves on the face of the waters—is not this to pass beyond the boundaries set around human invention? Is it not forbidden to man, who has no power over the winds and the waves, to tread so close on his Creator's heels?»[15] It is significant that at the end of his novels Verne destroys a goodly number of the fantastic creations he describes in such wealth of detail and for which he contrives so much scientific corroboration. He allots no fewer than three chapters to the end of the Mysterious Island, and devotes as much ingenuity to its destruction as he did to its creation. The *Nautilus* is sucked down into the maelstrom at the end of *Twenty Thousand Leagues Under the Sea*; she resurfaces in *The Mysterious Island* only to perish forever at the end of the book along with the Island itself—that artificial Paradise which its inhabitants (and the author) had taken forty chapters to create. The same fate befalls the steel giant in *The House of Steam* and the balloon in *Five Weeks in a Balloon*. The *Albatros* disappears in *Robur the Conqueror*: «I go, taking my secret with me,» declares the hero, but he reappears in *Master of the World*, along with *l'Epouvante*, which the author destroys in its turn because it has been witness and accomplice to Robur's insane ambition.

We should view this obsessive destruction of huge and wonderful creations in the light of Philippe Roger's analysis, in the epilogue to the present work, of the pictures of the Statue of Liberty destroyed. To the sculptor, on the contrary, the example of classical antiquity is seen as a pledge made to eternity, and at the same time a challenge to be taken up with the means available to him and to his age—means which owe everything to the inventive energy of men of unbounded genius.

27
Monument aux Aéronautes du siège de Paris . . .
Frédéric-Auguste Bartholdi
1904

28
The Question of Balloons
L. Benett and F. Delangle
From Jules Verne's *Robur le Conquérant*, 1886 ed.

29
The Balloon Ascent at the Chicago Exposition
Frédéric-Auguste Bartholdi
1893

Prelude

Frédéric-Auguste Bartholdi was born at Colmar, in Alsace, on August 2, 1834, the younger son of an affluent family that drew its income from real estate and commercial and professional endeavors. Protestants of long standing, the Bartholdis had risen over many generations from the lower middle class to the brink of real importance. Through Auguste his immediate family gained a glory beyond that of any other Bartholdis.

Auguste's father, Jean-Charles, appears in a Rossbach portrait (cat. 30) whose mediocrity is matched by the lack of expression on the subject's face. He owed his post as a counsellor at the Prefecture to his Army service at the time of the first Restoration, and lived in a large house at 30, rue des Marchands—now the Musée Bartholdi—handed down through his mother, Catherine-Dorothée Meyer, from her father, Étienne Meyer. Nearby was the pharmacy, Le Soleil, which Jean-Charles's paternal grandfather, Gilles-François, owned; the sculptor kept the pharmacy's signboard, which can still be seen in his reconstructed study (cat. 57).

1.
Bartholdi in His Context

Pierre Provoyeur with the assistance of Jacques Betz

30
Jean-Charles Bartholdi
Martin Rossbach
n.d.

31
Charlotte Bartholdi
Ary Scheffer
1855
reproduced in color
on p. 36

J. M. Schmitt has traced the family back to the first mention of a Barthold, in the Palatinate in 1578.[1] He was a Lutheran minister in Bavaria, his son a tailor at Frankfurt-am-Main, and his grandson a pastor in the region of Hesse. It was his great-grandson, Jean-Georges, who made the move to Alsace, first to Strasbourg, where he submitted his thesis in theology, then to Soultz-sous-Forêts, and finally to Wissembourg, where he died in 1733. Through him the family came to be called Barthold*i*, a Latinized form according to the custom of Protestant schools in the Rhineland.

The memory of these three Lutheran pastors[2] must have influenced their descendants, although the immediately following generations, beginning with Gilles-François, branched out into the fields of medicine and pharmacy or banking and shopkeeping. During the 1830s Auguste's father became the family's first civil servant. In Auguste's generation two cousins—Frédéric-Henri, born in 1823, and Philippe-Amédée, born in 1830—successfully pursued government careers, one as chief reporting official of the Audit Office and the other as Minister Plenipotentiary to Washington. Their sister married a Protestant banker, Alphonse Mallet, and her son married into a family of financiers, Poupart de Neuflize. Auguste's older brother had a brief career as an attorney. These flights to higher social levels led various family members to move to Paris, but not Jean-Charles, who remained at Colmar because of his post at the Prefecture.

The most remarkable career in the family, and one that affected the life of Auguste, was that of his great-uncle, Jacques-Frédéric, grandfather of Frédéric-Henri and Philippe-Amédée. He married an heiress to the cotton mills of Soehnée the Elder and Co., and when these mills passed into the hands of Hartmann and Son in 1818 he opened a bank in Paris, entered the fire insurance business, and became president of the Compagnie Royale d'Assurances Générales. He remained faithful to his church as a member of the Lutheran synod of Paris and an active member of various religious organizations. His daughter married Frédéric-Sigismond de Berckheim, a landowner from near Colmar and a member of the Chamber of Deputies from the Department of the Haut-Rhin; after his death she remarried, to Marquis

Adolphe de Boubers, a highly placed official and later councillor-general of the department under the Second Empire. Jacques-Frédéric was at the height of his influence during the 1860s, just when his great-nephew Auguste was looking for public and private commissions to further his career as a sculptor. Another supporter, who influenced Mme. Bartholdi's later decision to move to Paris, was the Countess Walthers, a cousin of Jean-Charles and mother of Frédéric-Henri and Philippe-Amédée; she was also prominent in Protestant affairs.

This network of family and social connections buoyed Auguste's rise both in his native province and in Paris, where he was taken as a child. His father, Jean-Charles, died at age forty-four in 1836, leaving his widow, Charlotte, and two sons, six and two years old. Charlotte emerged at once as a superior woman, well suited to face adversity. She was born in 1801 to the family of the mayor of Ribeauville, who was also a shopkeeper. The village, nestled against an old fortress overhanging the Alsatian plain, appears in a large portrait of Charlotte done after her husband's death in 1836 (cat. 31). The picture's composition expresses a sense of dignity, as well as a pretension to aristocracy reflected in the antique red draperies, the wide black satin gown, and the book, surely a Bible, evoking study and prayer, for Charlotte too was an ardent Protestant.

A sense of duty combined with business acumen marked Mme. Bartholdi's management of the family inheritance—the outlying land, the large house on the rue des Marchands in Colmar, the house next door with its ground-floor pharmacy.[3] Her prudence made possible a comfortable life for Auguste, who could pursue his career without having to depend on commissions, especially those from the state, which then as now were slow to be given and slow to be paid.[4] This freedom, however, increased the young artist's dependence on his mother, an emotional bond intensified by Charlotte's having lost two children in infancy in the years immediately preceding Auguste's birth,[5] the loss of the father, and the tragic rift between Charlotte and Auguste on one side and the surviving brother, Jean-Charles, on the other.

Jean-Charles was born in 1830, studied law in Paris, and was admitted to the bar in 1855. A photograph (cat. 32) taken at Colmar in 1860 (although he was then practicing in Paris) shows him to advantage. He enjoyed the arts and in Alsace published a review of historical studies. In his native city he entered into a liaison with a married woman, Fanny Spire, and incurred debts that his disapproving mother refused to pay. He suffered a breakdown in the early 1860s, and even tried once to shove Auguste off a moving train.[6] Stripped of his civil rights in 1863, he was shortly thereafter confined with an attendant to a small house at Vanves, where he died on April 1, 1885.

An uncompromisingly moralistic and authoritarian aspect of Charlotte Bartholdi appears in a photograph (cat. 33) taken late in life. Her notions about how her sons should marry were so unenlightened that she tried to arrange a match for Auguste while he was away on his second journey to Egypt in 1869; she had gone so far as to send out invitations when Auguste protested and escaped the match.[7] Despite her attempts to dominate him, Auguste did not rebel. An unusually full correspondence suggests the need mother and son felt for each other; they even sometimes wrote brief notes to say they lacked time for longer letters. The artist seems to have lived entirely for his work, using it and his filial devotion to compensate for the lack of a woman his own age. His mother, concerned, urged him, although more subtly than before, to visit the Protestant community during a trip to Bordeaux, in the hope that he might find a mate.[8] Auguste, now thirty-six, again turned a deaf ear.

32
Charles Bartholdi
E. Adam
1860

33
Madame Charlotte
Bartholdi
Frédéric-Auguste Bartholdi
n.d.

Two portraits of the young Auguste show him walled by silence behind a dreamy or fixed facial expression (cat. 34 and 35). A third portrait (cat. 36) shows him with his mother, pointing out something in a book and associating her visually, as he did in his letters, with his projects. The painting by Glück (1859) dates from a little after Auguste's first journey to Egypt; the photograph probably from before the second journey, near 1865; and the portrait with his mother perhaps from 1870, shortly before he joined the Garde National (cat. 77) and ordered cat. 76a–c, which are so close to it.

Given the extremely close ties between mother and son, the story of Auguste's marriage is amazing. He became involved with Jeanne-Emilie Baheux du Puysieux either just before Jeanne left France in 1871 or in America, where she took up residence as the adopted daughter of a Mrs. Walker. Her arrival in the United States coincided with Bartholdi's first trip there in 1871, and a letter from Auguste to his mother of October 30, 1876, suggests that the artist and his future bride met at that time. Until then Charlotte Bartholdi knew nothing of her son's daring and rather pathetic liaison; the letter was intended to appeal to her softer feelings and to prepare her for the marriage, which took place on December 20, 1876, before the couple's return to Paris. Mme. Bartholdi had just time enough to assure herself that her future daughter-in-law was a Protestant.[9] As to Jeanne's other qualities, her son urged her to take the word of the LaFarges, friends who may have been part of the conspiracy.

Auguste had chosen a woman who would give no trouble to him and no offense to his mother. In one letter he assured his mother that Jeanne was neither beautiful nor ambitious but merely warm-hearted.[10] That Jeanne understood the complexities of her new family is suggested by the line that Auguste took with his mother: «Her [Jeanne's] only concern is to have your affection. . . . On Christmas Day when we left church she told me: «I did not understand the minister, but I prayed all the time for your mother to like me.»[11] The official portrait of Jeanne, by Benner (cat. 37), accompanies that of Auguste, duly decorated with the Legion of Honor (cat. 98). A slightly later photograph (cat. 38) reveals the overwhelming good will of a woman

fated to live in an artist's shadow and present only to satisfy the needs of convention. The names of Auguste and his wife appear together on formal invitations (cat. 39) and a menu, but in daily life the couple yielded to his mother, not without clashes.

Bartholdi's biographers agree that his mother was probably his only love. This may explain his desire to protect her from information that might diminish him in her eyes, as when he tried to assure her that his meeting with Jeanne in America was a romantic accident, not a coolly calculated act designed to secure the marriage of his choice at a distance where his mother could not prevent it. Perhaps, also, a certain penchant for embroidery of the facts is not surprising in so ambitious a man. Years later he would skillfully make a show of the construction of the statue, offering to the public—with his mother the most privileged of the onlookers—the idealized image of a man in command of his projects and ready to use his inspiration to achieve success.

Apprentice Years

Mme. Bartholdi deserves full credit for encouraging the vocations of her two sons. They both showed an early talent for drawing, which was cultivated through school studies, although the courses that Auguste took at the Lycée Louis-le-Grand beginning in 1843 were mediocre (Schmitt has noted a sketchbook in which Auguste made retaliatory caricatures of his teachers).[12] Jean-Charles studied painting with Ary Scheffer, who played an important role in Auguste's training as well.[13] During holidays in Alsace, Auguste took drawing lessons from Martin Rossbach, who taught at the Collège de Colmar and was probably a family friend since he made the portrait of Jean-Charles reproduced here (cat. 30). Later Auguste sculpted a monument to his master; the plaster model (cat. 40) was still in his collection at the time of his death. Drawn equally to the brush and the chisel, Auguste painted the coast of Normandy during a holiday stay in 1847 and views of London in 1851. A taste for landscape that emerged at this time drew him to another family friend, the painter Gustave Jundt,[14] whose bust he sculpted in 1884 (cat. 41) as preparation for a funerary monument erected in 1886.[15] According to Gschaedler, Auguste's study of sculpture began with little bread figures and continued more seriously with a period in the Paris studio of Etex, where he was exposed to monumental art.[16] Etex, who was finishing the bas-relief of the Arc de Triomphe—a new expression of the First Empire's colossal style—taught at the École des Beaux-Arts and belonged to official art circles.

Among his master's creations, Bartholdi must have worked on the preparation, begun in 1842, of a *Monument à Vauban*, intended for the dome of Les Invalides, a sketch of which is in the Louvre (RF 2189). Etex sculpted many portrait busts of great men for public buildings and squares, among them a *Général Lecourbe* in 1852–57 for Lons-le-Saulnier; a *Puget* for a facade of the Louvre;[17] and a bust of Ferdinand de Lesseps in 1868. From Etex, Bartholdi must have learned not only the rules of art but also ways of obtaining government commissions. Then, in the early 1850s, he frequented the studio of Soitoux, another member of the École des Beaux-Arts, who was active in the design of the symbolic figure of *La République* and submitted a small-scale finished version to the competition of 1848.[18] Soitoux's prize-winning project represented a classically draped standing figure, the head surmounted by a star, wreathed with laurel, and bearing a band inscribed «République démocratique

39
Dinner Invitation from Frédéric-Auguste and Jeanne-Emilie Bartholdi
n.d.

38
Jeanne-Emilie Bartholdi
Frédéric-Auguste Bartholdi
n.d.

40
Maquette for the Monument to Rossbach
Frédéric-Auguste Bartholdi
1856

41
Bust of Gustave Jundt
Frédéric-Auguste Bartholdi
1884

du 24 Février.» With a sword the figure protects an altar topped by a hive and a mason's level, from which hangs a scroll bearing the words «Constitution française.» Critics commented on the work's classical inspiration while regretting its overdependence on the caryatids of the Louvre. Soitoux completed the work, but the Second Republic was swept away and the model went into a warehouse.[19]

There is no doubt that Bartholdi observed the master's work. The band that falls in two ribbons onto the shoulders and the double draping of the chiton and peplum both are reflected in the Statue of Liberty. The vicissitudes that befell Soitoux's works,[20] which were as famous in their day as Bartholdi's great statue was later to become, and the oblivion to which he was consigned after some of his statuary in the Tuileries was destroyed by the fire of 1871— none of this lessened the loyalty of his pupil, who helped create the *Monument funéraire de Soitoux*, topped by a cast of *La République* (cat. 42).[21] It was to Soitoux, Gautier, and his friend Simon that Bartholdi, in the will he drew up before leaving for the United States in 1876, confided the task of finishing the Statue of Liberty in the event of his death.

42
Tomb of J. Soitoux,
Montparnasse Cemetery
L. Villeminot
1892

In addition to his obvious indebtedness to academic sculpture, Bartholdi also owed much to other artists with whom he studied in Paris. The first was Ary Scheffer, the creator of the portrait of Charlotte Bartholdi mentioned earlier (cat. 31).[22] Scheffer was a Protestant from the Netherlands who settled in Paris in 1810 and was perhaps a friend of the Bartholdis living there. The reign of Louis-Philippe brought him political favor and great success, beginning in 1840, but after the king's abdication in 1848 he withdrew somewhat from public life, although he continued to entertain his artist friends—Chopin, Liszt, Rossini, and Gounod. In 1847 Jean-Charles Bartholdi entered his studio on the rue Chaptal and with him went the young Auguste, a student at the Lycée Louis-le-Grand.[23] Scheffer, who had a romantic ideal of Liberty during the Greek War of Independence—his *Femmes Couliotes* echoes Delacroix's *Massacres de Scio*—turned in 1840 to religious subjects.[24] In 1848, however, he participated in the competition for *La République*, as appears from a drawing, reminiscent of the Statue of Liberty, that resides in the museum of Dordrecht.[25] His political ideas ranged, then, from the liberalism cultivated before 1830 in the circles around Lafayette, whose lithograph portrait he made, to sympathy with the revolutionaries of the Three Glorious Days, insofar as they were responsible for the accession of Louis-Philippe d'Orléans to power. This sympathy enabled him to pass from the post of drawing teacher to Louis-Philippe's children to that of artistic advisor to the royal house and creator of several paintings for the new Galérie des Batailles. We cannot call Scheffer a republican, but his liberal monarchist ideas brought him close to Henri Martin, Charles Blanc, and Jules de Lasteyrie, who would later be members of the Franco-American Union;[26] the same ideas made him hostile to the Second Empire.

Of the works Bartholdi carried out in Scheffer's studio there remains cat. 43, copied after his master's composition *Les ombres de Francesca da Rimini et de Paolo Malatesta apparaissent à Dante et Virgile*. Since Scheffer copied or repeated this composition—here represented in the Louvre version (cat. 44), signed and dated 1855— some fifteen times, it must have been very successful at its first showing at the Salon of 1822. What is interesting for the present discussion is the translation from painting to sculpture and the way in which, through the depth of the cut and the use of relief in catching varying degrees of light, Bartholdi shaped the forms. Even more important is Ary Scheffer's teaching method: he in-

structed the young sculptor to copy not from nature (Bartholdi seems to have done no nude figures during this period) but from a finished work. Scheffer attached as much importance to drapery as to bodies, and began with the exterior envelope rather than internal structure. This follows the general trend of nineteenth-century painting. Earlier, in his *Serment du Jeu de Paume*, David showed himself a true heir of the classical school, which held that only a nude could reveal the movements of the body, but by the middle of the nineteenth century this theory was relegated to the past. The fact is relevant to the Statue of Liberty, for which it seems certain that no preparatory anatomical study was done: there is none in the Inventory of 1914 or in the Musée Bartholdi. Rather, like the *Françoise de Rimini*, the statue was inspired by ancient or contemporary models that were fully clothed. A brief review of Bartholdi's work reveals that it consisted largely of contemporary portraits that reflected the subjects' social rank and form of dress: Thiers (cat. 4) and Rossbach (cat. 40) are frock coats; Rapp (cat. 83) and Bruat, military uniforms. In essence, the Statue of Liberty is just drapery.

Along the same lines, Bartholdi's portrait of Scheffer (cat. 45), executed in 1862, four years after his death, is a collection of hints at the subject's greatness. The palette and brushes, the books, the nonchalant attitude, and the painstaking attention to dress all suggest the artist's exalted status. Indeed, he leans on a truncated column bearing the titles of all his works, listed like so many victories. The bronze's preparatory clay (cat. 46), which possesses an easier grace, reflects Bartholdi's earlier vision, that of a young man of twenty-eight.

The last teacher to influence Bartholdi (in the narrow sense, since he may have taken courses in architecture) was Eugène Viollet-le-Duc, whose name appears at various stages of the construction of the Statue of Liberty. No documentary evidence in the papers held by Viollet-le-Duc's descendants, no letters written by Bartholdi, allow a dating of their first meeting. Viollet-le-Duc's support to the government on the issue of reforming the curriculum of the École des Beaux-Arts in 1863 furnishes the earliest date when he could have met Bartholdi, who had signed a letter to the Emperor subscribed to also by Daubigny, Barye, Huet, and Baudet, and published in *Le*

Moniteur of November 29, 1863.[27] There is no reason to think, as some have suggested, that Edmond About introduced Bartholdi to Viollet-le-Duc in 1871 during About's visit to Colmar.[28]

If, as Trachtenberg says, Bartholdi was acquainted with Labrouste, the architect of the reading room of the Bibliothèque Nationale,[29] this may have marked the beginning of his interest in his two elders' metal architecture and its promise for the future. This would explain why Bartholdi called upon Viollet-le-Duc after 1869, when he had begun to concern himself with the supporting structure of his oversize monument.

It is clear from this survey of Bartholdi's apprentice years that he had little connection with the teaching methods of the École des Beaux-Arts. His studies were based largely on private lessons, doubtless because of his mother's jealous care and her financial means. We might regard him as a poor student condemned to make-up courses had he not won so much praise from his elders, who showed genuine interest in his curiosity, eagerness to learn, and achievements; his journey to Egypt in 1856 indicates that Gérôme and Bélly accepted him as an equal.

In the vast domain of monumental art Bartholdi made an early and fortunate choice: he selected the relatively unexploited field of colossal art, where a young man could produce original and spectacular results. Thus, paradoxically, the Statue of Liberty was created by a nonacademic Frenchman while its pedestal was designed by Richard Morris Hunt, the first American to enroll in the École des Beaux-Arts, where he was a brilliant student and an assistant to Lefuel on the Louvre additions in the mid-1850s. The best clue to Bartholdi's freedom from architectural canons, and also to the demands he made on them, an attitude derived from the practical consequences of Beaux-Arts teaching, lies in his drawings for *L'Égypte apportant la lumière à l'Asie* and for the pedestal of the Statue of Liberty. In 1881, when he was working with Hunt on the pedestal, Bartholdi let it be said about him: «Monsieur Bartholdi, like the artists of the Renaissance, believes that a sculptor is not complete unless he is also an architect.»[30] His whole work testifies to the degree to which he wanted to combine these two vocations.

43
Françoise de Rimini
Frédéric-Auguste Bartholdi, after Ary Scheffer
n.d.

44
Les ombres de Francesca da Rimini et de Paolo Malatesta apparaissent à Dante et à Virgile
Ary Scheffer
1855

45
Ary Scheffer
Frédéric-Auguste Bartholdi
1862

46
Ary Scheffer
Frédéric-Auguste Bartholdi
1862

In the discussion that follows, the word «studio» encompasses both the physical space and its contents, so that we may here combine and comment on a vivid collection of photographs of the artist, his residences, and his works. These photographs date from Bartholdi's middle and old age, and attest to his desire to «put himself on stage,» a practice common to nineteenth-century artists. The photographs also provide important information about his tastes, habits, and artistic methods.

By way of introduction, two photographs from his collection show Bartholdi during the years 1865–70, when men still wore the pencil mustache and short, narrow beard popularized by Napoléon III. A third photograph, in poor condition and therefore not included here, begins a trio that depicts a self-assured Bartholdi posing as an «artist»: first with books, then (cat. 47) with a statuette, and finally (cat. 48) with a portfolio. Most interesting of the accessories is the bronze statuette, a reduced model similar to the *Doryphore* of Polycletus in the National Museum of Naples.[31] The statuette quite possibly belonged to the photographer (it was customary at that time to pose the subject in an environment compatible with his social and professional status), since the statuette is not in the collection of the Musée Bartholdi at Colmar nor does it appear in any of the studio photographs discussed below. The statuette is important, however, for it is similar to the forms with which Bartholdi was experimenting in 1869–70 for the figures of *Égypte* and *Liberty*: free-standing and forward-leaning, though less so than the Tanagra figure (cat. 192) that the artist owned. These were the first professional photographs of the artist, intended to portray him to his contemporaries and also to posterity; a similar purpose attached to the photographs that follow, which are more personal.

Bartholdi had three main residences during his lifetime. First was the house at 30, rue des Marchands in Colmar, where he was born and which the family left in 1836, following his father's death; thereafter the family lived in Paris[32] but generally summered in Colmar. His mother eventually returned to Colmar, while her son remained in Paris, since, following the German annexation of Alsace in 1871, Bartholdi was reluctant to return to Colmar. When his mother turned eighty, she began to visit with her son and his wife for increasingly long periods; upon her death in 1891 Auguste inherited the Colmar house, which passed to his wife three years after his death in 1904.

Jeanne Bartholdi donated the house to the town on condition she be allowed to live out her life there. Jeanne died in 1914, but the transfer of the Bartholdi inheritance was not completed until 1918, following World War I, at which time Alsace was returned to France. The Musée Bartholdi, opened in the house in 1922, contains part of the contents of Bartholdi's last house in Paris, which have displaced some of the original furnishings, but only through photographs can we obtain any real impression of his Paris living and working arrangements.

Bartholdi's second Paris dwelling place, to which he moved in 1854, was at 40, rue Vavin, in the sixth *arrondissement*.[33] Several photographs of the interior of this house, which the artist left in 1892, following the death of his mother, were taken on the same occasion, judging from the attitudes of the human figures and other details, including Bartholdi's clothing, and can date from no earlier than 1886, since the *World* trophy that the sculptor received after the dedication of the Statue of Liberty appears mounted on a pedestal in one photograph (cat. 50). Charles Lefèbre offered a contemporary description: «Monsieur Bartholdi has settled on the rue Vavin, behind the Luxembourg, where he has built a small house, a real artist's nest, original in design, and inviting with its high windows and wrought-iron gratings. It has two entrances, one narrow, for visitors, the other very high, with double doors, which is opened only for the passage of statues. The studio is quite large and cheerful. The shelves are filled with a world of statuettes, reproductions, and sketches, which trace the artist's whole story.»[34] Indeed, the first photograph (cat. 49) reveals from left to right his 1858 project for a fountain for the Place des Quinconces at Bordeaux;[35] the statue of General Arrighi, erected at Corte in Corsica in 1868;[36] the *Vercingétorix* equestrian group, presented in 1870 and discussed below (cat. 66–69); the *Monument à les Victimes de Callao* (cat. 152);[37] and finally the project for a group sculpture entitled *Loisirs de la paix* or *Otia pacis*, interesting because it is one of the few Bartholdi works for which we have a nude study for a subject clothed in the final version.[38] On the cupboard to the right appears no. 124 of the 1914 inventory, a terra-cotta model 10¼ inches high that is at Colmar and «seems to represent,» according to its label, a *Projet de monument au Général Lafayette*.

47
Frédéric-Auguste Bartholdi with a Statuette
ca. 1865–70

48
Frédéric-Auguste Bartholdi with a Portfolio
ca. 1865–70

49
Bartholdi in His Paris
Studio
1886

50
Bartholdi Standing in Front
of His Sketches
1886

51
Bartholdi at His Easel
1886

A second photograph (cat. 50), showing another aspect of the studio and revealing part of the adjacent room (shown in cat. 51), presents several works connected with the Statue of Liberty: at the extreme left the *World* trophy; on the second shelf of the glass-doored display case a small model of *L'Égypte apportant la lumière à l'Asie* (a version mounted on a pedestal); and finally a Statue of Liberty, whose shading in the photograph suggests it is in clay, and one of the two *Modèles du Comité* still in the Musée Bartholdi.

The subject of cat. 51 is the next room, a veritable warehouse of sculptures as well as a study, where the artist had himself photographed while drawing. A bronze of his former teacher Ary Scheffer (cat. 45), with a filing cabinet as a pedestal, looks over his shoulder. On other pieces of furniture, from left to right, rest some trial bas-reliefs from the *Lion de Belfort*, a small version of the entire *Lion*, modelled in the round, and a small model of *La Saône emportant ses affluents*.[39] On the lowest shelf in front of the balustrade are a model for the *Jeune vigneron Alsacien*;[40] near the bust of Scheffer a small model of the *Égypte*; and the *Esquisse de la Statue allégorique de l'Alsace* (the final version is cat. 82).[41]

Against the balustrade, on the next shelf, from left to right, are a model (now lost) of the clock tower of the Brattle Street Church in Boston, for which Bartholdi in 1874 made the bas-reliefs illustrating «the four stages of a Christian life» (cat. 221); an unidentified bronze head; and then, side by side, *Vauban, Gribeauval*, the *Monument à l'Amiral Bruat*, the statue of *Rouget de l'Isle*, and, farther along, in the center, the *Monument au Général Lafayette*.[42] Perched on a little shelf to the left are the two models of *Jeanne d'Arc* (cat. 84 and 85), the *Tête du Général Rapp*—a reduced-scale model associated with Bartholdi's first public monument, designed at the request of his native city,[43] and the small project for a *Fontaine surmontée d'une arcature*, still in Colmar.[44] Finally, at the left a stool bears *Le Génie dans les griffes de la Misère* (cat. 58), the bronze currently on the stairway of the Colmar museum.

Some new pieces appear in a final photograph (cat. 52), in which Bartholdi had himself portrayed at work, although the work shown in the photograph is a finished piece: a *Buste d'homme* now in the storerooms of the Colmar museum.[45] The *Modèle du Comité* of the Statue of Liberty is a pendant to the less eclectic *Roesselmann* from the fountain built at Colmar in 1888.[46] The latter work is important as the first commission Bartholdi received after the Statue of Liberty; it was done for the Société d'Émulation et d'Embellissement of the city of Colmar, founded in 1883 and shortly thereafter presided over by Georges Kern, a member of the «Fidelity» Masonic lodge of Colmar and a friend of both Bartholdi and Colmar's Mayor Schlumberger. At approximately this time the sculptor had begun to choose his projects often on the basis of a covert desire to express or further the cause of Alsatian freedom from Germany. The statue of Roesselmann, a local hero who had once preserved the independence of Colmar from its neighbors' territorial ambitions, is an obvious allegory that bears the features of a former mayor, Peyerimhoff, who had ordered the *Fontaine Bruat* and had resigned from his post in 1877 out of hostility to the Germans.[47]

Other works also merit attention. In the lower part of the glass-doored sideboard are, from left to right, *La borne frontière*, the New York *Lafayette*, and the *Monument à Martin Schoengauer*.[48] Atop the sideboard sits a group of reduced models copied from Michelangelo—the *Moses* from the tomb of Julius II in Rome, the *Day* and *Night* from the Medici Chapel in Florence[49]—a commonplace trio in any nineteenth-century studio, yet also works that influenced several of Bartholdi's monumental forms, from the horizontal figures of the *Fontaine Bruat* to the *Neptune* of Bordeaux. The *Moses* was of interest to Bartholdi for its size; E. Lesbazeilles classes it, along with the *David* and the *Julius II*, as among Michelangelo's «colossal» works.[50] Aside from these objects, the storerooms of the Musée Bartholdi contain other important sculptures, including medieval figures from the tombs of Brou and Dijon and a head of Saint Louis from the Louvre; the *Agnes of Hergenheim*, Bartholdi's first known sculpture (ca. 1852), betrays the simplicity of his beginnings. In his Paris studio he gave an important place to the model of the *Monument funéraire de Paul Bert*,[51] which grew out of his friendship with a former cabinet minister of the Gambetta government. Bert, while resident general in Tonkin, Vietnam, was responsible for commissioning a 9-foot-high replica of the Statue of Liberty, furnished in 1887 by Thiébaut Frères for the city of Hanoi.[52]

These photographs give only a limited idea of the contents of Bartholdi's studio, all of which went to the museum in Colmar, where they remained virtually untouched until the reorganization of the museum in 1976. Some idea of the efforts made to give order to the collection when the museum opened in 1922 may be obtained from some old postcards in the collection of Jacques Betz. From them it is possible to determine that an arrangement of terraces enabled the visitor to see every model and thereby gain an immediate idea of the sculptor's extensive productivity. We, too, through one of the postcards (cat. 53) can see at a glance, from left to right and from top to bottom, the *Diderot*, the *Adieu au Pays*, the *Gambetta*, *Les loisirs de la paix*, the *Rouget de l'Isle*, the *Modèle du Comité*, *Lafayette* and *Washington*, and lower down an impressive collection of tombstones, preparatory models of the Statue of Liberty, and the *Malédiction de l'Alsace*. Up front appear the *Monument aux aéronautes du siège de Paris, aux héros des postes, des télégraphes, des chemins de fer et aux colombophiles de 1870–71* (cat. 27), *La Saône emportant ses affluents*, *Les grands soutiens du monde*, *le Travail*, *le Patriotisme*, *la Justice*, the *Lafayette*, the *Monument à la Mémoire des héros de l'Indépendance de 1830* (cat. 149), and finally the third version of *Vercingétorix* (cat. 66–69).[53]

A final group of photographs depicts the Bartholdi family in 1887–91. The three pictures were taken in what must have been the painting studio, but which was furnished as a music room, thus revealing Bartholdi as a musician, an interest not evident from his letters (Gschaedler records seeing Bartholdi's violin, an Amati, at Colmar sometime before 1966).[54] In one of the photographs (cat. 54), Bartholdi is accompanied at the piano by his wife or mother; the women wear dresses that look as heavy as the bulky furniture. In this photograph the *Lion de Belfort* has a conspicuous place; in cat. 55 it appears again but less prominently than the *Faunes et nymphes effrayées par un train* (cat. 13), which appears to be receiving its finishing brushstrokes at the

52
Bartholdi at Work on a Bust
1886

53
The Maquette Gallery at the Musée Bartholdi
Postcard photograph
n.d.

54
Bartholdi, His Wife, and His Mother in the Studio
ca. 1887–91

55
Bartholdi at His Easel
ca. 1887–91

56

Bartholdi with His Violin
ca. 1887–91

57

*The Colmar
Reconstruction of
Bartholdi's Studio, Rue
Vavin, Paris*
n.d.

artist's hand—some twenty years after its actual completion. The Statue of Liberty is there, of course, in the models (cat. 251 and 252) displayed for the admiration of visitors and seen by Charles Lefèbre in 1881.[55] Among new sculptures are the bust of William Maxwell Evarts,[56] a prominent member of the American Committee (see Chapter 8), and *La Petite Alsacienne,*[57] a tutelary figure recalling the sculptor's native area (cat. 56, at right).

Some of the atmosphere of the rue Vavin survives in the study as reconstructed in Colmar (cat. 57): the coat of arms sculpted by Bartholdi; the table; the mementoes of Bartholdi's journeys to Egypt; the books; the signboard from Le Soleil; and the models of the Statue of Liberty[58] and the *Lion de Belfort*. But we sense the absence of the spacious studios, the over-elaborate woodwork, and the Flemish pride of the decoration and embellishment that Bartholdi liked to surround himself with— frank expressions of a bourgeois artist's quintessence.

Bartholdi's Failures

Despite the considerable number of his creations, the honors showered upon him, and the authorship of two colossal works— the Statue of Liberty and the *Lion de Belfort*—Bartholdi has not come down to posterity as one of the great innovators of his century. Why has his name all but disappeared from historical and art-historical studies?

One answer lies, paradoxically, in the success of the Statue of Liberty. A work whose message was universal and whose image was powerful enough to withstand any attack, the statue far surpassed the intentions of its creator. However, after it left France, whose people had financed its construction and enthusiastically followed its progress, the statue was forgotten there. Three years later its place in the public eye was taken by another even more extraordinary colossus, the Eiffel Tower, which was solidly anchored on home ground. Once in New York, the statue no longer belonged to the

French. Its reassembly and pedestal had been financed by popular subscription and, once the inaugural lights were extinguished, it became the property of the American people. The power of the statue's symbolism soon supplanted Bartholdi's brief celebrity in the United States.[59]

Another reason for Bartholdi's eclipse lies in the nature of public statuary. Monuments in public squares and parks, sculptures on building facades, and funerary monuments—those specialties to which Bartholdi devoted his career—are conspicuous for the names of their subjects. The sculptor's name, usually consigned to the layer of bronze linking the sculptured figure to its base or pedestal, is not apparent to the viewer: the Statue of Liberty, according to Trachtenberg, bears the artist's signature hidden in a fold of the peplum.[60] Bartholdi is not the only creator of public monuments to be swallowed up by his works. The names of Carrier-Belleuse and Etex are enshrined only in the pages of art history, not in the fleeting attention of the public—and this despite their having altered cityscapes and thus influenced the local or national consciousness of a people.

There is yet another explanation: Bartholdi was not collected. His works have not made their way into, first, private collections and then into museums. The discussion above surveyed the models in Bartholdi's studio and reviewed the inventory of almost six hundred items drawn up after his death, and indicated that he had retained nearly all his preparatory sketches and models. The photograph of the Musée Bartholdi before its renovation (cat. 53) and the consignment of part of his work to storage offers a fascinating glimpse of the profusion of Bartholdi's works—half ultraconventional, half naïve. But it reminds us, too, that they are nowhere else to be seen. The pillage to which the Colmar collection was eventually subjected was a final blow. Bartholdi himself, the victim of mistaken calculations, made his work vulnerable in many respects, not the least of which was the gathering of it all in one place. It is somewhat ironic that when Bartholdi wanted to present something at the Salon of 1859, he chose a group entitled *Le Génie dans les griffes de la Misère* (cat. 58), a subject in no way autobiographical. This piece is an interesting variation on Auguste Dumont's *Génie de la Liberté* from the July Column in the Place de la Bastille. There are five clay models, four of which are included here (cat. 59).[61]

There is fine work in the torsions, the forward thrust, and the confrontation between the two figures, in the great tradition of Gian Bologna and his *Rape of the Sabines*. The style is more baroque than classical, as is often the case when the piece is to be in bronze. The modern eye, accustomed to seeing freshness and invention in a preparatory sketch, may overestimate these models. Nonetheless, they could «hold their own» in a museum and attract the attention of an art lover to an authentic effort and authentic skill.

Bartholdi's works include not only the Statue of Liberty, the *Lion de Belfort*, and a string of minor but far from negligible pieces—great men, portraits, funeral monuments, and patriotic allegories—but also several important but unrealized projects whose fulfillment might have modified our idea of the sculptor. Into this group fall at least eight projects, three of which were executed in a form different from that originally intended: the columns to the *Victimes de Callao*, to the *Indépendance de 1830*, and to the *Indépendance des États-Unis*; the Saint-Michel fountain; the fountain and decorative project for the Place des Quinconces at Bordeaux; the *Vercingétorix*; the decorative project for the Palais de Longchamps in Marseille; and the project for a *Monument à Gambetta* for the Palais Bourbon of Paris.[62] The connecting link among them is the mixture of architecture and sculpture and their colossal size.

The sculpture for the Place des Quinconces at Bordeaux was to be a great fountain 54 feet high and 72 feet in diameter, judging from the size of the two human figures placed in front of the model. The central *Neptune* draws on both Michelangelo's *Moses* and the Trevi Fountain in Rome; the figures on horseback are tritons, freely adapted from Roman models. The work suits the site of the Place des Quinconces, a large park dating from the eighteenth century, for whose hemicycle the circular fountain was intended, and it won first prize in the competition held by the city of

58
Le Génie dans les griffes de la Misère
Frédéric-Auguste Bartholdi
n.d.

59 a–d
Studies for *Le Génie dans les griffes de la Misère*
Frédéric-Auguste Bartholdi
n.d.

Bordeaux in 1858. The drawing (cat. 60) preserved in the Conservatoire National des Arts et Métiers, Paris, provides other details. Bartholdi collaborated with the architect Norbert Maillart, to whom, perhaps, are owed the columns that punctuate the perspective, and the lateral pavilions. Bartholdi displayed skill in adapting to the breadth of the hemicycle by embracing the tradition of the terraced basin, which knits the quiet horizontals of the background into a spiraled vertical. The sculptor drew upon classical Rome for the figures and Versailles for the terracing, while the basins derived directly from the *Rond d'Eau* of Hardouin-Mansart, all these styles being in harmony with the eighteenth-century character of Bordeaux. Unfortunately, the plan to recast the Place des Quinconces came to nothing, and Bartholdi was able to reuse his project, with considerable modification, only for the Place des Terreaux in Lyon. This was his first major defeat.

More misfortune awaited him in Marseille, where another fountain was the pretext for a gigantic project for ornamentation of the Plateau de Longchamp, terminus of the city aqueduct, where a new Fine Arts Museum and a Museum of Natural History were projected. The plan given to Bartholdi indicates that the first idea was to place the building on the plateau itself and to complete it with a water tower. Bartholdi upset this plan, combining the museums with the water tower around a fountain in the center, at the foot of the hill. He presented three projects, each one composed of a blueprint, an elevation, and a model. The choice was among different depths for the buildings and different sizes for the lateral wings or pavilions. In the progression from cat. 61 to cat. 62, Bartholdi increased the floor surface of the galleries but not that of the wings.

60
Project for the Decoration
of the Esplanade des
Quinconces, Bordeaux
Frédéric-Auguste Bartholdi
and Norbert Maillart
1858

Then, in cat. 63 he proposed two quadrangular wings, linked by the portico, and allowed for larger rooms in both museums. The first two projects were dominated by the water tower, behind them; the third gave greater importance to the central pavilion, which was to have a more ornate facade. The plan was not executed, and the embittered Bartholdi witnessed the arrival of a new architect, Henri Espérandier, who built first the church of Nôtre-Dame de la Garde, with a colossal Virgin atop it, and then an exhibition palace and water tower shamelessly derived from the designs of Bartholdi; Bartholdi brought a lawsuit, to which we owe the precious *Mémoire en défense* (cat. 64). The two museums are still housed there, but bear no mention of Bartholdi. Bartholdi had lost his first architectural project and the possibility of using it to obtain similar commissions. At the same time, the France of the Second Empire lost a talented architect, for in his projects for the Palais de Longchamp we can see his ability to add grandeur to the classical French line, a grandeur that, while not colossal, hints at it. As at Bordeaux, Bartholdi knew how to use a site to advantage.

In 1860 Bartholdi had another opportunity to create a monumental sculpture. The city of Paris held a competition for a fountain, six stories high, to ornament the point where the Boulevard Saint-Michel opens onto the Seine. In the storerooms at Colmar is a clay model that the Inventory of 1914 (no. 55; dated 1860) reveals as the *Projet de monument pour la Fontaine Saint-Michel,* Bartholdi's first equestrian monument. The terra cotta (cat. 65), like those of the preceding year, is vibrant and allusive; it has the same three features—a rock, a rider, and his horse—as Falconet's celebrated *Peter the Great* in Leningrad, but the serpent under the hooves of the Tsar's rearing horse has been transformed by Bartholdi into a dragon. The horizontal lines of the rock add to the power and invite the eye to travel upward. We do not know if the sponsors of the competition saw a more definitive model of Bartholdi's project; in any event, Francisque-Joseph Duret was declared the winner of the competition.

61
Maquette for the Palais de
Longchamp at Marseille
Frédéric-Auguste Bartholdi
n.d.

62
Maquette for the Palais de
Longchamp at Marseille
Frédéric-Auguste Bartholdi
n.d.

63
Maquette for the Palais de
Longchamp at Marseille
Frédéric-Auguste Bartholdi
n.d.

The challenge of an equestrian group maintained its interest for him. Before his first trip to Egypt nine years later, he presented to the Salon a *Vercingétorix* with the horse's hooves trampling a dead Roman soldier. The subject was not new; Millet had recently treated it, in chased copper from the Monduit workshop, on the summit of a hill overhanging Alix-Sainte-Reine, the ancient Alesia. The site left to Bartholdi was Gergovie, with its plateau and prehistoric dolmen raised toward the open sky. A photographic montage helps us imagine the composition (cat. 66), and a figure on the right demonstrates the size: the sculpted *Vercingétorix* is 36 feet high, the entire monument 57.

Two thoughts come to mind, both of them connected to the Statue of Liberty. The theme of the *Vercingétorix* is at once patriotic—the defense of Gaul, that is, France—and libertarian. In the context of 1869, on the eve of the Franco-Prussian War, the monument could be interpreted as a call for defense, congenial to Napoléon III. The title of the second model is, indeed, «A monument erected at Clermont-Ferrand to Vercingétorix and to the glory of Auvergne, where there arose the first cry of patriotism on French soil,» and a national subscription funded its erection. An alternative interpretation is that France, represented by the Gallic warrior, defeats the Roman, representing Caesar, making the group a cryptic protest against Caesarism and Napoléon III's Empire. Such an idea would appeal to the members of the liberal opposition with whom Bartholdi had been in touch since 1865, and to the dinner guests at Glatigny, where Bartholdi first met Edouard de Laboulaye. He surely took part in the effort of 1865–66 (suppressed by the authorities) to send Mary Todd Lincoln a medal «dedicated by French democrats to Lincoln»;[63] Michelet and Victor Hugo were among the most active proponents of the medal and signed the dedicatory letter. A monument the size of the *Vercingétorix* is not as discreet as a medal, but the sculptor's taste for the colossal spoke louder than politics or even prudence.

The monument in fact met with little enthusiasm. We do not know the verdict of the Académie des Sciences, Arts et Belles Lettres of Clermont-Ferrand, which initiated the idea; visitors to the Salon of 1870 held divided opinions about it. Bartholdi went on dreaming.

The documentation at Colmar shows his desire, if not to occupy the whole horizon, to continue his *Vercingétorix* in the vein of the colossal. We can reconstruct his next step, in an urban context, which he took of his own accord since he had no commission. The first version, obviously related to his earlier columns, produced a gigantic model (cat. 67) very close to the *Monument à l'Indépendance américaine*. The capitals and entablature are the same, but the effect of the whole is a bit ridiculous because of the

lack of proportion between the sculpture and its pedestal. Bartholdi divided it in two, gaining in depth what he lost in height (cat. 68). The model is in open work while the pedestal closely approaches that of Verrocchio's *Colleone* in Venice (cat. 69), with the horse suddenly carried away by enthusiasm. It was not only the pedestal that needed reduction, but the group as well. As erected in front of the University of Clermont-Ferrand (cat. 70), however, it is impressive. A series of models, which complete the project,[64] indicated that it steadily diminished in size, and when cast in 1901 made little effect on the square where it was inaugurated in 1903. Premier Emile Combes, with two of his Cabinet ministers, was there, but Bartholdi must have regretted the loss of the original site, at Gergovie. Of course, by then he had satisfied his aspiration to the colossal with the Statue of Liberty.

67

65

65
Project for the Monument for the St. Michel Fountain
Frédéric-Auguste Bartholdi
1860

66
Project for the *Vercingétorix*
Frédéric-Auguste Bartholdi
n.d.

67
Maquette for the *Monument élevé à Clermont-Ferrand à Vercingétorix*
Frédéric-Auguste Bartholdi
n.d.

68
Maquette for *Vercingétorix*
Frédéric-Auguste Bartholdi
n.d.

70
Monument à Vercingétorix
Postcard photograph
n.d.

CLERMONT-FERRAND
FAÇADE DE L'UNIVERSITÉ ET STATUE DE VERCINGÉTORIX (DE BARTHOLDI)

Bartholdi's last great setback, but perhaps his most ambitious staging, is the monument to Léon Gambetta in front of the Chamber of Deputies (now the National Assembly). A considerable number of drawings, photographic montages, and models suggest the breadth of the project and its vicissitudes.[65] It is large enough to be worthy of its subject, the republican hero Gambetta, whom Bartholdi may have met before the Franco-Prussian War, since Henri Martin, a member of the Glatigny group, later the core of the Franco-American Union, had since 1864 frequented the political salon of Mme. Adam, to which Gambetta also belonged. Bartholdi certainly could have approached his future subject when the sculptor volunteered his services to the republican government in Tours on October 4, 1870, three days before the arrival of Gambetta, fresh from liberating Paris by balloon, the first of those *Aéronautes* to whom Bartholdi dedicated a monument in 1904. The great man's death drove the artist to reflect on the republican mystique.

The development of nationalism in Europe at the end of the nineteenth century provoked the flowering of a number of «altars.» The *Bavaria* (cat. 119) of Munich is one; the monument to Victor-Emmanuel II in Rome is the most conspicuous and the closest to the great altars of ancient cities, stemming from the sanctuaries of classical Greece.[66] The reconstruction in Berlin of the Altar of Pergamon confirms the view, advanced without rash comparisons, that the phenomenon is, indeed, proper to the nineteenth century and its neoclassical roots.

Bartholdi lived through the period of the Republic's development and witnessed the efforts of liberal republicans on behalf of a system of constitutional law. Moreover, in 1875 he became a member of the Masonic lodge of Alsace-Lorraine; he was aware of a «secular mysticism» and obviously felt that he should furnish its shrines. The project for the Palais de Longchamp in Marseille exemplified this purpose, one pursued by all the architects of the century. We have clay models, dating from 1873,[67] of a major monument, of uncertain destination, which prefigures the *Gambetta* and indicates anew Bartholdi's desire to transcend pure sculpture by giving it a theatrical context. An earlier model, of his *Vauban*,[68] shows that he had the same concern in 1870. In the case of the *Gambetta* the proposed site—the facade of the Chamber of Deputies—made for its exceptional character; today the site

may seem inappropriate: the facade symbolizes an abstraction—the will of the people—that cannot be incarnated by any one political figure, even a national hero. A still later example shows the government consenting to the use of a universally significant and near-sacred public monument as the background for an individual artistic creation—the *Thinker* of Rodin, placed in 1906 in front of the Pantheon, on a base which, though less ambitious than the pediment Bartholdi proposed for his *Gambetta*, raised the mythical figure above the crowd and set it off against Soufflot's magnificent columns. It is true that the concern here was with the glory of Rodin, the sculptor, rather than the work itself, and that his abstract subject inspires loftier thoughts than the glorification of a single man.

Two photographs of Bartholdi's project provide an idea of his intentions. The first (cat. 71) is of a plaster model, placed in front of a canvas depicting the facade of the Chamber, created by Poyet.[69] The second (cat. 72) is of a drawing, probably engraved, of the monument as a whole in situ. A finished model exists in the museum at Colmar.[70] Bartholdi used the standard themes of his repertoire, such as the recumbent lion, symbol of resistance to invasion. Gambetta's arm is vehemently upraised in the projects for the Chamber of Deputies (cat. 71, 72, and 73 and the Colmar model, Inv. no. 54); it is folded against his chest, the artist's final choice, in cat. 74 and 75; and in both cases it is draped in the national colors. Bartholdi added the conventional Beaux-Arts symbols: flames, a tablet inscribed to Law, the female figure of the Republic wearing the Phrygian bonnet, and various ancient ornaments. Another photograph in the Musée Bartholdi bears the inscription: «Concours Gambetta—projet Bartholdi Devant la Chambre des Députés,»[71] which establishes that the sculptor did participate in an official competition, whose entries were all eventually discarded. Bartholdi's next model demonstrates more modest ambitions. The end product, in 1888, was a small monument, without access or flights of stairs and stripped of its character as a civic altar, which the people of Alsace-Lorraine, his official patrons, commissioned as a repository for the heart of Gambetta; it was financed by Mme. Paul Bert at Ville d'Avray.

We have seen how close Bartholdi was to
the Beaux-Arts tradition and how seldom he
was able to bear witness to it in the field of
his first vocation, architecture. Although his
funerary monuments resulted in little com-
pensation, they afforded him an opportunity
to utilize myriad references to great buildings of the past, and to give play to his
imagination in socles, pedestals, and columns. It is in the exploitation of sites, above
all, that he indulged in spectacular solutions: the *Lion de Belfort* and the Statue of
Liberty remain titles to glory, eclipsing by
far the *Vercingétorix* projected for Gergovie
and the apotheosis planned for *Gambetta*.
But they also overshadow a considerable
portion of his work that, although not
unique in the nineteenth century, could have
placed him among the greatest architect-
sculptors of his generation.

73
Maquette for the *Projet de
monument à colonnades
ornées de statues disposées
au haut d'un escalier à
double révolution*
Frédéric-Auguste Bartholdi
1873

69
Vercingétorix
Frédéric-Auguste Bartholdi
n.d.

74
Statuette of Gambetta
Frédéric-Auguste Bartholdi
n.d.

75
The Monument to
Gambetta at Ville d'Avray
Frédéric-Auguste Bartholdi
n.d.

73

74

69

75

71
The Monument to
Gambetta in front of the
National Assembly
Frédéric-Auguste Bartholdi
n.d.

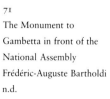

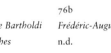

76c
*Frédéric-Auguste Bartholdi
in a Business Suit*
1870

77
*Frédéric-Auguste Bartholdi
in Uniform*
n.d.

76a
*Frédéric-Auguste Bartholdi
in Evening Clothes*
n.d.

76b
Frédéric-Auguste Bartholdi
n.d.

78
*Frédéric-Auguste Bartholdi
as a Garibaldean*
n.d.

79
*Bartholdi's Companions in
Arms in 1870*
Paul Bourgeois
1870

The change that overtook Bartholdi as a result of the Franco-Prussian War becomes apparent when we compare photographs of the well-mannered young man of thirty-six to those of the soldier and the veteran. The three shown here are from the same period as the photograph of the artist with his mother (cat. 36). Whether in evening dress (cat. 76a), dressed for a walk (cat. 76b), or in a business suit (cat. 76c), Bartholdi carries himself easily, as befits a man who has earned his Legion of Honor and is beginning to be well known. The Bartholdi of cat. 77, in a photograph taken shortly after he joined the Garde National, is another man entirely, tightly encased in his uniform,[72] rigid of countenance, and firm of carriage. The change is complete (cat. 78) after he joins the Free Corps and is attached to Garibaldi. The cocked hat has been replaced by a helmet and a beard modeled on those of Menotti Garibaldi, the great man's son, who inscribed a photograph (cat. 79), «To the worthy Major Bartholdi from his companion-in-arms, M. Garibaldi.»[73]

A photograph (cat. 80) of a watercolor, now lost, shows the artist as both actor and spectator in the tragic winter campaign of 1870–71. His letter to Edouard de Laboulaye from Colmar on May 8, 1871, after the war had ended with the loss of Alsace and Lorraine, sums up this period of military service better than any detailed narrative:

> I must begin by telling you that, like almost everybody else, I have had a pretty troubled winter. After doing my best to defend Colmar with the National Guard units under my command, I went through the whole campaign with Garibaldi. The Government in Tours sent me to join him, and he kept me by him as an aide-de-camp. I came out of that sound in wind and limb, and returned worn out with hope and effort to the house of my poor mother, who fortunately had not known exactly where I was and believed me to have been in Bordeaux. Life is tiresome here and everywhere else; by way of a rest I have six Prussians living with me in the house. So far I have been unable to accustom myself to the sight of these animals in a domestic setting, but it seems I shall have to. . . .

The purpose of the letter was to seek Laboulaye's help in obtaining the passport Bartholdi needed to leave the country. Caught between two horrors—a Prussian-occupied Alsace and a Paris thrown into confusion by the Commune—he determined to leave for the New World:

> I hope to get to know some art-lovers, and to procure some important commissions, but above all I hope to further my project for a monument in honor of independence. I have reread, and am rereading, what you have written on the subject, and I trust I shall do no discredit to the friendly patronage you are extending to me. I shall try to do honor to the Republic and Liberty over there, hoping all the time that I may one day find them again here, if that be possible! When I return, I trust I may find our poor France somewhat relieved from the plague of boils brought on her by the Imperial regime. . . .

The war, and its terrible aftermath for the people of Alsace, went far to determine Bartholdi's future, as well as the character of his work. From 1857, when he made his first appearance at the Salon, until 1870 he had exhibited only one work that could properly be called regional: the *Jeune Vigneron Alsacien* in 1869.[74] After 1872 his entries reflected an entirely new orientation: he exhibited the double bust of Erckmann and Chatrian (cat. 81),[75] whose writing celebrated the rich and independent tradi-tions of Alsace, and whose portraits he had done some time after 1869, and the *Malédiction de l'Alsace* (cat. 82),[76] an allegorical group that is nothing less than a latter-day *Pietà* in which Alsace represents a Virgin not overcome by grief but intent on vengeance—an allusion to the fate of Mme. Bartholdi in her enemy-occupied house in Colmar.

From this period on, Bartholdi makes in his work no clear distinction among the patriotic monument, the tribute to occupied Alsace, and the conventional commission in honor of a «great man.» It was in a regional spirit that Bartholdi undertook and completed his first monumental (not to say colossal) sculpture, 11 feet 6 inches high—too high, in fact, to be housed inside the buildings for the Universal Exposition of 1855: the statue of General Rapp on foot (cat. 83). This commission also marked the artist's first encounter with financing by public subscription. In the same vein Bartholdi paid homage to a new cult—at once political, religious, historical, and literary—of Joan of Arc. We know of his projects for Compiègne (a town also distinguished as the site of one of the Imperial residences) from

80
Sur la route d'Arnay-le-Duc
Frédéric-Auguste Bartholdi
1870

81
Maquette for a Double Bust of Erckmann and Chatrian
Frédéric-Auguste Bartholdi
1869

82
La malédiction de l'Alsace
Frédéric-Auguste Bartholdi
n.d.

two photographs of terra cottas, one showing the heroine on horseback (cat. 84),[77] while the other (cat. 85) has her standing alongside her horse in a romantic attitude inspired by the equestrian statuary of the Renaissance. For a still later patriotic work, the *Rouget de l'Isle*, cast in 1882 for his native town of Lons-le-Saulnier, the sculptor made several preliminary models including the one shown here (cat. 86). One of the attributes of the Statue of Liberty, the broken chains at her feet, suits the iconography of the author of the «Marseillaise,» and the whole recalls (perhaps with a little more vehemence) the *Lafayette* in New York (cat. 342).[78] Note should also be taken of the monument to Sergeant Hoff (cat. 87).

Bartholdi's patriotic Alsatian art, properly so called, includes certain works conceived in a broader national context. A painting, now lost, survives at Colmar in two copies of a photograph taken by the firm of Pierre Petit. *Le Droit prime la Force* (Bartholdi's own title) (cat. 88) is an allegory intended as propaganda without tears: a simple bouquet of cornflowers, daisies, and poppies in the French national colors tilts the balance maintained by the severely braided hair of the Alsatian women, and magnificently outweighs the Prussian helm and sword, while a watch counts down the hours of a condition the artist fervently hoped was temporary. Another piece of anti-Prussian propaganda, the *Tombe du Garde National* (cat. 89), placed in the Colmar cemetery at the end of the war, is a work intended to sting; it invokes the imagery of sixteenth- and seventeenth-century funerary sculpture through the partially opened tomb denoting forthcoming resurrection as well as present burial.[79] Bartholdi thus fell in with a national solidarity movement that took, at the Salons of 1872 and 1873, the form of a plethora of entries on the theme of Alsace in chains.[80] Out of this patriotic, anti-Prussian, and strongly regionalist movement came the artist's second major work (after the Statue of Liberty): the *Lion de Belfort*. The context in which it was conceived and executed makes it appropriate for consideration here, even though in some respects it is more properly seen as an episode in Bartholdi's pursuit of the colossal tradition.

83
Maquette for the
Monument to General
Rapp
Frédéric-Auguste Bartholdi
1856

84
Maquette for the
Monument to Jeanne d'Arc
at Compiègne, No. 112
Frédéric-Auguste Bartholdi
n.d.

The heroic defense of the town and citadel of Belfort, key to the passage across southern Lorraine that links France with Germany and Switzerland, was the occasion of a memorial monument. By the terms of the treaty signed in Frankfurt on May 10, 1871, Belfort and its environs escaped German occupation and remained French. The municipality, its independence thus ratified, readily voted to construct the inevitable monument, which was to celebrate both the resistance of Colonel Denfert-Rochereau and his troops, and the town's joy at finding itself still French; on December 5, 1871, a prize of Fr. 2,000 was offered for a competition by an approved list of artists.

Whether because of the meager reward, the forbidding location, or the nature of the assignment, only two of the artists submitted proposals. Consternation! Some artist of greater patriotic zeal had to be found—and relationships formed during the war led directly to Auguste Bartholdi, who on March 16 agreed to consider the proposition. The finished work, he said, must be «original in character, very special, and worthy of the patriotism of the City of Belfort» and «must not be hidden in some obscure spot, but should stand in the sight of all so that it may become an indispensable part of [the town's] landscape. It must partake of the city's public life, grow into a loved and needed element in its appearance, and become identified with it!» These remarks help to illuminate the sculptor's bargaining techniques: rather than present a potential client with a full-blown, detailed, and possibly daunting proposal, he began by offering some points of general principle to which the client could not possibly object; who in Belfort could have quarreled with the proposition that the city's future monument must stand «in the sight of all»? Earlier Bartholdi had handled Laboulaye in the same fashion: first sketching in with a broad brush the characteristics of an «ideal» monument to American independence; in subsequent letters dwelling on the enormous size of the country and the taste of its people for the colossal; later showing his patron a clay model and speaking of its form without mentioning its scale; then, finally, breaking to him the truth: the statue to American independence would stand more than 133 feet high.

On August 12, 1872, Bartholdi opened his mind to the Mayor of Belfort. He spoke highly of the site that he himself had chosen: a rock formation dominating the city,

«visible from every point . . . even to the passing traveler.» The well-worn themes of victory or defeat had no place here; what had to be celebrated above all was «the vigor of the defense,» for that was the quality occupied Alsace most needed if she were ever to be herself again. The figure would be that of «a lion, harassed and brought to bay but still terrible in its fury,» symbolizing the resistance of an entire people. It would stand 12 feet 5 inches high, carved from fine white stone and enthroned on a pedestal of 15½ feet. This precisely describes the model preserved in Colmar (cat. 90);[81] in its entablature and rustication it resembles some of Bartholdi's classical studies for the pedestal of *Liberty*, although in 1872 its design was still in the hands of Viollet-le-Duc. Accompanying the proposal were some very exact cost estimates, intended to allay the possible objections of the Municipal Council to the project's scope and attendant cost. As «a child of Alsace» the sculptor would ask no remuneration for himself; the sculpture's cost was estimated at Fr. 20,000 and the pedestal's at Fr. 12,000. In October 1873 the municipality anticipated a more realistic total expenditure of Fr. 50,000 and launched a national fund-raising campaign, designed both to relieve the burden on local contributors and to attract attention to the town of Belfort, at a time when each French city strove to outdo the others in its expression of unwavering national hostility to Germany. As the New York *World* was to do a decade later, the *Journal de Belfort et du Haut-Rhin* published the names of contributors. By 1875 the sum of Fr. 92,000 had been collected, and work could begin.

At this juncture some comment is required on two points. The first concerns the choice of subject, which Bartholdi could not have hit on without some recollection of Thorwaldsen's *Lion of Lucerne*, dating from the beginning of the century, about which Bartholdi and Lesbazeilles were to write so pejoratively in 1876.[82] At the same time he accepted the combined challenge of the *Arminius* and the *Bavaria*, by setting up on the frontier of France a colossal rival to them, a defiance in stone of the German national feeling they proclaim. The *Lion de Belfort* thus constitutes Bartholdi's reply to two kinds of provocation, the esthetic and the political. The second point requiring comment is the method of fund raising, which from *Belfort* on was the responsibility of Bartholdi's friend Augustin Juster, who

86
Maquette for the Monument to Rouget de l'Isle
Frédéric-Auguste Bartholdi
n.d.

87
Maquette for the Monument to Sergeant Hoff
Frédéric-Auguste Bartholdi
n.d.

88
Le Droit prime la Force
Frédéric-Auguste Bartholdi
n.d.

89
Maquette for the *Tombe du Garde National*
Frédéric-Auguste Bartholdi
n.d.

approached him on it. For the sculptor it represented a welcome trial run before the launching of *Liberty*. It could not have escaped Bartholdi's attention that to inaugurate a fund-raising campaign for the Statue of Liberty while the appeal for the *Lion de Belfort* was still short of its goal could only hurt both projects. Political considerations relating to the republicans' ascendancy in the Chamber of Deputies carried no little weight;[83] the sculptor must have understood that he was called on to make these problems his own, and to employ all his skill to ensure that his two projects should proceed without collision or competition.

When the field workshop for the *Lion de Belfort* was opened in 1876, on a piece of waste ground at the edge of the town,[84] some final models considerably modifying the project's initial form were produced. Several studies in clay (cat. 91) and stone (cat. 93),[85] identical in shape to the finished monument, mark the abandonment of the Beaux-Arts approach suggested by the presence of a pedestal. In placing his proud beast on the bare rock Bartholdi underlined the realism of his theme: here is a lion, sheltered by a chance overhang of rock, with a monstrous, invisible hunter on its track (cat. 91). The original white stone has been replaced by pink sandstone, and the statue has grown from 12 feet 5 inches to a height of 34 feet and a width of 68 feet. In its final form (cat. 92), as it came from the hands of busy stonecutters tirelessly supervised by Bartholdi (and, we may be sure, by his faithful associate Simon),[86] the *Lion de Belfort* typifies monumental statuary at the beginning of the twentieth century in its unadorned, smoothly finished, sweeping planes that contrast with the natural relief of the rock face. Since site and statue were already at odds, Bartholdi simplified his work in order to draw a clear image from the distracting background of citadel, rock, town, and vegetation. In New York the contrary situation obtained, so he multiplied folded surface textures until the draped body of his *Liberty* acquired its own inner vibrancy and the visual substance necessary to hold its own against the enormous, misty panorama of the harbor.

90

91

92

93

94

90
Le Lion de Belfort
Frédéric-Auguste Bartholdi
n.d.

91
Le Lion de Belfort
Frédéric-Auguste Bartholdi
n.d.

92
Le Lion de Belfort in Situ
Frédéric-Auguste Bartholdi
1880

93
Maquette for the *Lion de Belfort*
Frédéric-Auguste Bartholdi
n.d.

94
Lion on Which Is Seated a Figure Representing Alsace
Frédéric-Auguste Bartholdi
n.d.

Without waiting for the unveiling in October 1880, Bartholdi agreed to a request from the Municipal Council of Paris for its own *Lion*, to stand on a square that the city would name the Place Denfert-Rochereau in honor of the defenders of Belfort. According to No. 4030 in the catalogue of the Salon of 1878, he exhibited there a «plaster model on a scale of 1:3»; in 1880, No. 7238 was a «Model in beaten copper of the *Lion de Belfort*, done in the workshops of MM. Mesureur and Monduit Fils, the pedestal by M. Hergé,» undoubtedly the work in a photograph Bartholdi kept (cat. 95). The Paris version lies somewhere between animal art (which interested Bartholdi, judging from the Inventory of 1914, which shows his collection as including casts by Barye and Fremiet) and colossal art, a form that in the sculptor's opinion reached its apogee in the Sphinx of Gizeh. But the Paris work is subservient to neither genre, and in the weighty succession of symbolic lion-statues offers its own particular and effective symbolism. That Bartholdi regarded the resistance of Belfort as part of the resistance of Alsace in general is suggested by a terra cotta in the Colmar museum showing an Alsatian woman seated Amazon-fashion on the *Lion de Belfort* (cat. 94). It is clear, too, that the artist had come to see the resistance of Alsace as an aspect of the national patriotic cause—indeed, it was so regarded by the nation as a whole. Hence the popularity of the statue, copies of which (as would later be the case with *Liberty*) were adapted to every conceivable purpose.

The success of the *Lion de Belfort* inevitably reinforced Bartholdi's commitment to the special field of patriotic sculpture, as can be inferred from his submissions to a number of successive Salons. In 1878, along with the *Lion* (cat. 95), he exhibited a *Général de Gribeauval*—commemorating the man responsible for the modernization of the French artillery in the eighteenth century; the statue was therefore admitted to the courtyard of the Invalides in Paris.[87] Mention has already been made of the *Rouget de l'Isle* of 1881,[88] and there was also a series of representations of Lafayette bearing a double allusion to American independence and the French Revolution: besides the 1876 *Lafayette* in New York there were a bust in 1886, the *Washington and Lafayette* of 1892, the 1889 *Projet de monument à la mémoire de Lafayette et de l'Indépendance américaine*, and in 1901 another bust, of the young Lafayette.[89] At the Salon of 1891 Bartholdi exhibited *L'Alsace et la Lorraine se réfugiant au pied de l'Autel de la Patrie*, a group intended as a memorial to Gambetta (discussed above); in 1895, *La Suisse secourant les douleurs de Strasbourg pendant le siège de 1870*, a monument erected in Basel; the *Tombe du Garde National*, already standing in Colmar, and exhibited publicly in Paris in 1898; and in 1899, the *Monument des Soldats français morts à Schinznach (Suisse), 1870*.[90] In 1903 Bartholdi received a new commission from Belfort, for a *Monument des trois sièges soutenus par la Ville de Belfort dans le même siècle*, and in 1904 he executed a funerary monument to another hero of the war of 1870, Sergeant Hoff (cat. 87), at the Père Lachaise Cemetery in Paris.[91] In 1904 the sculptor was engaged on his last work, a patriotic monument dedicated *aux Aéronautes du siège de Paris, aux héros des postes, des télégraphes, des chemins de fer et aux colombophiles de 1870–71*,[92] which was exhibited again at the 1905 Salon before taking up its site on the Place des Ternes in Paris. No date can be found for the *Monument aux défenseurs de Brisach* (cat. 96), although it seems to be a late work; there is no model at Colmar. It shows Alsace shrinking away from an enormous bayonet sprung straight from the unbridled imagination of the sculptor; here his dreams of sculptural excess border on nightmare. On earlier occasions the sculptor's inspiration served him better; the impression left by this work is merely that he was a specialist in the genre.

95
The *Lion de Belfort* for the Place Denfert-Rochereau, at the Salon
Frédéric-Auguste Bartholdi
1880

96
Maquette for the *Monument aux défenseurs de Brisach*
Frédéric-Auguste Bartholdi
n.d.

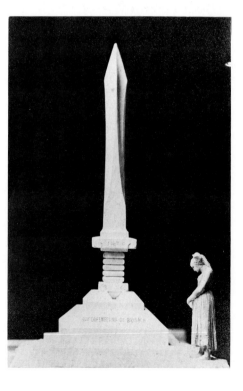

Bartholdi's patriotism greatly influenced his political and philosophical convictions. The liberal tendencies of his family had been stamped upon him as a young man; since 1865 he had been closely associated with the liberals in Paris, shared their endeavors, and witnessed with them the failure of Imperial France to rise above its Bonapartist origins; as an Alsatian, and thus a direct victim of the defeat of the Empire in 1870, he could not help sympathizing with the republican cause. This was the context in which, on his return from the United States in 1872, he learned of the establishment of a new lodge of the Grand Orient of France, entitled Alsace-Lorraine, and intended as a rallying point for patriots from the occupied territories. With his usual prudence he delayed joining the lodge until 1875, and a coincidence of dates might lead us to suppose that his personal decision had been conformed to the general strategy of the Franco-American Union. He was initiated on October 14, two weeks after the Committee's first announcement, on September 28. At least one other member of the Alsace-Lorraine lodge, Jean Macé, was active in the affairs of the Union, and several other members of the Committee were Freemasons.[93] Bartholdi was thus making the most of two different connections: provincial and political on the one hand, Parisian and social on the other.

The patriotic and Alsatian overtones are preeminent in understanding the sculptor's commitment, belated though it may have been, to Freemasonry, and his pursuit of personal ends proportionately less important. Only with much qualification may we invoke Masonic loyalties to explain his preferences, whether esthetic (his obsession with Egypt long antedated his initiation) or symbolic (the Suez and New York statues were both conceived as «enlightening» Asia, or the whole world, long before 1875). Lacking evidence to the contrary, we may see in Bartholdi's membership in the Grand Orient a visible sign of his patriotism and attachment to his native Alsace.

The system by which an artist's career was organized in the mid-nineteenth century left little room for personal initiative or choice of means. As we have seen, although Bartholdi lacked Beaux-Arts training, a private income, his active solicitation of political backing, the appropriation of a field in which he was without rival—colossal statuary—or one large enough to accommodate others—political statuary—all enabled him to rise above his limitations. And today, when art historians are beginning to investigate the circles of the Académie des Beaux-Arts and its École, Bartholdi's discoveries and innovations too will likely be reexamined.

As of 1886 his work had earned him a fame that existed quite apart from any debate over his talent. Although Jean Benner's portrait (cat. 97),[94] painted at the time of the statue's completion and erection in New York, shows a self-assured man prepared to take on new and colossal tasks, the portrait by Joseph Frappe (cat. 98),[95] which is contemporaneous with Bartholdi's receiving the Legion of Honor (cat. 99), is that of a man for whom it is all over: he is associated with his Statue of Liberty to the point of being devoured by it. A photograph (cat. 100) that may have been taken somewhat later, ca. 1900, does nothing to alter this impression, and this is how Bartholdi has come down to posterity. The German city administration tolerated the monument raised to him in Colmar (cat. 101)[96] because of the international renown of his statue, whose anti-German connotations were understood neither in 1906 when the city set aside the land, voted the money needed for the work, and authorized the fund-raising drive for it nor in 1907 at the time of the monument's unveiling, attended by German dignitaries and the president of the Haute-Alsace District, Albert von Puttkamer.

Bartholdi organized his own artistic fame—he himself planned the tomb and purchased space for it in the Montparnasse cemetery. His design for it (cat. 102) is a reworking of the Arica monument,[97] whose winged deity has here undergone a change of meaning and now represents the flight of the sculptor's soul. To see in it a vitality similar to that of the figure escaping «les griffes de la Misère» (cat. 58) and to read it as an allegory of genius requires only a small step, one eased by a body of angelic iconography. The sculptor has thus preserved his never-to-be-realized work by placing it as a Victory on his own tomb—a bitter revenge that reveals Bartholdi's extensive and continual frustrations. However, as if to deny this triumph of the unachieved work, the monument's pedestal bears the words «Author of the Lion of Belfort and of the Statue of Liberty Enlightening the World.»[98]

The glory of those monuments, ironically, has undermined that of their creator. Aside from those two colossi, we must still ask whether it is possible to discern in the remainder of the sculptor's work a significant nineteenth-century personality. The answer will be found in the Colmar museum when its collection has been restored and systematically examined. We noted above the extent to which the artist's fate was grounded in republican values, especially Liberty and Resistance. Each the product of conflict, revolution, or war, those values today represent, for those European generations raised in peace, struggles that were decided long ago. We know they could recur, but internal political struggle and national defense can perhaps no longer be as intertwined as they were in 1791 or 1870. It is in such conjunctions that the republican ideal was forged, and Bartholdi was to serve that ideal with his chisel. His fame declined as the meaning of the images inspired by that ideal became diluted. Republican iconography, even if founded in something sacred, is not Christian iconography—the *Lion de Belfort* is not decked with flowers, incense is not burned to the Statue of Liberty. The time has come when the virtue of such iconographies, dissected in the harsh light of research, will become diluted in the hands of the historians. The power of images interests them far more than does the fame of the artists to whom those images no longer belong.

*Translated, from the French,
by Frances Frenaye*

100

102

101

2.
Bartholdi and the Colossal Tradition

Pierre Provoyeur

It would not be difficult to place the Statue of Liberty in the context of the history of colossal sculpture, and to enumerate each and every masterpiece in the genre. However, it has seemed more useful here to view the subject through the eyes of Bartholdi himself, for not only has the artist left us several accounts of the technical problems involved in completing the statue, he has also written about the Colossus, thus shedding invaluable light on his entire artistic development.

We have four sources for Bartholdi's views on the examples of colossal statuary that he assigns to the artistic inheritance of humankind: a book published in Paris by E. Lesbazeilles in 1876, *Les Colosses anciens et modernes* (cat. 103); the 1883 article in *Le Génie Civil*, «La Statue de la Liberté Éclairant le Monde» by Charles Talansier (cat. 233); *The Statue of Liberty Enlightening the World*, translated from Bartholdi's original text by A. T. Rice (cat. 379); and eight glass-plate photographs from the sculptor's own collection (now in a private collection in Paris), several of which pertain to famous colossal sculptures that stood in Europe or the East in Bartholdi's day. We may infer a connection between these photographs and a lecture Bartholdi gave around 1890, at Boulogne-sur-Seine, on colossal statuary.[1]

Before turning to the history of the colossal art-form itself, we should acknowledge that each of our sources was, in a sense, taking dictation from Bartholdi. In describing the construction of the statue, Talansier brought to his task a command of the technical terms of architecture, but when he wrote of colossi the choice of references was not his own. Rice functioned purely and simply as a translator. Lesbazeilles, who is credited with authorship of the most ambitious of these works (the first, indeed, to treat of the colossi of antiquity since Quatremère de Quincy), extended himself so widely that we may legitimately doubt his competence in this specialized field: in 1881 he published *Les Merveilles du Monde Polaire*, and his last work, published in 1884, was *Les Forêts*. Clearly Bartholdi served as the literal inspiration for whole sections of the book— feeble enough when it deals with monuments in India, China, and Japan that the authors had obviously never seen; much better informed, and indeed almost autobiographical, in the passages on Egypt, Arona, the Statue of Liberty, and the *Lion de Belfort*. The book quotes at length from Bartholdi's friends, the critics Charles Blanc and Edmond About,[2] and its list of illustrations closely parallels Bartholdi's own picture collection.

Even the publication date of *Les Colosses anciens et modernes*—1876, when the fundraising appeal for the Statue of Liberty was well under way—indicates how Bartholdi had made it into a public relations instrument. The conclusion, which addresses the Statue of Liberty, clearly serves his purpose of putting the monument in a historical continuum of which it is itself the culmination. «This statue will rise to an extraordinary height; on its twenty-five-meter pedestal it will stand thirty-four meters tall from head to foot, or forty-four meters counting the upraised arm and its torch. Within a couple of meters this is the height of the Vendôme Column. The colossus will be unique: more than half again as tall as the Virgin of Le Puy; exactly half again as tall as the St. Charles Borromeo; taller than the Colossus of Nero; equal in stature (as tradition has it) to the famed Colossus of Rhodes, which was intended to remain forever unsurpassed.» And, in conclusion, «From the procession of masterpieces which has passed before our eyes, we can see that the art of colossal statuary retains the fullness of its vigor today.» In his eagerness to prove that he has surpassed all the rest, Bartholdi provides illustrations for his thesis: a photograph (cat. 104) compares the three «European colossi» referred to by Lesbazeilles (*St. Charles Borromeo*, the *Virgin of Le Puy*, and the *Bavaria* in Munich), as in a drawing (p. 61) from his 1885 work *The Statue of Liberty Enlightening the World*; this in turn foreshadows an engraving, possibly published the following year (cat. 105), showing the world's tallest monuments, with the statue preeminent among them—1 foot taller than the Battle Monument at West Point, New York.

With Lesbazeilles as his cover, Bartholdi passes from one work to the next and administers a shrewd dig to each of his predecessors: the *St. Charles Borromeo* in Arona is «a gigantic portrait rather than a great work of art» (p. 288); the face of the *Arminius* wears a «harsh and savage expression» (p. 309) and symbolizes «an odious and offensive German patriotism»; the *Lion of Lucerne*, to which Thorwaldsen gave an unduly human cast of countenance, fares no better: «. . . what exceeds the license allowed by poetic allusion, and by the art form, is that the grief expressed in its face properly pertains only to the human heart;

that to the appropriate and lifelike posture of the defeated animal there is superadded some counterfeit of melancholy. . . . Thorwaldsen's lion looks too well informed for its own good . . . and appears to commiserate, more than a creature of its kind should, with the woes of others and with its own» (p. 311). The case of Millet's *Vercingétorix* was more delicate, for Millet was a patron of the Monduit atelier which was then at work on the torch for Bartholdi's Statue of Liberty. The initial comments on Millet's work sound almost approving, but soon Lesbazeilles and Bartholdi assume a very different tone: «Vercingetorix, who overcame the Romans at Gergovia, might have been portrayed in the exultation of his triumph—the head upheld, scornful of eye, lordly of gesture, the sword brandished aloft; perhaps the Auvergne may one day boast such a statue . . .» (p. 325). There is no mistaking the allusion to Bartholdi's own *Vercingétorix*, conceived for the plateau of Gergovie (cat. 69) and exhibited at the Salon of 1870; there is a further allusion to the moral grandeur of the Gaul (that is, the Frenchman) face to face with the Roman Caesar—a moral grandeur not, apparently, to be found in the German *Arminius*.

At the other extreme, Lesbazeilles, no less clearly inspired by Bartholdi, bestows laurel wreaths to Etex for his bas-reliefs for the Arc de Triomphe on the Étoile: Etex was one of Bartholdi's teachers. But he gives the greatest care to assuring Bartholdi's own reputation, even as, while writing of the *Lion de Belfort*, he acquaints the reader with his working philosophy: «the good artist will have made himself master of the principles of colossal statuary; he will be seen to be familiar with the work of the Egyptians, who understood it so well; he is willing to sacrifice the niceties of detail, or rather to sum them up in simple masses, easy for the beholder to grasp; he looks for ample planes, seeks to set them at a marked angle one to another, and does not blunt the edges where they meet; he avoids deep hollows, which produce excessively dark shadows and attenuate the whole» (p. 330). These reflections extend the comment offered on the *Peter the Great* in Leningrad: «Falconet understood that a colossal statue must of its very nature be symbolic and approximative; if it sets out to be a precisely detailed copy from the life, it runs the risk of turning into a repellent monstrosity.»

104

Photograph of
Comparative Heights of the
Great Colossal Statues
without Their Pedestals
Frédéric-Auguste Bartholdi
n.d.

105

*The Highest Monuments in
the World*
ca. 1886

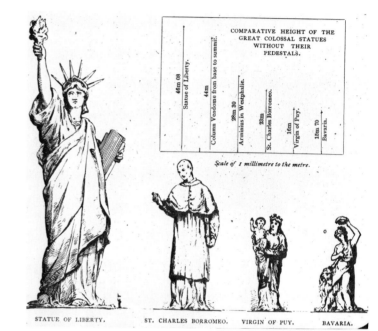

And further: «The requirement that a statue of great size must offer a wider meaning, and partake in character of the ideal, is so well understood by the sculptors of our own day that they have almost always reserved the form either for the portrayal of symbols, or for the depiction of personages who belong as much to legend as to history, and are in a fair way to become symbols themselves» (pp. 300–301).

No one could blow his own horn better than that. Bartholdi and Lesbazeilles, while purporting to make a list of the greatest human achievements in colossal statuary, have defined a single method as proper for its pursuit, and made that method into a kind of moral imperative: «So long as art endures, and there are men on earth, and deeds of men, whose memory requires to be perpetuated, so long—we may affirm—[the art of colossal statuary] cannot die; it will live for the discharge of its proper office, which is to pass down the annals of mankind to posterity in imperishable characters of stone or bronze» (p. 336). In fact this is the task of sculpture as a whole (it is significant that what Pierre Nora styles «places of remembrance» almost always take this form).[3] Sculpture is the preferred medium for expressing national rallying-cries, the frenzies of contemporary politics, or public grief. While it may be true that the function of sculpture is to «pass down the annals of mankind,» there is no reason that the sculpture must be colossal. Bartholdi has taken a law pertaining to sculpture as a whole and turned it to his personal advantage by proclaiming it as though the condition of colossal scale were self-evident. It is a bold generalization invoked in aid of a bold undertaking; the artist has searched history for ennobling precedents, and at the same time has imputed to history the very laws that he could claim to have followed.

The interpretation of certain great works is far more valuable, as a clue to the sculptor's sources, than the later etiological myths that have clustered around the statue. For example, writing of the Hera of Argos as described by Ottfried Muller, Lesbazeilles–Bartholdi might as well be writing about *Liberty*: «The whole body was chastely concealed by the clothing, except for the face, the neck, the upper part of the bosom and the arms . . . her features . . . expressed the bright and unchanging bloom of beauty; her curves, rounded without excessive fullness,

evoked admiration but did not compel it; the whole conveyed the impression of a woman in the full vigor of her youth, forever laved in her own cool, inexhaustible virginity.» Or again, of the Athena of the Parthenon, quoting M. Beulé: «What must be claimed for Phidias himself is this calm and powerful head, this mouth which knows not how to smile, but breathes wisdom and persuasion; these unalterably serene eyes, these severe features which convey only a pure and idealized femininity; these tresses which the helm cannot contain, so that their waves overflow to frame the forehead; above all the neck and the line of the shoulders, which evoke at once Hercules and the Blessed Virgin. All these I can easily conceive on a colossal scale, for the spirit which already informs the marble is too great to be contained by it» (p. 96).

Lesbazeilles' work is also remarkable for the way that architecture constantly creeps into it. In their eagerness to enumerate colossal statuary the authors become biased, and in the end are inclined to memorialize the colossal as such. One after another they mention and describe the ruins of Thebes, Karnak, and Luxor, the palaces of Assyria, the tomb of Mausolus of Halicarnassus, the grottoes of Elephantine Island, Eluru, Bor-obudur, the ruins of Palenque, the cathedrals of Europe, and the Arc de Triomphe in Paris. Our authors embrace the tradition of the Wonders of the World; their pleasure in dwelling on at least three of them—the Pyramids, the Mausoleum of Halicarnassus, and the Colossus of Rhodes—directs our attention to the Statue of Liberty, at the end of the book, as being yet another of their number, and the heiress of them all. It is not insignificant that the work was published by Hachette as one of a series entitled «The Library of Wonders,» and that Lesbazeilles followed his first venture with a book on «the Wonders of the Polar World.» But the obsession of both men with *mirabilia* can be profoundly misleading. We would like it to be poetic, nourished as we are on the Age of Fable, and by the profound awareness that implicit in these very masterpieces is the downfall of the civilizations that gave them birth.[4] In fact the obsession is practical and quantitative: the best way to convey the most exalted ideas to the greatest number of people is to construct the largest possible monument. Moreover, in their analysis of the body of colossal statuary, the authors frequently dwell on issues of technical skill and the challenge to conventional rules of equilibrium and construction that these works embodied. In this they are true children of their century, the century of the Universal Expositions and of the Eiffel

Tower—that abstract, arbitrary architectural exercise in the colossal, so opposite to the representational ideal of the Statue of Liberty.

Bartholdi's conception of the history of colossal statuary seems at once derivative, as far as the mythology is concerned, and cut off from the Greek and Roman roots of that same mythology. Derivative, as in his description of the Colossus of Rhodes, where he takes at face value all the texts of ancient fable, and marshals their figures with appalling precision: «. . . [the statue] was in bronze; it must have weighed 1500 quintals and cost 300 talents (Fr. 1,650,000)» (p. 7). Had he known more about the part played by the scholarship of the Italian Renaissance in resurrecting the Colossus of Rhodes, he might have been warier, and might have guided Lesbazeilles away from the assertion that «under the successors of Alexander . . . gigantic statues multiplied on every hand.» The work is as valuable to us when it completely misses the truth as when it grazes it: Lesbazeilles and Bartholdi assert without qualm that the bas-reliefs of Trajan's column are in bronze (p. 135); and they show a knowledge of Florence that is no more dependable, as on p. 275, where they assert that the copy of Michelangelo's *David* is a bronze, whereas it is stone (and to this day stands in the Piazza della Signoría). Elsewhere (pp. 28–29) they put a revealing comment into the mouth of a traveler, M. Ampère, who has visited Egypt «as both archeologist and poet»: «At this solemn moment the image of Rome, which had been the first to occur to me when I arrived, returned to my mind; but now that I had seen Thebes, now that I could recall to my imagination the ruins of temples, palaces, colossi, centuries past and gone, Rome no longer seemed equal to the grandeur of my impressions and my recollections; I cried out that «Thebes is Rome writ large!» Later the authors explain how Bartholdi held himself apart from the teaching of the École des Beaux-Arts, whose architecture and sculpture glorified the Greco-Roman inheritance to the exclusion of all else. We shall also see how the École, in 1874 at any rate, was supporting archeological research and, particularly in Rome, was taking systematic inventory not only of the ruined buildings of the ancient city but also of coins, sculpture, and manuscripts.[5] Since the sculptor had played no part in this work, he ignored it in his research into the history of colossal statuary. In fact, Rome could have afforded him some splendid colossi, starting with the eponym of them all, the Colosseum.[6] The colossal tradition owes much both to Rome and to the Roman Catholic Church, some of whose princes were among the first to assemble collections of antiquities and to refurbish (for obvious political reasons) the splendor of ancient Rome.

The reason that Bartholdi never went to Rome, and took no account of its treasures of Latin antiquity, is that, as the son of a family of devout Protestants, he mistrusted the Roman Catholic Church and all its works. Jean-Marie Schmitt quotes the artist as having said, «We must not fall into pessimism, but must always be a little wary. Hamon, the painter of olden times, said «Indeed, indeed I believe in God, but I mistrust Him!»[7] This cast of thought was reinforced in Bartholdi by his political stance—republicans held the Roman Catholic Church largely accountable for the defeat of 1870—and by a commitment, perhaps less spiritual than patriotic, to Freemasonry.[8] A pilgrimage to Rome would not have been consonant with the esthetic position he took in 1856 by electing to visit Egypt, nor with his political position in 1870 and 1875 as an Alsatian patriot and a Mason. Nevertheless, it was Rome, along with Florence, that had given birth to a new current of creativity and to a renewed infatuation with colossal sculpture and architecture. Michelangelo, the greatest artist of this renaissance, was author of a monumental *David* commissioned by the Medici, and of a huge architectural project for St. Peter's in Rome. Bartholdi's collection included reproductions of some of his work: the *Moses*, done for Julius II, and the statues *Day* and *Night*, for the Medici chapel of San Lorenzo. Michelangelo is the only sculptor of the Cinquecento, and indeed the only individual artist, to whom Lesbazeilles devotes an

entire chapter, and we sense Bartholdi's fascination with a creative artist who was at once the complete sculptor and the complete architect. For him, Michelangelo sums up the whole contribution of the Renaissance to colossal statuary.

We must look elsewhere to discover the source from which the art form drew its renewal in the sixteenth century. It was renewal rather than innovation, for the Middle Ages contributed yet another link to the chain in the form of cathedral carvings, the «mouths of hell» of the Christian mysteries, and the legendary giants whose literary avatar is Rabelais' Gargantua. From the early sixteenth century on, representations of the Wonders of the World were popularized in engravings; in 1521 C. Cesariano included the Mausoleum of Halicarnassus in the illustrations to his edition of Vitruvius' *De Architectura*; some time before 1572 (when P. Galle made engravings after his originals) Maarten van Heemskerck drew the Seven Wonders of the World according to Pliny. As we shall see, the Mausoleum served to inspire the graduated plinth for the Statue of Liberty which Bartholdi designed after the death of Viollet-le-Duc (cat. 398). These engravings would engender yet other works, such as Antoine Caron's tapestry (cat. 106) depicting the Colossus of Rhodes, from the *Tenture d'Artémise*, which shows that such subjects were popular at princely courts.

In this revival, the development of colossal statuary kept pace with the working out of an iconography of the Wonders of the World, which at first seems to have supported continuing research into «the art of the astonishing,» but on deeper study appears to have derived its sanction from the will of princes. The *Tenture d'Artémise*, ordered by Catherine de Medicis, tells the

story of the royal widow of King Mausolus who was moved by conjugal piety to build the famous Mausoleum of Halicarnassus as a memorial for her husband, and went so far as to swallow his ashes so that she herself might become his tomb. This is clearly an allusion to Catherine's having subsumed the power of the crown into her own person after her husband's death in July 1559. But there are other overtones as well. The Queen of France was a Medici, of a family that had traditionally placed grandiose commissions for colossal works of art with a series of artists, all tried and refined in the Florentine crucible. Leonardo da Vinci was the first to conceive of a gigantic equestrian statue, and although it was commissioned not by a Medici but by Francesco Sforza for Milan, it was undoubtedly intended to honor and glorify a prince. Along with Verrocchio's *Colleoni* in Venice,[9] it was, up to the end of the fifteenth century, the example of the genre most held up for emulation by other Florentine artists.[10] In its train came Michelangelo with the *David* referred to above and the colossal portrait of *Julius II* for Bologna; Bacio Bandinelli with the *Hercules and Cacus* on Piazza della Signoría; Ammanati with the *Neptune*, also on Piazza della Signoría; Benvenuto Cellini with a *Mars* destined for François I at Fontainebleau; and Giovanni Bologna with the portrait of Cosimo I in Florence.[11] All these are instances of a predilection for larger-than-life art, usually exercised on mythological figures whose virtues the prince might be held to share—David and Hercules for resourcefulness, intelligence, and power—sometimes in heroicized portraits and, toward the end of the century, sometimes in deliberately contemporary dress.

106

Le colosse de Rhodes

Antoine Caron

n.d.

107
Colossal Head of the
Emperor Constantine
Late Roman Empire

108
The Hand of Constantine
Late Roman Empire

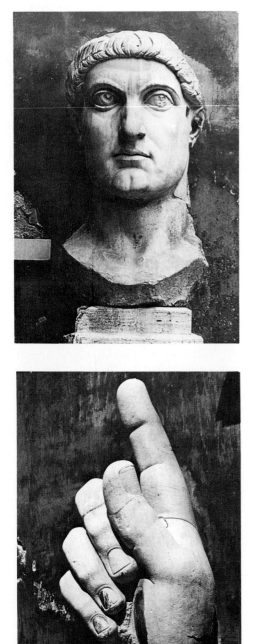

The commissioning of colossal sculpture as an expression of royal power is altogether characteristic of Renaissance Italy, and perhaps its most significant expression appears in the Capitoline in Rome, which Michelangelo designed and ornamented. For the benefit of his mighty patrons, the artist achieved a synthesis between the classical heritage—*Marcus Aurelius*, the *Tiber* and the *Nile*, the *Marforio*, the *Constantinian Colossi*, in bronze or in stone (cat. 107, 108, 109)—on the one hand, and a political decision, on the other, to invest Rome with the fullness of majesty due the principal seat of the Church. There is a logic connecting the elaboration of the colossal house of worship, intended by Julius II to replace the old basilica of St. Peter's, with the design of the new Capitol. The remains of the statues of Imperial Rome, reproduced by Lesbazeilles (p. 133), speak today with the same dramatic effect as the photographs of the face of the Statue of Liberty (cat. 440, 441). Even denuded of the rhetorical trappings of clothing and insignia, they remain true monsters, or fallen deities.

Still within the Medicean tradition, the Queen of France followed her commission for the *Tenture d'Artémise* with another; on November 14, 1559, she ordered from Michelangelo an equestrian portrait of Henri II, to be of the same height as the courtyard of one of her palaces. Daniele da Volterra undertook the work under his master's supervision, but only the horse was sent to France, where in 1639 it became a mount for a *Louis XIII* in the middle of the Place Royale; here the arrangement of the Capitoline is repeated, but the statue has become an explicit tribute to the king's majesty. Later Marie de Medicis ordered from Francavilla an equestrian statue of Henri IV, which was placed in 1614 so that its outline rose above the Ile de la Cité and the Pont Neuf. Historians tell us that there was a cannon in the melt from which

Giovanni Bologna's bronze of Cosimo I was cast; the *Henri IV*, on the contrary, was pulled down by revolutionaries in 1792 so that cannon could be cast from it—perhaps a fitting resolution to all the overtones of Power, and its powers, that resonate around colossal statuary. The same fate overtook Girardon's *Louis XIV*, cast in 1692 and erected in 1699 on the Place Louis-le-Grand in Paris, which survives only as a single foot of bronze (cat. 110), whose Roman sandal, openly echoing the *Marcus Aurelius* on the Capitoline, connotes an imperial portrait. This enormous foot was deliberately preserved in 1792 as a stick with which to beat the overweening ambitions of the Monarchy—an invitation to Frenchmen to reflect on «the littleness of their [the kings'] monuments, even in respect of what they esteemed the greatest.»

In her invaluable dissertation on the colossal statuary of the Cinquecento, Virginia Bush estimates that fully half of the works she enumerates originated in the patronage of the Medici.[12] The rivalry among artists seeking to take up the technical and artistic challenge of these commissions, and the family taste for «this extravagant and unsubtle means of advertising their power, their wealth and their magnificence» were the wellsprings of this artistic current that has flowed so strongly through the history of Western art. But in Florence and Tuscany it achieved an expression beyond the limits of the political: landscape architecture and the decoration of a number of Medici villas gave rise to works of an astonishing poetic force, such as the *Appenin* or *Jupiter Pluvius* of the Villa de Pratolino. This work of Giovanni Bologna, done in 1580–81,[13] surpasses in expressiveness and dramatic quality the sculptures Bomarzo executed after 1564. In the lineage of the river-gods of antiquity, it recapitulates the entire classical tradition, and its plastic affinity with the figures of the contemporary ballet—Time, Silenus, Winter, and so on—again evokes the court of the Medici, Buontalenti, and the Mannerist circle as a whole. Of more immediate concern to us is the interest that the sculpture seems to have held for Bartholdi; his glass-plate photographs include a view of *The Apennines*, annotated in his own hand as being in Florence (cat. 111). Lesbazeilles, of course, reproduces it and discusses it in a long excursus. After noting the disappearance of most of the hydraulic wonders that were originally placed in the grottoes around it, he observes that «what Time has not worn down, nor Man displaced, is the stone colossus . . .»—an endurance one might suppose to be typical of colossi. More relevantly, he notes that «Inside the body several rooms have been cut; the head encloses a splendid belvedere, with the eyeballs serving for windows.» Here we have the simultaneous birth of twin themes that lead directly to the Statue of Liberty and the aggrandizement of the colossal: the sculpture-as-habitation, and the mountain-as-sculpture.

The Apennines is a mountain-god, whose hair, beard, indeed, whole body, pertain to the mineral kingdom. Of secondary interest to us is the water that springs or trickles from head to heel and even from the lion's mask he tramples underfoot. Rather, here we see that a colossus has been built; there, it has been carved out of the living rock, and we cannot fail to recall the lunatic project of Deinocrates,[14] who according to legend wanted to carve Mount Athos into the likeness of Alexander the Great, and to place in one stone hand an entire town—the colossus as habitation—while he caused a river to rise from the other—the same watery theme as in *The Apennines*. The illustrations to Fischer von Erlach's *Entwurff einer Historischen Architectur*, published in 1721,[15] show how popular this

109
The Foot of Constantine
Late Roman Empire

110
Le Pied gauche de la statue de Louis XIV
François Girardon
1692

111
Photograph of *L'Appenin, Florence*
Frédéric-Auguste Bartholdi
n.d.

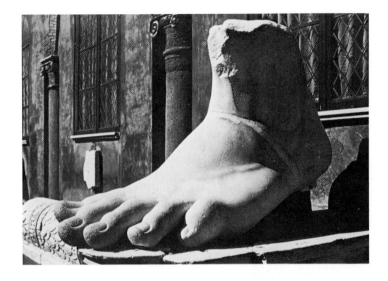

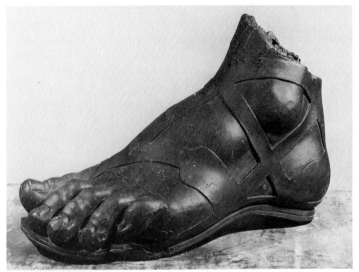

fable had become (cat. 112). Once again we are struck by the association between the colossus and the glorification of a sovereign—since Alexander withheld his consent, nothing was done—and the incorporation of both into a tourist attraction. The unbuilt masterpiece survived as a poetic dream-project handed down from century to century;[16] in Bartholdi's stone *Lion de Belfort*, built at the side of the cliff on which the citadel stands, it found an echo at least as sonorous as in Gutzon Borglum's two American monuments (cat. 132 and 133). Three other engravings from Fischer von Erlach draw from the same Grand Tour of classical antiquity. The Colossus of Rhodes (cat. 113), here again depicted with his rays, is a solar Apollo whose iconography cannot have been unknown to Bartholdi.[17] The Pharos of Alexandria (cat. 114), an exercise in the architecture of the unreal, is the other pattern for great maritime projects. Finally, the Jupiter of Olympus (cat. 115), dry as an architect's sketch, links Maarten van Heemskerck's drawing, or our panel from the *Tenture d'Artémise* (cat. 106), and the studies, as deserving as they are daring, of the École des Beaux-Arts in Bartholdi's day (cat. 120).

Michelangelo himself had not overlooked these two applications of colossal sculpture; Vasari relates that the Florentine wanted to carve the mountain of Carrara into a series of great statues,[18] while Ascanio Condivi

claims that in 1505, after passing some time there, Michelangelo thought of emulating antiquity by carving a lonely colossus, its face turned toward the sea.[19] As to the sculpture-as-habitation, in 1525, when Clement VII ordered a colossus to be placed opposite the Church of San Lorenzo in Florence, the sculptor made a study (perhaps not altogether serious) of a seated figure housing a barber-shop, with a Horn of Plenty for chimney! In the end the statue rose to its feet, so that it could serve as San Lorenzo's bell tower; the sound of the bells, issuing from its mouth, made it seem to bewail itself and ask for pardon.[20] Its tears make it akin not only to *The Apennines*, which moistens the earth around it, but even more to the Colossi of Memnon, which, according to Strabo, Pausanias, and Juvenal, weep at the rising of the sun.

While antiquity provides few examples of the colossus-as-habitation, modern times, especially since the end of the eighteenth century, have given us few colossi that do not conform to this application. The first of them, and the one which had the greatest influence on Bartholdi, is the *St. Charles Borromeo* (cat. 116). Lesbazeilles presents it without further ado as an outstanding tourist attraction («Few travelers to Italy fail to visit the colossal statue of St. Charles Borromeo, near Arona on the shores of the Lago Maggiore . . .») and stresses, in his deterministic way, that its scale is «as enormous as the honor it was intended to pay to him.» He praises «the excellent prospect spread out before the sculpture,»

and specifically advises that «the inner hollow of the nose is a little room of its own, big enough for the visitor to sit at ease» (p. 287). Quatremère de Quincy, in his *Dictionnaire historique d'architecture*, offers a similar evaluation: «Truth to tell, this colossus taken as a whole is remarkable less as a beautiful work of art than as a technical achievement, singular both in itself and by virtue of its position.» Paolo Farina, in a shrewd recent study, examines the different purposes and functions attributed to the saint's statue in a context of militant Catholicism.[21] In this light it becomes even more interesting that Bartholdi, the stubborn Protestant who so mistrusted Rome and its Church, was the most studious and observant of all the visitors to Arona quoted by Lesbazeilles. It may be that only the technical aspects of the work appealed to him, but in fact it had other characteristics prophetic of the Statue of Liberty: both were conceived as symbols, and both have become shrines. B. Manino in 1628 wrote a description of the Arona statue, denominating it «columna ignis per noctem» («a pillar of fire by night»), and once again there is a manifest allusion to the Colossus of Rhodes in its capacity of lighthouse. Farina thinks that the *St. Charles Borromeo* could not have been the navigation light for the harbor of Arona—an active lake port well placed on the inland waterways of Europe and the principal north-south axis of trade—and he therefore sees no need for the head to house, as at Rhodes, a light which shone out through the eye-sockets.

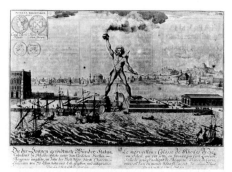

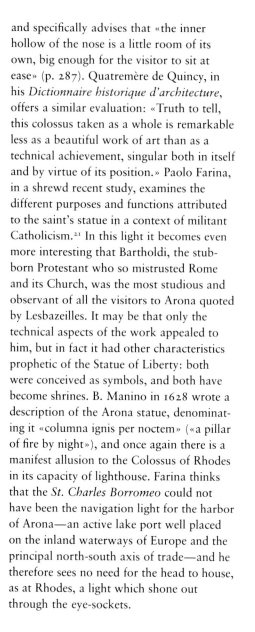

112
The Colossus of Mount Athos
Fischer von Erlach
1725

113
The Colossus of Rhodes
Fischer von Erlach
1725

114
The Pharos of Alexandria
Fischer von Erlach
1725

115
The Jupiter of Olympus
Fischer von Erlach
1725

The new resources made available to visionary architecture during the latter half of the eighteenth century fostered every kind of new conception in the realm of the colossal; they restored it to its place of honor from the sculptural ghetto to which it had been relegated, but at the same time they enhanced the importance of the distinction between interior and exterior. The *Cenotaph de Newton*, by E. L. Boullée,[22] one of the best-known and most important examples of a building with its own double meaning, is on the outside a vast spherical planet of stone, while its interior reveals a model of the universe, with little holes in the ceiling representing constellations seen on a dark night. Bartholdi seems to have overlooked this current of neoclassicism; on the other hand, he must have witnessed the demolition of the *Eléphant de la Bastille* (cat. 117),

made famous by Victor Hugo. It was the work of Alavoine, on a commission from the Emperor in 1809 or thereabouts; after the defeat of the Jacobins, who were inveterate enemies of colossal statuary because of its supposed associations with royal or aristocratic power, Napoléon ordered a number of such monuments,[23] among them the Arc de Triomphe on the Étoile. Once again the existence of the Monarch stimulated a spectacular enlargement in the scale of buildings and statues, keeping pace with the enlarged territorial ambitions of the Empire. Such ambitions had never since the days of classical antiquity rested so nakedly on military force: the Arc was dedicated to the Army of France, and its gigantic bas-reliefs had even greater influence on the young Bartholdi because two of them were from the hand of his teacher Etex.

Bartholdi and Lesbazeilles took pains to identify those tendencies that seemed to them, in the course of history, to have laid the foundations for the Statue of Liberty. They write of «the requirement that a statue of great size must offer a wider meaning, and partake in character of the ideal, [which] is so well understood by the sculptors of our own day that they have almost always reserved the form either for the portrayal of symbols, or for the depiction of personages who belong as much to legend as to history, and are in a fair way to become symbols themselves» (p. 301). This much said, they innocently include within this «category of subjects» the Westphalian *Arminius* (cat. 118) and the *Bavaria* of Munich (cat. 119). It is not an interpretation colored by subsequent events to say that these are, first and foremost, monuments to the grow-

116
Photograph of the *St. Charles Borromeo* at Arona
Frédéric-Auguste Bartholdi
n.d.

117
L'éléphant de la place de la Bastille
Jean-Antoine Alavoine
n.d.

118
Photograph of the *Arminius,* at Detmold, Germany
Frédéric-Auguste Bartholdi
n.d.

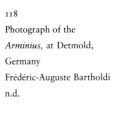

119
Photograph of the *Bavaria,* Munich
Frédéric-Auguste Bartholdi
n.d.

120
Projets de phares
(Concours de 2ᵉ classe à
l'École des Beaux-Arts,
Paris)
From *Revue Générale de*
l'Architecture et des
Travaux Publics
1852

123
Temple de Vénus et de
Rome, élévation restaurée
de la façade vers le Colisée
Ernest-Georges Coquart
1861

124
Temple de Jupiter à
Olympie, coupe
transversale
au 1/50°
Victor Laloux
1886

125
Coupe transversale du
Parthénon au 1/20°
Loviot
1880

ing nationalism of Germany. The *Arminius*, begun in 1838, was to be placed in «the very forest that witnessed the defeat of Varus» but was not finished until 1876, while the *Bavaria* was completed in the years 1844–50. What Lesbazeilles calls «the reassertion of national independence» was a reality of the period, and Arminius, or Hermann, was clearly one of its heroes. *Bavaria* is also a warrior; the sword at her side, and the laurel wreath «which she offers to him who deserves it most,» recall the proconsular triumphs of ancient Rome. Both sculptures are in bronze; one stands on a neogothic pedestal under an oppressive roof reminiscent of the Mausoleum of Theodoric in Ravenna, while the other rests on a classical base surrounded by stairways and colonnades that suggest the *Pergamon* in Berlin. Each is represented by a glass-plate photograph in Bartholdi's collection. Lesbazeilles further provides two little illustrations of the inside of *Bavaria*'s head, «furnished with a bronze bench and roomy enough to accommodate not, indeed, as has been claimed, twenty-five or thirty, but five or six persons. Openings have been contrived so that they offer a fine prospect of the city and the Alps» (pp. 304–305). Here the colossal statue-as-habitation is held up as a model to be followed, and although it does not appear that Bartholdi ever visited Munich to see the original, it is worth noting that the silhouette of both statues, standing with right arm upraised,[24] is identical to that of *Liberty*. She, however, has discarded their warlike trappings, and brandishes instead the torch of freedom.

The imaginative quality characteristic of the colossal statuary of France, which is lacking in the *Arminius* and the *Bavaria*, is most marked in Alavoine's *Elephant*, and also in a *Projet pour la colline de Chaillot* (cat. 121, 122). One of these drawings by Horeau, in a notable coincidence, has to do with a Statue of Liberty. The date is extremely important: 1868, before Bartholdi departed for Suez, at a time when he must have been evolving a form for the lighthouse project he intended to submit to the Khedive. The design echoes Horeau's project for a *Statue of the Emperor Napoléon I* in 1841 and his colossal statue of *Génie de l'Humanité* in 1851. The designs for a lighthouse (cat. 120) for the École des Beaux-Arts in some particulars prefigure the Statue of Liberty: from left to right, the rays of light above the figure of the Virgin, the drapery, and the lantern. The drawings themselves have disappeared, but

these pupils of the École would seem to have been much less accomplished than their successors, all winners of the Prix de Rome, to whom we owe drawings for the reconstruction of the Colossus of Nero with the Temple of Venus and of Rome, and the facade of the so-called Basilica of Maxentius, by Coquart (cat. 123); the Olympian Jove, by Laloux (cat. 124); and the Athena of the Parthenon (cat. 125). These drawings of colossal statues are admittedly incidental to the architectural studies of the artists, and because the original statues had long since disappeared without a trace, the three Fellows of the French Academy in Rome were left with no sources except the writings of the ancients and the opaque fabric of legend. In working out their ideas they provided us with the sources of Bartholdi's inspiration: in the Colossus of Nero, the rays which assimilate it to the sun and to Apollo, as well as the position of the legs; the gracefully raised arm of the Olympian Jove, and its hand, whose scepter Bartholdi replaced with a torch; and finally, the generously draped tunic of the only female figure among the three.

The innocent creations of these young Frenchmen, caught up in their nostalgic dream, prepared the ground for much grander reconstructions, whose eager customers included Universal Expositions, always careful about their scenery and prone to architectural theatricality. In Chapter 11, which concerns Richard Morris Hunt and the design for the pedestal, we will discern the beginnings of the ties that bound the architects of America to this same École des Beaux-Arts in Paris. They were strongest at the Universal Exposition in Chicago in 1893, whose *Columbia* (cat. 126) by now derived its inspiration from the Statue of Liberty. It is thanks to Bartholdi, who made a collection of photographs of the Chicago Exposition, that we can still contemplate the great sculpture of Daniel Chester French, standing amid its colonnades in a setting which could easily be a «reconstruction» from the École des Beaux-Arts—or from Hollywood. This particular photograph must have appealed to Bartholdi's professional pride as well as to his curiosity, for it illustrates a monument that conforms utterly to the principles he established for colossal statuary, in its nobility and amplitude of gestures, if not in economy of means. But the figure's slavish conformity to iconographic detail (or, rather, French's conviction that it did thus conform) shows how much the understanding of archeology had changed over a few decades, and what excesses might be committed in the future under the guise of evoking the classical antique.

126
Photograph of Daniel
Chester French's
Columbia
C. D. Arnold
1893

Bartholdi preserved for posterity evidence of another of his enthusiasms: Despradelles' monument «to the glory of the American people,» two photographs of which (cat. 127, 128) are in the Musée Bartholdi at Colmar.²⁵ Perhaps he saw in them a synthesis of his beloved Egypt (cat. 128)—teeming with obelisks, lions, Osiris, and pseudo-Pharaohs—and the familiar outline of the Eiffel Tower. An artist who never repudiated the style of the reign of Napoléon III, he may even have preferred this abundance of detail and historical reference to the stark simplicity of the Washington Monument as it stands today on the Mall in the capital. In cat. 130 we see the Father of his Country in an architectural and sculptural setting reminiscent at once of Halicarnassus, of Hunt's pedestal for the Statue of Liberty, and even of the statue itself. In the rayed diadem of the female figure driving the quadriga, the whole irresistibly recalls the monument to Vittorio Emmanuele II in Rome, another imposing shrine to patriotism, not unlike those which Bartholdi conceived for Gambetta (cat. 71–75) or Lafayette (cat. 339–342). In this same Beaux-Arts tradition must be reckoned the other temple of American national unity, Daniel Chester French's Lincoln Memorial (cat. 131). The gigantic seated statue of the President—a modern version of the Olympian Jove—provokes the question, whether Christendom did not lose something when the Church forsook the monumental icon of its God, the *Christos Pantocrator*, which dominates Byzantine churches, in favor of the mystical void arising from His absence. Because the Everlasting God has become Incarnate Man, the direction taken by dogma around the eleventh century was able to kindle in the West a devotion to Christ as a human being. Death takes Him away from us only so that He may return in his resurrection. But French's Lincoln is no god; he is simply a man who has died, but who has been immortalized as a colossal statue.

As if this did not amply affirm the immortality of America's national heroes—as if he felt the need to give them an eternity that would outlast even the architect's marble—

Gutzon Borglum (who remodeled *Liberty*'s torch in 1916) carved into the living rock of America the gigantic reliefs of Stone Mountain (cat. 132) and Mount Rushmore (cat. 133). Bartholdi, inspired by his transcontinental journey of 1871, had raised at America's gate a statue conceived on her own scale; Borglum, confronting the colossal tradition that Bartholdi and French had introduced to his country, sought to create a sculpture on the same grand scale, and took America's mountains for his material. Here a second ancient tradition found its American expression—that of the mountain-as-sculpture to which Deinocrates at Mount Athos, Michelangelo at Carrara, Giovanni Bologna at Pratolino, and finally Bartholdi himself at Belfort had all made their obeisance.

From this point on, the history of colossal statuary is largely an American matter, partly because the continent's boundless spaces invite projects proportioned to them, but also because this young society, functioning with its own terms of cultural reference but without any great burden of inherited memories calling for preservation, inevitably became an experimental laboratory of the arts. The unexecuted model for the Chicago Tribune Building of Adolf Loos demonstrates an unwillingness to recognize the skyscraper as a form of colossal architecture, and a desire to make it into an object that can be easily recognized as a specimen of the neoclassic style. Once the American building, in the hands of Mies van der Rohe and Walter Gropius, had attained maturity and become its own admirable kind of architecture, it remained for Claes Oldenburg to raise objects to a scale appropriate to the new city. *The Bat Column* (cat. 134) is a joke, but it is also the fruit of a readjustment by which we placidly accept the world in which we live. New York has assimilated the Brooklyn Bridge and the Statue of Liberty; this worries no one, and consummates Bartholdi's achievement.

Nevertheless, Borglum's reliefs and the Statue of Liberty contained the seeds of a change in the nature of colossal statuary—or, rather, of a return to its origins: an expression of power and an affirmation of authority. It is no coincidence that many of today's colossal heads (like the colossal

129
A Design for Washington Monument
From *American Architect and Building News*
November 8, 1879

130
Monument à Washington
E. Chifflot
1895

131
The Lincoln Memorial
Daniel Chester French
1915–22

132
Memorial Carving, Stone Mountain Park, Georgia
Gutzon Borglum
1915–25

133
Mount Rushmore
Gutzon Borglum
1927–41

134
The Bat Column
Claes Oldenburg
1977

Constantinian heads of antiquity) figure in the panoply of fascist or totalitarian governments in Europe and elsewhere. The Third Reich conceived a whole host of colossi; those of Arno Brecher have been destroyed, but those ordered by Mussolini for the Stadium in Rome still stand in the Foro Italico—no longer heroes from antiquity or holy writ, but the symbols of an ideal society of supermen. In the East, in the world of socialist realism, the huge *Motherland* (cat. 135) of Volgograd (formerly Stalingrad) is imbued with a collective emotion that no programmatic statue, not even the Statue of Liberty, can entirely escape. Other, less dynamic, but still dominating examples are the Christ on the Tagus in Lisbon and the Christ of Mt. Corcovado in Rio de Jañeiro. Most repellent of all is the recent colossal effigy of Ferdinand Marcos, a frivolous and impertinent tribute to a brutal and vainglorious government (cat. 136).

Despite all the correspondences we have noted between the world's inventory of colossal sculpture and the Statue of Liberty, it must be recognized that Bartholdi's undertaking has certain unique qualities—in its height, greater than that of any other nineteenth-century statue; in its inspiration, characterized less by nationalist allusions than any other work of the period; and by the context in which it was conceived and carried through by the united endeavors of two great peoples. Moreover, the Statue of Liberty, unlike Michelangelo's *David* or the Colossus of Nero, needed no prince or Pharaoh for her creation. That is why she has so readily become the vessel for the aspiration of peoples. It is more than probable that France's liberals and republicans, headed by Edouard de Laboulaye, were caught up in their enterprise unawares; none of them seems to have thought of anything beyond offering America a conventional statue in the middle of a square. When their intention fortuitously encountered the period's obsession with the colossal, *Liberty* was born. In the same way the tower of the Champ de Mars in Paris assumed its actual, surprising form because the technology of the pinnacle was enlisted to celebrate the centennial of the French Revolution. Both of these colossi have become dear to us because, more than any others, they have insinuated themselves into the fabric of History.

Translated, from the French, by Maxwell Vos

Genesis and Realization

Before looking over Bartholdi's shoulder as he conceives and develops a material form appropriate to the idea of Liberty, it will be worthwhile to review the long succession of images that Western civilization had made available to him. Some of these he may have absorbed from his cultural tradition; some may have lurked in his subconscious; of some he may have been wholly unaware—yet these too can help us determine the meanings conveyed by the form of his statue. The sculptor searched painstakingly for the attributes and the outline that would best serve to give human shape to an abstract idea. Fortunately for us, some of the many who have written on the statue have established parameters, if not for the entire evolving inventory of symbols, at least for that part of it which contributed to the artist's achievement: the combination of a torch with rays of light, tablets of stone, and broken chains marks the culmination of a centuries-old tradition.[1] The linkage of ideas—a colossal statue-lighthouse, in a beautiful harbor that became the gateway to the New World, with a flow of humanity around its feet reenacting the great migrations of history and myth—must have impressed a whole new image of Liberty on the collective unconscious of a full third of humankind.

Liberty has been a woman since the third century B.C. In Rome, in the temple dedicated to her on the Aventine, she is robed, wears the Phrygian cap of a freed slave, and holds a scepter denoting her independence. Her attributes are contradictory: the cat, which acknowledges no master; and the broken pitcher, a relic of her past imprisonment. Over the centuries Liberty never gave up her womanhood[2]—except when it was momentarily snatched from her by Dumont in his figure atop the Bastille Column (cat. 145) or again in 1876 when the statue of a freed slave (cat. 143) was exhibited at Memorial Hall in Philadelphia. In the seventeenth century, Cesare Ripa, in his *Iconologia*, derived the iconography, much as it stands today, from a study of ancient coins. Jean-Baptiste Huet's use of it in 1810 in *Le Trésor des artistes* demonstrates that the form not only persisted through the Revolution but derived from it the new aspect of the *sans-culotte* in the Phrygian cap. A print dated 1794, *Le Génie français adopte la Liberté et l'Egalité*, shows Liberty in classical garb with a Phrygian cap, ready to defend herself with the club of Hercules (cat. 137).

3.
Artistic Problems

Pierre Provoyeur

In America, following the Declaration of Independence in 1776, this same iconography, clearly European in origin and drawn from Ripa, developed in a parallel line. The young Democracy figures as the Infant Hercules taking suck at Liberty's breast (surely a novel association for this particular hero), under the protective wing of a *putto* carrying a Phrygian cap (cat. 138, *La Naissance de l'Amérique libre*). Three other works developing this theme of the infant America as Hercules—a drawing by Gibelin of 1783, *Libertas Americana* (cat. 139); and a terra-cotta (cat. 140) and a bronze medal by Dupré—equip Liberty with a lance, a helmet, and a shield to use in his defense, while the infant strangles the serpents as a tiger representing England watches. A drawing by Dupré (cat. 141) endows the warlike figure with new and more peaceful attributes: two tables, like those of the Mosaic Law, and the flag.

The American Liberty, as befitted her birth, was an Amazon, and is still encountered in that character many years later, for example, in 1863 on the dome of the Capitol (*Freedom*, bronze by Thomas Crawford). Her original headdress was the Phrygian cap inherited from classical antiquity; the present style dates back to 1786 and reflects the

influence of the Indian's feathers, which were by then a century-old attribute of the Americas. Thus an engraving by L. Roger (cat. 142), *Indépendance des États-Unis*, shows both the war-bonnet and the exotic headdress, intended by a double irony of history as a tribute to the French monarchy (under the setting sun of Louis XVI) and to the original inhabitants of America (soon to lose their own freedom altogether). In what Marvin Trachtenberg calls «a feat of unsurpassed iconographic hypocrisy,» the U.S. Mint in 1859 struck a medal that replaced the classical Liberty with an Indian woman in feathered headdress.[3]

The American image of Liberty evolved as did the European under conflicting pressures. From the first it related closely to the prestige of the State. In 1791 Giuseppe Cerrachi tried to sell Congress a 100-foot-high statue of Liberty, whose torch was to scatter the mists of error and illuminate the universe.[4] In 1805 the United States commissioned from Houdon a Liberty for the House of Representatives; it was destroyed in 1814, but a sculpture with the same theme (by Enrico Causici, a pupil of Canova) replaced it in 1825 and still stands there. The struggle against slavery contributed a new symbol, the broken chain (cat. 143).

139
Libertas Americana
Gibelin
1783

140
Libertas Americana
Dupré
n.d.

142
Indépendance des États-Unis
L. Roger after Duplessis-Berteaux
1786

141
La Liberté
Dupré
n.d.

138
La Naissance de l'Amérique libre
After S. Harding
n.d.

In France the iconography had been similarly enlarged by successive revolutions. Thus, when Bartholdi began his quest for the ideal form, it was already stamped by the concept of a liberating Liberty; the kinds of oppression had been different, but on either side of the Atlantic they were soon to be overthrown. Before the war of 1870 involving the fall of the Second Empire and the loss of Alsace, and also before the final repudiation of slavery in America in 1865, Bartholdi had been, like Edouard de Laboulaye, a republican in France and an abolitionist in America; he thus had a double reason for recalling the broken chain, symbol of slavery overthrown, which he placed both in Liberty's hand and beneath her feet.

A republican Bartholdi may have been, but with all the restraint which distinguishes the republican from the revolutionary. The place he occupies in both political and artistic theory in the nineteenth century is exactly indicated by a threefold evolution: from Delacroix's *Le 28 juillet 1830, la Liberté guidant le peuple aux barricades* (cat. 144) painted in 1830, to Dumont's *Le Génie de la Liberté* (cat. 145) exhibited at the Salon of 1836 and placed on the July Column in 1840, to the Statue of Liberty, which took its final shape at Bartholdi's hands in 1875.

The first of these works is outright revolutionary, and was rejected for the Salon of 1831. At about the same time, in 1835, Daumier and Grandville published a lithograph in *Caricature* in which Liberty holds out her torch to a group of unreconstructed bourgeois saying, «Puff as you will, you'll never blow it out!» At the Delacroix exhibition in Lyons in 1848 the picture was again rejected, and even when moderate republicans procured it for the Louvre in 1874 it was primarily because of its intrinsic merit. In the case of Dumont's *Génie*, its controversial force was tempered by a more allegorical style; it exhibited the broken chain rather than the musket—the illumination rather than the conflagration.[5] Bartholdi recapitulated both in his statue, and like Dumont omitted the Phrygian cap and the flag. Moreover, he whisked the broken chains to the ground beneath her feet; designed an architect's torch for her; and above all modified the entire rhythm of the composition.

What stands out in this succession of figures is, first, their decreasing immodesty: a naked breast is succeeded by a naked Mercury—then considered proper—and that in turn by an unassailably chaste matron from classical antiquity; and second, the decreasing vigor of their dynamic, culminating in a stately pace and an expressionless countenance. Delacroix stated his theme across a deafening tumult; Dumont stood on tiptoe and

whistled it; Bartholdi allowed it to develop on its own in the silence of an unbounded space. A gulf separates the «strong woman with great breasts, strident voice and coarse charms» conjured by Auguste Barbier in his poem of 1830 on Delacroix's painting, and the «mighty woman with a torch, whose flame / Is the imprisoned lightning, and her name / Mother of Exiles» of whom Emma Lazarus wrote in 1883. The same gulf separates an allegorical *Victory*—the inspiration of Delacroix and Dumont alike—and an image of *Faith* from whose diadem shoot the rays of light that link her to the Statue of Liberty.[6]

These works of Delacroix and Dumont were part of an everyday artistic environment to which Bartholdi paid scant attention. Much more important to him were the forms developed in a competition for a «Symbolic Figure of the Republic,» held in 1848 by Joseph Garraud, the young Republic's first Director of the Académie des Beaux-Arts.[7] Maurice Agulhon writes of the «understandable confusion of the symbols of the Republic and of Liberty. The philosophical and political ideal of realized Liberty was supposed to be held in common by the two nations, France and America, which had adopted the republican form of government; the form itself was esteemed up-to-date,

enterprising and progressive.»[8] Champfleury, describing the attributes that the competing artists assigned the Republic, hints at Bartholdi's sources: «there were Republics pink, green and yellow; Republics surrounded with the symbology of 1789— broken chains, egalitarian triangles, fasces, tablets of the law; Republics clad in silk, in dressing-gowns, in forest greenery, in militia uniform.»[9] Among the competitors were artists with whom Bartholdi was one day to collaborate, or whose work was to become known to him. Daumier renewed the symbology of Roman charity as well as embodying the popular Republic in the style of Delacroix (cat. 146). Gérôme used a star as a symbol of eternity. Janet-Lange heaped the instruments of industrial and agricultural prosperity behind the throne of a torch-bearing matron;[10] he even called his painting *La France éclairant le Monde* (cat. 147). Then there were Ary Scheffer's quick sketches (now in the Dordrecht Museum) of a standing figure with its right arm raised. The report of the jury reveals much about what the period required of an allegorical figure. Of Flandrin's painting the report says, «The Republic is pure and white, a virgin unspotted. . . . This countenance bears the stamp of distinction,»[11] which Daumier's did not.

146
La République
Honoré Daumier
1848

147
La France éclairant le Monde
A.-L. Janet-Lange
ca. 1848

143
The Statue of «The Freed Slave» in Memorial Hall
Smeeton Tilly
1876

144
Le 28 juillet 1830, la Liberté guidant le peuple aux barricades
Eugène Delacroix
1830

145
Model of the Colossal Statue *Le Génie de la Liberté* for the Bastille Column
Auguste Dumont
ca. 1836–40

Here we must take note of Bartholdi's introduction (by the ultra-republican Ary Scheffer) to the circle in which he found his future political affiliations. The time was ripe for a series of insensible alterations in the idea of Liberty itself. In 1830 a revolution was undertaken to change the form of government; in 1848, to improve it. The emphasis had shifted from Freedom to freedoms—of the individual no less than of religion and of the press which are inscribed on the throne of France in Janet-Lange's painting. By 1872 the march of ideas had reached those freedoms that could be assured only under law; there could be no more references to cat, pitcher, or Phrygian cap. Achille Deveria, in a lithograph (cat. 148) probably only a little later than the 1848 competition, already proclaims this profound change in iconography.

Bartholdi himself was to play variations on this theme of «The Republic.» One of them was his abortive project for a *Monument à la Gloire des Girondins*, several models for which are in the Musée Bartholdi, Colmar (Inv. nos. 60, 66, 103, 171). In one of these, dated 1887 and therefore almost immediately following the Statue of Liberty, the Phrygian cap reappears on the head of a figure that exactly copies the attitude of the New York statue, but without the same solemnity.[12] The *Monument à la Mémoire des héros de l'Indépendance, 1830* (cat. 149, 150, 151) is another variation on Liberty, probably later and certainly less colossal (though still twice life-size), perched on four disproportionately huge columns and looking very like the second project for a *Vercingétorix*.

149
Model for the Figure for the *Monument à la Mémoire des héros de l'Indépendance, 1830*
Frédéric-Auguste Bartholdi
n.d.

148
Étude pour une figure allégorique de la Liberté
Achille Deveria
n.d.

152
Maquette for the *Monument aux victimes de Callao*
Frédéric-Auguste Bartholdi
n.d.

154
La France couronnant l'Art et l'Industrie
Elias Robert
1855

Another columned project, preserved in a photograph (cat. 152), a *Monument aux victimes de Callao*, has a two-fold interest for us: it supports a winged Victory carrying crowns directly imitated from the Châtelet Fountain (cat. 153), which is itself derived from allegorical figures such as Elias Robert's *La France couronnant l'Art et l'Industrie*. This sculptural group, unveiled in 1855, stood above the entrance pavilion of the Palais de l'Industrie at the Universal Exposition. Its draperies and seven-rayed diadem foreshadow the Statue of Liberty. The old photograph reproduced here (cat. 154), from Bartholdi's own collection, confirms his indebtedness. The tradition of a Republic crowned with rays of light rather than the Phrygian cap was triumphantly incorporated by Auguste Barre in the new Seal of the State in 1848.[13]

The theme of the sun and its rays finds two echoes in Bartholdi's own background. His great-grandmother Marie Ursula Sonntag («*Sun*day») and her husband, Gilles-François Bartholdi, kept a pharmacy «At the Sign of the Sun» where the artist's studio now stands restored in Colmar. More significant, in 1875 the sculptor joined the Masonic lodge of Alsace-Lorraine, where he may have learned to stress the symbolic significance of rays of light.

Nonetheless, the rayed crown probably stems also from traditional iconography. Coquart's *Colosse de Néron* (1861), complete with rays, was this artist's entry for the Prix de Rome. S. A. Hardy's project for a lighthouse incorporated a Virgin and Child crowned with light. Bartholdi could not have failed to notice the figure of *Faith* (mentioned above), Protestant though he was. In any case, as Agulhon observes, «It was Bartholdi who first made popular the association of Liberty with the Sun. Thereafter one thing was certain: the old tradition of Liberty with her Phrygian cap had been effectively challenged.»[14]

In France most of Liberty's attributes evolved around the figure symbolizing the Republic. In the United States the evolution explored byways, and absorbed outside influences. Columbia, the personification of the United States that refers to Christopher Columbus and through him to Europe, rapidly assimilated with Liberty.[15] A work attributed to Bartholdi, a very free variation on the Statue of Liberty, has the attributes of a specifically American heroine but retains *Liberty*'s bearing, her torch, and her rays, transfigured into lightning-bolts which the figure tramples beneath its feet. *Liberty* as a statue, derived from many predecessors, has engendered its own host of successors. The popularity of the words «Statue» and «Liberty» together demonstrates that iconographic linkages (which may entirely escape the notice of the generality of humankind) are less important than the form finally achieved, or than the creative artist's own contribution.

*The Quest for Sources:
Bartholdi's Two Journeys to Egypt*

Bartholdi's journeys to Egypt are both milestones in his career. The first, in 1856 at the age of twenty-two, was a voyage of study and discovery, fulfilling a personal mission of Bartholdi's; he chose his own destination, covered his own expenses, and traveled with a group of artists who had come together for the purpose. The second journey, thirteen years later, was also taken on the sculptor's own initiative, this time for business purposes: in pursuit of a great commission, a long-cherished dream—the construction of a gigantic statue-lighthouse at the entrance of the new canal linking the Mediterranean with the port of Suez on the Red Sea.

This second journey is considered the more important to the genesis of the Statue of Liberty because it helped to establish Bartholdi's good relations with Ferdinand de Lesseps, with the court of Napoléon III, and with the Egyptian Khedive. It is, nevertheless, also important to consider how the expedition of 1856 may have enriched Bartholdi's imagination, and what it signifies in the context of the art of the period. Nor should we overlook Bartholdi's use of the camera on this trip, which anticipated the collection of photographs he assembled in the United States in 1871, and thereafter in the French and American workshops where the Statue of Liberty was constructed.

Prominent among the many objectives that may have drawn Bartholdi to Egypt was the desire to see the colossal sculptures and monuments of the Pharaonic period. Before treating this special motive and its consequences, however, we should consider some others.

Bartholdi's century witnessed something novel for the West: a peaceful intercourse with the East. The taking of Algiers in 1830 and the Narrows Convention of 1841 made the Mediterranean safer, both for the expansionist ambitions of Europe and for the individual traveler. Delacroix went to Morocco in 1832, Eugène Fromentin to Algiers, and Gérard de Nerval to Cairo in 1843, anticipating Flaubert who with Maxim Ducamp mounted the first photographic expedition to Egypt, the Levant, and Istanbul in 1849–51. Théophile Gautier was in Algeria in 1845 and in the Levant in 1853. When the French government dispatched Ignace Xavier Hommaire de Hell to record the wonders of Turkey and Persia (published in four volumes in Paris, 1854–57), David Roberts had already produced for the English market his *Views in the Holy Land, Syria, Idumea, Arabia, Egypt and Nubia* (1842–49). The increasing dominance of France and England in North Africa and the Middle East was attended by poetic and artistic accompaniments; Victor Hugo's *Les Orientales* of 1829 provides a useful *terminus a quo* for these. Perhaps the most significant *ad quem* is furnished by an episode of Europe's commercial and technical expansion—the undertaking of the Suez Canal by Ferdinand de Lesseps in 1854.

This background helps explain why the real or supposed invitation from the painter and sculptor Jean-Léon Gérôme went straight to the young Bartholdi's head, for it represented an opportunity to work in the forefront of contemporary artistic thought. There was perhaps another motivation for his making the journey. Bartholdi had watched students from the École des Beaux-Arts win the Prix de Rome, and leave for a five-year sojourn in Italy, Greece, and the

Middle East to complete their education. A vocal opponent of this system, he took pains throughout his career to avoid Rome; for example, from his second visit to Egypt in 1869 he returned by way of Venice.

More personal reasons may also have made travel attractive to him. As a Christian he was familiar with the Bible,[16] and its stories of colossal structures—the Tower of Babel, the Temple of Solomon—and the thought-provoking narrative of the Captivity in Egypt served as lodestones to draw him to the Middle East. Second, the oppressive atmosphere his mother imposed on her household may have planted in him an urgent desire to put as much distance as possible between himself and her, even if only for a few months.

Three other artists, two of whom already knew the Middle East, accompanied Bartholdi. Narcisse Berchère had visited Egypt, Asia Minor, the Greek islands, and Venice in 1849–50; Léon Belly had been part of the scientific expedition under the leadership of L. F. Caignart de Saulcy which in 1850–51 made the circuit of the Dead Sea and went on to Egypt. In April 1856 both men were back in the Sinai, and in July they were joined in Lower Egypt by Bartholdi and Jean-Léon Gérôme. Much the best known of the four, Gérôme had inaugurated at the Salon of 1855 a new career as an eth-nographic painter. Now, in Egypt, where his teacher Charles Gleyre had been before him in 1834–35, he sought a country that could bring him subjects worthy to succeed his first Greco-Roman compositions. Belly's *Oasis* (cat. 155) shows the village of Gizeh at the foot of the Pyramids where Belly made his headquarters; the treatment is reminiscent of the Barbizon School (he had worked at Fontainebleau in 1850 and 1855), and the atmosphere is like that found in Bartholdi's photographs. In the *Jeune homme coiffé d'une chéchia* (cat. 156), also by Belly, we may elect to discern a portrait of Bartholdi rather than of Edouard Imer, who is mentioned in a single letter of Gérôme's as a fifth member of the party but whose presence is otherwise undocumented. Imer was then thirty-six, and Bartholdi twenty-two, more plausible for the subject of the portrait, whose close-cropped mus-tache does not age a face dominated by its large black eyes and disordered hair. The silhouette resembles Bartholdi's photo-graphic self-portrait (cat. 166). Another drawing made by Belly on this trip (cat. 157) shows one of the artists studying in the ruins of the Ramesseum opposite Karnak.

155
L'Oasis
Léon Belly
n.d.

156
Jeune homme coiffé d'une chéchia [Portrait de Bartholdi]
Léon Belly
n.d.

157
Ruines de Karnak
Léon Belly
n.d.

The sketches for Gérôme's *Vue de la plaine de Thèbes* with the Colossi of Memnon (cat. 158), painted after the artist had returned to Paris in 1857, were made in the field. A comparison with Bartholdi's photographs illustrates the divergent concerns of the three painters on the one hand and the sculptor on the other. Belly, Berchère, and Gérôme were collecting impressions, from which they could later distill exotic paintings bathed in warmth and light, redolent of the Thousand and One Nights as revisited by trained ethnographers. Bartholdi's object was to inspect and reflect on the best-preserved remains of the colossal monuments of high antiquity.

Significantly, the young artist has left no painting «on my return from Egypt,» but rather a series of impressive camera studies worthy of any modern photojournalist. Leaves from a traveler's diary, apparently intended for his family (cat. 160–169), they are punctuated with careful documentary pictures. The view of the *Colossi of Memnon* (cat. 159a) has no purpose other than to bring out the superhuman scale of the figures, conveyed relative to two fellahin whom Bartholdi posed there. They appear again, this time in Western garb, at the foot of the gigantic columns in the model for the *Monument aux victimes de Callao* and the *Monument à la Mémoire des héros de l'Indépendance, 1830.* Bartholdi's approach is in a way the opposite of Gérôme's, for whom the Colossi of Memnon are «absorbed» into a setting on a scale commensurate with their own, in a landscape that overflows the edges of the canvas. For Bartholdi, their seated majesty overwhelms the standing figures at their feet; their mystery derives not from the space around them but from the innate power conferred on them by the mind, and the chisel, of the sculptor—from an inward tension with which he alone has endowed them:

> To all those who have studied it, Egyptian art has been the object of profound admiration, not only in view of the masses, the millions of kilogrammes moved by the Egyptian people, but on account of its concrete and majestic character, in design and in form, of the works which we see. We are filled with profound emotion in presence of these colossal witnesses, centuries old, of a past that to us is almost infinite, at whose feet so many generations, so many million existences, so many human glories,

158
Vue de la plaine de Thèbes—1857
Jean-Léon Gérôme
1857

159a
The Colossi of Memnon
Frédéric-Auguste Bartholdi
n.d.

159b
Statues of Memnon
Frédéric-Auguste Bartholdi
n.d.

160
Elephantine Island
Frédéric-Auguste Bartholdi
1855

161
Denderah
Frédéric-Auguste Bartholdi
n.d.

162
Ramesseum
Frédéric-August Bartholdi
1856

164
Cluster of Palms
Frédéric-Auguste Bartholdi
n.d.

163
Banks of the Nile
Frédéric-Auguste Bartholdi
n.d.

have rolled in the dust. These granite beings, in their imperturbable majesty, seem to be still listening to the most remote antiquity. Their kindly and impassable glance seems to ignore the present and to be fixed upon an unlimited future. These impressions are not the result simply of a beautiful spectacle, nor of the poetry of historic remembrances. They result from the character of the form and the expression of the work in which the design itself expresses after a fashion infinity.[17]

We do not know if Bartholdi's Egyptian photographs included studies of other colossi; those of Memnon must have fascinated him, because there is another view of them in his collection of glass plates (cat. 159b). He stopped also at Memphis, where he must have seen the colossal statue of Ramses II; the little band ascended the Nile as far as Aswan where Bartholdi photographed Elephantine Island (cat. 160), but apparently failed to cross the desert to Abu Simbel with its gigantic seated figures. He must also have seen the Pyramids of Gizeh and the Sphinx, since a watercolor by Thomas Seddon shows that by 1856 the excavations had progressed far enough to permit a magnificent view of the colossus. Bartholdi certainly had the Sphinx in mind when he conceived his *Lion de Belfort*. Later, when certain temples beneath the sand were uncovered, ideas about their vast scale were revised, but the photograph of the Temple of Hathor at Dendera (cat. 161) reminds us that even at the very beginning of the golden age of archeology, Bartholdi was careful to record the monumental heads that here serve as capitals. The temples of Luxor and Karnak (cat. 162) with their gigantic columns and obelisks impressed him no less than the enormous carved figures from the facades of Medinet Habu (Musée Bartholdi, Colmar, Inv. phot. 1P3/58).

Like all travelers, in our own day no less than his, Bartholdi fell under the spell of contemporary Egypt. His photographs of the banks of the Nile (cat. 163 and 164) are full of a humanity that contrasts with the heroic spirit of the earlier studies of architecture and sculpture.

Belly and Berchère, as well as Gérôme, who had his own camera, could guide Bartholdi's first steps in this landscape and open his eyes to it. But whereas for Gérôme the photograph seems always to have been prelude to a painting, for Bartholdi it was an end in itself, and almost every one carries his signature. It was the same with the American photographs of 1871.

165
Campground
Frédéric-Auguste Bartholdi
1855

166
Bridge of the Boat
Frédéric-Auguste Bartholdi
1855–56

169
Bartholdi in Oriental Costume
n.d.

Our travelers were careful to photograph each other to record their everyday doings for posterity; they documented the tents of their camp (cat. 165), the bridge of their boat (cat. 166), the native clothes (which they may have worn for a prank, no less than for protection from the heat of midsummer) (cat. 167).[18]

Bartholdi always looks serious in his fancy dress, standing with his friends Belly (cat. 168, right) and possibly Gérôme (cat. 169), and again in the center (cat. 168).[19] On their return to Cairo, they happily accepted the use of a house in the old city belonging to Suleiman Pasha, where Gérôme, Belly, and Berchère stayed for another four months. Bartholdi went home before the end of 1856 to prepare for the unveiling in Colmar of his *General Rapp*, a sculpture exhibited at the Salon of 1856. Before leaving he made some lithographs of picturesque views in and around Cairo; these have survived in photographic reproductions (Musée d'Unterlinden, Colmar: *Une Rue de Cairo*, no. 19; *Les Tombeaux des Califes*, no. 20; *Scène de rue*, no. 21). From this time also we may date his friendship with Léon Belly, whose portrait bust he made in 1877.[20] Finally, he brought back from this trip the notion of a group, *La lyre Berbère* (cat. 177, detail), which he exhibited at the 1857 Salon.

The true significance of this earlier journey, however, lies in Bartholdi's first encounter with the colossal sculpture and architecture of ancient Egypt, which stimulated his imagination and made real for him the legends of antiquity. Surrounded by Egypt's ruins, he must certainly have reflected on the Pharos lighthouse of Alexandria—gone forever, but preserved by architects and writers of classical times and of the Renaissance.

In the thirteen-year interval between Bartholdi's two journeys, the single most significant event for the history of the Statue of Liberty was Bartholdi's meeting with Edouard de Laboulaye in 1865. However, Bartholdi had already conceived a project for a monumental lighthouse and, immediately on his return from his first visit to Egypt, had set about considering how he could best become involved in the great Suez Canal undertaking.

Ferdinand de Lesseps had received the Canal concession in 1854 from Mohammed Sayyid, the viceroy of Egypt. Bartholdi and his companions must have known of it when they were in Cairo in 1856, for Berchère became the company's painter-in-ordinary, charged by de Lesseps with keeping a pictorial record of its work. His *Le Désert de Suez, Cinq mois dans l'isthme*, dedicated to Fromentin, appeared in 1863. In 1869 Berchère, Fromentin, and Gérôme, along with Frère and Vacher de Tournemire, were sent by the French government to participate at the opening of the Canal. It was in these very official circumstances that Bartholdi, who had come on his own, was reunited with his old traveling companions.

Bartholdi prepared his ground with the Egyptian authorities well before his second visit; the opportunity arose on the occasion of the Universal Exposition in Paris in 1867. The Egyptian pavilion was crafted of gilded wood so lavish that when the exposition closed King Ludwig II of Bavaria bought it for his castle at Linderhof, where it may still be seen. On the heels of this grand spectacle, which took Paris by storm, the Khedive himself arrived, bringing the mystery of the

East and a reputation for being up to date. Receptive to contact with the West, Ismail Pasha encouraged the industrialization of his country (of which the Canal was a prerequisite) while striving to preserve its historic inheritance; at the Exposition a second pavilion in the form of a temple displayed the discoveries of Mariette, the French archeologist who worked under the protection of the viceroy. Above all, the Khedive was an opponent of slavery; as such he paid a formal call on the Abolitionist Societies of France and England, whose president was Laboulaye. Finally, Bartholdi had made a careful presentation of his project to the Emperor and Empress,[21] perhaps with the help of Eugène Viollet-le-Duc, who had been Bartholdi's teacher in the 1850s, and on whom he was later to call for the structural engineering of his colossal statue. Thus, he did not lack means of introduction to the man who alone could give him his commission.

Bartholdi's acceptance of encouragement from the Empress[22] shows that he was politically uncommitted, although already closely linked to the liberal republicans around Laboulaye, whose opposition to the Empire was, however, still clandestine. The sculptor needed a commission from the Khedive as Head of State, which he could hope for only if he came recommended from the highest quarters. Uncertain that even such a recommendation would suffice, upon reaching Cairo, Bartholdi sought the help of two little-known men, M. Barrot and through him Dr. Burguières, who arranged for him to be received by the Khedive.[23] The meeting took place on April 8 at Ismailia, the new capital; what happened was immediately set out in a letter from the artist to his mother, from which we learn that Bartholdi carried with him a drawing and a model to explain his proposal.[24]

170
Project for the Suez Lighthouse
Frédéric-Auguste Bartholdi
n.d.

171
L'Egypte apportant la lumière à l'Asie
Frédéric-Auguste Bartholdi
1869
also reproduced in color,
p. 133

Of seven objects in the Musée Bartholdi that may reasonably be associated with this project, the most important is a photograph (cat. 170) whose mount bears a notation in Bartholdi's own hand: «Projet de Phare pour Suez.—Présenté au Khédive 1869.» The drawing which was the original for this photograph is lost, but it was certainly to this that Bartholdi referred in his letter: «I presented to His Majesty my drawings and the statuette, which he examined with interest.» The second drawing, a watercolor (cat. 171), is no doubt a preliminary sketch. The first offers a sternly frontal view of the monument, intended to impress with its symmetry and majesty; the second suggests a point of view moving around the statue. This considered approach was later to govern the drawings he made of the Statue of Liberty for publicity purposes; all were frontal views, the more grandiose for being wholly static. The most characteristic change between the first and the second rendering is the addition of rays of light springing from the figure's head, which confirm the annotation «Projet de Phare. . . .»

Bartholdi himself had entitled the project *L'Egypte apportant la lumière à l'Asie*, in an attempt to relate the storied heritage, historical and spiritual, that surrounds the very name of Egypt to the modernizing mission assumed by the Khedive, which was believed to be unique in Asia. Thence came the torch in the figure's hand—whose symbolism, however, became fainter and less certain when the sculptor caused rays to issue from the statue's forehead as well. But this was not the only solution that occurred to him. Of the five terra-cotta maquettes still at Colmar, only two (cat. 174 and 175) directly approximate the form of the final project. Two others (cat. 172 and 173), taking the most logical approach, place in the upraised arm a lantern so gigantic that it can contain the whole mechanism of a lighthouse.

172
Maquette for *Suez* with Socle
Frédéric-Auguste Bartholdi
1869

173
Maquette for *Suez*
Frédéric-Auguste Bartholdi
1869

174
Maquette for *Suez*
Frédéric-Auguste Bartholdi
1869

175
Maquette for *Suez*
Frédéric-Auguste Bartholdi
1869

Bartholdi cannot have overlooked the technical constraints on such a design nor the weight it would entail; perhaps for these reasons, between cat. 172 and 173 he introduced the unconvincing drapery that conceals the strong structural support, in metal or stonework, required by the weight of the enormous lantern. In this same version the forehead wears a simple fillet, later to evolve into a massive diadem; Bartholdi was on his way to eliminating the lantern by placing the lighthouse mechanism inside the figure's head, thus allowing him to be merciful to the raised arm. At the same time he balanced the composition by reversing the folds of the drapery, which now form a left-handed curve while the torch closes a curve to the right.

Unfortunately the sculptor's letters do not indicate which of the five maquettes was shown to the Khedive. It was most probably cat. 172, the most spectacular and, because of the human figures at the foot of the pedestal, the most indicative of the scale of the project. This maquette, moreover, is the only one to show the proposed dimensions, cut into its clay. On the other hand, Bartholdi may have decided, for convenience, to take only the smallest maquette, which is also the closest to the final design (cat. 175). A third possibility is that, like the drawing, the maquette shown to the Khedive was presented to him and is now lost. Of greater significance, Ismail Pasha exercised the customer's prerogative of choice: according to Bartholdi, the Khedive suggested that the lighthouse be placed atop the statue in a pitcher or a bundle of the kind that Egyptian women carry on their heads. Bartholdi, who feared losing the effect of his torch as well as any delicacy that still remained to the figure, replied that «it would be easier that way, but it would not look so well.»[25] Did this reserve prove fatal?

It was not that the viceroy of Egypt was ill-disposed; during his reign fifteen lighthouses were built at a total cost of $138,000.[26] Charles Pomeroy Stone, who was to play a leading role in the construction of the pedestal of the Statue of Liberty (see Chapter 12), took charge of the Khedive's Department of Works in 1870. The sculptor, fine diplomat that he was, did not ask for an answer until two months later, when the Pasha planned to visit Paris; if the answer

176

Ferdinand de Lesseps
ca. 1869

177

Detail of *La lyre Berbère*
Frédéric-Auguste Bartholdi
ca. 1856

was no, perhaps it had something to do with the negative attitude of Ferdinand de Lesseps (cat. 176), whom the sculptor had visited on his arrival in Egypt and who had tried to dissuade him from pressing his case with the Khedive, whom he knew well.[27] Or perhaps, after Bartholdi left, Stone moved to kill the project. If so, no grudges were borne; when the sculptor and de Lesseps met again the latter was president of the Franco-American Union (from 1883 on) and remained so through the unveiling of *Liberty* in 1886. The Suez lighthouse was only an episode in the history of their friendship.

There are questions the record cannot answer about the twin symbolisms of the Suez lighthouse project submitted to the Khedive. The first, intended by Bartholdi, uses the figure of a woman and the outline of an Egyptian fellah. She appears in his group *La lyre Berbère* (cat. 177), painted on his first return from Egypt, endowed with an unmistakably feminine bosom accentuated by clinging drapery and wearing a piece of traditional jewelry around her neck. Alas for all his pains! The final figure was more hermaphroditic (a criticism that cannot justly be leveled at the Statue of Liberty). But, significantly, the figure also proclaims a national theme in terms both historical and ethnological, mingling allusions to the dress of pharaonic Egypt (the diadem and veil together), the draped robe of classical antiquity, and the contemporary folk costume of the Nile Valley.

The idea of the lighthouse also had an eclectic derivation. Its greatest forerunner, the Pharos of Alexandria, was a gauntlet, so to speak, thrown down by Egyptian history which the sculptor eagerly took up. But, perhaps unconsciously, he flavored the historic original with his biblical learning; the rays issuing from the crown of the colossus are the same that shine from the forehead of Moses. In the final version, heavily Egyptian, the pedestal unmistakably recapitulates the trapezoidal doorway and straight cornice of a pharaonic temple. This pedestal, devoid of all superfluous elements, shows how careful Bartholdi was to reserve his finest effects for the draped figure and its curves. (Its starkness is prophetic of the artist's future problems with Richard Morris Hunt when the latter undertook a pedestal for the Statue of Liberty.)

178

L'Entrée du Canal à Port Said

Riou

n.d.

180

Project for a Mausoleum for the Khedive in the Classical Style

Frédéric-Auguste Bartholdi

1869

181

Project for a Mausoleum for the Khedive in the Egyptian Style

Frédéric-Auguste Bartholdi

1869

The second symbolism inherent in the project has to do not with its shape but with its position and orientation. If Bartholdi's lighthouse, facing the sea to mark the entrance to the canal, had been placed outside Port Said (cat. 178), rather than outside Port Tewfik (cat. 179), it would have looked westward over the Mediterranean, «bringing light» to the very continent on which its back was resolutely turned.

Unconcerned to read such excessive significance into his work, Bartholdi sought to present the image of a nation seen in all the grandeur of enlightenment. We are dealing here with a philosophy of light very close to Falconet's when he put Peter the Great, and all Russia with him, astride the irresistible momentum of his horse. In this case the momentum is signified by a physical light rather than by the shape of the figure, static and monumental as the colossi of Memnon and those masterpieces of Egyptian architecture which Bartholdi strove not to imitate but to equal.[28]

Whatever its various meanings, the canal lighthouse project broke new ground for Bartholdi, both in terms of sheer size and in its need for new technical resources that he probably expected to find in the enormous workshops of the canal itself. The figures on the model (cat. 172) indicate the scale of his ambition: the pedestal was to be more than 46 feet high; the figure almost 48 feet from head to toe and 86½ feet from the toe to the top of the lantern. At 133 feet overall, the monument would have been only 10 feet shorter than the Statue of Liberty (excluding its pedestal). Bartholdi's deepest concern, his dearest wish, was to build a colossus.

For the same patron he designed a monumental mausoleum that combined all his artistic convictions within an impressively logical framework. Did Bartholdi conceive this second project as an offering to Ismail Pasha when they met again in Paris, to flatter his patron—had not the Khedive given his own name to the new city of Ismailia?—and perhaps to furnish an alternative if the lighthouse were finally to be turned down? The two drawings reproduced here never left the sculptor's possession, and, like the later designs for *Liberty*'s pedestal, are variants on an artistic theme—based on a flight of steps—which recalls the tomb of King Mausolus of Halicarnassus. On a structure inspired by classical (cat. 180) or Egyptian (cat. 181) architecture the

seated figure of the Pasha leans on a lion—traditional architectural rhetoric used here to represent the living, peaceable animal (rather than the skin, as in the Nemean lion laid low by Hercules, which was evidently considered too warlike and «Western» for this purpose). The composition suggests a seated Buddha, and we know that Bartholdi possessed a glass plate of the *Bouddah of Kamakura* (cat. 182). Neither the Khedive nor the sculptor pursued this project.

The Suez lighthouse certainly provided the occasion of Bartholdi's first thoughts on a monumental sculpture, and thus the origin of the modeling for the monument to American independence. Twice Bartholdi had to defend himself against the charge that he had recycled the Egyptian project into the Statue of Liberty. Cut to the quick, he responded: «I never executed anything for the Khedive except a little sketch which has remained in his palace, and represents Egypt under the features of a female Fellah. Besides every one has seen the model of the Statue of Liberty made at Paris, and only evilly disposed persons are ignorant of what it has cost me. I have never answered these small cavilings. . . .»[29]

Replying to charges in the *New York Times*, Bartholdi told a reporter from *Argus*:

> . . . a colossal statue of an Egyptian female holding a light aloft . . . was declined on account of the expense. At that time my Statue of Liberty did not exist, even in my imagination, and the only resemblance between the drawing that I submitted to the Khedive and the statue now in New York's beautiful harbor is that both hold a light aloft. Now, I ask you, sir, how is a sculptor to make a statue which is to serve the purpose of a lighthouse without making it hold the light in the air? . . . My Statue of Liberty was a pure work of love, costing me the sacrifice of ten years and of twenty thousand dollars—little perhaps for Americans, but a great deal for me. The Egyptian affair would have been purely a business transaction. I declare most emphatically, and I defy anyone in the world to contradict me, that the Statue of Liberty was ever offered to any other government.[30]

The sculptor's declarations do not quite carry conviction, given the existence of watercolors and maquettes that provide visible proof of a line of descent. The real problem, then, is to determine just when the sculptor gave up on the Khedive and began to adapt his Egyptian form to the purposes required by the French liberals.

His correspondence offers the beginning of an answer; two letters in December 1869 mention discussions with an American, and a project worked out with him of which Bartholdi «has great hopes.»[31] Another clue appears in the inventory of his widow's estate after her death in 1914; it makes no mention of the Suez models, but lists so many maquettes for *Liberty* that we must conclude that the five maquettes for the Suez lighthouse project are listed under this heading. This suggests that Bartholdi himself had not thought it worthwhile to distinguish one group from the other.

Why did the sculptor wish the world to believe in two quite separate undertakings? Bartholdi's disclaimers occur late in the sequence of events. Perhaps, as has been suggested, by 1904 he would not have wanted the American people to suspect that the familiar shape might originally have been conceived for some other purpose. A more weighty reason, going back to the first clay maquettes fired by the artist on his second return from Egypt, is that he wanted to obliterate a failure, to wash away the bitter taste of rejection, and to merge into a new creation the remains of one that had miscarried. He threw himself energetically into the new project, and also launched yet another. In 1869–70 he made the first sketches for his *Vercingétorix* in its original, colossal form over 100 feet high, perhaps to ensure that one of the two would come to fruition. The Egyptian failure, far from discouraging him, kindled a furious urge to succeed.

Deliberately omitted in the commentary above is the fifth of the models (cat. 183) at Colmar, which certainly belongs to the Suez cycle since, like the others, it is initialed and dated «A B 1869.» It has been stripped alike of the characteristics of a lighthouse—no lantern, no torch—and of those of an Egyptian woman—no necklace, no head-dress but a rudimentary veil of no particular style. In this figure we may discern the archetype imagined by Bartholdi to express the idea—the gift of light—that the Suez and the New York projects have in common. From it we may trace two parallel lines of descent, one leading to *L'Egypte apportant la lumière à l'Asie* and the other to *La Liberté éclairant le Monde*. Leaving aside this and the *Modèle du Comité* of 1875, which must still be considered the definitive miniature before enlargement, we have eight maquettes in terra cotta or plaster to help us follow the sculptor's progress. This is few enough, compared to the number still in his studio at the time of his death, not to mention those that he may have given away in his lifetime (we are sure of two of these, one in Paris and one in New York) and those that have simply vanished.

We are at once struck by the pains Bartholdi took to endow his archetypal figure (cat. 183) with diverging tensions: one upward with the right fist raised in front of it; the other downward, left fist behind it grasping some fragmentary object, recalling the broken pitcher of traditional iconography. The diagonal thus created is balanced by the bust thrown backward and to the left and the right foot thrust forward, to form a second diagonal. The weight of the body falls on the left leg and its foot, which is placed toward the back of the plinth. The lack of drapery allows a clear view of the pattern formed by these lines. It is an allegory of revolution, declared by some resolute goddess of vengeance, whose fine face, for once, unequivocally matches the feminine figure.

The first model of *Liberty* (cat. 184) express-es the same tension between the two fists. The feet are now placed together, giving the figure more serenity; at the same time it has acquired the hipshot stance of one who has been standing for a long time. A new severity has crept into and hardened the face. New ideas have enriched the allegory with unambiguous symbols. The broken chain which the figure tramples beneath its feet clearly betokens resolution. The almost-Berber dress of the Suez figure has given place to the chiton and peplum of classical antiquity.

The historical sources are so numerous and so traditional that it would be pointless to give instances. In the storage-rooms of the Musée Bartholdi, however, we uncovered a little cast from an ancient statue that must have belonged to Bartholdi and may have served him as a model (cat. 192). The same drapery covers the two figures that are Bartholdi's exercises (cat. 185) on the theme Navigation, next to F. Jouffroy's sculptures at the Louvre (*Le Commerce* and *La Navigation*, 1861–64). Two other statuettes (cat. 186 and 187) show that the symbol of Alsace or of Agriculture could equally be embodied in a Greco-Roman matron. An-other project for the *Monument de l'Indépendance des États-Unis* shows a stele bearing the Declaration of Independence with two classically draped figures, one diademed. Finally, Bartholdi's composition for his *Monument allégorique aux victimes de 1870–1871*, entitled «In Clade Decus» («Glory in Defeat») and unveiled at Belfort in 1912, invokes the same associations, conferring the stoic virtues inherited from centuries of classicism and neoclassicism on

185
Study for *La Navigation*
Frédéric-Auguste Bartholdi
n.d.

184
First Idea for the Statue of
Liberty, Similar to *Suez*
Frédéric-Auguste Bartholdi
1870

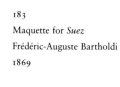

183
Maquette for *Suez*
Frédéric-Auguste Bartholdi
1869

figures representing national misfortune (Belfort, Alsace) or communal activity (Commerce, Legislation). Just as he designed for the Khedive an approximation of Berber costume, so Bartholdi submitted to Laboulaye, his patron in 1870, the noble dress of classical antiquity that must have been comfortably familiar to that distinguished professor of law.

The next maquette (cat. 188), now in the Museum of the City of New York, is particularly significant because we have reason to believe that it was brought to the United States by Bartholdi himself, left there, and rescued from oblivion by the increasing fame of its subject. It was certainly modeled in Paris before the artist left for America on June 10, 1871. Like its immediate predecessor it must have been conceived after the return from Egypt and the collapse of the Suez project in the fall of 1869, but before Bartholdi's posting as captain to National Guard G.H.Q. for the Seine in the spring of 1870. The Franco-Prussian War took him far away from his studio after August 13, when he joined the National Guard in Colmar. He moved to Belfort on September 30, and to Tours on October 4. On March 4, 1871, he was still at Bordeaux; the following May 8 he wrote to Laboulaye from Colmar. He did not return to Paris until the day before the surrender of the Commune, on May 31.[32] It is difficult to see how the statuette could have been finished between then and June 10.

This model has many of the characteristics of its predecessor; the body expresses the same rhythm on a scale almost exactly twice as large (cat. 184, 26.2 cm.; cat. 188, 56.0 cm.). The drapery is more detailed, and reveals more of the movement of leg and hip. The torch is lit, and its details of design are clear. The chain is still there, trampled under the left (or leading) foot. The right hand, less outthrust, grips the same fragment of a broken pitcher. The diadem is still of coffered design but, here and hereafter, carries seven rays angled somewhat upward.

These embody the same light whose rays Bartholdi had twice incorporated into his Suez project (cat. 170 and 171), but here they shine out above the diadem rather than through the coffered windows the sculptor had conceived earlier. The idea of the Pharos merges into the iconography of radiant figures, in both sacred and secular art.

Bartholdi's letter to Laboulaye of May 8, 1871, makes clear that his patron had not yet seen these preliminary sketches. The artist begins by lamenting the time he had been obliged to spend «restoring a little order to [his] confused affairs.» He continues, in another passage, «My house is almost untouched, except that it boasts not a single window . . .; otherwise nothing has been broken, stolen or damaged.»[33] Evidently his sketches and work in progress escaped harm, but were not ready to be shown to his patron. The sculptor asked for help toward his American journey, and it was probably only on his return that he sent

Laboulaye a model (cat. 189), similar to an earlier model (cat. 188) that had survived field tests in the United States—that is, both the confrontation with its future site in New York harbor, and the reaction of the Americans to whom Bartholdi, with the aid of the little clay model, had explained his project in detail.

The work was truly elegant. Bartholdi had lightened the folds of the peplum a little, disclosing the body beneath the fabric and perhaps even the life in his creation. In its left hand the figure held a fragment of the chain it trampled underfoot, in token of a victorious liberation. The high diadem with its rays appeared again; the face, less strained than in the preceding sketch, assumed an almost Roman nobility. Above all, Bartholdi carefully confined the figure within a parallelopiped extending from the square platform of the plinth. If the upraised arm was to be kept within this imagined boundary, anatomical accuracy demanded that the torso be flexed away from it. The left shoulder was drawn back and the right

188

Maquette for *Liberty*

Frédéric-Auguste Bartholdi

ca. 1871

189

Maquette for *Liberty*

Frédéric-Auguste Bartholdi

n.d.

knee thrust forward to achieve a dynamic balance. The effect of this flexion was that from different angles, the figure presented wholly different aspects to the spectator. A full-face photograph (cat. 196) shows clearly how the artist achieved a powerful surge on the right side, upward toward the torch, by concealing the right hip and the waist from frontal view while pushing the left hip and the pelvis strongly outward. But these anatomical and esthetic niceties concerned Laboulaye less than the inner meaning of the figure—which he soon set out to change.

From America Bartholdi kept his patron up to date on his travels and his contacts; his letters seem to urge Laboulaye to hold fast in the face of American indifference to the project. The sculptor recognized that if a true colossus was ever to grow from his models, a sustained effort would be required in France.

On his return from the United States Bartholdi met with Laboulaye on December 3, 1871.[34] Now his initial sketches must undergo two tests. First, how would they be judged by the one man who could ensure that the project was pursued? Second, how did the statue relate to the site he had chosen for it, and how effectively could he justify his choice to his patron? As for Laboulaye, just as liberal and republican as he had always been and now relieved of his underground struggle against the Empire, to what imperatives was he responding at the end of 1871? If we remember that both men took the Centennial of 1876 as a deadline for the monument to American independence, their dinner on December 3, 1871, must have seemed a last, crucial opportunity for reflection.

It seems certain that Laboulaye's reaction to the maquette (cat. 189) submitted to him was the main reason that a new form was conceived. It appears in another model of which the sculptor kept at least two copies, both now at Colmar; one is shown here (cat. 190). The downstretched left arm, its fist clenched around the broken chain, has given place to an arm bent at the elbow on which rests a tablet, presumably of stone, bearing the inscription «4 JULY 1776.» This reference to the American Declaration of Independence is certainly the work of Laboulaye. All writers agree that this liberal

political philosopher, an admirer of the American Constitution, regarded the shaking-off of the yoke of England (accomplished with powerful support from France) as less important than the popular initiative which created a new form of government and thereby assured the liberties of its citizens. This idea must have preoccupied Laboulaye in 1871 when his position as a deputy, and his influence as an authority on comparative law, combined to make him an important figure in the political negotiations over a new form of government for France. His liberty was not the liberty of the barricades, but liberty under (and assured by) law.

Bartholdi could cheerfully accept this point of view. From the Battery at the southern tip of Manhattan he had taken a long look at Bedloe's Island, where he hoped his statue would stand, and had been moved to eliminate some superfluous detail from his earlier design. The two links of chain falling one on either side of the clenched fist in the preceding model (cat. 189) could not have been seen or understood. The simple geometric outline of the stone tablet, although it could be clearly grasped, might attract the eye too strongly. The sculptor therefore put more emphasis on the torch, which he ornamented so that its line, continuing smoothly from the raised arm, provided balance for the weight of the draping. Since the head itself must not seem less important than the stone tablet, the sculptor gave it more substance, made the hair lie less closely to it, and added fillets which form a visual link between the face, the body, and the left arm. Above all he enlarged the diadem, gave it a patterned border, and made it a better support for the rays, which he thickened and flattened out. It must have been at this time that Bartholdi made and cast in bronze a sketch for the head which is reproduced here (cat. 191).[35] It is important as the first in the series of models which Bartholdi used for a purpose other than the search for an ideal form. The model of

190
Maquette for *Liberty*
Frédéric-Auguste Bartholdi
n.d.

191
Head of the Statue of Liberty
Frédéric-Auguste Bartholdi
n.d.

1871–72 (cat. 189) marks the point at which the statue's features finally emerged from the shadow of the Suez project and took shape. The serene countenance, deriving appropriate vigor from its arched brows, Greek nose, and willful chin, wears an elaborate diadem, freely sketched but arranged in scallops that foreshadow the arcaded decoration of the finished statue.

Before we turn to the last sketches, very different and refined, we must consider the question, addressed by all who have written on the statue, of Bartholdi's model. The bronze head and the three immediately preceding drafts share the treatment of the face and the emphatic presence of a real body beneath the clinging drapery. Such consistency, it is generally agreed, indicates that the studies were done from life. We, however, disagree.

Regarding the body, Bartholdi's perspective drawings of a colossal statue intended for Egypt are remarkable less for the statue's commanding appearance than for its national dress. The sketches at Colmar all show an androgynous figure and a harsh face; it is not ignorance of anatomy that makes the breasts look like an afterthought, but rather the compromise required of a statue forming part of a greater architectural whole. We have seen that Bartholdi was more concerned to cite a precedent from antiquity (cat. 172 and 175 are very reminiscent of Tanagra figurines) than to make reference to contemporary forms. His *Statue allégorique de la Douleur*, dated 1869 in the 1914 inventory but 1866 on the mount of the photograph in the Musée Bartholdi at Colmar (cat. 193), shows that, long before undertaking a representation of Liberty, he had looked to classical costume to convey the essence of nobility. Moreover, it is clear that cat. 190 was not done from a model posed in the same position: the stone tablet does not sit in the curve of the waist supported by the hipbone but lies much further back on the upper part of the thigh, in a position more graceful than natural.

The question of the face is more complex. Bartholdi's studio contains no clay study from the nude that could have served as a basis for our models,[36] but a sturdy tradi-

tion says that the face was inspired by the features of the artist's mother.[37] Bartholdi might have mentioned this notion to a friend, who could have repeated it. Trachtenberg offers an altogether more beguiling reason for subscribing to this legend. When Bartholdi worked on his models he had left Alsace, which was occupied by the Germans, but his mother was still there—and had become for him the very type and pattern of the captive crying for deliverance from oppression. In this case, the Statue of Liberty was inspired by a latter-day martyr. These tenuous indications cannot stand the test of the record preserved in Bartholdi's letters. We find there nothing to suggest that the artist acknowledged such a debt to his mother, although he shows himself to be a solicitous son who provided her with every possible emotional satisfaction. It also seems unlikely that he drew *Liberty* from his mother when among dozens of portrait busts of his contemporaries done from life he left not a single one of her.[38] In any case, he would probably have been reluctant to subject such a small-scale portrait to the successive enlargements needed to make it several yards high, which would have blurred the most striking resemblance into the vague likeness that we study today. Moreover, an artist so concerned with the universal symbolism of his creation would have taken care that it not resemble any one person.

At this point Bartholdi appears to have given up on the diadem of light which, in cat. 170 and 171, represents the legacy of the Suez projects. At the same time, in cat. 188–190 the torch has been adorned with a gallery, as if the artist had not yet decided to place a light in it, and allot to it alone the function of «illuminating the world.» Perhaps the idea was given to him by Laboulaye, who said in 1876, «This will not be liberty in a red cap, striding across corpses with her pike at the port. This will

192
Draped Figure, after a Tanagra Statuette
Frédéric-Auguste Bartholdi
n.d.

193
Statue allégorique de la Douleur ou le Génie funèbre
Frédéric-Auguste Bartholdi
1866

194
Colossal Head of Lucilla
Late Roman Empire

be the American Liberty whose torch is held high not to inflame but to enlighten.»[39] All the same, Bartholdi's designs of this period (cat. 198 and 199) show a statue from whose diadem issue powerful rays of light. Perhaps the next group of models, dated before or about 1875 (cat. 195 and 196) represent a variant line; in giving them a «blind» diadem or one decorated with stars Bartholdi might have been drawing a little closer to the traditional iconography that complements their altered style of dress. Or they may refer back to the *Colossal Head of Lucilla* (cat. 194) at the Louvre, which the artist must have known and which Lesbazeilles carefully reproduced in 1876 on page 137 of his book *Les Colosses anciens et modernes* (cat. 103).

b

The sculptor, in agreement with Laboulaye, had now resolved the iconographic problems; it remained to consider the consequences for his figure of enlargement to colossal size. This problem so preoccupied Bartholdi that (unless they have been lost) there are no models dating from 1873–74; the sculptor needed fully two years to negotiate with the architect and the workshop that were to undertake the project. At the same time he was helping to organize the Franco-American Union and was engaged in many other tasks, one of them being his other colossus, the *Lion de Belfort*.

c

a

196
The Statue of Liberty,
Variant of the *Modèle du Comité*
Frédéric-Auguste Bartholdi
1875

The first person Bartholdi approached for advice about the kind of structure that should underlie the copper cladding was Viollet-le-Duc, whose solutions are considered in Chapter 5. It may be that the architect, exerting all the authority that a teacher can on a former pupil, tried to dissuade Bartholdi from continuing work on a figure in such balletic motion. No doubt Viollet-le-Duc, who proposed to «prop up» the statue rather than to hang it as Eiffel eventually did, was afraid that its lopsided stance would produce a fatal structural imbalance. Perhaps it was he who advised Bartholdi to constrain the lifted arm of his colossi (yesterday's Suez lighthouse no less than today's Statue of Liberty) within a volume extended upward from the base.[40]

d

One thing is certain: Bartholdi must have approached Viollet-le-Duc before 1872. The two drawings reproduced here (cat. 198 and 199) show the statue at the stage where the left arm was pointing downward, the hand carrying a fragment of chain; this must have been before the dinner with Laboulaye on December 3, 1871, and certainly before the stone tablet made its first appearance on the statue's arm. All students agree that the pedestal shown in these drawings is from the hand of Viollet-le-Duc. It was not until after Viollet-le-Duc's death in 1879 that Bartholdi put forward his own drawings and designs, as in the double leaf (cat. 398) where the statue is scrupulously depicted in the final form of 1875. Here it stands on the pedestal of the sculptor's dreams—a stepped pyramid which evokes the Mausoleum of Halicarnassus or its gigantic Egyptian predecessors.

Other reasons as well caused Bartholdi to modify the form. On a small scale it was easy to make use of a specifically female figure to convey a lofty idea, even an aspiration toward the ideal, but, once enlarged above life-size, it was flirting with the grotesque. Bartholdi completely reworked his composition, imparting motion to the drapery rather than to the figure itself. Its folds now gave the statue a vibration, rather than a movement, in space, while the figure itself, in its fixed frontal hieratic attitude, carried the majestic message of the project. Now the statue comprised a series of juxtapositions of movement and stillness that were implicit in the 1872 model (cat. 190) but took on greater dramatic force once the whole figure had been struck motionless from top to toe: one foot firm, the other striding forward; the chiton smooth, the peplum in folds; the fingers of a hand clasping the tablet of stone; the head immobile, the light radiating from it; crowning the whole, the monumental torch and its flickering flame.

It took Bartholdi several models to reach this balance of opposing forces. One of them (cat. 195) suggests that at this stage the artist had already begun to popularize the statue. The plaster shows signs of hurried casting, the features and the drapery lack the delicacy of the other studies—everything points forward to the miniatures used to promote the subscription campaign opened in 1875. Much more carefully executed is a large bronze (cat. 196), similar to an original

in clay 49½ inches high,[41] which incorporates the final results of Bartholdi's research apart from the features, which are still those of the head in cat. 197. The star-studded diadem differentiates it from the latter version, in which the artist returned to the arcaded treatment. This model, leaving aside the absence of rays and the broken fillets, most closely resembles the statue as it stands today; the two faces are almost identical. But Bartholdi also made a clay model, in an edition of two hundred copies, which exactly recapitulated the attributes of cat. 196 except for the stars of the diadem, which here appears in its final arcaded form (cat. 282).

Why did Bartholdi finally return to this arcaded pattern? The most likely explanation is that he wanted to confirm the statue's function as a lighthouse, underlining its usefulness for the benefit of those weaker spirits who shrank from undertaking so vast an enterprise simply in the service of an ideal.[42] The rays which were to shine through these apertures may have carried a symbolism closely linked to the stone tablet that lay in the left arm. Here, our Protestant artist must have felt, was a second Moses; *Liberty* carried the Tables of the Law in her left arm, while her forehead shone with light like the prophet's on Mount Sinai. His thoughts may also have turned to his brothers of the Masonic lodge of Alsace-Lorraine, in the obedience of the Grand Orient of France. There, no doubt, the symbolism of light and illumination loomed large. Perhaps a taste for such mysteries led the sculptor to crown the statue with seven rays of copper and to draw in the heavens seven rays of light, suggesting that as sunbeams strike the seven planets so the beams shed by *Liberty* fall on the seven continents and seven seas of the world.

What is more demonstrable is that Bartholdi, who studied the works of Laboulaye with great care, could have found in them the metaphor of America enlightening the world.[43] Very soon after 1872 the two men must have agreed on the statue's title; *La Liberté éclairant le Monde* must clearly assume a form involving the physical shedding of light. This was the theme of publicity in 1875; Bartholdi's drawings, probably done before 1872 since they show the statue with its left arm pointing down and the hand clenched around a broken chain, and appropriately reworked in 1875 to serve as the Committee's «logo,» show both a nighttime (cat. 198) and a daytime (cat. 199) view of the statue with its rays.

The accompanying text says «. . . by night a halo of light will shine from her forehead far out across the boundless sea.» The cantata composed by Gounod (cat. 276) was set to words with a similar theme:

Je porte au loin dans la nuit sombre,
Quand tous mes feux sont allumés,
Mes rayons au vaisseau qui sombre,
Et ma lumière aux opprimés.[44]

[*In the dark night I cast afar*
When all my lamps are lit
My rays to help the foundering ship
And my light to lighten the oppressed.]

The lighthouse theme, going back to *L'Egypte apportant la lumière à l'Asie*, was to smolder for a long time; much effort was to be devoted, after the erection of the statue itself, to the problem of illuminating the torch. But another reason that persuaded Bartholdi to adopt an arcaded design for the diadem was the desire to open the statue to visitors.

Familiar as he was with Universal Expositions, the sculptor knew the public delight in climbing to a great height; the most spectacular ascents were those made in a balloon, but in 1889 the Eiffel Tower was to appeal to the same instinct. Bartholdi twice offered people a good climb: once into the torch at Philadelphia in 1876, and then into the head, at the Universal Exposition in Paris, in 1878. Once visitors had reached that head they must be offered a good view, but the experience of the monument itself must not be compromised by unsightly or inappropriate openings. The restricted volume of the head could not house both a lighthouse and a facility for visitors. The tourists won; the light was relegated to the torch, and they obtained the use of the space thus left free behind the arcading of the diadem. The work of construction could begin.

Translated, from the French, by Maxwell Vos

195
The Statue of Liberty
Frédéric-Auguste Bartholdi
n.d.

197
Maquette for *Liberty*
Frédéric-Auguste Bartholdi
n.d.

198
La Statue de la Liberté....
Henri Meyer, after Pierre Petit
Unidentified periodical illustration

199
La statue en place sur Bedloe's Island
Frédéric-Auguste Bartholdi
1875

La Statue de la Liberté
QUI DOIT ÊTRE OFFERTE A L'AMÉRIQUE PAR LA FRANCE ET ÉLEVÉE DEVANT NEW-YORK
Dessin de HENRI MEYER d'après les photographies de PIERRE PETIT — Voir les détails, page 323

4.
Voyage of Discovery: Bartholdi's First American Visit (1871)

Janet Headley

In the aftermath of the Franco-Prussian War, Bartholdi's beloved Colmar became a German possession. His house in Paris had been occupied by Prussian soldiers, and the city suffered through the traumatic final days of the Commune. Realizing his artistic skills were of little use in his homeland, where the new Republic struggled for survival, Bartholdi felt compelled to act, resolving that his deed would be charged with significance. Earlier in his career he had dreamt of visiting America; now, circumstances made the wish into a logical decision.[1] In the United States he could observe the character of the New World and its free citizens, seek new commissions, and make new contacts. Above all, he would search there for the proper environment for his greatest project, a monument that would celebrate the republican ideal of Liberty. Heartened by a reunion with Laboulaye at Versailles at the end of May, the sculptor completed preparations for his voyage.[2] On June 10 he boarded the steamship *Pereire*, bound for New York with Simon, his studio assistant and traveling companion. Bad weather and seasickness plagued the passengers throughout the eleven-day voyage, but once ashore, the artist immediately plunged into his mission.

On his first day in the new country, Bartholdi searched out potential sites for his monument, including the Battery, Central Park, and the islands in New York harbor (cat. 200), which possessed a special attraction. A thriving gateway to the New World, the port seemed to Bartholdi to symbolize the industrial modernity and ongoing progress of the expanding country. Entranced by the activity of this sprawling scene, the sculptor recounted his impressions in a letter:

> The first thing that strikes the eye is the immense steamers called «ferry boats.» The middle of the lower story is reserved for vehicles. They move this way and that across the bay, full of people and covered with flags, emitting deep-toned blasts from their whistles; they sound like huge flies. Elegant sail-boats glide along the surface of the water like *marquises* dressed in garments with long trains. Little steam-boats, no bigger than one's hand—busy, meddling, inquisitive—hurry after each other. . . .

> The East River and the Hudson . . . are covered with shipping as far as the eye can reach. The masts and spars of the vessels look like the cross-hatchings of a pen-and-ink drawing.[3]

The next day he narrowed his selection. Although the site was occupied by a fort, Bedloe's Island was perfectly situated[4]—isolated from the mainland but highly visible from the city and harbor approach (cat. 5). Bartholdi could already envision his monument towering over the harbor on Bedloe's Island, the hub of a bustling maritime commerce. Turning to his immediate business, in rapid succession he made arrangements to discuss his proposals with several of New York's prominent citizens.[5] Although he was received politely, the results were not promising; he found that liberated Americans were «hardly accessible to things of the imagination.»[6] Near the end of his first week abroad the discouraged sculptor concluded that he had to modify his approach, and quickly redirected his presentation:

> I spoke of my project from a new point of view. The French are going to offer a commemorative monument in 1876. We need a site and, if possible, the pedestal. This idea catches on![7]

From the American point of view, skepticism was justified. Relations between France and the United States had been strained by French support for the Confederacy during the American Civil War, and by popular American advocacy for a Prussian victory in the conflict with France.[8] Furthermore, both allegorical and colossal sculpture had encountered considerable public resistance in the United States. In such a climate, Bartholdi's new approach partially resolved a dilemma; rather than glorifying the abstract idea of Liberty, his proposed undertaking now celebrated the centennial of American independence. Nevertheless, the initial response to his scheme was lukewarm at best, and after a brief visit to the resort at Long Branch, New Jersey, Bartholdi and Simon proceeded south to test the political waters in the nation's capital and to observe American life in greater detail.

An observant traveler, the sculptor approached his experiences in America as an adventure combining novelty and strangeness. Hotels were efficient, he noted repeatedly in his letters and journal, but massive and expensive. One's shoes were never shined by the hotel staff, but baggage was transported automatically from train station to hotel. Americans consumed huge quantities of food, sometimes dining at very tall lunch counters rather than tables. Stagecoaches, trains, and enormous boats facilitated travel across vast distances, supplying endless images for the thumbnail sketches that abounded in Bartholdi's journal and letters. Americans also excelled at incredible technological feats. En route to Washington by rail, the visitor gazed in awe at the accomplished engineering of a giant timber truss bridge over the Susquehanna River.[9]

Arriving in Washington in time for the celebration of Independence Day, Bartholdi noted that the day was «spent in setting off firecrackers . . . as much as possible under the feet of people walking in the streets.»[10] To the foreigners the capital was reminiscent of Versailles, with its broad avenues and long, unimpeded vistas. They found the Capitol effective only from a distance, and the sculpture in Washington mediocre. The Washington Monument was poetic but ugly, and its truncated state must have sounded a note of warning.[11] Despite a busy sightseeing schedule, the artist did not neglect his professional role. On July 5 he presented his letter of introduction to Charles Sumner, the powerful Republican Senator from Massachusetts (cat. 201). Politically and artistically knowledgeable, Sumner responded enthusiastically to Bartholdi's ideas, supplying the sculptor with valuable letters of reference and personally acting as his host.[12] In the following days Bartholdi met a number of influential men in Washington, yet a week of political socializing left him frustrated.[13] His most promising connection was a journalist, Col. John W. Forney, the publisher of the Philadelphia *Press*.[14]

At Forney's invitation, on July 10 Bartholdi traveled north to Philadelphia, where he was warmly received. Carefully avoiding specific reference to his intended monument to Liberty, Bartholdi introduced himself as a competent sculptor from the art capital of Europe, seeking commissions to benefit artist and patron alike.[15] Forney provided a tour of the city, and presented his guest to the members of the Union League and the Fairmount Park Commission. Here Bartholdi encountered, for the first time, organizations renowned in the American art world, groups with sufficient power to assist his endeavors.

THE PORT OF NEW YORK.

200
The Port of New York. Bird's Eye View from the Battery. Looking South
Currier and Ives
1872

201
Charles Sumner
Darius Cobb
1877

Chartered in 1855, Fairmount Park provided a respite from the noise, dirt, and crowding that accompanied urban sprawl in Philadelphia. Although the park's development languished during the Civil War, interest revived thereafter, and by 1867 its land holdings amounted to three thousand acres. That year, the Fairmount Park Commission was established to preserve «the enjoyment of the quiet, doubly grateful to those who temporarily escape from the din of crowded city streets.»[16] From the outset, the Commission planned to display a permanent art collection within the grounds. When additional land acquisitions nearly doubled the size of the park, the task of development was too much for the Park Commission. As a result, in 1871 the newly created Fairmount Park Art Association assumed the task of adorning the grounds with «statues, busts, and other works of art, either of a memorial nature or otherwise.»[17] Given its philanthropic espousal of outdoor sculpture, the Art Association viewed Bartholdi as a potential contributor to its collection.

The Union League had a less immediate but ultimately more crucial effect on Bartholdi's career in America. Created in October 1862 in response to the Civil War, the Union League of Philadelphia spawned chapters in New York and Boston within the year. Dedicated to the abolition of slavery and the preservation of the Union, the League reinforced its expressed ideals by a program of positive action, including raising regiments and mounting a massive pamphleteering campaign. Framed in this political context, the club's charter somewhat surprisingly mandated establishing its own libraries and art collections in the progressive belief that education fostered good citizenship and art civilized society. Even after the war, the numerous branches of the Union League sought «to dignify politics as a pursuit» and «to enforce a sense of the sacred obligation of citizenship.»[18] Their patriotic zeal led to lobbying activities in the arena of political and social reform, and to a continuation of the original program of cultural enlightenment through art. The exhibitions sponsored by the League, to cite only one example, offered artists a rare opportunity to present their work to the public, at the same time affording the audience an equally rare glimpse of contemporary art.

While Bartholdi's political and artistic ideals sufficed to endear him to the Union League, his connection with Laboulaye guaranteed a lasting bond with the Philadelphia chapter. Few Europeans were so closely associated with the ideal of Liberty among educated Americans as Laboulaye, and in 1863 the society conferred honorary membership on the French republican for his pronounced advocacy of the united American Republic. A commemorative medallion struck for the occasion was gratefully acknowledged by its recipient in a letter, preserved in the League's archives (cat. 202).[19]

Bartholdi's Philadelphia experiences gave him an avenue of approach for his promotion. His appeal was aimed at a specific group of enlightened patriots—an elite inner circle of wealthy men, most of whom were active in the Union League and the Park Commission—whose support gave him a foothold from which to build his reputation: the Park Commission solicited a design for an entrance to the Park, and requested the sculptor's contribution to a monument planned for the Centennial Exhibition in 1876. In addition, he was offered the directorship of the sculptural programs of the

city.[20] Although he declined the post, Bartholdi agreed to prepare drawings for the Park entrance.[21]

With greater confidence, the sculptor returned to Long Branch, where Colonel Forney again furnished the introductions. On July 18 the journalist presented his foreign guest to President Ulysses S. Grant (cat. 203), with whom Bartholdi freely discussed his projected commemorative monument. Grant appeared receptive to the idea, adding that the dedication of Bedloe's Island presented no insurmountable obstacles.[22] Although Bartholdi acknowledged that Grant was informal and cordial, he found him «a cold man, like most Americans.»[23] Bartholdi pensively developed his perceptions of American character in a letter to Laboulaye:

American life seems to allow little time to live—their customs, their regimes, are not my ideal. Everything is big here, even the «petits pois» [little peas] are larger than those that I like. Everything is practical, but in a collective manner, the entire society marches like rail cars on tracks, but the isolated vehicle is obliged to stay on the rails if it is to move smoothly. The isolated individual cannot emerge; he is obliged to live in this collective society.[24]

Bartholdi's sense of American coldness and lack of originality was reinforced by another event. Following their interview with the President, Forney and Bartholdi attended a reception for a group of New York businessmen in Long Branch. In his enthusiasm for Bartholdi's projects, Forney pressured the reluctant artist to reveal his drawings to the assembled guests,[25] whose frigid response caused the humiliated sculptor to exit hastily.

Perplexed but undaunted, the artist returned to New York for another frantic week of interviews, including a chilly encounter with the landscape architect Frederick Law Olmsted.[26] Between business engagements he worked on the sketches for Fairmount Park, which he presented to the Park Commission on July 25. Their favorable reception led Bartholdi back to New York for a second conference with Olmsted. In light of the support of the Park Commission, Olmsted gave his approval of the plans for Fairmount Park.[27]

Soon after this meeting Bartholdi ventured north to Boston. Disgruntled and weary, he disliked the dirty old streets of the city, and thought that the ecclesiastical architecture seemed to be made of cork carved to resemble stone.[28] Visiting the celebrated Henry Wadsworth Longfellow, he gratefully basked in the poet's heartfelt enthusiasm for his artistic endeavors and remained for dinner at Longfellow's insistence.[29] Since many of his contacts had escaped the urban summer heat, Bartholdi headed for the resort of Newport, Rhode Island, to complete his introductions. In only four days he met John LaFarge, Charles C. Perkins, Richard Morris Hunt, and Henry Tuckerman, but the artist found these encounters even more restrained than previous ones.[30]

Returning to New York, Bartholdi determined that his business affairs on the East Coast were completed for the moment. During nearly two months of continuous travel between cities, he had politely presented himself to numerous strangers—including many prominent, powerful individuals whose support was crucial to the future success of his scheme—whose responses ranged from hostility to some degree of sympathetic understanding. But for the moment he could do nothing to further his project, so Bartholdi resolved now to focus on the other goal of his pilgrimage—to observe the country and the character of the people.

On August 10 the sculptor set out by train for the dazzling spectacle of Niagara Falls, the mecca of the nineteenth-century traveler.[31] Like other tourists after them, Bartholdi and Simon posed for souvenir photos (cat. 204) and donned yellow slickers for their descent to an observation point behind the Falls. On several visits to the site, Bartholdi struggled to convey the powerful sensation in watercolor sketches (cat. 205—see p. 13) and in words: «Our first view was similar to that which conveys the essence of a portrait . . . the spectacle of this ceaseless chaos and the perpetual noise, retained us for lengthy contemplation.»[32]

In addition to the natural majesty of the place, he was again struck by a demonstration of American technological ingenuity: a double-decked suspension bridge that spanned the Falls and fascinated the sculptor by its daring placement and its modern, streamlined beauty (cat. 206). Constructed by the brilliant engineer Augustus Jacob Roebling, this 821-foot masterpiece had an upper deck that served as a rail crossing and a lower level for pedestrian and vehicular traffic. Captivated by this wonderful piece of work, Bartholdi crossed the bridge several times, on both levels.[33]

After venturing farther into Canada by rail, the travelers returned to U.S. soil at Detroit, then stopped at Chicago (cat. 207—see p. 13). That city's wide streets and evidence of rapid growth and change (cat. 208) conveyed the essential element of urban progress that Bartholdi expected of American cities:

> One sees telegraph lines that look like spiders' webs, 126 churches, nearly a hundred journals, boat and train whistles make the constant music of an Aeolian harp, smoke blackens the sky, an enormous population runs about, pressed on by the colic of daily affairs. One cannot comprehend how all of this came about in so little time.[34]

A consistent absence of charm or any refined taste was the price extracted, it seemed, for this ceaseless industrial development (cat. 209). In an effort to compensate for the lack of urban beauty, Bartholdi presented himself to prominent community members and studied parks for potential sculpture sites. At once fascinated and repulsed by the strange character of the country, he decided to travel on to San Francisco.[35]

Simon returned to New York, while Bartholdi continued west alone. Crossing the plains of Nebraska, the artist from his train window viewed endless colonies of prairie dogs, herds of antelope, and an Indian woman with a papoose. In a watercolor sketch (cat. 210—see p. 17) he sensitively recorded the luminous emptiness of the prairie. At the entrance to the Rocky Mountains (cat. 211—see p. 17) the landscape became more awesome:

> After two days travel across the plains and the prairies, one arrives at the mountains. At the entrance to the mountains, they possess a most strange character, because of their tonality and their form; one senses that the character of the countryside has changed, there are

diabolical aspects about it, similar to those encountered in fairy tales. One begins to descend from high plateaus where we are 8,000 feet above sea level. One perceives a horizon filled with the vague forms of mountains, then the train descends, plunging into valleys and gorges, one passes through trenches, through tunnels flanked on one side by ravines and by massive rocks on the other. There are some magnificent views.[36]

In Salt Lake City (cat. 212), then a dusty frontier town, Bartholdi was astonished both by the elegant attire of the women and by Mormon polygamy.[37] He obtained an introduction to Brigham Young, whose bust he was asked to model, but departed indignantly when the Mormon leader repeatedly postponed his sitting.[38] As he continued west through the Sierra Nevada range, mining ventures rivalled the wildness of the scenery for spectacular effect (cat. 213). Finally winding through the fertile farmland around Sacramento and Oakland, the artist arrived in San Francisco on August 25 (cat. 214).

If he had hoped for an enthusiastic response in the western metropolis, Bartholdi was sorely disappointed, for he found less encouragement there than anywhere else. In the aftermath of the California Gold Rush,

San Francisco was scarcely typical of American cities, a fact Bartholdi astutely recognized, but his experiences reinforced his already negative impressions of American character: «In San Francisco, I think that they are more materialistic than anywhere else, and I think that, for the time being, the population does not have a very high moral education, there is an abundance of greed, there is no place for anything else; but this Babel is interesting to see and to study.»[39]

216

In five days of sightseeing, Bartholdi visited the Chinese theater, the Chinese district, and Seal Rock (cat. 215), a site he found particularly amusing.[40] During a side trip to Stockton, the carnival atmosphere of opposing political rallies delighted him with its array of bands, orators, and crowds (cat. 216).[41] He endured a long, filthy stagecoach ride to see and sketch the redwood forests of California, which awed him with their overwhelming size and beauty (cat. 217—see p. 17; cat. 218, 219).

221
Marriage: Relief for Brattle Street Unitarian Church, Boston
Frédéric-Auguste Bartholdi
1871–74

209
Chicago, Michigan Shore
Frédéric-Auguste Bartholdi
n.d.

212
Mormon Temple, Salt Lake City
Frédéric-Auguste Bartholdi
n.d.

Bartholdi's desire to see as much of the country as possible led him to choose a different route for his return. Departing on September 3, he passed through northern Nevada and Utah into southern Wyoming. From the flat prairie town of Cheyenne (cat. 220), Bartholdi proceeded south for a brief stop in Denver, then traveled through the vast herds of buffalo in Kansas. In St. Louis, Missouri, he presented himself to the dignitaries of the city, then continued his campaign in Cincinnati and Pittsburgh, returning to New York on September 16.

Over the next ten days, he shuttled between Boston, New York, and Philadelphia, then proceeded south to Washington for the opening of Congress at the end of September. At each stop he renewed old acquaintances and obtained new introductions, but made no concrete gains for his major project. Back in New York at the end of September, Bartholdi prepared to return to France.

His artistic skill had not gone unrecognized in America. Although the project for Fairmount Park never materialized, thirty members of the Union League of Philadelphia subscribed for the bust of Laboulaye that Bartholdi had brought to America. The portrait was presented to the Union League by Colonel Forney in December 1871.[42] The artist received a more substantial commission in Boston: a sculptural program for the steeple of Brattle Street Church was solicited by the architect Henry Hobson Richardson, and Bartholdi's design was approved on the final day of his American sojourn.[43] Richardson outlined the terms of agreement in a letter to the church council: a «complete model for the whole frieze 96 feet long—figures from 10 to 14 feet high—a separate study and composition for each of the four sides and models for the four angle figures—the whole modelled–delivered in this country with all expenses paid and approved by your committee and me for $4,000.»[44]

The reliefs occupied Bartholdi intermittently through 1874, when he exhibited the plaster maquettes at the Salon. The final commission entailed representations of the four principal stages of Christian life: Birth, Communion, Marriage, and Death (cat. 221). Formally and thematically, the task presented difficulties for the sculptor. To convey such abstract themes and to ensure their visibility from a distance, Bartholdi resorted to traditional Christian imagery. Birth alludes to the Christian birth of Baptism, but the image borrows heavily from scenes of the Presentation of Christ in the Temple. Similarly, Communion recalls representations of Christ among the Children, and Marriage conjures references to the Marriage of the Virgin. The demands of scale and distance combine in the reliefs to create a tense flatness, overriding symmetricality, and stasis. Classical drapery and figural style jar with realistic physiognomies that invite comparison with contemporary individuals.[45] At each corner of the frieze an angel sounds an elongated horn; this device earned the Brattle Street Church a nickname: the Church of the Holy Bean Blowers. When he returned to America in 1876, Bartholdi viewed his reliefs in situ, voicing some disappointment with the final appearance of his frieze: «The execution is not excellent, but for the most part, it is good, and I am content to see that I did not make a mistake in my handling of the subject.»[46]

During his five-month voyage of discovery, Bartholdi had lobbied intensively, sometimes presenting himself as a talented artist in search of commissions for projects to beautify American cities, on other occasions specifically advancing his idea for a monument to Liberty. At the end of his stay in America he had gained several friends and numerous acquaintances, but had received no official recognition of his great project, nor any definite assurance of its realization. Back in France, the sculptor planned his return to the United States at a time when his grand conception would be made known, not to a select few, but to an entire nation.

216
Sketch of Republican Rally
in Circus Tent at Stockton,
California
Frédéric-Auguste Bartholdi
In a letter dated September
8, 1871

220
Sketch of Town of
Cheyenne, Wyoming
Frédéric-Auguste Bartholdi
In his journal, early
September 1871

5.
Technological and Industrial Challenges

Pierre Provoyeur

The slow fabrication of the Statue of Liberty, between 1875 and 1884, represents one of the most impressive construction projects of the nineteenth century. The Monduit workshops, which had been taken over by Gaget and Gauthier, are in the heart of modern Paris, but lay outside it at that time; their location on the rue de Chazelles was on the far side of the toll barrier housed in Ledoux's rotunda at the Boulevard de Courcelles and the Parc Monceau. But they were near enough to be an object of Parisian curiosity. Chapter 6 recounts the masterly way in which Bartholdi turned the construction into a spectacle; by the time the finished statue finally loomed over the rooftops of the capital she had become so close to the hearts of its citizens that they wanted to keep her. History followed its course; the sculptor was stubborn in the management of his project, but one of his decisions had a happy consequence for modern scholars. By arranging for the workshop to be photographed at regular intervals, Bartholdi has left eloquent reference material on details of the construction that have now disappeared or can no longer be seen; at the same time he has provided a clear explanation of the links between successive phases of the project. These photographs are an archival treasure without which we could not hope to understand today how the monument was built.

The photographs of Pierre Petit and of Bartholdi himself provide a lively record of the «great workshop» and the many who labored there. Whether surprised at their work or posing for the photographer, these craftsmen still speak to us across the intervening century. They certainly understood what they were engaged in; the enthusiasm of the sculptor—not to mention the continual stream of official, or merely curious, spectators—must have heartened them in their work. They were actors in an enormous pageant, as well as the creators of the statue. Each photograph carries their collective signature, establishing the existence of the bountiful republican France of myth and legend—and the existence at her side of clever, hardworking Frenchmen devoted to her cause. Through the photographs, these men burst with salutary vigor into the story of the statue—a story that has otherwise tended to center around the lighthouses of the industrial age, or liberal ideology, or the power of the press, which is to say around Eiffel, Laboulaye, or Pulitzer.

Among these craftsmen one man stands out; his name was Simon. We know little more about him than that he appears in several photographs (cat. 222, 223, and 237). As early as 1871 he looks elderly, but he is always there, like an overseer keeping an eye on everything. He was very close to Bartholdi, a Mentor to his Telemachus, and accompanied him on his first trip to the United States, where he must have shared the sculptor's enthusiasm for the chosen site in New York harbor. In two letters, one left by Bartholdi on May 1, 1876, with Laboulaye in Paris, the other left with his mother in Colmar, Bartholdi asked that in the event of his death they consult, regarding the completion of the statue, «MM. Simon, Soitoux and Gauthier, sculptors, who will decide to whom the work should be entrusted, and will avail themselves of such other assistance as they see fit. . . . In case of disagreement the deciding vote should rest with M. Simon, who has long been acquainted with all my thoughts and all my studies in the matter. I request him to familiarize himself with what I did, and with the ideas I expressed, while in America.»[1]

A photograph (cat. 222) from Bartholdi's own collection, now at the Musée Bartholdi, shows Simon probably in the period 1880–85, when the statue was under construction in Paris. In this astonishing composition, a plaster figure stands beside the dignified patriarch, who wears his beret like a halo, an old workman embodying the tradition of the master-craftsman of the Middle Ages. Simon appears again with Bartholdi in front of a painting on canvas, dated 1873, of the *Lion de Belfort* (cat. 223).

Honoré Monduit (cat. 224) was already an old man when work began on the Statue of Liberty, but his business, apparently flourishing, had six hundred employees in January 1874, and enjoyed a high reputation for the many spectacular commissions it had completed. These included the figured finials for the Sainte Chapelle and Nôtre Dame de Paris, the restoration of the dome of the Invalides, the colossal figure of Vercingétorix at Alix-Sainte-Reine, the cupola and domes of Garnier's Opéra, and other works that have since disappeared, such as the figure of *Renommée* which crowned the old Palais du Trocadéro. The firm's catalogue (cat. 225) harks back to the Vendôme column, which it reerected after it was torn

222
*Portrait of Simon
Frédéric-Auguste Bartholdi*
n.d.

223
*Bartholdi, Simon, and a
Painter in Front of a
Canvas Representing the
Lion de Belfort*
1873

224
Portrait of M. Monduit
Th. Barenne
n.d.

225
Frontispiece of *La
plomberie au XIX° siècle*
Catalogue of Gaget,
Gauthier et Cie.,
ca. 1880

down by the Commune. The Monduit atelier owed its success partly to a mastery of the technique of beaten copper, described below, but also to the strong predilection, characteristic of most of the nineteenth century, for elaborate architectural decoration derived from the High Middle Ages or the Italian Renaissance. Garnier and Viollet-le-Duc, two architects catering to this taste, made the fortune of the Monduit concern between 1860 and 1874. They were active in all areas, from the restoration of historic landmarks to the construction of new buildings, public and private. It was commissions of the latter kind that created a demand for decorative elements—friezes, balconies, finialed ridge-tiles, corbels—which could be made from proprietary molds and sold at attractive prices. Monduit & Co. brought decorative sculpture within the reach of architects, and of their clients.

It is impossible to know today if it was Eugène Viollet-le-Duc who first brought Bartholdi and Monduit together, or if the sculptor, fascinated by the beaten-copper technique since his encounter in 1869 with the statue of *St. Charles Borromeo* at Arona, found his own way to the rue de Chazelles and there encountered his old teacher. The paths of Bartholdi and Viollet-le-Duc (cat. 226) had already crossed on several occasions. As suggested in Chapter 3, it may have been to Viollet-le-Duc that the sculptor owed such tepid encouragement as he received from the Emperor and Empress for his Suez lighthouse project. In 1875 Viollet-le-Duc attended the banquet at the Hôtel du Louvre, where a group of men gathered to celebrate the republican victory in the Chamber (see Chapter 6); he had opportunely remembered that long before he became the favorite of Napoléon and Eugénie, and architect of their chateau at Pierrefonds, he had manned the barricades in 1830 and had been the first to introduce radical politics into the Académie. In 1873–74 he had been active in republican politics, and it was probably this new commitment that led him to participate in the Statue of Liberty project. Over and above the friendly relations that may have linked him to the family of Bartholdi (they both knew Edmond About, who first introduced them), Viollet-le-Duc was a fellow-member of the generation now coming to power in France.

His influence on the design and construction of the statue shows itself in several ways. Two of Bartholdi's preliminary designs (cat. 188 and 189) exhibit characteristics linking them to models made before the artist's meeting with Laboulaye on December 3, 1871, since they show in the statue's down-pointed left hand the fragments of broken chain found also in the original design. This dating is significant, and at odds with the date written on the photograph of the drawing—1874 or 1875—except that the latter corresponds exactly with the project for the pedestal, which is itself very close in spirit to the neo-medievalism of Viollet-le-Duc. The octagonal tower with its machicolated outline was certainly not Bartholdi's taste. In cat. 397, as in the drawings now at the American Institute of Architects Foundation, he drew his inspiration not from the Middle Ages but from the ancient Egyptians, or from the Maya, or from legend, or from the Mausoleum of Halicarnassus. Chapter 11, concerning Richard Morris Hunt's pedestal, indicates a return, to some extent, to Viollet-le-Duc's medieval sources, at least in the bonding of the stone and the massive upthrust outline.

Viollet-le-Duc provided the earliest thoughts on the structure (and thus on the form) of the statue. Bartholdi's ambitions soared even above the scale of the colossal *St. Charles Borromeo* of Arona (cat. 227).[2] The height of 142 feet and more envisaged for his *Liberty* called for greater technical resources than the Italian statue, which consisted of a mass of stonework around which copper cladding had been molded. The masonry occupied all the interior space except for a narrow tube carrying the stairway to the top. Viollet-le-Duc suggested a different method of construction: «. . . in place of masonry there will be inferior coffers rising to about the level of the hips; they will be filled with sand. If an accident

226
Eugène Viollet-le-Duc
Nadar
1878

227
Saint Charles Borromeo at Arona
Postcard photograph
ca. 1985

The development of this structural plan also affected the statue's form. The lowering of the monument's center of gravity through the masonry coffers meant that the rest of the structure had to be self-supporting against all the torsional stresses to which it was exposed by its height and weight. When Viollet-le-Duc saw the model that evolved from Bartholdi's studies of 1869–71, and his new version of 1872, he must have been concerned at the wide, flat surfaces and their pronounced lopsided posture. It was probably he who inspired the major changes so evident in the models and drawings of 1875, as well as the multiple folding of the drapery that alone could give enough rigidity to the thin copper skin. It is no exaggeration to suggest that the Statue of Liberty owes its present form less to the Tanagra figurine that inspired it than to the constraints of structural engineering.

Another man, not referred to in earlier works on the Statue of Liberty, but as influential as he is attractive, was Pierre-Eugène Secrétan. Born in 1834, and by the 1870s wealthy from his business activities and from the production of copper, he used his fortune to assemble an art collection that included Millet's well-known *Angelus*. From him it was that the Franco-American Union and Bartholdi received the gift of the sheet copper used in the statue—a munificent action which the sculptor and his friends recognized appropriately by attempting to

arrange for the Legion of Honor.[4] As a mark of their friendship Bartholdi made a portrait bust of him (cat. 229); a copy cast in bronze has stood since 1900 in the courtyard of one of Secrétan's factories at Dives. Destiny, and the laws of competition, were unkind to Secrétan, who was ruined in the copper crash of 1889. His long piece of special pleading, *La Vérité sur l'affaire des cuivres*, was ineffectual against British dumping of the red metal, which completely destroyed his firm. Of Secrétan's copper there remains today one famous colossal statue, and a handful of snippings scattered around the world in the form of small plaques trimmed from the scrap left after cutting, and offered as souvenirs to visitors at the workshop (cat. 230a–b). The snippings show the thinness of the metal covering—2.5 mm.—which is not evident from the statue's appearance. The sheets were easy enough to work, but needed forming into complex three-dimensional curves to impart rigidity to each piece. Bartholdi had good reason to trust in this procedure: the copper covering of the *St. Charles Borromeo* in Arona is only 1.5 mm. thick, and had been beaten out not on molds but on the statue itself, without the deep and complex drapery folds that could have afforded additional stiffening.[5]

Once he had obtained his raw material, received the advice of a highly respected and imaginative architect, mastered the problems of form, gained the full support of his clients, and begun working with the finest craftsman of the period, Bartholdi could

should happen, stonework would have to be dismantled; with the coffers, simply open the flap-valve affixed to the inner surface of each coffer and the sand will run out by itself.»[3] This ingenious design presupposed a metallic superstructure, especially a metallic support for the arm (at Arona made of wood reinforced with metal). Foreshadowed in his earlier work and particularly that published in the *Entretiens*, this mode of construction was used for the first time in the torch exhibited in 1876 at Philadelphia, and the head exhibited in 1878 at Paris. A cross section of the head appears in a newspaper illustration (cat. 228), but is an inadequate substitute for the architect's drawings, now lost.

228
Cross Section of the Head
(detail of cat. 289)

229
Bust of M. Secrétan
Frédéric-Auguste Bartholdi
n.d.

230b
Copper Fragment of the
Statue of Liberty
ca. 1875–83

confidently proceed to the construction of his statue. He had to abandon the proposed date of completion—the centennial of American independence in 1876—but he still hoped to prepare some symbolic fragment of the whole in time for the proposed Centennial Exhibition in Philadelphia, so that an astonished world could contemplate the scale of the statue-to-be. It seems certain that a start was made at the Monduit establishment before the banquet at the Louvre, which marked the official launching of the fund-raising campaign. Sculptor and craftsman alike were taking a considerable risk in beginning their work before its financing had been assured, and before a number of technical problems had been resolved. Moreover, Monduit had brought Gaget and Gauthier into partnership in January 1874, and had handed the firm over to them in 1878, moving on to establish his own firm in Paris at 31, rue Poncelet. There Monduit Père et Fils maintained a sort of museum of their work, since moved to the Château de Pierrefonds, which includes nothing relating to the Statue of Liberty. Thus, the fabrication of the statue fell into three distinct stages: the construction by Monduit, Gaget, Gauthier et Cie. of the

torch, delivered to Philadelphia in August 1876; the construction by Gaget, Gauthier et Cie. of the head, delivered to the Universal Exposition of 1878 in Paris; and finally, following the death of Viollet-le-Duc in 1879, the arrival on the scene of Gustave Eiffel, which marked the turning point of the project and gave it the momentum that brought it to completion in 1884.

Four documents serve to explain how the sculptor and the workshop went about the sixteenfold enlargement from the original model, the clay *Liberty* 1.75 motes high (not quite 4 feet) which was also the *Modèle du Comité* introduced at the Louvre banquet of 1875. These are, first, the article on construction from *Le Génie Civil* written in 1883 by Charles Talansier but with the hand of Bartholdi discernible behind almost every line; second, and based on the foregoing, Bartholdi's own little book published in 1885 as a contribution to the fund-raising campaign (cat. 379); and finally, two graphics, one an engraving (cat. 231) taken from a newspaper, the other originally a drawing, subsequently lost but rediscovered in a private collection in the form of a print from a glass-plate negative (cat. 232).

The very detailed article in *Le Génie Civil* (cat. 233) provides the best discussion of the process of enlargement from the original model: «When the sketch was approved, M. Bartholdi made a figure measuring 2.11 meters from head to heel; this was the model on a scale of 1:16.» This is the model that appears at the left of cat. 231 and 246; it is now at the Conservatoire National des Arts et Métiers. «For the process of final construction the model was enlarged four times to a scale of 1:4; this new figure could still be taken in at a single glance.» This model has since been destroyed, but corresponds very closely to the statue that now stands on the Pont de Grenelle in Paris (cat. 499);[6] it may well have served as the original for the foundry mold, or at least suggested to the sculptor the appropriate scale for this site.

The scale of the finished work was arrived at by squaring up, after this fashion: the 1:4 scale model, when the artist had inspected it and made the necessary changes, was divided into sections. The *verticals* of the statue, taken with a plumb-line, were very precisely extended to a pedestal four times as large

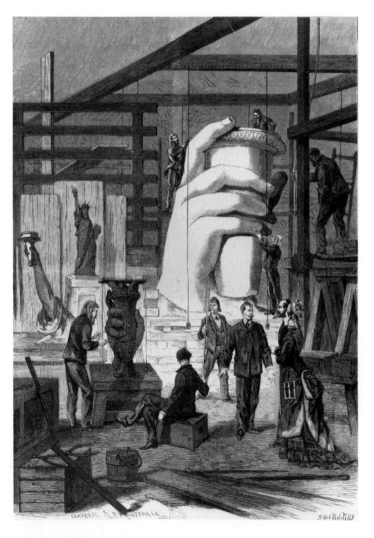

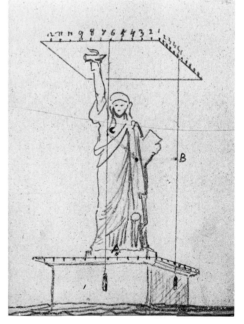

231
Taller de M. Bartholdi donde se ejecutan las differentes partes de la estatua
Claverie and P. Kauffmann
From *Del Correo de l'Ultramar*
n.d.

232
La mise au point
Frédéric-Auguste Bartholdi
n.d.

234
The Wooden Hand of the Statue
P. Petit
n.d.

235
Creating a Plaster Mold from a Wood Frame
Fig. 4 from Charles Talansier, «La Statue de la Liberté Éclairant le Monde» (cat. 233)

236
The Plaster Arm and Hand
n.d.

as the pedestal of the model. This procedure yielded a hypothetical solid bounded by the extended verticals and containing within itself the statue, or a part of the statue, on an enlarged scale. From this the position of the important points of the relief, relative to the verticals, could be determined by taking a series of imaginary sections across the 1:4 scale model. This is an elaborate version of the procedure used in transferring the elevations of a mountain to a map by means of contour lines. The cross sections were reproduced with mathematical precision in a fourfold enlargement. The procedure, simple enough in principle, demands consummate skill in practice. Six separate measurements—three on the model and three on the enlargement— were required to establish the position of each fixed point, and of course more were required to check it. The final sections averaged 3.4 meters in height, and in each there were 300 principal and more than 1,200 subsidiary reference-points, calling for some 9,000 measurements *on each section*. Sculptors worked on plaster models of the final size, each on its squared, sectioned, and numbered

pedestal. Measurements for the enlargement were calculated, with compass and ruler, from the plumb-lines. The principal reference-points of the cross sections once determined, they were joined by a framework of lumber and lath. The form thus sketched in wood was covered with a layer of plaster, the measurements were verified, details were finished and the surface relief completed.

This lath-and-plaster work is well illustrated in *Le Génie Civil* by an engraving (fig. 4 in the original; cat. 235), which is taken from the photograph reproduced here as cat. 234. The engraving omits the three human figures at the bottom, especially the plasterer, who cannot be distinguished against the edge of the drapery;[7] a solitary figure, standing in the hollow of the enormous hand, affords an idea of its size. This engraving is one of the finest visual images of the statue's construction, worthy to rank with the masterpieces of the nineteenth century. Equally striking is a photograph (cat. 236) laying out the vast panorama of the workshop, its activity frozen by the camera shutter. We have two slightly different versions of cat.

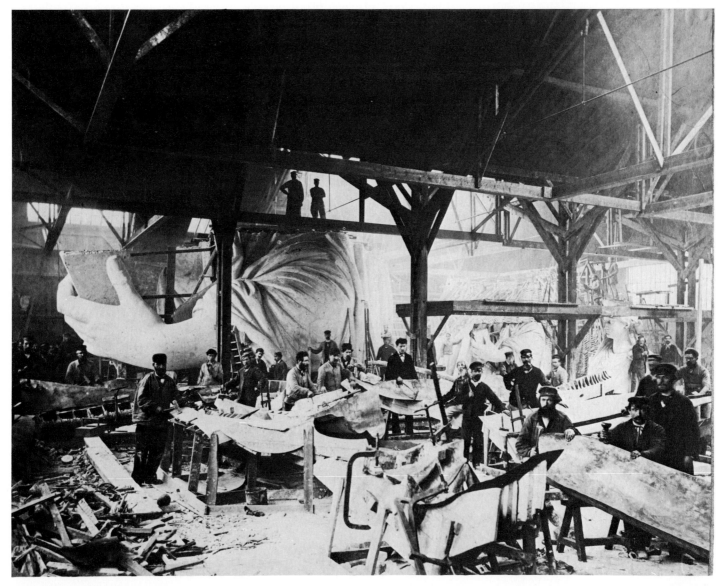

237, in which Bartholdi and Simon (at right) proudly contemplate the statue's left hand and the graceful line described by the finger (in copper, to judge by the tone of the print, like the one in the collection of the Conservatoire National des Arts et Métiers [see cat. 250] on which work is proceeding at the left of the photograph).

When the plaster model of definitive size was finished, the next step was to take a solid impression of it, in wood, against which could be hammered out the copper sheets which were to be the outer skin of the statue. This was a complicated exercise in joinery, presenting problems analogous to those of making a foundry-mold. The consistency of the forms had to be such that they could be easily detached from the model; later the sheets of copper which would be embossed onto the forms must also be readily detachable from them.

Following the least contorted curves of the model (generally those of its surface contours, like the rounded knolls of a range of hills) boards were cut to size and laid along the lines AA [see cat. 238], and connected to each other by boards laid transversely along the lines BB. The gaps between them were filled with smaller panels (CC) which were closer or farther apart in proportion as the part to be reproduced was more or less modeled. The sum total of these components, which had to match the plaster form exactly, constituted a rigid mold which resembled the contour-lines and hatchings on a military map.

The method of employing the laths appears clearly in a photograph (cat. 239) where they are laid over the drapery at left, or lean against another part of the plaster statue (cat. 240), or are shown in detail lying on the floor (cat. 241).

The molds were bigger or smaller according to the difficulty of the work. Sometimes several of them had to be joined together for the correct positioning of the copper sheets. These sheets had an average surface area between 1 and 3 square meters but could not be had in widths greater than 1.4 meters. The workers forced them into the molds with levers or by beating them with mallets. The finishing touches were added with goldbeaters' hammers or tamping-rods, and the whole was then carefully checked against wire templates or sheets of lead which had been impressed on the model.

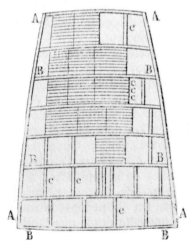

237
Construction of the Drapery and the Hand
P. Petit
n.d.

238
Outline of the Wooden Laths
Fig. 5 from Charles Talansier, «La Statue de la Liberté Éclairant le Monde» (cat. 233)

239
Laths Laid over Drapery
n.d.

240
Work in Progress on the Drapery
Attributed to P. Petit
n.d.

241
Hammering: Mold Making
Attributed to P. Petit
n.d.

242
Hammering the Drapery
P. Petit
n.d.

243
*Hammering a Copper Sheet
into a Mold*
P. Petit
n.d.

244
*Bartholdi at Gaget,
Gauthier et Cie.*
n.d.

245
*Assembly of the Copper
Segments*
Fig. 7 from Charles
Talansier, «La Statue de la
Liberté Éclairant le
Monde» (cat. 233)

246
*Destroying One Model to
Begin Work on the Next*
Attributed to P. Petit
n.d.

Cat. 242 clearly shows the hammered sheets and the heavy wooden mallet with which the copper was forced onto the form. Then comes the «skin»—the formed copper sheet being peeled away from its mold (cat. 243). In cat. 244, Bartholdi, at the left, examines the finished piece of copper ready to be riveted in place. Details on this operation, on the joining of the sheets, and on the final assembly are given in *Le Génie Civil*:

> When a piece has complex curves, or needs to be welded, the copper is heated in the forge and brazed with a blow-torch. At intervals, metal reinforcements are applied to the copper sheets in order to stiffen them; these fittings are wrought to follow the final shape of the copper, but are not to be affixed until the statue is finally assembled.
>
> *Assembling the Copper Segments.*—The copper envelope, hammered out as explained above, consisted of some 300 pieces with an aggregate weight of 80,000 kilograms. It was supported by an iron armature weighing 120,000 kilograms. . . . In the workshops of Gaget, Gauthier et Cie. the copper sheets were mounted to the armature with screws; the final assembly on site in America would be done with copper rivets, their heads hammered flat to make them invisible on the outer surface of the statue. These rivets were 5 millimeters thick, and inserted 25 millimeters apart. As the copper segments were butted together [see cat. 245], the technique of assembly could not be discerned even at close quarters, and the statue appeared to have been made from a single seamless sheet of metal.

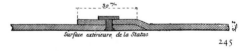

Surface extérieure de la Statue

245

The passage of time, taking its toll on the joints, rivets, reinforcements, and armature, would dispel this illusion, but it is still interesting to note the sculptor's concern that the finished work should appear as a huge bronze casting—a familiar form raised to a new order of magnitude. Furthermore, only with time did the statue acquire the now familiar patina of verdigris; the photographs taken in Paris, or the painting by Dargaud (cat. 317), show how she looked at first.

247

*La Construction de la
Statue de la Liberté*
Maurand and Claverie
From *Le Journal Illustré*
May 28, 1876

248

*The Torch at Monduit,
Gaget, Gauthier et Cie.*
n.d.

249

*The Completed Torch in
Front of a Canvas*
E. Flamant
n.d.

Once a batch of copper sheets had been worked into shape, and the artist had approved them, the plaster form and wooden molds were destroyed to make room for the next stage of the work (cat. 246). The scene possesses a kind of morbid poetry; a great work has been finished—and dismissed to oblivion. Today we could not begin to appreciate the heroic labor that brought these brittle shells of copper into being, had the camera not preserved a fleeting moment for all time, and turned the rubbish of the workshop into the celebration of a mighty task accomplished.

The assembly of the copper segments began in the early summer of 1876. An engraving (cat. 247) from May shows the flame and the torch being fabricated; the plaster head—bearing a windowless, unadorned crown—had been sculpted by Bartholdi a year earlier.[8] The torch made its first appearance in the cluttered workshop of Gaget, Gauthier surrounded by innumerable pieces of lead and copper roof ornament (cat. 248). In a second photograph (cat. 249), taken after more careful preparation, the formidable artifact stands out from its confusing background; the workshop has been tidied up and a backdrop hung behind the torch. The original model (lower right), and an enlargement of the arm and the hand, serve to measure the progress of the work, and evoke the scrupulous creative artist who in the process of enlargement refused to forego the slightest fine detail of the original. The ornate gallery of the torch, a masterpiece worthy of the Monduit atelier, was a rhapsody in metal basket-work, a demonstration of (decorative) art for art's sake—except that, as noted in Chapter 3, Bartholdi deliberately established a contrast between still surfaces, as of the arm, and surfaces in motion, as of the torch and its flame.

The arm then left for the United States, where it arrived in August 1876 and was mounted in Philadelphia. It became a popular attraction in New York as well, but this was not the only reason that delayed its return to Paris until August 10, 1882. Marvin Trachtenberg contends that Bartholdi was making changes in detail up to the last moment,[9] and Jacques Betz suggests that he even tried to sell this arm and torch in Philadelphia, so that he could start work on new and better ones. Time and money were not to be had, but the delays may have contributed to the problems of final assembly in 1884. In any case, it is appropriate here to call attention to the forefinger (cat. 250) of the gigantic hand, a feature of the exhibit of 1878 in Paris (see Chapter 6) astutely designed to astonish all beholders. Still more astounding are the two models Bartholdi made in connection with the lottery of 1879 (see Chapter 6). The first shows a plaster head (cat. 251):

> The little figures illustrate two different kinds of labor. The carvers, with their rules and plumb-lines, are taking measurements, doing the enlargement, and working on the full-scale model.

> The joiners are making hollow forms of wood, conforming precisely to the shape of the model (note the forms on the neck and bosom).

> Into these forms are hammered the copper sheets, as illustrated in the other exhibit. [Text of the explanatory plaque fixed to the side of the miniature scene.]

The other miniature shows the copper head (cat. 252):

> The metalwork is done by laying the copper sheet against the wooden forms, and applying pressure or beating it with mallets until it assumes their exact shape; when pieces are to be sweated together, or worked into a complicated shape, the metal is first softened in the forge. The finishing touches are added with a hammer.

> Assembly is done with plumb-lines on a sectioned framework, as for the plaster form. The sheets of copper are put in place and affixed to iron armatures wrought as required by the blacksmiths. [Text of the explanatory plaque fixed to the side of the miniature scene.]

These two scale models of the workshop, originally conceived as teaching aids, speak volumes about the artist's desire to explain his labors to others, and about his natural pleasure in so much organized ingenuity. Photographs (cat. 55, 56) show that in Bartholdi's studio on the rue d'Assas they held an honorable place beside the easel and the piano. They were a remembrance of past happiness for the artist, as well as a reminder for his visitors of past achievement. A watercolor by Bartholdi, which appeared in the press but now exists only in a photographic reproduction (cat. 281), shows the studio from the same angle, and seems to take its inspiration from these agreeable objects which resemble children's toys.

The death of Viollet-le-Duc in 1879 may have left Bartholdi at a loss. Even he, however, must have pondered the real problems that such an upward-thrust mass as the statue could create, especially wind resistance. The experiences of 1876 with the torch and of 1878 with the head may have provided some practical knowledge; what is certain is that Bartholdi confidently approached Gustave Eiffel and asked him to find a solution for just this problem.

Gustave Eiffel (cat. 253) is remembered today principally for his Tower, but to Bartholdi he was the leading designer of iron railroad bridges. His bridge across the Douro at Oporto was completed in 1877; at the time of Viollet-le-Duc's death in 1879 Eiffel had begun work on the viaduct at Garabit, which he was to finish in 1884. But it is not his bridges and their roadways which concern us, so much as it is the pylons that supported them, for in these Eiffel found the solution to the statue's problem. Bartholdi must have known Eiffel in another context as well, as designer of the iron structure of the Pavilion at the Universal Exposition of 1878, in front of which the sculptor had wished his head of *Liberty* to stand (cat. 286).

Eiffel may also have been linked to Bartholdi by common sympathies or political affinity. Trachtenberg points out that Eiffel may have had patriotic reasons for his involvement with *Liberty*.[10] In any case, Eiffel, who had failed to gain admission to the École Polytechnique and may have been attempting to avenge himself ever since by designing structures of the greatest technical daring, must have responded eagerly to the technical challenge, and admired Bartholdi's energy.

Le Génie Civil describes the project as it stood in 1883, when Eiffel disclosed his plans fully: «The iron scaffold on which the entire envelope of copper rests is formed like a great pylon,[11] attached at four points to the stone pedestal of the statue. Each point is a plate supported by three bolts; each bolt is 14 centimeters thick, and sunk into the foundation to a depth of 15 meters.» The «depth,» of course, was to be absorbed by the pedestal, as shown in a drawing formerly in Bartholdi's collection, now at Colmar (cat. 398). On this solid spar, whose footing may be seen in a photographic overview of the Gaget, Gauthier workshops (cat. 254), a lighter superstructure was mounted (cat. 255): «The envelope is tied to the pylon by flat armatures of iron, 50 millimeters broad by 8 millimeters thick; these are bonded to the interior surface of the copper to protect it from deformation. The armatures are bolted to one another at the points of intersection, and form a latticework resting directly on the scaffold.» Eiffel took every possible precaution against shifting of the structure or the envelope, by constructing a system of close but flexible linkage between the two:

> Two specific dangers had to be foreseen and averted in this phase of the work:

250

250
Copper Finger of the Statue
ca. 1876–78

251
Workshop Model with Plaster Maquette of the Head of the Statue
Frédéric-Auguste Bartholdi
1879
reproduced in color
on p. 133

252
Workshop Model with Copper Maquette of the Head of the Statue
Frédéric-Auguste Bartholdi
1879
reproduced in color
on p. 133

253
Gustave Eiffel
Crauk
1903
reproduced in color
on p. 133

254
The Gaget-Gauthier Workshop—General View
P. Petit
n.d.

255
Eiffel's Armature and the Head
n.d.

255

First, expansion. Expansion, of considerable magnitude, there must be, but it
need be attended by no inconvenience
because of the extreme elasticity of the
copper skin, and the effect of «expansion
bellows» provided by the folds of the
drapery. Moreover, so that each metal
could expand freely according to its own
coefficient, the iron armatures were not
riveted to the statue, but enclosed in
sleeves of copper which were themselves
riveted in place.

Second, and more serious, the effects of
electricity. Quite apart from any airborne
spray, the wind from the sea always
carries significant quantities of salt water
in suspension which can set up a powerful electrical gradient between iron and
copper juxtaposed, as in the statue. The
same effect can be produced by storm-
rain, heavily charged as it is with nitrates.
It could readily be foreseen that strong
currents would be generated in what
was, all said and done, a gigantic battery
of unknown potential.

To prevent this, the builders placed between the copper sheets and the iron
braces small plates of copper lagged with
rags which had been heavily smeared
with red lead. This is the same technique
which has been successfully employed by
marine architects in the sheathing of
hulls.

Clearly, the engineer foresaw precisely those
kinds of deterioration that concerned today's restorers (see Chapter 15). He took to
heart Viollet-le-Duc's strictures on the vertical rigidity of the envelope, while at the
same time imparting to it some flexibility
along the horizontal plane. Assembly, then,
was accomplished without modification of
the molded sheets; the arm and the head
had to be first dismounted, then remounted.[12]

254

Cat. 256, a photograph taken shortly after the first rivet was driven in 1881, shows how access to the interior was achieved through the sandal on *Liberty*'s foot. The pylon and its arm, now completely assembled (cat. 257) are carrying first half and then two-thirds (cat. 258, 259) of their cladding. A later photograph (cat. 260) shows how the skin was placed along the principal axes of the drapery (as is also the case with the replica at the Pont de Grenelle); there is an unavoidable hiatus across the bosom. Then the head was at last put in place (cat. 261)— but the inherent interest of this photograph goes far beyond the visual record of one

stage nearer completion; at this same moment other workmen are dismounting the arm which is to hold the torch, and we know now that an error in calculation had made this unavoidable. The arm had been placed too close to the head, but the structural logic of the original placement would not admit a simple readjustment of the arm and its drapery. This would be discovered in due course by today's restoration team, but it underlines the value of the photographs Bartholdi caused to be taken, in revealing the nature of the error. A sketch (cat. 262) helps explain the remedial procedures that now had to be undertaken.

Finally the first photograph of the finished statue was taken (cat. 263), immediately released, and made use of by newspapers, engravers, and painters. Its somber tint excited general admiration, as did the perfection of the final assembly (in spite of the mistake referred to above). But its contemporaries did not appreciate how far the work foretold the shape of things to come. Eiffel had created an envelope not standing but hanging, not bearing but borne. His inventive genius avoided the trap into which Viollet-le-Duc had fallen and opened the way to the curtain-wall (how apt the expression seems here!) and the highrise

256

257

258

259

260

256
Entrance to the Statue through the Foot
Frédéric-Auguste Bartholdi
n.d.

257
The Mounting of the Statue up to the Waist
n.d.

258
The Mounting of the Statue
n.d.

259
The Mounting of the Copper Pieces of the Statue
n.d.

260
The Mounting of the Statue, Three-Quarters of the Body
P. Petit
n.d.

261
The Mounting of the Statue with the Head and Arm
From *Album des Travaux de Construction de la Statue Colossale de la Liberté destinée au Port de New-York*
Paris: Gontrand, Reinhard et Cie., 1883

architecture from which the United States was to profit so greatly. Marvin Trachtenberg observes how timely the solution was, coinciding with the very first of these buildings, which were to become a specialty of Richard Morris Hunt.[13] The inaugural festivities once over, the disassembly of the statue began; each of the more than two hundred pieces was numbered and packed in its own portable case, and the whole was shipped by rail to Rouen, to be loaded (cat. 264) aboard the *Isère*. Construction had lasted almost ten years.

Translated, from the French, by Maxwell Vos

263
The Finished Statue, January 1884
Frédéric-Auguste Bartholdi
1884

262
Sketch Showing Eiffel's Original Design for the Arm and Shoulder; the Arm and Shoulder as Built; the 1932 Repairs; and the 1984 Repair Scheme
American Society of Civil Engineers
1984

261

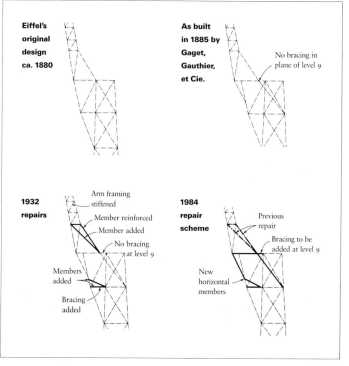

262

«America will very soon celebrate the centennial anniversary of her Independence. . . . We believe, as well as our friends of the United States, that it affords a solemn occasion to unite France and America in a common manifestation. . . . The question is to elevate . . . an exceptional monument. In the middle of the New-York harbour . . . a colossal statue . . . *Liberty enlightening the World.*»[1] This release to the French press, on September 28, 1875, opened the subscription list and launched the French fund-raising campaign (cat. 265).

The attempt to fund the construction of the Statue of Liberty between the fall of 1875 and the summer of 1876 was to prove a challenge. Moreover, Bartholdi's project—his «great work,» as he called it—had been the object of his 1871 journey to the United States. The four years since had seen no apparent progress. The complexity of the conception—a Colossus of Liberty—does not in itself explain this procrastination. Was there some reneging on the proposed method of financing? Perhaps so, but the idea of a national appeal for subscriptions, under consideration since 1871,[2] offered a classically appropriate solution. The explanation must be sought elsewhere: in the birth pangs of the French Republic itself.

6.
The French Campaign

Catherine Hodeir

In 1871, after the defeat of France by Germany and the fall of the Second Empire followed by that of the Commune, the country voted for a Republic: the Republic of Thiers, a conservative institution guaranteeing order and peace. Bartholdi returned from the United States while France was struggling to raise an indemnity of five milliards of francs, payable to Germany under the terms of the Treaty of Frankfurt. The bond issues launched to pay off this humiliating debt quite overshadowed the prospects of a subscription for a statue—and a gift to be offered to another country, at that. Patriotism is always a good approach, and Bartholdi thus began work on his other colossal statue, the *Lion de Belfort*. Rather than accept a compromise proposed at the time—a «large plaster-of-Paris model» of *Liberty*, which could later be made more serviceable by casting it in bronze[3]—the sculptor and Edouard de Laboulaye preferred to await more propitious circumstances. But in 1873, with the

last milliard paid over to Prussia, and France recovering little by little from the shock of her defeat, the Republic, still only provisional, seemed to collapse with the fall of Thiers on May 24. The rise to power of Marshal MacMahon, elected President of the Republic, and of the Duc de Broglie, named Prime Minister, opened the way to an attempted restoration of the Monarchy. The image of the Republic, and that of *Liberty* so closely linked to it,[4] did not enjoy a good press. The situation scarcely favored the launching of a promotional campaign for *Liberty*. «We may assume,» wrote Bartholdi in June 1873, «that the members of the Committee want nothing to do with this administration»—that of the Duc de Broglie.[5] The first obstacle had produced the first delay.

The structure of politics changed in 1875. Neither a legitimist nor an Orleanist restoration came to pass. On the other hand, the Bonapartist alternative, as fearsome to republicans as it was to monarchists, loomed closer. But what was the new regime to be like? On January 29, 1875, Edouard de Laboulaye proposed an amendment to the National Assembly: «that the government of the Republic consist of two Chambers and a President.» It was defeated, but the word «Republic» had been officially spoken. The next day the resolution was reintroduced by another Deputy, Henri Wallon, and passed by a voice vote. The Third Republic was born.

Under republican auspices, the campaign for the Statue of Liberty could at last begin. A committee was formed, calling itself the Franco-American Union. The honorary membership, international in nature, was a microcosm of Franco-American relations of the period. Three men in particular represented the official ties between the two countries. Elihu Washburne, as U.S. Minister Plenipotentiary in Paris, had been the first representative of a foreign power to recognize the French Republic. His French opposite number in Washington was none other than the sculptor's cousin.

Amédée Bartholdi, who agreed to join the Committee in April 1875,[6] was willing to use his influence to promote the project. John W. Forney, Commissioner in Europe for the Philadelphia Centennial Exhibition, stood slightly to one side of, but was nonetheless significant to, official French-

American relations. Forney's presence on the Committee was no small advantage: a monument intended for the U.S. Centennial could not but benefit from association with the Philadelphia Exhibition.

The honorary committee reflected another aspect of French-American relations: the traditional friendship between the two countries. Rochambeau, Noailles, and Lafayette served a symbolic function. They were there, first and foremost, because they bore names celebrated in the United States and France alike. These names had won their luster in the American ranks during the American Revolution, and were a storehouse of memories common to both nations. Two other descendants of the Marquis de Lafayette were also included: Jules de Lasteyrie and Paul de Remusat. At a slight angle to this tradition of French-American amity, but recalling the French obsession with the discovery of the United States in 1835–40, the name of de Tocqueville also adorned the Committee, in the person of the brother of the author of *De la Démocratie en Amérique*.

Another serious student of the American continent (although he had never been there) presided over the Steering Committee. Edouard de Laboulaye (cat. 266, 267) was the originator of Bartholdi's project, at least in respect of its symbol, Liberty, and its destination, America. It may have been at a dinner at Glatigny in 1865 that he suggested the sculptor make a statue to celebrate French-American friendship.[7] Regarding this first meeting, our sole source of information is Bartholdi's little book, *The Statue of Liberty Enlightening the World*, published only in the United States, twenty years after the event. According to that account, Laboulaye and Bartholdi met to discuss a possible commission from Laboulaye for his bust, intended perhaps for the Collège de France, on whose faculty he sat. (Bartholdi received the commission and exhibited the bust at the Salon of 1866.) At Glatigny, the two men would soon have discussed their mutual interest in seeing a more liberal French constitution. Assuming that they got on from the start, it is likely that Laboulaye approached the sculptor with his idea for a monument to be given by the French people to the United States to symbolize the friendship between the two countries as well as to celebrate the American political system.

No doubt Laboulaye intended a rather conventional type of public monument, of the kind represented by Bartholdi's *Lafayette and Washington* (cat. 12). The artist, for his part, was already prepared for something else. His discovery of colossal sculpture both at the Louvre and in Egypt in 1856 helped keep him open to any opportunity for realizing his dream: to build a colossus. After several years of thinking, traveling, and waiting, Bartholdi proposed to Laboulaye in 1872 a new idea, inspired partly by the site in New York harbor, partly by his own ambition. The new image must have puzzled Laboulaye, who would certainly never have envisioned challenging the legendary creations of the Greeks, Romans, and Egyptians, nor of giving birth to a totally new technical experiment. Still, Laboulaye played an important part in the subsequent story, especially since he is the one who gave final shape to the image, and since he held firmly to the whole symbolic meaning of the project. Bartholdi must have understood that immediately in 1865.

The overall composition of the Committee reflected a moderate republicanism, in perfect harmony with the spirit of the new regime. Several members of the Franco-American Union held public office: some, like Oscar de Lafayette, were nearing the end of a long parliamentary career; others, like the well-known historian Henri Martin, had entered public life after the war of 1870. Most were, or were to become, Deputies or Senators—Laboulaye in 1875, Jean Macé only in 1883 when he succeeded Jules de Lasteyrie. Some had been very belated adherents to the Republic, but all belonged to the left-center or to the republican left. Led by Laboulaye and William Henry Waddington, they were followers of Thiers and voted to reject his resignation on May 24, 1873. By 1875 they belonged to what might be termed the pragmatic majority, opposed alike to the right and to the radical-socialist left. The sole exception was one Cornélis de Witt, Guizot's son-in-law and an unsuccessful candidate of the right in the senatorial and legislative elections of December 1875 and February 1876, respectively. No doubt his authorship of *Études sur l'histoire des États-Unis d'Amérique* and his biography of Washington earned him his place among the supporters of *Liberty*.

265
Bilingual Subscription
Appeal of the Franco-
American Union
September 28, 1875

If republicanism was the Committee's keystone, other supporting influences could also be discerned. French Freemasonry was represented by an identifiable group; the sculptor's cousin Dietz Monnin, Jean Macé, and Bartholdi himself were, or were in process of becoming, brothers affiliated with the Grand Orient. All belonged to the Alsace-Lorraine Lodge, founded in 1872 in a dramatic gesture of loyalty after the two French provinces had been annexed to Germany. Bartholdi was received as an apprentice on October 14, 1875, a few months after future minister Jules Ferry and at the very moment that the Franco-American Union launched its campaign. Is it legitimate to infer a predominant Masonic influence on the Committee? Probably not, despite its inclusion of another Mason, V. Borie of the La Justice lodge. Toward the close of the nineteenth century it was both inevitable and unimportant that Masons should be found at the center of the bourgeois establishment and be closely linked to republican political circles. French Masonry,

moreover, had little or no interest in America, maintaining only superficial and intermittent relations with American Masons, whose obedience is not to the Grand Orient. The «predominance» of the Alsace-Lorraine Lodge within the Franco-American Union underlines the Committee's moderate-republican composition; the Grand Orient as a whole was reputed to be further left.[8] Of even less practical significance were some of the other ideologies represented on the Committee. Alongside liberal Catholics like Edouard de Laboulaye, or progressive Protestants like Waddington and Bartholdi, we find the founder of the Ligue d'Enseignement, Jean Macé, a militant proponent of secular education and of popular culture.

Not all members of the Committee brought to it the same degree of commitment. Laboulaye, Henri Martin, Dietz Monnin, Count Serrurier (a former Prefect), de Castro, Caubert (a former magistrate), Bartholdi, and Oscar de Lafayette were most prominent; other names figure less often in the Committee's proceedings. Over the years the Union evolved. Some members died: Wolowski, Count de Tocqueville, and Viollet-le-Duc were gone by 1879; Jules de Lasteyrie, Martin, and Laboulaye himself were not there to witness the inaugural ceremony on Bedloe's Island. New members joined the group: the iron-master Monduit, the «Americans» Thomas G. Appleton and Georges Glaenzer, and finally, in 1883, Ferdinand de Lesseps.

The Committee of the Franco-American Union, formed during the spring and summer of 1875, assumed official existence on September 26. The constitution of the Third Republic had been voted into law; although the political spring-tide had receded from its high watermark, it was still high enough to float the Union's project.

It was natural that the Committee should think in terms of soliciting subscriptions; since the beginning of the nineteenth century this had been, in France, the preferred mode of financing the erection of statues in public places.[9] Given the scale of the project it was decided that funds should be raised internationally: in America for the pedestal, and in France for the statue itself. Both the large sums of money required, and the concept underlying the project, made it appropriate that the French and American people unite their efforts to make the symbol of Liberty a reality.

The French campaign initially emphasized the national character of the appeal: the first object was to ensure that the Statue of Liberty should come into being. In 1875 a massive, urgent fund-raising program was envisaged, to end in 1876; no one suspected that it would drag on into 1880. The methods employed were, therefore, those suited to a short-term promotional effort.

The chosen instrument for inaugurating the campaign was the French press. The men of the Union, typical of the republicans of their era, saw clearly how effective an instrument the press was becoming—and they understood how to make use of it. On September 26, Laboulaye sent the Union's official appeal to every newspaper in France, with a covering letter to each editor stressing the patriotic nature of an undertaking «which is intended to do honor to the glorious memory of our fathers.» This approach, recalling the military achievements of France during the American Revolution, played deftly on the perceptible return of nationalist feeling after the humiliation of defeat by Germany.

Journalists developed this theme, recalling the exploits of the French army which, a century earlier, had set sail for America, and for glory. In some provincial papers it was not Laboulaye's letter that appeared, but one to the same effect from some other Committee member. Le Loir, for instance, served the Vendôme region, where the Rochambeau family was prominent; the appeal to that paper came more effectively from the hand of the Marquis de Rochambeau himself.

At just this point in time, the French press was entering a great period of expansion that was to make it, over the next few years, a mass medium. The appeal, and Laboulaye's letter, appeared in more than two-thirds of the forty daily papers in Paris, whose combined press-run was 1.5 million copies.[10] The papers that sold for 10 or 15 centimes (a high price at that time) rallied to Liberty's cause no less than their 5-centime contemporaries such as Le Petit Journal. The provinces did not lag behind: L'Echo des Cévennes, L'Eclaireur de Lunéville, La Volonté Nationale des Charentes, Le Moniteur Ardennais, Le Propagateur Picard—these among many others gave the subscription their blessing.

267
Bust of Edouard de
Laboulaye
Frédéric-Auguste Bartholdi
n.d.

In Paris and throughout France this press campaign was preponderantly republican, with the center-left papers in the vanguard. The venerable *Journal des Débats*, despite a modest circulation of 7,500, still had influence. At its side stood the ponderous daily *Le Temps*, the great organ of French liberalism, very close to Waddington, with a circulation of 15,000 copies. Like its contemporary *Le XIXe Siècle*, renowned for its embittered attacks on monarchists and radicals alike, *Le Temps* figured as a supporter in the amount of Fr. 500.[11] Other papers followed suit with varying degrees of enthusiasm; curiously, the venerable *Journal des Débats* sulkily declined to «associate itself with the subscription.»[12]

A second group of dailies supporting the Committee came from the republican left. *Le Siècle*, the business paper *Le National*, *L'Opinion Nationale*, and *La France* proclaimed a moderate republicanism cast in the very mold of Bartholdi's statue. On the other hand, it is a bit surprising to read the Committee's appeal in the columns of *La République Française*, which spoke for the supporters of Gambetta, or of *Le Rappel*, the only important radical paper of the day, with a circulation of 40,000. Somewhat out of the mainstream of the political press stood the «popular» newspaper *Le Petit Journal*, with its large (for 1875) circulation of 345,000 copies. It formed part of the «group» of Emile de Girardin, standing for a conciliatory ideal of republicanism, and at once took *Liberty* to its heart. Thomas Grimm, its celebrated «editorialist,» was «happy to be the first of our contemporaries to publish the subscription program.»[13]

At the other end of the political spectrum, the papers of the right, whether legitimist, Orleanist, or Bonapartist, held their peace. Only *Le Figaro* printed part of the Committee's appeal, adding a commentary, in its inimitable style, hinting broadly that American «friendship» for the French people was a delusion. Nevertheless, this attack by a popular daily selling 650,000 copies may not have worked altogether against the Committee's interests. Other opposition papers, such as *Le Gaulois*, eventually fell in behind *Le Figaro*. The provincial papers were less consistent than their Parisian counterparts; alongside the many republican organs that picked up Laboulaye's appeal were found some conservative publications.

Networks of influence began to form. Two journalists (or «publicists,» as they were called then), Victor Borie and Jules Simonin, were among the Union's members; Simonin worked for *La France*, another daily in the Girardin «group.» Edouard de Laboulaye was a fairly regular contributor to the *Journal des Débats*, while Henri Martin was a member of the supervisory board of *Le Siècle*. Several newspaper publishers, some very successful, were close to the Committee, among them the banker Cernuschi, a shareholder in both *Le Siècle* and *Le XIXe Siècle*; the chocolate magnate Menier, who provided a veritable horn of plenty to the republican press; and the influential Emile de Girardin, founder of the modern French press, who in the years 1875–80 was still very active.

Strengthened by such support, the Committee set out to win over the entire universe of French periodicals. Journalists were liberally invited to the events sponsored by the French campaign, and Laboulaye wrote to Gustave Janicot, owner of *La Gazette* and head of the publishers' association, who agreed to put the Statue of Liberty on the agenda of a meeting.[14] Most of the dailies did no more than publish Laboulaye's letter and the appeal for subscriptions, without comment—almost an unacknowledged advertisement. This impression is confirmed by Bartholdi's reference, in a letter to the president of the Committee dated December 14, 1875, to «an account which must be settled with the *Journal des Débats* for the insertion of leaflets.» Clearly the Committee paid to have its messages appear in the press, who were thanked again and again for their help. «With you» (journalists)—so Laboulaye summed it up—«we can do anything; without you we can do nothing.»[15]

The campaign once under way, it remained only to harvest the money. The Union made its headquarters at 175, rue St. Honoré in Paris, and opened an account at the Société Générale, a bank that handled both deposit and commercial accounts. Networks were set up for the collection of contributions; subscription forms were available at the Committee's headquarters, at branches of the Société Générale, and at newspaper offices (cat. 268, 269). Chambers of Commerce received coupon books to distribute to their membership. Bonds could be purchased «through your regular broker.» To accelerate the flow of subscriptions, the Union established subcommittees in Paris and the provinces, and set up a hierarchy of

subscribers. The Associate Members, «the General Staff of the Project, represent the Union and solicit donations according to the means at their disposal and their connections.»[16] Each Associate Member became responsible for selling at least one book of subscription coupons. Individual subscribers were also encouraged to multiply their personal contribution by networking; each was invited to recommend others who might be susceptible to the appeal. The would-be contributor could subscribe by money order, by check, or even at home, by completing and returning a form authorizing the Committee's agent to collect in person.

Who contributed for the Statue of Liberty? Everyone did—or at least the Committee hoped they would. «Let everyone bring a penny; small contributions will be gratefully received.»[17] The decision to solicit money from everyone arose less from financial calculation than from a determination to make the campaign national in scope. The Committee needed names no less than money: «every Frenchman, no matter what his politics,» can and should give «his signature»[18]—that is, his personal commitment to the work of a consensus. Throughout the nineteenth century, no matter what government was in power, every public subscription campaign had to establish its legitimacy by collecting signatures by the thousands.[19] In an attempt to lend the campaign a more republican flavor, the daily *Le Rappel* outdid the Committee in ingenuity: it suggested asking every Frenchman to offer a «republican nickel» to *Liberty*.

If every Frenchman had indeed brought his nickel, the target could have been reached quickly, perhaps even within the time limit imposed by the approaching U.S. Centennial, but as in all such undertakings, it was a long way from dream to realization. Through the newspapers urban France was kept informed of the Committee's progress; the poor could follow the campaign in the 5-centime press, because the urban working class had been generally literate since the middle of the century. The breadth of the coverage reached out to every audience, from the academics who followed *Le XIXe Siècle* to the craftsmen and skilled workers of Paris who read *Le Rappel*. Bearing in mind that each copy of every daily paper in France was probably read by several people, millions must have been following the progress of the appeal on behalf of Bartholdi's statue.

It appeared that all levels of French society presented themselves at the subscription counter: «the first lists bear the signatures of the Marshal President of the Republic (Mac-Mahon—Fr. 5,000), of the ministers (Fr. 1,000 apiece), of many deputies, and of bearers of illustrious names among the old aristocracy (Rochambeau—Fr. 1,000).»[20] The merchant princes, in the persons of Casimir-Perier, Cernuschi, and the brothers Lazard, fell in behind the project. The houses of Kinkelmann in Reims and Dormeuil in Paris contributed Fr. 1,500 between them. Employers «distributed around their firms» subscription forms through which their workers could participate.[21]

The reality of the subscription list offers a somewhat different picture. True, it was officially announced in July 1884 that there were now, in round figures, one hundred thousand subscribers, but where were the lists to be displayed proudly to American friends?[22] Where were the thousands of names supposed to be publicly acknowledged in the press? There were indeed individual subscribers, but it turned out that, as usual with subscriptions for public statuary, most of them belonged to the Establishment. This fact emerges clearly from a report sent to the Committee by one of the Union's associate members (cat. 270). «A Frenchman,» he wrote, «is likely to subscribe only if he is fairly well-educated.»[23] The letter is supported by the list attached to it. In the communes of St. Pol and Arras in the Pas-de-Calais, thirty-seven subscribers had given a total of Fr. 48: they were all local worthies, including a general councillor, attorneys, notaries, a tutor, a physician, a pharmacist, an auctioneer, businessmen, bankers, landlords, and men of means. This was the solid bourgeoisie of a small provincial town, people whose annual incomes would not fall far short of Fr. 10,000.[24] The middle classes, with incomes sometimes below Fr. 3,000 a year (a schoolteacher was paid Fr. 1,200), and workmen, whose daily wage was perhaps Fr. 4.50 in Paris or Fr. 3 in other places, could not with the best will in the world afford more than a few centimes.

As others had before them, the Committee sought the help of community organizations. At the spring session in 1876, local legislatures were invited to discuss modes of French participation in the forthcoming U.S. Centennial celebrations, one of these being the Statue of Liberty. In a debate on a vote for a subscription to Bartholdi's monument, conservatives aligned in opposition to a republican-sponsored proposal. In Vaucluse, a legislator recalled that the United States had supported Germany in the war of 1870. The response of the Bonapartists, on the other hand, was subtle: in Puy de Dôme they voted in favor of «this splendid proposal.»[25] Forty of the legislatures decided in the affirmative, but voted widely varying amounts: Meurthe-et-Moselle and Doubs voted Fr. 300 apiece; Rhône, Fr. 1,000.

Cities and towns were canvassed no less assiduously, Paris proving by far the most generous. Dietz Monnin, both a deputy from the Department of the Seine and a member of the Paris city council, proposed that the city «deposit Fr. 5,000» to the Committee's credit, but Parisian goodwill extended to a sum twice as large.[26] Le Havre offered Fr. 1,000, but the scale of municipal contributions was in general far more modest: Fr. 500, Fr. 200, Fr. 100, or even Fr. 50. By November 19, 1876, 125 towns and cities had sent in their remittances (cat. 271), to a total of a little more than Fr. 30,000; this was woefully short of the figure of Fr. 300,000 reported in a letter to the New York *Tribune*—but a little exaggeration might be expected to add momentum to the American fund-raising effort. In 1879 the Committee decided that it had not exhausted the potential of municipal liberality, and sent a follow-up letter to those mayors who had not yet replied; in the end, a total of 181 cities responded positively. The part played by the Chambers of Commerce is hard to quantify.[27]

No subscription is ever complete without its anonymous and exemplary act of munificence. The press announced that an anonymous donor, an industrial magnate, gave 25 tons of copper, valued at Fr. 64,000, for the statue's fabrication. History does not record whether or not this donation was raised to the full 80 tons required for *Liberty*, but the name of this mysterious benefactor was nonetheless to come down to posterity: Pierre-Eugène Secrétan. For his generosity he aspired to nothing less than an official recompense—perhaps even the Legion of Honor. The Committee and Bartholdi obligingly inquired of Laboulaye «if it might not be possible to do something» for the donor of copper «who so longed for a decoration. . .!»[28]

The hopeful beginnings of the campaign were orchestrated into three major events: an inaugural banquet at the Louvre on November 6, 1875; a *fête* at the Palais de l'Industrie on November 19; and a reception at the Paris Opéra on April 25, 1876.

At seven o'clock on the evening of November 6, 1875, in front of the entrance to «the great hall of the Hôtel du Louvre, which had just undergone a wonderfully timely redecoration,»[29] the invited crowd pressed forward. Little by little the dinner guests were sorted out from the general throng and were seated at five long tables set «with great splendor» (cat. 272, 273);[30] they included a few politicians of the right: Batbie, Admiral Fourichon, the Baron de Soubeyran. They were not there in force, and the presence of, for example, the Count de Bouillé probably reflected the part played by his ancestor in the American Revolution. In the great hall of the Louvre everything was «focused on America.»[31] The great hall «had been decorated with trophies, displays of weapons, and French and American flags.

272
Le Banquet Franco-Américain
H. Meyer
From *Le Journal Illustré*
November 21, 1875

274

Plan for the Socle of the
Statue of Liberty
Frédéric-Auguste Bartholdi
n.d.

Magnificent floral arrangements had been placed on the window ledges, and the portraits of Washington, Lafayette, Franklin, Rochambeau, Lincoln and Grant looked down from the walls.»[32] Amid this characteristically French-American decor, every eye turned to the silhouette of *Liberty*, now at last unveiled.

She stood at the end of the room opposite the head table, lit from behind, half-unreal on her still-imaginary pedestal (cat. 274) in New York harbor. The well-known photographer Pierre Petit had helped Bartholdi achieve the effect of an illuminated transparency thrown onto a large screen. *Liberty* was also present among the revelers in the shape of a very small statuette made by the sculptor. At nine o'clock dinner was served, the lavish and varied menu including filets de boeuf La Fayette and croustades Washington, all washed down with Haut Sauternes, Clos Vougeot, and Clicquot champagne. As glasses were raised to the Goddess Liberty, every festive lip carried its adornment of mustache or beard, for the social conventions of the nineteenth-century bourgeoisie kept public and domestic life in watertight compartments: wives had not been invited. This joyous masculine celebration of the official opening of the campaign followed a ritual of French conviviality popular among bourgeoisie and working class alike in the nineteenth century; the republicans were to invoke it again and again for various commemorations, such as the hundredth anniversary of Voltaire's death in 1878.[33]

In his address, Laboulaye stressed that «here . . . the old France no less than the new can find fulfillment, whether your dreams be of Louis XVI or of the Republic.» Such ecumenism, perhaps a little weighted toward the conservative position, points up the virtual absence from the banquet of the radical left; if that ardent republican Charles Floquet was invited, it was in his capacity as Chairman of the Municipal Council of Paris. The government of the new Republic, on the other hand, was abundantly in evidence. Although Marshal MacMahon did not attend, the Secretary to the President's Office, the Count d'Harcourt, and the Marshal's ADC, General Marquis d'Abzac, were there to respond to the toast to «The President of the Republic!» Léon Say, Minister of Finance, and Henri Wallon, Minister of Education and Religion and one of the founding fathers of the 1875 Constitution, were also there to sponsor the statue. Future political notables, destined to office in later governments, included Martel, Minister of Justice a few months later; Jules Simon, to become premier and Minister of the Interior in 1876; and Waddington, President of the Council in 1879. The Statue of Liberty was not undertaken as an act of State, but she derived useful publicity from ministerial, even presidential, support, of a kind somewhere between official and semi-official. The Americans were not slow to catch on. Although Washington generally frowned on public speaking by its diplomats abroad, the American Minister Plenipotentiary in Paris, Elihu Washburne, accompanied by his colleagues at the Courts of St. James' and Madrid, delivered an address in the name of President Ulysses S. Grant.

Around their minister clustered a group of Americans living in Paris. This group of bankers, industrialists, businessmen, and artists, which Laboulaye had set about cultivating, was a potential lobby that the Union strove to enlist in its cause. The American community in Paris, important enough under the Second Empire, had grown and flourished still further under the Third Republic.[34] It played a leading role that evening at the Louvre. Among the dinner guests were three of its most eminent members: Detmold, the venerable engineer and man of letters; Thomas Witberger Evans, a well-known and wealthy dentist, friend of Napoléon III and founder of the *American Register*, the first American newspaper in Paris; and Dr. Crane, editor-in-chief of the *Register*.

Politicians apart, the French and international press contributed the largest number of guests. Noteworthy among the foreign newspapermen were the famous Baron de Blowitz of the London *Times*, and his colleagues from the *Daily News* and the New York *Herald*. Press lords who accepted invitations included Emile de Girardin, Cernuschi, Menier, and Koechlin Schwartz; among the editors were Adrien Hebrard of *Le Temps*, Bapst of the *Journal des Débats*, Adolphe Gueroult of *L'Opinion Nationale*, De Pène of *Paris Journal*—not to mention Jules Simon, political editor of *Le Siècle* and *Le Petit Journal*. Present as well were the owners of many well-known by-lines: Fr. Charmes, Aurélien Scholl, Oscar Commettant, Detroyat, and above all the famous Thomas Grimm, who may have needed three or four seats at the table since his pen name concealed the identity of several persons, including the famous Escoffier.

The evening acquired additional luster from the presence of Alexandre Dumas fils (who was on the point of presenting his latest play, *The Foreign Woman*), and Jacques Offenbach, the Second Empire's most fashionable composer, who was preparing for his trip to the United States in 1876. There were none of the great names of painting or sculpture, despite the presence of Philippe de Chennevières, Director of the Académie des Beaux-Arts. The artistic establishment approached *Liberty* somewhat skittishly, but she enjoyed the support of successful art dealers like Goupil and Bing, who was to become a pioneer among those who launched Art Nouveau on a startled world.

Later, in the deserted banquet hall, the members of the Committee made a first accounting. Over and above the Fr. 130 contribution required from each Committee member, the dinner had brought in, «by way of donations,» some Fr. 40,000, or about one-tenth the projected cost of the statue.[35] Aside from the lavish and benevolent press coverage, perhaps the chief benefit of the occasion had been the unexpected opportunity for France to strengthen, semi-officially, her ties to her sister-Republic across the ocean at a time when she found herself relatively friendless in a reactionary Europe. A telegram signed by all the guests and sent to President Grant and Marshal MacMahon was an impromptu gesture signaling a turn in French-American relations.

THÉATRE NATIONAL DE L'OPÉRA

MARDI 25 AVRIL 1876, à Huit heures et demie du soir

SOLENNITÉ MUSICALE

ORGANISÉE PAR LE COMITÉ
DE L'UNION FRANCO-AMÉRICAINE

POUR L'ÉRECTION D'UN MONUMENT COMMÉMORATIF A L'OCCASION DU

CENTENAIRE DE L'INDÉPENDANCE DES ÉTATS-UNIS

Membres d'honneur :

M. WASHBURNE, Ministre plénipotentiaire des États-Unis à Paris.
M. AM. BARTHOLDI, Ministre plénipotentiaire de France à Washington.
Mᵐᵉ DE NOAILLES, Ambassadeur de France à Rome.   Mᵐᵉ DE ROCHAMBEAU.
M. W. FORNEY, Commissaire général en Europe de l'Exposition des États-Unis.
M. ÉDOUARD LABOULAYE, Président du Comité, Directeur.
MM. HENRI MARTIN et DIETZ - MONIN, Vice - Présidents.
MM. Oscar de LAFAYETTE, Jules de LASTEYRIE, Paul de RÉMUSAT, Comte de TOCQUEVILLE,
WADDINGTON, CORNÉLIS DE WITT, Jean MACÉ, Comte SERRURIER
L. SIMONIN, V. BORIE, A. BARTHOLDI, A. GAUBERT, DE LAGORSSE.

COMMISSION MUSICALE ORPHÉONIQUE

Docteur E. SAILLY, Président

Membres: MM. ARTAUD, E. DETOUCHE, E. D'INGRANDE, CH. LEFÈVRE, H.-A. SIMON, G. VÉLY

CONFÉRENCE SUR LES ÉTATS-UNIS
Par M. ÉDOUARD LABOULAYE, de l'Institut

Solennité avec le concours de

Mᵐᵉ ROSINE BLOCH   Mᵐᵉ ROUSSEIL   M. CARON

LES ARTISTES DE L'ORCHESTRE DE L'OPÉRA
Et les SOCIÉTÉS ORPHÉONIQUES du département de la Seine.

Sociétés chorales de dames environ, 600 Exécutants

PREMIÈRE PARTIE

1. Ouverture de la Muette de Portici......   AUBER.
   Exécutée par l'Orchestre de l'Opéra.
2. Discours-conférence par M.E. LABOULAYE
3. Les Rameaux (avec orchestre)......   FAURE.
   Chanté par M. CARON.
4. Les Martyrs aux Arènes......   L. DELILLE.
   Chœur chanté par toutes les Sociétés,
   sous la direction de l'auteur.

5. Ave Maria......   GOUNOD.
   Avec accompagnement de Violon, Orgue
   et Harpe par MM. Garcin, Benior, Sa-
   loman et C. Premier.
   Chanté par Mˡˡᵉ ROSINE BLOCH.
6. Ap de cent ma......   N. MAR.
   Poésie
   Dite par Mˡˡᵉ ROUSSEIL.

DEUXIÈME PARTIE

1. Ouverture de Guillaume Tell......   ROSSINI.
   Exécutée par l'orchestre de l'Opéra.
2. Caroline d'Arcen de l'embrasse......   ROSSINI.
   Chantée par Mˡˡᵉ B. BLOCH (orchestre)
3. Sur les Remparts......   SAINTIS.
   Chœur chanté par toutes les Sociétés,
   sous la direction de l'auteur.
4. Le Soldat......
   Poésie de M. PAUL DÉROULÈDE, mise en
   musique et orchestrée par......   A. COTTIN
   Chanté par M. CARON.

5. La Liberté éclairant le Monde......
   Chœur à 4 voix d'hommes
   Paroles d'ÉMILE GODARD, musique de CH. GOUNOD.
   Chanté par toutes les Sociétés chorales
   accompagné par l'Orchestre de l'Opéra.
   (Première audition, 700 chanteurs.)
6. Huit Columbia......
   Air national américain
   Orchestré par M. Victor Pont.
   Exécuté par l'Orchestre de l'Opéra.

L'ORGUE SORT DES ATELIERS DE LA MAISON ALEXANDRE

LE PRIX DES PLACES N'EST PAS AUGMENTÉ. — Les Dames sont admises à l'Orchestre.
Pour cette solennité, en dehors de l'abonnement. Les Loges de Rez-de-Chaussée, y compris rang, et Stalles des 1ᵉˢ Loges de
Face, ainsi que les dispositions du parloir.

LE BUREAU DE LOCATION EST OUVERT TOUS LES JOURS, DIX AUBER, DE 10 HEURES à 5 HEURES.

Paris.— Typ. Morris père et fils, rue Amelot, 64.

275
Program for the Solemnity
of Music at the Opéra
April 25, 1876

Thanks to the new-found speed of international communications Grant received the message as he sat down to dinner, and «was able to drink to France at the very moment that, in Paris, glasses were being raised to his health.»[36] This new handclasp across the Atlantic was affirmed when a friendly reception was accorded to overtures by Washburne and by Forney, who had come «to invite the participation of France in the American Exposition» in Philadelphia. «The Administration, the Legislature, the Cabinet, the press, manufacturers and workers join in expressing their pleasure in recognizing that America's Exposition of 1876 will offer an unparalleled opportunity to strengthen the friendly understanding which links the two countries, and to increase the flow of commerce between them.» Colonel Forney was able to add, in his after-dinner speech, that the National Assembly had already voted to fund this French participation, on a motion proposed by Edouard de Laboulaye. Washburne, originally skeptical of the Union's prospect of success, now (November 10, 1875) sent a dispatch to the Secretary of State urging that President Grant put before Congress the Committee's request for the Bedloe's Island site.

Liberty, the goddess who—most probably serving as a lighthouse—was to rule the waves of New York harbor, could choose no more appropriate occasion for launching her subscription than the closing ceremonies of the International Exhibition of Marine and Inland Navigation Industries. In the intervals between Universal Expositions, such theme exhibitions were given at the Palais de l'Industrie, built on the Champs Elysées in 1855. With one of these as its setting the Committee decided to give, on November 19, 1875, a French-American Fête. The occasion called for «a massive décor»[37] commensurate with the imposing Palais de l'Industrie, which had been designed to house huge pieces of machinery. Bartholdi entrusted the portrayal of the proposed statue to the decorative painter Lavastre. On a canvas almost 11 yards high, «the perspective shows Bedloe's Island and, in the background, New York, Jersey City, Brooklyn, the Hudson and the East River.»[38] The canvas was a kind of advertising poster, scaled to the needs of an urban environment; it had to be big, so it could be seen by everyone.

The fête began at 12:30 P.M. with a tour of the exhibition; this was followed by two concerts (one by the band of the Garde Républicaine) and the reading of a poem entitled «Navigation.» It ended at 4:30 P.M. with fireworks and marine flares. In spite of the rather high admission price (Fr. 5 a head) the organizers expected crowds—and, indeed, the ladies of the American colony were there in force. Still, the proceeds were meager: the fête «failed to produce the monetary results we had hoped for; nonetheless, there were results, and they were satisfactory.»[39]

For the months ahead the Committee envisioned a huge, fashionable *soirée* dedicated to the glory of the Franco-American Union. This time there would be no penny-pinching; the occasion was to take place in the world's largest theater, the brand-new Opéra, which Charles Garnier had completed in 1875. The Committee approached Halanzier, Director of the Palais de la Musique, who with his opposite number at the Comédie Française had been a dinner guest at the Louvre. He failed to evince the enthusiasm expected of him and «explains that he is unable to stage an entertainment»; nevertheless, Bartholdi hoped «to find a way of making him do something else and cooperate in spite of himself.»[40] This «something else» was to be «a great solemnity of music» (cat. 275).[41]

On the evening of April 25, 1876, the curtain at the Opéra rose on «a hall in a palace, with banners in the purest medieval taste, gilt figures of saints, and the flags of France and the United States.»[42] Lavastre's enormous canvas, already shown the previous fall at the Palais de l'Industrie, came out of storage for the occasion.[43] On stage were a score of men seated around a figure «dressed in a kind of high-necked tunic buttoned to the top and revealing only the line of the white neck; clean-shaven; the hair grey, worn long and brushed back.»[44] This «Quaker,» wearing, not a theatrical costume, but rather his everyday clothes, was Edouard de Laboulaye, standing among the members of his Committee. In an address that was «to the point, and often witty,»[45] he again recounted the part played by France in the heroic age of the United States. After much applause, the speech was followed by the performance, for which the Opéra had lent its orchestra and two prominent members of its cast.

The music offered something for every taste. First came pieces popular with the upper classes of the time: the overture to *La Muette de Portici* by Aubert (who had recently died); Rossini's *William Tell* overture and an extract from *Semiramis*; then Gounod's *Ave Maria*. A poem, set to music, had been commissioned from a young patriot-author whose verse-drama *Chants du Soldat* had recently been produced with moderate success; his name was Paul Déroulède, and he was not yet the writer-in-exile of the Third Republic. The hit of the evening, however, belonged to the creative genius of Charles Gounod. As announced in the newspapers, he had written the music for a «cantata,» *La Liberté éclairant le Monde*, scored for four male choirs (cat. 276).

Failing to secure Victor Hugo as his librettist (cat. 277), Gounod worked with one Emile Guiard (cat. 278), whose renown has almost failed to withstand the passage of time. An original feature of this choral opus (otherwise described as «too hurried and monotonous»)[46] was that it was sung by the massed choral societies of Metropolitan Paris. That evening on the stage of the Opéra, some six hundred to eight hundred male choristers, dressed in black with white ties and white gloves, intoned the piece a cappella.

The idea that choirs from the ranks of the people should perform the hymn to *Liberty* was ingenious; the unaccustomed conjunction of lyric art and amateur performers on the stage of the new Opéra could have been a triumph of public relations. Amateur choirs, recruited from the people at large, had enjoyed their heyday at the Universal Expositions of 1855 and 1867, and above all at the great performances by more than twenty thousand singers organized in Paris in 1859 and 1861.[47] Wagner and Berlioz had conducted them then, and Gounod had been their musical director in the 1850s. By 1876 populism was out of fashion, and choral societies had acquired a slightly clanking provincial overtone that the good citizens of Paris could not forgive. As it turned out, the experiment at the Opéra did not succeed. The newspapers, including the Committee's partisans, were unanimous in finding the musical part of the performance very tedious. In the acid words of *La Gazette*, a conservative paper accustomed to encountering choral societies in provincial competitions rather than as a cultural feature of the capital: «Had we but had the Mayor, his deputy and the town councillors» the occasion might have been mistaken for «All Fools' Day at Fouillies-les-Oies. . . . Choral Societies at the Opéra, indeed!» Even *Le Tintamarre*, a republican paper if there ever was one, expressed its astonishment. Not Mounet de Sully, the great tragic actor of the Comédie Française, not even the actress «in a white tunic and a crown of raw gold, carrying the American flag»[48] who depicted aspects of liberty in the charade fashion then popular, could draw a crowd. Only Laboulaye's speech «redeemed» the evening.

Even worse, the evening failed as a fund raiser. The box-office receipts were a mere Fr. 8,291, compared to the Fr. 22,000 to be expected from a full house. Many orchestra seats went unsold. The disastrous outcome of this occasion, on which the Committee had counted for so much, must be attributed to poor advertising. On April 22, a mere three days before the performance, the Union circularized the newspapers, expressing «its concern over the lack of publicity for its *fête* of April 25.» But the press no longer came readily to heel. On November 30, out went another of the Committee's letters to the newspapers: «the whole amount needed for the statue can be obtained with ease, if every French heart answers our appeal.» By December 8 only Fr. 37,500 had come in. The *Gazette de Cambrai* and the *Journal de Die* commented on the shortfall. The *Petit Journal* demanded that the Union's associate members now be required to sell, and remit the proceeds from, the books of subscription tickets for which each of them had accepted responsibility. Soon afterward the *Courrier de France* announced that it would begin to publish the subscriber lists on January 15, 1876. Another sales effort in March enjoyed scarcely greater success. In June the Com-

277

Letter of Charles Gounod

to Victor Hugo

March 1, 1876

mittee was warned that work on the statue was ahead of schedule. On July 4, Laboulaye seized on the occasion of the U.S. celebration of Independence Day to write to the newspapers again. Nothing helped; it looked as though the subscription campaign, like so many before and since, was burning out.

When Bartholdi left for the United States in 1876, the project of the Franco-American Union was at its nadir. The Monduit workshops were still busy with the torch, which, in the absence of the statue itself, was to be displayed at the Philadelphia Exposition. But the money had run out, or nearly so, and the estimates had risen. The figure discussed was no longer 400,000 but one million francs. Things were going so badly that before leaving France Bartholdi entrusted to his friend M. Jacob a last will and testament dated May 1, 1876 (cat. 279). If the Committee went into insolvency—no distant prospect at that moment—the sculptor instructed that «all expenditures entered into on his instructions . . . be covered, so far as may be necessary, from his personal estate.»[49] From America he set himself, in a series of long letters, to hearten Laboulaye, and encourage him to hold out until his return. It was the hopeful news he brought back from the United States that persuaded the Committee to continue its labors, and in mid-December 1876 the project was again «launched» in the press. The following March, Bartholdi was «occupied in patching up the tatters of the subscription.»[50] That same month the Committee reassured William M. Evarts, chairman of the executive committee of the American Committee: «In France, no one today has the slightest doubt that this gigantic undertaking will succeed.»

The campaign continued, but the style changed. What had at first been envisaged as a short-term effort was now seen as a long-term endeavor. The effort would have to extend into 1880. During those four years the organizers, headed by Bartholdi, worked tirelessly to evolve a series of new ideas, each more ingenious than the last.

The Statue of Liberty became familiar as an image before it was an object. It had already been displayed at the banquet at the Louvre, at the Palais de l'Industrie, and at the Opéra; now it was made available for the home. *Liberty*'s picture appeared in many illustrated magazines; thousands of copies were printed in the form of souvenir photographs signed by photographer Pierre Petit (cat. 280, 281). Every contributor received one of these prints, proportioned to the

281

Work on the Head
P. Petit
n.d.

281

285

Poster for the Diorama at the Tuileries
Chéret
1878

285

282

Modèle du Comité
Frédéric-Auguste Bartholdi
ca. 1876
reproduced in color
on p. 134

283

Model of the Statue of Liberty, with Diorama in the Base
Frédéric-Auguste Bartholdi
1875–1900
reproduced in color
on p. 134

amount of his donation: size 3 for contributions of less than Fr. 1; size 2 for contributions between Fr. 1 and Fr. 5, and size 1 for more than Fr. 5. The public was pleased with these premiums. At the same time, with its eye on a more select market—collectors of modern art—the Committee decided to produce a limited number of miniatures of the statue. The *Modèle du Comité* (cat. 282) was «one meter high, made of terra cotta and finished by the artist himself; each copy, bearing his signature, the seal of the Committee and a serial number, will be registered in the Golden Book of Contributions along with the name of its purchaser. Only two hundred will be made, after which the molds will be destroyed. The model will be priced at Fr. 1,000 in France or at $300 in New York.»[51] The firm of Goupil, art dealers on the Place de l'Opéra renowned for their fine reproductions of contemporary painting, undertook the distribution in France.

Business and industry were offered the statue as a logo. An insert in the *Union Nationale du Commerce*, the publication of the Paris Chamber of Commerce, read: «reproduction rights . . . for the Centennial statue will be granted to any manufacturer, sales agent or businessman who has dealings with the U.S. or elsewhere, and who would like his product to bear the mark which is to be the national symbol of American independence.» Champagne Delaunay of Reims labeled the bottles of its «Centennial Cuvée» with a miniature reproduction of the backdrop from the Opéra *soirée*, but this was an isolated example; in 1875 the Statue of Liberty had not yet caught on.

Marketing by reproduction did not imply neglect of marketing through the word. In newspaper articles and in speeches, the same slogans appeared over and over, with the same rhetorical flourishes. Bartholdi's statue was «colossal,» and could be compared with the great colossi of history; it was «at the cutting edge of technology»; it was «the type and symbol of the modern belief in universal progress,» down to the very material from which it was cast: «it has nothing in common with those gigantic bronze statues, which boast that they were cast from the metal of captured cannon. . . . Our statue is no monument to blood and tears such as these, but something far better—a work done in virgin metal, the fruit of peaceable labor.»[52]

By 1877 progress had encouraged the Committee to widen the range of its promotional techniques. The Opéra backdrop, having served its turn, was to be replaced with a diorama, the most fashionable kind of permanent display. *Liberty* was now to become a public attraction, accessible to all. To spend money on a diorama was to choose a new and very popular means of communication which in the 1870s ushered in «the age of the mass media.»[53] A small industrial venture on its own account, the project was undertaken in the spring of 1877.[54] Under Bartholdi's direction, on a canvas many yards long, several specialists painted an exact reproduction of New York harbor; meanwhile, the other elements of the composition were built and put in place.

The completed diorama was installed in the Palais de l'Industrie during the summer, where it was open to the public from 10 A.M. to 6 P.M. Once inside, the visitor was in the grip of a perfect illusion:[55]

> By some incredible feat of *trompe-l'oeil*, you are all of a sudden looking out over the stern of an American steamboat on her way out of New York harbor. Very near you, on the bridge, are life-sized people, dressed Yankee-fashion, smoking and talking; a little farther away more people are clustered together on the bridge, and farther off yet the pilot stands at the helm. Over his head floats the ensign with its silver stars. . . . But let us turn our eyes away from our ship to the spectacle which invites our attention. All around us, on the choppy waters, sailboats and steamboats of all kinds are moving, fast or slow, in all directions . . . the traffic is unbelievable . . . and now, from her island, rises the gigantic Statue of Liberty, illuminating the world with the rays of her electric beacon. . . . All around is the beautiful harbor; beyond it, the huge city . . . with its endless streets and avenues, an ocean of houses as big as the Atlantic itself.[56]

As Count Serrurier, secretary of the Committee observed, «The work speaks for itself, and anyone can understand it.»[57]

The Committee's costly gamble proved successful. The public flocked to the diorama. Soon the organizers were looking for a new site, and decided on the Jardin des Tuileries, in a neighborhood that was «affluent, densely populated and thronged by tourists,»[58] where other dioramas and panoramas were to be found. There was difficulty in obtaining a permit; Serrurier had to «make the rounds of the bureaucracy.»[59] The structure housing the diorama

was begun in June–July 1876. With a frontage of less than 11 yards, it was small; most dioramas and panoramas were built on a diameter of 130 feet. «The pavilion was crowned with two sheaves of French and American flags, on either side of two shields bearing the names of Washington and of Lafayette. Beside the main entrance stood a block of bronze as large as a man's body: it was one of *Liberty*'s fingers.»[60]

The diorama was as popular as its sponsors could have hoped. Everyone came to see it, «from the President of the Republic to the lowliest worker.»[61] The former received a personal invitation; the latter went because the price of admission was reduced from Fr. 1 on weekdays to 50 centimes on Sundays and holidays—as low a figure as could be found for this type of entertainment. The Statue of Liberty was democratizing itself; advertisements in color (cat. 284, 285) by Chéret, the inventor of the commercial poster, proclaimed that more than seven thousand people had seen the diorama in two months.[62] All the same, by the end of 1878 time had run out. The life expectancy of a diorama was never above two years; after that, the law of diminishing returns set in. According to the newspapers, various proposals were made to the Committee for moving the display out of Paris, either for a tour of France or abroad. If such a solution was ever contemplated, it was not implemented; in the spring of 1879 Bartholdi was still trying to get rid of the device, with only a month remaining before it had to be pulled down.[63] The only record of this extraordinary project is the diorama that still exists inside the pedestal made by Bartholdi in 1900 for his plaster reduction of the Statue of Liberty (cat. 283a). This actual diorama may even have been the model for the one that was displayed in 1878; in fact, the pavilion in the foreground (cat. 283b) corresponds to what we know of the general setting of 1878.

In 1878 many visitors, after leaving the diorama, went to the Champ de Mars for a close-up view of *Liberty*, or rather of her head, which was now finished. In a fashion made possible by the statue's enormous size, the Committee reenacted its part-standing-for-the-whole procedure: after the torch in Philadelphia in 1876, the head in Paris at the Universal Exposition of 1878. These two advance showings, one in America and the other in France, were a trademark of the Committee's publicity campaign.

On May 1, the opening day of the Exposition, workmen were still putting the finishing touches to *Liberty*'s head in the Monduit workshops. Its journey to the plinth reserved for it on the Champ de Mars was an event that defied description. «Suddenly, at about eight o'clock in the evening, a colossal head was discerned through the vault of the Arc de Triomphe, while salvoes of cheering—«Vive la République!»—echoed from far down the avenue. It was the head of the Republic!»[64] The head was «hauled on a cart which could have carried the Pantheon. . . . It was at once strange and moving to see that, at each turn of the wheels, the head swayed slightly, as though acknowledging the cheers of the inquisitive crowd. The effect was impressive and, in spite of ourselves, we tipped our hats to return the courtesy.»[65] This spectacle was not unprecedented: many times (particularly during the Second Republic) the streets of Paris had witnessed the passage of «Liberty floats,» carrying a woman representing the goddess.[66] Perhaps the passage of the great head of *Liberty* was seen as the echo, in contemporary imagination, of a scene once real and deeply charged with symbolic meaning.

Bartholdi, great theatrical producer that he was, at once thought of the best possible setting: in a design published in the press (cat. 286), he depicted the head, with its spikey crown, in front of the main entrance

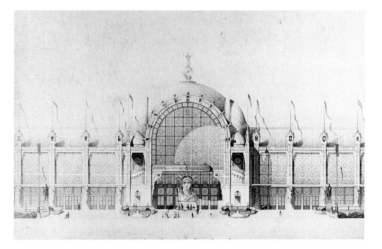

of the new Palais de l'Industrie, a masterpiece in metal conceived by Eiffel himself. But the authorities of the Exposition assigned the statue a home on the Champ de Mars, «surrounded by . . . a thousand curiosities more or less beautiful, more or less interesting—and more or less incongruous with herself.»[67] Her position did not detract from her popularity. At the beginning of July, when the statue of the French Republic was unveiled, its sculptor, the famous Clesinger, asked the Commissioner-General of the Exposition to draw the attention of the dignitaries present, especially the Minister of Education, to «the head of M. Bartholdi's colossal statue.»[68] The band of the Garde Républicaine played «Amour sacré de la Patrie,» from Auber's *Muette de Portici,* and the American national anthem. «La Marseillaise» rang out and the crowd joined in. Shouts of «Vive la République!» could be heard again and again.

This double ceremony may have appeared spontaneous, but it was probably planned in advance to benefit the two symbolic statues. The resemblance between Clesinger's *République* (cat. 287) and Bartholdi's *Liberty* did not go unnoticed. The Third Republic had not yet acquired an official symbol; the Universal Exposition of 1878, which was intended to display to the world the renaissance of France and the stability of her institutions, offered an appropriate opportunity to introduce the representation of a new Republic: «peaceful—but helmed; seated—but holding her sword upright.»[69] In her classical drapery, her left hand resting on the Constitution of 1875, Clesinger's work is, iconographically, close kin to Bartholdi's.

A pragmatic government had chosen the figure of a moderate Republic. The Municipal Council of Paris, more radical, would have preferred Marianne in her Phrygian cap[70]—in default of which it arranged for the playing of «La Marseillaise,» at a time when this was still the marching-song of the Army of the Rhine, rather than an officially acknowledged National Anthem.

After these preliminaries Bartholdi's statue rated its own official unveiling, on July 16. After a simple ceremony, at which Bartholdi and Monduit received the Commissioner-General of the Exhibition and two other dignitaries, *Liberty* became an official part of the Exposition and could be seen by the public, who came in force to gaze at the 30-foot-high face: «From the restaurant in the Belgian pavilion, one can discern on the features an expression of austere gravity, which disappears from closer at hand» (cat. 288)[71]—an effect attributable to light reflecting off the metallic surface. At the entrance to the head stood a scale model of the statue itself (cat. 289, 290). As with the torch in Philadelphia, the public was invited to come inside—to climb the thirty-six cast-iron and five wood steps and inspect, through the rays of the crown, a panoramic view of the Champ de Mars (cat. 291, 292, 293). Without being so presented, *Liberty* became a public attraction. The Committee obviously wanted to make money on this occasion as well, but no admission fees could be charged within the limits of the Exposition. How could the rules be bent? Very simply: every visitor who wanted to go inside the head had to produce the photograph that, as a contributor, he could obtain from the principal office of the Union. Alternatively he could get a free pass at the diorama, which itself had to be paid for. The public could also buy souvenirs: a blue satin badge embroidered with a small *Liberty* (cat. 294) or a miniature head of the statue (cat. 495).

The display of the head at the Exposition was well received by both the public and the government (cat. 295). Bartholdi wanted to maintain momentum by winning a mark of official esteem: the decoration of Officer of the Legion of Honor.[72] Aside from his own satisfaction, the glory would reflect on the project of the Franco-American Union, nor was it unprecedented for decorations to be awarded on the occasion of a Universal Exposition. Mme. Bartholdi was the first to plead her son's cause (did he know about it?) with Chauffour, a future Councillor of State from Colmar, asking him to make a

288

The Head at the Exposition
of 1878
Frédéric-Auguste Bartholdi
1878

289

Exposition Universelle—
Tête de la Statue de la
Liberté
Baude
From *L'Univers Illustré*
1878

291

Public Notice Concerning
Order and Ease of
Movement in the Head of
the Statue at the Paris
Exposition
1878

AVIS AU PUBLIC
POUR LE BON ORDRE ET LA FACILITÉ DE LA CIRCULATION

Les personnes qui montent sont priées de s'arrêter sur les palliers d'attente et de laisser passer, quand elles voient descendre.
On est prié de ne pas stationner trop longtemps dans la tête de la statue.
Les préposés du Comité étant chargés de veiller au bon ordre, doivent régler la circulation selon les nécessités qui se produisent.
La plus grande urbanité leur étant recommandée en toute occasion, le public est prié de faciliter leur tâche par sa bienveillance.

LE COMITÉ DE L'UNION FRANCO-AMÉRICAINE

direct approach to Dufaure, President of the Council. The request was denied on the grounds of untimeliness.[73] The Committee then explored a seemingly more promising avenue: Laboulaye, backed by all the political weight of the Union, approached Tesserenc de Bort, the Minister of Agriculture and Commerce, whose department had jurisdiction over the Universal Exposition. However, decorations were conferred on artists only by recommendation of the Minister of Education, so one more unsuccessful effort was made.[74]

The Universal Exposition of 1878 was the best possible physical setting for the Statue of Liberty, and the Franco-American Union was also very closely associated with American participation. Not until December 1877 did President Rutherford B. Hayes and the Congress officially accept the invitation delivered on May 20, 1876, by Amédée Bartholdi, then Minister in Washington. The delay most probably arose from problems in the Executive Branch consequent on a change of President. Throughout 1877 the American Committee for the construction of *Liberty*'s pedestal used their close ties to pressure the administration to commit itself. Its president, William Maxwell Evarts, who was also Secretary of State, met often with Forney and with another influential Committee member, Nathan Appleton, Jr., to effect U.S. participation.[75] Later, when the Commissioners were appointed, those re-

sponsible for the fine-arts sector included such Committee members as James W. Pinchot and Parke Godwin. The Paris jury that chose the paintings to be exhibited in the U.S. section included C. E. Detmold, one of Bartholdi's earliest supporters.

On three occasions Bartholdi's statue was linked to official events involving Frenchmen and Americans. On July 11, at Pierrefitte, Caubert, Commissioner Delegate of the Committee and one of the French representatives at Philadelphia in 1876, gave a splendid dinner for the American delegation. *Liberty* was present twice over: first and physically, in reproduction looming over the banquet hall; second and metaphorically, in a poem, «Les Deux Républiques,» declaimed by Senator Bozérian. Four days later, on July 15, the American Commissioner General, McCormick, officially welcomed the French directors of the Exposition to the American section; the procession ended its tour at the head of *Liberty*. This was the first indication that the head was soon to become the U.S. Commissioner's «reception hall.» Some time later an American exhibitor, Wilcox & Co., staged in front of its stand a mock «inauguration» of Bartholdi's monument, unveiling a scale model in candle-wax before a small invited audience.

The consolidated profit-and-loss statements of the diorama and the 1878 Exposition

showed a profit, but contributions still fell short of the goal by Fr. 200,000, «a situation which could endanger the entire project.» The Committee decided to apply «a brisk treatment.»[76] Why not a lottery? The idea was none the worse for being well-tried; witness the National Lottery of 1878, for which Bartholdi had proposed a reproduction of the Statue of Liberty in imitation antique silver. On January 8, 1879, Senator Henri Martin applied to Charles Lepère, the Minister of the Interior, for permission to organize a lottery.[77] Although this form of gambling was prohibited in France by a law of 1836, exceptions could be made for works of benevolence, or for the encouragement of the arts. Lepère, a radical republican but one of the staunchest supporters of the moderate administration, interpreted the law in *Liberty*'s favor: «we are dealing here,» he said at the banquet that closed the subscription campaign on July 7, 1880, «with brotherhood—indeed, the brotherhood of two great peoples; are we not, then, confronted with a work of benevolence? As for encouraging the arts,» he added, «a fine artist has conceived a colossal statue, which is great in genius no less than in size.» The official decree, signed on May 9, 1879,[78] established a «Commission for the Franco-American Lottery,» with Senator Bozérian as chairman, and including manufacturers like the watchmaker and jeweler Japy (who was related by marriage to Dietz Monnin), painters such as the American H.

293
Les Coulisses de l'Exposition.—Dans la Tête de la Statue de la Liberté, au Champ-de-Mars
Muller
From *Le Monde Illustré*
September 21, 1878

294
Souvenir Badge from the Paris Exposition
1878

295
La tête de la République américaine quitte Paris avec chagrin
Cham
From *Charivari*
November 18, 1878

Bacon and the Alsatian G. Jundt, and journalists like Véron. In less than two months, the Commission issued three hundred thousand tickets at Fr. 1 each, designed by Bartholdi (cat. 296, 297) and placed on sale at tobacco stores. They could be bought throughout France, and even in the United States. The lucky winners had a chance at seventeen grand prizes of Fr. 35,000 each, and more than five hundred prizes of Fr. 50 to Fr. 400 each (cat. 298), in addition to many other prizes: six pieces of porcelain from the factory at Sèvres were contributed by the government, and seven more by the Department of Fine Arts, which added «ten important engravings, after different originals by ancient and modern masters» such as Leonardo, Holbein, Ingres, and Gérôme.[79] The Ministry of Education donated twelve valuable illustrated books.

If the State expressed its patronage of the lottery in these tangible forms, the private sector was not far behind. At the height of the vogue for things Japanese, Cernuschi, the well-known collector of Far Eastern art, donated some of his most cherished Japanese pieces. As they had on other occasions, highly regarded painters and sculptors of the day contributed prints, drawings, and paintings. Among dozens of artists whose names no longer mean much to us were to be found Puvis de Chavannes, Gustave Doré, Cabanel, Detaille, and Etex.

Bartholdi himself parted with nine of his own works: a sketch of the *Lion de Belfort*, a statuette of Vauban, a terra cotta of Lafayette, and, above all, several of the *Modèles du Comité*, which were far from being sold out. The other lots included pieces of decorative art: faïence, expensive jewelry, and goldsmiths' work, the traditional épergne being from the house of Froment Meurice and valued at an impressive Fr. 20,000. By reason of the nature of the prizes, and the high price of the tickets, the lottery appealed only to the prosperous upper classes.

Bartholdi and the Committee were attempting, with success, to transform a simple game of chance into a prestigious public event. For several months the prizes were on show at the old Magasins Réunis, on either the Place Château d'Eau or the Place de la République. The sculptor took the opportunity to combine the lottery project with another, sponsored by the Société d'Encouragement aux Industries d'Art. He used the idea of «grouping art objects according to their use or their decorative function, thus forming a perfect whole from which many lessons can be learned about both utility and beauty.»[80] Bartholdi thus foreshadowed a museological style that would one day be proclaimed by the Musée des Arts Décoratifs. In addition to a Louis XIII bedroom and a Japanese interior, two great rooms at the Palais du Château d'Eau, decorated with French and American flags, contained some six hundred prizes on display. Amid the paintings, furniture, jewelry, and lace, three unusual objects recalled the purpose of the lottery. First were two small models of the workshop depicting progress on the statue (cat. 251, 252): the head, on a scale of 6:1,000, «was surrounded by scaffolding, ladders and templates, with workmen everywhere, taking measurements. . . . The proportions were so exactly observed that a man with his feet at the level of the nostrils would have his hat just above the eyelashes.»[81] The third special exhibit was «a little further away, a copper finger which shows the enormous scale of the monument . . . it could be one of Krupp's heavy guns aimed straight at the visitor.»[82] These three objects, exhibited only for publicity, were not among the prizes.

The exhibition of prizes opened on June 27, 1879, and the drawing was to take place at the end of the year. However, ticket sales fell short of the target. Perhaps the National Lottery, inaugurated the year before, had diminished the public appetite; moreover, three similar projects were competing with the Committee's in 1879.[83] So, despite a performance at the theater of the Château

d'Eau in November 1879—even despite an advertisement at about the same time offering free admission to the display of prizes to anyone carrying a newspaper—the Committee had to extend ticket sales into June 1880. The drawing was finally held on June 20, at the Trocadéro Palace built for the 1878 Exposition.

With the campaign now five years old and almost at its goal, Bartholdi and the Committee were overjoyed to receive a spontaneous proposal from the Société des Fêtes Versaillaises that the Statue of Liberty should figure in the procession at Versailles, in the tradition of Louis XIV, planned for May 11, 1879 (cat. 299). Past one hundred thousand spectators the Great Float of the World, drawn by sixteen horses, bore an enormous globe surmounted by the Statue of Liberty enlightening the world. Her silhouette, briefly outlined by fireworks in the evening sky, made another appearance at the end of the day's festivities.[84]

On the evening of July 7, 1880, at the Hôtel Continental, the Committee celebrated the closing of the French campaign. At 7 P.M. some sixty guests gathered around the members of the Franco-American Union and the U.S. Minister, General Noyes. Speeches washed down with champagne were delivered by Laboulaye, Noyes, Oscar de Lafayette, U.S. Consul-General Walker, and Senators Bozérian and Henri Martin. On behalf of the French government the former Minister of the Interior, Charles Lepère, proposed a toast to «old colleagues, with whom he had maintained close connections, and whose devotion to their shared ideals made it possible to work effectively together.» After dinner the banqueters were invited to append their signatures to «the official notification to the United States that the project undertaken by the Franco-American Union is now assured of completion» (cat. 300). The forty-one signatories included General Pittié (representing Jules

296
Design Sketch for Ticket for the Lottery of the Franco-American Union
Frédéric-Auguste Bartholdi
n.d.

300
Official Notification by the Franco-American Union to the United States of the Completion of the Fund-Raising Effort for the Statue of Liberty
July 7, 1880
reproduced in color on p. 136

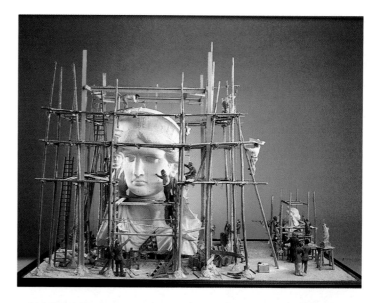

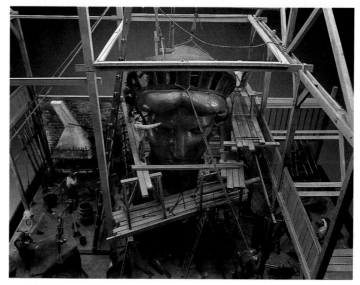

171
L'Egypte apportant la
lumière à l'Asie
Frédéric-Auguste Bartholdi
1869

251
Workshop Model with
Plaster Maquette of the
Head of the Statue
Frédéric-Auguste Bartholdi
1879

252
Workshop Model with
Copper Maquette of the
Head of the Statue
Frédéric-Auguste Bartholdi
1879

253
Gustave Eiffel
Crauk
1903

282
Modèle du Comité
Frédéric-Auguste Bartholdi
ca. 1876

283
Model of the Statue of
Liberty, with Diorama in
the Base
Frédéric-Auguste Bartholdi
1875–1900
a
Model and Base
b
General View of Diorama
c
Interior View of Diorama

317

La Statue de la Liberté,
Rue de Chazelles
Paul-Joseph-Victor
Dargaud
1884

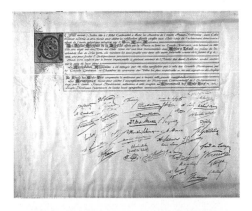

300

Official Notification by the
Franco-American Union to
the United States of the
Completion of the Fund-
Raising Effort for the
Statue of Liberty
July 7, 1880

319
Ferdinand de Lesseps
Léon-Joseph Florentin
Bonnat
1878

322
Deed of Gift of the Statue
of Liberty to the United
States
1884

Grévy, the President of the Republic), committee members Salmon and Stucklé, the construction magnate Gaget, the painter Jundt, Charles and Ferdinand de Lesseps, and others such as reporters from *Le Moniteur*, *L'Evénement*, *Journal des Débats*, the *Petit Journal*, and the Agence Havas. They «sought to express . . . to the Government and people of the United States, the completeness of their fellow-feeling.»[85] To the very end, French official circles and the French press loyally supported *Liberty*. The success of Bartholdi's statue—that symbol of a steadfast reality—was assured in the very year that the French Republic, by rediscovering its antecedents, took root in eternity: it was in 1880 that July 14 was proclaimed a national holiday.

At last the statue was to take on a body—a process begun on October 24, 1881. That Monday afternoon at 3 P.M. the new U.S. Minister, the influential banker-politician Levi Parsons Morton (cat. 301) arrived at the workshop of Gaget, Gauthier to preside over «the elevation onto its plinth of the first portions of Auguste Bartholdi's statue.»[86] In a courtyard hung with the colors of France and the United States, *Liberty*'s left foot, half-covered by a sketched-in panel of drapery, stood waiting to be fixed firmly in place. This honor went to Morton. Before the members of the Committee, the staff of the workshop, and dozens of invited guests French and American, he stood a few yards from the statue's head and, under her gaze, solemnly drove in the first rivet (cat. 302, 303). After the ceremony the witnesses «signed the following sworn statement, engrossed on a parchment illuminated with miniatures of Lafayette, Washington and Rochambeau: today, October 24, 1881, in honor of the anniversary of the surrender at Yorktown, the U.S. Minister Plenipotentiary Mr. Morton placed the rivet in the first part of the Statue of Liberty» (cat. 304).[87]

The construction now became an open-air public attraction followed by Parisians of all classes. As part of the Committee's public-relations strategy, the public had long enjoyed access to the Monduit (now Gaget, Gauthier) workshops. The press reported that during the 1878 Exposition the workshops would be open Monday and Thursday from noon to 5 P.M., on presentation of an admission ticket good for a party of four (cat. 305). The Committee also invited certain honored guests, the first of whom was former President Grant, on his unofficial visit to Paris in the fall of 1877. On November 2 the Franco-American Union showed him the diorama at the Palais de l'Industrie, and then brought him to the workshop. «The work was not very far advanced but the general outlines of the construction could be discerned»; Bartholdi had arranged for «some plaster casts, a few chairs, and some champagne with Liberty on the label.»[88] This visit from so prominent a personage had something of the force of a «consecration.»[89] The former President was

well received in France, with a *soirée* at the Opéra, a ball, and a banquet for 350 guests. Bartholdi and the Committee were there, as was *Liberty* herself: at the ball, as the *Modèle du Comité*[90] and at the banquet «as a painting.» The sculptor, ever mindful of «public relations,» had «arranged for the right people to be invited» to see his work.[91]

Another and unexpected visitor to the rue de Chazelles was the Comte de Paris, grandson of Louis-Philippe, pretender to the throne and Orleanist candidate for a restoration that never happened. First invited by Laboulaye in 1876, he found reason to refuse, but stayed in touch with him.[92] Perhaps he was of two minds about being seen in the company of so republican a lady. The crisis of May 16, 1877, which left the foundations of the Republic stronger, destroyed the Comte's hope of an illustrious career in politics. A true liberal, the Comte de Paris found time in 1878 to «express in person his fellow-feeling . . . with the defenders of the American constitution» and to acknowledge the great talent Bartholdi had brought «to the solution of his difficult task»[93]—the task, that is, of representing Liberty in a manner acceptable to moderate opinion (cat. 306, 307).

The most spectacular phase of the statue's construction was its assembly outside the workshop, which took two years and eight months. It was a kind of permanent attraction; as the copper robe made its way up the framework of iron, visitors came to the rue de Chazelles in ever-increasing numbers (cat. 308, 309). Some did not leave empty-handed, taking scraps of engraved copper with them (cat. 230a–b). In the summer of 1882, when the robe rose to knee-level, Bartholdi with his uncanny sense of impending occasion invited twenty-five people to dinner «in Liberty's right leg.»[94] At the height of the kneecap guests climbed ladders to a trestle-floor, on which stood a beautifully set table. In May 1883, when the draperies rose above the statue's waist, the President of the Republic, Jules Grévy, came to the workshop (cat. 310, 311, 312, 313). He was invited to admire the stupendous mass thrusting its torch-bearing arm toward the sky; then he was taken to see the craftsmen at work; finally he was offered the freedom of the statue, entering it through the right foot, whose sole was still a gaping aperture. About the same time the journalist and writer Jules Claretie re-

counted his experiences at the workshop (cat. 314), recalling Swift's *Gulliver's Travels*: «the statue is being built piece by enormous piece . . . as though carpenters or blacksmiths were dissecting Brobdingnagian bodies . . . bits of a bosom, of drapery, of arms, of hands. . . . Thus, little by little, the statue grows.»[95] The following year, in the spring of 1884, the statue was finished; strollers came to stare at it, towering over the rooftops of Paris, still in its scaffolding, while craftsmen put the finishing touches to the torch (cat. 315, 316, 317).

The time had come to celebrate a job well done. On May 21 the president of the American Exchange, Henry F. Gillig, an American businessman living in Paris, gave a dinner for fifty-three people (cat. 318). The dozens of after-dinner speeches showed how complex were the cross-currents of interest swirling around the statue. Two newspapermen, Molinari of the *Journal des Débats* and Jules Simonin, spoke first about commerce and industry. Dietz Monnin, echoed by representatives of French and American business and by the secretary of the Senate, made a plea for free trade and the abolition of tariffs; it was hoped that this freedom also would be subsumed in the

310

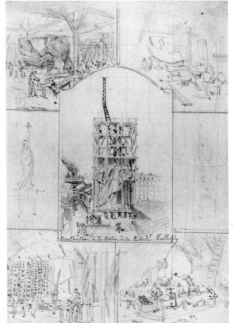

310

*Les travaux de la Statue
colossale de la Liberté*
Navellier de la Marie after
Karl Fichot
From *Le Journal Illustré*
May 1883

312

*Construction de la Statue
de la Liberté*
Karl Fichot
1883

312

symbolism of Bartholdi's monument. At the dinner Ferdinand de Lesseps (cat. 319) officially took his place as president of the Franco-American Union, succeeding Edouard de Laboulaye, who had died the previous year. His speech urged freedom of travel—for was he not soon to begin work on a Panama Canal? When the canal was finished, one of the guests suggested, a replica of the Statue of Liberty should stand at its entrance. It may have occurred to Lesseps that the presidency of the Union might ease his way in any future negotiations with the U.S. government, which in the light of the Monroe Doctrine was in no hurry to let a European dig a waterway across Central America.

The following July 4, American Independence Day, the official dedication ceremony took place in the Gaget, Gauthier workshops (cat. 320). The scaffolding was removed from the top of the statue and «the French and American flags streamed in the wind from the rim of the torch»[96]—though in proportion to the arm of the giantess the American flag looked like «a mere ornament of a bride cake.»[97] At 11 o'clock the officials and invited guests «took their places on a dais built in front of the monument . . . and the Harmonie de Batignolles played the American National Anthem» (cat. 321).[98] The proceedings began with the reading of a letter from Jules Ferry, asking forgiveness for his absence on the grounds of illness; as President of the Council and Minister of Foreign Affairs he was participating «in mind, heart and soul» in this celebration of the brotherhood of the French and American Republics.

After Lesseps had spoken, Morton, who had been carefully instructed from Washington,[99] accepted the statue on President Chester A. Arthur's behalf, with the gratitude of the government and the people of the United States. The minutes of the dedication ceremony were then signed by a long procession: the president of the Chamber of Deputies; the Ministers of Agriculture, of Commerce, of Finance, of the Navy, of Education; the representative of President Jules Grévy, and so on—so many of them that the quill pen passed from hand to hand wore out before the last signature was appended (cat. 322, 323). Then the invited notables undertook, under Bartholdi's guidance, the first public visit to the level of the crown and the torch, from where they could admire all Paris at their feet. The celebrations ended with a buffet set out in a marquee at the foot of the statue, thronged with French and American guests and with the artisans who had worked on the statue (cat. 324). Nine years after her conception, *Liberty* had at last become what she was intended to be: a public figure.

Originally she was to be disassembled in August 1884, but it was decided to postpone her departure for the United States until December 15. The job of labeling all the parts would be a long one; she would have arrived in New York in the middle of winter. Moreover, why hurry to deprive Parisians of their 50-centime climb to the top of the giantess (cat. 325)? History is sometimes made by delay: before she was taken to pieces and packed in her 214 crates, *Liberty* was visited by the most famous Frenchman of his day. Victor Hugo came to the Gaget, Gauthier workshop with his little daughter Jeanne and despite his advanced age climbed the statue's internal stairway as far as the second landing. Someone there said, «Behold! Two giants are regarding each other.»[100] But let the poet speak for himself: in *Choses Vues* (cat. 326) Victor Hugo wrote, under the date of November 30, 1884, «When I saw the statue I said «the turbulent estranging sea must now admit the linking of two great and peaceful lands.» They asked me to let them carve these words on the pedestal.»

Translated, from the French, by Maxwell Vos

316
The Finished Statue, Rue de Chazelles
n.d.

317
La Statue de la Liberté, Rue de Chazelles
Paul-Joseph-Victor Dargaud
1884
reproduced in color on p. 135

319
Ferdinand de Lesseps
Léon-Joseph Florentin Bonnat
1878
reproduced in color on p. 136

321
Official Presentation of the Statue to the Minister of the United States in Paris, July 4, 1884
Frédéric-Auguste Bartholdi
n.d.

322
Deed of Gift of the Statue of Liberty to the United States
1884
reproduced in color on p. 136

323
Official Attestation of Transfer of the Statue of Liberty from France to the United States
July 4, 1884

316

321

323

7.
Bartholdi's Second American Visit: The Philadelphia Exhibition (1876)

Janet Headley

For nearly five years Bartholdi clung to his vision for New York harbor with no assurance of the monument's favorable reception in America, no funds for statue or pedestal, and no officially sanctioned site. Since he had not widely publicized his plans in 1871, Bartholdi could have quietly relinquished the dream without damaging his reputation. Numerous commissions awaiting his attention in France rivalled an undertaking that must have seemed lunatic. Instead, Bartholdi plunged headlong into plans for another visit to America.

The Third Republic obligingly lent its assistance. Soon after his return to France in 1871, Bartholdi received a government commission for a monument to Lafayette.[1] On the surface a request for a straightforward historical portrait, the commission was exceptional for several reasons. *Lafayette*, the first commemorative statue of the French patriot,[2] was to be a gift to the citizens of New York, an official expression of gratitude for the city's aid following the Siege of Paris in 1870. Bartholdi accepted the commission in the hope that patriotic sentiments, as well as French generosity, would move the recipients to furnish a suitable site and subscribe funds to construct a pedestal, thus staging a miniature version of the campaign for the colossal tribute to Liberty.[3]

Thereafter, Bartholdi based his hopes for success on the International Exhibition known as the Centennial, scheduled to open in Philadelphia's Fairmount Park in April 1876. Through an extensive presentation of his works he planned to reveal his artistic genius before America, and thus obtain public support for his visionary idea for New York. To demonstrate France's commitment to the undertaking, he would arrange for a completed section of the copper statue—the arm and symbolic torch of enlightenment—to appear at the Exhibition. On the evident strength of his talent, a serious American campaign for the pedestal could then be initiated.

The herculean task of organizing the Exhibition belonged to a commission drawn primarily from the Union League and the Fairmount Park Commission, the very institutions that had welcomed the sculptor to Philadelphia in 1871.[4] Through a series of fortuitous events, the same contacts enabled Bartholdi to announce his campaign well in advance of his return to America.

Fearing that the great distance would jeopardize European participation in the celebration, Director General Alfred T. Goshorn authorized Col. John W. Forney (cat. 327) to act as Commissioner to Europe. Beginning in July 1874, for eighteen months the Philadelphian tirelessly and successfully promoted the Centennial throughout Europe. Forney also lobbied extensively on Bartholdi's behalf, visiting his friend on numerous occasions, and forwarding progress reports that appeared in the Philadelphia *Press*.[5] Through his accounts, the American public learned of the banquet that initiated the French subscription drive, the existence of the Lafayette monument for New York, and the development of Bartholdi's major works for the Exhibition—an iron fountain, and the completed arm of the colossal goddess. On the eve of 1876, the success of his Centennial enterprise appeared to exceed his expectations, yet Bartholdi had cause for grave concern in the months preceding his voyage.

In June 1875, the Republic of France officially pledged to participate in the Centennial.[6] Intermittent crises threatened the agreement throughout the year, and Commissioner Forney patiently courted the French, outwardly celebrating the harmony of French-American relations even as he privately relayed the stressful state of affairs to an anxious Goshorn.[7] At the heart of French resistance was E. du Sommerard, the circumstances of whose appointment to the position of French Centennial Commissioner remain somewhat mysterious. Sommerard actively disliked Americans and French liberals, and fought against France's involvement in the Philadelphia Exhibition, «but the grandiloquence of the American-mad lunatics in the Chamber of Deputies prevailed.»[8] Not surprisingly, Bartholdi earned a special place in Sommerard's anti-republican crusade.

The Commissioner did not initially appoint Bartholdi to the French delegation, but Bartholdi eventually received the powerless position of second adjunct secretary. The artist managed, however, to expand his duties to include an examination of decorative and industrial arts in the United States,[9] and wrote a *Rapport sur les arts décoratifs* when he returned to Paris (cat. 328).[10] The seventeen-page document encompassed the spectrum of decorative arts, including wallpaper, architectural ornament, furniture, and carriages. By balancing the Americans' lack of native style and ornamental creativity against their evident strength of artistry in technological design, the *Rapport* won American praise for its objectivity.[11]

At the Centennial, the outcome of Commissioner Sommerard's battle was evident in France's limited contributions to the Fine Arts Department.[12] On the other hand, although his troubled relationship with the French authority undoubtedly taxed Bartholdi, the outcome marked a personal victory for him. On May 9, 1876, the artist boarded *L'Amérique* with the delegation. Sommerard himself steadfastly refused to

attend the Centennial, and appointed a replacement.[13] The engraved tribute to «The Republic of France and the Centennial Exhibition» (cat. 329), which solemnly positions the absent Commissioner between busts of Bartholdi and Laboulaye, underscores an ironic contrast between public and private politics.[14]

En route to America, the artist sketched caricatures of his shipmates. Most of the drawings lightheartedly depict individual members of the jury, including the artist himself (cat. 330), but the ensemble appears in the curious sketch that opens the series (cat. 331). Suspended from the mast of *L'Amérique*, the group descends in a cauldron. Awaiting the arrival of their guests, two American Indians furtively fan the flames that surround the vessel. The caption, a witty pun on the uncomfortable summer climate of the New World and the obviously distressing condition of the delegation, may be extended to a third level, where Bartholdi acknowledged the political «heat» of the Centennial. The *Album du Bord* was published as a bound volume of thirty color plates in 1879, and the profits were applied to the French subscription for the statue.[15]

Once in the Centennial City, Bartholdi enjoyed a warm welcome from old acquaintances. At a private reception on May 18, the indefatigable Colonel Forney presented his distinguished guest to Philadelphia society. In a tour of the Exhibition, the visitor found seven of his entries (a remarkably large contribution from a single French exhibitor) already placed at the fairgrounds. Memorial Hall housed a life-size bronze fountain figure, *The Young Vintner*, along with paintings of *Old* and *New California*. The Art Annex contained three allegorical subjects—a figure of *Peace*, a *Génie funèbre*, and a composition entitled *Le Génie dans les griffes de la Misère*—as well as a study for a monument to George Washington.[16] Through this array, Bartholdi emerged as a serious composer of lofty, ideal subjects, and affirmed his patriotic ties with America. Despite his prolific showing in the Fine Arts Department, the sculptor was troubled by the progress of two other projects: the completed arm of his colossus, the essential component in his campaign, and the fountain cast for the Centennial.

327

329

327
John W. Forney
Frederick Gutekunst
n.d.

329
The Republic of France and the Centennial Exhibition
From *The Daily Graphic*
April 6, 1876

330
Passenger with Writing Tablet
Frédéric-Auguste Bartholdi
From *L'Album du Bord*
Paris: Bartholdi, Simonin, Fouret et Cie., 1879
reproduced in color
on p. 169

331
Le Jury Français Philadelphie
Frédéric-Auguste Bartholdi
From *L'Album du Bord*
Paris: Bartholdi, Simonin, Fouret et Cie., 1879
reproduced in color
on p. 169

The maquette for the Bartholdi Fountain, as it came to be known, originated in 1867 (cat. 332). The design incorporates three great caryatids on a triangulated base (cat. 333). Under the weight of a massive upper basin, the caryatids support three small tritons, which uphold the architectural motif that crowns the ensemble. Bartholdi's heroic females and aquatic creatures originate in French Renaissance designs for fountains of the Three Graces.[17]

In hopes of a sale, Bartholdi regenerated the fountain for the Centennial, asking only that the Commission furnish gas illumination and water power,[18] a request that indicates a degree of innovation within the traditional format. By using economical cast iron rather than bronze, the fountain paid a tribute to modern industrial power, the positive element of civilization in the New World. Through Forney, the artist eloquently advertised his concept before the cast was complete: the flowing water and gas illumination symbolized the «twin goddesses of a great city.»[19] A model of efficient beauty, the Bartholdi Fountain would inspire similar creations for «such places as Reading, Lancaster, Easton, Erie, and other towns of equal and even larger size in the States. . . .»[20]

Bartholdi intended to ship the fountain at the end of 1875, but cold weather hampered the foundry work. When the cast was still unfinished in March 1876, the artist petitioned Thomas Cochran, the Centennial Commissioner of Grounds, Plans, and Buildings, for an extension of his deadline and a reserved site for the fountain.[21] Wholeheartedly favoring the project, Cochran situated the fountain between the Main Building and Machinery Hall (cat. 334), where it commanded a vista of Belmont Avenue. This prominent location should have pleased the sculptor, but he had specifically requested that site for the arm and torch of his statue, and the substitution served as a grim reminder of another delinquent project.

Considerably behind schedule, the fountain arrived in April 1876, at which time Cochran experienced additional difficulties. As the month drew to a close, the work had not received its protective layer of paint.[22] The contractor for fountain installations failed to meet his deadline, and the beleaguered Buildings Commissioner lodged a letter of complaint.[23] Despite its prolonged absence from the Centennial, newspaper engravings soon brought the fountain to public attention.[24] But when the Exhibition closed in November, the tribute to modern progress had not been sold. Rather than pay return freight charges, Bartholdi offered the work unsuccessfully to the city of Albany, New York, and to the District of Columbia.[25] Frederick Law Olmsted personally advised Edward Clark, the Architect of the Capitol, that Bartholdi would relinquish the work for six thousand dollars, half its estimated value,[26] at which price the fountain was acquired in 1877.[27]

With Henri de Stucklé, the engineer of New York's waterworks, acting as agent, the fountain was reassembled in the Botanical Gardens in Washington. As Bartholdi's friend and representative, Stucklé noted that the base of the Centennial installation had been only half the proper height; the central motif was elevated accordingly in Washington.[28] Bartholdi's involvement ended with the sale of his creation, but he followed the subsequent history of his jinxed creation with interest. With funds for the construction exhausted, and with scaffolding still in place, the fountain remained inoperative until 1878.[29]

Bartholdi's concern for the fountain paled in comparison with his anxiety over the promotion of the colossal statue. He urgently wanted the great fragment to be erected in Philadelphia, and the unveiling was scheduled to coincide with the celebration of Independence Day on July 4. Problems arose in March when Commissioner Sommerard determined that the fragment exceeded space allocations within the French Department. Quickly dispatching a letter to Cochran, Bartholdi requested another site.[30] Since a French exhibitor in Machinery Hall had promised to furnish electric illumination for the torch, the sculptor suggested a location between the Main Building and Machinery Hall. Cochran evidently complied with this petition, but the space was subsequently relinquished to the Bartholdi Fountain.[31] The substitution resulted from a mishap during late March or early April, in which the mold of the colossal hand was destroyed. Bartholdi communicated news of his misfortune to Cochran:

> In removing the principal piece (the hand) to take it to the workshop where it was to be made in copper, the car on which it was placed has been upset, and that enormous pieces [sic] of 4 metres has been broken into a thousand splinters; therefore the assiduous work of two months has been unfortunately lost.
>
> I immediately recommenced the work, in hopes to be able to exhibit it before the 4th of July. . . . I fear it will be ready to [sic] late. . . .[32]

Both Laboulaye and Sommerard had been informed by Monduit that the arm and torch could not be shipped before mid-July, but Bartholdi was not immediately aware of this.[33] At the end of June, when it became clear that the piece would arrive much later than anticipated, he abruptly departed Philadelphia. Instantly regaining his characteristic ebullience, he channeled his energy into New York's celebration of American independence, making certain that his statue figured in the festivities: «Until now I've been distressed because things have not progressed. . . . However, today I obtained a result, and the monument of Independence will figure in the 4th of July festivities, I am busy with it at this moment. . . .»[34]

Under Stucklé's direction, the wall hanging that had formed the principal decoration at the Opéra gala in Paris was suspended on the New York Club Building at Madison Square, dramatically illuminated by a calcium fixture on the Worth Building (cat. 335).[35] For the first time, the monument generated widespread patriotic fervor, and Bartholdi relayed his excitement at the turn of events:

> I made certain that the Opéra decor figured in the Fourth of July festivities. It was exposed at Madison Square, it was hoisted up during the night, the place was thronged with people and a thunderous applause burst forth when the electric illumination struck it from below. A procession of some thirty thousand men filed past until two in the morning. The effect was excellent and since then, I've received the warmest encouragements. . . .[36]

His triumph was short-lived. Although the Opéra decor worked to his advantage, Bartholdi had in fact traveled to New York to oversee the installation of *Lafayette*. In contrast to his frustrating experiences at the Centennial, he anticipated no difficulty, since the sculpture was complete. In July, when he learned that the pedestal subscription had not advanced, and that his statue stood on a temporary base in Central Park, Bartholdi experienced a mounting sense of panic. The apparent lack of American enthusiasm, as well as the appointed site, aroused his fury. Passionately and sincerely, Bartholdi vented his rage in words that capture the idealism of his entire career:

> This work is a gift of the French government, and it is Lafayette! Neither the ministry, nor the consul, nor the minister is worried, it has been relegated to a French Committee that is going to erect it in a nook of Central Park (between O'Connell and Shakespeare). No one is concerned about the moral value of what they are doing, not even the French Committee, I intervened and stopped the work. I have seen the Minister and the Mayor on this matter and I've tried to make them understand, that this was not a simple art object.[37]

333
The Washington Fountain
Frédéric-Auguste Bartholdi
1876

334
The Bartholdi Fountain Installed at the Centennial Exhibition, Philadelphia
1876

335
The Opéra Decor at Madison Square, New York
After E. A. Abbey
From *Harper's Weekly*
July 22, 1876

Exhausted by Sommerard's political machinations, devastated by the arm's absence, and stunned by the cavalier arrangements for *Lafayette*, Bartholdi wandered between Boston, New York, Philadelphia, and Washington throughout July. Falling ill, he retreated to the LaFarge estate in Newport to recuperate.[38] Refusing to abandon the project, he began a painting of the statue in New York harbor, which he planned to exhibit at the Centennial. Rallying in mid-August at news of the arm's long-awaited arrival, the sculptor immediately returned to the Centennial to supervise the French workmen who were building the torch (cat. 337).[39] In early September, with the installation still incomplete, Bartholdi was again compelled to leave the Exhibition, this time for the dedication of the monument to Lafayette.[40]

Originally an incidental note in the sculptor's plans for his Centennial campaign, *Lafayette* assumed critical importance during his stay in America. Within New York City, French citizens appointed a committee to raise the sum necessary for the pedestal. With Frederic R. Coudert (cat. 338), a prominent New York attorney of French descent, as its president, the executive body of the committee included Charles Villa (secretary) and A. Vatable (treasurer); Adolphe Salmon, Louis Delmonico, Louis de Bebian, and Henri de Stucklé numbered among the general membership.[41] Although the tardy subscription angered the artist, in the end no widespread publicity was necessary to accumulate sufficient funds for the project, and at the final meeting of the pedestal committee, Vatable reported a surplus.[42] Coudert, incidentally, became a good friend of Bartholdi's. Years later, in 1888, they and Henry Spaulding gathered at the Villa Marguerite in Maisons-Alfort for a group portrait (cat. 336), in which the sculptor substitutes a lantern for the uplifted torch of his creation.

336
Bartholdi, Striking the Pose of the Statue of Liberty
1888

337
View of the Installation of the Arm and Torch at the Centennial Exhibition in Philadelphia
From *L'Illustration*
October 21, 1876

338
F. R. Coudert
n.d.

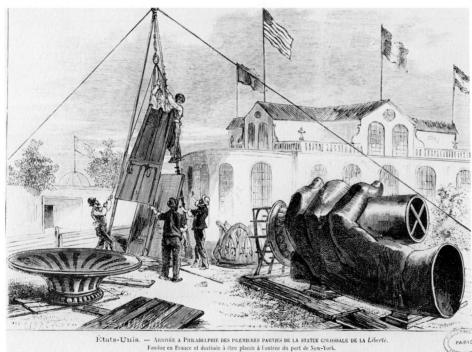

États-Unis. — Arrivée a Philadelphie des premieres parties de la statue colossale de la *Liberté*.
Fondue en France et destinée à être placée à l'entrée du port de New-York.

Responding to Bartholdi's objections to Central Park as a site, the committee moved to relocate the monument. With Olmsted's approval, Stucklé asked the city's Board of Commissioners for an alternate site at Union Square Park.[43] As a token of French gratitude, Stucklé reasoned, *Lafayette* should be placed near the center of daily urban activity rather than in the remote location of Central Park. The Union Square location, he continued, would situate *Lafayette* near Henry Kirke Brown's equestrian statue of George Washington, thereby linking the two Revolutionary heroes. Engineered by Bartholdi, the petition was approved.[44] Equally gratifying to the sculptor was the selection of the design for the pedestal. The committee's choice of Stucklé as architect, however surprising in light of Stucklé's profession as engineer, guaranteed Bartholdi's active collaboration in the matter.[45] Through sheer determination, *Lafayette*'s creator gained control of the diverse elements of sculpture, base, and site, ultimately securing a harmonious synthesis of the three elements.

Originally, Bartholdi conceived an elaborate program for the monument (cat. 339), in which two figures, presumably France and America, holding the Declaration of Independence, are housed in an ornate architectural structure surmounted by an equestrian statue.[46] It was typical of Bartholdi to think in such grandiose terms that the expense, obvious from the final sketch (cat. 340), probably led to its abandonment.

The final version of the monument consists of a single standing image. In authentic eighteenth-century costume, Lafayette gracefully extends his left arm, establishing a directional movement that is reinforced by the hero's gaze (cat. 341, 342). As he debarks from a tiny ship, the patriot steps forward, clutching his sword in a dramatic oath of allegiance. Countering this motion toward the figure's left, his forward stride and sword provide stabilizing vertical notes in the composition. The vitality of the image won critical acclaim in America.[47]

The severe square base on three granite steps tapers upward slightly. Checking the overall starkness, carved garlands echo the whimsical waves at the foot of the statue. From an oblique view to the right, an unbroken line passes from the pedestal through the advanced left leg, terminating in the hero's upturned gaze. Initially, the primary directional axis of the statue did not align with the surrounding streets; instead, *Lafayette* addressed Brown's equestrian *Washington*, whose reciprocal gesture affirmed the gift of France.

The elaborate unveiling ceremony (cat. 343) took place as scheduled, although the pedestal was unfinished. At 2:00 P.M. on September 6, the hero's birthday, the French honor guard, American and French troops from all branches of the military, and representatives of Masonic lodges and French societies assembled at the Brunswick House at 26th Street and Fifth Avenue, and proceeded south. Thousands viewed the

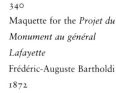

340
Maquette for the *Projet du Monument au général Lafayette*
Frédéric-Auguste Bartholdi
1872

343
Inauguration of the Statue of Lafayette at Union Square
1876

342
Maquette for *Lafayette* in Union Square
Frédéric-Auguste Bartholdi
n.d.

145

parade, and streets and houses along the route were decorated with banners. At Union Square the formal inaugural ceremonies included French and American anthems, and numerous addresses.[48] Following the unveiling, a twenty-one–gun salute triggered answering salvoes from ships anchored at New York harbor, Bedloe's Island, and the Brooklyn Navy Yard. The festivities concluded with a picnic and dance in Hamilton Park.[49]

If the display of the Opéra decor secured public recognition for Bartholdi in New York, the spectacular inauguration of *Lafayette* commanded serious recognition of his project for the harbor. Two days after the dedication, the sculptor boarded the steamer *Washington* with Stucklé; Bartholdi's Bostonian friend Nathan Appleton, Jr.; several key military personnel; and the Deputy Surveyor of the Customs House.[50] After ferrying to Bedloe's Island, the party examined the projected site for the Statue of Liberty.

Bartholdi then returned to the Centennial to oversee the installation of the colossal arm. Set into the simple square base that supported the fragment was a large rendering of the statue in New York harbor, quite possibly the product of Bartholdi's stay in Newport.[51] Although less than two months remained before the close of the Exhibition, the Centennial authorities nevertheless allocated a choice site on the shore of an artificial lake within the fairgrounds, where the isolation from the larger Exhibition buildings enhanced the colossal scale of the piece (cat. 344). Once the construction was complete, Bartholdi petitioned to sell «lithographs, photographs, medals, and small pieces of the copper specimens of the materials used for the execution of the Statue.»[52] Cochran readily acceded to this request, and the hollow base became a souvenir stand. Of all the mementoes, Centennial photographs of the arm and torch achieved the greatest popularity (cat. 345).[53]

Now in full command, Bartholdi demonstrated his skilled entrepreneurship on October 3, when the French exhibitors hosted a dinner at the restaurant Trois Frères Provençaux. At the conclusion of the meal, Forney toasted the statue as a unique gift from the citizens of one nation to another. The artist in turn saluted Philadelphia's hospitality. The subsequent events, unfolding before the entire French delegation, marked a personal vindication for Bartholdi's earlier embarrassment:

> On Mr. Forney's motion, a committee was appointed to take measures with a view to covering part of the cost of the figure, it being suggested that, as the arm at present on exhibit could be remodelled, Philadelphia would do well to secure it for herself as a work. . . .[54]

The journalist accurately recounted the proceedings, which had been orchestrated by Bartholdi.[55] It is possible that the sculptor simply wanted to dispose of some expensive freight. Had the proposal received serious consideration, Fairmount Park would possess a colossal monument composed of a truncated arm, an extraordinary conception even to an age accustomed to Claes Oldenburg's giant *Clothespin*. An equally likely explanation is that Bartholdi, a shrewd observer of American life, knew he could rely on the traditional, deep-seated rivalry between Philadelphia and New York—in which case his master plan worked beautifully. Forney served as president of the Philadelphia Committee, whose other founding members were drawn from the constituencies of the Union League, the Fairmount Park Commission, and the Centennial organizers.[56] Ignoring the literal account of events, Coudert asserted that the Centennial City was attempting to steal New York's statue, fueling local indignation over the imagined theft.[57]

Thereafter Bartholdi centered his campaign activities in New York. The unprecedented acclaim that greeted *Lafayette* led to a banquet in the artist's honor at New York's prestigious Lotos Club on September 16. On October 12, he addressed the equally esteemed Palette Club, where his speech was met with cheers.[58] The guest of honor was toasted at numerous testimonial dinners, many of which were held at Delmonico's restaurant at Madison Square. One invitation to Delmonico's, handwritten on the letterhead of the New England Society,

graciously requested the new celebrity's presence at the banquet on December 22 commemorating the two-hundred-fiftieth anniversary of the pilgrims' landing. Bartholdi seldom let slip such opportunities for professional socializing. In a painstakingly composed eight-page address for the festivities, the honored speaker doubtless charmed and amused his audience with his halting English:

> Your Society affords to me in respect of the mission which I have to perform a quite *prominent interest*. You are the *grandchildren* of the settlers of this grand metropolis of the *valorous men* who in gloomy times of trial came here in this immense desert to save the great principles of *human freedom*.

The body of his address, a combination of flattery, rhetorical inspiration, and information, conveys its author's jubilant spirit at the close of the Centennial year. The originators of the *Liberty* idea, he declared,

> having the joy to see France after long time of trial acquire the institutions for which they struggled in this country thought that it would be a splendid opportunity to . . . celebrate together the birth of the young French Republic and the Centennial of the American Liberty. They thought to edify together on this occasion the most colossal monument which has ever been executed and to erect a Statue of Liberty at the entrance of this great country . . . as a personification of hospitality to all great ideas and to all sufferings.

After reviewing the status of the French campaign, along with a more tentative affirmation of its American counterpart, and downplaying a direct appeal for funds, Bartholdi built his case on a consideration of the location of the monument:

> In Philadelphia they thought . . . that this monument could be in their City. In respect of the value of their patriotical feelings they would deserve it. . . . But I thought that that [sic] the conception was to locate that monument on a ground which would belong to all the United States and in the most conspicuous place possible at the entrance of the grand American Country.[59]

Bartholdi had other cause for buoyant optimism at this time. Two days before the New England Society address, he was married to Jeanne-Émilie Baheux de Puysieux at the LaFarge estate in Newport.[60] Underlying the decision to marry was the new-found security in his career that originated in a firmly established American Committee for the Statue of Liberty.

After the fulfillment of its initial mission, the *Lafayette* pedestal committee had voted to retain a provisional status. On October 17, the group convened at the Cercle de l'Harmonie Française and reorganized as L'Union Franco-Américaine, Comité français de New York, with Coudert and Villa continuing their respective roles as president and secretary.[61] The committee's first official move was to raise the sum necessary to transport the arm and torch from the Centennial to Madison Square, thereby guaranteeing that the City of Brotherly Love would not possess New York's colossus.[62] In October, a powerful body of New Yorkers formed the nucleus of Bartholdi's long-sought American Committee, which first met formally at the Century Club in January 1877. The event triumphantly climaxed a troubled year, and the new celebrity documented his social status with a formal photograph (cat. 346) taken at the end of his stay in America.

To inspire patriotic ardor for the cause, at its initial rally the Committee displayed the *Commerce of Nations Rendering Homage to Liberty* (cat. 347) by Edward Moran, an accomplished marine painter. Completed sometime in 1876, and acclaimed at the Palette Club reception in October, the work now served as a banner for the fledgling pedestal campaign, exhibited at social and business functions of the American Committee, at an art exhibition held at New York's Union League in 1880, and possibly at the banquet honoring Ulysses S. Grant held in Paris in 1877.[63] In 1880, Joseph W. Drexel acquired the painting at the reported price of ten thousand dollars—amply testifying to its appeal.[64]

Although the genesis of the *Commerce* is unknown, it may have sprung from a collaboration between Bartholdi and Moran. The two artists may have met as early as 1871, when the Moran brothers were the featured exhibitors at a Union League art show in Philadelphia. In Moran the French sculptor discovered a colleague who recognized the potential of fusing aesthetics and propaganda in art. From sketches of the monument and pedestal Moran created an effective vision that cleverly masked the specific details of the colossus. Fog obscures the low horizon line, thereby circumventing questions of scale, while small boats, asymmetrically massed in two broad groups in the harbor, open a path toward the right; a countering mass of fog returns visual movement to the base of the statue. Passengers, consisting of family groups as well as sailors, address each other as they traverse the harbor in busy concourse. Most conspicuously, the Commerce of Nations takes place beneath the Stars and Stripes and the Tri-Color. Barely acknowledged by the international flotilla that surrounds her, *Liberty* reigns protectively and serenely over this activity, gazing toward the viewer. The direct appeal compensates for the lack of specificity. Perhaps more than any other single image, Moran's *Commerce* embodies the entire network of complex associations inherent in the statue, from simple emotional patriotism and pride in a nationalistic ideal to thorny issues of international politics and economic disputes.

Moran recognized as fully as Bartholdi the value of art as a document for the public. On a more profound, personal level, the American painter identified a kindred spirit in the French sculptor. In the same year that he painted the *Commerce*, Moran created a very different image of the Statue of Liberty (cat. 348). Veiled in mist, the shadowy form of the goddess is rendered with even less clarity than her counterpart in the *Commerce*. In this evocative, Whistlerian atmosphere, the towering scale of the giantess belies the physical dimensions of the small canvas. Dwarf vessels maintain their activity in a hushed nocturne. Dramatic illumination, from no visible source, enhances a direct, unobstructed path from the edge of the painting to the base of the colossus. Out of the public eye, and removed from politics, Moran rendered intimate tribute to the compelling force of a personal artistic vision. For the rest of Bartholdi's life, it was this testimony to his undying dream that remained on his studio wall.

345
Bartholdi Standing at Torch Railing, Philadelphia Centennial Exhibition
1876

346
Bartholdi in New York
1876

347
Commerce of Nations Rendering Homage to Liberty
Edward Moran
1876
reproduced as frontispiece

348
The Statue of Liberty at Night
Edward Moran
1876
reproduced in color on p. 169

147

8.
The American Committee

June Hargrove

The overriding goal of Bartholdi's 1876 visit was the formation of an American Committee to assume responsibility for the statue. In addition to raising funds for the pedestal, the Committee would secure the site, oversee the construction and installation, and arrange for the dedication—goals that could be attained only by rallying the American public to embrace the statue as a symbol of their national heritage. This task required men of uncommon stature and vision, idealistic yet pragmatic. Bartholdi found such men through the New York Union League Club. His loose affiliation with its members generated in the fall of 1876 the core of the American Committee, which was to coalesce around John Jay, Richard Butler, and William M. Evarts.

Laboulaye had opened the doors, and, as Coudert observed, Bartholdi «knew how to create here a crowd of friends who would be delighted to cooperate in the success of your project, if only to be personally agreeable to him.»[1] By September the sculptor confirmed to his mentor (cat. 349):

> If you could send me a note for Mr. John Jay, the former minister who is one of your friends, it would be invaluable. He is President of the Committee organized by the Union League Club to pursue the work on the Statue of Liberty; you should simply tell him that our subscription has stopped, if no one in America helps us we cannot continue, that you count on him to organize his Committee on a grand scale with Sub-Committees.[2]

The news was a personal victory for Laboulaye. Almost without exception, the members of the American Committee, whose involvement was predicated on his own, belonged to the New York Union League Club (cat. 350).[3] Its commitment to nationalism and to art made the League a natural center from which to promote the Statue of Liberty. Its peacetime activities had included such diverse endeavors as breaking up the Tweed Ring and founding the Metropolitan Museum of Art,[4] but it had become increasingly social and politically conservative in more recent years.

John Jay (cat. 351), a son of the esteemed family of justices and himself a lawyer, had been one of the founders of the Union League. After the war he embarked on a diplomatic career, first as the American Commissioner to the 1867 Paris Exhibition, then as Minister Plenipotentiary to Austria. His position as the head of a preliminary American Committee lent credibility to the movement. This nominal committee served through the fall of 1876, until a more formal structure could be defined after the presidential election.[5] Although Jay was less conspicuous on the Committee thereafter, he remained a loyal partisan.

Richard Butler, a wealthy merchant who had recently developed the Butler Hard Rubber Company and the least publicly known of those involved, was pivotal behind the scenes. A frequent visitor to France and a discriminating collector, he chaired the Union League Art Committee more than once and joined in establishing the Metropolitan Museum. His son-in-law, Georges Glaenzer, secretary of the Franco-American Union, probably gave Bartholdi the letter of introduction that led him to Butler, who in turn presented him to Evarts, James W. Pinchot, and Joseph Choate, all of whom were central to the statue's future.[6] As secretary to the American Committee, Butler had the onerous charge of coordinating every step of its activities over the next decade. His close personal attachment to the sculptor reinforced his devotion to the statue, and he cheerfully persevered in his otherwise thankless duties. He proved a steadfast friend, persistently advancing the statue, encouraging the sculptor, and acting as his agent. In 1885 Butler sent a plaster cast of his profile from an old cameo cutting to assist Bartholdi in modeling his bust, for which this plaster (cat. 352) was the final study.[7] A touching photograph (cat. 353) of the two men, on Bedloe's Island, during Bartholdi's last visit in 1893, captures their mutual affection. As age pressed in on him, the artist paid tribute to his friend: «in the moment of dark thoughts, you are always among the dear souvenirs to which I like to refer to find comfort.»[8]

William Maxwell Evarts was preoccupied during the autumn of 1876 with vindicating the presidency of Rutherford B. Hayes before the Electoral College. He had combined a brilliant legal practice with distinguished public service. A staunch emancipationist, close to Sumner, he championed political, economic, and social reforms. His defense of Andrew Johnson against impeachment earned him national recognition. Augustus Saint-Gaudens' marble portrait (cat. 354) was first proposed when Evarts visited Rome after representing the United States at the *Alabama* claims hearings in Geneva.[9] Learned and witty, he was one of the most articulate men of his era.

Evarts epitomized the collective idealism of the American Committee; the conservative nationalism of the Republican party did not obscure the need for a more extroverted foreign policy. His appointment as Secretary of State was imminent, and the pedestal fund presented a timely opportunity to demonstrate international cooperation. He would be well placed to facilitate its progress, and it could enhance some of his personal goals.[10] This continued to be true after he left office. At the International Monetary Conference of 1881, the French were his strongest allies in supporting a bimetallic standard of gold and silver. While in France, he commissioned a portrait from Bartholdi (cat. 355).[11] As president of the Union League Club he concentrated on local civic and philanthropic responsibilities from 1882 until 1885, when he became a U.S. Senator.

At the Century Club, Evarts justified the formation of an American Committee to a large audience of prominent New Yorkers on January 2, 1877, and Bartholdi recounted the history of the idea. Evarts was elected to chair a committee of twenty, whom he chose carefully from among those powerful in politics, industry, finance, and art.

The New York Committee was to become *ipso facto* the American Committee. They convened later in January to devise their strategies. Evarts provided the philosophical direction, while Butler, as secretary, tended to the daily details of running the organization. James W. Pinchot, a merchant prince whose financial acumen allowed him to retire at age forty-four, accepted the post of treasurer. Five subcommittees divided the other responsibilities; the breakdown corresponds to the essential measures of the campaign:

350
The Old Union League Club,
Madison Square,
New York.
E. L. Henry
ca. 1870s

351
John Jay
Jared B. Flagg
n.d.

1. *Appeal*: to draft a national call for subscriptions. Evarts was seconded by Parke Godwin (cat. 356), who edited the *Evening Post*, the country's most respected newspaper, with his father-in-law, the poet William Cullen Bryant. A prolific author, Godwin wrote essays on subjects as diverse as German literature and constitutional law. *Ancient Gaul*, the first volume of his projected *History of France*, appeared in 1860. A man of towering intellect, who helped Evarts draft the public statements, he became one of the Committee's most dedicated members.[12]

2. *Ways and Means*: to assure the cooperation of the nation's various commercial institutions in raising the necessary sum.[13] Samuel Babcock, president of the Chamber of Commerce from 1875 to 1882, had directed half a dozen companies, including International Bell Telephone, and was a liberal supporter of local arts groups. He and his colleagues expected the nation's financial organizations to shoulder much of the responsibility for the pedestal, as similar groups in France had subsidized the statue. Babcock could guarantee the backing of the New York Chamber, but was unable to induce the support of local Chambers across the country. He himself pledged 1 percent of the pedestal's total cost. While the financial community was indispensable to the enterprise's success, Babcock's position as chair of Ways and Means also indicates big business's vested interest in furthering the statue as a sign of international good will. For this reason, the Chamber of Commerce sponsored the two official banquets to honor the French that were demanded by contemporary protocol.

3. *Publicity and Printing*: to supervise printing and distribution of flyers, and to maintain relations with the press. Art dealer Samuel P. Avery was entrusted with the delicate mission of spreading favorable mentions in the appropriate journals.[14]

4. *Site*: to procure the site and provide for maintenance of the statue. Evarts coordinated this subcommittee.[15]

5. *Artistic*: to oversee practical and aesthetic matters. Theodore Weston, an architect and engineer, had the technical expertise that his co-members lacked. A veteran of civic boards, he had previously worked with most of the Committee.[16]

The Franco-American Union envisioned a series of committees in major cities across the United States cooperating in raising funds for a truly national monument. The American Committee pursued this goal with frustrating results to the end. While distant communities occasionally promised aid, very little materialized. The Philadelphia Committee looked to enhance their own city with the torch, but Boston formed a bonafide association to assist Evarts' group.

The same week that the New York Committee met, Joseph Iasigi, a Bostonian with international connections, including some formal ties to the French Consulate in Boston, invited a dozen Bostonians to second the wishes of the Franco-American Union.[17] Although the Boston Committee did little more than collect contributions, its existence helped to project a more national image for the pedestal effort. Robert Winthrop (cat. 357), president of the Massachusetts Historical Society, after touring the atelier of Gaget, Gautier in 1882, promised Laboulaye to «do everything in my power» to see the statue through. And in an equally personal exchange of February 1885, Evarts gratefully acknowledged additional monies from Winthrop.[18]

352
Bust of Richard Butler
Frédéric-Auguste Bartholdi
n.d.

356
Parke Godwin
John White Alexander
1886
reproduced in color on
p. 169

353
Frédéric-Auguste Bartholdi and Richard Butler at Bedloe's Island
1893

354
Bust of William Maxwell Evarts
Augustus Saint-Gaudens
1874

The men who constituted the American Committee were politically, financially, and socially related to each other. In the simplest terms, they were the American equivalent of Laboulaye's circle. As businessmen and statesmen, they wielded enormous power, which they viewed as a sacred trust, compelling them to public service. They saw international accord as a corollary to national prosperity. Most had visited France, and many had specific professional attachments there. But what deeper rationale prompted these men, whose time was much in demand, to apply themselves to the erection of a colossal statue?

The Centennial of the American Revolution was a momentous occasion for the United States. If Bartholdi indeed manufactured the association of the Centennial and the statue to entice Americans, it was a stroke of genius. The nation had firmly resisted encroachments on its fundamental liberties, and the first democratic government of the modern world saw itself as the model to which other peoples could aspire.

The Centennial also awakened the old ties between France and the United States. The Declaration of Independence was indebted to the same enlightened French thinking that led Lafayette to cross the Atlantic. The theme of Liberty struck a mutual chord, evoking the shared ideals that had only recently become a reality in France. Relations had deteriorated during the Second Empire, but now that France was a sister Republic, both nations were eager to mend

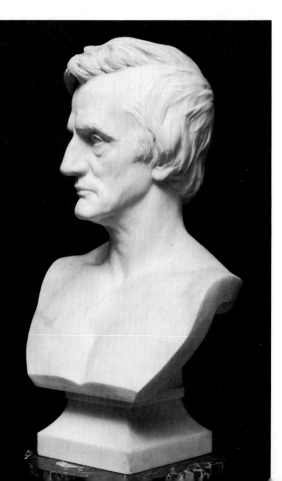

fences. After the dates pertinent to the Centennial passed, the monument evolved into a broader statement of enduring French-American amity. As a joint venture, it would serve as the visual incarnation of a future rapport strengthened by past history.

Naturally the Americans were flattered by the magnanimous recognition of their status as a beacon of Liberty—to have instigated it themselves would have been immodest, if not indecent. They hoped too that this example of international fellowship would inspire other nations to emulate the love of Liberty, for the greatest legacy of the Enlightenment was a profound faith in the progress of mankind. What better illustration of their ideals than a magnificent colossus embodying the highest achievements of their civilization? The fires of her torch, the literal and figurative emblem of progress, «joined with answering rays, . . . shall pierce the darkness of ignorance and man's oppression, until liberty enlightens the world.»[19]

Combined with the international rationale was a more tacit, national one. The commemoration of the American Revolution affirmed the principles of freedom, and for many, the Statue of Liberty obliquely glorified the preservation of the Union. Just as the French republicans found it expedient to extol the virtues of Liberty abroad, the American Committee welcomed the monument as a de facto expression of their ideals in the convenient guise of a gift to the nation. The wounds of the Civil War were too fresh for it otherwise not to appear to be a celebration of victory over the Confederacy. The pacific nature of Bartholdi's image was crucial to this message. Aware of the explosive potential of certain iconographic aspects, he eliminated the Phrygian bonnet and downplayed the broken chains. Evarts bluntly equated the statue with the war's outcome: «the liberty-loving people of France hailed the triumph with an immense and vivid enthusiasm. Nor was this . . . to be satisfied but by some adequate and permanent expression of their sympathy in our fiery trial. . . .»[20]

Underlying the symbolic meaning of the statue was the motif of commerce. When Moran entitled his painting *Commerce of Nations Rendering Homage to Liberty*, he was not indulging in rhetoric. New York was the commercial gateway to America, and the financial community had everything to gain by a display of French-American good will. The statue became a metaphor for commercial relations between the two Republics.

Some indication of the complexities of the liaisons between the French and American financial worlds may be gleaned from the career of Nathan Appleton, Jr. (cat. 358). From an old Boston family, Appleton joined the Paris branch of Bowles Brothers, an investment firm, in 1868. He soon became a quasi-diplomat representing U.S. financial interests in France, particularly the Board of Trade, in conjunction with Iasigi. A measure of his status was his appointment to the Franco-American Union in 1875, and he was certainly instrumental in Iasigi's initiative in calling for a Boston Committee. His genuine sincerity for French-American friendship was not disinterested.[21]

357
R. C. Winthrop
Daniel Huntingdon
1885

358
Nathan Appleton
ca. 1883

Through the Franco-American Union, he joined forces with Forney to attract French exhibitors to the Philadelphia Centennial Exhibition. They then worked together to persuade Americans to take part in the International Exposition or World's Fair of 1878. Besides providing the setting to display a nation's wares, these fairs were gestures of good faith between governments. Grant's administration had hesitated over participation in the Paris fair, but a belated application might yet be admitted. To arrange this, newly appointed Secretary of State Evarts conferred with Appleton, Forney, Stucklé, and Salmon, all of whose association with the statue «will greatly facilitate the necessary negotiations. . . .»[22] At Evarts' behest, Congress agreed to subsidize American exhibitors, for whom Salmon and Stucklé became the intermediaries.[23] Their company's publicity also grandly advertised the statue and the sale of merchandise for its benefit.

Concurrently, a move to revive a version of the 1778 Treaty of Alliance, Amity, and Commerce was underwritten by a group whose names, not surprisingly, recur in the statue's history: Laboulaye, Lafayette, Dietz Monnin; Evarts, Appleton, Iasigi, and Anthony Pollock. They arranged a conference during the World's Fair to draft a proposal for a ten-year commercial treaty. Although both governments were favorably inclined, the treaty's opponents were vociferous, and negotiations were postponed indefinitely in 1880.[24] The treaty's failure aggravated already strained French-American trade relations.

The treaty was a disappointment, but the Panama Canal was a thorn in Evarts' term. Appleton was equally involved in this venture: when he had encountered Lesseps in Suez in 1869, they discussed future cooperation in the Isthmus of Panama.[25] Although Lesseps' company was a private enterprise, the United States feared it might revert to the French government, in violation of the Monroe Doctrine. Evarts personally thought Lesseps a scoundrel, and avoided him during the latter's promotional tour with Appleton in 1880, but a number of Americans invested with the Frenchman. The debacle over the Canal would occur after *Liberty*'s inauguration, but Evarts must have tasted the irony of feting Laboulaye's successor.

If the ramifications of the statue went beyond the realm of art, art was still a primary issue for all concerned. They believed profoundly in the spiritual and civilizing benefits of art that corresponded with Bartholdi's aim to create a work of «great moral value.» The magnificent colossus would instruct all who passed of the glory of Liberty; she would incarnate the values of the nation at whose threshold she stood. It was an extension of their endeavors to bring art to the people—through institutions, exhibitions, and, increasingly, public monuments. On a more personal level, many of them were serious collectors.

To these positive motives must be added one converse. From the beginning, the point was stressed that to refuse or to fail to provide for the statue would be an «ineffaceable stain.»[26] While such a fear was premature until 1884, the press harped relentlessly on the repercussions of a «monument to indifference,» legitimizing French anxiety. Bartholdi begged Evarts to use his influence to avert failure, which would be very painful for his important patrons.[27] The pressure of a sluggish subscription eroded the Committee's confidence, until they too pleaded with the nation «to prevent so painful and humiliating a catastrophe!»[28] Failure would be as humiliating for Americans as it would be insulting to the French. But in 1877 failure seemed highly unlikely.

Sure of Grant's agreement, on February 1, 1877, the Committee addressed to Grant their request that the French gift be accepted by the President in the name of the nation. Grant forwarded the Committee's resolution to Congress with his own, desiring «your very favorable consideration.» The Joint Resolution authorized Grant «to designate and set apart a site for the colossal statue of «Liberty Enlightening the World,» and to provide for the permanent maintenance and preservation thereof. . . .»[29] Swift passage of the bill enabled Grant to sign it as law on March 3, his last day in office.

President Rutherford B. Hayes, no less receptive to a project patronized by his Secretary of State, ordered Gen. William Tecumseh Sherman to choose the site. Sherman graciously deferred to the known wishes of the sculptor.[30] Securing congressional approval of the statue and the site was a coup for the American Committee, which was not so fortunate with future legislation.

Meanwhile the Committee released its first appeal for funds, explaining the purpose of the statue, «which will not only form an impressive ornament to the entrance of the commercial Metropolis of the Union, but answer a useful purpose as a beacon or a signal station, and prove an enduring record of the early and lasting friendship of the two great Republics of the nineteenth century.»[31] Drafted by Evarts and Godwin, the statement summarized contemporary ideas about art: beauty and symbol allied with function and commerce. The retarded progress in France, however, soon stymied the American campaign, which gradually sank into inertia.

The American Committee languished from 1877 until the autumn of 1881. French consternation quickened after the 1880 proclamation met with no response. Early in 1881, from Paris, Pinchot communicated to Butler the Franco-American Union's alarm; Butler was at a loss to imagine why the parchment had never reached the Committee.[32] Before matters could be resolved, Evarts arrived in Paris for the International Monetary Conference. After meeting with Laboulaye and Bartholdi, he wrote to Butler:

> In this position of the work on this side of the water, it behooves the committee in New York to be moving with promptness and energy toward raising the necessary funds. . . . The opinion you expressed to me as I was leaving New York, that no difficulty and no delay would be met with in raising funds in our country, I do not doubt was correct. I beg to suggest, with some emphasis, that the moment has arrived for putting this to the proof.[33]

Still, nothing could be done until Evarts returned to the United States in the fall. The assumption that it would be easy to find money explains why the Americans delayed starting a vigorous campaign; optimism rather than procrastination seems to have misled them.

Butler conveyed this to Morton (cat. 359) on the eve of taking up «the statue business in blood earnest.» He had «no doubt» over the outcome, but, he explained, they «could not go on until we could be assured of its completion at a certain time—I had to relinquish my enthusiasm and bide my time.»[34] Ambassador Levi P. Morton, who accepted the invitation to serve on the Committee, shared this faith.

The meeting on November 22, 1881, that heralded the renewed campaign was less well attended than expected. Evarts explained that since 1877 the Committee had postponed a strenuous campaign in order to allow the French time to conclude theirs. Now it was hoped to have all ready by the centenary of the Treaty of Versailles, in 1883. The size of the Committee more than doubled following this meeting, adding eminent men outside of New York to emphasize the national scope.[35]

The next year saw little visible accomplishment. Richard Morris Hunt was chosen as architect of the pedestal, but no public measures were taken. The American Committee's inaction «has led to some impatience on the part of the French Committee. . . . The rumor that the latter committee were contemplating an offer of the statue to Boston has stirred the NY committee a little; but they are still debating whether to attempt to raise the money by popular subscription or to solicit a few large contributions from the more wealthy citizens.» If New York was not going to come through, it «ought to decline in favor of Boston or some other more deserving city.»[36]

A distressed sculptor wrote to Butler on October 31, 1882, after meeting with the Franco-American Union:

> . . . the sarcastic articles of the newspapers have worked up these gentlemen's feelings. This letter addressed to the New York Committee must be given by us to the newspapers in order to cover our responsibility with the public at large; this however we will only do in a month, so as to give the American Committee time to send their reply which would be published as soon as received thus avoiding the continuation of the ridiculing by the press.
>
> In short, we consider it high time for the US to act. The Committee here is about to make applications to the Government for the official transport of the Statue, but as you well understand we must be first assured of the feelings of the Americans on this subject.[37]

In more moderate words, both Bartholdi and Laboulaye communicated their anxiety to Evarts, who returned a lengthy reassurance that the Committee had deferred action to coordinate the pedestal campaign with the completion of the statue.[38] The Americans still clung to the belief that money would be quickly found.

The Committee shook off its lethargy with a mass meeting on November 28, 1882, at the Academy of Music, held to «arouse public sentiment.» Six hundred prominent men sat on the dais, and the packed auditorium included the Grant family and the city's patriarch, Peter Cooper. If success could be predicted by the number of influential supporters, *Liberty*'s was assured.

The Committee's size was expanded to four hundred members. Henry F. Spaulding replaced Pinchot as treasurer, and an executive committee was created, chaired by Joseph W. Drexel, with Godwin and Pinchot joined by V. Mumford Moore and Frederick Potts. The subcommittees were also modified. Weston remained head of the pedestal (formerly the artistic) committee, and a finance committee replaced the site committee, which was no longer needed.[39]

360
Bust of Joseph W. Drexel
J.Q.A. Ward
1889

Drexel followed the banking tradition of his Philadelphia family, whose European firms he oversaw. Drexel, Harjes, and Company opened in Paris in 1867. After establishing Drexel, Morgan & Co. in New York, he chose in 1876 to devote his life to philanthropy. He was a partner in the *Public Ledger*, Philadelphia's largest newspaper, with his brother and George W. Childs. Anthony J. Drexel and Childs, his closest friend, joined the American Committee in 1881, but Joseph Drexel's name first appears in 1882, by which time he owned Moran's painting.[40] His widow commissioned a classicizing bust (cat. 360) from John Quincy Adams Ward shortly after Drexel's death in 1888.[41]

Drexel's role in the Committee was probably far greater than existing documents suggest. A letter to his wife, Lucy, of October 4, 1883, gives some insight into the tensions within the Committee:

> Owing to a protracted meeting this afternoon caused by a quarrel between our Engineer and Contractor on the Bartholdi Statue which I had to settle I could not go out to see the children. . . . I shall have to go down to Bedloe's Island at least once a week until the work is finished as I find all hand [sic] including the Committee are very much inclined to quarrels. Hence all is left to me.[42]

Over the next four years, the Committee would have woes enough to rue the day they vowed their concurrence. Besides the burden of raising an ever-increasing sum of money, they supervised countless details, ranging from the construction and installation to the numerous ceremonies, the most lavish of which was the inauguration.

Well aware of the sacrifices that these men had made for the statue, the French thanked them with a new medal designed by Oscar Roty for the Paris Mint (cat. 361a–b). Butler's bears the added inscription, «A. Bartholdi / To his dear friend / Richard Butler.»[43] The French government further acknowledged the hospitality extended to the inaugural delegation with magnificent Sèvres porcelains. Bartholdi was «very angry» when he learned that the Ministry «struck out several names,» and that there was «nothing for Messrs. Pulitzer, Hunt, King and the friends of the Executive Committee.»[44] His response had an effect, and these names were listed at Sèvres, along

with the Union League Club, the Chamber of Commerce, and others.[45] Butler received a sumptuous Vase Parent (cat. 362), designed by Albert Carrier-Belleuse, the renowned sculptor and artistic director of the manufacture of Sèvres porcelain.

Despite its past struggles, the Committee chose to continue its role in the statue's welfare after the dedication. It operated a ferry for tourists, hoping to devote the profits to make the island «famously attractive.»[46] In the nineties, Bartholdi was gratified to learn that the depleted Committee had been reconstituted «with the most sympathetic names» to continue «the noble tradition of the Statue of Liberty.»[47] But time took its toll, and Butler's death in 1904 left Cornelius Bliss as the Committee's sole member.[48]

The workload had been staggering, and the members had much else to occupy their time; the unforeseeable problems and the manifold costs left the members to absorb an untold amount of incidental operating expenses. The American Committee has been overshadowed by the more dramatic events of the statue's history, yet it was the perseverance of its members that truly made Bartholdi's dream a reality.

361a–b
Medal for the Franco-American Union Commemorating the Dedication of «Liberty Enlightening the World» presented to Richard Butler
Louis Oscar Roty
1886

362
Vase Parent
Albert Carrier-Belleuse (modeler) and Alfred Thompson Gobert (decorator)
1883–85

9.
The American Fund-Raising Campaign

June Hargrove

Raising the pedestal funds proved more arduous than anyone had expected. Into the eighties, Evarts believed that «our people will cheerfully furnish the means for the pedestal and that we can complete its structure in time. . . .»[1] The assumption that money would be readily found was not as naïve as it might seem. The Union Defence Fund, which Evarts chaired during the Civil War, had raised well over a million dollars (the New York Art Fair alone accounted for that amount). Americans had organized impromptu subscriptions in aid of other causes, most recently for the flood victims in the Midi, just as French artists magnanimously held a sale of their works in sympathy for the victims of the great Chicago fire.[2] But these were all reactions to crises; the slow momentum of the pedestal fund robbed it of a sense of urgency. The idea of a gigantic personification of an abstract concept might be intriguing, even appealing, but hardly compelling enough to prompt a midwestern farmer or a confederate veteran to dig into his pocket.

In 1876 Bartholdi's presence in America sparked «wildcat» appeals that brought a promising response.[3] To encourage subscriptions, Coudert's French Committee gathered funds to ship the arm and torch from Philadelphia to New York. The installation in Madison Square (cat. 363) in February 1877 was subsidized by the Department of Public Works.[4] The pedestal (cat. 364), of «solid masonry, covered with wood to represent cut stone,» was enhanced with a reduction of the statue and a view of the monument in New York harbor.[5] Only subscribers could ascend the torch; further profits were generated from the sale of photographs.[6]

The audacity of this move characterizes Bartholdi's knack for winning attention, and the fragment must have been quite a curiosity in those pre-Rodin days. Among the numerous notices that it inspired was a parody, entitled «Serial Statues,» which supposed that segments of the colossal lady were to be scattered through the city's parks as they arrived.[7] Although the torch was supposed to remain in New York only until 1880, Bartholdi was content to leave it. In October 1881, just before the first rivet was driven in Paris, he asked Pinchot to arrange for its return, but it arrived in his studio only in August 1882.[8]

The American Committee's first official appeal, in February 1877, merited sporadic mention through the spring, but the protracted schedule in France discouraged more high-powered undertakings, and an indeterminate sum was collected before efforts tapered off entirely.[9]

After the Committee revived in 1881, it stalled for a year, confident that a short, intense drive when the statue neared completion would be more effective, particularly with a specific pedestal design. In the meantime, spiraling construction costs had doubled the earlier estimate of $125,000.

A more aggressive phase began with the mass meeting of November 28, 1882. The appeal to the American people was renewed, but as a *Times* editorial aptly warned, «Everyone's business, nobody's business.»[10] The sums were recorded in booklets held by the members, and later donations were acknowledged by an elaborate subscription certificate (cat. 365), with an engraved variant of Moran's painting.[11] The members of the Committee came forth generously, and eventually paid one-fourth of the direct costs themselves. Drexel, Evarts, Godwin, Spaulding, Cornelius Vanderbilt, Pinchot, Delmonico, and others each gave $1,000;

363
Erecting, on a Temporary Site, in Madison Square, February 22d, the Hand of Bartholdi's Statue of Liberty
From *Frank Leslie's Illustrated Newspaper*
March 17, 1877

Drexel, Morgan & Co., $5,000; and many others $500.[12] The Chamber of Commerce arranged for the balance in the Union Defence Fund to be applied to the pedestal.[13]

The Chamber of Commerce persuaded local businesses to house contribution boxes, and early in 1884 a «Subscription Department» was organized to divide New York into districts for a systematic personal canvass.[14] The Committee supplemented the subscriptions with entertainments and souvenirs, both of which served a dual purpose: fund raising and publicity. Among the more popular measures were a public ball and mass concerts, played by Gilmore's Band, and even a «monster entertainment.» All manner of memorabilia were sold to benefit the treasury. The Root and Tinker lithograph (cat. 366) of 1883, the «Only Official Authorized Edition,» was almost certainly the one used to augment the fund. Photographs and stereopticons of the construction were produced in quantity (cat. 419, 420). The rights to these photographs, «by authorization» only, were jealously guarded.[15] Profits from the sheet music of Kennedy's «Liberty» (cat. 367) went to the Committee's coffers. Bartholdi dutifully sent three thousand signatures, which were offered to autograph collectors.[16] An «agitator» in the person of Mahlon Chance stumped in the West to stimulate national interest. Even the reigning divas volunteered their talents. The Committee's resourcefulness was matched by their industriousness. «What with fairs, raffles, shows, and contribution boxes the gigantic female of Bartholdi's dream may have at least a leg to stand on before the arrival of the Greek kalends.»[17]

Benefits were increasingly in vogue and lucrative. Visual traces of these events are scarce—justifying the appellation «ephemera.»[18] The «Fete of Nations» on May 12, 1884, at the Brooklyn Academy netted $12,000 with great flair, but no photograph or souvenir captures the much-touted merriment.

The most frequent type of benefit was the amateur theatrical. The Academy of Music and the Madison Square Theatre, generously lent by the proprietor, housed at least four in 1883. The wives and friends of the Committee threw themselves heart and soul into such productions. While these events raised thousands of dollars and kept the campaign in the public eye, they inadvertently did a disservice to the fund by

364
The Torch in Madison Square, New York
n.d.

365
Certificate of Subscription
1883

366
Liberty Enlightening the World
Root & Tinker
1883
reproduced in color
on p. 170

perpetuating the impression that the statue was the preoccupation of the rich. A review of *The Princess* announced that «the Bartholdi Statue Pedestal Fund has been rescued from disgrace by a committee of ladies, who are determined to give . . . the prettiest amateur entertainment ever. . . . Many of the costumes which appeared at the Vanderbilt ball will be worn by their owners on the stage.»[19] Tickets to the ultra-fashionable tableaux vivants were unabashedly advertised as for «recipients of the circular only, so that, as nearly as possible, the audience should be select and private.»[20] Well meaning, and in their own way effective, such benefits implied that the fund was the latest divertissement of the New York 400.

Still, there was a genuine sensitivity to public welfare in the Committee. The Art Loan Exhibition (cat. 368), held at the National Academy of Design, was in itself a major accomplishment. As the preface to the catalogue states, beyond increasing the fund the exhibition's purpose was the «awakening among us a potent influence in art.»

The idea for this mammoth display was suggested by Montague Marks, editor of the *Art Amateur*, to Constance Cary Harrison.[21] The scale and the scope were to be encyclopedic, and several hundred people diligently organized it for months. When «The Venetian Palace of Art» opened its doors on December 3, 1883, it was

> filled to overflowing with one of the rarest collections of paintings and art-objects ever brought together. Rich old tapestries make a background for medieval arms and armor; the patient and elaborate art of the Orient is brought into juxtaposition with the crude fabrications of the American aborigines; seven hundred characteristic paintings by the greatest modern artists hang upon the walls of the south gallery; another room is filled with the most exquisite embroideries and women's decorative work; old miniatures, historical relics, musical instruments, carved and painted fans, cobweb lace, old china, stained glass, illuminated missals, and all kinds of choice *bric-a-brac*, are crowded together in a rich profusion. . . . All of these treasures are private loans. . . .[22]

Mrs. Harrison, a renowned author herself, conceived of the «Portfolio,» containing original works of art and literary manuscripts, to be auctioned at the gala opening. She recalls that Emma Lazarus was paying a call «when I begged her to write something for my «Portfolio.» She declared she could think of nothing suitable, . . . when I reminded her of her visits to . . . the newly arrived immigrants whose sad lot had so often excited her sympathy.» Miss Lazarus soon sent her neighbor the manuscript for «The New Colossus,» first published in the exhibition catalogue.[23]

One reason for the exhibit's quality and coherency was the number of professional artists in key positions. On the Executive Committee sat William M. Chase (charged with «Admission of Objects»), Augustus Saint-Gaudens, John LaFarge, Eastman Johnson, and Olin Warner. Among the dozens of others named are Louis C. Tiffany, Albert Bierstadt, and Albert P. Ryder. All agreed not to mount any work of art previously shown publicly.

The show demonstrated a sophisticated awareness of contemporary European trends. While much of it was devoted to landscape and genre scenes, it was a revelation for Americans; Manet was exhibited here for the first time in America. Some complained that there was no Bouguereau or Cabanel, and too much Millet and Courbet, «a painter whose rough brush sends a cold chill down the average American's back.»[24] If the point of the exhibit was to make money, it was a mistake not to cater to American collectors and the public. Such observations did not, however, deter the visitors, forty thousand of them. Although heavy expenses cut into the $25,000 received, almost $15,000 profit was left.

Despite the glamour of the exhibition, the show aroused heated controversy with its Sunday opening, which violated the Blue Laws. The Sunday Closing League was roasted for not distinguishing between «a place where dissolute women exhibit themselves» and «a decorous and refining exhibition.»[25] The friction extended into the ranks of the committee, half a dozen of whom numbered among the vehement protesters. F. Hopkinson Smith, the director, justified the decision on the grounds that «education is next to religion.» The organizers desired that the working classes «shall see for themselves what constitutes the surroundings of a refined home life and what education results in. . . . Sunday is the only day left to these people, and they

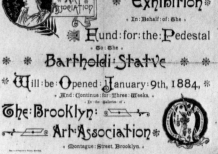

370
The Tortoise and the Hare: An Old Fable Reversed
Unidentified cartoon
ca. 1885

believe they are doing the greatest good to the greatest number of our citizens. . . .»[26] Sunday attendance, «unmistakably drawn from the working people,» was the highest.[27] An amusing cartoon of «Smith as the Statue of Liberty,» with the National Academy of Design as his pedestal, touted his plucky fight against the Closing League.[28]

The Brooklyn Art Association sponsored an exhibition of oil paintings in the new year (cat. 369), which raised an additional several thousand dollars. Over one hundred of the works came from the collection of banker George I. Seney. Special tickets were issued for the press, teachers, and students, underscoring the pedagogical role of art exhibits.[29]

Idealistically, in accordance with the wishes of the French, the Americans aspired to a national subscription, but, pragmatically, they realized that New York would have to furnish the bulk of the money.[30] They were torn between mounting an energetic popular campaign and concentrating on fewer, more substantial donations. Hesitation within the Committee may have dulled its effectiveness on both scores. Succumbing to the temptation to twist a few rich arms, Parke Godwin solicited Tilden, Vanderbilt, and Astor for $10,000 to no avail.[31] By the fall of 1883, when spontaneous largesse was not forthcoming from the public, Evarts and Drexel fired off a new round of letters to monied New Yorkers, asking for contributions of at least $5,000; the results were equally dismal.[32]

Something of the campaign's underlying political complexities may be deduced from this correspondence. Godwin contacted Tilden without reference to Evarts, surely because the latter may be credited with Tilden's loss of the presidency to Hayes. Likewise, although the form letter bore the signatures of both Evarts and Drexel, only the latter wrote to Hamilton Fish, as a carefully masked antipathy clouded the rapport between the two former Secretaries of State.[33] Disapprobation of the statue may have been directed at Evarts, whose opinionated politics inevitably made enemies. One disgruntled Brooklynite labeled the canvass «Evartsania.»[34]

The correspondence of Fish yields additional insight. Fish declined Drexel's request without comment, but he subsequently denounced the statue harshly:

[It has] nothing but its colossal exaggerations of size to recommend it. I had this opinion of it when the design was first shown to me when I was in the Department of State by the French Minister and have not been able to change it. And I have therefore abstained from all effort to place in the harbor of New York what *I* believe to be neither an object of Art or of Beauty.[35]

Such virulent assaults on the aesthetic merits of the statue were rare, but not unique. Others found its novelty disturbing:

. . . there was . . . a lurking doubt how the statue would look, and whether it would not be likely to reflect the reverse of glory upon those who were conspicuous in procuring its erection, and this doubt was calculated to repel even public-spirited capitalists who were on the lookout for safe aesthetic investments.[36]

Despite optimism over events staged by the Committee, its flagging finances were painfully obvious. The first spurt of donations augured an easy victory, but contributions dwindled rapidly. Although $97,102.46 had been subscribed by December 4, 1883, all but $23,463.49 of that amount had been pledged prior to January 17, 1882.[37] From the outset, the press admonished its readers for their tardiness in subscribing.[38] The torch was hardly up in Madison Square before journalists started to carp on its

pathetic gesture «imploring alms.»[39] The criticism was unwarranted in the first phase, and over the years the constant accusations of public apathy damaged the campaign, as people were put off by the negative tone. As the public subscription became increasingly crucial, the public tired of the monotonous appeals and dire forecasts. Cartoonists poked fun at the tardy pace: reversing the old fable, the French hare beat the tortoise Committee (cat. 370). Many satirized the statue as an old crone, decrepit from waiting for her «footstool» (cat. 371).

The local press was loyal, but condescending editorials from outside New York were unsparing. One began, «a panic seems to have fallen upon the unfortunate committee . . . with the news that the statue is completed. . . .»[40] One can sympathize with Spaulding, who announced on a pitching ferry ride to inspect the foundation that he felt terribly sick. When his companions shrank back, he hastened to explain, «it's only because I'm treasurer.»[41]

Everyone but the American Committee seemed to be profiting from the statue—so much so that *Puck* concluded it would be wise to «Let the advertising agents take charge of the Bartholdi Business» (cat. 372). The Committee may have attempted to market the reproduction rights to the statue, as the French had, as advertising such as that for Pratts Astral Oil on the Root and Tinker lithograph (cat. 366) could hardly

371
The «Statue of Liberty»
One Thousand Years
Later; Waiting
From *Frank Leslie's*
Illustrated Newspaper
August 30, 1884

372
Let the Advertising Agents
Take Charge of the
Bartholdi Business, and the
Money Will Be Raised
Without Delay
From *Puck*
April 8, 1885
reproduced in color
on p. 170

THE BARTHOLDI STATUE.

The republican spirit of the French people has been again signalized by their presentation to us of the most magnificent statue ancient or modern civilization has ever seen.

upon the sea. Our citizens have been asked for $250,000 to erect a fitting pedestal. Only $120,000 have yet been raised. To stimulate subscriptions we made the following proposition:

182 Fulton Street,
New York, March 25th, 1884.

Hon. Wm. M. Evarts,
Chairman of Pedestal Fund Committee:

Sir,—So far as we know the largest single subscription for the Pedestal Fund is $5000. To promote the good work, we tender you a subscription of twenty-five thousand dollars, provided that for the period of one year you permit us to place across the top of the pedestal the word "Castoria." Thus art and science, the symbol of liberty to man, and of health to his children, would be more closely enshrined in the hearts of our people.

Very respectfully, yours,
The Centaur Company.

When about thirty years ago Dr. Pitcher, warring against dangerous narcotic medicines, discovered the formula of vegetable Castoria, he recorded a scientific advance, which has been adopted by millions of mothers, and by liberal physicians everywhere. Castoria is not, as some suppose, a secret remedy. It contains no morphine or other injurious ingredient, and is now as regularly prescribed as paregoric and Castor oil once were. Mothers who thus loan money to the Goddess of Liberty will be rewarded by the enlarged patriotism of their children.

Liberty Enlightening the World

is to be of bronze, and, when mounted upon its base and pedestal, will catch the breeze at the height of three hundred and twenty-nine feet! The head measures 14½ feet; the index finger 8 feet, and the nose 3¾ feet. Twelve persons can sit within the torch, and forty persons within the head.

This figure is to stand upon an island in the bay of New York, and cast its beacon light sixty miles

373
Liberty Enlightening the World
From *Harper's Magazine Advertiser*
July 1884

374
*The «Sons of the Revolution» Collecting Money for the Bartholdi Statue Pedestal,
October 4th*
After a sketch by C. Upham
From *Frank Leslie's Illustrated Newspaper*
October 24, 1884

have escaped notice.[42] Otherwise there is little evidence that the pedestal fund benefited from the abundance of trade cards (cat. 511, 512, 565, 568) exploiting the image. The statue became so popular an advertising ploy that one company, Castoria, wrote Evarts with an offer of $25,000 for the privilege of hanging its banner from the future pedestal (cat. 373).

In September 1884, the Sons of the Revolution, a new social organization comprised of the descendants of the men who fought for American independence, volunteered to go after the nickels and dimes that eluded the Committee's grasp. Their subscription book indicates that their appeal reached the small benefactors. Among their endeavors was to provide twenty-five–cent ferry rides to Bedloe's Island. They literally took to the streets (cat. 374), parading from the Battery to Madison Square, gathering donations from the crowd.[43]

To broaden the support beyond New York, they tackled a nationwide mail campaign for one dollar contributions, only to meet with the same resistance that had discouraged the Committee. As one Indiana resident lamented, «Our people will not understand this as a national matter and will insist upon it it is [sic] a New York affair. . . .»[44] The Sons ran afoul of Evarts because they contacted such people as President Chester A. Arthur, «who were most able to contribute in tens and hundreds» and who supposed that they had thus «discharged their patriotic duty.» «Mr. McDowell (chairman) is credited with having displayed much energy and self-reliance,» but the scheme was suspended as «more detrimental than beneficial.»[45] Evarts and McDowell were caricatured as squabbling while *Liberty* stood by the empty coffers (cat. 375). The tiff blew over quickly.

Overcoming its scruples against tax dollars, the Committee pinned great hope on legislation as a solution to its dilemma.[46] In the spring of 1884, the state legislature approved New York City's request to add $50,000 to the pedestal fund. Evarts took the precaution of personally expressing his hope that Governor Grover Cleveland would «be able to pass upon this . . . without delay. . . .»[47] In a move that stunned the Committee, the scrupulous Cleveland vetoed the appropriation as unconstitutional.[48]

The Committee fared no better with Congress. In December 1884, Representative S. Cox, seconded by a petition from the Sons of the Revolution, introduced a joint resolution «that in recognition of the spirit which has prompted this gift, and in aid of the timely completion of the pedestal upon which it is to be placed, the sum of one hundred thousand dollars, . . . be . . . appropriated out of any money in the Treasury. . . .»[49] There was a grudging consensus that Uncle Sam would have to compensate for New York's flagrant stinginess (cat. 376). Then, in a fateful twist of events, the Senate attached Cox's proposal to the Deficiency Appropriation Bill, fervently opposed by the House. Referred to a Conference Committee on March 3, 1885, the bill was quietly smothered by Representative S. Randall, permanently at loggerheads with the Republicans.[50]

Spaulding's report of March 12, 1885, disclosed that of the $182,491.40 received to date, less than $3,000 remained, leaving the fund well over $100,000 shy. Money was trickling in, but not fast enough to keep pace with expenses. The Committee's desperation is apparent in a poignant missive from the treasurer to Evarts: «I have begged until I am ashamed until now, the more I beg the less I succeed.»[51] A house-to-house canvass was planned to coincide with a final, impassioned bid to New Yorkers, «in the name of our country, in the name of civilization and of art, not to neglect this last opportunity for securing to yourselves and to the Nation an imperishable glory.»[52]

Given the prestige of the American Committee, its financial and political clout, and the concentration of energies and talent brought to bear in the fund raising, its predicament may seem incredible. In fact, the Committee raised a very large sum of money in a relatively short time, an accomplishment that has been overlooked in light of the deficit. At least one writer of the time pinpointed part of the difficulty:

Instead of venting bile on the United States in general, it would be in better taste if certain French and American journals would make allowance for exceptional circumstances about the scheme, among which were public uncertainty whether the Nation, the State, or the city was to be responsible for the pedestal, the extreme size and cost of the structure, the complete novelty of the idea, the remoteness of the site from the parks and thoroughfares of the city, the long-continued financial depression.[53]

The newness of the concept was an obstacle in the United States; the inception of the Statue of Liberty slightly predated the advent of public sculpture erected through popular subscriptions. Although the decade of its realization saw the proliferation of commemorative monuments, the American public was not yet accustomed to furnishing the wherewithal. The Bunker Hill Monument was inaugurated eighteen years after the cornerstone was laid, and Congress had

376
The Monument Finished—
Next. The Missing
Pedestal—The Nation
Should Supply What
Niggard New York Refuses
Unidentified press cartoon
December 1884

to pass legislation for the completion of the Washington Monument; both memorials had commenced with public subscriptions that withered soon after the fanfare died down.[54] The Association for Grant's Tomb had a very erratic start, «which by the way,» Spaulding noted to Evarts, «appears to be quite as apathetic an affair as ours. . . .»[55] The American Committee pioneered in the popular subscription as a means of funding sculpture, and its techniques were soon imitated across the United States.

375
The Arrival of «Liberty.»
Uncle Sam to Bartholdi
Statue—«Here, you sit
down and hold what we
have of your Pedestal,
while I settle the
Committee dissensions. Jay
Gould thinks we have too
much Liberty here now.»
Unidentified newspaper
cartoon
ca. November 1884

THE EVENING TELEGRAM.

VOL. XVIII.—NO. 5,866. NEW YORK, SATURDAY, JULY 19. 1884.—DOUBLE SHEET. PRICE THREE CENTS.

THE BATTERY PARK OF THE FUTURE—A STUDY FOR THE CONSIDERATION OF NEW YORKERS.

377
The Battery Park of the
Future—A Study for the
Consideration of New
Yorkers
From *The Evening
Telegram*
July 19, 1884

378
*A Hint to the Public. The
work is being done well
and rapidly, but time flies
and the master mason must
have help*
From *The Daily Graphic*
May 22, 1885

379
*The Statue of Liberty
Enlightening the World
Described by the Sculptor
Bartholdi*
Frédéric-Auguste Bartholdi
(ed. A. T. Rice)
New York: North
American Review,
1885

The failure to establish a definitive national identity for the statue also plagued the Committee. To reinforce the national import of their cause, they received congressional permission to exhibit a model of the statue and pedestal in the Capitol in June 1884. A terra-cotta reduction (cat. 407 and 494) stood in the Rotunda on Hunt's model of the pedestal until 1887. Whatever cachet the monument thus acquired, the display had little impact on subscriptions.[56] An attempt to emphasize that the statue was a gift from the people of France to the people of the United States, this idea failed to convince the rest of the nation. «The plain truth appears to be that the pedestal . . . must be paid for by those for whom the statue was made, the citizens of New York,» and the Committee was accused of trying to persuade «the people of Chicago and Connecticut that they ought to pay the expense which those of New York would like to avoid.»[57] While 90 percent of the money had come from the New York area, the donation of tiny sums from elsewhere indicated that some interest had penetrated beyond the Hudson.[58] Given the sprawling, regionalized character of the nation, this perhaps merits more recognition than condemnation.

No less detrimental to the pedestal fund was the «feeling . . . that the committee represents wealth.»[59] Incidents such as the dinner party for presidential candidate Blaine, labeled «Belshazaar's Feast,» attended by Evarts, Morton, and others, reinforced the impression that «the work was in the hands of a few rich men of the city of New York, who would contribute the amount required.»[60] An aura of elitism emanated from the American Committee. Accustomed to the elegances of power, the members advocated reform but were unlikely to fraternize with the masses. Consequently their approach to fund raising betrayed a patrician bias. For example, the idea of publishing the names of subscribers to give impetus to others was sound, but the amount of the initial sums unfortunately implied that small donations were superfluous.

The frequent complaints of hard times were legitimate. As many fortunes were lost as made in the decades following the Civil War, and the Wall Street panic of 1873 left even wealthy men pinched. The working class was caught between inflation and unemployment. Strikes and political dissension exacerbated the division between rich and poor and generated a fear of radical movements. Although it is difficult to assess the direct impact this had on the pedestal fund, one ramification certainly was the fear of subversive «liberty.» As if to quell a tacit suspicion that the celebration of liberty might be an invitation to anarchy, the statue's advocates cast the image in the role of a «law-abiding liberty,» resisting radical assaults (cat. 552).[61]

On a less abstract level, the remoteness of the site may have hampered the cause. The *Evening Telegram* (cat. 377) contended that if the more accessible Battery were substituted for Bedloe's Island, people would be more willing to contribute.[62] The *Times* justified Bartholdi's choice, but conceded that a change of venue might «enlist [to] the poverty-stricken cause of the fund many who at present are, as the adder, deaf to him who charms for contributions.»[63]

When prospects looked bleakest, Joseph Pulitzer appeared. However unlike a «knight in shining armor» he may have seemed to the Committee, he rescued their good works from coming to naught (cat. 378). His spectacular crusade to raise $100,000 through the *World*, described in the next chapter, is justly hailed as a tour de force. Although Pulitzer saved the imperiled pedestal, the Committee must have felt some rancor over being upstaged.

Nor were the trials over. Since all of the $300,000 received by September 1885 would go for construction, at least $40,000 more had to be found to assemble the statue.[64] The Committee hoped to cover this through two recent money-makers, both of which had gone on sale in late spring. First, to aid the foundering fund, Bartholdi wrote *The Statue of Liberty Enlightening the World* (cat. 379), offering a comprehensive, illustrated account of the statue; it was published by Allen Thorndike Rice's *North American Review*.[65]

Statue of "Liberty Enlightening the World."

THE Committee in charge of the construction of the base and pedestal for the reception of this great work, **in order to raise funds for its completion**, have prepared a miniature Statuette, *six inches in height*, the Statue bronzed, Pedestal nickel-silvered, which they are now delivering to subscribers throughout the United States at **One Dollar Each.**

This attractive souvenir and Mantel or Desk ornament is a *perfect fac-simile* of the model furnished by the artist.

The Statuette, in same metal, *twelve inches high*, at **Five Dollars Each,** delivered.

The designs of Statue and Pedestal are protected by U. S. Patents, and the models can *only* be furnished by *this Committee.* Address, with remittance,

RICHARD BUTLER, Secretary,

AMERICAN COMMITTEE OF THE STATUE OF LIBERTY,

33 MERCER STREET, NEW YORK.

380
*Statue of «Liberty
Enlightening the World»*
American Committee flyer
1885

381
6" American Committee
Model
1885

382
12" American Committee
Model
1885

The second was the American Committee Models.

> M. Bartholdi sent Max Baudelot, the sculptor, from Paris to model the figure, and granted permission to Brundage and Newton . . . to manufacture them under his patent rights. The statuettes stand a little more than a foot high, the pedestal resting on a foundation of plush. The modelling of the statue was done under the suggestion of M. Bartholdi. Instead of a clay cast of the completed goddess a model of a nude figure was first made, and on this the draperies were placed. In this way a graceful effect is gained which is lacking in other statuettes. Besides the small figure a large model measuring three feet from the pedestal to the torch has been made . . . to be utilized as a gaslight or lamp. . . .[66]

The tin statuettes were advertised (cat. 380) in two sizes, 6 inches for one dollar (cat. 381) and 12 inches for five dollars (cat. 382); the large version (cat. 383) sold for ten dollars.[67] A long list of cooperating merchants made these miniatures readily available; they are the forerunners of the replicas in souvenir stands today. Sales were brisk, and orders came in faster than they could be filled; an estimated fifty thousand of the 6-inch version were sold.[68] Butler issued a press release in September 1885, explaining that the «sale of the Statuettes, on a liberal scale . . . , will produce the needed amount,» and a confidential circular tempted jewelers with a 20 percent discount, payable in statuettes.[69]

Despite the all-out efforts, Spaulding confessed to Evarts on March 20, 1886, «I am very sorry to say that there have been very few responses to the last appeal—less than $1200. To keep you posted, I have to advise you that at the last meeting of the Executive Committee it was voted to go on and finish the pedestal, obligating [us] for any deficiency in receipts to pay the bills.»[70] The Committee elected to prevail on Congress to defray the expenses of refurbishing the island, installing the lighting, and providing for the inauguration. Their checkered past with legislators notwithstanding, they reasoned that the $323,000 of voluntary

contributions warranted federal recognition.[71] Moreover, the 1877 resolution could be interpreted as legal obligation for the remaining costs. Aware that the request arrived late in the session, the treasurer declared to Evarts, now a Senator, that «a failure to make a prompt appropriation [would be] a monument of disgrace to Congress and of humiliation to the nation. . . .»[72]

President Cleveland, «most happy to cooperate,» recommended the appropriation to Congress in May.[73] Butler pleaded with Evarts «to leave no stone unturned,» adding, «I know you will pardon my frankness in this matter. When I assure you my anxiety to end our long struggle is so great . . . which you can readily appreciate.»[74]

Forewarned that Randall, the Committee's *bête noire*, hoped to whittle down the $106,000 estimate, Spaulding urged Evarts that «should a difference between the Senate and the House Committees in this matter lead to a conference, I trust that you will use your influence. . . .»[75] Evarts reassured his colleagues that «the Senate will restore the items struck out.»[76] After passing the subcommittee unanimously, the amendment was defeated through some skullduggery in the House.[77] Butler admitted, «the vote . . . quite set me back,» as «now it is a case of restoring the whole Bill.»[78] Evarts managed to have a modified version of $56,500 inserted. After a week of finagling, it was adopted on August 4.[79]

The American Committee had raised over $300,000 (one-third of which came from the *World* campaign) in less than four years. Although they lacked the $50,000 to harmonize the statue with its surroundings as befitted «a monument of Art,» they could at last fix a date for the inaugural ceremonies.

383
36″ American Committee
Model
1885

10.
Power of the Press

June Hargrove

The power of the press made *Liberty* a star. The printed page was the indispensable conduit to the public. Only after the statue's presence was established in the public eye could the specific goal of fund raising proceed. The very notion of a national subscription presupposed mass communication. Indeed, had not a dramatic rise in the number of publications and their circulation occurred after the Civil War, the idea would have been scarcely feasible.[1]

The American press embraced the cause of *Liberty* almost unanimously. The range of publications documents the widespread interest in Bartholdi's statue. The modern notion that the statue was maligned in the press is a distortion of the truth. Acrimonious jibes and misunderstandings filled the news, but reactions to the gift of the statue itself were overwhelmingly positive. The American public was lambasted for its apathy, the American Committee was chastised for being laggard, the rich were vilified, New York was ridiculed, but Bartholdi and his «daughter» were hardly grazed. Even those who objected to the statue as a heathen goddess praised Bartholdi for «his genius and his skill.»[2]

Bartholdi was acutely conscious of the potency of the press. From the start he cultivated prominent figures of the Fourth Estate. In 1871 he sought out such giants of the press as Horace Greeley and William Cullen Bryant, and he became fast friends with John Forney. During his second visit, he claimed (cat. 384), «almost all the papers are with us, and I thanked them in the name of the [Franco-American Union] with a medal.»[3] He gave frequent interviews, charming his questioners with his gallic warmth. He brought to America the atmosphere of a «happening» that was proving so effective for public relations in France. He cleverly staged newsworthy activities, encouraging his friends in the press to publicize them. He subscribed to the Argus clipping service in order to monitor from across the Atlantic the public status of his enterprise in America.[4]

Bartholdi did not hesitate to call on his friends to counter pejorative commentaries. Forney (cat. 385) proved a faithful ally in the crucial early days of the campaign. Shortly after the torch had been erected in Philadelphia, the *New York Times* belittled the future statue. Not only did the editor ridicule the idea of the gift, he also suggested that the Americans would have to pay for the completion of the statue:

> It would unquestionably be impolite to look a gift-statue in the mouth, but . . . when a nation promises to give another nation a colossal bronze woman, and then, after having given one arm, calmly advises the recipient of that useless gift to supply the rest of the woman at its own expense, there is a disproportion between the promise and its fulfillment which may be forgiven but which cannot be wholly ignored.[5]

Bartholdi's vulnerability in 1876 made the *Times* attack more than he could let pass. Slurring the intentions of the Franco-American Union might jeopardize the nascent American campaign. The sculptor replied with a letter, no doubt drafted by Forney, in the Philadelphia *Press* concluding that Philadelphia would welcome the statue should New York decline. Pugnaciously the *Times* seized upon «A Philadelphian Conspiracy,» blaming pretensions to pirate *Liberty* on Philadelphia's recent presumption to be a steamship port. This of course falsified the spirit of the Philadelphians, who recognized that Bartholdi himself preferred the site in New York harbor, but any hint of competition for the honor of receiving the statue provided an ideal opportunity to exploit the traditional rivalry between cities. Bartholdi's letter to Laboulaye written only four days after this reveals how clearly he understood the rules of the game.

JOHN W. FORNEY.
An "Occasional" Contributor to the Press.

This exchange has been the basis on which subsequent authors have argued that the press opposed the statue.[6] The *Times* unquestionably denigrated the idea in this instance, but the editorial should be viewed in context. The *Times* published other articles favorable to the project, but its editorials were famous for a Mark Twain–brand of humor in which nothing was sacred. Some of their deliciously witty defenses of *Liberty* have been similarly taken as serious slander.[7] Most other New York newspapers unequivocally promoted the statue, even if they occasionally quibbled over details.[8]

Attuned to the importance of the press for mobilizing support, the American Committee designated Samuel P. Avery (cat. 386) to lead the subcommittee for Publicity and Printing. Since his appointment as Commissioner of the Fine Arts for the 1867 Paris World's Fair, Avery had become the most respected art dealer in America. His affable personality drew him into the city's prestigious social clubs, where he served willingly to advance the cultural climate of New York. As secretary of the Art Committee of the Union League, he was a founding trustee of the Metropolitan Museum of Art. His judgment on all matters artistic was a certified endorsement in the minds of his contemporaries, and his experience in publicizing his gallery had familiarized him with the process, by which he «was able to whisper in a great many good ears.»[9]

The Committee's affiliations with the New York press formed a tight network that guaranteed support. With the exception of the two Pulitzers' papers, the common bond was the Republican party, but less obvious ties were even stronger. Of the thirteen major newspapers, all of which favored the project, ten can be linked to the personalities surrounding the statue:

• COMMERCIAL ADVERTISER was edited by Parke Godwin, after he sold the EVENING POST in 1881.
• The COURRIER DES ÉTATS-UNIS, the city's largest French newspaper, predictably hailed the project in glowing terms. The owner, Leon Meunier, was on the New York French Committee until he retired to Paris in 1883. He was an official delegate to the inauguration.

- The DAILY GRAPHIC changed ownership frequently until it went out of business in 1889. The only copiously illustrated daily of its era, it took advantage of the visual possibilities of the subject. Beyond a decidedly Republican slant, no known connection between the paper and the Committee exists.
- The EVENING MAIL, previously owned by Clark Bell, on the original Committee, and the EXPRESS were consolidated in 1882 by Cyrus Field, who purchased them with Evarts' help. Field was a lifelong friend of Evarts, who expedited federal financing for Field's Trans-Atlantic Cable. Field was informally involved from the start, offering money and hospitality.
- The EVENING POST, made famous by William Cullen Bryant, was published after his death in 1878 by Parke Godwin. When the latter sold it in 1881, two of Evarts' long-standing friends, Carl Schurz and E. L. Godkin, became the editors.
- The HERALD and the EVENING TELEGRAM were both owned by James G. Bennett, Jr., whose residency in Paris predisposed him to the Franco-American Union. Bartholdi asked that he be sent a cable to express «hearty greetings, and to convey the regret of all that he should be absent» from the inaugural ceremonies.[10]
- The MERCANTILE JOURNAL was managed by Robert Allen, Jr., to whom Bartholdi wrote a note of thanks in April 1885.[11]
- MORNING JOURNAL was begun by Albert Pulitzer in 1882. Although he resented his brother's competition, he did not let his sibling rivalry affect *Liberty*. His coverage was limited but favorable.
- The SUN had been the organ of the Union League Club since Charles A. Dana acquired it through capital provided by the Republican aristocracy, notably Evarts, in the late sixties.
- The NEW YORK TIMES, despite its editorial irony, was unequivocally active in promoting the pedestal campaign. Many of the Committee members—Evarts, Spaulding, Jay, Godwin—had collaborated with the *Times* in breaking up the Tweed Ring, in which the strategy of the «crusade» was introduced to American journalism. George Jones, who was the largest stockholder from 1876, later served on the American Committee.

387
The Statue of Liberty as It Will Appear by the Time the Pedestal Is Finished
From *Life*
January 17, 1884

389
Sculptor Bartholdi—«Vell, Mees Boston, If Ze Gentlemen Vill Not Pay for Ze Pedestal Maybe You Vould Like Ze Statue»
From *The Daily Graphic*
October 6, 1882

391
Joseph Pulitzer
Leopold Horowitz
1902
reproduced in color
on p. 170

THE STATUE OF LIBERTY
AS IT WILL APPEAR BY THE TIME THE PEDESTAL IS FINISHED.

Les deux Jullien et Bartholdi,
C'est le distique qui le dit.

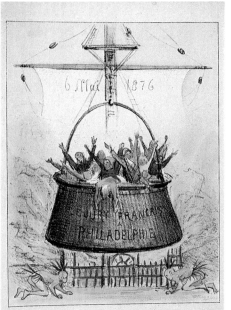

C'est le jury qui cuit dans la marmite,
Tant il fait chaud en Amérique.

330
*Passenger with Writing
Tablet*
Frédéric-Auguste Bartholdi
From *L'Album du Bord*
Paris: Bartholdi, Simonin,
Fouret et Cie., 1879

331
*Le Jury Français
Philadelphie*
Frédéric-Auguste Bartholdi
From *L'Album du Bord*
Paris: Bartholdi, Simonin,
Fouret et Cie., 1879

348
*The Statue of Liberty at
Night*
Edward Moran
1876

356
Parke Godwin
John White Alexander
1886

366
Liberty Enlightening the World
Root & Tinker
1883

372
Let the Advertising Agents Take Charge of the Bartholdi Business, and the Money Will Be Raised Without Delay
From *Puck*
April 8, 1885

391
Joseph Pulitzer
Leopold Horowitz
1902

395
Testimonial Torch
Presented by the *World* to Frédéric-Auguste Bartholdi
James Whitehouse, Tiffany and Co.
1885

428
Reception of the French
S.S. Isère in New York Bay
Edward Moran
1885

397
La Statue de la Liberté en phare
Frédéric-Auguste Bartholdi
n.d.

453
Judge's Compliments to Bartholdi and the Monument Committee
From *Judge*
October 30, 1886

455
Certificate of the Freedom of the City Presented to Bartholdi by the City of New York
October 28, 1886

- The TRIBUNE, upon Greeley's death in 1872, was controlled by Whitelaw Reid, a member of the American Committee after 1881.
- The WORLD was purchased in 1883 by Joseph Pulitzer, who took an immediate interest in the pedestal fund. A Democrat, removed from the social milieu of the American Committee, he gravitated to the cause out of a mixture of idealism and enlightened self-interest.

George W. Childs owned Philadelphia's two strongest papers, the *Public Ledger*, with the Drexels, and the *Press*, bought from Forney. Childs joined the Committee in 1881 and spoke at the Inaugural Banquet.

In addition to the dailies, *Harper's Weekly*, with the largest readership in America, unfailingly reported on the statue's progress. William G. Curtis, its editor-in-chief, was involved from the start and officially belonged to the Committee after 1881. *Frank Leslie's Illustrated Newspaper* took full advantage of the subject's visual appeal, but had no particular association with the Committee.[12]

With such connections, it is little wonder that Evarts acknowledged «the press has hitherto been very kind in its notices on different occasions of the pending project, and we have derived substantial support in our work from this source. . . .»[13] Nonetheless, things were not all roses with the press. As enthusiasm for the colossal lady grew, criticism over the financial dilemma waxed increasingly virulent. Sometimes the Committee was accused of indolence: Evarts had to admit that the press «stirred us up once or twice for not opening our subscription books . . . sooner.»[14] More often the public was censured for behaving «in a manner as churlish and contemptuous as the intention of the givers was delicate and generous.»[15] *Liberty* was portrayed as the victim of the indifference or ineptitude of others.

Satirists had a field day with the paucity of funds, frequently depicting *Liberty* as a decrepit hag (cat. 387), and the *Evening Telegram* (cat. 388) sanctimoniously touted its chronic reminders. The chance to take a pot shot at New York was irresistible to cities across the nation, which boasted how quickly THEY could raise the funds that New York seemed so reluctant to furnish.

Rumors that Boston aspired to lure *Liberty* away triggered a response in Manhattan (cat. 389). The *Times* retorted with mock outrage:

> Boston has probably again over-estimated her powers. This statue is dear to us, though we have never looked upon it, and no third-rate town is going to step in and take it from us. Philadelphia tried that in 1876, and failed. Let Boston be warned in time that she can't have our Liberty. . . . If we are to lose that statue it shall go to some worthier and more modest place—Painted Post . . . or Glover, Vt.[16]

This repartee reflects the battle of the presses more than the facts. If these skirmishes were not concocted by the journalists, they were certainly fueled by them. The defensive stance of the New York papers aggravated the accusatory remarks from other cities. And if the American Committee magnified these deliberately as a «scare» tactic, the manoeuvre backfired. The harangues did little to motivate the Americans and a great deal to irritate the French. The Parisian journals interpreted the slow progress of the pedestal fund as a lack of enthusiasm for the gift. The satirical *Charivari* lampooned the Yankees, declaring that the pier of Le Havre would be more worthy of the statue. Godwin's *Commercial Advertiser* retaliated, «while there is no harm in a French writer's amusing himself by flinging ink at an alleged American indifference to the fine arts, . . . he should remember that it took the French public five years to raise the sum required. . . .»[17] Bartholdi complained to Butler (cat. 390):

> . . . we have had trouble with newspapers that have reproduced gossip from America but have also a great many friends in the press and need only to rectify the misrepresentations.

> I avoid to do so in person, but have an answer given in an indirect manner when they are as silly as the article that appeared in the «Voltaire.»[18]

Despite Bartholdi's intrigues, the French press persisted in taking a hostile view of American reports. After the congressional denial, the American Committee's gloomy forecast of March 1885 incited new venom, such as the anonymous letter to the *Journal des Débats* insisting that the statue «must remain in France.»[19] The volleys between the presses continued until the arrival of the *Isère*, by which time the pedestal was assured through the *World* campaign.

Joseph Pulitzer (cat. 391) had been sympathetic to the pedestal's cause since he bought the *World* in 1883. His first attempt to aid the fund, ending in June of that year, was dubbed the «Great Phizzel»—neither his reputation nor his circulation could sustain it.[20] By 1885, however, when the fund was in dire straits, he had significantly aggrandized both. He masterminded a brilliant campaign that raised $100,000 in five months, while his readership soared.

Pulitzer had come to America from Budapest in 1863. After fighting for the Union, he settled in St. Louis to build his fortune through an astute blend of journalism and Democratic politics. When he acquired the *World*, he assumed the mantle of spokesman for the common man. He transformed the paper's staid intellectualism into a lively forum. In refining the technique of the crusade, he founded «new journalism.» His first triumphant venture put Grover Cleveland in the White House.

He believed sincerely in the people, and his faith in liberty undoubtedly attracted him to Bartholdi's statue. His genius lay in convincing the public that the responsibility to save the pedestal was truly theirs. He launched his campaign on March 16, 1885, with an editorial «meant for every reader of the WORLD»:

> *We must raise the money!* The WORLD is the people's paper, and it now appeals to the people to come forward. . . . the statue . . . was paid [for] by the workingmen, the tradesmen, the shop girls, the artisans—by all irrespective of class or condition. Let us respond in like manner. Let us not wait for the millionaires to give this money.

He gave the drive excitement, the pizzazz it had sorely lacked. It became a race to save the nation's honor before the statue arrived. His editorials flattered, cajoled, and exhorted the people, as they bombarded the millionaires with insults. This was the poor man's chance to one-up the rich. The *World* circulated a flyer (cat. 392) encouraging individuals to canvass and promised prizes for the largest amounts. After importuning dowagers, he attempted to get $250 each from one hundred affluent citizens for the last quarter of the goal.[21] Cartoons seasoned the texts. Under logos of «Liberty» or «Uncle Sam,» the *World* printed the names of contributors, followed by touching letters from widows, pensioners, immigrants, and tots, which filled the story with human interest. It is not unlikely that this correspondence was partly contrived. The letters sparkle with Pulitzer's ability to engage the reader's emotions, and they have the articulate flow and rhythmic range of the editorials.[22] Pulitzer was not the first to publish the names of subscribers, but he characteristically made such a listing popular rather than elitist. Letters from other papers throughout the country, congratulating the *World* on its initiative, soon occupied another column—furthering the national reputation of both the *World* and the statue. Pulitzer cleverly focused on the daily gains, rather than the amount lacking, until the drive topped the midway point (cat. 393).

The ingenious variety of tactics, a decided contrast to the dignified restraint of the official appeals, whetted public anticipation. What would happen next? Read the *World*. Circulation rose as fast as the Committee's coffers, and Pulitzer, justifiably proud of both achievements, alternated the statistics in boxes by the masthead. He eventually incorporated *Liberty* into the masthead, flanked by two globes.

The trend toward sensationalism in journalism, emerging in the early 1880s, was hastened by Pulitzer. Competition for readership among the growing number of alternatives accelerated the tendency to spice the news with innuendoes. The fierce struggle among newspapers spilled into their reporting on the pedestal fund. Pulitzer remonstrated Bennett, who had funded the expedition to the North Pole, that he would advertise the *Herald* better by paying for the pedestal outright than by spreading painted signs over an ice-cap.[23] The *Tribune* sniffed, «it's a cold day when the *World* doesn't get at least 13 cents for the Bartholdi Statue Pedestal.»[24] Even the *Times*, which had given $250 to the *World*'s fund, parodied the occasional snares that its competitor encountered, as in «Mr. Vandergilt's Check.»[25] Attacks between papers have often been misconstrued as opposition to *Liberty*.

Victory came on August 11 (cat. 394). Before it closed, the campaign collected $102,000 from more than 121,000 people. The elated Committee sent the publisher a parchment attesting to the *World*'s aid.[26] Among the ironies of the situation was that Pulitzer, the man of the people, now dined with the millionaires he had derided. He hobnobbed with the social and political establishment on a new footing that few situations could have supplied him. That he was well regarded and remained friendly with such men as Chauncey Depew, with whom he had previously feuded, attests to the substance of the man.

The *World* applied the campaign's surplus toward an elaborate testimonial (cat. 395) honoring Bartholdi, commissioned from Tiffany Studios. The hand and torch surmount a silver globe resting on an ornamented base of petrified wood. Bartholdi's profile floats above the figure of Columbia and a printing press. France and the principal rivers of the globe are outlined in gold. The inscriptions read:

> All Homage and Thanks to the Great Sculptor, Bartholdi.

> A Tribute From the New York WORLD and over 121,000 Americans to AUGUSTE BARTHOLDI and The Great Liberty-Loving People of France. 1886.

Because the sculptor cut short his stay after the inauguration, the trophy had to be sent on to him later by sea.[27] As one of the few tokens of gratitude that the sculptor received for *Liberty*, it was placed conspicuously in his studio.

Bartholdi entangled Pulitzer the following year in the web of his ambitions. The saga of the *Washington and Lafayette* epitomizes how the sculptor's obsession with making a great career exceeded his good judgment. In 1887 Bartholdi cabled to ask if the *World* would undertake a subscription for a monument of Washington and Lafayette, with their comrades around the base, as a gift of the Americans to the French. The ensemble would be inaugurated near the Opéra in 1889, the centennial of the French Revolution, at a cost of $37,000. Pulitzer refused, offering only his personal commitment of Fr. 40,000.[28] They struck a compromise; Pulitzer agreed to finance a single figure for Paris, which Bartholdi elevated to two for the price of one. Bartholdi finished the maquette in 1890, and the next year announced to Pulitzer that the completed bronze could be seen at Barbedienne.[29] Holding the flags of the two nations, Lafayette steps toward Washington, who clasps the hand of his new ally.

Not content to leave well enough alone, the sculptor determined to send the pair to the Columbian Exhibition in Chicago. When the city of Paris denied him permission to exhibit the bronze, on the grounds that that would interfere with its permanent installation, the irrepressible artist reasoned that a second copy would surely find its way into a Chicago park. A short-lived subscription was instigated by the Mayor of Chicago, but sharp criticism of the stolid portrait of Washington in contrast to the lively French officer seems to have deprived the Windy City of the monument.[30] To add insult to injury, the second bronze was back in Paris in storage before Pulitzer's gift was erected on the Place des États-Unis in 1895.[31] Finally «the good Salmon» freed his old friend «of that elephant,» persuading Charles B. Rouss to offer it to New York. It remains at 114th Street and Morningside Drive, where it was dedicated on April 19, 1900.[32]

Pulitzer considered embellishing the *World*'s new building, opened in 1890, with the artist's work.[33] Bartholdi kept a bond with him to the end, yearning on Christmas Day 1903 for a reunion, since he too was not well.[34] When the ailing journalist named his yacht *Liberty*, he was alluding less to his role in the statue's history than celebrating a lifelong principle.

Exploitation by the press seems an obvious tactic in the twentieth century, but the manipulation of public opinion through the printed page was only dawning in the second half of the nineteenth century. The press made its audience aware of the statue's existence, without awakening the patriotic conscience with regard to its fate. The Committee appreciated the press as a means of communication, without grasping the nature of a mass appeal. It took a man of Pulitzer's vision to bring the matter to the people. The very tone of his campaign broke with the circumspect format of his competitors: to animate public sentiments, he challenged their more passive traditions. In championing *Liberty*, he had concomitantly demonstrated the power of the press.

392

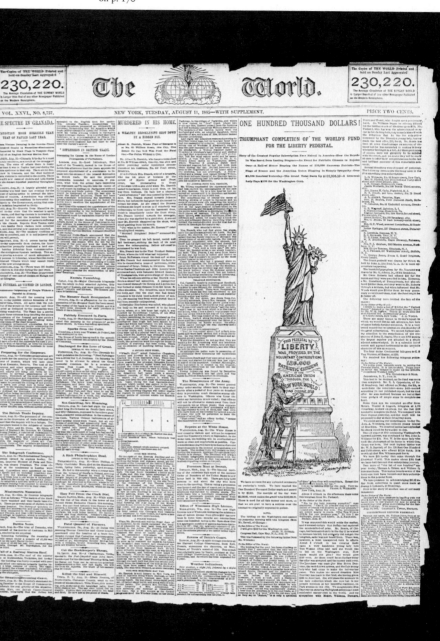

394

393

11.
Richard Morris Hunt and the Pedestal

Susan R. Stein

The activity surrounding the design and construction of *Liberty* herself, along with the fund-raising efforts on both sides of the Atlantic, tended to overshadow an ever-more-pressing concern: the nature of the pedestal on which *Liberty* would stand. This was no small matter, for it involved issues basic to the visual impact of the statue; because the choices made in creating the pedestal—including height and shape—would have an enormous and dramatic effect on the final appearance of the monument, the design would have to be exactly right.

No precedents existed to help in the search. Bartholdi himself was unsure about the exact design of the pedestal, and had received suggestions from Viollet-le-Duc and others. Responsibility for the selection of a designer for the pedestal fell to the American Committee, but little is known of the exact circumstances of their decision. It is known that after an informal competition involving a number of drawings (presumably by several architects), the Committee, on December 6, 1881, selected as its designer Richard Morris Hunt (1827–1895), one of the best-known American architects of the day. In addition to his portfolio of highly regarded commissions, Hunt boasted social and professional ties with several members of the Committee and a thorough knowledge of monumental architecture in France.

Hunt became the first American to study architecture in France when he enrolled in the *section d'architecture* at the École des Beaux-Arts in 1846.[1] His older brother, the painter William Morris Hunt, was enrolled in the atelier of Couture at the same time and thus Dick Hunt, as he was called, came to know both French architects and artists. At the École, Hunt chose the small and new atelier of Hector Martin Lefuel, probably because Lefuel and Samuel Darier, Hunt's tutor in Geneva, had studied together under J. N. Huyot. Lefuel had achieved some recognition in 1839 as the winner of the Grand Prix de Rome, and after Louis Visconti's death in 1855, Lefuel was chosen to carry out the remaining work on the additions to the Palais du Louvre. As an assistant to Lefuel, Hunt was the only American to play a part in the design of the Louvre.

Much as architects had done since the seventeenth century, Hunt began his studies by familiarizing himself with classical and Renaissance sources. Later he studied engineering and construction techniques in wood, iron, and stone, and then spent most of his time in Lefuel's atelier preparing designs according to the specifications described in *programmes* distributed at the École for competition in *concours*.

Generally a student was encouraged to conceive of a design as part of a larger whole, since the relationship between a building and its context, whether it be garden, street, or another structure, was essential to the success of the building. A site plan was often a requirement of the *programme*.

The buildings described in the *programmes* were essentially public in nature, because training at the École was intended to prepare students for the practice of architecture in France, a country whose dominant force in the 1840s and 1850s was government. Hunt witnessed the dramatic transformation of Paris from a medieval city to a modern and monumental capital. Consequently, at the École less attention was devoted to the kinds of projects that beginning architects in the United States were most often asked to design—houses and small commercial buildings—than to such projects as a ministry of justice, a theater, a national archives, and a large public winter garden, or conservatory.

After traveling throughout Europe and Egypt and completing his studies at the École, Hunt returned to the United States in 1856. His first commission, the Rossiter house in New York City, was dramatically different from the typical, comparatively simple houses underway in New York at the time. The lively Rossiter facade, in which Hunt consolidated into a single facade much of what he had absorbed at the École, was embellished with sculpture and elaborate stonework. His proposed southern gateways for New York's Central Park also presented a characteristically classical and French solution;[2] conceived in 1861 as grand entrances to the park designed by Frederick Law Olmsted and Calvert Vaux, the gateways incorporated terraces, fountains, plazas, and figural sculptures. These classical designs were rejected as too radical and «European» by Central Park's governing Board of Commissioners, who preferred the more popular, rustic Gothic solution. Thus, Hunt had prepared a monumental design emphasizing sculpture very early in his career.

Hunt achieved wide success in the 1860s and 1870s through a wide variety of accomplishments. He designed two pioneering apartment dwellings in New York; houses, chiefly in New York City and Newport, Rhode Island, a chic summer resort; commercial and office buildings including one of the earliest skyscrapers, the New York Tribune building (1873–76); a large hospital; many pedestals for sculpture; and a superb Neo-Grec structure, the Lenox Library (1870–77), which was as up to date as any building in France.

Hunt's practice of architecture was augmented by a lifelong interest in architectural education, and a generation of important architects such as Henry Van Brunt, George B. Post, and Frank Furness were schooled in his office, which functioned much like an atelier; his student William R. Ware, who established the first department of architecture in the United States at the Massachusetts Institute of Technology in 1868, acknowledged that Hunt's office was his model. Hunt also possessed the largest, and finest, architectural library of his day in America, which included, along with Serlio and Palladio, the latest English and French publications. Hunt was known for his generosity and, as his biographer has written, Hunt was an ambassador of art, bringing his wider experience and knowledge to the United States.[3]

Hunt also found time to keep in touch with the artistic community both in France and the United States. Painters such as Frederic E. Church, John LaFarge, Albert Bierstadt, Emanuel Leutze, and Winslow Homer rented space in the Hunt-designed Studio Building (1857–58), where the architect had his own office. Frequent visits to France enabled Hunt to stay current on art and architecture there, and his wife, Catharine Clinton Howland Hunt, later wrote of Hunt's enjoyment of dinner parties with the likes of Bonnard, Baudry, Gérôme, Bougereau, and Baron Haussmann.[4]

396
Sketch of Proposed Domed Pedestal for the Statue of Liberty
Richard Morris Hunt
January 4, 1882

397
La Statue de la Liberté en phare
Frédéric-Auguste Bartholdi
n.d.
also reproduced in color, p. 172

Given these impressive credentials, it is not surprising that the American Committee chose Hunt to design the pedestal of *Liberty*. If they required any additional persuasion, they may have received it from Levi P. Morton, the American Minister to France, who had engaged Hunt to design a ballroom for his Newport home in 1869 and a stable in New York in 1871. Hunt seems only to have met Bartholdi and perhaps did not know Laboulaye until after he received the commission for the pedestal. However, Hunt's client and family friend, the poet Thomas G. Appleton, had known Laboulaye in Paris years earlier.

Long a member of the Union League Club, an influential organization that had supported *Liberty* from the start, Hunt was also connected to prominent members of the American Committee. In 1869 and 1879 he drew up plans for the headquarters of the Union League Club, and in 1872 he prepared a design for the Drexel Bank on Wall Street for Joseph W. Drexel, chairman of the American Committee's executive committee. Henry G. Marquand, for whom Hunt had designed a large townhouse on Madison Avenue, a house in Newport, Rhode Island, and a chapel at Princeton University, was a member of the finance committee. Two years after his selection as pedestal architect, in 1884–86, Hunt designed Grey Towers in Milford, Pennsylvania, for James Pinchot, the American Committee's first treasurer.

Hunt's experience with the design of pedestals for sculpture was as instrumental in his selection as were his personal connections to the American Committee. He had an unequalled reputation, among American architects, for working with sculptors, especially in the design of bases for public monuments. Before 1880, Hunt's recognition as a designer of civic monuments stemmed largely from his association with the sculptor John Quincy Adams Ward (1830–1910).[5] Their collaboration began with a monument to Commodore Matthew Calbraith Perry (1868) in Newport, and came to include a total of thirteen works including the Seventh Regiment Memorial (1869), a monument to Major John Fulton Reynolds (1871), and the Yorktown Monument (1879), all of which were either completed or well under way by the time of Hunt's selection in 1881.

399
Sketch for the Pedestal of
the Statue of Liberty
Showing a Pre-Columbian
or Mexican Influence
Attributed to Frédéric-
Auguste Bartholdi
ca. January 1882

400
Sketch for the Pedestal of
the Statue of Liberty
Showing a Pre-Columbian
or Mexican Influence
Attributed to Frédéric-
Auguste Bartholdi
ca. January 1882

401
Sketch for the Pedestal of
the Statue of Liberty
Showing a Tower-Like
Scheme
Attributed to Frédéric-
Auguste Bartholdi
ca. January 1882

Finally, Hunt must have appeared to the informed members of the American Committee as an architect sympathetic to the use of sculpture in his buildings. Sculpture on building facades (for example, Visconti's and Lefuel's Palais du Louvre additions) and interiors was characteristic of Hunt's training and, later, of Hunt's own work. His drawing of the Rossiter house showed two sculptures adorning niches on the third story, and an early proposal for the New York Tribune building showed a seated Horace Greeley above the main entrance. Together with Hunt's proposed gateways for Central Park, such early ideas, although few were executed in their entirety, represented the first Beaux-Arts schemes in America and prefigured the City Beautiful movement of the late nineteenth century.

Even before his official selection, Hunt on November 25, 1881, requested a survey of Fort Wood on Bedloe's Island from the U.S. War Department in Washington, D.C. Hunt later contacted Bartholdi on January 4, 1882, enclosing a sketch (cat. 396) of a domed base surmounted by a short pedestal; this sketch probably resembled one that Hunt had shown to the American Committee. Bartholdi's written reply to Hunt's inquiry has been lost, but the drawings that he enclosed with it survive (cat. 399, 400, 401). The Pre-Columbian or Mexican-inspired forms suggested here, despite their symbolic connection to the New World, were eclipsed by the tower-like pedestal with loggia that both Hunt and Bartholdi came to prefer. Earlier, in a drawing thought to be dated about 1880, Bartholdi showed *Liberty* atop a Doric pedestal placed on a stepped pyramid (cat. 397, 398). The tower-like scheme (cat. 401) is the one that Hunt

pursued in subsequent designs, since a tall pedestal was considered necessary to dominate Fort Wood's existing star-shaped fortifications.

Three early undated sketches in one of Hunt's sketchbooks explore the tower-like theme (cat. 402, 403, 404). Cat. 402, the flattest of the three compositions, uses two large pilasters with only a minimal suggestion of a loggia. Without any loggia, cat. 403 is a three-storied square tower placed over a colonnaded base. In cat. 404, which relates directly to Bartholdi's sketch (cat. 401), Hunt has added rustication to Bartholdi's somewhat undefined idea, extended the loggia all the way across the top, and eliminated the stepped entrance at the base.

402
Early Study for the Pedestal
of the Statue of Liberty
Richard Morris Hunt
ca. 1882–83

403
Early Study for the Pedestal
of the Statue of Liberty
Richard Morris Hunt
ca. 1882–83

404
Early Study for the Pedestal
of the Statue of Liberty
Richard Morris Hunt
ca. 1882–83

The famous Pharos design (cat. 405), so-called from its resemblance to the ancient lighthouse at Alexandria, emerged from these drawings (cat. 401 and 404), and a model of it was ready for exhibition on July 22, 1883.[6] Hunt's first Pharos design, square in plan, tapered slowly toward the top. The heavily rusticated base with its unusual projecting stone pattern sat on a low Doric socle, or plinth, and the tripartite loggia, smaller than those in earlier drawings, was repeated on the pedestal's four faces. Straight stairs led up the center of each side. A variation of the Pharos scheme (cat. 406) shows the pedestal without stairs at the base and with two alternate schemes for the cornice.

Before the Pharos plan was finally rejected in 1884, a number of interesting variations were investigated (cat. 407, 408, 409), mainly in 1883 and early in 1884. An alternate version of the Pharos plan (cat. 407) eliminated the Doric frieze in the socle, widened the loggia, and added a parapeted cornice. A lithograph (see cat. 366) published by Root and Tinker in 1883 to raise funds for the pedestal is a hybrid of the two Pharos schemes.

The Pharos plan raised a storm of controversy. Nathan Appleton, Jr., a member of the Boston pedestal committee, complained that «the design of the pedestal is exactly what it ought not to be. I have before me a photograph of the Statue and pedestal published in Paris in 1875, in which the pedestal is not as high as the Statue. It seems to me entirely opposed to good art and architecture to have a colossal figure like that of Liberty perched upon a pedestal twice the height where it will be dwarfed and its effect greatly diminished.»[7]

In response to Appleton and other critics, Hunt probably argued to the Committee that the pedestal and statue were suitably proportioned. A revised Pharos version (cat. 408) was placed on a heavily rusticated base and compared in height and massing to a pier of the just-completed Brooklyn Bridge. With the height of the bridge's pier at 273 feet and the statue at 309 feet, it was obvious, at least to Hunt, that the pedestal was not too high. The Statue of Liberty, many of its supporters thought, must dominate the Brooklyn Bridge, for the statue, after all, represented Liberty while the Brooklyn Bridge was simply a great engineering feat.

Nevertheless, Hunt prepared three quite different but related schemes at about this time, one of which demonstrated a close link with the earlier Pharos plans. Some radically different pedestal alternatives were proposed before the height of the pedestal was reduced; one involved the use of a cylindrical, circular pedestal. In another drawing a cylindrical pedestal, complete with parapet, was placed on a rusticated base (cat. 409). Here, the 321-foot statue on its cylindrical base has been pierced by a tier of round openings over three tiers of medieval-like slitted windows set in recessed bays. Cat. 410 also incorporates a rusticated base and slitted windows, but is sleeker, lacking a parapet. The cylindrical idea, lacking the strength of the Pharos concept, was dropped.

405
The First Pharos Proposal
Richard Morris Hunt
August 16, 1883

406
Variant of the First Pharos
Scheme, Showing Two
Alternate Treatments for
the Frieze
Richard Morris Hunt
1883

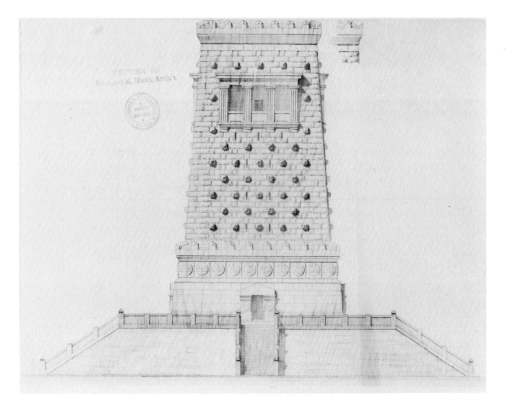

409
A Variation on the
Rounded Tower Theme
Richard Morris Hunt
1883

410
A Variation on the
Rounded Tower Theme
Richard Morris Hunt
1883

407
Model of the Revised
Pharos Scheme
Richard Morris Hunt
1883

408
Revised Version of the
Second Pharos Scheme,
Compared to a Pier of the
Brooklyn Bridge
The Office of Richard
Morris Hunt, probably
drawn by Henry Ogden
Avery
1883

Henry Ogden Avery, a draughtsman in Hunt's New York office through most of 1883 (and son of Samuel Avery), worked on many different, apparently tangential alternatives, most of which were not pursued beyond the stage of early studies.[8] One study (cat. 411) divided the support for the sculpture into two distinct parts, a low classical pedestal placed atop a stepped pyramid, but Avery's pyramidal base was penetrated by a straight run of stairs to the pedestal. The pedestal itself had a powerful profile but lacked the embellishment characteristic of Hunt's designs.

Some of Avery's designs were very distinctive (cat. 412a–b, 413a–b). Cat. 412a–b shows a smoothly rusticated base, an ornate ironwork parapet, and a large eagle bearing

the inscription «Independence»; although the U.S. Centennial had long since passed, Avery (perhaps following Hunt's instructions) here again related *Liberty* to the 1876 celebration, as Laboulaye had originally intended. Or perhaps *Liberty*'s meaning had already begun to be transformed by America to suit her own needs, in this case a celebration of «independence.» In cat. 413a the meaning of *Liberty* and her pedestal have been further altered; *Liberty* celebrates the American Centennial with a sculpted eagle on a stepped tower instead of a stepped pyramid. A smaller tower (cat. 413b), echoing the Centennial, possesses smooth stonework and a more sizable entrance at the base.

Neither these designs nor Hunt's powerful Pharos and its variations, the cylinder and the stepped pyramid, were accepted. The Committee demanded that the height of the

a

b

411
Proposal for the Pedestal
Showing a Stepped
Pyramid Similar to
Bartholdi's 1880 Design
Henry Ogden Avery
1883

412a–b
Sketches for the Pedestal
Demonstrating a
Connection with the
Celebration of the U.S.
Centennial and American
Independence
Henry Ogden Avery
1883

pedestal be reduced. The concern that *Liberty* would be overwhelmed by her pedestal persisted, but what probably foiled Hunt's design was its anticipated cost. The Committee members thought that if the height of the pedestal were reduced, the cost would also be reduced; in fact, the new, shorter pedestal was to cost at least as much as the projected Pharos.

Hunt had to rework the entire design in order to shorten the pedestal, and the result was far different from the powerful Pharos scheme. An apparently early and obviously problematic attempt at the reduced pedestal, seen in cat. 414, retains the Doric socle and projecting rustication of the Pharos plan; the design was so squat and unsatisfactory, however, that it must have been rejected speedily. What was Hunt to do?

a

b

413a–b
Sketches for the Pedestal
Demonstrating a
Connection with the
Celebration of the U.S.
Centennial and American
Independence
Henry Ogden Avery
1883

414
Model for the Greatly
Reduced Pedestal
Richard Morris Hunt
1884

415
Sketch for an
Unornamented Pedestal on
a Doric-Order Socle
Richard Morris Hunt
July 1884

416
Winning Design for the
Pedestal of the Statue of
Liberty
Richard Morris Hunt
July 1884

417
Sketch for the Pedestal
Resembling the First
Pharos Scheme in Rough
Rustication but Lacking Its
Projecting Stonework
Richard Morris Hunt
July 1884

415

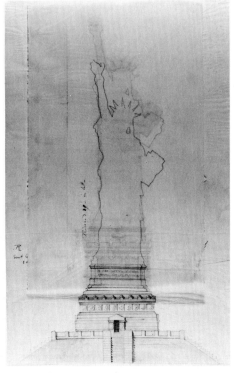

416

417

By the end of July 1884, Hunt and his office had prepared three closely related alternate designs. These pencil drawings on tracing paper (cat. 415, 416, 417), affixed to one another for easy comparison, were submitted to the Committee on July 31, 1884. One of these designs became the final choice. The shortest, least interesting, and simplest of the three (cat. 415) placed the sculpture on an unornamented pedestal sitting upon a Doric-order socle, which rests on a very low-pitched, stepped pyramid. The resulting composition's lack of grandeur was perhaps the reason for its quick rejection by the Committee.

The choice between the remaining two designs, however, presented a challenge because they were so similar. One (cat. 416) resembled the first Pharos scheme (see cat. 405) in its rough rustication but lacked the projecting stonework of the first scheme. Not quite as tall as the winning design, it also featured a pedestal with a metope directly beneath *Liberty*'s feet.

The winning design (cat. 417, 418), the tallest and most distinguished of the three late designs, perfectly suited *Liberty*. The pedestal was at once bold and noble, classical and straightforward. The somewhat rough overall stonework contrasted with the smooth-finished stone of the loggia, socle, and parapet. The pedestal and statue sat on a smooth-sided pyramid with steps, much as Bartholdi had suggested in 1880. Hunt had persistently included the Doric socle virtually throughout the design process, and in the finished pedestal the socle proved to be one of the most successful elements.[9]

Erection of the pedestal proceeded slowly, in part owing to the stonemasons' difficulties in carrying out the complex work. On May 16, 1886, five months before the dedication ceremony, the nearly completed pedestal awaited the installation of *Liberty* and her armature. Sometime before the dedication on October 28, 1886, Hunt received his one thousand dollar fee, which he contributed to the fund to erect *Liberty*.[10]

Hunt's role as architect of the pedestal had truly made the Statue of Liberty a cooperative artistic venture between France and the United States. Hunt, subsequently named a chevalier in the French Legion of Honor, had been well served by his training in France. No other American architect could have created a pedestal so attuned to the Beaux-Arts classicism that harmonized with Bartholdi's allegory.

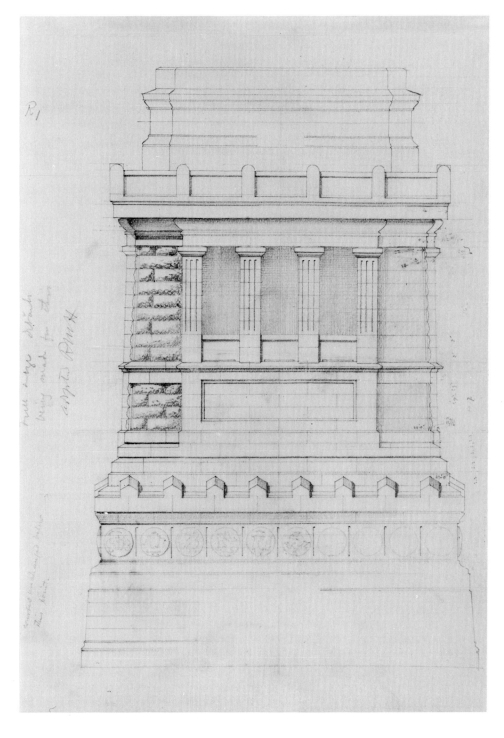

Charles Pomeroy Stone (cat. 419) brought to the position of chief engineer the multiple skills of his many careers. An 1845 graduate of West Point, he spent a decade in the Army. He left to explore commercial ventures in Mexico, and was a banker in California on the eve of the Civil War. Shortly after he entered the Union Army as a colonel, Congress unjustly blamed him for the defeat of Ball's Bluff. Despite the staunch support of his fellow officers, he found his military career blighted. Resigning his commission, he became the engineer for a Virginia mining company. Upon General Sherman's recommendation, Ismail Pasha summoned Stone to Egypt in 1870. As the Khedive's chief of staff, he was decorated for his role in modernizing the Egyptian Army.

When Stone returned to the United States in 1883, Sherman again intervened on his behalf, convincing his old friend Pinchot that Stone, «a man of stainless character,» was «the very man» to oversee the work on Bedloe's Island.[1] He added that Stone «attaches little importance to the matter of pay—what he now needs most is the recognition of such men as compose your committee. But in truth and fact you will do a wise thing in putting him in charge. . . .»[2] To Stone the appointment represented a public refutation of the allegations that had haunted him for twenty years.

Sherman's faith was merited; Stone proved himself a second time in meeting the challenges of combining the components of Bartholdi, Eiffel, and Hunt in the definitive construction.[3] Faced with unexpected difficulties, chronic shortages of funds, and false accusations from the press, he persisted in his duties. Stone would later boast that not one man was killed on the job, in contrast to the twenty-seven men he claimed lost their lives in building the Brooklyn Bridge, completed just as he began the foundation on Bedloe's Island.[4]

Brigadier-General Charles P. Stone
Frontispiece from Pierre Crabites, *Americans in the Egyptian Army*
London: George Routledge and Sons, Ltd., 1938

The pedestal would rest on a foundation platform built in the center of the fort. From the parade level within the walls, a 15-foot-deep pit was excavated.[5] General Stone broke ground in mid-April 1883 to discover a honeycomb of hidden masonry that was to cause costly delays. Laborious as the removal of these prior defenses proved, the pedestal ultimately gained soundness from being nestled into this massive substructure.

The foundation mass was begun on October 9, 1883, as the statue in Paris neared completion.[6] Stone designed a truncated, stepped pyramid in concrete (cat. 420);[7] the wooden forms which held the shape until the concrete hardened were still in place when this photograph was taken, shortly after the foundation was completed on May 17, 1884. Two arched passageways at parade level (the concrete extends below another 15 feet) intersect in the middle of the mass, where a 10-foot-square shaft rises to the top, to be continued by the shaft of the pedestal, destined to house the elevator.

12.
Reassembly on Bedloe's Island

June Hargrove

An «army» of Italian workmen, who lived on the island, labored through the winter, landing materials, building the wooden forms, and pouring the concrete.[8] Railroad cars on high wooden trestles, which extended into the water, hauled supplies to the construction site.

The total height of the foundation was almost 53 feet, tapering from 91 square feet to 67 square feet, making it the world's largest solid mass of above-ground concrete.[9] The top of the pyramid, which rose 22 feet above the parapets (cat. 421), was originally to be joined to the walls of the fort by a series of arches, which when covered with sod would hide the entire foundation with an «artistic touch of green» (cat. 422).[10] The final cost, $93,830.94, was almost double the estimate, due to the unforeseen expense of the excavation.[11]

Pouring rain dampened the spectators, but not the grandeur of the Masonic rites at the laying of the cornerstone (cat. 423). A crowd of over five hundred gathered near where a 6-ton granite block hung, ready to drop into position with a touch (cat. 424).[12] Beneath its destined resting place was deposited a copper box, containing commemorative medals and parchments. Grand Master Brodie, wearing his ceremonial apron (cat. 425), spread the mortar with his silver trowel (cat. 426), and the stone was solemnly lowered into position. The Masonic officers then tested the stone with their jewels, the symbolic instruments of their time-honored craft. The Deputy Grand Master judged the stone «by the square of virtue.» The Senior Grand Warden assured it was level, «to remind us of equality,» followed by another, who verified it to be plumb, teaching «rectitude of conduct.» Three blows of the gavel declared the stone duly laid. As the Masonic brethren replied with the traditional «so mote it be,» the stone was consecrated with the corn of nourishment, signifying plenty; the wine of refreshment, for joy and gladness; and the oil of joy, for peace.

420
Foundation Mass of the Pedestal
ca. 1884

421
View of the Foundation Mass from the Trestle
1884

The Free Masons originated with «operative» masonry, that is, the actual craft, and although the organization has become «speculative,» it continues through the laying of cornerstones, perpetuating a tradition that dates from antiquity. Ever since George Washington laid the cornerstone of the Capitol with Masonic rites, the ceremony has been customary for public edifices in the United States. The ritual on Bedloe's Island, as the Grand Master explained, had particular relevance for the brotherhood:

No institution has done more to promote liberty and to free men from the trammels and chains of ignorance and tyranny than freemasonry, and we as a fraternity take an honest pride in depositing the corner-stone of the pedestal of the statue of «Liberty Enlightening the World.» And which we pray God may deserve to prosper by becoming a beacon light of liberty to all men and promoting harmony and brotherly love throughout the world till time shall be no more. Amen.[13]

Laying the cornerstone initiated actual construction of the pedestal. Bids had gone out in the spring, but they had all been rejected as prohibitive. General Stone's proposal to economize by using concrete faced with granite, instead of a solid masonry core, was accepted. David H. King, Jr., a wealthy contractor, offered to build the pedestal for $132,500, munificently promising to return any penny of profit to the Committee.[14]

The granite at Leete's Island Quarry combined the desired color and strength. Every stone was individually cut because it had its own pattern and was numbered to indicate its placement.[15]

Completion of the pedestal was predicted for October, but the treasury's coffers were too bare for work to progress rapidly. In September, Butler wrote Jay that they were proceeding «as if [they had] money in hand,» but the following month the Committee was notified that work would soon be suspended.[16] The island was silent, the site abandoned during the winter, while the Committee banked on the ill-fated congressional appropriation. Hunt was asked to

lower the height to save money. The drastically revised design, aesthetically an improvement, was even more expensive. Only after the World's campaign augured well did construction resume, and the granite facing reached the level of the stringcourse (cat. 427) just in time to save face with the arrival of the Isère.

While the pedestal's fate hung fire, Bartholdi nervously proceeded to dismantle the statue in Paris and to crate it for its voyage. Each of the 214 wooden cases was numbered and labeled to guide the reinstallation. On May 1, 1885, the first of seventy railroad cars carrying Liberty pulled onto the quay in Rouen, where the crates were transferred to the French naval transport, the frigate Isère. The boxes ranged from 150 pounds to 3 tons, totaling over 150 tons of dead weight; complicated by the varied dimensions of the cases, the loading took a fortnight.[17] Commander Lespinasse de Saune set sail on the morning of May 21, accompanied by the Bartholdis, the Gagets, and Richard Butler, who all debarked at the coast.[18]

422

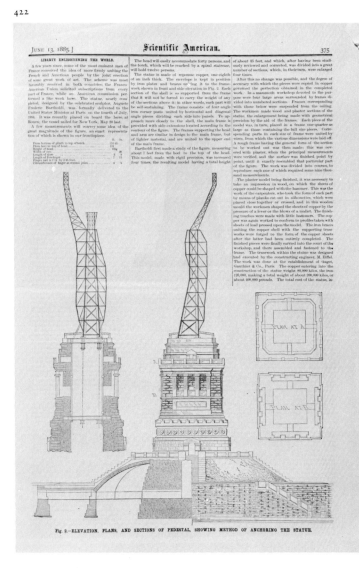

423

422
*Elevation, Plans, and
Sections of Pedestal,
Showing Method of
Anchoring the Statue*
From *Scientific American*
June 13, 1885

423
*Platform for Cornerstone
Ceremony, August 5, 1884*
Pach Brothers
1884

The *Isère* was expected on June 10, but after encountering heavy seas and rough weather, she dropped anchor off Sandy Hook a week later. The next day, she was joined at Gravesend by Rear Admiral Lacombe on the *Flore*, flagship of the French North Atlantic Squadron, which came up from the French Antilles to lend magnitude to the occasion.[19]

The splendor of the official reception of the *Isère* (cat. 428), despite its hasty organization, surpassed all expectations. On the morning of June 19, a deputation headed by Evarts and Mayor Grace boarded the *Atlantic*, the pride of the Union Ferryboats, to greet the French. General Stone, «despondent» over the apparent lack of interest, grew «exultant» at finding the bay filled with ships. American naval vessels, large excursion boats, millionaires' yachts, steam launches, tugs, and no end of small craft «seemed to be pouring out in the wake of the *Atlantic*.»[20]

The entourage reached the *Isère* about 10 A.M. The only hitch was that the gangplank from the *Atlantic* was too low to reach the *Isère*. In desperation, a board was thrown across from the top deck, forcing the honored dignitaries to scramble unceremoniously onto the French vessel. After the requisite champagne toasts of welcome, Commander de Saune transferred responsibility for his unusual cargo to the American Committee.[21] Evarts, Stone, de Bebian, and members of the Chamber of Commerce were privileged to remain on the *Isère* as the U.S.S. *Dispatch* sounded the departure for Bedloe's Island.

The impressive flotilla (cat. 429) began with the *Dispatch*, followed by the *Omaha*, the *Powhatan*, and the *Flore*. The *Isère*, flanked by the *Patrol* and the *Atlantic*, led the escorting fleet. Over one hundred ships gracefully conducted the statue to its new home. The booming cannonades of the forts along the banks were returned with 18-gun salvos from the French frigate. «For the next hour, during which the fleet sailed up the harbor, there was a constant din of steam whistles, and every few minutes or so the roar of salutes.» When they reached the

426
Ceremonial Trowel of
Grand Master Brodie
1884

424

427

424
Placing the Cornerstone,
August 5, 1884
From *Harper's Weekly*
August 16, 1884

427
Pedestal for Bartholdi's
Statue of Liberty on
Bedloe's Island, New York
Harbor
W. P. Snyder
From *Harper's Weekly*
June 6, 1885

428
Reception of the French
S.S. Isère in New York Bay
Edward Moran
1885
reproduced in color
on p. 171

island, the tumult was «something terrific» (cat. 430).[22] Spectators crowded onto the island to catch a glimpse of the marine panoply (cat. 431).[23]

With the *Isère* safely and ceremoniously anchored, the French officers joined their hosts for a land parade from the Battery to City Hall (cat. 432). The Tricolor and the Stars and Stripes hung in profusion, and bunting lined the route, above a crowd so dense that pedestrians were compelled to walk in the roadway. Counting the military escort, over two thousand people proceeded to City Hall for a reception.[24] The luncheon table was decorated with elaborate sugar confections, including a 2-foot model of the *Isère*, replete with sailors and rigging.

Even more sumptuous was the banquet at Delmonico's, «almost as colossal in its proportions as the statue . . . itself,» offered by the Chamber of Commerce on June 24.[25] On a humorous note, Evarts congratulated Saune for «keeping liberty under the hatches,» a task few nations would dare.[26] The Minister of Foreign Affairs, de Freycinet, promptly communicated his government's «gratitude for these demonstrations of friendship which respond so well to the sentiments of understanding and cordiality that unify the two nations.»[27]

During the week of festivities, the crates were transferred from the *Isère* to lighters, which brought them to the trestle, where they were lifted by a crane to the tramway. Soon the grounds of the fort became «highly picturesque, for the crates are of every

conceivable size, and the structural fragments of iron are each painted a bright vermillion» (cat. 433).[28]

While fortune smiled on the Committee, the summer found Stone under the censure of the press. The *Evening Telegram* published in June a rather embarrassing, chauvinistic interview concerning the American Committee's alleged annoyance with the technical challenges that Stone was left to resolve, namely the anchoring system and the potential galvanic reaction. In the interview, the Americans expressed concern about the stability of the torch arm, apparently aware of modifications during assemblage in Paris. The newspaper asserted that Drexel believed that «the French were getting all the credit, that the Americans were doing much the greater part of the work and making far greater outlay.» Stone purportedly had to

429
*Arrival of the Isère
Carrying the Statue into
New York Harbor*
1885

431
*Arrival of the French
Transport Steamer «Isère,»
with the Bartholdi Statue
on Board, at the Base of
the Pedestal, Bedloe's
Island, Friday, June 19th—
The Salute of Welcome by
the Fleet*
From *Frank Leslie's
Illustrated Newspaper*
June 27, 1885

432
*Arrivée à New York de
l'Isère, Portant à son bord
la Statue de La Liberté par
Bartholdi*
H. A. Ogden
From *Le Monde Illustré*
June 27, 1885

434
Project for the Monument
to the Memory of Lafayette
and American
Independence
Frédéric-Auguste Bartholdi
n.d.

compensate for «the blundering of Bartholdi,» of whom the engineer spoke slightingly. Drexel and Stone denied that the interview even took place, while the reporter swore the piece was accurate.[29]

Charges of mishandling expenses made Stone further indignant: «all this is the work of a disconsolate contractor who got one contract but didn't get another.»[30] Finally, the general demanded action on his behalf from the Committee, depending on the support of Pinchot: «I would consider it a personal favor if you would kindly be present. I am weary of being made the newspaper scapegoat of the pedestal and the committee.»[31]

Meanwhile Bartholdi spent his summer wavering about another trip to the United States. He was eager to consolidate the commission for a monument of Lafayette for Washington, D.C. The *Lafayette* was truly a sorry affair, in which Bartholdi received shabby treatment; however, it was characteristic of the man that his deception was the greater for his earlier overconfidence. Although legislation for a *Lafayette* competition was passed on March 3, 1885, Bartholdi somehow imagined that the commission was to be offered outright to him:

> The plans of the committee have changed in character; after having begun by talking of giving me the work to do, it appears that (unknown to me) the committee has organized a competition. . . . I first thought of being courteous in going to the U.S., now my trip would have all the appearance of an intrigue which is repugnant to me.[32]

By October, he rationalized his trip on the basis of «a great desire to see how the work is getting on and to settle with Genl. Stone about the erection of the statue.» More to the point, he added how willing he would be to explain his model of the *Lafayette* (cat. 434) should that committee «wish to invite me to do so.»[33] Among those waiting to greet the sculptor at the pier on November 4 was his friend Anthony Pollock, representing the *Lafayette* committee. Pollock hosted his subsequent visit to Washington to present the two models for the proposed monument. Since it was commonly understood that Secretary of War Endicott had «virtually decided upon one of the Bartholdi models,» Bartholdi was understandably furious when the extended competition resulted in a commission to his compatriots Falguiere and Mercie.[34]

To Richard M. Hunt Esq.
Architect in Chief.

Construction of the
Pedestal of the Statue of Liberty
"The last position of the Derricks"
Photographed March 6. 1886

Engineer in Chief

Otherwise, at Bartholdi's request the stay was more private than his previous visits. With the fate of his «big daughter» secure, the artist confined his socializing to those organizations and individuals who had helped him, reciprocating with his own dinner party before he sailed again on November 25.

By March 1886 forty of the forty-six courses of granite were in place (cat. 435), and the following month the pedestal was at last ready for the statue. Eiffel had solved the structural challenges of the statue, leaving the Americans to attach his system to the pedestal. With nearly 4,000 square feet of surface exposed to the wind, the elemental stresses on the structure would be massive.[35] Stone devised an ingenious system (cat. 436) into which the four corner-posts of Eiffel's pylon were set. Horizontal pairs of steel I-beams, at right angles, were embedded into the concrete walls of the pedestal shaft, 60 feet apart. They were joined by steel girders, set against the four walls, which gain tensile strength from them, while they reinforce the anchoring system. The statue's main frame was bolted into the upper cross-yoke.[36] The final solution was so solid that it was claimed that it would be necessary «to upturn the island itself before the pedestal could be unseated.»[37]

Misunderstanding between the engineer and contractor clouded the site, and Stone fretted that «Mr. King has undertaken something in setting up the statue that he knows nothing about.»[38] Despite his fears, assembling the pylon was under way by May (cat. 437), and the internal frame, with its secondary extensions, conforming more to the statue's silhouette, was completed in August (cat. 438).

The copper sheets had been under preparation during the year (cat. 439); portions damaged in transit were restored.[39] Some of the pieces were riveted together into larger sections and refinished while still on the ground. The island was strewn with a surreal array of *Liberty*'s anatomy. Her austere countenance hung aloof in a wooden frame (cat. 440), exposing the iron armature bars that reinforced the thin copper skins (cat. 441) and the perforated edges where the rivets would join the seams. Her feet stood by a parapet (cat. 442) to the great amusement of the press, who could not resist pleasantries on the «titanic tootsies.»

437
The Great Statue
From *The Daily Graphic*
May 22, 1886

438
*Interior Armature
Completed*
July 1886

439
*The Statue of Liberty. The
Progress of the Work on
the Great Statue*
From *The Daily Graphic*
September 2, 1885

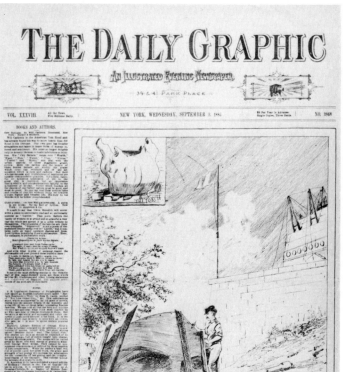

440
View of the Face of the
Statue of Liberty Hung in
Wooden Frame
ca. 1885–86

441
Interior View of the Face
Hung in Wooden Frame
ca. 1885–86

442
Toes and Torch of the
Statue near the Parapets
ca. 1885–86

As the skeleton advanced, two rivets, christened «Bartholdi» and «Pulitzer,» attached the first plate of the copper skin to the frame. Each piece was hoisted in a wooden box to the top of the pedestal, then wrestled into position. Effaced or inaccurate numbering meant several hauls to find the correct piece; bent edges had to be smoothed out to align perfectly with neighbors.[40]

The shell was assembled in horizontal stages (cat. 443). Scaffolding such as had served in Paris was not feasible in the final erection because of the awkward size of the base, so workers hung from the armature itself. Their ordeal of assembling a 200-ton jigsaw puzzle was thus compounded by being suspended mid-air. By early October, the bizarre specter of a headless *Liberty* towered over the harbor (cat. 444):

> Workmen are at present moving like industrious ants over the classic draperies and uplifted arm of the mighty figure. They remind one of the Lilliputians swarming over Gulliver in the picturebooks; or, if they will pardon the comparison, like New Jersey mosquitoes attacking a Summer boarder.[41]

Meanwhile, no practical consideration had been given as to how *Liberty* was literally to «enlighten» the world. Early engravings show beams of light, like a halo, echoing the rays of her crown (see cat. 199). A later description claimed that «a great light will be placed in the torch, and the pointed diadem, encircling the head, will be studded with electric lights.»[42]

As the dedication rapidly approached, no provision for the lighting had yet been made. The congressional allocation did not provide sufficient funds to cover the installation of a system, and the American Committee began to fear that another campaign would be necessary to light the statue.

443
View at Top of Pedestal,
Showing the Shell and
Bracing
From *Scientific American*
August 14, 1886

444
[*Last Stage of Mounting*
Copper to the Armature]
Unidentified German-
American newspaper
October 1886

445
*Le Flambeau électrique de
la statue de «La Liberté» à
New-York*
From *L'Illustration*
October 29, 1887

446
*Now Liberty Wants to Be
En-light-ened. And the
Whole World Knows It*
Thomas Nast
From *Harper's Weekly*
November 20, 1886

447
*Statue before Mounting of
the Torch*
October 1886

448
*The Great Statue—
Sketches of the Interior*
From *The Daily Graphic*
October 18, 1886

449
*Completing the Bartholdi
Statue of Liberty—View of
the Interior of the Upper
Portion of the Statue*
From *Frank Leslie's
Illustrated Newspaper*
October 23, 1886

LE FLAMBEAU ÉLECTRIQUE DE LA STATUE DE « LA LIBERTÉ »
A NEW-YORK

NOW LIBERTY WANTS TO BE EN-**LIGHT**-ENED.
AND THE WHOLE WORLD KNOWS IT.

Sometime in September, Edward Goff, President of the American Electric Manufacturing Company, volunteered to furnish the electrical plant and system, a gift worth about $7,000. The design of the system was then turned over to Lt. John Millis, in the name of the Light-House Board. The intention was to place arc lamps with reflectors in the balcony around the flame and incandescent lamps in the diadem. Further arc lamps were to be suspended at the corners of the pedestal to illuminate the statue and base.[43]

In mid-October, Millis informed the Committee that the torch could be more effectively lit from within. He ordered two staggered rows of circular holes to be cut around the base of the torch and covered with glass.[44] The solution proved a disaster, not only ineffective as a beacon for all but migrating birds (cat. 445), but also causing accelerated deterioration of the statue that would require future restorations. Objections to Millis' mutilation of the statue were raised before work was completed.[45] According to the *World*, the result resembled a glowworm; Bartholdi recommended gilding the statue to reflect the light.[46] The problems extended into November since no one could agree as to which authority was to assume the costs of operating the electric plant (cat. 446), but finally President Cleveland directed the Light-House Board to maintain it as a beacon.[47]

The torch was the last major portion to be placed (cat. 447). On Saturday, October 23, the last plate of copper, the sole of the right foot, was secured; it had been held aside to allow the workmen access to the interior and to provide some natural light for the dark interior.[48] Ultimately three hundred thousand rivets, binding the copper sheets together, had been discretely hammered into place so as not to disfigure the unified surface. Frederick Law Olmsted supervised the landscaping, the only visual evidence of which until spring would be the clearance of the debris.[49]

To expedite the completion of the interior, a forge (cat. 448) was manned inside the figure. Barely in time for the dedication, workers were bolting the last of the thousands of flexible rods on the interior (cat. 449), joining the strapwork braces to the secondary trusswork. *Liberty* was ready.

While the iron skeleton was dressed in its copper garments, letters sailed between France and America to work out plans for the unveiling. The fiasco in Congress precluded some of the finishing touches, but the ceremony itself would not be lackluster. When the anniversary of the Treaty of Versailles, September 3, proved unrealistic, the date of October 28 was fixed.

Just in time for the official invitation to read «Inauguration by the President of the United States» (cat. 450), Grover Cleveland (cat. 451) deigned to accept the Committee's invitation. Cleveland had never opposed the statue, but his meticulous definition of the government's proper role in its erection had tested the Committee's endurance more than once. His appointment of Gen. J. M. Schofield as his «representative» for the ceremonies had implied his absence. His subsequent decision to participate elevated the event to one of national stature.

Ink flowed thick over the ticklish question of official invitations. Bartholdi began prodding in April, because «we must not forget that Diplomatic people are very slow moving.»[1] President Cleveland refused to authorize invitations from the government, using the familiar excuse of «unconstitutionality,» but finally allowed them to be issued by the American minister in the name of the Committee.[2] After much deliberation, seventeen guests were selected to represent the Franco-American Union, the French government, commerce, and the press.[3] The name of Ferdinand de Lesseps was as familiar to Americans as Bartholdi's. Despite the U.S. government's distrust over the Panama Canal, Lesseps charmed most Americans with his vivacity and awed them with his entrepreneurial daring. The Canal had yet to go sour, and Lesseps, although he was quite short, was dubbed «le grand français» in the press. His globe-trotting teenage daughter, «Tototte,» accompanied him to America.

In anticipation of his stay, Bartholdi made numerous tiny watercolors of his statue, presumably to give to friends and admirers as personal souvenirs of his *Liberty*, but on October 25, when the *Bretagne* steamed past bearing the French delegation, *Liberty*'s

13.
Unveiling the Colossus

June Hargrove

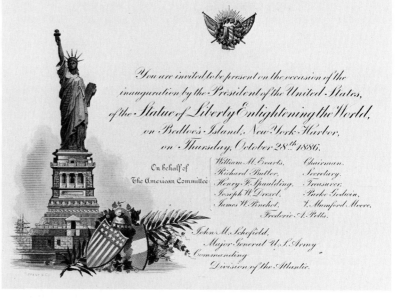

450
Invitation to the Statue's
Inauguration
October 28, 1886

silhouette was hardly perceptible in the morning mist.[4] The American Committee's intention to whisk the French from Quarantine earlier went awry, and the gaily rigged yacht *Tillie* ended up chasing the ocean liner across the bay to the pier.

Rays of sunshine broke through the clouds to illuminate the joyous reunions on the quay, and the festive party set off immediately to visit Bedloe's Island. The canvas veil that masked *Liberty*'s face (cat. 452) was lifted in honor of Bartholdi's arrival. The sculptor found the walls of the fort a trifle high, a problem easily remedied with graded earth, but he refused to comment on the controversial lighting. Overall, he was immensely pleased. «The dream of my life is accomplished. In this . . ., I see the symbol of unity and friendship between two nations—two great republics.»[5]

The guests were housed at the luxurious Hoffman House, the type of American hotel that Bartholdi had marveled at in 1871. The artist found himself lionized like a war hero—a comparison he would have found singularly fitting. While the sculptor basked in the limelight, all of the principals (cat. 453) were extolled across the continent.

Official festivities commenced the following evening at the Academy of Music, where Coudert presided over the public reception in the visitors' honor offered by the French Committee.[6] On Wednesday, the 27th, Mayor Grace presented Bartholdi with the Freedom of the City (cat. 454, 455), on behalf of New Yorkers, in «gratitude to the . . . creator of the statue which will forever remain a splendid ornament of their metropolis.»[7] A hasty visit to the Produce Exchange left little time to rest before the formal gathering at the Union League Club.

It was deemed only appropriate that the Club, which had remained faithful throughout *Liberty*'s trials, should have the honor of receiving the distinguished French visitors on the eve of the inauguration. Evarts, putting aside his personal aversion, gallantly escorted Lesseps on his arm through the prestigious throng. In the center of the sumptuous table decor stood a reduction of the statue, holding aloft her electrified torch (cat. 383). On the morrow she was to illuminate the harbor.

The pageantry, promising a parade, flotilla, and fireworks, brought out a crowd estimated at one million spectators.

> In every direction extended the crowds up and down Fifth Avenue. House-tops were dense with them. Every window was filled with pretty faces. Flags and streamers fluttered heavily in the slight breeze from the roofs and windows of nearly every building. A French flag and an American was the common combination. Men climbed up the telegraph poles and lodged themselves on the crosspieces to see the pageant. Every street lamp was surmounted by a small boy. They climbed the trees and the statuary and even crept between the close ranks of the horsemen to the imminent peril of their lives and to the annoyance of the police. . . .[8]

454
Mayor Grace Presenting the Freedom of the City to Bartholdi
From *The Daily Graphic*
October 29, 1886

The day was declared a public holiday, but unpropitious weather robbed the occasion of its shining splendor. A fine drizzle left the decorations bedraggled, and it was hard to see much through the interstices of the umbrellas. Undeterred, «Mr. Gotham simply buttoned up his overcoat, Miss Gotham took out her rainy-day hat and her Winter pelisse, and the little Gothams didn't care a button for the rain anyhow.»[9]

General Stone, as Grand Marshal, led the parade to the reviewing stand where Cleveland and all the luminaries were waiting (cat. 456). The President hailed Bartholdi as «the greatest man in America today,» to which the modest Frenchman replied, «Through your courtesy, sir.»[10] Twenty thousand individuals marched by, including one hundred bands, crack regiments, zouaves, veterans, national guards, police forces, firefighters with the latest equipment, state delegations, civil authorities, social clubs, and colleges. «Fifth Avenue is like a river bed. . . . Black and drabbled, shining in the dull light like the back of a monster python, [the parade] stretches downward between banks composed entirely of human masses.»[11] It was over two hours before the Sons of the Revolution, marking the tail of the parade with George Washington's old carriage, passed the stand at Madison Square.

To proceed to the Battery (cat. 457), the route crossed onto Broadway.[12] In front of the *World* Building, the parade passed under a triumphal arch of evergreens (cat. 458). Crowned with the newspaper's masthead—two globes flanking the Statue of Liberty—the arch bore canvas panels reading «La Belle France,» «The United States,» and «Vive l'entente fraternelle des deux Républiques.» Because the rain had delayed its construction, the arch had to be completed during the night with electric lights, a novelty in itself that drew a crowd of sidewalk supervisors.

Souvenirs multiplied beyond the Committee's control as hawkers peddled trinkets and ephemera. Among the scarcest reminders are copies of the official *Souvenir Programme of the Unveiling . . . of the Bartholdi Statue of Liberty* and the deluxe edition by John Garnett of *The Statue of Liberty* (cat. 459). Printed on fragile paper, mauled and mulled over, copies have all but disappeared.

Clouds turned the flotilla into a Dutchman's phantom, with glimpses of ships through great trailing mists. Admiral Luce, who commanded the North Atlantic Squadron, presided, accompanied by seven men-of-war, but all were disappointed that the French fleet was located too late for them to come. The poor visibility made the navigating hazardous, and the flagship for the naval parade, the sleek *Gedney*, was nearly rammed before the 250-vessel argosy was under way.

456

FRANK LESLIE'S
ILLUSTRATED
NEWSPAPER

No. 1,624.—Vol. LXIII.] NEW YORK—FOR THE WEEK ENDING NOVEMBER 6, 1886. [Price, 10 Cents,

NEW YORK CITY.—THE GRAND DEMONSTRATION ON "LIBERTY DAY," OCTOBER 28th.—THE MILITARY AND CIVIC PROCESSION PASSING DOWN LOWER BROADWAY, WITH THE NAVAL PAGEANT IN THE DISTANCE.

Twenty abreast the fore-running tugs, snorting and coughing, sea-devils that they are, out for a frolic and no work, and determined for this day to paint the harbor red. Behind them huge bulks moved stately; steamers bearing their thousands; scows plebeian and yachts aristocratic; dredges fresh from delving; non-descripts fished from some aboriginal canal; proud warriors of the sea; ferryboats; freighters, coasting steamers and river craft—everything that could float . . . was there, a world of shipping, flying every flag the ocean knows. Such . . . churning as whipped the waters . . . into yeast, as they took their places, has never in the wildest pilot's dream been seen before. . . .[13]

«Liberty embodied as a woman» transmitted a special meaning to some that was not to pass without action. The New York State Woman's Suffrage Association, cordially excluded from the more conventional festivities, rented a boat to circle the island during the unveiling. Speeches by leading suffragettes protested the indignities suffered by women in a society that, at least in this case, was literally putting a woman on a pedestal.

458

459

The President boarded the *Dispatch* to cross to Bedloe's Island, switching to the launch *Vixen* for the last few hundred yards.[14] Jolly tars manned the rigging at attention (cat. 460), while Gilmore's Band played «Hail to the Chief»; a 21-gun salute announced the Chief Executive's arrival, accompanied by booming cannons, whose smoke obscured the statue in smoke and mist (cat. 461). Steam whistles and sirens added to the chorus, out of any maestro's control, delaying the ceremonies until 3:15. Lesseps joked that «steam which has done so much good in the world is just now doing us a good deal of injury!»[15]

The speakers assembled on a festooned dais (cat. 462) against the side of the pedestal, above a broader platform for distinguished guests. Another several thousand people were below on the parade level.

Lesseps began with a speech praising American «go-ahead» resulting in a century of fearless progress. Evarts followed with the presentation address. The tri-color veil was to be lifted at the Senator's conclusion, but during a critical pause in his speech a premature signal was given to the sculptor, who released the flag, baring *Liberty*'s brow. The immediate response was as confused as are the historical accounts of this mishap. The most precise contemporary description claimed that a cord was strung down the interior of the pedestal to the entrance passage, level with the roof of the speakers' box. D. H. King, Jr., was to stand on this roof, where he was to receive a signal when Evarts' address ended. On King's sign, Bartholdi pulled the cord, stripping the flag to reveal the goddess's face.[16] Pandemonium ensued. At the sight of *Liberty*, the tooting, whistling, and bellowing joined the *feu de joie* of ten thousand rounds of Gatling guns from the Battery, punctuated by cannonades from the forts and salvos from the surrounding fleet. The cacophony drowned out Evarts, who turned his back on the audience in desperation to deliver his final words to the President.

When the crowd calmed down, Cleveland accepted the statue in the name of the United States, in a short, eloquent statement. He was jovial and gracious throughout the day, giving no indication of any second thoughts he might have had over his past reluctance to subsidize the glorious lady at whose feet he now stood.

460
Inauguration de la Statue de la Liberté Éclairant le Monde
H. A. Ogden
Unidentified press illustration
1886

462
The Dedication of the Great Statue. The Ceremonies at Bedloe's Island
From *The Daily Graphic*
October 29, 1886

When Bartholdi reemerged on the rostrum, the cheering crowd demanded a speech, but the sculptor deferred to the General Consul, Albert Lefaivre. Chauncey Depew, president of the Union League Club, gave a lengthy oration in the florid language of the era. He was one of America's most sought-after speakers, and his intricately crafted review of French-American friendship can still capture a reader's imagination. The entire ceremony was recorded in the *Inauguration of the Statue of Liberty Enlightening the World. . . .*[17]

The mad scramble for the boats scandalized the officials, whose boat laden with delectable collations debarked with a pack of unknowns aboard, quaffing champagne. The press blamed the police, and it was the fortune of *Liberty* that no one was seriously injured.

The dismal, wet evening necessitated the postponement of the much-anticipated fireworks (cat. 463) until November 1, when the staid earth was «bounced from her peaceful orbit and shot pellmell into a shower of meteors.»[18] The pyrotechnical extravaganza offered 120 different displays, such as asteroids, harlequinades, wagglers, tourbillions, snakes, peacocks, spreaders, and streamers.

Any fear that the French would find the inaugural banquet meager as a result of congressional economies was quickly dispelled. The Chamber of Commerce regaled 243 notables at Delmonico's (cat. 464, 465). Louis Delmonico, compatriot of both nations and original Committee member, outdid himself. With Babcock and Bliss in charge of the program, the great restaurateur commanded a magnificent decor and an incomparable feast to distinguish the occasion. Bartholdi was celebrated as the «Columbus of Bedloe's Island.» George William Curtis, who had had to decline as orator for the dedication, elaborated on the words of an English scholar, «Above all nations is humanity.» Convivial toasts required reciprocations, and words flowed with champagne into the night.[19]

La Liberté éclairant le Monde had been welcomed to her permanent home with great fanfare and genuine affection. Sightseers flocked to the island to experience for themselves the colossal monument, beginning the next phase of the statue's history, when *Liberty* would gain the emblematic preeminence that her votaries had so earnestly anticipated for her. To commemorate the event, Moran painted *The Unveiling of the Statue of Liberty* (cat. 466), modifying the format of his earlier oil (cat. 347). Rather than depicting the specific occasion, his painting communicates the festive grandeur of the Grand Finale.

Taken from Steamer "Patrol", 28 October, 1886.   Copyright 1887, H. O'Neil, 31 Union Square, New York

"LIBERTY ENLIGHTENING THE WORLD"
INAUGURATION OF THE BARTHOLDI STATUE, HARBOR OF NEW YORK.
MILITARY AND NAVAL SALUTE, THE PRESIDENT'S ARRIVAL AT LIBERTY ISLAND.

466
*Unveiling of the Statue of
Liberty, 1886*
Edward Moran
1886

477
Scaffolding around the
Statue
1985

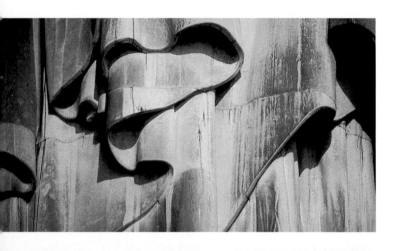

476
Drapery of the Statue
1984

478
The Old Flame of the
Statue
1983

482
The New Flame
1985

483
*Test Lighting of a Model of
the Flame*
1985

485
*Interior View of Work on
the Statue*
1983

490
Model of the Monument
Showing Statue Structure
and Stair System in
Pedestal
Swanke Hayden Connell,
and The Office of Thierry
W. Despont
1985

497
Avoiron et Cie.
Cast, «C» size
Frédéric-Auguste Bartholdi
ca. 1883

504
Replica of the Statue of
Liberty, Jardin du
Luxembourg, Paris
Frédéric-Auguste Bartholdi
1900

One Hundred Years

14.
A National Monument Emerges: The Statue as Park and Museum

Barbara Blumberg

As French and American dignitaries gathered in New York on October 28, 1886, for the long-awaited dedication of the Statue of Liberty, President Grover Cleveland proclaimed, «We will not forget that Liberty has here made her home; nor shall her chosen altar be neglected.»[1] In the years that followed, the federal government's administration and care of the statue and its surroundings often belied Cleveland's solemn pledge. This is not surprising given that in the nineteenth and well into the twentieth century, the United States, more than any other nation, subscribed to the philosophy of limited government. Thomas Jefferson had preached in his First Inaugural Address that good government was frugal and confined to a narrow range of actions. Almost all nineteenth- and most early twentieth-century political figures interpreted his argument to mean that the federal government had no business erecting and/or maintaining monuments to national glory, supporting the arts, or providing the citizens of a particular city with parks and pleasure gardens. These activities, if they were to be undertaken at all, lay in the sphere of local and private action.

Conversely, it was primarily in those periods of American history when the prevailing philosophy of limited government came under question and was modified, particularly the progressive and New Deal eras, that the federal government remembered «the great symbol of Liberty that has here made her home» with significant efforts to maintain and protect it, beautify its surroundings, and interpret its meaning. Aside from federal action in those periods, whatever moves have been made to preserve, restore, and amplify the statue have come from the initiative of private citizens and have often been financed through voluntary contributions.

The philosophy of limited government responsibility influenced Washington's actions concerning the statue almost from the moment of its conception. In 1877, a joint congressional resolution accepted the gift from France and authorized the Chief Executive to «designate and set apart a site» for its future home. Further, Congress instructed the President to «cause suitable regulations to be made for its future maintenance as a beacon, and for the permanent care and preservation thereof as a monument of art. . . .» No appropriation accompanied this measure, however. Indeed, Senator Simon Cameron of Pennsylvania reassured his colleagues that the measure «costs no money.»[2]

The federal government played no part in the subsequent efforts to raise funds for a pedestal for the statue and supervise its construction. Only in the final months prior to the dedication did the lawmakers agree to a $56,500 appropriation to cover the cost of the ceremony at the Army's Fort Wood on Bedloe's Island.

In keeping with the 1877 congressional resolution, in November 1886, a month after its dedication, President Cleveland ordered the statue to be placed «under the care and superintendance of the Light-House Board and that it be from henceforth maintained by said Board as a beacon.» The President's directive placed only the statue and pedestal under the jurisdiction of the board. The Army controlled Fort Wood, the military reservation that occupied most of Bedloe's Island, and assumed responsibility for guard functions around the monument. The American Committee continued to provide the public with ferry service from Manhattan to the Statue of Liberty and purportedly was to contribute profits therefrom toward maintenance of the monument. In fact, they did very little to beautify or care for the statue.

These administrative arrangements worked poorly. For the next twenty years, Congress rarely voted specific appropriations for upkeep of the statue. The Light-House Board made do with the general departmental monies it received, and eventually admitted that the monument was useless as a «navigational aid» because of its inland location. In addition, the three guardians of the monument and its site were soon accusing each other of neglecting the property. The Army commander at Fort Wood claimed in 1901 that neither the Light-House Board nor the American Committee had expended money or done work on the monument since its dedication. As a result, he wrote, «inside and out, the statue of Liberty . . . is a distinct disgrace to our country.» He predicted that «this grand work of Art» would steadily deteriorate unless the divided authority ended.[3]

Others voiced their dismay as well. Joseph Pulitzer's *World* editorialized, «The National Government has been shamefully indifferent to the great monument of Liberty from the first. It has never done anything for it except to light it.» After the *World* objected to the possible location of an immigrant-screening station on Bedloe's Island, Ellis Island was chosen for that purpose instead. The newspaper urged Congress to protect permanently the home of the statue and develop it as «a pleasure ground for the people.»

In 1890 the Senate did consider a resolution providing that the Secretary of War should «control, use, and improve the whole of Bedloe's Island . . . as a free public park. . . .» Several Senators objected, however, that the resolution would commit Congress to future appropriations. In addition, they argued, «to furnish to the people of New York a public park and pleasure ground» would set a «dangerous precedent» of federal largesse to a particular city. The upper house therefore allowed the measure to die in committee.[4]

Modification of the general pattern of divided authority and neglect came finally with the first small move away from the philosophy of limited government. In 1901, Theodore Roosevelt, the first «progressive» President, entered the White House. He questioned the traditional hands-off approach and preached instead the doctrine of federal activism in a broad range of areas, including the conservation of the nation's natural resources and heritage. In the years from 1901 to 1917 other progressive reformers were elected to Congress and to the presidency, among them Woodrow Wilson. Their activist politics produced change for the nation and for the administration of the Statue of Liberty.

Theodore Roosevelt's first Secretary of War, Elihu Root, in 1901 requested transfer of jurisdiction over the statue from the Light-House Board to his department. The Chief Executive agreed, and signed the order on December 30, 1901. Root's successor, William Howard Taft, urged Congress to appropriate funds for improved lighting of the monument and for repairs. With some hyperbole, he claimed that «the condition of the statue is such that it may collapse unless the repairs are made soon.»

Taft's warning must have impressed the lawmakers since the General Deficiency Act of 1906 provided $62,800 for the monument. The War Department used the funds for filling and grading inside the fort walls, repairing the wharf, constructing a wharf-house, repairing and facing with granite the pedestal and terreplein, repairing and painting the interior of the statue and pedestal, and altering stairways to permit installation of the first electric elevator in the pedestal. Unfortunately, after these first-priority jobs were completed, no money was left for improving the lighting (cat. 467).

Here again private initiative intervened to bolster government action. The New York *World* in 1915 submitted to the War Department a plan to improve the torch light and install a permanent floodlighting system. The paper proposed to conduct a campaign to raise $30,000 in public donations if the federal government would agree to vote an annual appropriation for maintenance of the lighting equipment. The War Department urged Congress to make the commitment, which it did with an amendment to the Rivers and Harbors bill of 1916. President

467
Statue of Liberty from the East Wharf
Office of the Chief Signal Officer, «Redbook Series» December 1907

468

The Statue of Liberty As
Now Illuminated at Night
Central News Photo
Service
December 22, 1916

Wilson signed the bill in July; within six months the *World* had its $30,000 in contributions, and by December, Wilson turned on the new lights that bathed the statue in a golden glow (cat. 468).[5]

Another development of the progressive era, with its heightened interest in conservation, would have great bearing on the administration of the Statue of Liberty. The full impact would not be felt, however, until after 1917. During Theodore Roosevelt's administration, Congress passed the Antiquities Act of 1906, which gave the President power to proclaim and protect as national monuments any landmarks, structures, and/or objects of historic or scientific interest found on federal property. To help the Chief Executive carry out the provisions of this law, the Secretaries of Interior, Agriculture, and War issued instructions to field officers to report from time to time on any objects situated on or near the areas they administered which might be suitable for designation. Subsequently, the captain in command at Fort Wood called the Statue of Liberty to the attention of his superiors, and

in 1915 the War Department listed the statue as one of fifty objects under its jurisdiction that should be regarded as national monuments. The War Department's action was not, however, followed by the expected presidential proclamation, in part because of World War I. Not until 1924 did the Army prepare a final draft of a proclamation designating the Statue of Liberty and structures on four other military reservations as national monuments. It was President Calvin Coolidge, not a noted supporter of conservation, who signed the proclamation on October 15, 1924.[6] At first the elevation to national monument status made little difference: the Army continued to care for the statue. The 1920s saw a return to peace and an emphasis on federal frugality. The War Department received limited funds and certainly no special appropriations for preserving the new national monument.

The resulting lack of finances in the twenties prevented the War Department from making in the illumination of the statue those improvements that it believed were necessary. Spokesmen for the department testified in 1922 at congressional appropriations committee hearings that the lights installed in 1916 caused unflattering shadows around the face of *Liberty*. The army proposed that the «now obsolete system of lighting» be revamped to remove these shadows. The lawmakers declined to finance the improvement, and in fact the Army did not possess even the wherewithal to repair the existing system. A 1928 Army report stated that half the floodlight projectors had faulty reflectors, and that due to erosion many were becoming unmounted.

In 1931, after two years of serious decline in the nation's economy, Congress, hoping that some spending on public works might halt the downward economic spiral, authorized an emergency appropriation of $58,000 for improvements to the Statue of Liberty. The War Department used this fund to replace the twenty-five-year-old elevator, strengthen the structure of the raised arm, steam clean the monument and pedestal, and make other minor repairs. The most dramatic change was the installation of a new floodlighting system. Ninety-six 1,000-watt lamps were placed on the terreplein in the eleven starpoints of Fort Wood; twenty-four 200-watt lights were installed on the pedestal balcony and at the copper base of the statue; and twenty-two 50-watt Mazda flashing lights were situated in the crown. The illumination of the torch was increased by replacing the 200-watt lamps with fourteen 1,000-watt lights. On October 26, 1931, the completed 500,000-candlepower system was formally dedicated.

Here matters stood at the deepening of the Great Depression and the coming of the New Deal. The breakdown of the nation's economy produced bank failures, ruined farmers, bankrupt businesses, and millions of unemployed. To alter these conditions, Franklin D. Roosevelt and his advisors abandoned to an unprecedented degree the philosophy of limited government. In an attempt to pull the country from the depths of depression, the administration and Congress traded frugality for «pump-priming» and set millions of jobless to work on massive construction and conservation projects. All of this would directly affect the administration and care of the Statue of Liberty.

An executive order of June 10, 1933, greatly enlarged the scope of a federal conservation agency that had been created during Woodrow Wilson's administration. According to Roosevelt's Executive Order 6166, the Department of the Interior's Office of National Parks, Buildings and Reservations—renamed the National Park Service (NPS) in 1934—was to take jurisdiction over all national parks, national monuments, national historic sites, and national cemeteries. The following month the directive became more explicit with a second executive order listing the areas formerly administered by the military that were to be transferred to the Interior Department's Office of National Parks. These included the statue, pedestal, and fort, but not the remainder of the Army base on Bedloe's Island.[7]

The Park Service immediately undertook a study of its newly acquired property and started to plan its future development. NPS officials announced as early as December 1933 that they wished to remove the Army base entirely in order to create on Bedloe's Island «a national park, thus providing a dignified and fitting frame for the celebrated statue.» What they found in 1933 was a far cry from such a «frame.» The island was cluttered with warehouses, barracks, and miscellaneous structures. Visitors debarking from the ferry «had to pass by a warehouse located on a dilapidated, one-hundred-year-old dock, and adding to the inappropriateness of Liberty's setting were a prominently placed «comfort station,» a metallic frankfurter stand, and sixteen unsightly buildings.»

469

The Statue of Liberty
McLaughlin Air Service
ca. 1938–39

470

View of Crown Showing
Reconstruction of Spikes
Collins
August 31, 1938

471

Repairing Interior—
Workmen Replacing
Section of Band Iron
Supporting Sheet Copper
Cover
June 8, 1938

To effect the change the NPS desired, Secretary of the Interior Harold Ickes, an aggressive, committed conservationist, began negotiations with the Secretary of War. The transfer ran into some resistance and temporary legal difficulties, but by 1937 was finally accomplished. On September 7, President Roosevelt issued a proclamation adding the entire island to the national monument because that was «necessary for the proper care, management, and protection of the colossal statue of «Liberty Enlightening the World.» By the end of the month the Army removed its personnel and equipment and turned over the former base to the NPS.[8]

As soon as it had gained possession of the statue's setting, the Park Service drafted a General Development Plan that proposed improvements estimated to cost more than $1.5 million. That plan, officially approved in 1938, called for demolishing twenty army barracks and other structures and situating all necessary administrative, utility, and residence buildings at the northwest end of the island in a landscaped area away from the statue. This would necessitate adding landfill to that area and building a new seawall. The east dock, immediately in front of the statue, would be abandoned, to be replaced with a new one on the west side, which would afford visitors the best view of the monument. Wide walks would be built, leading from the boat landing to the statue (cat. 469).

The Park Service, lacking the funds in its own budget to carry out this extensive work, turned instead to two New Deal organizations created to stimulate the economy and employ the jobless: the Public Works Administration (PWA), headed by Ickes, and the Works Progress Administration (WPA). Over the next four years these two emergency agencies supplied money and labor that went a long way toward implementing the General Development Plan.

Between 1937 and 1941 WPA laborers repaired or replaced rusted sections of the statue's armature and removed the crown's rays in order to replace their rusted supports (cat. 470). The cast iron stairs in the pedestal were so corroded as to be structurally unsafe. This led the NPS to close the monument to the public temporarily while the WPA measured the statue and pedestal and investigated their physical condition. Structural faults, due primarily to water seepage, were found in the statue, its copper base, and the pedestal. To remedy and repair these the WPA constructed a copper apron

around the bottom of the statue to keep water out (cat. 471), repointed and painted the pedestal, and removed the old cast iron steps, replacing them with a reinforced concrete stairway to the foot of the statue. The WPA demolished most of the old Army buildings, regraded and seeded the eastern end of the island, began to construct a new seawall to prevent erosion, and repaired the old east dock to make it look presentable until it could be replaced by a new one. The last WPA construction projects included excavating for a flagpole foundation and building granite steps for the new entrance at the rear of the statue (cat. 472). In addition, when the NPS superintendents at the Statue of Liberty National Monument complained that they did not have sufficient staff to clean the whole island properly and maintain the utilities, the WPA supplied five laborers to augment the NPS crew. Private construction companies under PWA contract laid a new waterline to New Jersey and built a Park Service administrative center and a concessions building on the island. After the Japanese attack on Pearl Harbor, the planned development came to an abrupt standstill.[9]

472
Pedestal Stairs—Statue of
Liberty
Collins
August 8, 1939

During World War II, the bulk of the nation's resources were devoted to the war effort, and almost all public and private construction stopped; materials and labor for maintenance and repairs on the home front became scarce. The only work done on the island was improving the illumination of the statue by the addition of sixteen mercury-vapor lamps to the floodlighting system and six vapor lamps in the torch. On May 7, 1945—V.E.–Day—the brilliant new lights were switched on for the first time.

Following the war, in 1946 the neglected condition of the statue began to arouse protest. The New York *World-Telegram*, successor to Pulitzer's paper, charged that «the unkempt condition of this revered monument borders on a national disgrace. From the dilapidated, sea-worn east dock to the grassless terrace, littered with partly eaten fruit, sandwiches and soda glasses, Miss Liberty's environs reflect Washington's apathy toward a once beautiful shrine. . . .» Such civic groups as the National Life Conservation Society and the New York City Federation of Women's Clubs passed resolutions calling upon Congress to appropriate money to complete the planned improvements that had been started by the WPA and PWA. Sixteen members of the New York and New Jersey congressional delegations declared the statue was «standing in a slum» and petitioned the House Appropriations Committee to vote $1 million for «slum clearance on Bedloe's Island.»

The public pressure induced Congress to act. During fiscal years 1947 through 1957, the lawmakers appropriated about $1.3 million to finish implementing the General Development Plan adopted in 1938. The dilapidated east pier was finally removed. Under contracts let by the NPS, construction firms dredged a new channel and turning basin for the ferries and built a new west pier on which visitors landed, and used the fill from the dredging to enlarge the western end of the island. It was then landscaped, and living quarters were built for the superintendent and other NPS personnel. The statue received a new heating system and some interior structural repairs. New utility lines were laid between the mainland and the island, while the concessions building (containing a restaurant) and the administrative center were enlarged and remodeled.[10]

Throughout these years of alternating government neglect and improvement, the public's interest in the statue and desire to see it had steadily grown. Eighty-eight thousand visitors arrived in 1890; by 1957, some eight hundred fifty thousand debarked from the ferry. From the mid-1960s onward, over one million visitors would come annually. Was it part of the function of the administrators of the statue to inform these people of *Liberty*'s creation, history, and symbolism? The Light-House Board and the Army offered no interpretive programs since their primary mandates were, respectively, to operate a lighthouse and a military post, not to educate the public. The NPS, upon taking over in the 1930s, had initiated some interpretation in the form of small, temporary exhibits about the statue's creation and creators, its history, and the history of Fort Wood. It had also placed a tablet bearing Emma Lazarus' famous poem inside the pedestal. The Park Service, although desiring to do more than this, could not do so because of lack of funds and personnel and above all because there was very little space inside the pedestal for exhibits.

Then, in the early 1950s, a group of prominent New Yorkers active in the American Scenic and Historic Preservation Society approached the NPS with an offer that seemed to present a solution to the dilemma. William H. Baldwin, Walter Binger, Gardner Osborn, and Alexander Hamilton (great-great grandson of America's first Secretary of the Treasury) told Park Service officials they would like to raise money through private donations to create a museum depicting the story of the millions of immigrants who had flocked to the United States in search of liberty and opportunity. They initially suggested housing such a museum in another NPS-administered site, Castle Clinton. The representatives of the NPS with whom they met convinced them that the pedestal of the colossal monument on Bedloe's Island offered a better location, by arguing that Castle Clinton was too small and unsuitably shaped a location for a decent-sized museum. Second, they felt a museum of immigration would complement interpretation of the statue; as they put it, «The foot of our great symbol of the American ideal was the most appropriate place for presenting the fruits of that ideal.»

Third, housing a museum of immigration in the monument's base would provide the excuse and funds for enlarging the pedestal in a manner that the NPS had advocated since at least the 1930s.

In the 1880s, Richard Morris Hunt, architect of the pedestal, had prepared several designs. The American Committee had rejected Hunt's preferred design and instead selected a smaller and, it hoped, less expensive one that did not fill all of star-shaped Fort Wood. The remaining space between the pedestal and the fort walls had never been used. The rejected Hunt design had envisioned a stepped-terrace pedestal that completely filled the area of the fort and was bounded by its walls; the NPS believed, as had Hunt, that this was the better plan. Park Service officials reasoned that the Preservation Society group could raise the money to enlarge the pedestal according to Hunt's original design, and have ample room to house their immigration museum within it.[11]

Once the regional NPS officials and the New York–based promoters had agreed to build the museum within *Liberty*'s base, Baldwin and the other original backers formed a National Committee for the American Museum of Immigration. They persuaded industrialist Pierre S. du Pont III and retired Maj. Gen. Ulysses S. Grant III (grandson of the eighteenth President) to become its chairmen. Du Pont led a committee delegation that in August 1954 obtained the endorsement of President Dwight D. Eisenhower, who understood them to be offering a fine museum at no cost to the taxpayers.

Congress, on the same understanding, subsequently gave its approval. In 1956, a joint resolution officially changed the name of the statue's home from Bedloe's to Liberty Island because the meaning of the monument was «to be made more brilliant by the establishment at its foot of the American Museum of Immigration as the gift of individual Americans to the American people for all future generations»[12] (cat. 473).

In 1955, the National Committee was chartered by the State of New York as a nonprofit corporation, known as AMI, Inc.; signed a cooperative agreement with the Department of the Interior; and began its fund-raising campaign. Unfortunately, AMI, Inc.'s drive went badly—it failed to attract substantial corporate and foundation backers, and its efforts were so inept that at some points its administrative and public relations overhead consumed nearly 73 per-

cent of the many small contributions it did receive. Although it persisted in its solicitations for nearly a decade, it raised less than half a million dollars.

The corporation's directors, realizing that their fund-raising campaign was in trouble, began to adjust their plans. They had initially spoken of a 50,000-square-foot museum that would fill the entire enlarged pedestal, but by 1959 had accepted a scaled-down design for a museum occupying about 7,500 square feet of a third level in the base, and devoting another 1,690 square feet, on the second floor, to a Statue of Liberty Story Room.[13]

The AMI, Inc. directors also began to seek modification of their cooperative agreement. They were successful in September 1957 when the agreement was amended to read that the Park Service, in consultation with the AMI, would build and develop the museum out of funds contributed by AMI «and by other sources and funds made available by Congress.»

The Park Service was able to raise most of the money to pay for excavating the landfill between the base and the walls of Fort Wood and for building the stepped-terrace pedestal (cat. 474). It did this with funds from «Mission 66,» the NPS's ten-year conservation program aimed at improving and expanding facilities and visitor services at the national parks, monuments, and historic sites to accommodate the greatly increased tourism of the 1950s and 1960s. By the summer of 1965, then, the concrete stepped-terrace pedestal, granite faced and with a new massive stonework entryway, was finished. The Park Service entered into no further contracts to complete the interior and lay out the museum because the «Mission 66» funds were exhausted and no additional private donations were forthcoming. Over the next seven years, the work proceeded fitfully. As the cost of the Vietnam War rose relentlessly, Capitol Hill inclined toward cutting back on nonessential domestic spending.[14]

473
A Donation to Build the American Museum of Immigration
October 1956

474
Excavation for the American Museum of Immigration
November-December 1961

475
*Statue of Liberty—Back
View (Showing American
Museum of Immigration
Addition)*
Jett Lowe
1984

Bitter controversy over the content of the museum further delayed its opening. Afro-, Italian-, and Polish-American groups objected that they did not receive adequate or appropriate coverage in the proposed exhibit plan. Such complaints proved extremely difficult to satisfy, and escalated after financial considerations necessitated a drastic reduction in the museum's size. Historians and other specialists in the field of immigrant and ethnic studies criticized the exhibit plan for being based on inaccurate information and outmoded concepts. They accused the NPS and the AMI of ignoring the advice and findings of the best scholars in the discipline. The Park Service modified the exhibit plan to try to quiet the protests, but succeeded in pleasing neither the ethnic spokesmen nor the academic specialists.[15]

Twenty years after the little band from the Preservation Society first approached the Park Service with the idea, the American Museum of Immigration was ready to open. President Richard M. Nixon arrived on Liberty Island on September 26, 1972, to dedicate this $5 million addition to the Statue of Liberty National Monument. It had been paid for primarily by the taxpayers of the United States; in addition, approximately $450,000 had come from private donations, and the City of New York had contributed $50,000 (cat. 475).

Besides opening the museum in the 1970s, the Park Service also proposed to upgrade the illumination system in time for the nation's bicentennial celebration. When the NPS budget proved inadequate to cover the planned improvement, the electrical contracting company scheduled to do the work donated its services and equipment. On July 3, 1976, the new lamps were switched on for the first time; they threw four times more light on the statue than the earlier system, but used 33 percent less energy. Inside the torch, high-pressure sodium lamps, rich in yellow, simulated a flame. Within the crown, mercury lamps provided a blue-green effect. Metal halide lamps bathed the remainder of the statue in white light, while lamps on the pedestal contained a blend of yellow sodium and white halide to reveal the warm color of the granite masonry.

The American Museum of Immigration and improved lighting were not the statue's only new attractions. On May 11, 1965, President Lyndon B. Johnson signed Proclamation 3656 making Ellis Island a part of the Statue of Liberty National Monument, ending a decade of controversy over the wisdom of joining the two historic sites.[16]

The Immigration and Naturalization Service had in November 1954 removed its famous immigrant admitting and detention center from Ellis Island, announcing that it no longer wanted the facility. The General Services Administration (GSA), failing to find another government agency to use it, declared the island surplus property and offered it for sale. No private buyer made an acceptable offer, and the hundreds of protests that greeted the announced sale persuaded President Eisenhower to hold off on disposing of the former immigration station.

Most of those who objected to the sale suggested instead that the federal government develop the island as a museum or monument commemorating the immigrants who had been screened there. The GSA specifically asked the NPS if it would like to take over Ellis for that purpose, but from 1954 to 1964 the Park Service declined, largely because AMI, Inc., with which it had signed a cooperative agreement, viewed development of Ellis Island as a duplication of and a rival to their proposed immigration museum.[17]

Meanwhile, Congress was also trying to answer the question of what to do with Ellis Island. In 1962 the Senate Subcommittee on Intergovernmental Relations began a series of hearings on the issue. Among those who testified before the committee were representatives from New Jersey who told about the Garden State's intention to transform the run-down waterfront of Jersey City into Liberty State Park. In light of this, in September 1963 the subcommittee urged the Department of the Interior «to review the proposal for Ellis Island as a national park, monument, or recreation area in conjunction with the New Jersey shoreline.» In a 1964 report, the Park Service reversed its earlier position and called for designation of the former immigration station as a national monument to be joined administratively to the Statue of Liberty. The NPS attempted to minimize the opposition of AMI, Inc., by stressing that Ellis Island must be developed in a way to augment, not duplicate, what was done in the American Museum of Immigration.[18]

Before Congress could act on these recommendations, President Johnson jumped in with his proclamation of May 1965. By August, Congress had authorized an appropriation of no more than $6 million for repairing and preserving the former immigration station. However, as happened also in the case of the American Museum of Immigration, cuts in nonessential domestic spending resulted in Congress's decision not to appropriate the authorized funds.

By the time the Park Service took over the former immigration station, its more than thirty buildings were suffering badly from neglect and decay. Without money the NPS could do little to arrest the deterioration. The structures lacked heat or other utilities, the roofs leaked, whole chunks of plaster fell from the ceilings, some buildings were no longer structurally sound, and the seawall was cracking. Such conditions made it unsafe to allow access to visitors, and so this important part of the Statue of Liberty National Monument remained off limits to the public.[19]

Only the intervention of a group of concerned and determined citizens effected a change in this dismal situation. Dr. Peter Sammartino, president of Fairleigh Dickinson University, founded the Restore Ellis Island Committee. He and his organization lobbied extensively to convince the lawmakers that at least parts of the main building on Ellis Island should be opened to the public in time for the country's bicentennial. Their efforts paid off when Congress appropriated $1 million for limited rehabilitation. As soon as the money was voted, the Park Service undertook repairs essential to making a carefully laid out tour of the Great Hall and other portions of the main building safe for visitors, arranged ferry service to the island, and developed an interpretive program. In the summer of 1976 the public was finally admitted.

While a part of the main building could now be seen, Congress appropriated little additional money to stabilize the rest of the complex, let alone preserve or restore it; therefore it continued to deteriorate. By 1980 the Park Service had presented a number of alternative plans for management and development of Ellis Island, but the estimated costs ranged from $33 million to $78 million, depending on the extent of the work.[20]

As the centennial of the Statue of Liberty approached, its guardian, the Park Service, faced prodigious problems. The Ellis Island part of the monument was rapidly crumbling. The American Museum of Immigration, inside the pedestal, had never developed into a first-rate interpretive facility because it was too small, underfunded, and understaffed. The statue, despite periodic repairs, was showing clear signs that nearly a hundred years of exposure to the salt air of New York harbor and to millions of tourists had taken its toll. Major restoration must be performed in the very near future if Liberty was to continue to hold her lamp aloft into the twenty-first century. The question now was whether or not the federal government would carry through with President Cleveland's pledge of 1886 that Liberty's chosen altar would not be neglected.

If such action would require tax monies, the answer was almost definitely no. The political climate in Washington by 1982 had swung sharply back in the direction of limiting government responsibilities. The Reagan administration was attempting a wholesale cutback on domestic spending and vigorously pushing the idea that reduction in federal financing would be compensated by increased private-sector contributions to the arts, science, culture, and welfare. In line with this, President Ronald Reagan, instead of asking Congress for an appropriation for the rehabilitation, announced in May 1982 the formation of a twenty-one-member Statue of Liberty–Ellis Island Centennial Commission, chaired by Lee Iacocca, head of the Chrysler Corporation, to serve as «an umbrella group coordinating private activities on behalf of both installations.» Its members would also advise the Secretary of the Interior on «preservation needs, the projected use of facilities and the programs associated with the upcoming centennials.» The Commission in turn created a strictly private fundraising foundation to coordinate a massive subscription campaign to pay for saving the lady.[21]

Thus, over a century, when it came to administration and care of the statue and its island home, not much had changed. Back in the 1870s the government of the United States had accepted the gift from the French people, but left it to private initiative to build a pedestal. In the 1980s, Washington favored restoration and development to preserve the beautiful national monument and symbol, but again placed the job of paying for the work in private hands. Once more the future of the statue depended on the voluntary contributions of thousands of American and French citizens.

15.
Restoration of the Statue of Liberty, 1984–86

Richard Seth Hayden
and Thierry W. Despont
Architects for the Centennial Restoration

As latter-day colleagues of Bartholdi, Eiffel, and Hunt, the members of the restoration effort sought merely to complete the work begun a century earlier. Proper restoration, however, was to require a thorough familiarity with the thoughts of the statue's creators. Like archeologists, the restorers—architects, engineers, and other specialists—studied all aspects of the construction and subsequent transformations of the statue. The statue's documentary history was completed by a careful diagnostic survey of the monument itself to assess its current condition. On the basis of these two preparatory steps, it was possible to draw up a comprehensive plan of restoration and improvements, not only for the outside surface of the statue but for its interior as well.

Studying the statue's documented history as a structure proved in itself a major undertaking, since the piecemeal evidence is scattered all over the world in obscure books and magazines, in museums and private collections. Bartholdi's notes and correspondence are available, but there are no detailed drawings. Although some of Eiffel's calculations and sketches exist, they reveal nothing about his attitude toward a section of the statue—the shoulder of the torch-bearing arm—built at variance with his original design.

Richard Morris Hunt's drawings for the pedestal do not fully reflect a structure greatly modified during construction. The members of the current restoration effort thus had to give special care to the interpretation of the surviving evidence.

Insights gained from the historical documents helped refine the scope and nature of the restoration effort. The three areas of the statue's outside fabric that seemed most in need of further examination were the copper skin, the shoulder of the torch-bearing arm, and the torch itself.

Bartholdi decided that to save weight the statue should be a mostly hollow structure covered with a thin skin of copper. He asked his former teacher, Eugène Viollet-le-Duc, to design the internal structure and the system for connecting that support with the skin.

Viollet-le-Duc proposed supporting the 151-foot-tall figure with sand-filled masonry compartments, and also devised an armature system of iron bars to support the copper envelope like veins of a leaf, based on the system he had previously used for Millet's statue *Vercingétorix*.

In 1879, before most of the figure had been built, Viollet-le-Duc died, and Bartholdi then approached Gustave Eiffel, who was well known for his long-span iron bridges, to design the definitive internal structure. Eiffel, adapting concepts developed for his bridge designs, proposed a central iron tower for the primary support. His most original contribution to the design of the statue, however, was the system of flat bars or springs that connect Viollet-le-Duc's armature system to the secondary structure that emanates like a tailor's mannequin from the primary structure, the central iron pylon. Those bars allow the skin-support system to behave independently of the primary and secondary structures while transferring gravity and wind-induced loads to them.

Viollet-le-Duc's skin-attachment system, which placed dissimilar metals in contact with each other, was retained. Since copper and iron in the presence of moisture produce an electrolytic reaction that causes the iron to corrode and disintegrate (cat. 476), this decision would plague the statue and provide the main impetus for the centennial restoration.

During the diagnostic phase of the restoration, it was discovered that the head is offset some 24 inches, and the shoulder framing approximately 18 inches, from the axis of the central pylon, in defiance of Eiffel's drawings. This explained why the shoulder framing has always been weak, but raised other questions: when, and by whom, was the change made? Two years of painstaking examination of historic photographs established that the change was probably made during assembly in Paris, not New York.

The torch assembly, too, showed deviations from the original design. In 1876, the torch, flame, and a portion of the arm had been completed and sent to the Philadelphia Centennial Exhibition; later they went to New York, where they remained on display at Madison Square until shipped back to Paris in 1882. A comparison of photographs taken of the flame in the United States and after the return to Paris revealed that one of the flares had been altered radically and relocated so that it projected away from the main body of the flame. This modification was the first of many changes to the flame over the years. Subsequent ones, however, were made in the United States and not authorized by Bartholdi. They plagued the statue as well as the restoration.

While the documentary and diagnostic examinations were proceeding, the restoration team began to consider how the work on the exterior fabric would be accomplished, especially how to gain access to all parts of the statue without damaging the fragile copper skin. The scaffolding necessary to wrap so gigantic a piece of art would have to be able to withstand even the most ferocious winds—the so-called hundred-year storm that was possible although extremely unlikely.

The selected scaffolding (cat. 477)—a free-standing system—began at the base of the pedestal and rose more than 300 feet above the island, belted around the base at four levels with tension ties. The upper 150 feet never touched the statue itself; this giant vertical cantilever remained at a distance of approximately 18 inches from every part of the statue to allow for movement under strong winds. It was made of aluminum, for even painted ferrous metal would rust in the salt air of the harbor and drip harmful residues onto the copper patina.

To gain access over the walls of Fort Wood, which surrounds the pedestal and is considerably broader than the base of the statue, a 400-foot ramp was built from the water's edge over the fort to the pedestal base. There, an elevator rose the height of the scaffold in an area adjacent to the torch and flame. The trip upward ended 300 feet above the water, at the upraised arm, with Manhattan in all its glory as a backdrop and the world around in miniature. In strong winds the scaffold sang as if it had a life of its own and gave us a feeling eerie yet exhilarating.

484
Model of Entrance Doors to the Monument
Swanke Hayden Connell and The Office of Thierry W. Despont
1985

Close examination of the copper skin revealed many surprises: from birds' nests to graffiti, torn rivets to hidden cracks. During the restoration we were repeatedly asked if the exterior would be cleaned and the green patina removed. Quite the opposite, we made great efforts to preserve the patina, which had developed uniformly and protected the copper from corrosion and deterioration. Left intact, it would allow the copper to weather several hundred more years.

Despite its generally clean condition, the statue showed many stains, some quite ugly when seen close up, although they blended into the overall texture when viewed from afar. It was decided to pressure-wash the entire statue and to scrape away only those stains and bird droppings visually and chemically detrimental to the fabric.

Cracks, tears, and blemishes were tackled next. The most numerous were dimples and stretch marks caused by rivets that had

pulled away. While replacing the armature, the restorers installed new prepatinized rivets using the existing holes. In the process, the copper was gently hammered to soften the most obvious dimpling. Of more serious concern were some large cracks, tears, and missing pieces encountered at various points: cracks in the right eye, lips, and chin; a damaged nostril; missing hair curls; badly patched plate assemblies at complex folds; and broken foot chains found completely detached from the statue. To correct the most serious cracks, like the one in the nostril, a mold was taken of the original part and a replacement *repoussé* piece prepared. Minor tears were simply hammered back together and sealed from the inside.

The spikes of the crown were removed and cleaned and the armature replaced. Upon examination we discovered that the outside edge of the spikes was made of bronze and the top and bottom of brass, not of copper as we had expected. One of the crown's spikes was in contact with the upraised right arm, probably because of the sway resulting from the displaced and weakened shoulder. The spike's position was adjusted by a few inches to gain clearance.

The most exposed and battered part of the statue was the torch—especially the balustrade, made of a thinner-gauge copper because it has intricate ornamentation—

which required complete replacement, as did the flame (cat. 478). After exhaustive research on the successive transformations of the flame and replacement alternatives, we decided to replicate Bartholdi's original idea of a gilded copper flame illuminated from outside. Historic photographs gathered by the National Park Service and the restoration team provided the specifications (cat. 479a–b) for one-half-scale clay models of the flame. Plaster casts from the models were made in much the same way that Bartholdi had worked in sculpting the flame.

Only craftsmen skilled in ornamental and sculptural copper *repoussé* could replicate the torch and flame. A French firm was selected and a team of twelve craftsmen from Reims came to build the new torch, balcony, and flame on Liberty Island. Work on the torch replica began after removal of the existing torch from the statue, during a public ceremony on July 4, 1984. With the aid of computers (cat. 480a–b), the restoration team developed a half-scale plaster model of the flame. Photographs of the flame and the model were digitized; same-scale drawings of the old flame and the new model were produced (cat. 481), and the two shapes were compared in every detail. A full-size plaster mold was then prepared.

For months, advising the French craftsmen as Bartholdi must have done, members of

pp. 220–223
Working Designs for the
Restoration of the Statue of
Liberty
Swanke Hayden Connell
and The Office of
Thierry W. Despont

479a–b
Torch and Flame Working
Drawings
1984

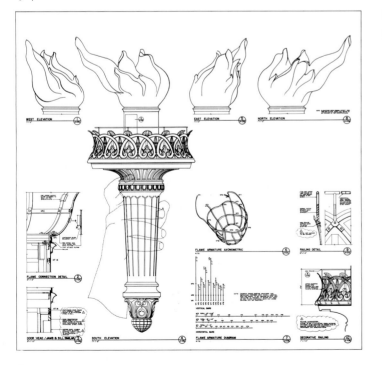

a

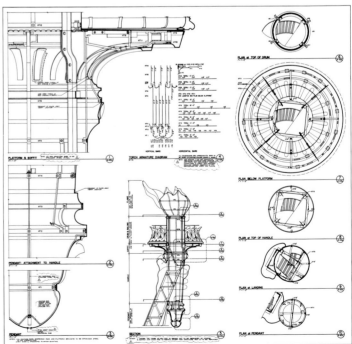

b

a

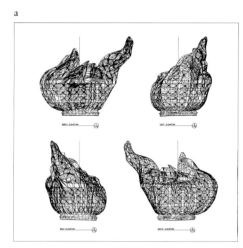

b

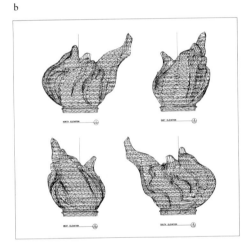

the restoration effort added, chipped, re-moved, and added again until the shape was finally approved. Small pieces of sheet metal were fitted together to cover the final model. These pieces were spot-welded to form a mold, and exterior bracing and concrete backing provided reinforcement. The crafts-men then hammered the copper against the interior surface of the mold to recreate the flame. The formed sections of copper were overlapped and riveted, and joints were smoothed and soldered to fill any gaps that could cause the still-to-be-applied gilding to crack. For the reflective surface of the flame we chose gold leafing for its luminescent quality, its beauty, and its historical ac-curacy as well as its durability (cat. 482).

Lighting the flame required special atten-tion. Using projectors on the torch balcony and in lighting pits on the ground, the half-scale gilded mockup was illuminated in numerous tests. Today's technology in re-flective lighting allows the flame to be as bright and intense as one could wish. Bartholdi's original intention and the dreams of those wanting to see a torch burning in the night have finally been realized (cat. 483).

The overall lighting design enhances the sculptural quality of the statue and rein-forces its scale within New York harbor. The fort walls are lit softly, the pedestal a

bit more brightly, the hem of the robe even more. Gradually the level of illumination increases, culminating with the brightest intensity at the crown and torch.

With the lighting completed, only one major element of the exterior needed attention—the statue required a proper entrance. The utilitarian entrance added in 1960 was replaced by an opening 21 feet high and 9 feet wide, rescaled within the massive rusti-cated walls. A pair of newly designed monumental doors (cat. 484) now fill the opening and provide an imposing entry to the statue. The doors are made of bronze bas-relief panels that tell the story of the statue's construction and centennial restora-tion through the work of the artisans and the tools of their trades.

As with the exterior fabric, the interior of the statue, including not only its supporting structures but also its routes of public access, required an initial documentary and diagnostic examination, followed by a com-prehensive and thoughtful plan of action.

The structure itself needed repair. The iron armature (cat. 485, 486, 487) that connects the skin to the framework was badly de-cayed: when the statue was first surveyed during the restoration, almost 30 percent of

486

Drawing of Armature

1983

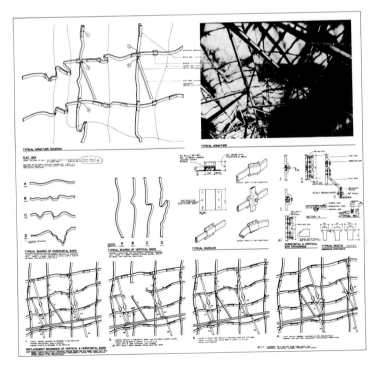

487

Full Section of Statue Only

Showing Structure

1983

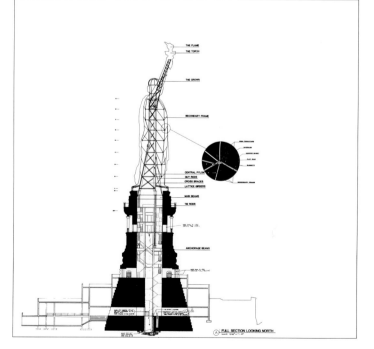

the riveted saddles that attach the armature network to the copper envelope were found to be loose or damaged. To prevent such deterioration from recurring, we tested various replacement materials and concluded that stainless steel 316L was the most suitable for the armature bars. Ferallium was chosen for the replacement flat bars because of its springlike quality, and teflon tape with pressure-sensitive silicone backing was used as an isolator between saddles and flat bars. Before replacing the armature, the entire system of some 1,800 individually shaped bars, 325 springs, 2,000 saddles, and 12,000 rivets had to be surveyed and delineated to define the scope of the work.

Because of the need to preserve the overall integrity of the copper envelope during the work, only bars from small portions of the statue could be replaced at any one time. Once removed, the bars were stripped of paint and asbestos, then duplicated using heat and forming presses. After annealing and passivation, the new bars were installed using new copper saddles fabricated to match the old ones and new conical, pre-patinized rivets.

After the armature bars, the most serious condition within the statue was the displaced and weakened right shoulder. Whatever the reason for the displacement, from a structural standpoint the modification of Eiffel's original design was incorrect.

The connection of the right arm to the central pylon was eccentric, too flexible, and overstressed. The joints lacked continuity, which allowed twisting and excessive movement. Previous repairs had compounded the problem.

The design team faced the choice of repairing or replacing the shoulder framing. It proved to be one of the most difficult philosophical and structural dilemmas of the project, pitting restorationists against preservationists, architects against engineers. Over a twelve-month period, the design team prepared tests and concepts for both replacement and repair schemes. Ultimately, we decided that the shoulder would be repaired rather than replaced.

There were other unequal stresses on the statue, which concerned the functioning of the anchorage in the pedestal (cat. 488). The anchorage, which like a bridge anchorage keeps the structure from overturning, consists of two sets of massive cross-members, called dunnage beams, interconnected by giant vertical tension bars. The upper set of dunnage beams takes all downward loads, and the lower set resists the uplift resulting from lateral loads, including wind forces. For best operation, the tension bars should be pretensioned to keep them from stretching out like rubber bands. This can be done

by turning the bolt at the bottom of each bar. During the restoration, 30-ton hydraulic jacks were used to retighten the bolts to balance and tune the tension bars.

An investigation of the statue's framework revealed that several of the five head-support arches were not directly attached to the central pylon. The restoration team reinforced and properly connected them to the pylon. Finally, damaged portions of the lattice girders which receive and frame the bottom folds of the draping copper robe, to form an outline for the pedestal cap, were replaced.

The general condition of the statue's interior space needed improvement. Many coats of lead-based paint that covered the iron framework and the inner surface of the copper skin were removed—without damaging the copper—using the freezing characteristics of liquid nitrogen. Masked workers applied the liquid nitrogen under pressure at a temperature of −320 degrees Fahrenheit, in a frigid spray that caused the paint to shrink and fall away like sheets of paper. A black layer of coal tar underneath the paint could be removed only through blasting with sodium bicarbonate. After the coal tar was removed, the interior skin was washed with deionized water. Paint still had to be removed from the central pylon and the secondary structure and the metal blasted to a «white metal» condition to eliminate the chance of hidden corrosion.

489

Head Section Showing Stair

1983

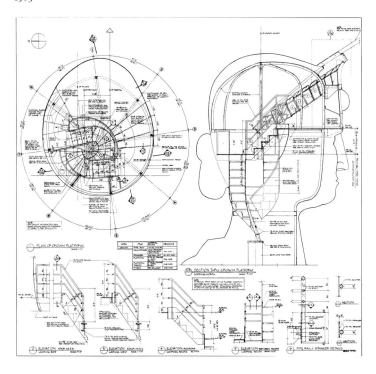

491

Section Through the

Museum

1985

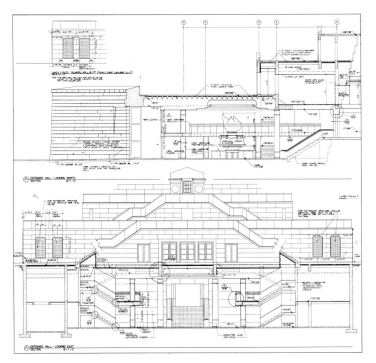

The restoration team's last task was to improve public access within the statue's interior (cat. 489, 490). On October 29, 1886, the day after its inauguration, the statue was opened to the public in response to popular demand, and it has remained open ever since. The familiar double-spiral stair was later built in Brooklyn and installed for visitors who wanted to climb to the head. Later, an elevator and stairs were installed in the pedestal; still later, a museum was added to the base. Plans for each change, however, were made more in response to pressing need than in fulfillment of any long-term plan. One by one, alterations chopped up the original interior, making the sensible incomprehensible. This jumble of failed spaces—intimidating, mysterious, and rather dizzying—was returned by the restoration team to its original, unobstructed state, and the visit route was reorganized (cat. 491) to offer views and vistas never before possible.

The original Richard Morris Hunt drawings were studied (cat. 492) in developing a proposal (cat. 493) for the renovation of the pedestal's interior; the revised concept for visitor circulation reflects the order of his designs. Visitors now enter through the new monumental doors in the renovated two-story lobby containing the old torch and flame. Continuing straight toward the

monument, they walk up a new grand stair, to either side of which the stepped walls of the statue's foundation have been exposed to reveal the very base of the monument. The statue's interior core was returned to its original 90-foot-high space by removing the concrete floor slabs added at various times during the last one hundred years. This allowed the installation of an appropriate stair system and a new glass-enclosed double-deck elevator that climbs within the cavernous interior. Through glass walls of the double-deck elevator, visitors can see the statue's massive anchorage system and the rough-hewn, board-formed concrete walls of the pedestal. The new elevator provides handicapped access. For the first time, physically challenged individuals can experience the interior of the monument and reach the colonnade level to enjoy harbor views.

Above the balcony level, the visitor suddenly discovers the beauty and mystery of the statue's interior: a magnificent volume—a 110-foot-high «room» of copper and metal, of light and shadows. The restored double-spiral stair takes the visitor through this most unusual space. At five different levels during the climb, the visitor can step off and walk around the helical stair to view the interior spaces. The steps to the head platform and the platform itself were modified to ease visitor flow. A small but crucial emergency elevator now gives Park Service personnel prompt access from the base of

the pedestal to the platform immediately below the statue's neck. Mechanically circulated air ventilation is provided. The air is dehumidified by a refrigeration plant at the base of the statue. New interior lighting enhances the views. As with the exterior, the lighting allows a gradual revelation of spaces as one moves through the monument.

Throughout the project the restoration team sought to expose, glorify, and enhance what existed: the drama of the spaces, the beauty of the structure, the excitement of the climb. They have succeeded if the visitor leaves the statue marveling at Hunt's boldness, Eiffel's ingenuity, and Bartholdi's vision.

This essay is based on an extract from Restoring the Statue of Liberty *by Richard Seth Hayden and Thierry W. Despont (New York: McGraw-Hill, 1986).*

490
Model of the Monument
Showing Statue Structure
and Stair System in
Pedestal
Swanke Hayden Connell
and The Office of Thierry
W. Despont
1985
reproduced in color
on p. 207

492
Section of Pedestal Only,
before Restoration
1983

493
Section of Pedestal Only,
After Restoration
1984

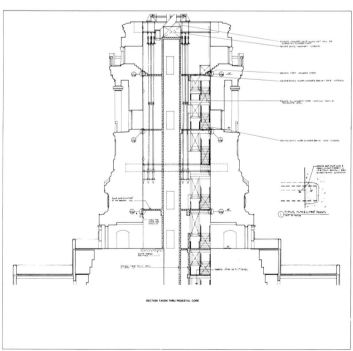

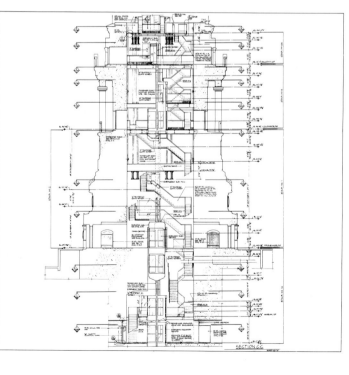

16.
Models and Reductions of LIBERTY

Edward L. Kallop, Jr.
with the assistance of
Catherine Hodeir

Although there is only one true Statue of Liberty, many thousands of smaller replicas, created for varying reasons and audiences, pay homage to the original. A comprehensive look at these models and reductions would require a work of considerable length, but some hint of their range and quality can be gained by examining representative examples of four kinds: sculptor's guides; commercial replicas; outdoor reductions; and folk artifacts.

From the beginning of his work on the statue in the studio, models served its creator, Auguste Bartholdi, as working studies (called maquettes) and were used in the process of enlargement for construction of the statue. Aside from these maquettes, *Liberty* in cast reproduction centered on the 4-foot model frequently mentioned by Bartholdi.[1] In 1875 the sculptor wrote to his mother of the time «when I will have finished the first model of the statue.» Bartholdi's reference distinguishes between the already existing maquettes and the still unfinished «first model,» a distinction emphasized by the term *modèle d'étude* (study model), signifying for Bartholdi a definitive version for the design of all subsequent models.[2]

The 4-foot *modèle d'étude* for *Liberty* is best represented in a terra-cotta cast once in the Musée Bartholdi and now in the collection of the Statue of Liberty National Monument.[3] Firmly documented, the cast was pictured in early photographs of maquettes and models of *Liberty* on display in the museum at Colmar, with design features identical to one depicted in the photograph accompanying Bartholdi's application to the U.S. Copyright Office.

Of the same size and probably from the same mold is a terra-cotta figure in the collection of the National Museum of American Art, Smithsonian Institution, Washington (cat. 494). Displayed until early 1887 in the Rotunda of the United States Capitol, the cast appears to be the same model used in 1883 by Richard Morris Hunt, the architect for the statue's pedestal, to demonstrate to the American Committee how the completed statue would appear in relation to his several pedestal designs.[4]

Both these models, along with the earlier maquettes, were undoubtedly made in Bartholdi's studio. Located on the rue Vavin in Paris, his residence and studio were one, and probably closely resembled the premises to which the sculptor and his wife moved shortly after 1890; a description of the latter premises is provided in an inventory made in 1914. From room descriptions it is apparent that Bartholdi was able, certainly in the latter and presumably in the earlier location, to practice almost all aspects of his profession, including the reproduction of models in cast.[5]

Bartholdi's 9-foot *modèle d'étude* is probably the plaster figure of *Liberty* now in the Musée National des Techniques, Paris. Pigmented brown to resemble the color of the copper statue, the model was certainly made in 1875, as were the examples of the 4-foot *modèle d'étude*, and represents a model of the same height seen in photographs of the interior workshop of Gaget, Gauthier and published in the Gontrand *Album*.[6] Like the 9-foot model described by Bartholdi, the cast was probably produced by mechanical means from the preliminary 4-foot study model, and was used in the process of enlargement that produced the subsequent 36-foot model.

Contemporaneous with the construction of the Statue of Liberty, but unrelated as either preparatory studies or as models used in the process of enlargement, were casts reproduced in France principally for public sale. By 1876, when the arm and torch of *Liberty* was already on its way to Philadelphia for display at the Centennial Exhibition, Bartholdi had recognized the possibilities of small-scale reproductions of the statue as a source of income, necessary since the statue's construction was an enormous drain on his finances. Casts in metal were made beginning probably in 1878 when a small bust of *Liberty* was reproduced by Avoiron et Cie. as a souvenir of the Universal Exposition: this bust duplicated in design the full-scale head of *Liberty* that was placed on public view (cat. 495).[7]

Avoiron et Cie., specialists in «imitation bronze» (zinc with surfaces treated to resemble bronze),[8] had a contract with Bartholdi that began probably in 1878 and ended in the fall of 1886.[9] Avoiron's casts of *Liberty* in full figure are distinguished from casts by other foundries by their distinctive circular self-base. Moreover, they are the only casts that include a U.S. copyright number and date as part of the inscription on each model (cat. 496, 497). Bartholdi's copyright, 9939 G, dated August 31, 1876, is registered in official records of the U.S. Copyright Office under the title *Statue of American Independence*.

Avoiron can be identified with none of Bartholdi's numerous projects apart from *Liberty*, and is a name unknown among foundries of the period generally associated with cast reproduction of sculpture. While in the smaller two of four sizes the foundry cast *Liberty* with a flame as part of the cast, the two larger sizes usually feature, not a cast flame, but fittings for either gas or electrical illumination. In designing the cast with this added feature, Avoiron produced a figure outside the conventions of sculpture, one that in embracing the latest technology (electrical illumination was in its infancy) was consistent with the structural innovations of the colossal statue itself and was an entirely apt, if literal, symbol of *Liberté éclairant le Monde*.

494
Study Model (cast), *Liberty (or) Liberty Enlightening the World*
Frédéric-Auguste Bartholdi
ca. 1875

495
Avoiron et Cie. Cast
Frédéric-Auguste Bartholdi
1878

496
Avoiron et Cie. Cast, «A» Size
Frédéric-Auguste Bartholdi
ca. 1883

497
Avoiron et Cie. Cast, "C" Size
Frédéric-Auguste Bartholdi
Ca. 1883
reproduced in color on p. 208

498
Thiébaut Frères Cast
Frédéric-Auguste Bartholdi
ca. 1884–86

499
Replica of the Statue of
Liberty, Pont de Grenelle
1907

501
Le Pont de Grenelle en
1927
Paul Signac
1927

502
La Vue du Quai d'Auteuil
et le Pont de Grenelle
Emile Béjot
n.d.

402. PARIS — Pont de Grenelle

Liberty cast in bronze was reserved by Bartholdi «to himself,» and for the purpose he turned to the firm of Thiébaut Frères.[10] Among the better-known foundries in Paris, the firm, founded in 1789, had a distinguished history throughout the nineteenth century, and Bartholdi appears to have reserved his use of this foundry for special commissions. Small-scale models, cast in differing sizes like those by Avoiron, were made by the firm beginning probably in 1884 and continuing intermittently until perhaps 1900 (cat. 498). Unlike Avoiron, Thiébaut Frères appears to have reproduced casts largely on individual command and to have no contractual agreement with Bartholdi.[11] As casts by Avoiron have their identifying characteristics, so do those by Thiébaut Frères: a square self-base, usually without the canted corners normally found in examples of the *Modèle du Comité* or of the American Committee Model (see below) and shared by the statue itself, and a tablet inscription in Roman, not Arabic, numerals. The latter is a feature not found in models by any other foundry, and among historical models is paralleled only in the tablet inscription of the statue in New York harbor.

Visually, the casts by Thiébaut Frères represent the founder's craft at its finest: the intricate pattern of the figure's robe (a loose, flowing garment commonly worn by women in classical antiquity) is delineated with infinite attention to detail, and is matched in quality by the rich patination originally produced and on a few examples still intact on the bronze surface. These casts display the most refined artistry of all reproduced versions of the statue and present *Liberty* in small scale as the noble figure envisioned by her creator.

The smaller models by the firm were almost certainly linked to the process of enlargement by the foundry as part of the project for the Ile des Cygnes.[12] Of all the outdoor reductions of *Liberty*, the best known and most frequently photographed is the replica (cat. 499) that stands on the narrow strip of land in the middle of the river Seine, not far from the Eiffel Tower, in Paris. Thirty-six feet in height and in bronze—the largest statue in Paris—the replica was installed in its present location in 1968 when the adjacent Pont de Grenelle, on which the statue originally stood, was completely rebuilt. Prior to 1968, the replica was mounted on a smaller base that stood at the edge of a semi-circular projection part of the original bridge, a location it had occupied, with a change in position in 1937, since its dedication on July 4, 1889.

In November 1875, to acknowledge the fund-raising campaign of the Franco-American Union, a Dr. Evans, a well-known dentist living in Paris, proposed that the American community offer a monument to France. Evans began the project with a personal contribution of $10,000,[13] but this promising beginning was not followed up, and a new start had to be made eight years later. The end of 1883 saw the formation of the American Subscription Fund for the Purchase of the Original Model of Liberty Enlightening the World, with H. F. Gillig as treasurer, and E. King and T. Stanton as honorary secretaries. The Fund sought to purchase the original 1:4 scale model of the finished statue—that is, the final enlargement that served as the model for construction in the Gaget, Gauthier workshops. Early in 1884, Levi P. Morton, U.S. Minister to France, offered a guarantee of one-third of the Fr. 75,000 to be raised by subscription; he also personally contributed Fr. 5,000.[14]

Six months later the project had changed its nature and come under new auspices. The American colony decided to offer the city of Paris a bronze cast from Bartholdi's plaster, as being more likely to withstand the ravages of time. The Committee of Patronage for the Presentation to the City of Paris of a Reduced Copy of Mr. Bartholdi's Statue of Liberty had as its president the American painter Henry Bacon. The cost of the casting was to be Fr. 10,000; Morton contributed Fr. 1,000.[15]

The casting was entrusted to Thiébaut Frères for completion by the beginning of May 1885. A few privileged spectators attended by invitation to watch the fantastic spectacle of 10 tons of bronze being poured, but on the great day the work had reached only the hem of *Liberty*'s skirt. Since the statue would not be ready in time, the committee decided to unveil the plaster original; the city of Paris had graciously made a site available on the Place des États-Unis. The unveiling took place on May 13 in the presence of Brisson, President of the Council; Morton; Poubelle, the Prefect of the Seine; a deputation from the City Council of Paris; and members of the Franco-American Union. Victor Hugo sent his compliments.

The bronze statue, like its sister in New York harbor, experienced a series of delays. In 1887 the casting had still not been poured; it appears that the Thiébaut firm had not received timely payment. Consideration had also turned to a different site, the Ile des Cygnes or the Pont de Grenelle.[16] Rising from the Seine and facing toward America, the smaller colossus would form part of a panorama reminiscent of New York harbor, though on a smaller scale.

July 4, 1889, was the doubly auspicious date chosen for installing the bronze *Liberty* on her site. The Universal Exposition was in full swing, and the day itself commemorated the two dates carved on the pedestal: 1776 and 1789—the former, that of American independence; the latter, of the French Revolution, and of Washington's nomination to the presidency. Below the dates were carved these words of Morton's: «France and America are as one in the cause of a government of free men.» No other words could better have conveyed French-American friendship. French officialdom, headed by President Carnot, attended the inauguration in force. The statue was turned to face inward, toward the center of the bridge, with its back to New York, so that a boat would not be required for the inaugural ceremonies conducted by French President Carnot.[17]

The Paris Statue of Liberty has inspired painters such as Henri Rousseau (cat. 500), Signac (cat. 501), and Béjot (cat. 502), and also photographers, particularly Robert Doisneau (cat. 503). Like the statue in New York, the one in Paris has been surrounded with scaffolding and given a facelift, in preparation for the ceremonies of 1986.

503
Replica of the Statue of Liberty, Pont de Grenelle
Robert Doisneau
ca. 1961

Less dramatic in setting is a 9-foot bronze reduction of *Liberty* from the same foundry, located in the Jardin du Luxembourg in Paris (cat. 504). Positioned at the far end of the gardens, the replica occupies a location near the site of the now-demolished house and studio in which Bartholdi lived at the end of his life. The figure, specifically commissioned by Bartholdi for the Centennial Exposition of 1900,[18] is apparently the sole survivor among a group of identical reductions produced by Thiébaut Frères between 1887 and 1900. Earlier casts, known only from photographs and historical accounts, once stood in Bordeaux, Lunel, and Saint-Affrique; a companion cast was reportedly installed in Hanoi, but is said to have disappeared in 1945.[19] The Bordeaux statue, designed by Bartholdi and cast in bronze by Thiébaut, was erected during 1887 or 1888 on the Place Picard, where a Liberty Tree once stood. The 9-foot-high statue was melted down for German armaments in 1942 by order of the Vichy Government's Non-Ferrous Metals Commission;[20] its pedestal, which was a fountain, survives in a few postcards (cat. 505) and a poorly preserved terra-cotta model in the Musée d'Aquitaine in Bordeaux (inv. 12499). The statue at Lunel memorialized the centennial in 1889 of the French Revolution; the statue at Saint-Affrique, also erected in 1889, was equipped with a lantern built into the torch.

Reductions of *Liberty* in the same 9-foot size as those produced by Thiébaut Frères were made for outdoor installation during the years immediately following the turn of the century by another Parisian foundry, the Société du Val d'Osne, in association with the foundry of Antoine Durenne.[21] The names are associated with at least four reductions which, although bearing independent foundry inscriptions, are identical in design and height, and which were all made about the same time in cast iron, probably from the same molds. They are located in Poitiers, Roybon, Saint-Cyr-sur-Mer, and Buenos Aires. The Poitiers statue (cat. 506) bore a lantern built into the torch; the still-standing replica at Roybon was dedicated in 1906 to the memory of Saint Romme, a member of the republican Chamber of Deputies in 1848. Saint-Cyr-sur-Mer unveiled a *Liberty* to celebrate the opening of the first network of irrigation canals. The Val d'Osne and Durenne replicas share design characteristics, most noticeable in facial expression and complexity of drapery arrangement, with the casts produced earlier by Thiébaut Frères. Val d'Osne, like Thiébaut Frères, probably acquired directly from Bartholdi a *modèle d'étude* for its foundry production.[22] Val d'Osne acted independently in soliciting commissions; the figure of *Liberty* was advertised in catalogues of its products published after the turn of the century.[23] Certainly Val d'Osne maintained a continuing interest in the subject, producing a reduction installed at Saint-Etienne in 1915, and in the 1950s

reviving production with two replicas: one for a then-American military base at Semoutiers, the other, from a design unrelated to the original *modèle d'étude*, commissioned for the Liberty National Life Insurance Company in Birmingham, Alabama.[24]

In addition to these replicas were several others, which served diverse purposes. An ephemeral one of wood and cloth, erected in 1909 in the village of Bazoches les Gallerandes, lasted for only a single July 14. A replica at Izon, like many of those mentioned above, carried a lantern built into the torch. At Cambrin Bartholdi's masterpiece served as a monument to the dead.

In America, small-scale models of *Liberty* were reproduced in quantities far greater than those in France. The American Committee Model (see cat. 381, 382, 383) was reproduced under contract to the American Committee of the Statue of Liberty, with two of three sizes sold in 1885 to raise funds for the statue's pedestal.[25] Apart from models made under contract to the American Committee were others manufactured solely for commercial purposes. Although Bartholdi had obtained a U.S. copyright in 1876 and in 1878 was granted the first of two patents (the second was issued a year later),[26] his design for *Liberty* was soon imitated by others and sold as souvenirs (cat. 507).[27]

506

23. BORDEAUX. — Place Picard

507

504
Replica of the Statue of Liberty, Jardin du Luxembourg, Paris
Frédéric-Auguste Bartholdi
1900
reproduced in color on p. 208

505
Replica of the Statue of Liberty, Place Picard, Bordeaux
Postcard
n.d.

506
Replica of the Statue of Liberty, Poitiers
n.d.

507
Model (cast)
Hermann Follmer
1883

Possessing a different appeal and wholly unconnected with commercial production are folk replicas, single examples that are handmade in almost every case by an anonymous, untrained craftsman. Other single examples are certain works made for specific commission; these, unlike folk pieces, are usually highly refined pieces, often produced by jewelers associated with well-known houses.[28]

As works created for their own sake, labors of love fashioned in materials understood by untrained but accomplished craftsmen, folk replicas of *Liberty* rarely come to public attention. They generally remain in anonymous custody, kept by the families of their makers as mementoes, and in every instance are works unique in both design and example. A typical folk work without documentable origins and by an anonymous craftsman is a 32-inch-high model of *Liberty* in carved wood (cat. 508). Comparatively refined in the rendering of drapery folds, and with a self-base that includes the canted corners of the original statue, the figure offers evidence that its maker was familiar with the statue in sculpted form. Of an uncertain date, the model is inscribed «VIVAT AMERIKA» on the front of its base, and on the reverse, «At Bartholdi.» «At» represents «August,» a German rendering of Bartholdi's forename; this, coupled with the German spelling «Amerika,» suggests that the model's maker was German, probably an immigrant newly arrived about the turn of the century.

In another material and also made about the turn of the century is a unique work in metal that can be identified as an authentic folk piece (cat. 509). Acquired by its present owner in St. Louis, Missouri, the model may be linked with the American Woman's League, a remarkable organization founded about 1905 in St. Louis by a publisher who built the Woman's Magazine Building, from which he promoted a number of worthy but financially unsound endeavors, including the American Woman's Republic, which possessed a written constitution and an organizational structure similar to that of the federal government. Among its activities the League sponsored an art academy with which the folk work may be associated.[29] Standing 55 inches high, the figure and its pedestal are in hammered copper, duplicating in both technique and material the Statue of Liberty itself. Whether the piece was made by an anonymous student at the League's academy or is an altogether unrelated work cannot be determined.

Two copper Statue of Liberty weathervanes, both dating from the late nineteenth century, are not precisely replicas but, rather, folk adaptations of the figure. The larger of the two, privately owned and on view at the Museum of American Folk Art in New York, is of molded copper and is mounted on a large arrow that serves as wind indicator. Made by the J. L. Mott Iron Works of New York and Chicago, the vane was advertised by the company and may have been made to order. With no companion examples so far identified, the vane can be regarded as a unique, remarkable example of *Liberty*'s image turned to utilitarian purpose.

The second weathervane is in the collection of The Abby Aldrich Rockefeller Folk Art Center in Williamsburg, Virginia. Different in design from and slightly smaller in height than the vane made by J. L. Mott, this example is identified as having been discovered in the Penobscot Valley, Maine, but is otherwise without indication of maker; no further information exists to document its origins.

The creation of such folk-art replicas of *Liberty* continues to the present day. Many are the product of the amateur craftsman inspired to create *Liberty*'s image for a particular purpose and always in an entirely personal manner.

Among replications of *Liberty*, souvenirs are those most familiar to the public and have been in continuous demand since before the statue's inaugural in 1886. Least familiar are the large-scale reductions in outdoor settings. In nearly every instance, the outdoor reductions were initially endowed with a sense of mission, generally commemorative and directly sharing in the symbolic virtues for which the Statue of Liberty is universally recognized. Thus, from the largest of these outdoor replicas to the earliest study designs by the sculptor himself, all replications of *Liberty* were created in the shadow of the original. Some are of greater historical and technical interest than others, and a few possess an artistic refinement which gives them a rightful place of their own among the arts.

508
Model, Folk Replica
ca. 1900

509
Model, American Woman's League Folk Replica
ca. 1905

17.
Proliferation of the Image

*Anne Cannon Palumbo
and Ann Uhry Abrams*

THE GREAT BARTHOLDI STATUE,
LIBERTY ENLIGHTENING THE WORLD.

WITH THE WORLD RENOWNED AND BEAUTIFUL

STAR LAMP,

«Image-making has to supplement form-giving in public sculptures,» declared critic Lawrence Alloway, who offered the Statue of Liberty as a prime example of a public monument that achieved popularity because it was «legible and learnable» as an image.[1] Taking Alloway's assessment a step further, we might say that it is the image itself, appearing with amazing frequency in an astonishing variety of forms and contexts, that has brought Bartholdi's statue a celebrity unparalleled by any other work of art of its day or ours. Long before *La Liberté éclairant le Monde* had reached completion, pictures were appearing in newspapers and magazines, sometimes depicting the progress of the work, often representing artists' conceptions of the finished statue. This was a relatively new phenomenon. A half-century earlier, visual information in such profusion would have been unthinkable, but by 1886, when Bartholdi's statue was installed on its pedestal in New York harbor, «the explosion of imagery» was well underway, spurred on both by revolutions in the technology of printing and pictorial reproduction and by the adoption of mass-production techniques. Pictorial journals like *Harper's Weekly, Frank Leslie's Illustrated Newspaper*, and France's *L'Illustration* had recently sprung up, carrying the statue's image to thousands who had not seen, and perhaps never would see, the great copper figure itself. The daily press, which formerly consisted of grey pages of unbroken type, also sprouted pictures to give the statue further popular exposure. And inexpensive lithographs bearing the statue's likeness, issuing from a spate of publishers, such as Currier and Ives or Root and Tinker, were eagerly snapped up by a public as yet innocent of pictorial saturation.

Modern technology and mass production made possible the manufacture of inexpensive three-dimensional replicas as well. The thousands of miniature versions of *Liberty* distributed by the American Committee of the Statue of Liberty to raise money for the pedestal began the process of three-dimensional replication that went on to give us Statues of Liberty in every conceivable material: metal, glass, china, and, eventually, plastic (cat. 381, 382, 383). A recent film about the legendary labor radical Joe Hill opens with the hero's landing in turn-of-the-century New York City where he is met at the dock by a peddler with a tray of miniature Statues of Liberty. Hill's purchase of one of these to keep by him as a symbol of the promise held out by his new homeland is heavily ironic, but the scene graphically illustrates the phenomenon of the mass-produced replica and serves to remind us of the vast numbers of these little models that found a place on the shelf in the homes of countless individuals.[2]

Besides drumming up support for the statue and its pedestal, much of the imagery spawned during the early years of the statue's history met the demand for information about the celebrated monument or satisfied the desire to possess a memento of it. However, another category of images emerged with quite a different objective. In another of those fateful coincidences, the Statue of Liberty happened upon the American scene at just about the time that the advertising agent made his appearance. The new statue's celebrity quickly engaged his attention, and before long its image, often substantially altered, appeared in advertisements, hawking everything from patent medicines to sewing thread. Sometimes an existing image was simply changed to accommodate the sponsor's product. A lithographic view of the statue published by Currier and Ives in 1883 reemerged the following year with a «Star Lamp» replacing *Liberty*'s torch (cat. 510), and the name «Astral Oil» showed up on the statue's base in a reissue of the Root and Tinker print that had originally been commissioned by the American Committee (cat. 366).

Even more substantial changes materialized on trade cards bearing the statue's image. Typically consisting of a brightly colored picture on one side and a printed sales pitch on the other, this advertising device was extremely popular during the last quarter of the nineteenth century. Of a convenient size (usually about 3″ × 5″) for tucking into the pockets of aprons and overalls or pasting into scrapbooks, these cards were inserted into products or handed over the sales counter to make their way to virtually every part of the farflung continent. Occasionally there was an observable tie-in between the advertised product and the statue—Liberty Flour shared a name; Parisian Sauce a (somewhat tenuous) French association (cat. 568)—but more often the advertiser found it necessary to strain to create a connection. What the statue had to do with sewing machines was ingeniously spelled out in a message on the back of the card put out by the Singer Co., which read:

> . . . if the WOMEN of the world were to build a monument to commemorate that which had afforded them the greatest liberty, and given them the most time for enlightening their minds and those of their children, they would build one to the SEWING MACHINE, which has released the Mother of the Race from countless hours of weary drudgery, and has in the truest and best sense been quietly but steadily *Enlightening the World*.

Designers of trade cards blithely replaced the statue's accessories with spools of thread, cookie tins, and other products, sometimes going so far as to do away with the statue altogether. In one instance, the monkish figure representing St. Jacob's Oil assumes the statue's pose atop the pedestal with a bottle of the touted pain killer held aloft and, in another, the presumed consumer of Dr. Haas Hog Remedy, suitably draped and brandishing torch and tablet, reposes atop a wholly imaginary pedestal studded with the product's name (cat. 565).

510

The Great Bartholdi Statue
Currier & Ives
ca. 1884

Judging from the frequency with which it appeared in advertisements and cartoons, the favorite comic variation of the statue's pose was the one which produced a disgruntled matron raising her lamp to chastise errant spouses or offspring (cat. 511). In part because the monument had acquired few associations that readily lent themselves to parody, comic advertisements usually confined themselves to making sport of material elements such as pose or accessories. An advertisement for laundry soap that features an Irish washerwoman striking the pose while straddling two laundry tubs (cat. 512) conforms to the rule, but is notable because it makes a rare allusion to the statue's symbolic meaning: by linking the statue to immigrants it promulgates an association that would become an essential part of the statue's symbolism, even though the comic treatment tends to deny it any genuine significance.

The prevalence of the advertising spoof suggests that the Statue of Liberty was initially regarded by the American public as little more than a particularly imposing piece of sculpture. Had it been invested with compelling spiritual or patriotic meaning, it is unlikely that advertisers would have risked offending potential customers by such cavalier treatment. France provides an instructive contrast. While *Liberty* was used to promote French goods as often as American ones, Gallic commerce handled her image with more respect. This may signify regard for the statue's higher meaning, or, perhaps, having to pay for the privilege of using *Liberty*'s image, French advertisers felt less inclined to joke about it. Whatever the reason, distortion for comic effect seems to have had little vogue in France.

The ephemeral nature of advertising makes it easy to underestimate its importance to the creation and popularization of images of the Statue of Liberty. While she was new, advertisers contributed greatly to her celebrity; but when her novelty wore off, her image soon faded from the marketplace. It was seen only in the occasional advertisement until World War I returned *Liberty* to prominence, once again rendering her image appealing as an adjunct to product promotion. But the emotion-charged atmosphere of the war precluded the earlier free-wheeling approach. A patriotic symbol could not safely be made an object of humor, however

511

T. W. Perry Trade Card

ca. 1886

reproduced in color

on p. 241

512

G. A. Shoudy & Son Trade Card

n.d.

513

Your Glass of Coca-Cola....

World War I advertisement

good-natured. The advertising industry reached a compromise, introducing the statue into its copy to suggest the sponsor's contribution to the war effort, but studiously avoiding any alteration to the image that might be construed as disrespectful (cat. 513).

Such comic distortions of the statue as were pervasive in advertising in the 1880s and early 1890s reappeared briefly in the 1920s, but returned in force only after the iconoclasm of the 1960s stripped away the protective aura from all such sacred national symbols. A seemingly irreverent poster in which the statue joins with Uncle Sam in advertising Haig whiskey (cat. 514) is not so much an example of «roaring twenties» iconoclasm as it is a reminder of *Liberty*'s brush with Prohibition, when «Wets» called upon her image to protest what was in their view an unwarranted abridgment of personal liberties. Today, however, the statue is regularly seen carrying cocktail trays, sporting blue jeans, and extolling the virtues of underarm deodorant with an abandon that suggests the wheel has come full circle.

Commercial exploitation has not gone unremarked by critics of the consumer culture. What happens to the meaning of symbols like the Statue of Liberty when they are regularly employed to push merchandise is the issue raised by the poster entitled *Yankee Flame*, created by Ben Schonzeit for the American Bicentennial (cat. 515). The easily recognizable shape of a glass of Coca-Cola occupies the foreground, marking it as a new icon that all but obliterates the traditional ones of George Washington and the Statue of Liberty. The irony of Schonzeit's poster is compounded when seen in conjunction with soft-drink advertisements, which have not infrequently employed the statue's image to tout their wares. Interestingly, the cover of the paperback edition of Frederick Lewis Allen's *The Big Change: America Transforms Itself, 1900–1950* hits upon a similar visual device to suggest a shift in national allegiance, depicting a figure whose upper body is that of the Statue of Liberty, but whose lower portions are those of a soft-drink bottle. Attesting to the currency of the theme is French artist Jean Lagarrigue's satirical painting *Liberté-Cola* (cat. 516) which likewise questions American priorities by conflating the same two recognizably American symbols. Less sharply critical, but an equally relevant commentary on contemporary icons, is the playful drawing by Robert O. Blechman, captioned «Over 17 Billion Served,» in which *Liberty*'s crown is metamorphosed into the «golden arches» of McDonald's (cat. 517).

Of course, the inexhaustible flood of pictorial material trading on the image of the Statue of Liberty cannot be wholly attributed to advertising, nor is it necessarily inspired by a desire for commercial advantage, yet the net effect may be the same—a leaching of meaning and an inevitable slide in the direction of the banal. Implicit in Andy Warhol's painting *Liberty Enlightening the World 24 Times*, with its serial images of the famous monument, is the suggestion that an image constantly repeated loses its power to evoke an emotional response. To make his point, Warhol deliberately imitates the characteristics of the mass-produced image, a strategy employed in his well-known depictions of media celebrities such as Marilyn Monroe and his chillingly repetitive images of an electric chair. The issue is fraught with irony, ambiguity, and complexity. The Statue of Liberty owes much of its fame and success to the readiness with which it became an image and the ease with which that image could be multiplied, but the same circumstances threaten to reduce it to a meaningless bromide.

Artist Cosmos Sarchiapone's collage *Statue of Liberty Centennial 1886–1986* also calls attention to mass-produced imagery by focusing on the mundane but not inconsequential phenomenon of the postcard (cat. 518). In assembling cards issued over a period of a century, each different and yet all significantly alike, the artist invites the viewer to ponder the extent to which such images have come to pervade our consciousness. When we reflect that each individual card stands for thousands more exactly like it, we begin to appreciate that even the homely postcard represents the proliferation of the image of the Statue of Liberty on a monumental scale.

As Sarchiapone's collage attests, the postcard characteristically emphasizes the statue's distinction as a landmark, one of New York's premier tourist attractions, although this hardly exhausts its possibilities. *Liberty* has been featured on a host of novelty cards, her outline traced in sparkle dust, stamped on wood, leather, even aluminum, and cards with transparent inserts have «illuminated» her form when held to the light. Some of the most colorful of the early Statue of Liberty cards were printed in Germany, but their patriotic character makes it clear that they were designed for

514
Spirit of Haig
Guillaume
ca. 1928
reproduced in color
on p. 241

515
Yankee Flame
Ben Schonzeit
1976
reproduced in color
on p. 242

516
Liberté-Cola
Jean Lagarrigue
1974
reproduced in color
on p. 242

518
*Statue of Liberty
Centennial, 1886–1986*
Cosmos Sarchiapone
1976
reproduced in color
on p. 243

517
Over 17 Billion Served
Robert O. Blechman
1974

the American market. Postcard views of Paris provide an interesting variation in showing the replica of Bartholdi's statue erected in the Seine, and thereby demonstrating that it was possible for *Liberty* to function as a landmark of both Paris and New York.

The image of the Statue of Liberty made its way through the mails in another capacity—the postage stamp—an additional example of a single image multiplied by the thousands and hundreds of thousands (cat. 519). As might be expected, American issues are numerous, and France, too, has found occasion to honor the statue and its sculptor in philatelic fashion. Less expected, however, are the scores of other nations, from the tiny Republic of San Marino to such Communist-bloc countries as Bulgaria and Poland, that have employed the image and thus facilitated its proliferation throughout the entire world—«Liberty Enlightening the World,» indeed.

It was not until 1922 that the Statue of Liberty made its appearance on a U.S. stamp, thirty-six years after its installation on Bedloe's Island. Why did it take so long for *Liberty* to be officially recognized as the symbol of the nation? The images of *Liberty* produced during the intervening decades help to answer the question. Although frequently pictured at the time of the

inauguration, and never entirely out of sight thereafter, the statue was typically featured in the context of abstractions such as «Liberty» and «republicanism,» as a celebrated landmark, or occasionally in connection with immigration. Only after the turn of the century did the statue begin to be seen more often in an American, sometimes a specifically patriotic, context, as in a series of patriotic postcards dating from the first decade of the twentieth century. Although the monument had not yet become the symbol *of* America, it was in the process of collecting significant American associations.

The process was various, multiform, and impossible to catalogue, but an exploration of the statue's participation in the brand-new and exciting field of aviation gives some idea of how it worked. Over the years the statue has been pictured in conjunction with virtually every type of aircraft—dirigibles, helicopters, and airplanes ranging from the open-cockpit monoplane to big-bellied clippers to sleekly supersonic jets (cat. 520, 521)—but the convention was established during aviation's pioneer period and began, appropriately, with Wilbur Wright. In 1909, a canoe strapped to the underside of his craft as a precaution, Wright made the first American flight over water, taking off from Governor's Island and making a circuit around the Statue of Liberty (cat. 522). This was a featured event of the Hudson-Fulton celebration of the tricentenary of Henry Hudson's voyage and the centennial of the successful navigation of the Hudson to

Albany by Robert Fulton's steamship *Clermont*.[3] A flight over the route taken by the *Clermont* was accomplished the following year by another American pioneer aviator, Glenn H. Curtiss, who capped his performance by taking a turn around the Statue of Liberty, and received in return one of the most extravagant triumphal parades New York ever accorded a celebrity. A third historic flight involving the statue occurred in 1910, in connection with the famous air exposition held at Belmont Park, which concluded with a spectacular race around the monument. American John Moisant captured the prize and memorialized his feat with a poster advertising his troupe of fliers, the Moisant International Aviators (cat. 523).[4]

In practical terms, the Statue of Liberty was ideally suited to early aviation exploits. Her location—free of the clutter of buildings yet near a suitable landing site and sizable population—and her size—easily visible from the air and providing, like an aerial yardstick, a sense of scale and rough measurement of altitude—assured her a role in the history of American aviation. And because of the intense international competition marking the early years of aviation, and the early lead that the achievements of the Wright Brothers gave to the United States, *Liberty*'s association with aviation became an important part of her Americanization.

520
Liberty for All. Keep 'em Flying
Works Projects Administration
1932

521
Alouette Helicopter Circling the Statue of Liberty
Fairchild Republic Co.
1957

519
Selection of Stamps reproduced in color on p. 244

From this time forward, the statue was a regular feature in aerial events: acting as a beacon to fliers, as in the historic nonstop, transcontinental race undertaken by Lieutenants John A. Macready and Oakley G. Kelly in 1928; or as a showcase, as in the spectacular nighttime flight made by aviatrix Ruth Law, who flew over the statue with the word «liberty» spelled out in lights on the underside of her plane on the occasion of the 1916 floodlighting of the statue.[5] When the new French helicopter the *Alouette* was introduced in the United States in 1957, its revolutionary capacity for hovering was demonstrated by a performance undertaken alongside the head of the statue (cat. 521). The statue even became a part of the history of events in which it had no part: Charles Lindbergh's transatlantic flight was memorialized with a tapestry (cat. 524), manufactured in France, showing *The Spirit of St. Louis* winging above the Statue of Liberty, although Lindbergh did not actually fly over, or even very near, the monument.

The statue's relation to aviation, though frequently pictured, has seldom been noted. Not so its association with immigration. Scarcely an article or book, film or television show concerned with immigration—factual or fictionalized—lacks its obligatory reference to the Statue of Liberty, often in the guise of a picture of tired and shabby pilgrims on the deck of a ship sailing past the majestic monument. Countless personal testimonies describe the rapturous first glimpse of the symbol of American freedom and asylum. The story of American immigration and the Statue of Liberty are by now inextricably fused. The American Museum of Immigration is housed within the statue's precincts, and jet-age immigrants, who no longer sail past her island refuge, are nonetheless greeted by the words of Emma Lazarus' «New Colossus,» written in the statue's honor and now affixed to the entrance of John F. Kennedy International Airport. So firm is the association that it is natural to assume that Bartholdi's statue was created to serve as a symbol of welcome to those seeking refuge and a new life on American shores.

This was not at all the intention of the statue's creator, nor of its sponsors, French or American. Few at the time perceived any connection between the mounting numbers of newcomers swamping the Castle Garden receiving station and the splendid republican «goddess» destined to tower majestically on nearby Bedloe's Island. Emma Lazarus was the exception, and, as her fellow poet James Russell Lowell remarked, she gave the statue its «*raison d'être*»[6] with her ringing words:

Not like the brazen giant of Greek fame,
With conquering limbs astride from land to land;
Here at our sea-washed, sunset gates shall stand
A mighty woman with a torch, whose flame
Is the imprisoned lightning, and her name
Mother of Exiles. From her beacon hand
Glows world-wide welcome; her mild eyes command
The air-bridged harbor that twin cities frame.
«Keep, ancient lands, your storied pomp!» cries she
With silent lips. «Give me your tired, your poor,
Your huddled masses yearning to breathe free,
The wretched refuse of your teeming shore,
Send these, the homeless, tempest-tost to me,
I lift my lamp beside the golden door.»

A NEW KIND OF GULL IN NEW YORK HARBOR

522
[*Wilbur Wright Circling the Statue of Liberty as He Makes the First American Flight over Water*]
From *Harper's Weekly*
October 9, 1909

524
Tapestry Commemorating Charles A. Lindbergh's Transatlantic Flight
1928

523
The Moisant International Aviators
Guerra
1951
reproduced in color
on p. 244

Daughter of a wealthy Sephardic Jewish family, the Boston-born poet had little in common with the poor and dispossessed refugees fleeing from Russian Tsarist pogroms who attracted her notice about the time that the cornerstone was being laid for the statue's pedestal. But their plight excited her sympathies and prompted her to imagine the statue as representing the promise of asylum to the world's «huddled masses.» Although Lazarus' poem was featured in the fund-raising art exhibition hosted by the National Academy of Design, the sentiment failed to take hold, and the poem was soon forgotten. It had no place in the unveiling ceremonies, where keynote speaker Chauncey Depew felt compelled to warn that while the statue would teach the immigrants that «there is room and brotherhood for all who will support our institutions and aid in our development, those who come to disturb our peace and dethrone our laws are aliens and enemies forever.»[7]

Depew's cautionary remarks reflect an uneasiness that was becoming increasingly widespread. As immigration historian Maldwyn Allen Jones has noted, «the Statue of Liberty arrived at precisely the moment that Americans were beginning to doubt the wisdom of unlimited immigration.»[8] Several factors contributed to their skepticism. The «new immigration,» stemming principally from southern and eastern Europe or from Asia, consisted of peoples of vastly different cultural backgrounds, who many feared could not readily be assimilated into American society. Their numbers strained urban resources, creating massive housing and hygiene problems. Moreover, as Depew's remarks indicate, some viewed them as harbingers of social unrest, carriers of radical political ideas, violence, and crime.

Such fears found expression in the storm of protest that greeted a proposal put forward in 1890 to establish a new immigrant-receiving station on Bedloe's Island. The suggestion, which Bartholdi denounced as a «monstrous plan,» prompted *Judge* to portray *Liberty* in two cartoons. In one she lifts her skirts to avoid contamination from the immigrants being dumped at her feet, and in the other she is disfigured by a tenement-style fire escape and clothesline hung with washing.[9] *Puck*'s Louis Dalrymple took the theme a step further, conceiving a ruined statue lying amid the debris of ramshackle sheds thrown up to handle the needs of the immigrants. To indicate at whose door the «latest outrage» should be put, the figure of

New York State's Republican leader, «Boss Platt,» strikes an imperious pose on the vacant pedestal (cat. 564). Reactions such as these forced a change of plan, resulting in the substitution of the swampy marshes of Ellis Island for the old Fort Wood site, thus sparing the Statue of Liberty the threat of immigrant «desecration.» Two years later a cholera scare elicited a similar negative reaction in which the statue's image also figured. Earlier, Thomas Nast had laid the epidemics that plagued New York at the doorsteps of corrupt politicians and city officials who failed to provide adequate facilities for the city's teeming population. He conjured a spectral Statue of Liberty greeting visitors with the warning Dante encountered at the entrance of the gates of Hell—«Leave All Hope, Ye That Enter» (cat. 525a). Little more than a decade later, Nast and other cartoonists were blaming the immigrants, to whom such epithets as the «Dregs of Europe» were applied, for disease and death (cat. 525b).

After these contretemps, the tendency to identify the Statue of Liberty with immigration, negatively or otherwise, slipped into the background. A 1912 piece of Yiddish sheet music pairing the statue with the arrival of a young immigrant and the remarkable replica erected by a Russian immigrant in 1902 to crown his West 64th Street warehouse suggest that the immigrants themselves endeavored to keep the association alive.[10] If their scattered efforts failed to make much of an impact, the persistence of the association is also attested to by a few pictures, usually illustrating articles on immigration, and occasional literary references, like O. Henry's short story «The Lady Higher Up,» which describes *Liberty* as having been «made by a Dago and presented to the American people on behalf of the French Government for the purpose of welcomin' Irish immigrants into the Dutch city of New York.»[11]

The Great War helped to reinforce the association through propaganda posters aimed at winning the support of the nation's foreign-born population. The inspirational poster *Remember Your First Thrill of American Liberty*, with its clean lines and its patriotic red, white, and blue coloration, is particularly attractive (cat. 526). Although the poster makes use of the conventional motif of the Statue of Liberty seen by the immigrants from the deck of a ship, these passengers have nothing of the «huddled masses» look about them and, if picturesquely dressed, are neat and altogether presentable. Another shipboard scene, this one with Manhattan's tall buildings in the background, is equally inspirational, urging food conservation with the slogan «You came here seeking Freedom/Now you must help to preserve it,» issued in English as well as in Yiddish, Italian, Hungarian, and Spanish (cat. 527). As it turned out, the positive view of the immigrants' special relation to the Statue of Liberty was shortlived, scarcely extending beyond the Armistice. After the war the foreign born were frequent targets of the «Red Scare» that opened the postwar period, and in 1924 America's open door was abruptly slammed shut with the institution of a quota system that slowed the tide of immigration to a trickle.

It fell to the immigrants, or, in many cases, their sons and daughters, to establish the Statue of Liberty's special significance to the foreign born, a movement that gained momentum in the 1930s.[12] Ida Abelman's lithograph *My Father Reminisces*, a product of the Depression era's Works Projects Administration, graphically expresses the often poignant and bittersweet feelings characteristic of second-generation Americans, as they reflected on the trials and hardships experienced by their parents (cat. 528). Images of struggle and work—the union placard, the sewing machine—alternate with those of joy and hope—a ghetto gathering and a radiant Statue of Liberty. Increasingly the statue was featured in the literature of immigration—in novels, in immigrant memoirs, and in the books and articles written to bring to notice the contributions of the nation's ethnic minorities.[13] Philip Reisman's 1954 painting of a shirtwaist-makers' strike meeting presided over by Samuel Gompers and strike leader Clara Lemlich (commissioned by the Emma Lazarus Federation of Women's Clubs to commemorate the tricentenary of Jewish settlement in the New World) takes up this theme (cat. 529), although the introduction of the Statue of Liberty into a scene otherwise filled with images of labor strife and oppression raises a question: does she act as a protective deity sheltering her immigrant charges or as a helpless witness to their sufferings?

World War II, with its horrifying revelations of persecution, tended to intensify the idea of the statue as a symbol of refuge, but it did not immediately result in a change in immigration policy, as an R. A. Lewis cartoon illustrates. Inspired by the Hungarian uprising of 1956 and the American response

527
Il Cibo Vincerà la Guerra!
[*Food Will Win the War!*]
C. E. Chambers
1917

528
My Father Reminisces
Ida Abelman
1937

to its victims, Lewis replaces the statue's tablet with a weighty volume of «Immigration Red Tape,» which contradicts the welcome emanating from her torch. But images like Lewis' had their effect in the eventual passage of a new immigration bill, signed by President Lyndon B. Johnson in 1965 in a ceremony at the base of the Statue of Liberty. Today, as the works of contemporary image-makers demonstrate, the Statue of Liberty is firmly wedded to the topic of immigration. Commenting on recent immigration issues, Gene Basset sends his «illegal aliens» charging over a hapless and helpless *Liberty* (cat. 530). The association is so firmly cemented that it invites parody. It is not the «huddled masses» but an entirely different set of «new immigrants» who look to Johanna Vogelsang's jewel-bedecked statue for asylum, as the accompanying paraphrase of «The New Colossus» makes clear (cat. 531).

The name «The Immigrant City,» which is often applied to New York, highlights one of the factors that helped to wed the statue and the city, yet it was but one element in the web of associations that made the statue the special symbol of the metropolis. Recently a columnist observed that «the Statue of Liberty, the Empire State Building, the World Trade Center, these are New York,»[14] thereby drawing attention to another circumstance that entitled the statue to represent the city. Artists have long noted the correspondence between the skyscrapers and the statue and treated them as visual analogues. Joseph Pennell, a noted turn-of-the-century illustrator and printmaker who returned to New York after living abroad for most of his career, confessed his delight at the vista created by the juxtaposition of statue and skyscrapers. «As the steamer moves up the bay on one side the Great Goddess greets you,» he exclaimed, «a composition in colour and in form, with the city beyond, finer than any in any world that ever existed, finer than Claude ever imagined or Turner ever dreamed.»[15] He channeled his excitement into the mezzotint *Hail, America*, picturing the Statue of Liberty dramatically silhouetted against a moonlit sky with tall buildings clustering along the shoreline beyond (cat. 532).

Even before the advent of the skyscraper, the statue's size had recommended it as an emblem of the nation's largest city. Its forward-looking technology—as modern as the gleaming steel cables of the Brooklyn Bridge, which spanned the East River only a few years before Bartholdi's goddess rose to dominate the Narrows—furthered the correlation of statue and city. Printmakers of that era often coupled the two structures in bird's-eye views, picturing them cheek by jowl, as if they occupied adjacent sites. A city bounding into the modern world eagerly appropriated such engineering marvels as emblems of its own energetic pursuit of modernity. But although the statue was structurally up to date, its outward aspect increasingly seemed hopelessly old-fashioned, an artistic relic that, unlike the bridge or the city itself, both of which fired the imaginations of the artists of the new century, inspired no modernist masterpieces.

As a landmark, however, the statue proved indispensable to artists. No other feature of the landscape could so readily guarantee instant recognition of the scene as that of New York. The statue inhabits the Impressionist-inspired views of Theodore Butler

and William Glackens, the sketchy visions of Louis Eilshemius, and the sophisticated naivetes of Florine Stettheimer. By virtue of her site alone, the «lady in the harbor» bespoke the nature of the city as a great port, which Reginald Marsh commemorated in a mural for New York's Bowling Green Customs House. Marsh, whose art was devoted to explorations of New York, selected the Statue of Liberty to symbolize the port, devising a novel presentation that shows the statue from behind, facing the city as though to introduce Manhattan's teeming shoreline.

Predictably, the statue's eminence as a landmark made it a tourist attraction, a facet of its appeal captured on canvas by Arnold Friedman. Friedman, too, was a New York artist, and no doubt often witnessed the Circle Line ferries plying their cargo of sightseers. As the focus of New York's tourist industry, the statue adorns postcards, travel posters, and souvenir guidebooks. It has also been a never-failing resource for photographers seeking to interpret the metropolis, a Beaux-Arts complement to the sleek glass and steel facades of modern skyscrapers, and now, thanks to the magic of technology, *Liberty* can be photo-

graphically relocated to stand alongside the World Trade Center and other giant landmarks. Some matings of the Statue of Liberty and Manhattan's famous buildings have been playful. Saul Steinberg placed a barber pole/Indian/Statue of Liberty at the foot of the Chrysler Building. The design of the Art-Deco structure repeats the projecting rays of the statue's crown, while the figure acts as an amalgam of sign-post symbolism. In his parody of Manet's *Dejeuner sur l'Herbe*, Hudson Talbott provided a nude Statue of Liberty with the companionship of anthropomorphic Chrysler and Empire State Buildings, transposing the famous picnic scene from the Tuileries to Central Park (cat. 533).

Acquiring associations such as those with American aviation, immigration, and New York City certified the statue's American citizenship and even granted it a place among American symbols, but this did not suffice to make the Statue of Liberty the symbol of America. That was accomplished by World War I. Since the emotions stirred by such crises find release in patriotic symbols, it was to be expected that one of

532
Hail, America
Joseph Pennell
1908

533
Luncheon on the Grass
Hudson Talbott
1982
reproduced in color
on p. 246

535
Pour la Liberté du Monde
Sem
1914–18

536
America Calls, Enlist in the Navy
J. C. Leyendecker
1917

539
Czechoslovaks, Your Allies
1945

511
T. W. Perry Trade Card
ca. 1886

514
Spirit of Haig
Guillaume
ca. 1928

America: the third century

515
Yankee Flame
Ben Schonzeit
1976

516
Liberté-Cola
Jean Lagarrigue
1974

518
*Statue of Liberty
Centennial, 1886–1986*
Cosmos Sarchiapone
1976

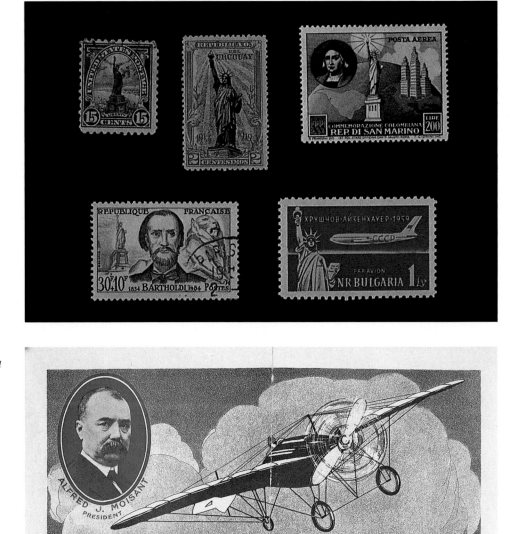

523
*The Moisant International
Aviators*
Guerra
1951

526

Remember Your First Thrill
of American Liberty
World War I Liberty Loan
Poster
1917

533
Luncheon on the Grass
Hudson Talbott
1982

THAT LIBERTY SHALL NOT
PERISH FROM THE EARTH
BUY LIBERTY BONDS
FOURTH · LIBERTY · LOAN

537
*That Liberty Shall Not
Perish from the Earth*
Joseph Pennell
1918

534
French Handkerchief
1918–19

538
July Fourth, 1934
J. C. Leyendecker
1934

540
Liberation
R. Doumoulin
1944

R. DUMOULIN

LIBÉRATION

541
We, too, have a Job to do.
Join a Boy Scout Troop
1942

547
Two French Girls
Sheila Elias
1984

548
Ms. Liberty
Mutz
1975

549
Women and the Arts in the
1920s
Seymour Chwast
1978

552
Our Statue of Liberty.—
She Can Stand It
C. J. Taylor
From *Puck*
October 27, 1886

A REPUBLIC.

AN EMPIRE.

554
[Untitled lithograph]
Grant Hamilton, from an
idea of William Jennings
Bryan
From *Judge*
January 26, 1901

553
*Rushing to Their Own
Destruction*
Louis Dalrymple
From *Puck*
November 23, 1887

557
[Soviet Desecration of the
Statue.]
Kukrinisky
1968

563
*Liberty Inviting Artists to
Take Part in an Exhibition
Against Leftist Terrorists
(IRA PLO FALN Red Brigade
Sandinistas Bulgarians)*
Roger Brown
1983

BOSS PLATT'S LATEST OUTRAGE.

564
Boss Platt's Latest Outrage
Louis Dalrymple
From *Puck*
March 19, 1890

565
Dr. Haas Hog Remedy
Trade Card
1884

ENLIGHTENING THE WORLD.

OVER

J. H. LE GRANDE GROCERY
GROCERIES — MEATS — VEGETABLES
Open Daily: 7 AM 'til 10 PM

Phone 32-631   BRADENTON, FLA.

566
Le Grande Grocery
Calendar
1950

568
Parisian Sauce Trade Card
ca. 1886

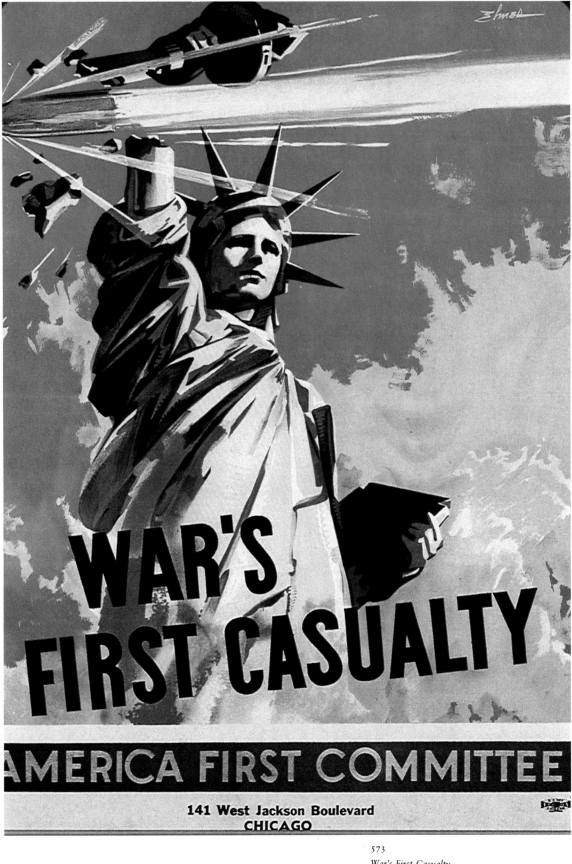

573
War's First Casualty
Elmer
1939

542
Life Magazine cover
June 5, 1939

543
Saboteur
Universal
1942

544
Funny Girl
Columbia/Rastar
1968

the war's by-products would be a new prominence for the statue. Certainly it had several factors to recommend it as a wartime symbol. It was not only useful in securing the allegiance of foreign-born citizens, but uniquely suited to popularize the French-American alliance (cat. 534). Much more important, however, in catapulting *Liberty* to the status of symbol of the nation was the fortuitous choice of the name «Liberty Loan» to designate the war bond campaigns and the inevitable appropriation of *Liberty*'s image to promote them. By war's end, *Liberty* had taken her place beside Uncle Sam, displacing Columbia, who had long been the female symbol of America.

The Liberty Loan was launched with an arresting poster by G. R. Macauley picturing a finger-pointing Statue of Liberty demanding, «YOU Buy a Liberty Bond,» which was soon joined by a spate of others promoting support of the war. When the Division of Pictorial Publicity was formed under the chairmanship of famed illustrator Charles Dana Gibson, hundreds of artists, many of them also well-known illustrators, volunteered their services, which resulted in high-quality poster designs like those of J. C. Leyendecker and Joseph Pennell, although perhaps the most aesthetically satisfying of the Statue of Liberty posters was produced in aid of France's war effort by the French artist Sem (cat. 535). Leyendecker's recruitment poster for the Navy (cat. 536) is particularly noteworthy as an example of «Columbia-Liberty,» a hybrid figure that emerged during the war and represents a stage in the eventual displacement of the traditional Columbia by the progressively predominant *Liberty*. Joseph Pennell's poster, unique among his many views of the statue, is also significant: because he had previously employed the image to extol American progress and the majesty of the New York skyline (cat. 532), his chilling rendering of the magnificent ruin, a victim of the destruction of war (cat. 537), resonated with ominous implications.

While bringing *Liberty* to the forefront as a symbol of the nation, recalling her French origins, and reinforcing her association with immigration, the war also furnished *Liberty* with new roles. To counter the fears and insecurities aroused by the hostilities, the statue was portrayed as an impregnable bastion, a metaphorical fortress defending the nation's values as well as its shores. Its location, significantly both entry and point of embarkation, gave rise to touching images of the grand lady sending the troops off to fight and welcoming them home on their return. She was a comforting beacon, a secure haven in time of trouble, and by war's end unquestionably accepted as the symbol of the nation. When Americans were confronted with economic crisis a decade later, it was only natural to call upon the image of *Liberty* to lift the Depression gloom. Applying an up-beat, Art-Deco style, J. C. Leyendecker pictured a thirties goddess as though triumphantly risen from the sea (cat. 538).

By the time the world was plunged once more into war, *Liberty* had become the symbol by which America was identified both at home and abroad (cat. 539). Hardly anyone remembered her Gallic origins except in France where, despite enemy occupation, the memory persisted to emerge at last in posters celebrating the Allied victory in Europe (cat. 540). In America *Liberty*'s official role was not as significant as it had been in World War I, but her duties were much the same, and much of the imagery made familiar by the earlier conflict reappeared, sometimes suitably updated. She still sold savings bonds, although Daniel Chester French's statue *The Minuteman* was the officially designated logo this time around; she promoted the war effort once more, but was occasionally allowed to assume a more active persona, akin to that of «Rosie the Riveter» (cat. 541). She welcomed home the troops, although some now returned by air; and once again her image was appropriated to serve in both patriotic and commercial contexts.

Perhaps most important among the many World War II roles assigned the statue was that of «fortress of freedom.» Throughout the war and into the Cold War period that followed, *Liberty* was depicted as an impregnable bastion, the stalwart guardian of democratic values. Three times during the war (first in 1939 at the onset of the European conflict) *Life* featured the same picture of *Liberty* on its cover. Abandoning its usually inflexible black-and-white photographic rule, the magazine pictured her arrayed in patriotic hues of red, white, and blue, the camera angle emphasizing her monumental grandeur (cat. 542). Silhouetted against a dramatically dark background, the statue glowed like a shrine. The editors explained their selection with the comment, «It is fitting enough that in these days when the light of freedom burns ever lower in Europe, Liberty stands out with new brightness against the American sky.» In the imagery of war, *Liberty* could be many things—a comforting symbol of home, a defender of freedom, and a transcendent mother-goddess.

Liberty's ascendancy to patriotic icon did not mean that she abandoned her earthier roles. She had often descended her pedestal to appear behind the footlights, as often showgirl as goddess. Before she could be properly said to be a statue at all she was starring in such entertainments as the Philadelphia Centennial and the Universal Exposition. Her effigy, displayed on the facade of Fifth Avenue's New York Club, stole the show at the gala Centennial Fourth of July celebration, and her appearance as a sculpture made from the novel medium of hay, corn, and grain delighted visitors to the 1885 New Orleans World's Fair (cat. 570). Subsequently she was to capture the lead in a Broadway musical, star in wartime radio dramas, and perform character roles and walk-ons in a variety of films. She has graced innumerable parade floats, pageants, and tableaux vivants, and furnished inspiration for entertainment publicity as well as caricatures of stage and screen luminaries.

Liberty made her debut as a Broadway star in 1949, when postwar patriotic fervor still guided national taste. A product of the joint efforts of songwriter Irving Berlin, playwright Robert E. Sherwood, director Moss Hart, and choreographer Jerome Robbins, *Miss Liberty* revolved around a make-believe rivalry between two New York newspapers, Joseph Pulitzer's *World* and James Gordon Bennett's *Herald*, each trying to scoop the other by uncovering the supposed mystery girl who posed for Bartholdi's masterpiece. Stars Eddie Albert, Allyn McLerie, and Mary McCarthy romped through songs and dances, backed by sets of New York and Paris in the 1880s, and assembled with the entire cast before a spectacular silhouette of the Statue of Liberty to sing «Give Me Your Tired, Your Poor» for the grand finale. Except for the dramatic finish, New York critics thought *Miss Liberty* «a pedestrian tale» that was «put together without sparkle or originality,»[16] but the public responded enthusiastically and made several of the songs—«I Love You,» «Let's Take an Old-Fashioned Walk,» «Only for Americans,» and the musical version of Emma Lazarus' poem, «Give Me Your Tired, Your Poor»— popular hits.

Filmmakers have been even more inventive in finding uses for the Statue of Liberty, employing it as both scene and symbol. Alfred Hitchcock's 1942 film *Saboteur* concludes with a chase up the statue's interior and a hair-raising struggle that results in the villain's dangling suspensefully from the statue's arm before his fatal plummet to the star-shaped base of the pedestal (cat. 543). Less gratifying, but equally symbolic, was the ending of *Planet of the Apes*, in which the remnants of a ruined Statue of Liberty signify the destruction of human civilization. The collapse of civilization is the theme as well of the film *Escape from New York*. Manhattan, cordoned off as a maximum-security prison, is patrolled from Liberty Island, the Statue of Liberty acting as «control central» for policing the penal colony of New York.

In contrast to such dark imaginings are the film musicals in which *Liberty* contributes to a more lighthearted fantasy. She provides a backdrop for Gene Kelly, Frank Sinatra,

and Jules Munshin, the sightseeing sailors of *On the Town*, and for the song «Don't Rain on My Parade,» performed by Barbra Streisand as *Funny Girl* Fanny Brice (cat. 544). In *Yankee Doodle Dandy*, the film biography of George M. Cohan, a suitably draped showgirl, with *Liberty*'s torch and spikey crown, joins James Cagney and a star-spangled cast in a spirited rendition of «You're a Grand Old Flag.»

Liberty's brush with show business serves to highlight another dimension of the statue's persona: *Liberty* is a she. On stage and screen, more often than not, she is «Miss Liberty»—even *Supergirl*. And, however incongruous a «sexy» Statue of Liberty may seem, caricaturists have delighted in provocatively converting noted theatrical «sex symbols»—Marilyn Monroe and Mae West among them—into the Statue of Liberty. The world of entertainment merely brings into sharp relief a factor that has continuously influenced the way in which the monument is presented. That *Liberty* is a woman inevitably suggests certain roles and situations appropriate to her sex, which vary in accordance with changes in cultural ideas regarding the roles of women in general. Evidence of this is pervasive: we see it in the creations of cartoonists and satirists; we find it in advertising when *Liberty* is made to sport a fashionable bustle, or, a century later, hip-hugging jeans—changes in fashion making no perceptible difference in the convention. The assimilation of the statue to the arena of fashion is in itself sex-related, connoting a cultural assumption that personal adornment is of greater interest and relevance to women than to men. By contrast, Uncle Sam is seldom supplied with an up-to-date wardrobe or seen to recommend male sartorial accouterments. *Liberty*'s relation to Uncle Sam is also instructive. When she appears as his consort, it is usually he who takes the active (masculine) role, and she the passive (feminine) one.

Gender was crucial to the part the statue was to play in the Women's Rights campaigns. It should have been foreseen that a statue dedicated to liberty and personified as female would be readily embraced by proponents of woman's suffrage, a subject of hot debate in the period when the Statue of Liberty made its American debut. Not having received an invitation to the dedication ceremonies, the suffragettes managed to attend anyway, although only written evidence survives to document their presence.[17] But the Women's Rights movement persisted in identifying *Liberty* with their cause: in 1915, with victory in sight, a group headed by Carrie Chapman Catt assembled at the base of the monument to demand the vote, with one of their number, arrayed to resemble the statue, striking the distinctive pose for the benefit of photographers (cat. 545). A half-century later, the granddaughters of the suffragettes would coopt *Liberty* for their cause and, like their forebears, choose the statue as the site for demonstrations (cat. 546). Several of Sheila Elias' multimedia painting/reliefs, such as the suggestively titled *Two French Girls*, affirm her commitment to the feminist viewpoint by including the Statue of Liberty in their richly textured, otherwise abstract surfaces (cat. 547). Although the statue is frequently a target for lampoon (cat. 548), its association with the Women's Liberation Movement occasions subtler humor too. Wittily bringing together *Liberty* and the «liberated woman» of the twenties, Seymour Chwast gives us a flapper Statue of Liberty (cat. 549). Once an image has become established and its meaning or meanings agreed upon, it lends itself as readily to parody as to advocacy.

This is nothing new. Indeed, the statue has been an unfailing resource of satire for most of its history. Comic renderings have always accounted for a substantial portion of the imagery devoted to it, to such an extent that we can trace the development of the image and discern the meanings and sentiments evoked by it simply by investigating the ways in which it has been used by satirists and humorists. Since no very compelling meanings attached to the statue at first, much of the early humor derived from events directly related to the monument or its site—jibes at the dilatory progress of the pedestal fund, for example. Even the early satires inspired by the immigration issue were more concerned with the physical than the symbolic character of the statue. In such cases, surprise and incongruity provide the humor. In two examples, which feature the statue in a New York context, comic effect

545
Suffragette Margaret Wycherly Striking the Pose of the Statue of Liberty
July 1915

546
Women's Liberation Demonstration at the Statue of Liberty
Jill Krementz
August 1970

547
Two French Girls
Sheila Elias
1984
reproduced in color
on p. 250

548
Ms. Liberty
Mutz
1975
reproduced in color
on p. 251

549
Women and the Arts in the 1920s
Seymour Chwast
1978
reproduced in color
on p. 251

is obtained by rendering the statue as human, or altering it in a startling way. Lyonel Feininger's 1906 comic strip showing a handkerchief-waving Statue of Liberty seeing off the Kin-der-Kids as they embark for Europe has no satirical edge (cat. 550); devoid of allusion to values or meaning, it simply focuses upon the statue's role as a harbor landmark. More critical is W. A. Rogers' humorous drawing protesting the proposal to build an elevated railway on Broadway (cat. 551). He applies a like excrescence, snaking its way up the statue, in a comic but effective jab at the aesthetic merits of the scheme and at promoters who might be expected to go so far as to deface the Statue of Liberty if the profit motive so dictated.

Less common, but nonetheless significant in the early period, were forays into political and social satire where *Liberty*'s meaning and the values implied by her image were uppermost. Officially the statue stood for a special kind of liberty, embodying the idea of the Republic—the lawfully constituted state under the sovereignty of the people. Reflecting this understanding are cartoons issued in conjunction with the unveiling that complacently show monarchs fleeing the light of *Liberty*'s torch, as well as satires that warn against dangers to the Republic. C. J. Taylor expressed his concern by depicting the Statue of Liberty besieged by the forces of «anarchism,» «socialism,» and «Georgeism» (a slap at the economic theories of single-taxer Henry George) (cat. 552). A very different treatment of essentially the same theme involved reworking an illustration that documented a bizarre occurrence connected with the lighting of the statue: thousands of birds flew into the lights and were killed (cat. 445), which moved Louis Dalrymple to picture avian anarchists «rushing to their own destruction» (cat. 553) just as the unfortunate birds had done. A third example of the republican theme comes from the pen of Grant Hamilton, but was suggested by William Jennings Bryan. Invited by the humor magazine *Judge* to supply his version of America in the period following the Spanish-American War, Bryan directed the artist to represent the Republic as the Statue of Liberty and to contrast it to Empire, in the guise of a Roman centurion, with the broken statue on the ground beneath (cat. 554). Common to each of these examples is the tendency in the early years to equate *Liberty* with the Republic rather than with the nation.

World War I changed that usage. In broadening the associative character of the image to embrace the idea of the nation in its entirety, it blunted its edge as an instrument of satire. Wrapped in the mantle of patriotism, the statue discouraged irreverence. High-jinks involving the statue's image were relatively rare in the decades immediately following the war, with the exception of prohibition cartoons, notable because they represent the first popular use of the statue's image to advocate individual liberty in opposition to the constitutional authority of government. Since, prior to the passage of the 18th Amendment, political satirists characteristically pictured the Statue of Liberty as the symbol of lawful authority, this represented a considerable deviation from the norm. Roughly contemporaneous is another challenge to the law in behalf of individual liberty from the pen of German-born artist George Grosz (cat. 555), its

scathing satire in sharp contrast to the bantering humor of the prohibition cartoons. Grosz's *Liberty* is spattered with blood, her torch replaced by an electric chair, and the flag behind her reversed in a signal of distress. The notorious executions of Sacco and Vanzetti inspired this powerful image, as rare in its intensity as in its characterization of *Liberty* as corrupt. It would not see its counterpart for several decades.

Grosz's drawing indicates that *Liberty*'s starring role as the personification of the nation caused her image to resonate with new meaning and significance, made all the more intense by another war following close behind. Once the statue was understood as both the symbol of the nation and the

552
Our Statue of Liberty. She Can Stand It
C. J. Taylor
From *Puck*
October 27, 1886
reproduced in color
on p. 251

553
Rushing to Their Own Destruction
Louis Dalrymple
From *Puck*
November 23, 1887
reproduced in color
on p. 252

550
The Kin-der-kids abroad. Triumphant departure of the kids, in the family Bathtub!!
Lyonel Feininger
From the Chicago *Sunday Tribune*
May 6, 1906

551
Grand Completion of the Broadway Elevated Railroad System
W. A. Rogers
1887

554
[Untitled lithograph]
Grant Hamilton, from an idea of William Jennings Bryan
From *Judge*
January 26, 1901
reproduced in color
on p. 252

555
Sacco and Vanzetti
George Grosz
1927

550

551

556
Un-American Committee
William Gropper
n.d.

558
Ship of State
Saul Steinberg
1959

557
[Soviet Desecration of the
Statue]
Kukrinisky
1968
reproduced in color
on p. 252

personification of Liberty in its broadest sense, it became a doubly effective weapon in the hands of satirists, especially when aberrations like McCarthyism seemed to call American values into question. Among the Americans critical of the Senator's relentless pursuit of «un-American activities» was artist William Gropper, who charged the «thugs» of McCarthy's committee with clubbing and gagging *Liberty* (cat. 556). From abroad came such barbs as that of the distinguished British cartoonist Leslie Illingworth, who caricatured Joseph McCarthy himself as the statue in a powerfully menacing drawing that shows the Wisconsin Senator engulfed in black smoke issuing from the torch and clutching a tablet labeled «Report of the Senate Investigating Committee.» Russian artists positively reveled in depicting *Liberty* violated by the «police state» (cat. 557). Even the French, heretofore generally respectful of the handiwork of their countryman, found *Liberty* in her new role an irresistible target.

The whimsical genius of Saul Steinberg brings to light still another consequence of *Liberty*'s ascendance. He shows us that her image had become so familiar that the merest indication of torch and spikey crown sparked instant recognition. Steinberg's *Liberty* is as radically simplified as an Egyptian hieroglyph or a child's stick drawing, but we have no trouble identifying it or what it represents. With equal economy Steinberg playfully encompasses the range of *Liberty*'s symbolic roles. She is the masthead of his 1959 *Ship of State*, leading a crew made up of other American symbols—among them, the eagle and a Lincolnesque Uncle Sam, a cowboy, Indian, and majorette, along with baseball players representing the Democratic and Republican parties (cat. 558). Although an element of political satire may be read into Steinberg's «Jules Verne» fantasy, it is allusive rather than pointed.

Far more direct and bitingly sharp were the images of the statue created by artists at work in the turbulent 1960s. The civil rights movement inspired harsh criticism of the disparities between the American ideal of Liberty and its realization, an issue in which the Statue of Liberty, symbolic both of Liberty and the United States, could hardly escape becoming involved. *On the Right*, Benny Andrews' mixed-media composition of rags and other found objects, bodies forth a frighteningly battered and belligerent Liberty, clenched fist raised menacingly in the «Black Power» salute (cat. 559). French artists, too, fastened on *Liberty*'s image to

559
On the Right
Benny Andrews
1972

560
*Food Is Not a Weapon, It
Is a Human Right*
Leon Klayman
1975

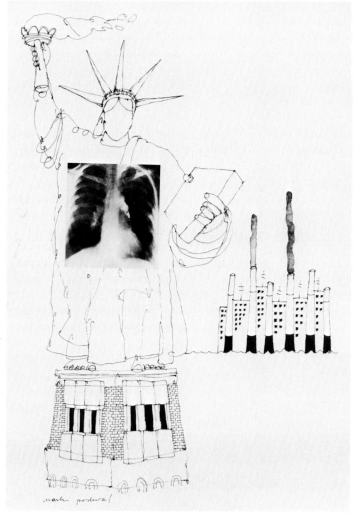

561
Fun City
Mark Podwal
1970

562
*«What Are a Couple of Nice
Guys Like You Doing in a
Place Like This?»*
Draper Hill
1976

563

Liberty Inviting Artists to Take Part in an Exhibition Against Leftist Terrorists (IRA PLO FALN Red Brigade Sandinistas Bulgarians)

Roger Brown

1983

reproduced in color

on p. 253

comment on the civil rights issue, Jean Lagarrigue by characterizing black activist Angela Davis as the statue.

Foreign-policy issues affected the statue's image in the 1960s as decisively as domestic ones. The war in Vietnam was responsible for renderings commensurate in force and scathing wit with those to which the civil rights protests gave rise. Along with constructions, like Benny Andrews' *Trash*, where the statue is portrayed as a «war bitch,» and Red Grooms' *Patriot's Parade*, where she wears a banner designating her «Miss Napalm,» were numerous cartoons and posters, several of which included unflattering caricatures of American officials—Henry Kissinger was a favorite target—masquerading as *Liberty* (cat. 560). It is worth noting that satire was not the exclusive preserve of the protesters. An officially sponsored promotion for the Peace Corps (cat. 576) shows the monument directing viewers to «Make America a Better Place . . . Leave the Country,» a clever paraphrase of the taunt—«If you don't like the country, leave it»—often leveled at dissidents. The statue's image entered the fray in the context of other issues, such as that of the environment, inspiring Mark Podwal's *Fun City*, which visualizes the Statue of Liberty afflicted with black lung (cat. 561). A decade of protest subjected the image of the statue to treatment unparalleled in its history, which to many seemed to veer perilously close to desecration. Paradoxically, however, the period also saw the image charged with new energy and relevance. Seldom had artists found the Statue of Liberty so fertile an inspiration.

In recent years—the Bicentennial provides a conveniently symbolic juncture—the statue has continued to occupy a large place in the imagery of satire and humor, although a lighter touch prevails. Contemporary cartoonists such as Draper Hill make use of the statue to lampoon the foibles of society and government with cleverness, but without rancor (cat. 562). Hudson Talbott's multifarious renditions of *Liberty* as shopper, homemaker, and New York sophisticate are gaily upbeat, suitable accompaniments to his equally lighthearted parodies of familiar masterpieces, in which the Statue of Liberty occupies the scenes made famous by artists such as Andrew Wyeth, Manet, or Henri Rousseau.

At one level Roger Brown's painting *Liberty Inviting Artists to Take Part in an Exhibition against Leftist Terrorists (IRA PLO FALN Red Brigade Sandinistas Bulgarians)* is also a parody of a work by Rousseau (cat. 563). Both its title and its organization make reference to the naive master's 1906 painting *La Liberté Invitant les Artistes à Prendre Part à la 22e Exposition des Indépendants.* Making use of the same toy figures, who march in obedient rhythm with their canvases under their arms, Brown pays homage to his French predecessor while at the same time subtly subverting the childlike simplicity of the earlier work with doses of modern irony and ambiguity. «But what is he saying?» asks critic Kim Levin. «Is he playing the devil's advocate to the left-leaning art world in order to provoke debate, being a sour satirist, or flaunting a simplistic patriotism?»[18] The question remains unanswered, and viewers are left to ponder the artist's intended message. On another level, however, the message is clear. Brown's painting is the consequence of one hundred years of image-making, to which the artist himself draws attention by selective borrowing. Although he updates and simplifies the convention—in Brown's painting, smokestacks represent the New Jersey shore and the twin towers of the World Trade Center stand for Manhattan—he makes use of the stylized format favored by nineteenth-century printmakers who grafted an outsized Statue of Liberty onto bird's-eye views of the New York harbor (see cat. 366). Striking an even more intriguing note, Brown substitutes for Rousseau's allegorical Liberty—part angel, part goddess—the Statue of Liberty. And this, too, results from a century of image-making. Like Rousseau, Bartholdi drew on centuries-old allegorical conventions to embody the ideal of Liberty. Bartholdi's creation, however, has succeeded in driving out competing images, as Brown's painting makes us newly aware. The meaning of Liberty may elude final definition, but about Bartholdi's statue there is this certainty: *La Liberté éclairant le Monde*—the Statue of Liberty—has become the image of Liberty.

Epilogue

The tribulations of Bartholdi's statue did not end with its official unveiling on October 28, 1886—indeed, that event was but the beginning of its greatest adventure: the accretion of meaning. Once the structure was built, it had then to be read, its legend established—a superhuman task, one that could be accomplished only through the efforts (now a century old) of a whole community in search of its own identity. When it comes to cultural significations, creators propose (a name, a form, a hospitable edifice), but societies, with their histories and their image reservoirs, dispose.

Bartholdi's statue is perhaps the finest example of the operation of the eternal law according to which the communal receptor is the final and sovereign interpreter of any work offered it. A successful monument is the one that escapes its creator, like the Golem of Cabalistic tradition: a single letter altered in the inscription on its forehead drew it out of its sleep of death to that excessive state, Life, and endowed it with the uncontrollable powers that even its creator himself could not control. Bartholdi's colossus (we shall call it simply the statue) was to become a semiological Golem. The manipulation of its name, the distortion of its «text,» begun even prior to its departure for the shores of America, liberated it from its promoters' intentions from its very inception. The writer O. Henry was one of the earliest to understand this and say it in a brief and humorous passage of dialogue entitled «The Lady Higher Up»;[1] or, rather, he endowed the statue itself—mature enough at the turn of the century to reflect upon effects and causes—with speech. Here she is chatting with her colleague who towered over the City, the statue of Diana,[2] who is somewhat surprised at «Aunt Liberty's» Irish accent: «Ye must know, Miss Diana, that 'tis with statues the same as with people—'tis not their makers nor the purposes for which they were created that influence the operations of their tongues at all—it's the associations with which they become associated, I'm telling ye.» O. Henry's Aunt Liberty must have read Locke—who was of her age: the Enlightenment—as well as William James—who was of her period, in whose atmosphere both idealism and pragmatism combined and flourished. However, she also deserves to be included among the pioneers of structural semiology. One might perhaps criticize her for somewhat overrating «associations,» for being a bit too functionalist, and for being ungrateful to her «creator,» to whom she owes more than an «intention»: a *form*, with which the work of reinterpretation must come to grips.

The statue's semiological fortunes are, indeed, fraught with paradox. Rarely has an emblematic object been so quickly corrupted, had imputed to it significations it does not contain: first and foremost, the «association» with immigration, officially attached to the monument as early as 1903, the year Emma Lazarus' famous poem was carved on its pedestal. At the same time, however, the statue continued to demonstrate enormous resistance to iconographic «deformation»; and this for reasons that are undoubtedly in part cultural (the manipulation of the national symbol it was tending to become being impossible without risk of iconoclasm), but, even more, formal: as a colossus, the statue does not lend itself to distortions of detail; the deviant narratives it inspires can have only a limited number of sequences, of episodes; if the meaning changes, it is only massively, in accordance with the massive quality of the object itself.

From a formal point of view, in fact, we could gather all (or nearly all) the «readings» presented by a century of—variously unfaithful—citations into two *figures*, in the rhetorical sense of the word: a play of substitution, total or partial, or a labor of displacement (a change of perspective) operating on the visual and semantic context of the object. Each of these formal procedures can, in turn, assume different, antagonistic, meaning values. For example, substitution most often *signifies* a usurpation—and Miss Liberty is dethroned by a Democratic party «boss» (cat. 564), a policeman, the Kaiser, the Golden Calf, Mussolini, or even General De Gaulle. However, the statue can also be supplanted by a positive figure—a reciprocal exchange then takes place, an interchange of qualities between it and its famous doubles: André Breton, Mae West, Angela Davis. Advertising, for its part, obviously favors partial substitution that makes *Liberty* herself the saleswoman for the product. And on rare occasions the article being advertised can physically replace the goddess on her pedestal: such was the case with the glowing pig whose blooming good health proclaims the virtues of Dr. Haas's porcine elixir (cat. 565). The principle of substitution can also spare the statue's body and work on its allegorical attributes. Torch and crown are the obvious targets of such appropriations. The former can become a ballpoint pen (in Evelyne Noviant's 1982 drawing *Le Point*), the pull of a toilet flush (in Siné's 1963 cartoon «La Statue de la Liberté»), a gasoline drum, or various canned goods according to the taste of the

**18.
The Edifying Edifice**

Philippe Roger

admen. As for the crown, it seems to lend itself to bellicose metamorphoses: an American cartoon against U.S. entry into World War I transforms the rays into bayonettes and, this time in an anti-American sense, a 1974 pen-and-ink drawing by Michel Guiré-Vaka replaces them with smoking guns.

Both highly economical and extremely eloquent, substitution is therefore the process that has presided over almost all the image's «deformations.» (One quantitatively important series during the years 1885–1900 seems free of it: these are the statue's «leave-takings»—because it has grown weary of waiting for its pedestal, and, later, because of its disgust at the downtrodden and woebegone appearance of the arriving immigrants; structurally speaking, however, that series is still derived from the same figure: such caricatures merely replace the statue with an absence that then becomes the sign of its wrath.)

A spectacular procedure, substitution enjoys (and makes the reader enjoy) the force of the uplift created by any metaphorical figure. However, it must be added that «deformation» does not exhaust all the

possibilities of rereading: indeed, even the most sober lithograph, the most placid photograph, is still an exercise in reinterpretation. Every vantage point selected, every choice of this one particular angle over another, modifies the symbolic, ideological, message. The most banal calendar, one showing the statue in the 1950s against the green background of a quasi-pastoral New Jersey, can be a sociological and historical document of the Golden Age of suburbia (cat. 566). The manner in which the statue is located in space, the choice made by the draftsman or photographer in associating it with the maritime element or with the urban landscape—making it materially consubstantial with the city—also draw upon an image rhetoric but are based upon another «figure,» playing upon contiguousness, which we can contrast with «substitution,» in the same way as the linguist Roman Jakobson contrasted the «metonymic» pole with the «metaphorical» pole.[3] The operation of metonymy, as Jakobson noted, is always more secretive—which does not prevent it from taking over, on occasion, historical and ideological sequences that are just as extensive as those manipulated by the action of substitution. Hence, any aerial view taken from almost straight above, by accentuating—or, better,

by revealing—the monument's isolated character, manages to insinuate an isolationist message that the legend then need only confirm: «Peace and security in a war-torn world» (cat. 567).[4]

Thus the two axes along which we could order an exhaustive (or aimed at being exhaustive) description of the statue's semiological manipulation. And yet, if we are to make any attempt at all to interpret such readings as a *corpus*, we must go beyond the stage of formal description and reinscribe such a description within a larger context. For the «meanings» proffered by iconography are preceded by a complex polysemy, that of the statue itself: figurative monument and unassigned symbol, compact allegory and overt signifier, work of art and sumptuous, ostentatious gift, marvel of technology and useless monster.

Ideally, therefore, we should concurrently decipher those images and the myth they continually refashion: on the one hand, as O. Henry's Aunt Liberty learnedly opines, «the history of art in its foreign complications,» and, on the other, a semiological history of the statue's formal appropriation by and absorption into the collective American image repertory.

567

Her Torch Held High, the Statue of Liberty Symbolizes Peace and Security in a War-Torn World
U.S. Army Air Corps
From *National Geographic Magazine*
June 1940

The statue is first of all a symbol, a symbol in the most basic etymological meaning of the word. In ancient Greek, the *symbolon* was the sign of recognition (most frequently a ring broken into two pieces) handed down from generation to generation, signifying the link between two families foreign to each other—«foreign,» meaning «from different cities.» It was a linkage that crossed legal frontiers. Later, the word came to designate a pact between States, especially for the settlement of trade disputes; and this latter meaning was to acquire an ironic tinge over the course of the quarrelsome history of French-American relations.

At its origins the imposing gift was at once the product of a personal initiative and a private undertaking by a small group of men desirous of renewing strained ties of friendship with their American counterparts. There was probably some desire to thaw the diplomatic chill created by the Mexican adventurism of Napoléon III's reign; even more, however, there was the desire to offset the effect on the public created by demonstrations organized by the German-American community—indeed, Bartholdi made specific reference to them in the presentation brochure for his colossus.[5]

The statue had an official reception in the United States only at the cost of considerable struggle: the final skirmish arose out of Congress's refusal to foot the bill for the refreshments at the unveiling ceremony. Above all, however, from Joseph Pulitzer (of whose role no one needs reminding) to New York's Free Masons (who got up the parade), there was a convergence of individual or group efforts designed to force the hand of the authorities by achieving a victory on the field of public opinion. The *World* subscription echoed that of the French Committee, and the propaganda in favor of the monument on both sides of the Atlantic got under the public's skin to a degree that lifted the matter onto a level that freed it from the ups and downs of diplomatic or political history.

If we examine the century of the statue's iconography, however, it is clear that the symbolism of the bond between countries, the upsurge of what Bartholdi himself was to call a «tradition» of mutual good-feeling, remained, semiologically speaking, a dead letter. The statue's French nationality is almost never referred to in pictures, in any manner, even in the earliest days of its American residence. A cartoon such as the one (published in *Frank Leslie's Illustrated Newspaper* in 1885) showing her asking directions in her «native tongue»—«Ah! Monsieur Oncle Sam, escort me to my pedestal, s'il vous plaît»—is the exception that proves the rule. From the shock of having been thrown into the melting pot, over which it was soon to preside as guardian spirit, the statue was immediately to speak English, albeit with a heavy accent, as in O. Henry. And its Frenchness re-emerges only when summoned by powerful—and equally unusual—gastronomic appeals, such as the trade card showing «La Belle France» presenting Columbia and the New World with her «Parisian Sauce» (cat. 568). Forgetfulness of the statue's origins is otherwise nearly total. As for a Milton Haggard song that in 1917 attempted to recall it in a lyric, the title of the song—«France, We Have Not Forgotten You»—has more than a hint of well-intentioned disclaimer.

On the French side, of course, there was a greater propensity during the 1920s and 1930s to link the Eiffel Tower and the Statue of Liberty. However, this for the most part took the form of topographical messages to illustrate steamship routes, advertising invitations to travel; the value of «alliance» is lacking. It took the special charisma of a Maurice Chevalier to reunite in the imagination what had come to be increasingly separate and apart: the last beneficiary of the hospitable *symbolon*, we see him on a sheet music cover stepping lightly across an ocean reduced to the narrowest of rivulets: one of his arms is still crooked around the Eiffel Tower, while Miss Liberty is already laying her hand familiarly on the other.

That's about all, and it isn't much. Of course, we could make a historical and political investigation into the reasons for this rapid—better, this almost instantaneous—eradication of the French referent. It was helped along, in France, by a dormant anti-Americanism that was soon to become more lively and, after 1918, across the Atlantic, by the upsurge of isolationism that put an end to the Wilsonian ideals of collective action. The irony of the statue's symbolic trajectory is patent from the aerial view cited earlier, which isolates the inhabitant of Bedloe's Island from a world threatened by the horrors of war. In this extreme example the statue has ceased to represent the Alliance and has become the Ark: the chosen land, the new Zion of Puritan culture, alone fit to survive in a universe dominated by Evil. That it can be so identified at the brink of World War II reveals fairly clearly the distance the statue has traveled toward its assimilation—and away from its roots.

Yet we must beware of overemphasizing the political or ideological explication of this «forgetfulness,» for which other—and otherwise profound—motives can be found in anthropology and, closer to hand, in semiology. Since Mauss's analyses of «potlatch» (that Indian intertribal competition in which victory was won by whichever side gave or «spent» the most), we have better understood the repugnance social groups feel at being indebted. Through another irony of history, the lowest point in French-American relations during our statue's lifetime was reached in 1932, created by the question of those very war debts France had decided to cease repaying when American diplomatic and financial manoeuvres (the Dawes Plan) led to Germany's stopping the payment of sums «owed» to France as reparations. With regard to the statue itself, the ill humor of the American press was early manifested against the cumbersome «gift» and its colossal «uselessness.» Did this represent some obscure recognition, underlying the offering's uniqueness, of the disturbing power of the «sumptuous gift,» the constraining prestige of the «symbolic expense»? In any event, such a gesture was obviously contrary to the traditional phrase in the light of which the new world intended to conduct relations—economic, social, human, and international—the «give and take» that might well be, after all, no more than an exorcism through accountancy of the ancient fear of the Gift of the Other.

However that may be, the statue had, if only for the sake of acclimatization, to cease being foreign; and what better way of naturalizing it than to assign it the job of welcoming foreigners—all foreigners. «'Tis what I've been doing night and day since I was erected,» says O. Henry's statue, whose notions of her genealogy are very odd indeed: «I was made by a Dago and presented to the American people on behalf of the French Government for the purpose of welcomin' Irish immigrants into the Dutch city of New York.»[6] Such a role reversal was made possible by the basic semantic data: the universality of the concept of liberty that its creator had assigned it as meaning. And the primordial reason for the disappearance of the French-American *symbolon* from its iconography is also—semiologically—the simplest: nowhere is that character inscribed in the object itself. Nothing points to it, nothing recalls its origin. Aunt Liberty gives not so much as a hint. The «abstraction» that Bartholdi viewed as being inherent in the colossal project was paradoxically responsible for his work's rapid Americanization. As he was to write, paraphrasing Lesbazeilles, «colossal statuary ought to be used only to symbolize figures of thoughts which are grand in themselves, and as far as possible, abstract.»[7] To offer a *Liberty*—that pure Kantian concept—was indeed a grandiose idea, because it entailed offering at the same time total liberty to reinterpret it. More fortunate than the forgotten *symbolon*, the allegory would survive all the better in that it was basically open to being invested with «foreign» significations.

This is not the place to dwell upon all the anecdotes (they have been related elsewhere) about the emblematic choices made by Bartholdi in creating his *La Liberté éclairant le Monde*, nor to go into the long history of semantic stratification that has left it with two major significations: Immigration and National Identity. Rather, we shall attempt to describe how the play of «deformations» in extremely diverse iconographic areas contributed to the popularization of those «added values,» which enabled the United States to assimilate the statue.

It is important to emphasize that the metamorphoses imposed on the statue are basically sober-minded and, so to speak, structurally edifying, even when apparently the most disrespectful. Sacrilege (systematically cultivated in the 1960s and 1970s) has only the effect of confirming the sacred it is jeering at. That is true of the mustache on the Mona Lisa and just as true of the mustache on the male figure that replaces the statue in Michael Rock's 1980 montage *Mr. Liberty*. The message is not without ambiguity: men's liberation, along with women's liberation? Or discreet revindication, under the implicit aegis of the solid Matron, of the right to those heterodox forms of «the pursuit of happiness» for which New York is both shelter and harbor? In both instances it is less a matter of insulting Miss Liberty than of bringing under her protection a gesture that, far from being nihilistic, is more like an affirmative action. On the American side, indeed—some French drawings are much more aggressive—we find a kind of graphic tenderness even in the least gallant incarnations: from Dr. Haas's pig (after all, the great Thomas Paine himself proposed replacing the predatory eagle with the nutritious turkey as the Republic's symbol) to Pol Bury's ingenious constructions of moving plates, image-deformers *par excellence*, little aesthetic racks for the statue's torture. The underlying morality of the procedure can be discerned even more clearly in the political cartoon. The statue

can be replaced, as in the Tammany Hall days, with a petty Democratic tyrant holding sway over the enslaved city with a whip, or even, in our own time, a Ronald Reagan brandishing dollars and money-box over urban poverty—in each instance the satire of the vices of the day is a backhanded tribute to the symbol's timeless virtue. Parody is always the discreet encomium of the original. Every distortion, wink, or grimace strengthens the permanence and enhances the consistency of the structure of which it becomes a variant. And we can even go so far as to say that the vast growth in iconoclastic images in the agitated decade from 1965 to 1975 constitutes the surest indication of the statue's total acceptance as a shared referent, the site of a mythic consensus; imaginary lesions on the national-maternal body, such minute graphic alterations confirm more surely than the iconography of allegiance created in wartime the consecration of the «Mighty Matron» as the major totem of the North American tribe, its «best mascot,» as a 1939 poster affirms.

Now, such an investment of the allegory did not come about unaided. The overt «given» of the symbolism of *Liberty*, the ability of the object to lend itself to a condensation of meaning, are only partial explanations of the success of the collective assimilation of this semiologically foreign body into a culture that had more than one reason to reject it—or to keep it at a distance. The figure who came to poach on Columbia's terrain at the end of the last century is, first, a pagan goddess, and was denounced as such by a number of preachers. It was also a creature from contaminated Europe, the political and moral foil in the founding myths of the American nation; significant in this connection is the malicious rumor that the artist's model had been a prostitute—a rumor so persistent that as late as 1950 a relative of Bartholdi made a point of reminding the press that the noble figure had been that of the sculptor's mother.[8]

Even those whom a Jeffersonian tradition predisposed to look kindly upon the Goddess *Liberty* ran up against other problems, semantic in character, when it came to

HUMAN STATUE OF LIBERTY
18,000 OFFICERS AND MEN
AT
CAMP DODGE, DES MOINES IA.
COL. WM. NEWMAN, COMMANDING
COL. RUSH S. WELLS, DIRECTING

MOLE & THOMAS
915 MEDINAH BLDG.
CHICAGO, ILL.

569
Human Statue of Liberty
Mole & Thomas
1918

popularizing the entity—beginning with its title. *La Liberté éclairant le Monde* does not translate easily, and O. Henry poked fun at the «enlightening of the world» by which «our learned civic guardians» had sought to English the statue's proud name. Indeed, the muddy word «enlightening,» which is unduly pedantic, has been the source of countless graphic-textual plays on words, both commercial—«Liberty Feeding the World,» an advertisement for biscuits, ca. 1885—and racial in nature, as in the example of Thomas Worth's 1884 *Liberty Frightenin' the World*, in which the statue is transformed into a black woman.

Where, when, and by what means then did the statue enter into the image reservoir of the American people? War propaganda and its «melting-pot» associations are only the most visible signs of a long process, a kind of mythic tussle to Americanize the very substance of the statue. That is the deep meaning to be discerned in the famous reproduction (a literal reincarnation) of Miss Liberty by «18,000 officers and men at Camp Dodge,» Iowa, in 1918 (cat. 569). The totemic giantess becomes a fabulous conglomeration of flesh and blood, her body a mosaic of human bodies. And that extraordinary tableau vivant is a mythic realization of the desired fusion of the foreign colossus and the social corpus, embodied in its military avatar by the troops. Even more kitsch, perhaps, and in any case a product of the same «substantial» image reservoir, is a cereal replica of the statue displayed in 1885 in the Nebraska Pavilion at the New Orleans World's Fair (cat. 570). According to the magazine that reproduced it for the delectation of its readers, it was made entirely of «hay, grain and corn.» This early initiative, highly symbolic in nature, continentalizes the giantess and simultaneously endows her with the nutritive values (and religious, and national: the first corn harvest is the myth that underpins the ritual of Thanksgiving) appropriate to «Middle» America. And the same fantasy would appear to reemerge, albeit in a very mild form, in a photomontage of nearly a century later: the statue is depicted standing in an ocean, but in this case it is an ocean of ripe wheat in the Corn Belt.

The appropriative urge is clearly being given voice in such symbolic reconstructions; however, it emerges on a broader scale, on the scale of (potentially) the entire community, in quite another context—in that activity so specifically associated with monuments since the eighteenth century, namely, the *visit*, itself inseparable from its representation. For although the visit, as a «tourist» activity, appears to go beyond the iconographic framework, it is nonetheless closely linked to it. There are countless engravings and photographs depicting the statue's being visited: entering at the foot, the climb up the inside, the arrival at the top, et cetera; and here the private iconography contained in the millions of photographs taken by visitors plays a more important sociological role than the public imagery.

As Roland Barthes has remarked, to visit a monument is to «make the rounds» of an interior, a little in the manner of an owner: every exploration is an appropriation; this tour of the *inside* corresponds, moreover, to the question raised by the *outside*: the monument is a riddle, to enter it is to solve it, to possess it.»[9] Marvin Trachtenberg, one of the statue's best exegetes, gives us a description of this experience that, apart from the difference in viewpoint, matches up with Barthes' analysis when he speaks of the visitors: «like Lilliputians atop Gulliver, they can fancy themselves titillatingly perched on a giant—or even for a moment *become* the giant goddess. The experience fuses the modern love of spectacular amusements like ballooning with the sense of some ancient rite, perhaps a visit to an oracle across distant waters.»[10]

Indeed, the initiatory image reservoir (Barthes compares the tourist to «the neophyte who, in order to accede to the initiate's status, is obliged to traverse a dark and unfamiliar route») is redoubled in the case of the statue: the pilgrimage «to the inside» is preceded by the maritime journey from the mainland to the island; and the ferry trip in a modest way extends the most traditional of rites of passage: a water crossing, not only an experiencing of the frontiers between worlds (as the Styx separates the realm of the dead from the land of the living) but also the spiritual stripping away of everyday, worldly values, which are left behind on the other shore.

Although from Bartholdi's point of view the site fulfilled quite different requirements, it is nevertheless remarkable to note that the sculptor took pains to emphasize his edifice's ease of visitation. In the 1885 pamphlet he published for apologetic and publicity purposes he boasts of the interior layout of the structure he has conceived, which can be exhaustively and ascentionally visited all the way to the head, and even to the torch; and he is explicit about the number each can hold: head, forty; torch, twelve.[11]

That the tour of the monument awakens powerful mythic echoes is uniquely confirmed by the way it is depicted in painting, as well as by the cinema. At the top of the edifice, in a work by De Mejo, we find the true arcana of America: «Doctor Merck» and his stiff companions, in the torch, see a gigantic, half-submerged Indian going by, like the Great White Whale of the American historic subconscious, this too an initiatory encounter, which the artist places under the sign of shamanism. Even stranger, *Miss Liberty* by James Morlock turns the statue's head into the headquarters for a lesbian club; and in a disturbingly strange reduplication the statue's face, outside, is seen looking in through the porthole with an impassive voyeur's gaze. Behind the modern Bacchantes, the Great Goddess seems to be rapt in contemplation of her own Mysteries.

At the end of the pilgrimage, in the heart of the Idol, one finds another world, one that is also the «inner world» of the best-hid secrets—with, as its price of entry, the danger inherent in any sacred place. Disturbing to the profane, the statue will be pitiless to the profaner. This is the lesson of Alfred Hitchcock's film *Saboteur* (1942); when, with an unbelievable arrogance (and an undeniable lack of foresight) the Nazi master spy decides to seek sanctuary on Bedloe's Island, his fate is obviously sealed, the more cruel will be his downfall—from the top of the monument defiled by his presence (cat. 543). The distance from totem to taboo is never far.

570
At the New Orleans Exposition. [3. Corn Statue of Liberty]
Charles Graham after sketches by John Durkin
From *Harper's Weekly* January 17, 1885

The statue is not, therefore, all that *sure.* Initiatory, it participates in the mystery to which it introduces . . . belonging. Identificatory, it goes through the same identity crises as does the American nation. In 1974 the trauma of Watergate drove the statue to the couch in a comic strip by Robert Grossman; the treatment is doubtful: her psychoanalyst, whose features are familiarly presidential, indicates to her that she has come to the wrong place by reminding her of his own identity: «I am Ford, not Freud» (cat. 571).

However, the threat emanates from a greater distance. In spite of all the reassuringly alliterative soubriquets—«Mammoth Mother of Exiles,» «solid matron,» «mighty matron,» and even «comfortable matron»[12] —Americans from the beginning fantasized the statue as being fragile, threatened. This, indeed, constitutes the major difference between American representations and French depictions, particularly contemporary ones, which are replete with «imperialist» caricatures of a delinquent and menacing *Liberty*: Michel Guiré-Vaka turns the statue into a millionaire with cigar and guns, Mordillo repaints it as a female convict, and Folon turns it into a prison.

And finally we must mention the astonishing iconography that plays numerous variations on one single theme: the statue's demise. It is striking that this obsession with the *perishable* should be as old as the statue itself. Indeed, this funereal premonition goes very far beyond the historical framework of «interesting eras,» as Camus sarcastically dubbed them, those times when war makes the spectacle of annihilation familiar. From 1886 up to today, the leitmotiv has been a constant one, indifferent, or nearly so, to current events. And even when inspired by them, the phenomenon seems to rewrite events at another depth, that of the deep waters of oblivion beneath which the forsaken statue lies. Propaganda (national or partisan) has the monopoly on this death-bound image that has, in its durability, its pictorial violence, and the diversity of its forms, managed to create a Narrative, a Legend, with some of the resonance of the great myths of sunken cities, the City of Ys, Atlantis.

571
. . . *I'm Ford not Freud*
Robert Grossman
From *New York Magazine*
December 9, 1974

572
The Next Morning
From *Life*
February 26, 1877

Some of these representations of course have a fairly simple «primary message.» Some, as we have seen, *denounce*: Democratic party bossism, rampant plutocracy (incarnate in the Golden Calf to whose feet the dethroned statue has wandered), et cetera. Others *prophesy* some imminent catastrophe: «The Next Morning» of 1887 anticipates the destruction caused by an attack by a «hostile fleet» (cat. 572); in later years, a propaganda poster of the America First Committee would show the statue as the first victim of the nascent world war (cat. 573). The best known quite simply *admonish* in order to mobilize («Lest I Perish,» poster for the first war loan, 1917; «That Liberty Shall Not Perish from the Earth, Buy Liberty Bonds» [cat. 537]).

However, the fantasy of destruction, here exploited for political or patriotic purposes, would appear to spring from a deeper image reservoir, one that has been explored by artists (or filmmakers like Franklin Schaffner in *Planet of the Apes*) whose ideological concerns are null—or nonsensical: one outstanding example is the «New Liberty of Venice,» showing the statue

sinking into the lagoon: Ludovico de Luigi, its creator, oddly imputes the cause of this contagious collapse to the «republican form» of the Most Serene's government! Thus the impetus behind the statue's execution can be derived from highly disreputable institutional linkages.

Even though well set forth in political cartoons or patriotic posters, the recurrent theme of the statue's demise has in fact occurred autonomously; it pervades every «iconographic» genre and forms a ground bass in the semiological score. In the 1930s Grace Clements used it in a surrealist-inspired painting: the statue's head is connected by limp supports à la Dali to a whitened bovine skeleton. In 1975, a collage by Eric Seidman employed it, as well as the Dantesque referent that has for so long accompanied the statue's mythic life. As early as 1881 Thomas Nast had inscribed the famous line «Leave all hope, ye that enter . . .» at the base of a *Liberty* whose head is a skull, an allegory of the Epidemic (cat. 525a);[13] as for Seidman, he borrows from Gustave Doré his foreground showing the poet of the *Divine Comedy* and his

· LIFE ·

THE NEXT MORNING.
BEING A VIEW OF THE U. S. NAVY AND THE CITY OF NEW YORK TAKEN AFTER THE ARRIVAL OF A HOSTILE FLEET.

guide contemplating the last remaining traces of New York: the lone torch emerging from the harbor's waters (cat. 574). Even more recently, a 1982 work by Susan Backman shows the statue pierced like a voodoo fetish with mysterious, other-worldly needles. And advertising, too, has found ways of using this dread of loss: a 1984 advertisement for Kellogg (a «sponsor» of the monument's refurbishing) threatens every young cereal consumer with the loss of this symbolic nourishment and urges parents to prevent, by their judicious purchases, their cherished offspring from being reduced to drawing Miss Liberty «from memory.»

Can we make an interpretation of this destructive iconographic passion, this determination to represent the statue's mutilation, collapse, or slow disappearance beneath the waters? Analysis of the iconography suggests one answer: there is a mythic condensation underlying allegorical condensation (Liberty–Immigration/Melting Pot–Homeland), and it unites three separate, not to say contradictory, cultural areas: a magic attitude, a religious vision, and a historical perception.

The depiction of destruction is magic in the sense that it refers back to the apotropaic practices used in archaic rituals to avert any evils threatening the city. But it also stems from the religious heritage of a civilization imbued with biblical culture: it can either illustrate a new Flood (as Eric Seidman's collage suggests) or be a graphic image of some apocalypse, like the «petrified New York» of Jean Lagarrigue that appeared in *Esquire* magazine in 1968. Yet, in what is perhaps a basic paradox, one that creates the statue's greatest semantic ambivalence, this latter theme (the End of History) must always in the statue's «mortuary» iconography involve its symmetrical inverse: historical awareness.

An odd little volume appeared in 1966; it purported to be an archeological study of the Weans (a vanished race whose members had referred to themselves by the pronoun US), and it sets forth the meager hypotheses suggested by the discovery of a «holy figure . . . of what appears to be a giantess, or possibly a goddess, with one arm upraised in a threatening attitude. Within what is left of the shell, heavily encrusted with bird-droppings and worm-mold, our diggers uncovered a fragment of script, in blocked letters or signs, which Bes Nef has translated: «Keep off the. . . .»[14] Conclusion: the Weans must not have been a very hospitable nation.

It is interesting that the statue should bear the principal weight of this archeological fantasy, whose narrative schema is exemplary. (Another futuristic novel that looks backward to the past, J. G. Ballard's *Hello America*, covers the same, but more action-filled, terrain: the story opens with the sinking of a boat come to reconnoiter the abandoned site of New York when it rams into the submerged arm of the former «Dame of the Narrows.»)

Now, this archeological topos is in no way a recent phenomenon indicative of contemporary America's discovery of its own defects and cracks. Association of the statue with the notion of decrepitude began in the very year it was erected, and the best illustration of it is an 1886 engraving by Hamilton for *Judge*, «A Peep into the Future» (cat. 575). The theme of the archeological dig is already being treated humorously: «ancient» pottery is represented by a collection of glasses designed to hold every kind of alcoholic beverage, and the 1884 City Council is shown sculpted into a vaguely Assyrian frieze. However, our attention is particularly drawn to the figure on the left, the abandoned statue, bathed in a glaucous, crepuscular light and festooned with what looks to be seaweed. Even as early as that time, Bartholdi's young giantess had ceased to reign over anything more than a stretch of muddy and filth-strewn flats whose sole inhabitant, a melancholy owl, watches over the cadaver of a cat. This old familiar owl— the one Hegel described as setting forth at twilight—is the last witness to the tragedy we call History. And it is not the least paradoxical aspect of this offering in the name of the values of the Future, of Progress, that it should have brought to the shores of America the unhappy awareness of the historicity of its fate.

What is a national identity? Perhaps it is the identity that can be expressed only by the fear of its loss. This monumental gift was also the gift of an image reservoir of decline: behind the poetry of the colossal we can always glimpse a poetics of ruin. The United States certainly did not need Bartholdi's statue to know that its moral life was bound up with a certain notion of liberty. However, it is perhaps through the statue and the imagery to which it has given rise that this young civilization began, in Valéry's words, to «know that it was perishable.»

Translated, from the French, by Richard Miller

574
Untitled collage by Eric
Seidman
From the *New York Times*
September 19, 1975

575
A Peep into the Future
Grant Hamilton
From *Judge*
October 30, 1886

573
War's First Casualty
Elmer
1939
reproduced in color
on p. 256

Notes

The following short titles and abbreviations are employed in the notes:

Bartholdi	Frédéric-Auguste Bartholdi (ed. A.T. Rice), *The Statue of Liberty Enlightening the World Described by the Sculptor* (New York: North American Review, 1885); reprinted in facsimile with an introduction by Jeffrey Eger (New York: New York Bound Books, 1984)
Betz	Jacques Betz, *Bartholdi* (Paris: Les Editions Minuit, 1954)
CNAM (plus number)	refers to the album of Bartholdi's clippings at the Conservatoire National des Arts et Métiers, Paris
Dard and Blanchet (New York)	Bertrand Dard and Christian Blanchet, *Statue of Liberty: The First Hundred Years*, trans. Bernard A. Weisberger (New York: American Heritage, 1985)
Dard and Blanchet (Paris)	Bertrand Dard and Christian Blanchet, *Statue de la Liberté* (Paris: Comet's Edition, 1984)
Gschaedler	André Gschaedler, *True Light on the Statue of Liberty and Its Creator* (Narberth, Pa.: Livingston Publishing Company, 1966)
Inv. no. _____	refers to the Inventory of the contents of Bartholdi's house in Colmar, made in 1914 after the death of Bartholdi's widow
Journal	refers to the journal of Bartholdi's 1871 visit to America; Chemical Bank, New York
Lesbazeilles	E. Lesbazeilles, *Les Colosses anciens et modernes* (Paris: Hachette, 1876)
Schmitt	J.M. Schmitt, *Bartholdi, une certaine idée de la liberté* (Strasbourg: Editions de la Nuée-Bleue-D.N.A., 1985)
Stone	Ross Conway Stone, *A Way to See and Study the Statue of Liberty Enlightening the World* (New York: Bullion Press, 1887)
Trachtenberg	Marvin Trachtenberg, *The Statue of Liberty* (New York: Viking Press, 1966). The revised edition (New York: Penguin Books, 1986) became available too late for inclusion here.

Letters to and from the following individuals are located as indicated below, except where otherwise noted:

Frédéric-Auguste Bartholdi	letters to his mother from his American trip in 1871 are in the collection of Chemical Bank, New York; other letters cited, except those to Butler and Laboulaye, are in the Archives Municipales, Colmar; in some instances, noted below, only an English transcription of Bartholdi's letters, by Rodman Gilder, survives—these transcriptions are in the Chemical Bank, New York
Richard Butler	The New York Public Library, Rare Books and Manuscripts Division, American Committee Papers
William Maxwell Evarts	Library of Congress, Manuscript Division, Evarts Papers
Hamilton Fish	Library of Congress, Manuscript Division, Fish Papers
Edouard de Laboulaye	Collection François de Laboulaye, Saint-Saens
Levi P. Morton	The New·York Public Library, Rare Books and Manuscripts Division, Morton Papers
Gifford Pinchot	Library of Congress, Manuscript Division, Pinchot Papers, Series 3, Family Correspondence (Box numbers are indicated in the notes)
Joseph Pulitzer	Columbia University, Pulitzer Papers

1.
See Louis Girard, *Les Libéraux français, 1814–1875* (Paris: Aubier, 1985), p. 188, and André Jardin, *Histoire du libéralisme politique* (Paris: Hachette, 1985), p. 387. Marcel Prelot, in his *Histoire des idées politiques*, 3rd ed. (Paris: Dalloz, 1966), p. 487, correctly affirms that the influence of Constant was broader and stronger than that of Tocqueville.

2.
Laboulaye went so far as to accuse Tocqueville of not having read Constant. «To mention only Tocqueville,» he wrote in the Introduction (p. VII) to his *Cours de politique constitutionnelle*, «this noble-minded man would have spared himself much hard work and trouble if he had read the liberal writer. In Constant's pamphlets, which plainly he did not know, he would have found his own thoughts expressed with equal subtlety and vigor.»

3.
L'État et ses limites, 2nd ed. (Paris: Charpentier, 1864), p. 139.

4.
Ibid., pp. 181–182, 18. It is true that Tocqueville's *Souvenirs*, where he spoke in detail of the Commission for the Constitution, were published only posthumously, in 1893. But Laboulaye could have consulted oral tradition by questioning, for instance, Dufaure. On the 1851 debate, it is surprising that Laboulaye should have read Tocqueville's speech so inattentively. «As the voice of a divided Commission he came to no conclusion,» said Laboulaye. Actually, Tocqueville pleaded for revision, but without great conviction. On this point see the *Mémoires* of Odilon Barrot, IV: 137, and Paul Bastid, *Doctrines et institutions de la seconde République* (Paris: Hachette, 1945), II: 293.

5.
Benjamin Constant, *De la liberté chez les modernes* (Paris: Pluriel, 1980), p. 502.

6.
Ibid., pp. 501–502.

7.
L'État et ses limites, p. 110.

8.
See the Introduction and Chapter II of *La Démocratie en Amerique*.

9.
Tocqueville to his friend Eugène Stoffels, June 24, 1836.

10.
The modern republican opposition of the period was divided on this problem. For Jules Simon, God was the foundation of liberty and morality (see *La Liberté*, 1859). The moral and political philosophy of Vacherot, on the other hand, did not call upon the idea of God (see *La Démocratie*, 1859).

11.
L'État et ses limites, p. 152.

12.
Ibid., p. 157. Laboulaye even said: «The Atlantic is less of a separation than the Channel.»

13.
Friedrich Karl von Savigny (1779–1861) was the creator of the German historical school and author of a monumental treatise on Roman law. Wilhelm von Humboldt (1767–1835) was a German statesman, linguist, and philosopher. His essay on the limitation of State action was written in 1792 but published only in 1851. John Stuart Mill (1806–1873) was the English economist and philosopher. Laboulaye refers to only one of his works, *On Liberty* (1859). William Ellery Channing (1780–1842) was a great Unitarian preacher. Laboulaye made a French translation of Channing's works of social interest, preceded by an essay on his life and thought.

14.
See Jean de Soto, «Edouard de Laboulaye,» *Revue Internationale d'Histoire Politique et Constitutionnelle* (1955), 114–150. This substantial article is to this day one of the most remarkable studies of Laboulaye.

15.
Thanks to Channing, Unitarianism reached the height of its influence in the United States between 1825 and 1840.

16.
See de Soto, pp. 124 and 126.

17.
La Liberté religieuse (Paris: Charpentier, 1858), p. 428.

18.
L'État et ses limites, pp. 76, 95.

19.
Le Parti libéral, 8th ed. (Paris: Charpentier, 1871), pp. 109 and 122. Such liberties, says the writer, are «the common heritage of Christianity» (p. 128).

20.
Ibid., pp. 24–30. See Emile Ollivier, *Commentaire de la loi du 25 mai 1864 sur les coalitions*.

21.
Le Parti libéral, Chapter IV, pp. 37–40.

22.
Ibid., Preface to the 1st ed., p. VII.

23.
Ibid., pp. 307, 272.

24.
Histoire des États-Unis, 3rd ed., 3 vols. (Paris: Charpentier, 1868), I: 6, 23.

25.
Ibid., III: 3.

26.
Esquisse d'une Constitution républicaine (Paris, 1872), pp. 31 and 35.

27.
Benjamin Constant, *Cours de politique constitutionnelle* (Paris: Guillaumin, 1872), I: 263, the chapter entitled «Of That Which Is Not Constitutional.»

28.
Sismondi, *Études sur les constitutions des peuples libres*, quoted in Laboulaye's *Questions constitutionnelles* (Paris: Charpentier, 1872), p. 57.

29.
Questions constitutionnelles, Preface, p. ii.

30.
See *Considérations sur la Constitution*, Chapter IV; *Histoire des États-Unis*, Vol. III, first lesson; *Le Parti libéral*, Chapters XII and XIV; *Esquisse d'une Constitution républicaine*, 6th Letter.

31.
Already at the time of *L'Acte additionel* Constant was in the wrong. Napoléon gave in to him for tactical reasons, but his initial opposition to the idea of setting up a paymaster's office was well founded. This is the only instance in which Laboulaye lends reason to Napoléon rather than Constant. See *Histoire des États-Unis*, III: 24.

32.
La Revision de la Constitution, originally published in 1851, is among the texts gathered together in *Questions constitutionnelles*.

33.
Esquisse d'une Constitution républicaine, 5th Letter. Laboulaye demanded the «sanction of the country» for the constitutional laws of 1875 and maintained his teachings on the right of revision during the debates of that same year (*Annales de l'Assemblée Nationale*, 39 [June 22, 1875]).

34.
Esquisse d'une Constitution républicaine, p. 2.

35.
Ibid., 2nd Letter, p. 22.

36.
Questions constitutionnelles, p. 65. However, Laboulaye's admiration for the United States was not blind. Thus, for instance, he recommended for France the irremovability of judges and not their election, American style.

37.
See, for example, *Histoire des États-Unis*, III: 25, and *Esquisse d'une Constitution républicaine*, 2nd Letter, p. 19.

38.
Le Parti libéral, Chapter X on universal suffrage and Chapter XI on public education; quotation from Preface to the 1st ed., p. XII.

39.
Pierre Guiral, *Prévost-Paradol (1829–1870): Pensée et action d'un libéral sous le Second Empire* (Paris: Presses Universitaires de France, 1955), pp. 164–170.

40.
Ibid., pp. 296–297; see also *L'État et ses limites*, pp. 323–391; and Laboulaye, *Études morales et politiques* (Paris: Charpentier, 1862), pp. 150–175.

41.
He never failed to pay tribute to liberal Catholics and to Monsignor Dupanloup.

42.
On Laboulaye in the Union Libérale, see Louis Girard, *Les Libéraux français* (Paris: Aubier, 1985), Chapter XXII, especially pp. 188–190.

43.
Jules Simon, *La Liberté* (1859) and Vacherot, *La Démocratie* (1860).

44.
Preface to the 1st ed., p. VII; see also Chapter XVIII, pp. 274–275.

45.
See the last page of *Le Parti libéral*.

46.
Ibid., p. 5.

47.
In a letter to Baroche (quoted by Guiral).

48.
Guiral, p. 518.

49.
Esquisse d'une Constitution républicaine, 1st Letter, p. 12; *Le Parti libéral*, p. 281. Constant's text is in the *Cours de politique constitutionnelle*, II: 70.

50.
On the basic character of this demand see *Le Parti libéral*, Chapter XIII, p. 171.

51.
Questions constitutionnelles, Appendix: «Le Plébiscite de 1870,» pp. 255–309; quotation from pp. 259–260.

52.
See *Esquisse d'une Constitution républicaine*, 7th Letter.

53.
Annales de l'Assemblée Nationale, 39: 475.

54.
See Gabriel Hanotaux, *Histoire de la fondation de la IIIe République* (Paris: Plon-Nourrit et Cie., [1926]), 4: 10. Rémusat presided over the Commission.

55.
Charles de Rémusat, *Mémoires de ma vie* (Paris: Plon, 1967), V: 513.

56.
Marcel Prelot, *Institutions politiques et droit constitutionnel* (Paris: Dalloz, 1984).

57.
Le Parti libéral, Preface to the 1st ed., last sentence. Laboulaye died in 1883. Since 1873 he had been the administrator of the Collège de France.

1.
Speech of Edouard de Laboulaye at the banquet at the Hôtel du Louvre, Paris, November 6, 1875.

2.
Bartholdi to Butler, February 18, 1887.

3.
Bartholdi to Evarts, February 5, 1884.

4.
Bartholdi to Butler, June 2, 1886.

5.
Bartholdi to Butler, April 20, 1890.

6.
Trachtenberg, p. 143, implied this synthesis when he wrote that «the unity is that of the universal methods of the civil engineer, Eiffel solving the structural needs of Bartholdi's sculptural envelope, and Stone providing the support for Eiffel's armature.»

7.
Deborah Nevins used John Gast's painting to illustrate her discussion of the bridge as a symbol for «Manifest Destiny,» in *The Great East River Bridge 1883–1983*, catalogue of an exhibition at the Brooklyn Museum (New York: Abrams, 1983), pp. 10–11.

8.
James Goode, *The Outdoor Sculpture of Washington, D.C.* (Washington, D.C.: Smithsonian Printing Office, 1874), p. 257.

9.
Trachtenberg, pp. 146–147, elaborates on the «love of immoderate amusements» that large nineteenth-century monuments catered to with their visiting platforms. The Brooklyn Bridge, also a popular platform, is deliberately included in the illustration of the torch.

10.
Jules Verne, *Robur le Conquérant* (Paris: Hetzel, 1886; 2nd ed., 1891; reprinted Paris: Hachette, 1979), pp. 31–32.

11.
Quoted by Robert Taussat, «Le Malheureux Destin du «Great Eastern,» in Jules Verne, *Ouvrage collectif* (Paris: Hachette, 1982).

12.
Robur le Conquérant, pp. 31–32.

13.
Jules Verne, *Autour de la lune* (Paris: Hetzel, 1872; reprinted Paris: Le Livre de Poche, 1978), pp. 3–4.

14.
Robur le Conquérant, p. 240.

15.
Jules Verne, *L'Ile à Hélice* (Paris: Hetzel, 1895; reprinted Paris: Hachette, 1980), p. 440.

1.
Schmitt, pp. 9–17 and genealogical tree, p. 18.

2.
Four, if we count a brother of Gilles-François Bartholdi, pastor at Oberbrunn.

3.
Charlotte Bartholdi's father-in-law died in 1830 and his brother, Gilles-Engelhard, the pharmacist, in 1822, leaving no children. Gschaedler, p. 6, mentions a list of the Bartholdis' land holdings in the Musée Bartholdi, Colmar, which we have not found. However, the inventory of his possessions, drawn up after his widow's death, in 1914, gives a clear idea of Auguste's land holdings, to which we shall return.

4.
During the 1860s Mme. Bartholdi sent from Colmar (to which she had returned) money to be invested by Auguste in Paris (in 1865 Fr. 11,500 were placed in an Italian government loan) as well as foodstuffs and household linen. Letters show that she saw to renting her houses and selling land. At the end of 1865 Auguste asked his mother for help: «Send me some money, whatever you can. We said that we'd end the year with Fr. 3,000 and that, beginning in 1866, you'd send me Fr. 1,500 a month.» This amounted to a real allowance» (quoted in Schmitt, pp. 32–33).

5.
A little Frédéric-Auguste had died, at six months, in 1832; Augusta-Charlotte, at one month, in 1833.

6.
Nevertheless, on November 6, 1869, Auguste wrote to his mother expressing the wish that the future Musée Bartholdi should contain at least one picture, a Christ, painted by his brother. This is interesting because it shows that Bartholdi was already planning a museum dedicated to his works.

7.
Bartholdi to Mme. Bartholdi, November 14, 1869: «If I let myself be carried along by the matrimonial current I am running great risks, and I would not like to be involved incautiously by you. I beg you therefore to be careful in what you say or do, because I reserve for myself all freedom. I would prefer if you want to reconcile me with marriage that you made it possible for me to see and meet the person you have in mind instead of talking about marriage or making compromising overtures» (quoted in Gschaedler, pp. 17–18, who also cites a letter of December 27, 1869, from Auguste to his mother).

8.
Mme. Bartholdi to Bartholdi, December 1870.

9.
Bartholdi to Mme. Bartholdi, November 18, 1876.

10.
Bartholdi to Mme. Bartholdi, October 30, 1876.

11.
Bartholdi to Mme. Bartholdi, January 22, 1877, from Albany (quoted in Gschaedler, p. 59).

12.
Schmitt, p. 20. Doubtless this is the Physics Notebook from the collection of Mme. Golliez, Antibes, annotated by Bartholdi: «Extracts from my physics notebook, 1851–1852—Auguste Bartholdi.»

13.
Schmitt, p. 19. Jean-Charles may have been in Scheffer's studio around 1846, when he was sixteen.

14.
Gustave Jundt painted a portrait of Jeanne Bartholdi in 1877 (Inv. no. 467).

15.
The bust is Inv. no. 386. The model of the monument is in the storerooms of the Musée Bartholdi. The sculptor decorated this monument with a palette and a little Alsatian girl paying her respects.

16.
Gschaedler, p. 8. Similar objects were to be found himself in the collection of Mme. Golliez, Antibes.

17.
A trace of this commission is in the Archives Nationales, Paris, under the number F^{21} 1753.

18.
A notice from the Beaux-Arts director, J. Garraud, of March 18, 1848, specified that models for the sculpted figure should not be more than 19½ inches high (Jacques Lethève, «Une statue malchanceuse, «La République» of Jean-François Soitoux,» *Gazette des Beaux-Arts* [October 1963]).

19.
The Commune (of 1871) considered rescuing Soitoux's statue from the warehouse.

20.
The project failed again in 1878, when there was a question of placing his *République* in front of the Universal Exposition building on the Champ de Mars in Paris. Clésinger received the commission instead, and his *République* was inaugurated on June 30, on the spot where Bartholdi had thought of placing his statue's colossal head. Soitoux and Bartholdi competed against each other, but were reconciled, no doubt, after the success of Clésinger, who was backed by the Minister of Industry.

21.
The decidedly unlucky *République* of Soitoux was placed in front of the Institut de France in 1880, but Premier Jules Ferry, for political reasons, was unable to inaugurate it (a similar mishap marked the inauguration of the Statue of Liberty). Soitoux's statue was taken down in 1960 during a reordering of the Seine embankment and the restoration of the Collège des Quatre-Nations. The bronze grave monument was recently stolen from the Montparnasse cemetery.

22.
Ary Scheffer was known to be a close friend of Etex, and even his biographer.

23.
A small painting by Arie Johannes Lamme in the museum of Dordrecht shows Ary Scheffer's studio in 1851, when Bartholdi knew him. See *Catalogue Institut Neerlandais* (Paris, 1980), pp. 4–5.

24.
It is possible that *Le Bon Samaritain*, the first work presented by Bartholdi to the Salon, in 1853, and turned down, was influenced by Ary Scheffer, who was at work on several New Testament subjects between 1850 and 1854.

25.
Trachtenberg, p. 50.

26.
Henri Martin published an «Ary Scheffer» in the *Annuaire des artistes et amateurs* in 1860. Charles Blanc wrote an article on him in his *Histoire des peintres de toutes les écoles, École Française* (Paris, 1865), III: 17.

27.
Trachtenberg, p. 208, n. 9, credits Albert Boime with this discovery.

28.
Ibid.

29.
Ibid., p. 74

30.
Charles Lefèbre, «L'Oeuvre de Bartholdi,» *Revue Alsacienne* (Paris, 1881) (quoted in Gschaedler, p. 66).

31.
There are several versions of Polycletus's *Doryphore* or copies of it. The closest to that of Naples, which includes the lance, is at the Munich Glyptotheca; there is a Roman version in the Uffizi in Florence and another in the Vatican (Museo del Biaccio Nuovo).

32.
We have little information about the place where Mme. Bartholdi established her family in Paris. One letter is sent from the «rue denfer.» Today there are a passage d'Enfer, an avenue Denfert-Rochereau, and a square of the same name, where there is a reduced version of Bartholdi's *Lion de Belfort*, all three in the same *arrondissement*.

33.
Jacques Betz, «Les Demeures parisiennes de Bartholdi,» *Annuaire de la Société d'Histoire et d'Archéologie de Colmar* (1979), pp. 74–75. Betz proposes 1854 as the date of occupancy of the house on the rue Vavin, counting back thirty-eight years from 1892, the date of expropriation. Charles Lefèbre wrote in the *Revue Alsacienne* of February 1881: «Monsieur Bartholdi has been on the rue Vavin for more than twenty years,» which points to an occupancy date before 1861, but not necessarily in 1854.

34.
Quoted in Schmitt, p. 71.

35.
The Colmar museum still has the overall drawing of the Quinconces project, reproduced and commented upon here under cat. 60. We shall see that the projected fountain was never completed, although it won first prize in the competition of 1856 and was adapted by Bartholdi for the Place des Terreaux, Lyon.
36.
The model is doubtless Inv. no. 344, «Statue of General Arrighi, duke of Padua, 67 cm. high, on a monumental quadrangular base.» Inv. no. 277 mentions a slightly taller model of the monument, installed at Bastia in 1865.
37.
This monument, which is not mentioned in the Salon catalogues, commemorates the Peruvian victory over a Spanish squadron on May 2, 1866. A work with the same subject was exhibited by L. C. Cuynot at the Salon of 1872 (No. 1628).
38.
Presented at the Salons of 1868 and 1873, this «bronze group» was preceded by a series of sketches (see «Essai d'iconographie bartholdienne» in Betz). There is a certain confusion about this matter in the inventory. No. 68 describes a plaster group 13 inches high, a model for a bronze monument to the *Loisirs de la paix* erected in New York in 1868 and presented at the Salon the same year. But Bartholdi never received a commission for such a monument in New York. Under No. 379 there is a «large plaster group,» 29½ inches high, marked «Salon of 1868» and bearing on the base the Latin version of the title, *Otia Pacis*. This cannot be the model in this photograph, since the figures are nude whereas No. 379 shows them in antique dress, he a Roman soldier and she wearing a tunic. This model is presently in the museum at Colmar, which also possesses a second model, in bronzed plaster, unnumbered, and doubtless very close to the bronze shown at the Salon of 1873, now lost.
39.
This is the project designed for Bordeaux in 1858 (see n. 35) and redone by Bartholdi for the Place des Terreaux in Lyon, where it stands today, spectacularly impressive, a perfect variation of the sculpture of Versailles and the Bassin d'Apollon. The work was presented at the Salon of 1898 as a model one-quarter completed (No. 3127). We have three photographs of this presentation, one a three-quarter view (Musée Bartholdi, Colmar), the two others affording a front view (one at Colmar, showing also the *Tombe du Garde National*, exhibited the same year, as No. 3128, plate 5 of the album *L'Art décoratif aux expositions des Beaux-Arts*; the other at the Conservatoire National des Arts et Métiers, Paris, no. 13768–8–34). Two other photographs, also at Colmar, show two models that place the fountain in two different architectural contexts. Finally, we found in the Colmar storerooms three little plasters of the main grouping of *La Saône*, one of which is marked Inv. no. 178 as well as «Salon of 1898.»
40.
A fountain erected at Colmar in 1869. There is an undated model in the storerooms of the Musée Bartholdi. The bronze was presented at the Salon of 1869, No. 3239.
41.
Inv. no. 36: «Allegorical terracotta statue of Alsace, offered in silver to Msgr. Bergmann of Strasbourg, dated 1873, 37 cm. high.»
42.
The *Vauban* was commissioned by the town of Avallon. (We may note that Etex received a commission for a piece on the same subject.) Bartholdi's work was presented at the Salon of 1870. The Musée d'Unterlinden, Colmar, has a photograph of it, taken perhaps at the Salon (Unterlinden, no. 32). Two plaster models are still at the Musée Bartholdi: one of the face (no. 319, signed and dated 1870, 22¼ inches high), the other of the architectural context (no. 278, 13¾ inches high, 25½ inches wide). Finally, four similar subjects (now lost) are mentioned in the inventory: no. 275, a bronze reduction, and no. 351, three small bronze statuettes, which recall the large number of likenesses of Marshal Vauban throughout France; Vauban was popular because the fortifications he designed had defended the country from invasion.

The *Monument à Gribeauval* was preceded, in 1876, by a version in clay (Inv. no. 91, now in the storerooms at Colmar). A plaster presented at the Salon of 1878 (No. 4031) was bought by the government. This monument to «the promoter of French artillery in the eighteenth century» (according to Schmitt, p. 69) was placed in the courtyard of the Hôtel des Invalides in Paris. A second, more accurate model, in plaster, is still at Colmar, Inv. no. 32.

Regarding the *Bruat*, Schmitt, pp. 26 ff., reprints the extraordinarily detailed description Bartholdi sent to the mayor of Colmar. The artist had this text printed in order that no one should fail to understand the meaning of the sculpture's symbolic references: the four parts of the globe, the combat dress of the soldier and sailor, the attributes of each of the continents. The fountain was inaugurated on August 21, 1864; it won him the rank of Chevalier of the Legion of Honor and increased his local glory, which dated from the installation of his *Général Rapp*, not far away. A model is in a glass case at Colmar, but the one shown here is more likely the small plaster, more simply ornamented, in the storerooms. We have brought together two recumbent figures for the *Africa* (Inv. no. 87) and another continent (likewise no. 87) as well as four clay models of the main subject, Admiral Bruat (Inv. nos. 47, 62, 63, and 90). Finally, under Inv. no. 284 are listed four terra-cotta models, statuettes of a man (or a woman) personifying «rivers among those of various continents,» which may belong to the same project. Finally, the head we see in the photograph, on the same shelf, may be that of *Asia*. Since the monument was destroyed by the Germans on September 9, 1940, and reconstructed in 1957–58 with sculptures by Gérard Choain, it is difficult to verify this identification.

Schmitt, p. 69, says the *Rouget de l'Isle* was presented at the Salon of 1881. It is certain that it was unveiled at Lons-le-Saulnier, native town of the great patriot and author of "La Marseillaise," in 1882. We reproduce the model (Inv. no. 295) as cat. 86. A photograph of the completed statue in the artist's studio is at the Conservatoire National des Arts et Métiers, Paris, no. 1913 (another print is no. 1914). Other models are in the Colmar museum. Inv. no. 89 is signed and dated 1881 (terra cotta, 11¾ inches high); no. 70 is a variation (terra cotta, 12¼ inches high), as is a last statuette, in plaster, unnumbered and in very poor condition.
43.
Inv. no. 259 speaks of this head as «reduced» in size, although it is quite large in comparison to that of Bartholdi, who is also in the photograph. It was made for the statue of General Rapp erected on the Champ de Mars in Colmar in 1850 and is 13½ inches high. There is an old photograph at the Conservatoire National des Arts et Métiers, Paris (no. 137688–33). The inventory also lists a small plaster statuette, actually in the storerooms of the Musée Bartholdi; the figure and its pedestal, perhaps the definitive model, are displayed elsewhere in the museum. The bronze statue was destroyed in Colmar in September 1940, then remounted and reinaugurated, February 3, 1946.
44.
Inv. no. 162.
45.
The subject of this bust is impossible to identify. The beard, features, and lack of insignia or decorations suggest that the subject is an American. Bartholdi did so many portraits of French government officials and notables that he must have almost automatically sculpted the rosette of the Legion of Honor into the subject's buttonhole.
46.
The architectural context was a product of Bartholdi's imagination but was executed by the marble-sculptor Hatz of Colmar. The plaster model, photographed here, is in the Colmar museum.
47.
Schmitt, pp. 74–75.
48.
La borne frontière, no. 328, a reduced plaster model, 20½ inches high. Bartholdi made numerous highly patriotic preliminary watercolors, which are on display in the Colmar museum. The child laying a wreath of flowers on the frontier marker resembles the one on the funerary monument Bartholdi made for his friend Gustave Jundt.

It was apparently through his brother, Jean-Charles, at this time a practicing lawyer in Colmar, a devotee of medieval history, and a friend of Louis Hugot, founder of the Schongauer Society, that Auguste Bartholdi received a commission for a fountain memorial to the Colmar painter whose famous *Vierge au buisson de Roses* is conserved in the city. The figure of Schongauer, in its typically flamboyant curve, resembles that of the *Agnès de Hergenheim*, which dates from the early years of Bartholdi's career. He finished the statue in 1861 and showed it at the Salon with the rest of the project (No. 3169: «Monument in memory of Martin Schoen [sic], fifteenth-century painter, engraver, and goldsmith, a group in sandstone from the Vosges. This fountain is to be set up in the courtyard of the Museum of Colmar»). And so it was, in the same year. The Colmar museum has the first model (Inv. no. 249), two definitive models (no. 169, in the storerooms, a number not found in the museum itself), and four figures of the *goldsmith* (no. 362, Room O and a reduced plaster in the storerooms); the *wood engraver*; the *painter* (no. 282 and a reduced copy in plaster, unnumbered), and the *poet* (in a museum room and a reduced copy in plaster, unnumbered). A small bronze of the *goldsmith* is in the storerooms. Finally, a contemporary photograph shows the entire monument as exhibited at the Salon (Unterlinden, no. 31).
49.
Now in the storerooms: *Day* and *Night*, unnumbered, and *Moses* (Inv. no. 337).
50.
Lesbazeilles, p. 273.
51.
Inv. no. 30, plaster, dated 1887; it was placed by mistake in Angers and inaugurated in Auxerre in 1888.
52.
Schmitt, p. 64.
53.
The *Diderot* was ordered by the city of Langres and inaugurated on August 3, 1884, two days before the laying of the cornerstone for the Statue of Liberty in New York. A plaster model is in a glass case at the Musée Bartholdi; another, including the pedestal, in the storerooms (Inv. no. 648, 25½ inches high). A contemporary photograph shows the statue on display at the Musée d'Unterlinden, Colmar (no. 34).

Betz considers that the *Adieu au pays* was presented at the Salon of 1900; this is confirmed by Schmitt, p. 79, but he confuses the Salon and the Universal Exposition. The Salon catalogue mentions only the «Christopher Columbus, aluminum statue» (cat. 11). A reduced-size sketch, unnumbered, is in the storerooms of the Colmar museum; there is also a clay form, intended to shape the mold for casting. Bartholdi used this group to complete, in the same patriotic spirit, the monument offered to the city of Basel by the Baron de Gruyer to celebrate *La Suisse secourant . . . Strasbourg*. The first model dates from 1891 (Inv. no. 317, in the storerooms of the Musée Bartholdi, as is another unnumbered model). A reduced bronze version of the monumental group is in a private collection in Franche-Comté. One of the female figures, representing Switzerland, seems to derive directly from the Statue of Liberty: the same diadem, the same dress, and, above all, the same thrust of the leg and foot under an accumulation of folds. A bas-relief by Bartholdi, *Nirsbrey*, completed the monument in 1896; a plaster is in the storerooms of the Musée Bartholdi (Inv. no. 360). The artist also drew from this a cylindrical bronze vase, in the storerooms (Inv. no. 305), with three plaster molds (no. 306).

A first model of the patriotic *Monument aux Aéronautes* was shown at the Salon of 1904, No. 2646; then a full-size plaster, at the Salon of 1905, after Bartholdi's death. The Salon catalogue indicated that it would be located on the Place de la Révolte at Neuilly, but it was actually set up at the Porte des Ternes in 1906. The Germans destroyed it during World War II. Six models are mentioned in the inventory. Three are lost: no. 177, in plaster (that of the 1904 Salon), and terra cottas nos. 141 and 69. The others survive, in the storerooms: no. 41, in plaster (bearing the title «Paris, 1870»); no. 327, another plaster; and, finally, no. 321 (cat. 27). The storerooms contain also a bronze, mounted on Algerian onyx (Inv. no. 311, 28¾ inches high). An old photograph shows the monument set up at the Porte des Ternes. At some point Bartholdi considered making it into a street light, with an alabaster or glass globe.

Of *Les grands soutiens du monde*, the Colmar museum displays, in the courtyard of the former house, the final bronze monument, presented at the Salon of 1902, No. 2231, and two models in plaster, one with the terrestrial sphere (Inv. no. 41), the other without it (no. 174), as it was presented at the previous Salon, in 1901 (No.2978).
54.
Gschaedler, p. 4.
55.
Gschaedler (p. 66) writes: «Lefèbre went to see Bartholdi in his studio on Vavin Street and admired a miniature reproduction of the whole workshop where the head [of the Statue of Liberty] had been made. It [the workshop model] was complete, including the modest broom used to sweep the shop, with the workers and Bartholdi himself giving instructions.»
56.
Inv. no. 164, presented at the Salon of 1883, No. 3319, a terra-cotta «Portrait of W. M. Evarts, former head of the Council of Ministers.»
57.
The description given in the inventory is «A little girl, standing, with flowers in her apron, dated 1883.» The plaster is described as «dyed,» and it is likely that the flowers were originally colored red, white, and blue since the child represents patriotic Alsace, resistant, despite the German occupation, to assimilation.
58.
An Avoiron cast, probably the «C» size.
59.
A Bartholdi Club was founded in New York in 1885; a hotel bore his name and his portrait appeared on medals and plates.
60.
Trachtenberg, p. 201, n. 26: «there appears to be a crypto-signature of Bartholdi on his colossus in the depths of the folds of the lower front cascade, visible from a front-right oblique viewpoint, in the form of a raised «B» (a frequent monogram on his sketches).»
61.
The fifth, of less interest, is Inv. no. 122. The bronze (no. 287) was modeled in plaster and is also in the storerooms at Colmar.

Chapter 2

62.
We know the *Callao* column through a photograph in the Musée Bartholdi (cat. 152). It can also be seen at the upper right of a photograph of the studio on the rue Vavin. We must look elsewhere to observe its close relationship to the Châtelet fountain. Here it is enough to underline that this was indeed the model. The four figures at the foot of the shaft, hand in hand and forming a chain, have simply been centered on the four sides of the base. The angles of the base, under the stylobate, ornamented with the upturned prows of ancient ships, recall the ornamentation of the base of the Statue of Liberty which Bartholdi made for the Chicago Exposition of 1900 (cat. 283a) and allow us to date this model from very late in the artist's life.

The model of the *Indépendance de 1830* is still at Colmar. The four columns are assembled on a square stylobate, set on an embossed base and a stairway. The cluster of flags and the eagle, probably meant to be in bronze, respond to the figure perched atop a globe. There is here thus a later version of the Statue of Liberty from around 1890—this is the only column that is not in the photograph of the studio—showing an important stylistic modification, by the artist, of his original concept.

We know the column to the *Indépendance des États-Unis* from a photograph in the museum at Colmar and as Inv. no. 61. It is amusing to see the artist return to the original title of the Statue of Liberty, and even more so to find him reusing the winged spirit at the top for his own funeral monument.

The Saint-Michel Fountain, Inv. no. 55, is dated 1860.

Besides the large drawing for the Place des Quinconces project that we show here, the Musée Bartholdi contains photographic plates of two models, preliminary and definitive; plaster models for one of the basins and for the group topping the monument, and a *Neptune*. Two 20-inch-high plaster models appear in the inventory as nos. 338 and 339. The pedestal of the *Neptune* has ships' prows, which were to appear again in the *Callao* column.

There are, at Colmar, thirteen pieces—photographs and models—relating to the *Vercingétorix*, among them two imaginary views of it installed at Clermont-Ferrand. The large plaster is shown in the museum at Colmar. A bronze version is in the Musée Bargoin at Clermont-Ferrand. The equestrian subjects in plaster, which we treat here, were not listed in the inventory and are kept in the storerooms at Colmar.

Four models are listed under Inv. no. 279, *Projet du monument pour la décoration du Plateau de Longchamp à Marseille.* Only three—reproduced here—have been found, including the first (cat. 61), with which we are acquainted through the *Mémoire en défense*, published by Bartholdi in order to defend his work against the misappropriation on the part of Espérandier. A comparison of maps, drawings, and models suggests that there was only one project, with two variations. The lost model may be of the site.

63.
Trachtenberg, p. 28.

64.
This is a project with double columns (Inv. no. 175). This model has disappeared but we have the photograph shown here (cat. 67), and further witness is borne by a 48-inch-high model (Inv. no. 185). The medium-size model for Clermont-Ferrand is cat. 68, and there is another copy in the storerooms. There are three photographs of the modeled socle: one of the front, one side view, and one at an angle (cat. 70). A small model is in the Musée d'Orsay, and two bronzes are listed as Inv. nos. 353 and 301. A medallion shows the sculpture, as no. 471. The large plaster model, perhaps the final study, is located in the large room of the Musée Bartholdi.

65.
We know the *Gambetta* project through some nineteen photographs, montages, and models in the museum at Colmar, all in the storerooms, and through the monument in situ, at Ville d'Avray. The list is as follows:

Project for the Chamber of Deputies: a large overall model (Inv. no. 369); a small model of Gambetta with upraised arm (Inv. no. 54); a model of the figure of the *République* (Inv. no. 73), incorrectly called «a Roman Emperor, draped and helmeted, sitting on a bench»; and three photographs of a model in front of a mock facade of the Chamber of Deputies: one front view, one three-quarter view, and one bird's-eye view, a drawing.

Project for Ville d'Avray: eight small models of the entire structure, more or less reduced in size in relation to the foregoing (Inv. nos. 253, 80, 80b, 80c, 80[4], 80[5], 81, and 161); a model of Gambetta with folded arm (Inv. no. 293; cat. 74); a photograph of the definitive model (Inv. no. 149, dated 1888; a second copy is in the Musée d'Unterlinden, Colmar); a photograph of the finished monument (cat. 75); and a rear photograph, with a handwritten notation of its destination.

66.
We regret that we cannot draw upon Catherine Brice's forthcoming work on the monument to Victor Emmanuel II in Rome, in which she relates the uses to which the monument was put by successive Italian governments.

67.
Inv. no. 269, *Projet de monument à colonnades ornées de statues disposées au haut d'un escalier à double révolution,* signed *B*, dated 1873; Inv. no. 142, *Projet de fontaine monumentale*; Musée Bartholdi, Colmar.

68.
Inv. no. 278, at Colmar.

69.
The facade dates from 1804–05. The pediment was sculpted by Cortot and the lateral sculptures are by Rude and Pradier.

70.
Inv. no. 369, presently in storage.

71.
The handwriting does not seem to be that of the artist.

72.
No doubt the same uniform which André Gschaedler noticed in a cupboard at the Musée Bartholdi in the 1960s, and which appears in the inventory.

73.
Menotti Garibaldi is the standing figure, center.

74.
A plaster cast of this work is to be found in the Musée Bartholdi.

75.
A plaster cast on the scale of the completed work is in storage at Colmar, and appears as Inv. no. 105, dated 1869 (cat. 81).

76.
This piece (Inv. no. 378) may also be found in tinted plaster, in storage at the Colmar museum. The museum at Unterlinden has a photograph (Bartholdi collection no. 26) of the group exhibited at the Salon, under the title «La Malédiction d'Alsace—Salon 1872,» and of its socle, to which is affixed a plaque reading «Souscription Alsacienne.» In the end the work was presented to Gambetta by the Alsatian community in Paris.

77.
Inv. no. 112, noted as «Jeanne d'Arc—Compiègne» and dated 1863. It may be observed in passing that the myth of Joan of Arc as patriot was already established in 1819, when a critic reported that there was «a throng of Maids at the Salon,» and that Ary Scheffer treated the subject more than once in his paintings around 1839.

78.
In the same vein Bartholdi completed in 1870 a *Vauban*, then regarded as the worthy defender of his country's frontiers, for his native town of Avallon.

79.
Emplaced in 1872, this sepulcher was sculpted by Bartholdi to house the remains of two National Guardsmen who fell while under his command at Colmar in 1870, Adolphe Voulminot and Joseph Wagner. Their funeral occasioned notable popular demonstrations of patriotism.

The best-known example of funerary sculpture in Alsace is the tomb of the Maréchal de Saxe at Strasbourg; its Parisian counterpart is the tomb of le Brun's mother at St. Louis en l'Ile.

80.
At the Salon of 1872: John Lewis Brown, *Journée du 6 Août 1870: Reischoffen* (No. 219); Anne Henriette Browne, *Alsace!* (No. 221); Emile Charles Chanson, *L'Alsace d'après M. Henner* (enamel, No. 288); Gustave Doré, *Alsace* (No. 521); François Ehrmann, *Strasbourg, Août 1870* (No. 587); Frédéric-Théodore Lix, *Les Adieux à la Patrie* (No. 1033); Charles François Marchal, *Alsace!* (No. 1061); Ortès, *Le Trésor de l'Alsacienne* (No. 1188); Théophile Schüler, *Le Berceur, souvenir d'Alsace* (No. 1401).

At the Salon of 1873: Henry Bacon, *L'Option: l'Alsace* (No. 46); Charles Emile Matthis, *Au bord du chemin, souvenir de Froeschwiller* (No. 1023); Pierre-Louis Détrier, *Alsace!* (No. 1617); Louis Grégoire, *L'Alsace* (No. 1699).

81.
No. 365c (reserve) in the inventory; we propose 1872 as a date for this study in clay.

82.
In *Les Colosses anciens et modernes*; see Chapter 2 for a discussion of this work.

83.
See Chapter 6.

84.
Schmitt, pp. 65–69; several of the points made in this paragraph are drawn from Schmitt's book.

85.
The 1914 inventory includes more models attributable to studies for the *Lion de Belfort* than have survived from the studies for the Statue of Liberty.

86.
See cat. 92, showing the two men in front of the *Lion*.

87.
The plaster was exhibited at the Salon of 1878 (No. 4031) and the bronze the following year (No. 4783).

88.
Betz dates this 1882; like the present writers he has been unable to find it in the Salons of 1881–82.

89.
The two busts, both marble, are Nos. 3477 and 2979, respectively. *Washington and Lafayette* is described in the Salon catalogue as «Group in bronze, no. 2261, presented to the city of Paris by Monsieur J. P. of New York»—quite certainly Joseph Pulitzer. The 1889 project, No. 3190, is the great monument with the statue of Lafayette on horseback.

90.
These works are, respectively, a group in marble, No. 2256; a group in marble, No. 2845; No. 3128; and No. 3189.

91.
The *Monument des trois sièges* is No. 2509. A bronze of this group (perhaps the very one exhibited at the Salon) still exists in a private collection in Franche-Comté. The plaster *Sergeant Hoff* is No. 2645.

92.
1904: No. 2646, in plaster; 1905: No. 2821 (a fragment of the monument to be erected at the Rond-Point de la Révolte in Neuilly-sur-Seine).

93.
For additional discussion, see Chapter 6.

94.
Inv. no. 15, 1886. A companion piece to the portrait of the sculptor's wife by the same artist (cat. 37).

95.
Inv. no. 465. A smaller copy of this portrait is in the Musée Bartholdi.

96.
Hubert Louis-Noël, the statue's creator, was a long-time collaborator and friend of Bartholdi. Assisted by Rubin for the sculpture and by the architects Georges Bloch and Charles Winkler at Colmar, he created a large-scale monument (63½ inches for the statue, 76 inches for the base), flanked by the figures of Painting and Poetry, Sculpture and Architecture on two bronze bas-reliefs.

97.
The Arica Monument is known from a photograph in the Colmar museum showing the plaster model. It is a reworking of those colossal columns of which Bartholdi was fond, similar to the monument to Independence or the Callao column (cat. 152).

98.
Bartholdi's tomb in the Montparnasse cemetery bears a medallion by A. Rubin, signed and dated 1905 and dedicated to «Mes amis Bartholdi.» It depicts the artist and his wife in profile bust. The winged bronze figure is signed »Bartholdi.»

1.
See, in the Archives of the Association Philotechnique de Boulogne-Billancourt, a study with commentary by Dr. Bezançon dated December 5, 1964. The meeting on «The Colossi» took place in March 1903 in the Salles des Fêtes, which still stands today. The records contain only a summary of the meeting. Dr. Bezançon believes that Bartholdi was in Boulogne at the time because he had a studio there at 45, rue Gutemberg, where he had taken over the business of the painter Théodore Gudin, who died in Boulogne in 1880.

2.
For Charles Blanc, on the Sphinx of Gizeh, see Lesbazeilles, p. 20; for Edmond About, on the defense of Belfort with reference to the *Lion*, see Lesbazeilles, pp. 328–329.

3.
Les Lieux de Mémoire (ed. Pierre Nora) (Paris: Gallimard, 1984).

4.
Kolossos, in the original Greek, signifies stele or funerary monument; as far back as pre-Hellenic times the word was used of a terra-cotta statuette representing a person's double. An article in the *Revue des Études Anciennes* LXII (1960), 5–40 contends that the legs of such a statuette may be joined or may take the form of a pillar or column. Herodotus uses the word indiscriminately for small as well as large statues. Virginia Bush in *The Colossal Sculpture of the Cinquecento* (New York and London: Garland Publishing, Inc., 1976) says that by 304 B.C. the term was applied only to statues of great size.

5.
In 1874 the École Française was founded in Rome; its department of ancient history was given jurisdiction over French archeological research in Rome and Italy.

6.
The Colosseum, or Flavian Amphitheater, was called «Colosses» by the Romans, who confused it with the nearby colossal statue of Nero.

7.
Schmitt, p. 42.

8.
It should be noted here how well Bartholdi's overt cult of the Egyptian conformed to the Masonic tradition—at least since Mozart's *The Magic Flute*—and how much the artist's works *L'Égypte apportant la lumière à l'Asie* and *La Liberté éclairant le Monde* owe to the mythology of light.

9.
Verrocchio, whose workshop in Florence was often visited by the young Leonardo, erected his equestrian statue of the condottiere Bartolommeo Colleoni in Venice at the end of the fifteenth century.

10.
Bush, pp. 166 ff.

Chapter 3

11.
We know that the *David*, commissioned in 1501, was intended as a challenge to the artists of the time: how to make proper use of the great, magnificent block of marble, cut at great expense from the quarries of Carrara, which neither Agostino, Duccio, nor Antonio Rossellino had dared to carve (Bush, pp. 98 ff.).

Michelangelo's colossal statue of Julius II was commissioned in 1506; in 1508 it was placed above the great door of San Petronio in Bologna. A symbol of Papal authority over Bologna, it was destroyed in 1511 when Annibale II Bentivoglio recaptured the city.

Hercules and Cacus was ordered by Clement VII (de' Medici) in 1525 (Bush, p. 123).

The competition sponsored by the Medici was won by Ammanati in 1560 (Bush, p. 134).

The *Mars* project was submitted to François I in 1542, but not executed on its intended scale until 1546. The king's death in 1547 put an end to the work.

The portrait of Cosimo I was commissioned by Ferdinand I de' Medici in 1587 (Bush, p. 193). The horse, cast in one piece, was the crowning achievement of Giovanni Bologna. The statue was unveiled in 1595. In 1601 Ferdinand commissioned his own equestrian statue, placed in the Piazza sta Annunziata in 1608.

12.
Bush, pp. 204–205.

13.
Ibid., pp. 288 ff.

14.
Bush attributes this unrealized project to one of two authors: Deinocrates (whom Lesbazeilles [p. 121] had already derived from Vitruvius) or Stasicrates.

15.
Fischer von Erlach, *Entwurff einer historischen Architectur in Abbildung unterschiedener berühmten gebäude des Altertums und fremder Völker* (Vienna, 1721).

16.
Semiramis is supposed to have had portraits of herself and of her soldiers carved into the mountain of Bagistan (quoted by Bush, p. 8, from Herodotus and Diodorus). It should be remembered that the Sphinx of Gizeh, and above all the temples of Abu Simbel, Elephantine Island, and Ellora, are all carved from the living rock—and all three are mentioned by Lesbazeilles.

17.
See Lesbazeilles, p. 134.

18.
Bush, p. 20.

19.
Ascanio Condivi, *Vita di Michelagnolo Buonarroti* (Florence, 1926), p. 34.

20.
Bush, p. 21.

21.
Paolo Farina, «Un altissimo Monte a un monte sopra,» *Psicon* (Florence, 1976), pp. 64–77.

22.
Étienne-Louis Boullée was, along with Claude-Nicolas Ledoux, the most visionary of French architects of the eighteenth century. He conceived the *Cenotaph de Newton* in 1784 as «a continuous surface without beginning or end»: Newton having demonstrated that the earth is a sphere, Boullée wanted—he said—to entomb him in his own discovery. All the projects of Boullée (none of which, any more than those of Ledoux, were ever realized) were on a gigantic scale; however, he systematically excluded colossal sculpture in favor of pure architecture.

23.
Bush says (p. 231) that Napoléon I not only commissioned colossal portraits (Canova's is at Apsley House in London) but also ordered that the statues of the Doria be restored to Genoa and supplemented by gigantic portraits of two of the city's favorite sons—Christopher Columbus and himself.

24.
The engraving accompanying the text (Lesbazeilles, p. 303) is disturbing because the arms are reversed from their position in the photograph, and the error is repeated in the text. It is conceivable that, by mistake, the photograph was inverted or that the text was written from the engraving without reference to its original.

25.
Constant Désiré Despradelles (1862–1912) was a French architect trained at the École des Beaux-Arts. In 1893 he settled in Boston, where he became a professor at the Massachusetts Institute of Technology. In France, Bartholdi came across his series of eight projects for the *Flambeau du Progrès* or *Beacon of Progress*, two of which were purchased by the French government for the Musée du Luxembourg. The sculptor wrote to the architect: «I remarked with great interest at the last Salon the project of the monument conceived by you for the glorification of the american [sic] people, and was much struck with the powerful character of its symbolism. It stamps itself on the mind by its impression of aspiration towards the infinite pervading the entire conception, whether in the detail or the ensemble. Accept my sincere compliments and best wishes for the realization of your noble thought, together with the expression of my most distinguished sentiments.» The following drawings were published in *Pencil Points*, No. 6 (May 1925), 58–70: a frontal view cut off at half-length, an overall view, a detail of the left corner, and a comparative view of the monument beside the pyramid of Gizeh, the Washington Monument, the Eiffel Tower, St. Peter's in Rome, et cetera. The *Beacon of Progress* was to be built on the shores of Lake Michigan, not far from Chicago; it displays in such concentrated form all the preoccupations of the Beaux-Arts in the year 1900 that it provokes us to ask whether the weight of History has not here overwhelmed Progress. A short biography of Despradelles may be found in the *Technology Architectural Record*, V, 3 (June 1912).

1.
See especially Trachtenberg, p.79.

2.
Trachtenberg (p. 216, n. 20) makes the point that, paradoxically, women were excluded from the unveiling of the Statue of Liberty, and adds—pursuing a divergent train of thought—that this allegorical and respectable female, visited by throngs of tourists, «for a fee . . . is open to all for entry and exploration from below» (p. 196).

3.
Ibid., p. 64.

4.
Ibid., pp. 80–81.

5.
The torch as an attribute signifying movement and force appeared everywhere during this period. According to Trachtenberg, its dramatic character made it easy to reconcile, in the years after 1848, with the neobaroque esthetic. It is a dynamic element in Carpeaux's *La Danse* in the Paris Opéra. We encounter it again in Jouffroy's design for the wicket-gates at the Louvre. There are many precedents from antiquity; Bartholdi himself, drawing inspiration from the Colossus of Rhodes, placed a torch in the hand of his Suez lighthouse figure.

6.
Reference may be made to two statues by Canova: *La Foi* of 1787–92, a monument in St. Peter's to Clement XIII, and *La Religion* of 1814 at Possagno; also to Santo Varni's *La Foi*, ca. 1850, in the Staglieno Cemetery, Genoa.

7.
Albert Boime, «The Second Republic's Contest for the Figure of the Republic,» *Art Bulletin*, 53 (1971), 68 ff.

8.
Maurice Agulhon, *Marianne au combat (L'Imagerie et la symbolique républicaines de 1789 à 1880)* (Paris: Flammarion, 1979), pp. 169 ff.

9.
Boime, p. 74, n. 46.

10.
Two little terra cottas from Bartholdi's hand treat similar subjects: *Le Travail* and *Les Sciences* at the Musée Bartholdi (Inv. no. 49).

11.
In the Archives Nationales, Paris, F 21 566.

12.
Agulhon, p. 177, observes that the Phrygian cap was «one of Liberty's classic attributes for two millennia, and an optional attribute of the French Republic from 1792. After 1871 it fell into disrepute for [a decade] or two, as carrying associations of violent social revolution. It lost this unsavory connotation fairly quickly after about 1890, perhaps because workers' and socialist movements were acquiring other symbols, perhaps because the centennial of 1789 served to remind the Republic of Sadi Carnot of the panoply of its great forerunners.»

13.
Ibid., p. 174.

14.
Ibid., p. 180.

15.
See Blanchet and Dard (New York), p. 42, for an illustration of Columbia in a Phrygian cap.

16.
The first work presented by the young Bartholdi at the Salon of 1853 was a *Bon Samaritain*.

17.
Bartholdi, p. 36.

18.
The Inventory of 1914 lists several sets of exotic apparel that the sculptor doubtless brought back from these journeys, as well as some small canvas studies, none of which, it appears, was developed on his return into a full-scale painting (nos. 17, 19–22, 25–26, 228–229, 412).

19.
In the Bibliothèque Nationale, Paris (85B 107443), there is a photograph of Bartholdi on the bridge of the boat that carried the travelers on the Nile, wearing the broad-striped burnous which appears in the photograph reproduced here (cat. 169). This unmistakable dress, along with other details such as the construction of the ship's bridge, confirms Bartholdi's presence among the members of a mysterious «Mission Fouqué, groupe européen (du Musée de l'Homme).» The curators of the museum's photograph collection, whom we take this opportunity to thank, were unfortunately not able to uncover any information on it.

20.
In the Musée d'Unterlinden, Colmar.

21.
«I showed my project to the Emperor and the Empress who lavished on me their good wishes for my success.» Bartholdi to Mme. Bartholdi, March 23, 1869.

22.
Trachtenberg, p. 54.

23.
Gschaedler, p. 13.

24.
Bartholdi to Mme. Bartholdi, April 8, 1869.

25.
Ibid.

26.
Pierre Crabites, *Americans in the Egyptian Army* (London: George Routledge and Sons, Ltd., 1938), p. 94.

27.
Bartholdi to de Lesseps, April 15, 1869.

28.
The reference here is certainly to the statue still to be found in Leningrad. The *Vercingétorix* designed by Bartholdi for the plateau of Alésia tends toward a kind of equestrian figure even more dynamic than its probable antecedent in Leningrad, since here the horse leaps not *from* the rock but *over* it. Trachtenberg, p. 49.

29.
Bartholdi, p. 37.

30.
Quoted in Gschaedler, p. 15.

31.
December 16, 1869, and December 20, 1869, both to Mme. Bartholdi.

32.
This chronology is based on the work of Schmitt.

33.
Schmitt, pp. 45, 42. The same idea is expressed by Laboulaye as quoted in Bartholdi, pp. 16–17: «Go to see that country. . . . You will study it, you will bring back to us your impressions. Propose to our friends over there to make with us a monument, a common work, in remembrance of the ancient friendship of France and the United States. We will take up a subscription in France. If you find a happy idea, a plan that will excite popular enthusiasm, we are convinced that it will be successful on both continents, and we will do a work that will have a far-reaching moral effect.» Even if Laboulaye had seen Bartholdi's models before he left for the United States, the sculptor's story is intended to persuade us that the «good idea» was hit on only after his return. This is a courteous acknowledgment of the importance of America; it is also certainly true in respect of Laboulaye's knowledge of the project.

34.
According to Gschaedler, pp. 33–34, who cites no source.

35.
The inventory of 1914 includes (no. 352) two small bronzes, «Heads of the Statue of Liberty Enlightening the World.» Only one survives in the Musée Bartholdi, and there is no mention in the literature of any original in clay.

36.
The inventory of 1914 is very valuable here; it makes no mention of a male or female nude, and in fact we have seen no studies or sketches in the museum at Colmar. This is less surprising when we recall that the sculptor never attended the

École des Beaux-Arts, and that he stayed so short a time with Etex and Soitoux that he could not have done much work of this kind. The studies we have collected in this catalogue for *Le Génie dans les griffes de la Misère* show that Bartholdi had a talent for the nude when he chose, but was too drawn to contemporary subjects to exercise it often.

37.
Trachtenberg (p. 60) goes so far as to find similarities between the photographs of the portrait of Bartholdi's mother and the countenance of the statue as it appears in cat. 440. His argument is not conclusive, but his ideas about the reasons for the resemblance, which are noted in the body of this chapter, are not without interest. Reference is also made to two press clippings from the archives of the Conservatoire National des Arts et Métiers, Paris—from the New Orleans *Daily City*, September 27, 1884: «The Bartholdi Statue must be modelled after some Ohio girl. The ears are three feet long»; from an unidentified newspaper, August 5, 1884: «It is said that Bartholdi's Statue of Liberty was modelled after his mother. It will be noticed, by examining the picture of the statue, that Mrs. Bartholdi used to hold the shingle in her left hand.»

38.
The inventory of 1914 mentions only two painted portraits of the artist's mother (nos. 13 and 430). There are only three busts of members of his family: of M. Meyer, his uncle and godfather (no. 484); of Mme. Mathieu, done in 1857 (no. 336); and of the artist's father, Jean-Charles Bartholdi (no. 382).

39.
Gschaedler, p. 39.
40.
Trachtenberg, p. 112.
41.
A similar work in clay is at the offices of the Société Miège et Buhler in Paris.
42.
Trachtenberg, p. 212, n. 17.
43.
Ibid., p. 82.
44.
Trachtenberg (p. 83) also quotes President Cleveland at the unveiling ceremony in 1886: «We will not forget that *Liberty* has made here her home, nor shall her chosen altar be neglected. Willing votaries will constantly keep alive its fires and these shall gleam upon the shores of our sister Republic in the East [France]. Reflected thence and joined with answering rays, a stream of light shall pierce the darkness of ignorance and man's oppression until Liberty enlightens the world.»

1.
Bartholdi's journey to America has been considered by Gschaedler, pp. 19–33, and Betz, pp. 101–117. The sculptor's responses to his American experience are discussed in Paul-Ernest Koenig, «Bartholdi et l'Amérique,» *La vie en Alsace*, VIII (August 1934), 169–178. Since these works contain occasional errors, the principal sources for this section are the primary documents.

2.
Bartholdi wrote to Laboulaye on May 8, announcing his plans for the American pilgrimage, and requesting letters of introduction to American societies and press organizations. His meeting with Laboulaye took place at Versailles, noted in *Journal*, May 29, 1871.

3.
Bartholdi to Mme. Bartholdi, June 24, 1871. Only the English transcription of this portion of the letter survives.

4.
The alternate sites were mentioned briefly in *Journal*, June 21, 1871. Bartholdi indicated his preference for Bedloe's Island in *Journal*, June 22, 1871.

5.
His first introduction was to Mary Booth, who had translated a number of French texts, including Laboulaye's writings in support of the Union cause; she had written independently on the same subject. She maintained a correspondence with Laboulaye through the 1880s; a letter from Laboulaye to Booth is published in the *French-American Review*, II (1949), 235–236. Booth presented Bartholdi to the sculptor John Quincy Adams Ward, and to Charles Parsons, a watercolor painter who directed the art department at Harper's publishing company. She may also have furnished the introduction to Michael Knoedler, the owner of Knoedler Gallery in New York, where Bartholdi exhibited some of his bronzes. Among other introductions, these are listed in *Journal*, June 23, 24, 26, and 27.

6.
Bartholdi to Mme. Bartholdi, June 24, 1871.

7.
Journal, June 28, 1871.

8.
Even in liberal circles the Prussian army received tacit, if not active, American endorsement. Americans sympathetic to the plight of the citizenry of France directed opposition at the government of the Second Empire.

The Philadelphia *Press*, later Bartholdi's champion, voiced widespread popular sentiment in an article on March 21, 1871: France was «the victim of the mob, the slave of the despot, or the spoil of the conqueror. As she would not be instructed by us, let us be warned by her. . . .» Nine days later, the newspaper announced a fund-raising drive to provide relief for wounded German soldiers and French peasants. In the early days of the Third Republic, the daily sustained its anti-French tirade: «at present, France is as entirely under the one-man power [i.e., Thiers] as it was during the reign of the Napoleons (uncle and nephew), and of Louis Philippe d'Orleans.» See *Press*, January 16, 1872.

9.
Constructed by George A. Parker between 1862 and 1866 at a cost of $1.5 million, the bridge traversed the Susquehanna River at Havre de Grace, Maryland. The letter in which Bartholdi described the structure to his mother, dated July 4, 1871, is lost. In the English transcription, the quoted dimension of the bridge is 3,000 meters. In actuality, the Susquehanna River crossing at Havre de Grace, the lengthiest span in the region, measured 3,192 feet, which Bartholdi or the translator mistook for metric dimensions.

10.
Bartholdi to Mme. Bartholdi, July 4, 1871. This letter survives only in an English transcription.

11.
Construction of the obelisk was interrupted in 1854 for lack of funds, at a height of 150 feet. Construction was resumed following a government appropriation in 1876.

12.
The Senator met Laboulaye in the 1850s, and the two politicians maintained a mutual respect thereafter. Sumner was profoundly sensitive to the struggles of American artists, but his taste inclined toward European art, especially French painting. His death in 1873 deprived Bartholdi of a potentially powerful ally.

13.
Sumner arranged a dinner at his home for Bartholdi and the publisher George W. Curtis on July 6. Subsequently, the artist obtained introductions in Washington to Bancroft Davis and Charles W. Eliot, the president of Harvard University, probably at Sumner's instigation.

14.
Forney blended politics and journalism throughout his career, serving as Clerk of the House of Representatives in 1853, 1855–57, and 1860.

During the Pierce and Buchanan administrations, he edited the Washington *Union*. At the time of the Kansas Secession, Forney shifted from the Democratic to the Republican party, ardently championing the Lincoln administration and the Republican cause. Relocating to Philadelphia, Forney used the popular Philadelphia *Press* as a vehicle to express his political views. In 1867, Sumner presented Forney to Laboulaye, who deeply impressed the journalist.

15.
After his experiences in New York and Washington, Bartholdi was reluctant to discuss his idea for the monument in New York harbor. Eventually, he revealed the drawings for his project to Forney in confidence. See *Journal*, July 25, 1871.

16.
Esther M. Klein, *Fairmount Park: A History and a Guidebook* (Bryn Mawr, Pa.: Harcum Jr. College Press, 1974), p. 23.

17.
Banker and philanthropist Anthony Joseph Drexel served as the first president of the organization. Although Klein dates the inception of the Fairmount Park Art Association to February 1872, the Philadelphia *Press* carried a notice of the formation of the Association in June 1871. See Klein, p. 26; and Philadelphia *Press*, June 22, 1871.

18.
The passage is quoted from *The Union League's History, a Brief Summary*, published by the Union League of New York (n.p., n.d.). The origins and activities of the Philadelphia League are discussed at length in Maxwell Whiteman, *Gentlemen in Crisis: The First Century of the Union League of Philadelphia* (Philadelphia: Winchell Company, 1975).

19.
The letter, dated February 7, 1864, remains in the archives of the Union League of Philadelphia. We are grateful to Mr. Maxwell Whiteman, the League's archivist, for access to this and other unpublished material from the collection.

20.
His successes in Philadelphia are enumerated in a letter to Mme. Bartholdi, July 12, 1871.

21.
For unknown reasons, Bartholdi's projects in Philadelphia never materialized. Subsequent letters and journal entries do not mention the commissions for Fairmount Park or the Centennial.

22.
In his journal entry for July 18, 1871, Bartholdi noted, «Very good reception. I show him the project. He approves of it [and states] that the site will not be a problem, that it will be submitted to Congress.» He seems to have realized that Grant's verbal acquiescence held little promise for presidential action.

23.
The description is found in a letter to Mme. Bartholdi, July 21, 1871.

24.
Bartholdi to Laboulaye, July 15, 1871.

25.
Journal, July 18, 1871.

26.
Bartholdi's journal entries from July 18 to July 25 chronicle his ceaseless promotional endeavors, recounting meetings with the mayor of New York, a wealthy industrialist named Butler, and the colonel in charge of the fort at Bedloe's Island, in addition to Olmsted. The tone of the entries preserves the exasperation of the author.

27.
At the time, Olmsted, the most famous landscape architect of the day, was under consideration for the role of developer of Fairmount Park. Heinrich Schwarzmann's subsequent appointment to this position in 1872 terminated Olmsted's relations with Philadelphia.

28.
Journal, July 31, 1871. Bartholdi developed this characterization in a letter to Mme. Bartholdi, August 1, 1871: «In general, the architecture here is distinguished by great carefulness in execution, and shows a great quest for originality; but it lacks taste and seems to ignore the essential laws of art; wooden houses and brick structures are the best buildings in America, they have some charm.»

29.
Journal, August 2, 1871. Strangely, although Longfellow lived until 1882, he and Bartholdi apparently never met again.

30.
Bartholdi's journal entries from August 3 to August 6, the dates of his stay in Newport, list only surnames. Nearly all of the «restrained» New Englanders, however, were later involved in the campaign. Hunt, the designer of the pedestal for the Statue of Liberty, is mentioned briefly as an «architect from New York, a bit arrogant, self-contented» in the entry of August 6. Perkins, described as a «rich man who knows many artists, a knowledgeable analyst, but not an artist himself» in the entry for August 4, must be Charles Perkins, who served on the Boston Committee for the statue. Tuckerman was an art critic. The widespread belief in a friendship between Bartholdi and LaFarge dating from the latter's days in Paris is apparently erroneous. Bartholdi mentioned the American painter for the first time in his journal entry for August 4, at which time he described LaFarge as «obliging, intelligent, somewhat ecclesiastical, a painter whose paintings I do not see.» Two days later, the two men dined together; the journal entry for that date briefly adds that LaFarge «seems very obliging.»

31.
The phenomenal popularity of the site is examined by John Sears in an essay entitled «Doing Niagara Falls in the Nineteenth Century,» published in Jeremy Elwell Adamson, et al., *Niagara Falls: Two Centuries of Changing American Attitudes*, exhibition catalogue (Washington, D.C.: Smithsonian Institution Press, 1985), pp. 103–115.

32.
Bartholdi to Mme. Bartholdi, August 16, 1871. Niagara Falls held a lasting attraction for Bartholdi, who planned to return to the spot during his second visit to America in 1876. A third visit is documented in a letter from Bartholdi to George W. Childs, November 2, 1886, in the Historical Society of Pennsylvania, Dreer Collection.

33.
Roebling's bridge consisted of two 821-foot decks suspended from 10-inch cables and connected by wooden trusses. On March 8, 1855, a locomotive crossed the upper rail deck for the first time, marking the official completion of the bridge. In 1877, the decay of the limestone piers that supported the span necessitated repairs; steel elements replaced the stone pylons and wooden trusses. Further decay of the structure led to its demolition in 1896.

34.
Bartholdi to Mme. Bartholdi, August 16, 1871.

35.
Bartholdi's letters to his mother give no indication of this decision, probably because he sensed her concern for his well-being in the uncivilized New World. He first mentioned the possibility of extending his journey in a letter to Mme. Bartholdi on August 16, at which time his plans were complete; he departed the next day.

36.
Bartholdi to Mme. Bartholdi, August 22, 1871.

37.
Journal, August 22, 1871.

38.
Journal, August 23, 1871. Brigham Young, the Mormon missionary and preacher, led his followers to the desert region surrounding the Great Salt Lake in 1847, and actively participated in the architectural design of the Salt Lake Temple. Beginning in 1850 he served as the governor of the Territory of Utah. To develop the area around Salt Lake, he worked to improve farming techniques, established telegraph and railway lines (notably the Union Pacific Railroad), and founded the University of Deseret (today the University of Utah) and Brigham Young University.

39.
Bartholdi to Mme. Bartholdi, August 29, 1871.

40.
Journal, August 27–29, 1871.

41.
Bartholdi to Mme. Bartholdi, September 8, 1871. Bartholdi observed competing Democratic and Republican rallies in a gubernatorial race. Noting similarities in the rhetoric of both candidates, he acknowledged that the Republicans had a larger following and much better installation than their opposition.
42.
The cast, bearing a date of 1866, measures 30 inches in height. The presentation ceremony was published in the *Ninth Annual Report of the Board of Directors of the Union League of Philadelphia, December 11, 1871* (Philadelphia: Harry B. Ashmead, 1871), pp. 22–29. In the mid-1950s, the cast was sold at auction, after which time its whereabouts were untraced until recently, when it was reclaimed by the American Museum of Immigration.
43.
At the time, Brattle Street Church was Unitarian. The original congregation disbanded in 1876 (the year in which Bartholdi's reliefs were installed), and the church was purchased by the First Baptist congregation early in the 1880s.
Bartholdi mentioned Richardson for the first time in *Journal*, August 7, 1871. In *Journal*, August 8, the sculptor recorded a meeting with Richardson, cryptically noting, «Richardson shows up at last to speak of the work to be done.» A second meeting took place August 9, one day before Bartholdi's departure for Niagara Falls. On that day he noted, «things seem to progress.» While the specifics of the project are not developed in journal entries or letters, it is likely that the Brattle Street commission was under consideration. In *Journal*, October 1, 1871, the sculptor noted the completion of drawings for Richardson. With evident excitement, he recorded LaFarge's arrival in New York and the prospect of his meeting with LaFarge and Richardson; *Journal*, October 5, 1871. This conference took place on October 6, and the commission was confirmed at that time.
44.
H. H. Richardson to Franklin Haven, September 5, 1871, Massachusetts Historical Society, Haven Papers.
45.
Gschaedler, p. 32, notes the resemblance of some of the figures to specific persons Bartholdi had met in America. The observation warrants more careful consideration, since the modern, portrait-like character of many of the faces is striking.
46.
Bartholdi to Mme. Bartholdi, July 18, 1876.

Chapter 5

1.
Bartholdi to Laboulaye.
2.
Bartholdi returned from his second Egyptian journey by way of Venice, no doubt intending to pass by the Italian Lakes and there make a personal assessment of this construction technique. He had just had a setback at the hands of the Khedive, and his dearest wish was to make a new beginning on his project. He was accompanied by a mysterious American (Gschaedler finds traces of him in the letters, but cannot put a name to him), and no doubt he had already formed the intention of switching to a collaboration with his compatriot and protector Edouard de Laboulaye. The stop at Arona in 1869 was prophetic.
3.
Eugène Viollet-le-Duc, *Entretiens sur l'Architecture* (Paris: A. Morel et Cie., 1863–72; reprinted Paris, 1980), p. 249.
4.
Bartholdi to Laboulaye, March 25, 1877.
5.
Pure copper, after its molecular structure has been compacted by rolling, has long been recognized as offering advantages over the alloy of copper and tin, which is less ductile and more expensive. The Monduit firm may have advised Bartholdi on this point as well. *Le Génie Civil* of 1883, in a thorough study of the beaten-metal technique, stresses that it works particularly well when executed in pure copper. Those who appealed to the generosity of Secrétan knew what they were about.
6.
Gschaedler, p. 94.
7.
On the other hand, he is clearly visible on the glass-plate print (Private collection, Paris).
8.
The head here closely resembles the *Colossal Head of Lucilla* in the Louvre (see Chapter 3).
9.
Trachtenberg, p. 110; p. 206, n. 10
10.
Ibid., p. 129.
11.
The iron pylon is 92 feet high; its cross section is 16 feet 6 inches × 13 feet at the base and 6 feet 10 inches x 5 feet 10 inches at the top. The posts are of iron, L-shaped, 28 × 24 inches. The arm, set out of plumb, measures ca. 61 feet 6 inches, of which 38 feet 5 inches rise above the level of the pylon.
12.
The arm was a construction project in itself, when account is taken of the procedures of mounting and dismounting to which it was subjected: mounted at Monduit's in 1876; dismounted; remounted in 1876 in Philadelphia; dismounted; remounted in New York; dismounted; remounted in Paris in 1884 on the finished statue; dismounted; remounted (for the last time) in New York in 1886.
13.
Trachtenberg, p. 140.

Chapter 6

1.
Appeal for contributions (CNAM 7, 8, 9, 10).
2.
Bartholdi to Laboulaye, July 15, 1871.
3.
Ibid.
4.
See Maurice Agulhon, *Marianne au combat (L'Imagerie et la symbolique républicaines de 1789 à 1880)* (Paris: Flammarion, 1979).
5.
Bartholdi to Mme. Bartholdi, June 12, 1873.
6.
Bartholdi to Mme. Bartholdi, April 12, 1875.
7.
According to Bartholdi in his 1885 book. This piece of hagiography is not contemporary with the subscription; between 1875 and 1880 no mention by any author serves to support this story, plausible though it is.
8.
In the archives of the Grand Orient there is no evidence of support for the fund-raising campaign by the Masonic community in France. Bartholdi did not speak on the Statue of Liberty until the sessions of November 13, 1884, and March 10, 1887, after the campaign was over. It should be mentioned, however, that according to Mme. Février Ritter (personal communication), one of his heirs, his papers dealing with Freemasonry were thrown into the Seine at the time of the German occupation.
9.
Chantal Martinet, «Erigé par souscription,» a catalogue of the exhibition *From Houdon to Maillol* at the Grand Palais in Paris, April–July 1986 (Paris: Réunion des Musées Nationaux, 1986).
10.
J. Godechot, P. Guiral, and F. Terrou, *Histoire générale de la presse française*, 5 vols. (Paris: PUF, 1969–72).
11.
Le XIX Siècle, December 10, 1875; *Le Temps*, December 8, 1875.
12.
Bartholdi to Laboulaye, December 14, 1875.
13.
Le Petit Journal, September 28, 1875. «Thomas Grimm» was a pseudonym shared by several writers.
14.
Le Rappel, November 20, 1875. According to Dietz Monnin's speech at the close of the campaign on July 7, 1880, the Committee of the Franco-American Union had had dealings with the press; there is no documentary evidence beyond that.
15.
Le Rappel, November 20, 1875.
16.
The Committee's press release of July 14, 1876.
17.
Appeal for contributions (CNAM 7, 8, 9, 10).
18.
Press clipping (CNAM)
19.
See Agulhon, *Marianne au combat*.
20.
Le Bien Public, November 6, 1875.
21.
La Gazette de Cambrai, December 10, 1875.
22.
See the appeal for contributions of September 28, 1875, and the official closing of the campaign in 1880. There is no evidence to confirm or deny the figure of one hundred thousand contributors.
23.
Louis Lecomte to Laboulaye, November 12, 1876.
24.
E. Levasseur, *Questions ouvrières et industrielles en France sous la IIIème République* (Paris, 1907).
25.
Le National, April 30, 1876.
26.
Le Temps, October 6, 1875.
27.
The records of the Chambers of Commerce relating to their participation in the campaign have not so far come to light, so their role is unclear. They transmitted money collected from others, but it was also open to them to contribute under their own identity. Ten of them in fact did; that of Valenciennes contributed Fr. 500, while that of Paris could scarcely escape donating since its president, elected in 1876, was Dietz Monnin himself.
28.
Bartholdi to Laboulaye, March 25, 1877.
29.
A. Caubert to Laboulaye, October 25, 1875. Caubert was the Committee's Commissioner-Delegate.
30.
Le Petit Journal, November 8, 1875.
31.
Laboulaye's speech at the Louvre banquet, November 6, 1875.
32.
Paris Journal, November 6, 1875.
33.
Maurice Agulhon, *Le Cercle dans la France bourgeoise 1810–1848* (Paris: Armand Colin, 1977); Madeleine Rébérioux, «Le Mur des Fédérés» in *Les Lieux de Mémoire* (ed. Pierre Nora), Vol. I, *La République* (Paris: Gallimard, 1984).
34.
S. Jeune, *De F. T. Graindorge à A. O. Barnabooth, les types américains dans le roman et le théâtre français 1861–1917* (Paris: Didier, 1961).
35.
Caubert to Laboulaye, November 12, 1875.
36.
Compte rendu du Banquet de l'Hôtel du Louvre (Paris, 1875).
37.
Bartholdi to Mme. Bartholdi, November 21, 1875.
38.
Le Bien Public, November 22, 1875. The writer was the same François Favre who was a signatory of the *Compte rendu*.
39.
Bartholdi to Mme. Bartholdi, November 21, 1875.
40.
Bartholdi to Laboulaye, December 14, 1875.
41.
L'Evénement, April 27, 1876.
42.
Le Figaro, April 26, 1876.
43.
La Gazette, April 12, 1876. The decor would be used again in Madison Square in New York on July 4, 1876.
44.
L'Evénement, April 27, 1876.
45.
Le Figaro, April 26, 1876.
46.
La France, April 26, 1876.
47.
Philippe Gumplowicz, *L'Orphéon (Pour une histoire sociale de la musique)*. Thesis, Université Paris VIII.
48.
Le Tintamarre, April 30, 1876.
49.
Will of Frédéric-Auguste Bartholdi, dated May 1, 1876, Collection François de Laboulaye, Saint-Saens.
50.
Bartholdi to Laboulaye, March 8, 1877.
51.
Advertisement of the Franco-American Union (CNAM 694).
52.
Laboulaye's speech at the solemnity of music at the Opéra, April 25, 1876.
53.
François Robichon, «Le Panorama, spectacle de l'histoire,» No. 131 of *Le Mouvement Social* (Paris: Les Editions Ouvrière, April–June 1985). The *Liberty* diorama should probably be classified as a panorama. The diorama, properly speaking, is much less complex than the panorama and does not create the same order of illusion, since the spectator looks from the outside at a scene represented on a flat surface. Here the «diorama» of the statue, being semicircular, is really a half-panorama.
54.
Bartholdi to Mme. Bartholdi, April 23, 1877.
55.
This apparently simple method of communication-by-illusion in fact concealed a good deal of complexity. To reach the diorama the viewer had to mount a flight of steps leading to a platform, which here took the shape of a ship's upper bridge, forming part of the spectacle. Standing in the center of the «stage,» and leaning over the bulwark, the viewer saw in the foreground the vessel's lower bridge, populated by life-size dolls. In the background, his eye could encompass New York harbor, painted on a semicircular canvas lit through a skylight. Various devices, such as a screen protecting the viewer from direct daylight, ensured a realistic congruity among the various parts of the scene.
56.
Undated press clipping (CNAM 652).
57.
Serrurier to Laboulaye, June 28, 1877.
58.
L'Univers Illustré, July 1880.
59.
Serrurier to Laboulaye, February 23, 1878.
60.
Press clipping (CNAM). The finger, in copper, not bronze, was to indicate the real size of the statue.
61.
Serrurier to Laboulaye, June 28, 1877.
62.
Serrurier to Laboulaye, February 23, 1878.
63.
Bartholdi to Mme. Bartholdi, March 3, 1879.
64.
Le Républicain, July 1, 1878.
65.
Le Petit Journal, June 30, 1878.
66.
See Agulhon, *Marianne au combat*.
67.
Serrurier to Laboulaye, May 19, 1878.
68.
Le Goulois, July 2, 1878.
69.
Le Temps, August 14, 1878.
70.
See Agulhon, *Marianne au combat*.
71.
La France, October 17, 1878.
72.
Bartholdi had been made Chevalier of the Legion of Honor in 1864.
73.
Mme. Bartholdi to Chauffour; Chauffour to Senator Swinzer, April 6, 1878, Private collection.
74.
Bartholdi to Laboulaye, August 2; October 7; and October 20, 1878. Bartholdi received his promotion to Officer in 1882, when his statue of Rouget de l'Isle, the author of «La Marseillaise,» was unveiled at Lons-le-Saulnier.
75.
For further discussion of the relations between the French and the American financial worlds, notably Nathan Appleton, Jr. (cat. 358), see Chapter 8.
76.
Senator Bozérian's speech at the opening of the exhibition of lottery prizes, June 27, 1879.
77.
Serrurier to Laboulaye, January 8, 1879.

Chapter 7

78.
Serrurier to Laboulaye, May 10, 1879.
79.
Senator Henri Martin's speech at the opening of the exhibition of prizes, June 27, 1879.
80.
Le Progrès Universel, May 16, 1880.
81.
Le Rappel, July 1, 1879.
82.
Le Temps, July 7, 1879.
83.
The three projects were a lottery for the construction of a crèche in the Gros Caillou district; another for an orphanage for the children of soldiers; and a third for the relief of flood victims in Murcia in Spain.
84.
Program of the Grand Cavalcade of May 11, 1879 (CNAM); Victor Bart, President of the Société des Fêtes Versaillaises, to Bartholdi, May 7, 1879, Bibliothèque Municipale, Versailles.
85.
Official communication (see cat. 300).
86.
Laboulaye to Levi P. Morton, October 14, 1881.
87.
L'Illustration, November 5, 1881.
88.
Bartholdi to Mme. Bartholdi, November 7, 1877.
89.
Laboulaye to Grant, November 22, 1877, released to Agence Havas November 24, 1877 (CNAM 599).
90.
Jeanne Bartholdi to Mme. Bartholdi, October 12, 1877.
91.
Bartholdi to Mme. Bartholdi, November 7, 1877.
92.
Louis-Philippe d'Orléans to Laboulaye, June 9, 1876.
93.
Louis-Philippe d'Orléans to Laboulaye, April 2, 1878. The Comte de Paris contributed Fr. 5,000 to the Statue of Liberty; see Serrurier to Laboulaye, undated.
94.
Bartholdi to Mme. Bartholdi, July 16, 1882.
95.
Jules Claretie, *La Vie à Paris* (Paris, 1883).
96.
La Petite République Française, July 1884.
97.
The Morning News, July 5, 1884.
98.
La Petite République Française, July 1884.
99.
There was an exchange of cables between Morton and Secretary of State F. T. Frelinghuysen on June 28 and 30, 1884.
100.
Evening Star, January 7, 1885.

1.
The commission is recorded in Paris, Archives Nationales, F214289 3, November 30, 1871. The plaster maquette, for which Bartholdi received Fr. 6,000, appeared at the Salon of 1873. A bronze cast, commissioned from Barbedienne foundry on January 30, 1874, at a cost of Fr. 8,000, was furnished in March 1875.
2.
As late as 1875, the New York *Herald* noted the absence of a monument to Lafayette in the United States. Responding on November 18, 1875, the *Messager Franco-Américaine* chided the *Herald* for its failure to acknowledge Bartholdi's monument. Although Bartholdi's was the first sculptural tribute to the hero, the idea was timely—B. H. Kinney of Boston exhibited a model for an equestrian Lafayette at the Centennial (No. 3447).
3.
Whether the campaign was intended from the outset to be a jointly sponsored French-American project remains unclear. Early in 1875, Forney stated that the site in Central Park had already been designated, and a committee of French residents of New York had been appointed to raise funds for the pedestal. See John W. Forney, *A Centennial Commissioner in Europe* (Philadelphia: J. B. Lippincott, 1876), p. 139.
4.
The principal figures involved in the Centennial were Alfred T. Goshorn, Thomas B. Cochran, and John Welsh. Goshorn, a Cincinnati lawyer, was the Centennial delegate from Ohio, and Director General of the Exhibition. A member of the Cincinnati City Council, he organized the city's annual industrial exhibitions, and later served as the first director of the Cincinnati Art Museum. John Welsh, the Centennial's Director of Finance, mobilized a committee of sixteen to raise the funds, drawn mostly from private sources, for the Exhibition. Cochran, the Commissioner of Grounds, Plans, and Buildings, collaborated with the painter John Sartain and Heinrich Schwarzmann, the Centennial architect, in the task of arranging the exhibition grounds, placing works, and allocating space to the exhibitors. All three were members of the Union League of Philadelphia, Welsh serving as treasurer of the institution for years, and Cochran as secretary.
5.
The accounts were assembled and republished in Forney, pp. 137–140, 223, 226–227, 331–333, 368–372.
6.
The outcome of the vote is recorded in Philadelphia, City Hall Archives, series 230.26, Foreign Bureau, Foreign Correspondence, cable, Sommerard to Cunliffe-Owen, June 21, 1875. These archives are hereafter cited as CHA, followed by series number.
7.
The exhibition catalogue *1876: American Art of the Centennial*, Smithsonian Institution, National Collection of Fine Arts, May 28–November 28, 1976, p. 9, n. 15, cites the frequency of steamship accidents involving French shipments to the Centennial as the source of the difficulties. Goshorn's papers reveal an ongoing debate over the exhibitor's responsibility for freight charges. See CHA, series 230.26, February 8, 1875, and December 16, 1875.
8.
The quotation is taken from an English transcription of a letter dated October 1, 1876, from Sommerard to an unnamed friend in Vienna. Evidently the letter was published. Goshorn's papers preserve a cable from Aupry that denies Sommerard's authorship of the damaging document. The translated letter and the cable are in CHA, series 230.26, Foreign Correspondence.
9.
The definitive list of French jurors, dated May 4, 1876, exists among Goshorn's papers in CHA, series 230.26. Bartholdi's name does not appear, yet his appointment was reluctantly confirmed earlier by the Ministère de l'Agriculture et du commerce: «My keen desire to please you leads me to revoke the decision of the Superior Council of the Philadelphia Exposition, and to appoint M. Bartholdi secretary to the Franco-American Jury.» Since the French delegation already included two secretaries, «the Jury will have three secretaries and as our resources are practically exhausted, I have to limit M. Bartholdi's remuneration to Fr. 5,000.» F. du Bord to Laboulaye, April 19, 1876.
10.
Rapport sur les arts décoratifs (Paris: Imprimerie Nationale, 1877).
11.
New York Times, August 24, 1877.
12.
Many critics complained of the unlimited size of the French Fine Arts Department, without mentioning the underlying causes.
13.
R. du Gage acted as French Centennial Commissioner until his resignation on July 31, 1876.
14.
Daily Graphic (New York), April 6, 1876.
15.
L'Album du Bord (Paris: Bartholdi, Simonin, Fouret et Cie., 1879).
16.
French shipments to the Centennial commenced in March and continued through May. Most of Bartholdi's contributions were earlier, studio projects. *The Young Vintner*, dated 1867, was acquired by Anthony Joseph Drexel, and remains in the collection of Drexel University. The paintings, variously described in Centennial catalogues as oils and watercolors, are unlocated. In all probability, the allegorical subjects were shown in the form of plaster maquettes: *Le Génie dans les griffes de la Misère* was exhibited at the Salon of 1859 (No. 3073); the maquette for a *Génie funèbre* appeared at the Salon of 1866 (No. 2626). *Peace* may be the sculpture entitled *Les Loisirs de la paix*, displayed at the Salons of 1868 (No. 3409) and 1873 (No. 1512).
17.
Francis Kowsky, «The Bartholdi Fountain: «A Model for All Our Cities,» *Gazette des Beaux-Arts*, 6e période, 93 (January 1979), 231–232, compares Bartholdi's design to the fountains of Charles Lebourg; however, the graceful liveliness of Bartholdi's conception is closer in spirit to Renaissance prototypes. For a discussion and catalogue of French Renaissance designs for fountains of the Three Graces, see Naomi Miller, *French Renaissance Fountains* (New York: Garland Publishing, Inc., 1977), p. 309 and figures 195, 211–214, 218.
18.
Forney, p. 139.
19.
Forney, p. 138. This idea is explored by Kowsky, p. 235.
20.
Unfortunately, no additional casts were produced for American cities. In 1885 the city of Reims obtained a cast of the fountain without illuminating fixtures. This copy was damaged during World War I, dismantled in 1923, and vanished during World War II. See Kowsky, pp. 235–236.
21.
The delay was explained by Bartholdi in a letter to Thomas Cochran dated March 15, 1876; Forney noted the arrival of the fountain in a letter to Cochran on April 17. Both letters are in CHA, series 231.12, Records of the Commission on Grounds, Plans, and Buildings.
22.
Bartholdi stated that the person responsible for this task, Mr. Harnelle, had been contacted, but added that he would personally attend to the matter as soon as he arrived in Philadelphia. See CHA, series 231.12, April 23, 1876.
23.
The base for the fountain was constructed from specifications that Bartholdi forwarded to Forney. Subsequently, the sculptor notified Cochran that «Provided the foundation be solid and in the exact measures, it is all that is necessary. . . .»
The information is contained in Bartholdi's letter to Cochran dated March 15, 1876, in CHA, series 231.12. Cochran's letter of protest to the contractor is preserved in the same series, Cochran to Quackenboss, April 19, 1876.
24.
The engravings appeared in the *Daily Graphic* on June 7, 1876, and in the *Press* on June 17, 1876, suggesting that the fountain was operative beginning in early June, more than a month after the opening of the Centennial.
25.
Kowsky, pp. 233–234.
26.
Olmsted to Clark, Office of the Architect of the Capitol (hereafter cited as AOC), November 22, 1876.
27.
AOC, March 3, 1877.
28.
Stucklé to Clark, AOC, March 29, 1877.
29.
The Washington *National Republican* reported the halted construction work in an article dated September 15, 1877, which Bartholdi carefully preserved. The modern fate of the project would undoubtedly have interested the sculptor. In 1927, the expansion of the Botanical Gardens necessitated the dismantling of the fountain. Stored for five years, the work was relocated to its present position at 1st and Independence Streets S.W. at a cost of five thousand dollars, nearly the original purchase price. The graceful gas lanterns of the original design, which were replaced with the stark white electric globes in 1932, are presently being restored to the fountain.
30.
Bartholdi to Cochran, CHA, series 231.12, March 15, 1876. The letter contains a rapid sketch of the fragment mounted on a simple square with the dimension of 8 meters per side specified for the base.
31.
The arm and torch are not indicated on Schwarzmann's early plans of the Centennial grounds, and the Bartholdi Fountain is roughly sketched on the final plan. Copies of Schwarzmann's four undated development plans for the Centennial are in the Maps Division of the Free Library of Philadelphia.
32.
Bartholdi to Cochran, CHA, series 231.12, April 23, 1876.
33.
This information was transmitted to Laboulaye in an unsigned letter dated June 26, 1876.
34.
Bartholdi to Mme. Bartholdi, July 1, 1876.
35.
A description of the occasion was published in the New York *Herald*, July 6, 1876. The engraving, based on a sketch by E. A. Abbey, appeared in *Harper's Weekly* on July 22, 1876.
36.
Bartholdi to Laboulaye, July 8, 1876.
37.
Ibid.
38.
On July 29, 1876, the *Evening Telegram* reported an illness brought on by the hot weather. Attendance at the Centennial dwindled during the exceptionally warm months of June and July 1876, and many of those who did attend fell ill. While Bartholdi complained frequently about the American summers in 1871 and 1876, the strains of the previous year apparently extracted a toll at this time.
39.
Inexplicably, the freight was sent to New York, arriving there on August 15. The New York *Tribune* initially reported that of a total of eight sections, two had arrived. The *Tribune* subsequently revised this total, recording the completed shipment of twenty-one sections on August 18. A statement issued on the letterhead of the Franco-American Union on September 21 placed the freight costs at 2,975 francs 25 centimes.
40.
Ongoing construction of the arm was noted in the Philadelphia *Press*, September 7, 1876. On September 18, the *Daily Graphic* stated that the arm had been «placed on view,» suggesting that the installation was complete at that time. *L'Illustration* published an engraving of the construction on October 21, 1876.
41.
Salmon was president of the French society Cercle de l'Harmonie Française. Delmonico owned the famous restaurant that bore his name, and Louis de Bebian controlled the French ocean lines to America.
42.
Some discrepancies exist in the reported figures. The most reliable account seems to be that which appeared on October 9, 1876, in the *Courrier des États-Unis*, which placed the total subscription amount at $3,707.00, of which $27.00 was not received. According to the same source, the expenditures for the pedestal amounted to $3,434.84, and the excess was distributed among French benevolent societies.
43.
The letter was published in the *Evening Telegram*, July 20, 1876.
44.
Bartholdi forcefully articulated his preference for Union Square in a letter to Laboulaye on July 14, 1876.

Chapter 8

45.
Villa later reported that the committee sponsored a competition for the design. See *Courrier des États-Unis*, October 9, 1876. However, the meticulous conception of the base and the care with which the figure was placed strongly suggest Bartholdi's personal involvement.
46.
The photograph and the maquette of the earlier designs are in the holdings of the Musée Bartholdi, Colmar.
47.
A few writers voiced objections to inaccuracies in costume and to the tiny boat at the base of the sculpture. Generally, criticism of the work accorded with the opinion voiced in the *Home Journal* on September 13, 1876: «The action is greater than our artists usually attempt in sculpture; but is managed in a masterly manner, and the effect is at once life-like, spirited, elegant, and eloquent. . . .»
48.
The speakers included E. Breuil (the French Consul), Mayor William Wickham, W. C. Cattell (the president of Lafayette College), Coudert, and Villa. The speeches followed similar lines: French-American unity, the history of Lafayette's involvement with America, and the glorification of the French and American Republics. An exhaustive account of the dedication was published in the *Courrier des États-Unis*, September 7, 1876.
49.
In 1913 the Lafayette monument had to be relocated because of subway construction in Union Square. The enduring power of Bartholdi's image is attested to by the report of the committee on relocation. Chaired by Karl Bitter, the committee recommended that the interaction of the Washington and Lafayette monuments should be preserved during relocation. See Art Commission of the City of New York, Submission 1771, September 15, 1913. Unfortunately, subsequent relocations have destroyed the spatial relationship between the two monuments.
50.
Herald, September 8, 1876.
51.
This embellishment appears to be a painting in three sections, measuring over 5 feet in height.
52.
Bartholdi to Goshorn, CHA, series 231.26, Foreign Correspondence, September 20, 1876. Earlier, some memorabilia pertaining to the statue had been sold in the Exhibition buildings. In his letter to Goshorn, Bartholdi added that the articles were manufactured within the fairgrounds, thereby circumventing an excise tax on imported goods.
53.
Institutions that possess photographs of the arm and torch at the Centennial include the Conservatoire National des Arts et Métiers, the Musée Bartholdi, the Free Library of Philadelphia, and The New York Public Library.
54.
Press, October 5, 1876.
55.
In a letter to Laboulaye on October 10, Bartholdi verified his role: «I have given Philadelphia the idea of buying the arm. This will save money for the Committee, it will also guarantee expenses made and permit changes to be made during execution.»
56.
Among the fourteen charter members were Thomas Cochran and General Hector Tyndale, a close friend of Bartholdi's and a champion of the Union League. The subsequent activities of the Philadelphia Committee are difficult to determine. Publicly, the group proposed only to consider the acquisition of the arm, yet Bartholdi viewed the organization with some seriousness, commenting in his letter to Laboulaye on October 10, 1876: «There is a very active committee in Philadelphia.» Thereafter, little interest was evidenced by the city that had once welcomed the Statue of Liberty with such enthusiasm. The philanthropic banker Anthony J. Drexel, publisher George W. Childs, and financial wizard John Welsh served on the Philadelphia branch of the reformulated American Committee in 1882, but apparently without the zeal of the original members. Cochran had relocated to Washington, where he acted as Chief Clerk of the Senate from 1877 to 1889. Sadly, neither of Bartholdi's principal supporters in the city lived to share the realization of his dream. Hector Tyndale died in 1880, and Forney's death in December 1881 deprived the sculptor of a singular companion who had fully participated from the outset in his idealistic vision.
57.
Times, October 8, 1876.
58.
The reception toasted three foreign artists who gained special recognition from the Palette Club for their contributions to the Centennial. Besides Bartholdi, recognition was accorded the Spaniard Ignacio Léon y Escosura and the German Carl Schlesinger. See *Herald*, October 18, 1876.
59.
The speech, edited by Bartholdi and an unknown proofreader, is undated and undirected, but the quoted passages establish the audience as the New England Society. The grammatical errors and emphatic underlined passages presumably remained intact in his delivery. The text is in the collection of Mme. Golliez, Antibes.
60.
The circumstances of Bartholdi's courtship and marriage, as well as specific biographical information on his bride, are difficult to trace with any pretense of accuracy. A brief account of the wedding ceremony is supplied by Betz, p. 136. For a touchingly romantic, but contradictory, description of the courtship, see Gschaedler, pp. 52–56.
61.
Courrier des États-Unis, October 17, 1876.
62.
The relocation of the fragment to New York had been planned since mid-1876, but Coudert's role in Philadelphia's alleged attempt to steal the statue probably figured in the expediency with which the move was accomplished. Alternative sites for the piece—including the vestibule of a New York building, Central Park, and Union Square—were mentioned intermittently in the press throughout 1876.
63.
The history of Moran's *Commerce* in America, insofar as it is known, is recounted in Paul D. Schweizer, *Edward Moran: American Marine and Landscape Painter*, exhibition catalogue, Delaware Art Museum, April 27–June 3, 1979, p. 44. The presence of this version in Paris, or a lost copy of the painting, is documented in J. F. Packard, *Grant's Tour Around the World* (Philadelphia: William Flint Company, 1880), pp. 145–146.
64.
Schweizer, p. 44, establishes Joseph W. Drexel's ownership of the *Commerce* by 1880, at which time it was displayed in the art gallery of the New York Union League.

1.
J. M. Coudert (Frederic's brother) to Laboulaye, October 3, 1876.
2.
Bartholdi to Laboulaye, September 10, 1876.
3.
The Union League's Madison Square Clubhouse was the scene of many important functions between 1868 and 1881, when the Club moved into a Queen Anne–style building at Fifth Avenue and 39th Street, where it remained until the present location, 38 East 37th Street, was finished in 1931. We are particularly grateful to Jane Reed, Librarian of the Club, for her assistance in our research. The New York chapter commissioned Laboulaye's portrait in 1865 and collected his published works.
4.
The Tweed Ring had politically strangled New York City in the early seventies; many of the members of the future American Committee had cooperated in squashing this corrupt combine. The Metropolitan Museum was founded with the strong support of the Union League under the leadership of John Jay; other members of the American Committee who participated were William Cullen Bryant, Samuel P. Avery, Richard Butler, J. T. Johnston, A. P. Stokes, Theodore Weston, and Worthington Whittredge; those founders closely associated with the statue but not directly on the Committee were Christian Detmold, George W. Curtis, John LaFarge, Richard Morris Hunt, and Henry Marquand.
5.
New York Times, September 7, 1876. Jay's committee seems to have been intended as a temporary measure to prepare for a more specific plan. Bartholdi wrote to Laboulaye (October 10, 1876) that his friend General Dix would direct a committee of fifty New Yorkers. According to an unidentified clipping of December 27, 1876 (CNAM 542), Dix presided over a meeting on November 17 that named the president of the New York French Committee to take charge of subscriptions. The correlation between the various preliminary committees remains unclear.
6.
Evening Post, November 18, 1884. Joseph Choate, Evarts' law partner, was not on the official committee until 1881, but his name appears in letters and clippings from 1877. The collection of Richard Butler's papers, most of which are letters from Bartholdi, is the most important body of original archives on the American Committee. Butler, N.J., the site of the company plant, was named for him in 1901. The main street is Bartholdi Avenue.
Glaenzer, whose father was German, was born in Paris in 1848. After receiving a diploma in architectural design from Stuttgart, he practiced this profession in Paris. He married Alice Cary Butler in 1876. He was secretary of the Franco-American Union until the family moved to New York around 1881. He worked as a negotiant in fine wines and fancy groceries while establishing an interior design firm. Among his better-known commissions were rooms of the Vanderbilt Mansion at Hyde Park. Glaenzer translated when necessary for his father-in-law, who did not read French. We are grateful to Glaenzer's descendants for assisting our research.
7.
The accompanying letter from Butler to Bartholdi of July 16, 1885, is one of several original manuscripts in the CNAM album. The final bronze has disappeared.
8.
Bartholdi to Butler, December 2, 1897.
9.
I am grateful to Kathryn Greenthal, who directed me to the Evarts bust and generously allowed me to read the manuscript of her *Augustus Saint-Gaudens: Master Sculptor* (New York: Metropolitan Museum of Art, 1985). Ms. Greenthal documents Evarts' early patronage of Saint-Gaudens and his interest in classical sculpture, which encouraged the use of an antique herm base. See also John H. Dryfhout, *The Work of Augustus Saint-Gaudens* (London: University Press of New England, 1982), p. 74, no. 51.
10.
Perhaps the earliest American image of *Liberty* with political connotations is a *Daily Graphic* cartoon of May 19, 1877, showing the statue enlightening Hayes about needed reforms—most of which views Evarts shared.
11.
The bust's present whereabouts is unknown. Although Bartholdi notified Evarts in a letter of April 27, 1882, that the bust had been shipped, he exhibited this terra-cotta model in the Salon of 1883 (No. 3319).
12.
E. D. Morgan, a former governor of New York, seems to have been a figurehead for the American Committee.
13.
The largest subcommittee, it included W. H. Appleton, William Cullen Bryant, Frederic Coudert, J. T. Denny, J. T. Johnston, J. S. Page, Theodore Roosevelt, Henri F. Spaulding, A. P. Stokes, and William H. Wickham.
14.
Members included William H. Appleton and Clark Bell. Appleton was head of the prestigious publishing house D. Appleton, as well as the director of boards of several financial institutions. Bell, a corporate lawyer, was publisher of the *Evening Mail* until Field purchased it, and president of the Palette Club, which had given Bartholdi support early on.
15.
Other members were Morgan, Jay, Godwin, and Bell.
16.
Avery was also on this subcommittee, along with Worthington Whittredge, a famous landscape painter active in Union League Club art exhibitions.
17.
An example of Iasigi's circular, dated January 8, 1877, is in the Massachusetts Historical Society. Laboulaye had been made an honorary member of the Society in 1863. Politically, the Boston Committee paralleled their New York counterparts—Republican emancipationists. Among the members were Charles Perkins and the poet Thomas G. Appleton, both of whom Bartholdi had met in 1871; and Charles Francis Adams, Jr. (Henry's brother), a close friend of Evarts, whom he brought into the Cave of Adullam, a short-lived conspiracy to reform the Republican party in 1873. Appleton may have become involved because of his brother, Nathan Appleton, Jr. (see n. 21).
18.
Winthrop to Laboulaye, October 9, 1882. Letter from Evarts, February 9, 1885, Massachusetts Historical Society, Winthrop Family Papers, Reel 33. The total sum furnished by Boston is not known, but this correspondence is one of the proofs that Boston has been unfairly accused of giving nothing toward the pedestal. Iasigi is mentioned here in relation to the Boston Committee for the first time since 1877. Evarts also consoled Winthrop for the illness that prevented him from giving the oration for the inauguration of the Washington Monument. The *Courrier des États-Unis*, April 12, 1877, claimed that the Bostonians met several times before disbanding.
19.
Stone, p. 46, quoting President Cleveland's acceptance speech.
20.
This is excerpted from a much longer passage on the Civil War in Evarts' speech at the dedication, cited in Stone, p. 44. The French likewise associated the two, as did the Consul Albert Lefaivre, who spoke of «the momentous war which . . . ended in the emancipation of five millions of human brethren. This religious faith [in liberty] was perfectly justified . . . and . . . it entrusted to Liberty the task of healing the wounds caused by the war» (Free and

Accepted Masons of New York, *Grand Lodge of New York Proceedings* [1884], pp. 48–56).

Trachtenberg, pp. 213–214, n. 2, notes that Bartholdi's supporters in the United States were abolitionists, but he felt that by 1877, with the Reconstruction over, «American energies turned elsewhere.»

21.
Personal information about Appleton, including his autobiography, is found in the Appleton Family Papers at the Massachusetts Historical Society. After he returned permanently to Boston in 1881, Evarts thanked him for his support (letter of November 9, 1881, Appleton Papers, Box 10), and the following year he assured Evarts that the Boston Committee still existed (letter of November 21, 1882). He worked on the Art Loan Exhibition, but after an acrimonious exchange with Parke Godwin fell out with the committee. He remained devoted to Bartholdi, who sent him a warm letter on July 4, 1889 (Appleton Family Papers, Box 10).

22.
Philadelphia *Press*, March 17, 1877. Salmon remained in Paris, a devoted friend to Bartholdi, whose art he continued to champion.

23.
Times, March 11, 1877. At Bartholdi's urging, both Stucklé and Salmon wrote to Laboulaye, on January 30, 1877, asking for his benevolent support.

24.
National Archives, Washington, D.C., Diplomatic Courier, #223, Noyes to Evarts, May 16, 1879, confirms that the French are divided, but it is a «favorable time.»

The American policy of «protectionism» riled the French as much as it exacerbated domestic strife in the 1870s and 1880s. Capitalists demanded high tariffs to protect their goods, while labor felt that tariffs inflated the cost of living. Complaints of «hard times» and strikes intensified the antagonism. At the same time, the growing need to export more products split the business establishment into two camps. A free-trader like Nathan Appleton differed with Evarts, who spoke for the Association for the Protection of American Industry, «virtually a branch of the Union League Club,» yet both agreed that a mutually advantageous commercial treaty with France would ease these tensions. Quoted in Brainard Dyer, *The Public Career of William Maxwell Evarts* (New York: Da Capo Press, 1969), p. 246.

Hardly anyone spoke of the statue without mentioning tariffs or commerce. The French Consul Lefaivre neatly summarized the relationships among these diverse threads at the inaugural banquet: «The ceremonies of today will tend to diminish the quarrels between capital and labor, and will undoubtedly result in the increase of commerce between the sister republics» (New York *World*, October 29, 1886).

Bartholdi was certainly aware of the role that commerce played in his affairs; among the few clippings in the CNAM album not directly pertaining to the statue are cartoons from the *Daily Graphic* related to tariffs.

Anthony Pollock, a Washington lawyer who was later affiliated with the French legation, became a lifelong friend of the sculptor. Bartholdi had Pollock invited to Glatigny before the treaty negotiations began (letter to Laboulaye, August 2, 1878). Pollock attempted to ensure the *Lafayette* commission in Washington for his friend.

25.
Appleton's visit to Egypt may have coincided with Bartholdi's. One wonders if Appleton is the «mysterious American» who turns up in Bartholdi's letters in 1869; see Gschaedler, p. 14. He had known Gambetta since 1866, so he could conceivably have known the sculptor before either was in Egypt.

26.
Daily Graphic, July 19, 1876.

27.
Bartholdi to Evarts, April 27, 1882.

28.
Times, March 23, 1885. Later, when the installation was menaced, haunting reminders were again common; e.g., *Harper's Weekly*, February 6, 1886, p. 83, stated that to leave the pedestal destitute of the statue would be a «permanent and laughable discredit.»

29.
Congressional Record, 44th Cong., 2nd Sess. (February 27, 1877), p. 1960, from the Senate discussion. The resolution had passed the House on February 22, 1877, p. 1824, Joint Resolution 196. The Committee's letters and Grant's are printed in that session, Ex. Doc. No. 36.

30.
Courrier des États-Unis, February 11, 1877 (CNAM 1154). Sherman preferred Governor's Island, because it offered sufficient space for a park. Evarts, who dropped by the War Department on March 10, 1877, for no reason of «extraordinary significance»—according to the *Herald*, March 10, 1877—no doubt ensured that the sculptor's choice was respected.

31.
Times, February 6, 1876.

32.
Pinchot to Butler, January 10 and 20, 1881. The document arrived at the Department of State on July 29, 1880, as Noyes's accompanying letter to Evarts, of July 15, proves (National Archives, Diplomatic Courier, #368). As Evarts could hardly have ignored it, the implication is that it was somehow misplaced or filed without his having seen it.

The American Committee changed addresses several times. In 1877 the office was listed as Municipal Hall, 67 Madison Avenue; in 1881, at 33 Mercer Street, the headquarters of Butler's American Hard Rubber Company. By June 1884, and probably earlier, it was at 55 Liberty Street, where it remained until the end of 1885, when it returned to 33 Mercer Street.

33.
Evarts to Butler, May 5, 1881, from Paris. This letter was reprinted in the *Evening Post*, November 18, 1881.

34.
Butler to Morton, November 18, 1881, Morton Papers, Box 1.

35.
See the printed flyer included in Butler's less personal letter to Morton of November 16, 1881, Morton Papers, Box 1.

36.
Scientific American, 47 (October 14, 1882), 249.

37.
Glaenzer's translation in the American Committee Papers.

38.
Both French letters are dated October 31, 1882; the copy of Evarts' reply is dated November 17. Bartholdi specifically mentions an article in the *Herald* that the *Journal des Débats* reprinted: in a seemingly innocuous article of October 4, 1882, Butler regrets that so little has yet been done, but doubts that the statue will go to Boston (see Chapter 10, n. 16). Five prior letters were addressed to Evarts concerning the statue's progress, including one from C. E. Detmold of October 16; at Evarts' request, Detmold had visited the ateliers to verify the progress. Evarts' letter was sent to the French press, as Laboulaye's and Bartholdi's replies were published in the *Times*, January 10, 1883.

39.
No complete record of the reorganization exists, as it does for the 1877 committee. It appears that only the size changed, not its social fabric. The artistic was renamed the pedestal subcommittee, according to Weston's letter to Butler, August 10, 1883. A finance committee, consisting of William Strong, Henry Marquand, Louis de Bebian, Charles Lanier, Edward Kemp, S. V. White, and Henry Hentz, was listed in the *Times*, March 23, 1885. There were additional men who supported committee activities, such as Cyrus Field, Chauncey Depew, and Carl Schurz, whose names never appear on the official lists.

40.
Times, November 27, 1882.

41.
Lewis I. Sharp, *John Quincy Adams Ward, Dean of American Sculpture* (Newark: University of Delaware Press, 1985), p. 232, no. 86. Drexel bequeathed his music library to The New York Public Library and his collection of musical instruments to the Metropolitan Museum of Art.

42.
The letter is in The New York Public Library's Rare Books and Manuscripts Division.

43.
The medals here were given to S. P. Avery, 93.10.21, and Butler, 02.11.2. See John J. Gabriel, *Exonumia of Liberty Enlightening the World* (N.p.: Bellmore Books, 1983), for a list of all the medals. This one, listed GO–3, misleadingly identified Bartholdi as the recipient, when in fact he was the donor.

44.
Bartholdi to Butler (in English), January 21, 1887.

45.
The initial list had been submitted by a zealous member of the Franco-American Union without the Committee's authority, making it difficult to add names. I am particularly indebted to Mme. Tamara Preaud, the Archivist of the National Manufacture at Sèvres, who kindly did this research for me. The list, as well as pertinent correspondence, is found in the Archives, Carton U23, folder 2. This is obviously in the second list, as Butler is not mentioned; however, an official «urgent» memorandum from the Director of Fine Arts, October 26, 1886, requests three vases, of an exceptional value, for Butler, Spaulding, and Stone. Perhaps their names were additions to a first list, as other key names, e.g., Evarts and Drexel, are conspicuously absent.

46.
Spaulding to Evarts, letter of March 20, 1886.

47.
Bartholdi to Butler, November 9, 1894.

48.
Major A. C. Taylor to Adjutant General, June 30, 1901, National Archives, Washington, D.C., RG 26, Light-House Board 1901–1910.

Chapter 9

1.
Evarts to Laboulaye, December 3, 1881, Collection François de Laboulaye, Saint-Saens.

2.
Courrier des États-Unis, October 30, 1875 (CNAM 108–109). Blanchet and Dard (Paris), p. 53 and p. 184, n. 19—who cite it as November instead of October—misunderstood this article entirely, claiming that it was a subscription for the State of Liberty, instead of a natural disaster in the south of France. The error was compounded by placing the $65,000 of the Midi fund in the context of American indifference to the statue. If their interpretation had been accurate, two-thirds the amount necessary at the time would have been raised within two weeks of the Franco-American Union's announcement, which could hardly be called indifferent.

As for the Chicago monies, Bartholdi lobbied for the unspent $35,000 under the control of Committee member E. D. Morgan. This sum, first refused by Chicago, was the subject of three letters to Laboulaye, July 8 and 21; September 10, 1876. See also the *Courrier des États-Unis*, November 22, 1876, and the *World*, December 7, 1876. Given that Chicago later reclaimed the money for sewers, the *Times*, December 20, 1883, considered the city's offer to buy the statue «rather impertinent.»

3.
The earliest call seems to be the *Tribune*'s, September 20, 1876, to which the Teacher's Association responded with $100, announced in the *Tribune*, September 23, 1876.

4.
World, February 22, 1877. The department allotted $972 to W. F. Croft, the architect of the pedestal; however, this probably covered only the installation proper. In contrast to the electric illumination of the torch planned in Philadelphia, gaslight, furnished by the French Committee, was to illuminate it on national holidays in New York. The lack of evidence suggests that neither was done.

According to the *Evening Telegram*, July 29, 1876, the display of the torch in New York was already under consideration.

5.
Evening Telegram, March 14, 1877. Unidentified periodical illustrations of the torch are taken from the photograph in the collections of the Bibliothèque Nationale and the Conservatoire National des Arts et Métiers, Paris.

6.
Gschaedler, p. 61, states that a charge of fifty cents allowed visitors «to ascend the steel ladder leading to the balcony,» but offers no source. Many different types of photographs exist of the torch in Madison Square, most as stereopticons, at The New York Public Library, the New-York Historical Society, and the Library of Congress.

7.
Times, February 26, 1877.

8.
October 7, 1881, and August 16, 1882, Library of Congress, Manuscript Division, Pinchot Family Papers.

9.
According to the *Times*, February 18, 1878, Nathan Appleton, Jr., arranged for the receipt of subscriptions in local post offices, an excellent idea that was never pursued.

10.
Times, November 28, 1882. The *Appeal to the People of the United States in Behalf of the Great Statue, Liberty Enlightening the World* was published as a brochure by the *Evening Post* in 1882 and reprinted in 1883 and 1884.

11.
The American Bank Note Company of New York had a copyright registered in 1883. The pedestal depicted in this engraving resembles Hunt's design rather than the painting of 1876. An example of a member's record of subscribers, the *Subscription Booklet, Liberty Enlightening the World Pedestal Fund. Algernon S. Sullivan*, is at the New-York Historical Society.

12.
Times, December 7 and 13, 1882.

13.
According to the Chamber of Commerce, *Twenty-Seventh Annual Report* (New York, 1885), Part I, p. 92, meeting of December 4, 1884, several hundred dollars remained in this fund. As one of the Fund's trustees, Hamilton Fish consented grudgingly; see also letters to Fish from A. A. Low, February 11, 1884, and George Wilson, December 10 and 13, 1884, with Fish's reply copies of February 13 and May 10.

14.
Times, February 20, 1884. This plan may have remained on paper, as there is no subsequent mention of it.

15.
An illustrator for *Frank Leslie's Illustrated Newspaper* complained of being run off the island; June 27, 1885, p. 303. The Committee may have made money from the sale of their photographs to the press, or at least wished to control their distribution. This is suggested by the quantity of press illustrations that are taken from a limited number of photographs.

The inscription «Official Authorized» on the Root and Tinker lithograph lends credence to the hypothesis that it was the one sold by the Committee. Currier and Ives published a contemporary view of the monument, with no mention of the Committee. See below, n. 42.

16.
Bartholdi to Butler, October 14, 1883.

17.
Times, January 3, 1884.

18.
The only collection of such memorabilia seems to be the New-York Historical Society's copy of *France's Old New York*, into which Lucy Drexel inserted some of her husband's programs and invitations.

19.
Frank Leslie's Illustrated Newspaper, April 21, 1883, p. 146.

20.
Herald, January 27, 1884.

21.
Constance Cary Harrison, *Recollections, Grave and Gay* (New York: C. Scribner's Sons, 1912), p. 314. The *Art Amateur* devoted the January 1884 issue to Bartholdi and the exhibit. The exhibit was the forerunner to the Amory Show in 1913. The exhibition will be reconstituted in the fall of 1986 at the Parrish Museum, Southampton, N.Y., and the National Academy of Design.

22.
Frank Leslie's Illustrated Newspaper, December 15, 1883, p. 262.

23.
Harrison, pp. 313–314. Mrs. Harrison had been active with many earlier benefits, e.g., the Mount Vernon Aid Society, with Committee members. Bartholdi sent her a medal, deposited at the Virginia Historical Society. Linda Leazer, curator there, kindly brought the autobiography to our attention.

24.
Times, December 16, 1883.

25.
Times, December 30, 1883.

26.
Herald, December 31, 1883.

27.
Times, December 31, 1883.

28.
Members of the Kit-Kat Club dashed off «comicalities» one evening at the Lotos Club, described in the *Art Amateur*, February 1, 1884, p. 58. Smith, a collector and amateur artist, was also the contractor for the cement foundation.

29.
Madeleine Fidell-Beaufort pointed out that Seney's loan was not all altruism, since he sold many of the works shortly after. The catalogue in The New York Public Library collection has extensive press clippings about both the exhibit and the sale attached. The name of Samuel Avery is conspicuously missing from both of the exhibitions, yet his involvement with the Committee had not changed. He was probably behind the scenes by choice, as he had sold many of the works to the collectors in the first place, and perhaps felt a more visible role would be in bad taste.

30.
Times, November 27, 1882.

31.
John Bigelow, ed., *Letters and Literary Memorials of Samuel Jones Tilden*, 2 vols. (New York: Harper Brothers, 1908), II: 625 and 629. Godwin's letters are dated October 3 and 12, 1882, and Tilden's reply, January 11, 1883. The results were discouraging enough for Evarts to state to a *Times* reporter on November 28, 1882, that they could not find ten rich men to give $25,000 each.

32.
The standard letter, of January 1884, among Butler's papers, provides for both men's signature.

33.
The form letter of January 1884 is in The New York Public Library, Rare Books and Manuscripts Division, American Committee Papers. The letter from Drexel, November 12, 1883, and reply copy, January 24, 1884, are in the Fish Papers. Spaulding also omitted Evarts in his «stirring appeal» to Tilden, which he described to Butler in a letter of February 9, 1886.

34.
World, December 26, 1884.

35.
Copy of June 17, 1885, to John Readie of the *World*, replying to Readie's letter of June 12, concerning the *World*'s attempt to get $250 each from one hundred men for the last $25,000. The French Minister that Fish refers to was Amédée Bartholdi. Fish attended the cornerstone ceremony, but declined the inaugural invitation.

36.
Times, August 5, 1884.

37.
Times, January 4, 1884. The date was probably a misprint for January 1883, but the point remains the same—gifts dropped off rapidly. The fund was brought to the halfway mark in January 1884, but most of that addition was from the Art Loan Exhibition and other benefits that required enormous energies.

38.
Evening Telegram, March 14, 1877. These remonstrances appeared dozens of times in newspapers across the country.

39.
Evening Telegram, October 25, 1881.

40.
American Architect and Building News, December 1, 1883, p. 253, which an «Observer» refuted in the December 15 issue, p. 285.

41.
Herald, May 24, 1884.

42.
The identical lithograph was used to advertise handkerchiefs by «Low's Jersey Lily.» A trade card for Pratts Astral Oil was also printed by Root and Tinker in 1883, showing the statue in the moonlight; a blurb on the back promotes the statue, taken «From the American Committee's Official Circular.»

43.
Their demonstration earned a disappointing $659.57, which was attributed to the novelty and disorganization of the event. Undaunted, they intended to stage similar attempts to collect money.

44.
Letter to Austin Huntington, October 16, 1884, The New York Public Library, Library Americana, Box 39.

45.
Times, November 23, 1884.

46.
From the first meeting, according to the *Times*, January 3, 1877, members of the Committee, particularly Godwin, opposed going to the legislatures.

47.
Copy of letter to Cleveland, May 20, 1884.

48.
Tribune, July 5, 1884.

49.
Congressional Record, 44th Cong., 2nd sess., H. Res. 296 (December 8, 1884). H. Res. 294, introduced the same day, was absorbed into H. Res. 296. A similar bill, H.R. 3038, 48th Cong., 1st sess. (January 9, 1884), seems never to have surfaced from the Library Committee to which it was referred. The petition from the Sons of the Revolution, December 12, 1884 (preserved in the National Archives, Papers of the Library Committee, HR 48A–H15.2) was presented in the House on December 15.

50.
The *World*, March 16, 1885, blamed the failure on Randall and Long, of Philadelphia and Boston, respectively, because of their cities' jealousy of New York. The Senate, *Congressional Record* (March 3, 1885), pp. 2444–2446, attached it to the Deficiency Appropriation Bill. The favorable recommendation from the House is recorded in *Serial* 2328, 48th Cong., 2nd sess., H.Rp. 2259 (January 10, 1885). The French paper *Le Soir*, March 30, 1885, accused Congress of «ladrerie» (stinginess). During the later conflict over the inauguration appropriation, Spaulding advised Evarts to «be on the alert to see that the Senate does not give way to Mr. Randall as it did in the same matter last winter»; June 21, 1886.

51.
Spaulding to Evarts, January 15, 1885.

52.
Times, March 23, 1885. The house-to-house plan is presented in the *Times*, March 29, 1885. Like the previous plan for an individual canvass (see n. 14), this one seems never to have been implemented; however, the reason now was the success of the *World* campaign.

53.
Times, November 25, 1884.

54.
Harper's Monthly Magazine (August 1885), pp. 475–476, compares the Bartholdi statue to Bunker Hill, which took from 1825 to 1843, and was reportedly finished with the contribution of Fanny Elssler, the famous dancer. See the *World*, August 11, 1885.

55.
Spaulding to Evarts, January 15, 1885. The Grant Association included many members of the American Committee.

56.
The finished model was announced in the *Times*, July 11, 1883, the gift of David H. King, Jr., the contractor; the pedestal and model were described as 15 feet tall, but since the terra cotta is only 4 feet high, it is unlikely that the pedestal ensemble was another 11 feet. The terra-cotta model is probably a variant of 1875. It was moved to the Smithsonian Institution in 1887, according to correspondence in the Office of the Architect of the Capitol; it is now in the National Museum of American Art. The head is a replacement, and all of the damage to the statue is quite old, possibly dating from when it was in Hunt's studio. Nothing indicates the fate of the pedestal model. *Congressional Record*, 48th Cong., 1st sess. (February 18, 1884), p. 1194. H. Res. 167, authorizing temporary exhibit in the Capitol, was introduced; June 24, 1884, p. 5545, it was approved by President Arthur. The legislation usually refers only to the pedestal, but the discussions prove that both were included from the start. See also Chapter 16, n. 4.

57.
American Architect and Building News, December 1, 1883, p. 253.

58.
See, for example, *Times*, July 11, 1883, and March 13, 1885. The figures give the collective amounts raised in smaller communities, including the dime subscriptions at local military posts.

59.
Times, March 26, 1885.

60.
Quoted from the *Call for Subscriptions to the Pedestal Fund of the Statue of Liberty*, September 20, 1884, found in the subscription book of the Sons of the Revolution in the New-York Historical Society.

61.
Oration by Hon. Chauncey M. Depew at the Unveiling . . . (Privately published, 1886), p. 33.

62.
Evening Telegram, July 19, 1884. While the article was entirely favorable to Bartholdi's statue, it described Bedloe's Island as «a miserable, barren island graveyard.»

63.
Times, July 27, 1884.

64.
Times, September 4, 1885, treasurer's report. The *World*'s campaign was probably kept to $100,000 for fear that $150,000 would seem too great, jeopardizing its chances. During and after the *World* campaign, the benefits continued; see, for example, *Times*, April 25 and May 7, 1886. General C. P. Stone issued his own appeal, «to the wealthiest 200 men and women in the cities of New York and Brooklyn»; it appeared in the *Times*, March 2, 1886.

65.
The Statue of Liberty Enlightening the World has been faithfully reprinted by New York Bound, 1984. Jeffrey Eger, the editor, remarked that the 1885 book provided a lucid introduction from which journalists could work, noticeably improving their articles.

66.
World, October 27, 1886. Edward L. Kallop, Jr. discovered that the manufacturer was Newton Bottle Stopper of Britannia Co.

67.
Kallop provided information about these models, which were first treated in depth in the exhibition *Images of Liberty: Models and Reductions of the Statue of Liberty, 1867–1917*, at Christie's, New York, January 25 to February 16, 1986. See Chapter 16, nn. 25 and 26. A full-page advertisement based on the brochure appeared in the *World*, June 7, 1885, with subsequent advertisements in the major papers and illustrated periodicals. Another version adapted for lighting was produced by Star Lamp (see cat. 510).

According to legend, the tiny American Committee Model gave rise to the word «gadget,» derived from Gaget, Gauthier; however, all dictionaries list the word's origins as unknown. Michael Lesk of Bell Laboratories, who generously shared the results of his research on the word's etymology, affirms that the association is apocryphal.

68.
Herald Tribune, October 4, 1936. Mr. Layley, who worked for Butler, recalled that orders for the models «were coming in so fast that even with help . . . it was hard for me to keep up. . . . I was busy at 8 o'clock in the morning and often until 2 and 3 the next morning.»

69.
The press release was quoted almost verbatim in *Harper's Weekly*, February 6, 1886, p. 83. It and the circular, dated October 5, 1885, are in the collection of Jeffrey and Miriam Eger.

70.
Spaulding to Evarts, March 20, 1886.

71.
This sum is taken from Spaulding's letter, printed in *Serial* 2361, 49th Cong., 1st sess., S.Rp. 1280, p. 6.

72.
Spaulding to Evarts, May 28, 1886.

73.
Serial 2401, 49th Cong., 1st sess., H.Ex.Doc. 232. Following the prescribed protocol, Drexel addressed the request to the Secretary of State, who transmitted it to the President, who passed it on to Congress on May 12, 1886.

74.
Butler to Evarts, June 20, 1886.

75.
Spaulding to Evarts, June 21, 1886. General Stone prepared the estimate, printed in *Serial* 2401, 49th Cong., 1st sess., H.Ex.Doc. 249, forwarded by the Secretary of the Treasury, May 29, 1886.

76.
Butler to Evarts, July 8, 1886.

77.
Congressional Record, 49th Cong., 1st sess., pp. 6421–6422. The amendment was attached to the Sundry Civil Appropriation. The appropriation failed on a vote of 103 to 107. For comments on the procedural confusion, see *Times*, July 2, 1886; *Herald*, July 6, 1886.

78.
Butler to Evarts, July 8, 1886.

79.
Congressional Record, 49th Cong., 1st sess. (July 20, 1886), p. 7219; on August 4, 1886, both houses passed it, and on August 5, H.R. 9478 was signed by President Cleveland. Most of the deleted $50,000 was needed to cover the foundation, landscape the surroundings, and improve the landing dock; $2,500 of it was to provide refreshments for the inaugural guests.

Chapter 10

1.
The point of departure for all the research on the American press was Frank L. Mott, *American Journalism* (New York: Macmillan, 1950).

2.
«Our Great Goddess and Her Coming Idol,» *American Catholic Quarterly Review*, 5 (1880), 587. The article criticizes the widespread use of «Libertas» imagery in America, particularly on coins.

3.
Bartholdi to Laboulaye, October 10, 1876. Bartholdi had written Laboulaye on September 10: «There is not a single paper here which is not now ready to give us its support in some measure.»

4.
Among the articles that Bartholdi saved (now in the CNAM album) is one pertaining to the growing importance of newspapers and advertising in the United States.

5.
Times, September 29, 1876.

6.
Jennie Holliman, *The Statue of Liberty*, part II, manuscript at American Museum of Immigration, Civil Works Administration for the Office of National Parks, 1934, pp. 1–2; Blanchet and Dard (New York), p. 58; Gschaedler, pp. 47–50. In 1875 and 1876 there was some skepticism (e.g., an unidentified article in the CNAM 105, pointing out that American sympathies were with Germany); what is surprising is that there was not *more* resistance. See also n. 10 below.

7.
For more straightforward reports in the *Times*, see September 17 and 25, 1876. «A Gift Statue,» in the *Times*, December 26, 1883, which begins with «the painful Parsimony of the French . . .,» exaggerates the French obligations to their «gift» to parody the Americans' parsimony. Gschaedler, p. 85, for example, takes it for legitimate opposition. The *Times* editor in 1876 was Louis Jennings, and by 1883, Charles Miller.

8.
The *Courrier des États-Unis*, October 21, 1876 (CNAM 1057), reprints, in French, articles from New York papers, providing a broad sample of the favorable press. It includes the article from the *Tribune* cited by Blanchet and Dard (New York), p. 58, arguing that the statue was «almost too fantastic and poetic to ever be realized,» which they contend attests to American antipathy to the statue. The key to the phrase is «almost»: the substance of the article is quite positive, stating that «our French brothers have the right, in fact, to expect a prompt and cordial response.»

9.
This comment was made to the present author by Madeleine Fidell-Beaufort in explaining why Avery was the perfect choice for such a responsibility. In *The Diaries of Samuel P. Avery*, edited, with an introduction, by Fidell-Beaufort, Herbert Kleinfield, and Jeanne Welcher (New York: Arno Press, 1979), pp. 419, 666, and 672, Avery records two visits to Bartholdi, in 1877 and 1882, when he saw the statue at Gaget's studio.

10.
Herald, October 26, 1886. Holliman, pp. 39–40, claims that both newspapers opposed *Liberty* in 1885, citing editions of June 23, 1887 (sic for 1885) as an example. The *Herald* of that date had only positive words to say; the *Telegram*'s article, «The Great Image, Bartholdi's Imperfect Ideas to Be Completed,» dealt primarily with technical problems of anchoring the pylon; however, an unnamed sculptor was quoted in the last paragraph as saying the statue was balanced on the wrong leg. The *Telegram* was obviously trying during the *World* campaign to sensationalize news about the statue in the hope of drawing away some of the *World*'s readers, as the two publishers, Bennett and Pulitzer, were locked in bitter competition for circulation. Comments in both papers are directed at each other more than at the statue.

11.
This note is on Glaenzer's calling card at the New-York Historical Society.

12.
After the inauguration, Mrs. Leslie bought a stock of American Committee Models for use in the magazine's promotionals; see *Life*, December 9, 1886, p. vii, for an advertisement for *Leslie's* offering a 6-inch model for a year's subscription.

13.
Times, November 27, 1882, p. 8. One very telling reference is Butler's note to Evarts, after the brouhaha over the inauguration amendment: «the Press of N.Y. are very indignant about the lack of interest shown the Nation or France. . . . I have met here [the Union League Club] Reid of The Tribune, Jones of Times, the World people, Mail & Ex [sic] etc and all regard the action of the House as pretty unpatriotic and unAmerican.» July 8, 1886, Library of Congress, Manuscript Division, Evarts Papers.

14.
Ibid. Examples of two sharp criticisms are found in Chapter 8, n. 37, and Chapter 9, n. 40.

15.
The *American Architect and Building News*, XII, no. 353 (September 30, 1882), 154.

16.
Times, October 3, 1882. See Chapter 8, n. 36, for other comments on the Boston incident. It is not clear what started these rumors, but Butler replied to them in the *Herald*, October 4, 1882. The following month, Appleton reaffirmed the Boston Committee's support; see Chapter 8, n. 21.

17.
Albany *Express*, July 6, 1884 (CNAM 1412).

18.
Bartholdi to Butler (translated by Glaenzer), August 3, 1883. The specific article in *Voltaire* to which Bartholdi referred is not clear. Another example of «gossip» alarming the French is cited in Chapter 8, n. 38. Both committees answered their critics in the press, anonymously or not, and published each other's letters.

19.
This article was reprinted in the Franco-British paper *Galignani's Messager*, April 2, 1885 (CNAM 1573).

20.
Anonymous letter to *World*, December 26, 1884 (CNAM 1539).

21.
World, June 14, 1885. It was in response to this solicitation that Fish returned his condescending refusal; see Chapter 9, n. 35. The *World*, June 24, then proclaimed that the millionaires did not understand *Liberty* as a work of art. His editorials established the myth that the rich gave nothing. Pulitzer was perfectly aware that among the millionaires, Jay Gould, Tilden, and Fish were exceptions in not having given money. Besides the wealthy men on the Committee, W. K. Vanderbilt, Henry Villard, Pierre Lorillard, Chauncey Depew, Cyrus Field, and one of the Astors are among those who contributed.

22.
There is no evidence to substantiate this, nor—as collector Jeffrey Eger observed (personal communication)—has any trace of the letters been found. While today this might be considered unethical, in Pulitzer's day it would have been a creative method for achieving a good end.

23.
World, June 2, 1883.

24.
Tribune, March 19, 1885.

25.
Times, July 12, 1885. This was based on a real incident, described in the *World*, August 11, 1885, in which a check for $30,000 signed «Wm. H. Vanderbilt» was received in the *World*'s offices but was proven a forgery before any public announcement was made.

26.
World, February 21, 1886. Pulitzer wrote to Butler, January 12, 1886, American Committee Papers: «Permit me to thank you for the elegant frame, which you sent to the house with the testimonial. I think it is altogether too expensive; still I appreciate it very highly.» Holliman, pp. 44–45, describes it in detail.

27.
World, November 13, 1886.

28.
October 26 and 31, 1887.

29.
Bartholdi to Pulitzer, November 15, 1891, copy in American Committee Papers. The cast cost Fr. 27,000, and Bartholdi was anxious to have from Pulitzer the «25000 francs, which make out the balance of our agreement.» Bartholdi asked Butler, letter of January 14, 1892, to learn if Pulitzer ever received the original letter. He added that the journalist «had asked to me only a singel [sic] statue, but I *ask nothing else* than what he promised for the singel [sic] statue.» The sculptor cabled on the 26th, «Pulitzer has written all is settled.» The bronze was exhibited in the Salon of 1892, No. 2261.

30.
Times, September 24 and October 8, 1893. A bronze reduction by Barbedienne was on display in New York at Tiffany's.

31.
Bartholdi wrote to Butler, outraged because «I would have escaped the mistake which I made in having done a copy in bronze for Chicago.» He claimed that the erection was to be «*next month*,» but the dedication was not until December 1895; Bartholdi to Butler, October 14, 1894.

32.
Bartholdi to Butler, December 2, 1897. The *Herald*, November 13, 1897, announced that the merchant would offer the bronze to the city in memory of his son, but the inscriptions make no mention of this.

33.
The building eventually received a stained-glass window of the paper's masthead; the window, now in the World Room, Columbia School of Journalism, is signed «Heinigke and Bowen, NY.» Bartholdi had a different window of *Liberty* in his studio; it has since disappeared. Bartholdi wrote Butler, April 21, 1892, that Pulitzer «asks if I would not come over to execute a project group for the World, on place, to have it done there.» This never materialized.

34.
Bartholdi to Pulitzer, December 25, 1903.

Chapter 11

1.
For a rich and complete account of Hunt's studies in France, see Richard Chafee's essay in *The Architecture of Richard Morris Hunt*, ed. Susan R. Stein (Chicago: University of Chicago Press, 1986).

2.
See Francis R. Kowsky's essay «Hunt and the Central Park Gateways» in *The Architecture of Richard Morris Hunt*.

3.
Paul R. Baker, *Richard Morris Hunt* (Cambridge: The MIT Press, 1980).

4.
Catharine Clinton Howland Hunt, unpublished manuscript biography of her husband, Richard Morris Hunt, a gift of Richard Baron Hunt to the American Institute of Architects Foundation, Washington, D.C. The Hunt Collection at the AIA is the chief repository for documents relating to the pedestal's history.

5.
The definitive work on Ward is Lewis I. Sharp, *John Quincy Adams Ward: Dean of American Sculpture* (Newark: University of Delaware Press, 1985). For more information about Hunt and Ward, see also Sharp's chapter «Richard Morris Hunt and His Influence on American Beaux-Arts Sculpture» in *The Architecture of Richard Morris Hunt*.

6.
In *The Statue of Liberty*, Marvin Trachtenberg has carefully analyzed the sources, the Pharos of Alexandria and the Colossus of Rhodes.

7.
Daily Graphic, December 20, 1883.

8.
Many of these sketches are preserved in the collection of the Avery Architectural Library at Columbia University.

9.
This was not Hunt's first such use of the Doric order. In about 1870 Hunt had proposed a monument to the Union Army's Seventh Regiment of New York, to be placed in Central Park. Although this particular design was not realized, the Doric order on the base is immediately recognizable and indicates that Hunt must have held it in the back of his mind for many years. Furthermore, Hunt must have liked the repetition made by the discs, since he used a similar treatment but with stars on the Abraham Lincoln memorial he collaborated on with Henry Kirke Brown.

10.
Catharine Clinton Howland Hunt, unpublished manuscript biography of Hunt.

Chapter 12

We are grateful to Carole Perrault, who collaborated on the organization of this section and brought to our attention the Pinchot and Lockett documents as well as material she had gathered for the National Park Service.

1.
Sherman to Pinchot, March 6, 1883, Pinchot Papers, Box 52. Stucklé was designated in 1876 to take charge of the pedestal, but no mention of him is made after 1878. Since he and Bartholdi were very close, one suspects that he was deceased.

2.
Sherman to Pinchot, March 25, 1883, Pinchot Papers, Box 52.

3.
Trachtenberg, p. 143, observes: «the unity is that of the universal methods of the civil engineer, Eiffel solving the structural needs of Bartholdi's sculptural envelope, and Stone providing the support for Eiffel's armature.»

4.
World, April 23, 1886; cited in Holliman, p. 48.

5.
Herald, August 5, 1884, copied from the records of the American Institute of Architects Foundation (AIA).

6.
Specifications for the concrete were issued on August 3, 1883; an example is in The New York Public Library, Rare Books and Manuscripts Division. F. H. Smith, the collector who directed the Art Loan Exhibition, was designated the concrete contractor. According to Drexel's letter of October 4, 1883 (see Chapter 8), Smith and Stone did not get along.

7.
The AIA has the identical photo without inscription, and the Pinchot Papers include an example of cat. 421 with an inscription.

8.
Vignettes of the workmen on the island are found in *Frank Leslie's Illustrated Newspaper*, May 10, 1884, p. 189.

9.
Trachtenberg, p. 141, points out that the use of concrete here «marked a turning point in the United States in the revival of the ancient Roman building material.» General Stone took every precaution to ensure the stability of the structure, including making briquettes of the concrete with which to test strength and durability. According to the *Times*, May 20, 1884, «the weight of this foundation mass is 24,000 tons. There will be a pressure at the bottom of the mass, when the statue is in place, of five tons to the square foot. . . .» Trachtenberg says 27,000 tons.

10.
Times, May 20, 1884. This was not done.

Chapter 13

11.
Times, September 1, 1885.
12.
Frank Leslie's Illustrated Newspaper, August 16, 1884, p. 405, gives a different view, as does the unidentified scene in the Cooper-Hewitt Museum, Kubler 1552.
13.
Grand Lodge of New York Proceedings, 1884, pp. 48–56, 52–53. We are very grateful for the cooperation we have received from the Free and Accepted Masons of the State of New York, particularly Deputy Grand Master of the Grand Lodge Robert Singer, who generously assisted our research in every way. We are also grateful to Allan Boudreau, Lodge Librarian, and Robert Waring of the Geneseo Lodge.
The possibility of a larger role for the Masons in the pedestal's history has been raised, but no evidence exists to substantiate the connection. The *Herald*, August 6, 1884, states that «the inward significance of the rites that were observed was doubtless appreciated by nearly all who were there, as nearly all were Masons,» but this would be expected at a ceremony over which they presided.
14.
Times, September 1, 1885.
15.
S. H. Lockett to Stone, March 28, 1884, *Calculations for Anchoring Statue. Specifications for Stone and Anchoring System*, University of North Carolina, Chapel Hill, S. H. Lockett Papers.
16.
Butler to Jay, September 9, 1884, Columbia University, Jay Family Papers; Greenough to McDowell, October 23, 1884. The New York Public Library, Library Americana, Box 39.
17.
We are very much indebted to Mrs. Ulane Bonnel for her assistance. In addition to verifying our discussion of the arrival of the *Isère*, she provided information from the Archives of the Navy, Paris, which she was to publish subsequently in the *Cols Bleus*. According to Commander de Saune's letter to the Minister of the Navy, May 21, 1885, Archives of the Navy, BB4 186, «after the average draft I estimate a charge of 150 to 170 tons instead of the 220 tons announced by Mr. Bartholdi. . . .» De Saune had to add more coal in order to obtain «an average draft of 3m 95; but we are lightly charged.»
In the same letter Saune reported that the loading was well and rapidly done, given the nature of the «freight»; loading began on May 5, and was completed on May 20. *L'Illustration*, June 13, 1885, shows the loading at Rouen.
18.
Journal de Rouen, May 22, 1885. The passengers probably debarked at Caudebec en Caux.
19.
Mrs. Bonnel clarified the frequent misconception that the *Flore* came with the *Isère* from France. Admiral Lacombe came up from the Fort de France de la Martinique, leaving on June 9, to await the *Isère* at Newport, R.I. The U.S. Navy offered the *Isère* a better port at Gravesend, where the frigate was joined on June 18 by the *Flore*.
20.
Evening Post, June 19, 1885.
21.
Commander de Saune carried a letter from Lesseps, now at the New-York Historical Society, dated May 15, 1885, on the Franco-American Union letterhead, ordering him to deliver his cargo to Drexel and Stone.
There is some question about what document commemorated this transfer. The deed had already been presented and sent to the Secretary of State, but the description of the transfer papers in the press, e.g., the *Scientific American*, June 27, 1885, p. 400, sounds like the deed, a «parchment [that] bears the seal of the French Republic. It is decorated with a picture of the statue and pedestal, and, very appropriately, with the heads of Washington and Lafayette.» It may simply have been a facsimile.
22.
Evening Post, June 19, 1885.
23.
L'Illustration, July 11, 1885, repeats the engraving from *Frank Leslie's Illustrated Newspaper* (see above, n. 12). Another scene by Jo Davidson, from an unidentified newspaper, is at the Cooper-Hewitt Museum, Kubler 5430.
24.
Planned for the 15th, this reception was postponed when the *Isère* did not arrive. An invitation to the original ceremonies is at the Museum of the City of New York.
25.
Times, June 25, 1885.
26.
The quotation from Evarts' speech is from printed pages, without number, inserted in vol. 34, 1885, of his papers at the Library of Congress.
27.
The French minister's letter was forwarded by Robert McLane, the American minister to France, to the Secretary of State, June 23, 1885, No. 28, «Despatches from United States Ministers to France, 1789–1906,» National Archives, Washington, D.C., General Records of the Department of State, RG 59.
28.
Frank Leslie's Illustrated Newspaper, July 4, 1885, p. 324. *Harper's Weekly*, August 9, 1884, p. 522, also illustrates this.
29.
Evening Telegram, June 23, 25, and 29, 1885.
30.
Times, August 19, 1885.
31.
October 17, 1885, Pinchot Papers, Box 53.
32.
Bartholdi to Butler, July 21, 1885, taken from Glaenzer's English translation.
33.
Bartholdi to Butler, October 15, 1885, Glaenzer's translation.
34.
CNAM 1605. See also CNAM 1604 and 1832. Endicott was the head of the competition committee. Paul Goldener, of the National Park Service, kindly informed us that on November 11, 1885, Bartholdi was paid $500 for the competition.
It is not certain which «design» and «model» Bartholdi submitted. At the Musée Bartholdi in Colmar are two plaster maquettes, nos. 124 and 130; there is also a photograph (CNAM 1913) of a full-sized plaster.
On the choice of the other two Frenchmen, a letter from McLane to Bayard, January 7, 1886, no. 142, «Despatches from United States Ministers to France, 1789–1906,» National Archives, Washington, D.C., General Records of the Department of State, RG 59, refers to Endicott's request to approach Antonio [sic] Mercie, Alexandre Falguiere, Paul Dubois, and Ernst Barrias—the four leading academic sculptors of Paris. Bartholdi, in a letter to Butler, June 30, 1887, suspected that Hunt had connived against him to «be *persona grata* to his friends of the French Institute,» that is, Falguiere and Mercie.
35.
Holliman, p. 51, citing the *World*, April 22, 1885.
36.
Lockett, *Calculations*. Lockett collaborated with Stone in working out the final calculations. Some of the more incredible suggestions for stabilizing the statue were printed in *Scientific American*, e.g., a pendulum hung from the head (March 31, 1883, p. 192) or raising the statue up as the pedestal is built (May 26, 1883, p. 320).
37.
Stone, p. 30. Trachtenberg, pp. 143–144, who paraphrases this, offers the most lucid account of the system. He also points out that there are elements here that are a transitional stage of reinforced concrete. See also *Scientific American*, June 13, 1885, p. 376, for a detailed description of the system.
38.
Scientific American, June 1, 1886. Bartholdi sent a Mr. Bouquet from Paris to assist in the erection of his work, which he discussed in a letter to Butler, April 16, 1886.
There are three photographs of the completed armature in the collection of the AIA, numbers P 79.57, 79.58, and 79.60.
39.
Tribune, October 24, 1886: «Many of the huge pieces boxed up so long, shaken about in so many handlings and exposed to a great variety of temperatures, had flattened out of their original shape. There was a great deal of delay . . . in reforming them. . . .»
40.
The *World*, August 19, 1886, gives a more detailed explanation of these delays. The best contemporary description of the installation is «The Statue of Liberty Nearing Completion,» *Scientific American*, August 14, 1886, pp. 100–101, which also describes the precautions taken to prevent a galvanic reaction that would make the statue a «battery»: «no part of the ironwork is in direct contact with the copper, a thorough insulation being obtained by shellacking the adjoining surfaces and interposing a strip of asbestos.»
41.
Frank Leslie's Illustrated Newspaper, October 9, 1886, p. 123, which repeats the cat. 437 image.
42.
Charles Barnard, «The Bartholdi Statue,» *St. Nicholas Magazine*, XI (July 1884), 732.
43.
Annual Report of the Light-House Board to the Secretary of the Treasury (Washington, D.C.: Government Printing Office, 1887), «Report upon the Installation of the Electric-Light Plant . . . and an Account of the Operations of the Plant,» by John Millis, Appendix no. 1, pp. 119–127. The «Report,» a detailed statement about the plans and their modifications, was the source for our research.
44.
Ibid., p. 123.
45.
World, October 18, 1886.
46.
World, November 5, 1886. Millis, pp. 126–127, prints Bartholdi's reply of April 1887. Bartholdi reiterated this idea on his last trip to the United States in an interview with the *Times*, September 4, 1893.
47.
Ibid., p. 122. See also *Times*, November 5, 1886. Contention over the jurisdiction of the statue after 1886 arose between the Committee, the War Department, and the Light-House Board.
48.
Unidentified newspaper clipping, ca. October 25, 1886, New-York Historical Society, *Statue of Liberty*, album of clippings. For the same reasons the sole was not fitted in Paris, and therefore was the only part of the colossus that had to be bored for rivet-holes in situ.
49.
World, October 8, 1886.

1.
Bartholdi to Butler, April 16, 1886. His letter of June 25 discusses the guest list in detail, and implies that the French Line, undoubtedly through Bebian, subsidized the transatlantic crossings. See also his letters of July 6 and October 8.
2.
National Archives, Washington, D.C., Senate Foreign Relations Committee Papers, telegram from McLane, Minister in Paris, July 6, 1886: «It is the earnest desire of those concerned in the Bartholdi statue movement that the French government be invited by ours to attend ceremony of inauguration. Such invitation would be well received and would have a good effect here.» The Secretary of State, Bayard, had forwarded the telegram to the Senate committee, with a note of July 8: «In the present condition of the appropriation bills, the President is reluctant to address any additional communication to congress on the subject . . ., and yet as there is no authority of law for the invitation suggested by him, nor any fund out of which [to pay] the expenses necessary incidental to the proper reception and entertainment of the official guests . . ., I lay [it before the committee] for such action as may be deemed proper.» McLane to Bayard, October 15, 1886, no. 292, «Despatches from the U.S. Ministers to France, 1789–1906» (National Archives, Washington, D.C., General Records of the Department of State, RG 59), outlines the previous month's exchanges and details the guest list; McLane to Bayard, October 20, 1886, no. 297, states, «all invitations made by me in the name of American Committee.» See also September 8, 1886, no. 273.
3.
The official delegates were as follows: Count Ferdinand de Lesseps; the Bartholdis; Admiral Jaures and General Pelissier, representing the French Sénat; Eugene Spuller and Desmons, the Chamber of Deputies; Lt. Villegente, the Ministry of the Marine; Colonel Bureau de Pusy, the Ministry of War; Colonel Laussedat, Director of the French École des Arts et Métiers; Léon Robert, the Ministry of Public Instruction; Deschamps, of the Paris Municipal Council; Hielard, the Chamber of Commerce (and old friend of Chauncey Depew); Giraud, the Ministry of Commerce; Charles Bigot, the press; Napoléon Ney, President of the Société de Géographie Commerciale; and Léon Meunier, corresponding member of the Franco-American Union and for twenty-five years the publisher of the *Courrier des États-Unis*, before returning to Paris. Additional guests were invited by the French Committee.
4.
Bartholdi gave an almost identical watercolor to Mrs. Rosetta L. Lumley; it is now in the New-York Historical Society.
5.
World, October 26, 1886.
6.
Charles Bigot wrote a detailed account of the trip, *De Paris au Niagara, Journal de Voyage d'une Délégation* (Paris: Dupret, 1887).
The same day, October 26, without ceremony, two bronze Tiffany plaques were put on the southern entrance to the pedestal. On the right: «This pedestal was built by voluntary contributions from the people of the United States of America. Construction and Executive Committee—William M. Evarts, Richard Butler, Secretary; Henry F. Spaulding, Treasurer; Joseph W. Drexel, V. Mumford Moore, Parke Godwin, Frederic A. Potts, James W. Pinchot, Richard M. Hunt, Architect; Gen. Charles P. Stone, Engineer-in-Chief; David H. King, Jr. Builder. Completed A.D. 1886.» On the left: «A gift from the people of the Republic of France to the people of the United States. This Statute of Liberty Enlightening the World commemorates the alliance of the Two Nations in achieving the independence of the United States of America, and attests their abiding friendship. Inaugurated Oct. 28, 1886. Auguste Bartholdi, sculptor.»
7.
Times, October 28, 1886.
8.
Morning Journal, October 29, 1886.
9.
Ibid.
10.
Ibid. General John M. Schofield's papers concerning arrangements for the dedication are in the Library of Congress, Manuscript Division.
11.
Herald, October 29, 1886.
12.
This view of the parade also appears in *Frank Leslie's Illustrated Newspaper*, November 6, 1886.
13.
Times, October 29, 1886.
14.
Frank Leslie's Illustrated Newspaper, November 6. 1886, p. 181, illustrates the last leg of his trip, shown over the shoulders of the sailors on the rigging.
15.
Sun, October 29, 1886. Additional photographs of the island during the ceremony are in a private collection.

16.
As every version differs in detail, and none are firsthand, the exact circumstances of who transmitted the signal and how, as well as where Bartholdi was waiting, may never be determined with certainty. The cited version is from the *Sun*, October 29, 1886. The *Herald*, October 29, 1886, claimed that Bartholdi, Glaenzer, Butler, and King ascended into the statue, and on a mistaken signal one of them drew the string, whereas the *Times*, October 29, 1886, had Bartholdi, Butler, and King on *Liberty*'s head, waiting for the white handkerchief of a young boy. The legend that the signal was given by David H. King's son may have some basis in fact.

17.
Bartholdi to Butler, February 18, 1887, asked for a copy bound in the «chic Américain,» to give to the President of the Republic. See also the private publication of the *Oration by Hon. Chauncey M. Depew at the Unveiling . . .* (1886).

18.
Times, November 2, 1886. Charles Graham's drawing of the fireworks also appeared in the London *Illustrated News*, November 6, 1886, and the *Daily Graphic*, November 3, 1886. Since the congressional appropriation was not enough to finance the fireworks, Bliss, Drexel, Evarts, Cyrus Field, and Morton covered most of the expense themselves. See also the *Tribune*, October 23, 1886, and the *Times*, October 24, 1886.

19.
A complete account of the banquet is found in the *Twenty-Ninth Annual Report of the Chamber of Commerce, of the State of New York*, 1886–87, part I, pp. 46–70.

We are grateful to Carole Perrault for her assistance with research and selection of photographic materials for this chapter.

1.
Walter Hugins, *Statue of Liberty National Monument: Its Origin, Development and Administration* (U.S. Department of the Interior, National Park Service, 1958), p. 6. This is the definitive work on administration of the statue from 1886 to 1952. Readers wishing to find original sources for this period should see its endnotes and bibliography.

2.
Congressional Record, 44th Cong., 2nd sess. (February 23, 27, 1877), pp. 1822, 1824, 1960, (Index) 190; Hugins, p. 9.

3.
Congressional Record, 49th Cong., 1st sess. (July 24, August 3, 5, 1886), pp. 7456–7458, 7473, 7939, 8027; Annual Report of the Light-House Board (1887), pp. 8, 30; Hugins, pp. 13–14, 17–18, 21.

4.
New York *World*, March 1, 2, 4, 5, 1890; *Congressional Record*, 51st Cong., 2nd sess. (March 2, 1891), p. 3628; Hugins, pp. 20–21.

5.
Hugins, pp. 21, 24–25, 27–28; *World*, May 24, 1916; *Congressional Record*, 64th Cong., 1st sess. (May 23, 1916), pp. 8490–8492; *World*, November 27, 1916.

6.
Hugins, pp. 30–32, 35; Bulletin No. 27, War Department, July 17, 1915, *General Orders and Bulletins, War Dept.*, 1915; *U.S. Statutes at Large*, vol. 43, part 2 (December 1923–March 1925), pp. 1968–1969.

7.
Hugins, pp. 36–37, 40–41.

8.
New York Times, December 7, 1933; Paul Weinbaum, *Statue of Liberty: Heritage of America* (Las Vegas, Nev.: KC Publications, 1979), p. 38; *Times*, December 29, 1933; Proclamation No. 2250, dated September 7, 1937, *Federal Register*, vol. 2, no. 174 (September 9, 1937), p. 1812; Hugins, pp. 43–45, 48–50.

9.
Hugins, pp. 50–56, 57, 60; Weinbaum, p. 40.

10.
New York *World-Telegram*, June 20, 1946; Hugins, pp. 62–64, 66–69; Barbara Blumberg, *Celebrating the Immigrant: An Administrative History of the Statue of Liberty National Monument, 1952–1982* (Washington, D.C.: U.S. Department of the Interior, National Park Service, 1985), pp. 20–21. Readers wishing to find original sources for the period 1952–82 should look at the chapter notes and bibliography of this work.

11.
Hugins, pp. 106, 76–77; «Statue Annual Visitation Figures,» Office of Superintendent; Blumberg, pp. 28–29; Thomas Pitkin, *Keepers of the Gate* (New York: New York University Press, 1975), p. 181.

12.
Times, August 11, 1954; Blumberg, p. 30.

13.
Charter and Bylaws of the AMI, Inc., January 28, 1955; Cooperative Agreement Between the Secretary of the Interior and the AMI Relating to the Establishment of the American Museum of Immigration at the Statue of Liberty National Monument, October 7, 1955, NPS Papers, Liberty Island; Blumberg, pp. 31–44, 51–53.

14.
Blumberg, pp. 34–57, 44; New York *Daily News*, October 3, 1971.

15.
Blumberg, pp. 63–72.

16.
Blumberg, pp. 44, 82–83, 22; *Daily News*, September 27, 1972; *Times*, September 27, 1972; Proclamation No. 3656, dated May 11, 1965, *Federal Register* (May 13, 1965), pp. 6571–6572.

17.
Blumberg, pp. 95–98.

18.
Blumberg, pp. 99–102; Harlan D. Unrau, *Ellis Island Historic Resources Study* (Washington, D.C.: U.S. Department of the Interior, National Park Service, 1984), III: 1153–1165.

19.
Blumberg, pp. 102–104, 108–109, 111; Unrau, III: 1176–1177; «Ellis Island at Low Point in Its History,» *Times*, March 5, 1968.

20.
Blumberg, pp. 119–123, 129–132; Unrau, III: 1188–1191, 1194–1195; Newark *Star-Ledger*, October 23, 1974; *Times*, December 6, 1978.

21.
Blumberg, pp. 23, 134–135, 138–142; *Times*, July 30, 1984, and November 4, 1985; Bergen (N.J.) *Record*, June 27, 1985.

1.
Bartholdi described the process of construction for the statue as beginning with «a model of four feet»; the description is in Bartholdi, p. 37. Other references to the 4-foot model appear in various of his letters, principally those to Richard Butler.

2.
Bartholdi to Mme. Bartholdi, July 24, 1875. On public display in the Musée Bartholdi, surrounded by a dozen or so maquettes for the same subject, is a representation of Bartholdi's *Lion de Belfort* labelled «Premier Modèle d'Étude du Lion de Belfort,» a model clearly the definitive design for the completed work in situ.

3.
In 1976 the model was given by the city of Colmar to the Timken family, which has industrial interests in Colmar, in recognition of contributions through the Timken International Fund that made possible renovation of the Musée Bartholdi in 1977. The model was recently given by the family to the Statue of Liberty National Monument through the Statue of Liberty–Ellis Island Foundation.

4.
Correspondence among various authorities beginning in February 1887 details the circumstances of the model's display in the Rotunda and of its transfer to the then United States National Museum, Smithsonian Institution; this correspondence is in the Office of the Architect of the United States Capitol. On October 10, 1883, the *New York Times* reported that the American Committee had «viewed Hunt's model.» Contemporary photographs of models representing the preliminary designs prepared by Hunt show each with the same model of the statue, a figure which in design features can be identified as the cast now in the National Museum of American Art; these photographs are in the collection of the American Institute of Architects Foundation, Washington, D.C.

5.
Titled *Catalogue de la Collection Auguste Bartholdi*, the document is in the Archives Municipales, Colmar, together with a document prepared in 1907 by Bartholdi's widow donating upon her death the family home in Colmar and its contents, as well as the contents of the house and studio in Paris, to the city for use as a museum. Contents are listed room by room with each identified by its function. Among the rooms are two studios and a third studio for casting (*atelier de moulage*).

6.
Album des Travaux de construction de la statue colossale de la Liberté destinée au port de New-York (Paris: Gontrand, Reinhard et Cie., 1883).

7.
Avoiron's reproduction of *Liberty* in cast is fully documented in E. L. Kallop, Jr., *Images of Liberty: Models and Reductions of the Statue of Liberty, 1867–1917* (New York: Christie, Manson & Woods, 1986), pp. 19–23.

8.
A contemporary description of the development of zinc as a medium for reproduction of sculpture, and of techniques for the alteration of the surface appearance of zinc, is in P. Poiré, «Bronzes d'Art et d'Ameublement, Fontes d'Arts Diverses,» *La France Industrielle* (Paris, 1875), pp. 608 ff.

9.
Beginning in 1883, Bartholdi attempted to sell *Liberty*'s contractual rights to an American manufacturer, an effort detailed in letters to Richard Butler. In one letter Bartholdi states that Avoiron «was bound towards me . . . until the 1st of October, 1885.» The effort dragged on, however, and not until September 1886 was the sale finally effected; Bartholdi to Butler, March 10, 1886, and September 23, 1886. Further discussion of the contract and its sale in Kallop, p. 28.

10.
References to Bartholdi's right to reproduce *Liberty* in both terra cotta and bronze, as distinct from Avoiron's rights, are in letters to Richard Butler dated March 10 and September 23, 1886.

11.
Only five casts by Thiébaut Frères have so far been identified. Of these, the documented histories of three indicate they were clearly commissioned by Bartholdi himself as presentation pieces or were subsequently given by him as gifts to friends or to those who otherwise rendered him assistance during the statue's period of construction. Further discussion of individual casts is in Kallop, pp. 24–26.

12.
The process of mechanical enlargement and reduction in the reproduction of sculpture was common practice among foundries and was based on the device invented in 1836 by Achille Collas. Utilizing the principles of the pantograph, the device helped to revolutionize sculptural reproduction during the second half of the nineteenth century.

13.
Le Courrier des États-Unis, November 18, 1875.

14.
Levi P. Morton to The American Subscription Fund for the Purchase of the Original Model of Liberty Enlightening the World, June 1, 1884.

15.
Le Matin, 1885. Morton to the Committee of Patronage for the Presentation to the City of Paris of a Reduced Copy of Mr. Bartholdi's Statue of Liberty, July 31, 1884. Had the committee really changed, or simply been reorganized to exclude Gillig? Apparently the Fr. 10,000 were to be added to the initial Fr. 75,000 for the purchase of the plaster model and the construction of the pedestal.

16.
Bartholdi to Morton, April 24, 1887. According to Bartholdi it was Gillig who was responsible for the delay. Morton favored the Place des États-Unis while Bartholdi preferred the Pont de Grenelle.

17.
Account in F. Bournon, «La Voie Publique et Son Décor» in the series *Les Richesses d'Art de la Ville de Paris* (Paris, 1909), p. 181. In 1937 the figure was turned around on its then pedestal to face in the direction originally intended.

18.
The history of the cast, beginning with its commission for the Centennial Exposition, is detailed in correspondence initiated by Bartholdi, and continued after his death by his widow, addressed to the Sous Secrétariat d'État des Beaux-Arts; this correspondence is in the Archives Nationales, Paris.

19.
While the replicas in France are known through photographs, no record of the replica in Hanoi exists other than in writing; see Betz, p. 213.

20.
The campaign to melt down all nonferrous metals for the Germans' use is commonly referred to as «lors de l'enlèvement des métaux non-ferreux.»

21.
A detailed account of the two foundries and their interrelationship is in Kallop, pp. 54–57.

22.
News accounts of casts produced by Val d'Osne during the 1950s contain a reference to the foundry's possession of a «modèle même «petri» des mains de Bartholdi»; see *La Haute-Marne Liberée*, June 25, 1958.

23.
Val d'Osne's cast of *Liberty* is illustrated in the company's catalogue «Fascicule No. 21,» Pl. 624 C.

24.
The cast at Semoutiers was commissioned by the U.S. Air Force 48th Tactical Fighter Wing, since moved to a base in England, and was produced from the original molds or from the same model as the earlier casts in the same size. The

second cast, a 30–foot bronze reduction produced from a model prepared by the American sculptors Archie and Lee Lawrie, was commissioned by the life insurance company for its headquarters building.

25.
In advertisements placed by the American Committee throughout 1885 in newspapers, chiefly in the *World*, which was *Liberty*'s principal advocate, the American Committee Model was offered for sale as a «suitable souvenir» of the statue to be erected in New York harbor.

26.
Patents issued to Bartholdi by the U.S. Patent Office are Design No. 10,893 dated November 5, 1878, and Design No. 11,023 dated February 18, 1879. Both dates appear in abbreviated form on the upper surface of the pedestal that accompanies the American Committee Model in both the 6- and 12-inch sizes.

27.
On December 6, 1885, the *Times* reported that «Various parties have infringed [Bartholdi's] patents» and noted that an injunction had been granted to prevent unauthorized manufacture of imitations of the statue. However, in 1883 a copyright had been granted to a Hermann Follmer to produce a model of *Liberty*, about which Bartholdi complained in a letter dated July 28, 1883, to Richard Butler. Bartholdi was unable to prevent Follmer from exercising his copyright, and Follmer produced a model, a single example of which has been documented. Further discussion of Follmer and others who produced replicas unrelated to Bartholdi is in Kallop, pp. 35–38.

28.
An example is a unique replica of *Liberty* made in 1917 by Tiffany & Company and presented to Marshal Joffre, the French «Hero of the Marne,» who was in the United States to enlist American help with the war. Commissioned by the *World* and financed through public subscription, the model and its presentation were fully documented in the daily press, e.g., *World*, May 11, 1917. The model is today in the collection of William M. Gaines, New York.

29.
Further discussion of the American Woman's League is in E. Fendelman, «An Empire of Women,» *American Heritage* (October 1984).

1.
Lawrence Alloway, *Topics in American Art Since 1945* (New York: W. W. Norton & Co., Inc., 1975), p. 247.

2.
Bo Widerberg (writer-director), *Joe Hill*, Sagittarius Productions, Inc., 1971. The promise turns out to be an empty one, and Hill's pursuit of liberty ends before a firing squad.

3.
Edward Hagaman Hall, *The Hudson-Fulton Celebration, 1909* (Albany, N.Y., 1910), 1: 486–497.

4.
Lloyd Morris and Kendall Smith, *Ceiling Unlimited: The Story of American Aviation from Kitty Hawk to Supersonics* (New York: Macmillan, 1953), pp. 101–104.

5.
Ibid., p. 107.

6.
Quoted in H. E. Jacob, *The World of Emma Lazarus* (New York, 1949), pp. 179–180.

7.
Chauncey Depew, *Oration by Hon. Chauncey M. Depew at the Unveiling . . .* (Privately published, 1886).

8.
Maldwyn Allen Jones, *American Immigration* (Chicago: University of Chicago Press, 1960), p. 247.

9.
On the proposed immigrant station, see Ann Novotny, *Strangers at the Door* (Riverside Conn.: Chatham Press, 1971), p. 54; for cartoons, *Judge* 17 (March 22, 1890), cover; and 18 (April 12, 1890), 16.

10.
On the warehouse replica, see Gay Talese, «Miss Liberty— Uptown,» *New York Times Magazine*, October 2, 1960.

11.
O. Henry [William Sydney Porter], «The Lady Higher Up,» *Sixes and Sevens* (New York: Doubleday, Page & Co., 1916), p. 216.

12.
John Higham, *Send These Unto Me: Jews and Other Immigrants in Urban America* (New York: Atheneum, 1972), pp. 78–87.

13.
See, for example, Henry Roth's novel *Call It Sleep* (1934); and the memoirs of Edward Corsi, *In the Shadow of Liberty* (1936); and Emma Goldman, *Living My Life* (1936).

14.
Lisa DeNike, «Taking a Bite of the Big Apple,» Baltimore *Evening Sun*; reprinted in Atlanta *Journal*/Atlanta *Constitution*, February 12, 1984, p. 1F.

15
«New York» in Charles Holme, ed., *Sketching Grounds* (London: Studio, 1909), pp. 31–38.

16.
See, for example, Brooks Atkinson, *New York Times*, July 16, 1949, sec. 5, p. 6, and July 24, 1949, sec. II, p. 1; and Richard Watts, New York *Post*, July 17, 1949, p. 12.

17.
The New York Woman's Suffrage Association chartered a boat to take its members to the ceremonies, as the New York *World* reported in «The Doings of Women Folk,» October 31, 1886, p. 12. Alongside was printed the sonnet «A Woman to Liberty,» by the Rev. Phere A. Hannaford, which contained the following lines:
As Freedom's welcome to this favored land,
And as a prophecy of Equal Rights
This bronze [sic] presentment of the truth must stand
More loyal to woman than the crusade Knights.

18.
Village Voice, February 28, 1984, p. 79.

1.
O. Henry [William Sydney Porter], «The Lady Higher Up,» *Sixes and Sevens* (New York: Doubleday, Page & Co., 1916), p. 216.

2.
This statue of Diana topped (at 365 feet above the pavement, as O. Henry points out) the tower of the original Madison Square Garden. O. Henry was not the only one to bring the two goddesses together: an 1891 *Harper's* caricature depicted Miss Liberty startled at the sight of the bow pointed in her direction by her mythological sister («Murder. Miss Liberty catching glimpse of Diana on the New Madison Square Garden Tower»).

3.
See Roman Jakobson, «Deux Aspects du langage et deux types d'aphasie,» *Essais de linquistique générale*, trans. A. Adler and N. Ruwet (Paris: Editions de Minuit, 1963).

4.
It is worth pointing out that this photograph, which is copyright «National Geographic Magazine» and bears the credit «Official Kodachrome U.S. Army Air Corps,» accompanies an article by Major-General H. H. «Hap» Arnold, Chief of the U.S. Army Air Corps, entitled «Aerial Color Photography Becomes a War Weapon.» The European conflict, to which very discreet allusion is made, is considered, but from far away and above.

5.
Bartholdi, pp. 14–15.

6.
O. Henry, p. 216.

7.
Bartholdi, p. 40.

8.
Letter from Albert Bartholdi to the New York *Herald*, October 28, 1950.

9.
Roland Barthes, *The Eiffel Tower*, trans. Richard Howard (New York: Farrar, Straus & Giroux, 1979), p. 14.

10.
Marvin Trachtenberg, «The Statue of Liberty: Transparent Banality or Avant-Garde Conundrum,» *Art in America*, No. 3 (May–June 1974), 39.

11.
Bartholdi, p. 52.

12.
New York *Sunday News*, May 29, 1955.

13.
Thomas Nast is referring to the scarlet fever epidemic that, it seems, began in the Bronx and assumed catastrophic dimensions because of the deplorable conditions of public sanitation in most of New York's neighborhoods (*Harper's Weekly*, April 2, 1881).

14.
Robert Nathan, *The Weans* (New York: Knopf, 1966).

The Catalogue

All dimensions are given in centimeters; height precedes width precedes depth (in the case of some sculpture, only height is indicated). Except where otherwise indicated, dimensions do not include frames.

Items included in The New York Public Library, Musée des Arts Décoratifs, and National Touring exhibitions are designated by the respective symbols NY, P, and T at the end of the entry. Except where indicated T*, touring items are facsimiles rather than originals.

Photo credits are indicatd in the entries only when they differ from the collection or institution that holds the item.

1
Edouard de Laboulaye
n.s.; ca. 1865
Oil on canvas
80.0 × 63.0
Collection Gerard de
Laboulaye, Paris
NY, P, T

2
Benjamin Constant
Esbrard
n.d.
Engraving
Bibliothèque Nationale, Paris
P

3
Alexis de Tocqueville
Théodore Chassériau
Signed and dated: *Thre
Chassériau, 1850*
Oil on canvas
16.3 × 13.0
Château de Versailles, Inv.
M.V. 7384
P

4
*Maquette for a Monument to
Thiers*
Frédéric-Auguste Bartholdi
n.s., n.d.
Terra cotta
21.5 × 13.0 × 17.0
Musée Bartholdi, Colmar, Inv.
1914 no. 107
P

5
New-York & Environs
Bachman
1850
Lithograph
Diameter: 60.2
The New York Public Library,
Art, Prints and Photographs
Division (Photo: Robert D.
Rubic)
NY, P, T

6 (not illustrated)
Letter of Frédéric-Auguste
Bartholdi to Edouard de
Laboulaye, July 15, 1871
Collection François de
Laboulaye, Saint-Saens
P

7
*La Statue de la Liberté en
place*
Frédéric-Auguste Bartholdi
n.s., n.d.
Watercolor on paper
12.0 × 21.0
Musée Bartholdi, Colmar
(Photo: Christian Kempf)
T*

8 (not illustrated)
*La Statue de la Liberté en
place*
Frédéric-Auguste Bartholdi
Signed: *A. Bartholdi*; n.d.
Watercolor on paper
12.6 × 21.0
Inscribed: *a Mr Mariani
souvenir cordial*
Collection Philippe Bisson,
Paris
P

9
La Statue vue d'un bateau
Frédéric-Auguste Bartholdi
n.s., n.d.
Watercolor on paper
11.0 × 18.5
Musée Bartholdi, Colmar
(Photo: Christian Kempf)
P

10
*«Liberty Enlightening the
World»—Bartholdi's Colossal
Statue on Bedlow's Island,
New York Harbor*
Harry Fenn
n.s.; October 30, 1886
Engraving
34.4 × 103.8
Musée Bartholdi, Colmar
(Photo: Christian Kempf)
P

11
Christopher Columbus
Frédéric-Auguste Bartholdi
1893
Sterling silver casting by
Gorham Co. Founders; dated
on base: *1975*
66.0
Sunset Memorial Park,
courtesy of the Graham
Gallery, New York
NY, P

12
Washington and Lafayette
Frédéric-Auguste Bartholdi
n.s., n.d.
Photograph
25.5 × 18.5
Musée Bartholdi, Colmar, Inv.
phot. no. 2P17

13
*Faunes et nymphes effrayées
par un train*
Frédéric-Auguste Bartholdi
n.s., n.d.
Oil on canvas
57.0 × 74.0
Musée Bartholdi, Colmar
(Photo: Christian Kempf)
NY, P

14
*Wrapped Coast—Little Bay
Australia 1969 (One Million
Square Feet)*
Christo
1969
Co-ordinator John Kaldor
Photograph
17.1 × 24.1
(Photo: Harry Shunk;
© Christo 1969; courtesy of
Christo)

15
Dedication of *Album des
Travaux de Construction de la
Statue Colossale de la Liberté
destinée au Port de New-York*
Paris: Gontrand, Reinhard et
Cie., 1883
The New York Public Library,
Rare Books and Manuscripts
Division (Photo: Robert D.
Rubic)

16
*Bartholdi's Design for the
Statue*
From *The Daily Graphic*,
October 27, 1886, p. 944
(Photo: Simon Taylor)

17
Genius of Electricity
Antonio Rosetti
From Edward Strahan [Earl
Shinn], *The Masterpieces of
the Centennial International
Exhibition*, I: Fine Art
Philadelphia: Gebbie and
Barrie, 1876, facing p. 108
The New York Public Library,
General Research and
Humanities Division (Photo:
Robert D. Rubic)

18
American Institute
51st Grand National
Industrial Exposition
1882
Announcement card
Collection Jeffrey and Miriam
Eger

19
*American Progress (Manifest
Destiny)*
John Gast
1872
Oil on canvas
The Congoleum Collection,
Portsmouth, N.H. (Photo:
Robert D. Rubic; reproduced
from Deborah Nevins, *The
Great East River Bridge
1883–1983*, catalogue of an
exhibition at the Brooklyn
Museum [New York: Abrams,
1983], p. 11)

20
*The Torch of the Statue of
«Liberty,» as It Will Appear
When Completed, on Bedloe's
Island*
From *Frank Leslie's Illustrated
Newspaper*, June 20, 1885,
p. 288
Collection Ed Hotaling, NBC
News (Photo: Robert D.
Rubic)
NY, P

21
*Puck's Patent Plan for a
Tremendous Tower at the
Great Fair*
Undated cartoon from *Puck*,
ca. 1889
The New York Public Library
(Photo: Robert D. Rubic)

22
Great Eastern
Signed, bottom center:
Pannemeker; bottom left:
P. Ferat
From Jules Verne. *Une Ville
Flottante*
Paris: Ed. Hetzel, 1926, p. 1
Bibliothèque de l'Heure
Joyeuse, Paris (Photo: Jean-
Loup Charmet)
P

23
Albatros
Signed, bottom left: *L. Benett*;
bottom right: *G. Roux*
From Jules Verne. *Robur le
Conquérant*
Paris: Ed. Hetzel, 1886, p. 117
Bibliothèque de l'Heure
Joyeuse, Paris (Photo: Jean-
Loup Charmet)
P

24
*Transcontinental Train on
Bridge*
Frédéric-Auguste Bartholdi
n.s., n.d.
Glass positive, gelatin-silver
process
10.0 × 8.0
Inscribed on the mount:
initialed *B*; *Chemin de fer
transcontinental. Pont
métallique*
Former collection of Frédéric-
Auguste Bartholdi; Private
collection, Paris
P

25
Snowplow Train
Frédéric-Auguste Bartholdi
n.s., n.d.
Glass positive, gelatin-silver
process
10.0 × 8.0
Inscribed on the mount:
initialed *B*; *Chasse neige,
chemin de fer du Pacific*
Former collection of Frédéric-
Auguste Bartholdi; Private
collection, Paris
P

26
Epouvante
Signed, bottom left:
F. Duplessis; bottom right:
G. Roux
From Jules Verne. *Maître du
monde*
Paris: Ed. Hetzel, 1904, p. 109
Bibliothèque de l'Heure
Joyeuse, Paris (Photo: Jean-
Loup Charmet)
P

27
Maquette for *Monument aux
Aéronautes du siège de
Paris . . .*
Frédéric-Auguste Bartholdi
1904
n.s., n.d.
Plaster
68.0 × 22.0 × 23.0
Musée Bartholdi, Colmar, Inv.
1914 no. 321 (Photo:
Christian Kempf)
P

28
The Question of Balloons
Signed, bottom left: *L. Benett*;
bottom right: *F. Delangle*
From Jules Verne. *Robur le
Conquérant*
Paris: Ed. Hetzel, 1886, p. 17
Bibliothèque de l'Heure
Joyeuse, Paris (Photo: Jean-
Loup Charmet)
P

29
*The Balloon Ascent at the
Chicago Exposition*
Frédéric-Auguste Bartholdi
1893
n.s., n.d.
Glass positive, gelatin-silver
process
10.0 × 8.0
Former collection of Frédéric-
Auguste Bartholdi; Private
collection, Paris
P

30
Jean-Charles Bartholdi
Martin Rossbach
Signed, bottom center: *Dessiné par Mtin Rossbach*; n.d.
Drawing on paper
Framed
Musée Bartholdi, Colmar
(Photo: Christian Kempf)
NY, P

31
Charlotte Bartholdi
Ary Scheffer
Signed and dated, bottom left: *Ary Scheffer 1855*
Oil on canvas
151.0 × 102.0
Musée Bartholdi, Colmar
(Photo: Christian Kempf)
NY, P, T

32
Charles Bartholdi
n.d.
Albumen print visiting card
8.7 × 5.5
Printed by E. Adam, Colmar
Musée Bartholdi, Colmar, Inv.
phot. no. 3P1/24 (Photo:
Christian Kempf)
NY, P

33
Madame Charlotte Bartholdi
Frédéric-Auguste Bartholdi
n.d.
Albumen print visiting card
13.7 × 10.4
Printed by P. Petit
Musée Bartholdi, Colmar, Inv.
phot. no. E42 (Photo:
Christian Kempf)
P

34
Frédéric-Auguste Bartholdi at Sixteen
Glück
Signed and dated, bottom left:
Glück; 1859
Oil on canvas
32.5 × 24.5
Musée Bartholdi, Colmar, Inv.
1914 no. 224 (Photo:
Christian Kempf)
T*

35
Frédéric-Auguste Bartholdi
n.s., n.d.
Salt print from a paper
negative
14.6 × 10.5
Musée Bartholdi, Colmar, Inv.
phot. no. 3P1/1 (Photo:
Christian Kempf)
P

36
Madame Bartholdi and Her Son Frédéric-Auguste Bartholdi
n.d.
Albumen print
14.5 × 17.1
Printed by Marck
Musée Bartholdi, Colmar, Inv.
phot. no. 3P1/28 (Photo:
Christian Kempf)
NY, P, T

37
Jeanne Bartholdi
Jean Benner
n.s.; 1884
Oil on canvas
93.0 × 73.0
Musée Bartholdi, Colmar
NY, P, T

38
Jeanne-Emilie Bartholdi
Frédéric-Auguste Bartholdi
n.d.
Albumen print
9.3 × 6.0
Printed by Sarony's, New York
Musée Bartholdi, Colmar, Inv.
phot. no. 3P1/18
P

39
Dinner Invitation from
Frédéric-Auguste and Jeanne-
Emilie Bartholdi
n.d.
Collection Doin, St. Denis de
Jouhet
NY, P

40
Maquette for the Monument
to Rossbach
Frédéric-Auguste Bartholdi
n.s.; 1856
Plaster
27.0 × 18.0 × 23.0
Musée Bartholdi, Colmar
(Photo: Courtauld Institute of
Art, London)
P

41
Bust of Gustave Jundt
Frédéric-Auguste Bartholdi
n.s.; 1884
Plaster
72.0 × 57.0 × 41.0
Musée Bartholdi, Colmar, Inv.
1914 no. 386
P

42
Photograph of the Tomb of
J. Soitoux, Montparnasse
Cemetery
n.d.
Albumen print
23.0 × 14.6
Printed by V. Pennelier, Paris
Musée Bartholdi, Colmar, Inv.
phot. no. 2P20
P

43
Françoise de Rimini
Frédéric-Auguste Bartholdi,
after Ary Scheffer
n.s., n.d.
Plaster
40.0 × 54.0 × 55.0
Musée Bartholdi, Colmar
P

44
*Les ombres de Francesca da
Rimini et de Paolo Malatesta
apparaissent à Dante et à
Virgile*
Ary Scheffer
Signed and dated, bottom left:
Ary Scheffer, 1855
Oil on canvas
171.0 × 239.0
Musée du Louvre, Paris
(Photo: Musées Nationaux,
Paris)
P

45
Ary Scheffer
Frédéric-Auguste Bartholdi
n.s.; 1862
Bronze
87.2 × 33.0 × 24.0
Musée Bartholdi, Colmar, Inv.
1914 no. 296 (Photo:
Christian Kempf)
P

46
Ary Scheffer
Frédéric-Auguste Bartholdi
n.s.; 1862
Terra cotta
23.0 × 8.0 × 7.0
Musée Bartholdi, Colmar, Inv.
1914 no. 65
P

47
*Frédéric-Auguste Bartholdi
with a Statuette*
n.s.; ca. 1865–70
Albumen print
25.4 × 19.4
Musée Bartholdi, Colmar, Inv.
phot. no. 3P1/5 (Photo:
Christian Kempf)
P, T

48
*Frédéric-Auguste Bartholdi
with a Portfolio*
n.s.; ca. 1865–70
Albumen print
28.6 × 21.9
Musée Bartholdi, Colmar, Inv.
phot. no. 3P1/4 (Photo:
Christian Kempf)
P

49
Bartholdi in His Paris Studio
n.s.; January 1886
Albumen print
27.5 × 22.0
Inscribed in ink, bottom left:
Atelier, Janvier 1886
Musée d'Unterlinden, Colmar,
Inv. phot.: M.U.C. no. 37
(Photo: Christian Kempf,
© Musée d'Unterlinden)
NY, P

50
*Bartholdi Standing in Front of
His Sketches*
n.s.; 1886
Albumen print
19.6 × 24.5
Musée Bartholdi, Colmar, Inv.
phot. no. 3P2/9 (Photo:
Christian Kempf)
NY, P, T

51
Bartholdi at His Easel
n.s.; 1886
Albumen print
20.5 × 26.5
Musée Bartholdi, Colmar, Inv.
phot. no. 3P2/7 (Photo:
Christian Kempf)
P

52
Bartholdi at Work on a Bust
n.s.; 1886
Albumen print
26.9 × 20.4
Musée Bartholdi, Colmar, Inv.
phot. no. 3P2/1 (Photo:
Christian Kempf)
P

53
*The Maquette Gallery at the
Musée Bartholdi*
n.d.
Postcard
9.0 × 14.2
Printed by Christophe,
Colmar. Braun et Cie Editeurs,
Dernach, Ht Rhin
Collection J. Betz, Paris

54
*Bartholdi, His Wife, and His
Mother in the Studio*
n.s.; ca. 1887–91
Albumen print
20.3 × 20.1
Inscribed on the print, bottom
left: *A son ami Simon,
souvenir affectueux, Bartholdi*
Musée Bartholdi, Colmar, Inv.
phot. no. E4 (Photo: Christian
Kempf)
NY, P

55
Bartholdi at His Easel
n.s.; ca. 1887–91
Albumen print
20.7 × 26.8
Musée Bartholdi, Colmar, Inv.
phot. no. 3P1/33 (Photo:
Christian Kempf)

56
Bartholdi with His Violin
n.s.; ca. 1887–91
Albumen print
18.6 × 26.8
Inscribed on the print, bottom
left: *A son ami Simon,
souvenir affectueux, Bartholdi*
Musée Bartholdi, Colmar, Inv.
phot. no. 3P1/32 (Photo:
Christian Kempf)

57
*The Colmar Reconstruction of
Bartholdi's Studio, Rue Vavin,
Paris*
n.s., n.d.
Albumen print
20.4 × 20.6
Musée Bartholdi, Colmar, Inv.
phot. no. 3P2/8 (Photo:
Christian Kempf)
NY, P

58
*Le Génie dans les griffes de la
Misère*
Frédéric-Auguste Bartholdi
n.s., n.d.
Bronze
114.0 × 52.5 × 49.3
The plaster was exhibited at
the Salon of 1859, No. 3073.
Musée Bartholdi, Colmar, Inv.
1914 no. 28 (Photo:
Courtauld Institute of Art,
London)
P

59a–d
Studies for *Le Génie dans les
griffes de la Misère*
Frédéric-Auguste Bartholdi
n.s., n.d.
Terra cotta
From left to right: a: 20.5 ×
9.3 × 8.5; b: 22.5 × 8.8 ×
7.5; c: 17.5 × 10.5 × 9.5;
d: 17.0 × 10.0 × 8.0
Musée Bartholdi, Colmar, Inv.
1914 nos. 44, 113, 108, 43
(Photo: Christian Kempf)
P

60
Photograph of the Project for
the Decoration of the
Esplanade des Quinconces,
Bordeaux
Signed, bottom right: *Par
A. Bartholdi et Norbert
Maillart*; 1858
37.0 × 46.0
Inscribed, bottom left: *Projet
de décoration de l'esplanade
des Quinconces à Bordeaux*
Bibliothèque du Conservatoire
National des Arts et Métiers,
Paris, Musée des Techniques,
13768/8
P

61
Maquette for the Palais de
Longchamp at Marseille
Frédéric-Auguste Bartholdi
n.s., n.d.
Plaster
14.0 × 47.0 × 52.5
Musée Bartholdi, Colmar
(Photo: Christian Kempf)
P

62
Maquette for the Palais de
Longchamp at Marseille
Frédéric-Auguste Bartholdi
n.s., n.d.
Plaster
12.5 × 47.5 × 40.5
Musée Bartholdi, Colmar, Inv.
phot. no. E4 (Photo: Christian
Kempf)
NY, P

63
Maquette for the Palais de
Longchamp at Marseille
Frédéric-Auguste Bartholdi
n.s., n.d.
Plaster
12.5 × 49.0 × 41.0
Musée Bartholdi, Colmar
(Photo: Christian Kempf)
P

64 (not illustrated)
*Mémoire en défense sur le
Palais de Longchamp*
Frédéric-Auguste Bartholdi
Bibliothèque Nationale, Paris,
Département des Imprimés
P

65
Project for the Monument for
the St. Michel Fountain
Frédéric-Auguste Bartholdi
n.s.; 1860
Terra cotta
24.0 × 14.0 × 8.7
Musée Bartholdi, Colmar, Inv.
1914 no. 55
P

66
Project for the *Vercingétorix*
Frédéric-Auguste Bartholdi
n.s., n.d.
Albumen print and watercolor
14.5 × 26.5
Musée Bartholdi, Colmar, Inv.
phot. no. 2P5/1
P

67
Photograph of the Maquette
for the *Monument élevé à
Clermont-Ferrand à
Vercingétorix*
Frédéric-Auguste Bartholdi
n.s., n.d.
Albumen print
25.4 × 15.8
Musée Bartholdi, Colmar, Inv.
phot. no. 2P5
P

68
Maquette for *Vercingétorix*
Frédéric-Auguste Bartholdi
n.s., n.d.
Plaster
35.5 × 34.5 × 12.5; with
pedestal: 100.0 high
Musée Bartholdi, Colmar, Inv.
1914 no. 184 (Photo:
Christian Kempf)
P

69
Photograph of *Vercingétorix*
Frédéric-Auguste Bartholdi
Signed: *A. Bartholdi*; n.d.
Gelatin-silver process
16.0 × 23.5
Musée Bartholdi, Colmar, Inv.
phot. no. 2P5/25
P

70
Monument à Vercingétorix
n.s., n.d.
Postcard
9.0 × 14.0
Musée Bartholdi, Colmar

71
The Monument to Gambetta
in front of the National
Assembly
Frédéric-Auguste Bartholdi
n.s., n.d.
Albumen print
20.1 × 20.4
Musée Bartholdi, Colmar, Inv.
phot. no. 2P8

72 (not illustrated)
The Monument to Gambetta
in front of the National
Assembly
Frédéric-Auguste Bartholdi
n.s., n.d.
Albumen print
9.5 × 15.1
Musée Bartholdi, Colmar, Inv.
phot. no. 2P8
P

73
Maquette for the *Projet de
monument à colonnades
ornées de statues disposées au
haut d'un escalier à double
révolution*
Frédéric-Auguste Bartholdi
Signed: *B*; 1873
Terra cotta
39.0
Musée Bartholdi, Colmar
P

74
Statuette of Gambetta
Frédéric-Auguste Bartholdi
n.s., n.d.
Plaster
74.5 × 31.0 × 30.0
Musée Bartholdi, Colmar, Inv.
1914 no. 293
P

75
Photograph of the Monument
to Gambetta at Ville d'Avray
n.s., n.d.
Albumen print
14.0 × 9.7
Musée Bartholdi, Colmar, Inv.
phot. no. 2P8
P

76a
*Frédéric-Auguste Bartholdi in
Evening Clothes*
n.s., n.d.
Albumen print
11.0 × 6.0
Collection Doin, Saint Denis
de Jouhet

76b
Frédéric-Auguste Bartholdi
n.s., n.d.
Albumen print
11.0 × 6.0
Collection Doin, Saint Denis
de Jouhet
P

76c
*Frédéric-Auguste Bartholdi in
a Business Suit*
n.s.; 1870
Albumen print
11.0 × 6.0
Collection Doin, Saint Denis
de Jouhet
P

77
*Frédéric-Auguste Bartholdi in
Uniform*
n.s., n.d.
Albumen print
13.1 × 8.9
Musée Bartholdi, Colmar, Inv.
phot. no. 3P1/12 (Photo:
Christian Kempf)
P

78
*Frédéric-Auguste Bartholdi as
a Garibaldean*
n.s., n.d.
Albumen print
11.0 × 6.0
Collection Doin, Saint Denis
de Jouhet
NY, P, T

79
*Bartholdi's Companions in
Arms in 1870*
n.s.; 1870
Albumen print
12.7 × 9.8
Printed by Paul Bourgeois.
Châlon sur Saône
Inscribed at bottom: *Au brave
Commandant Bartholdi: son
compagnon d'armes
M. Garibaldi*
Collection J. Betz, Paris
P

80
Sur la route d'Arnay-le-Duc
n.s.; 1870
Photograph of a lost
watercolor drawing by
Frédéric-Auguste Bartholdi
8.9 × 15.7
Drawing inscribed by
Bartholdi: *Sur la route
d'Arnay-le-Duc*
Collection J. Betz, Paris

81
Maquette for a Double Bust of
Erckmann and Chatrian
Frédéric-Auguste Bartholdi
n.s.; 1869
Terra cotta
14.0 × 19.0 × 8.0
Exhibited at the Salon of 1872
Musée Bartholdi, Colmar, Inv.
1914 no. 105 (Photo:
Courtauld Institute of Art,
London)

82
La malédiction de l'Alsace
Frédéric-Auguste Bartholdi
n.s., n.d.
Plaster
44.0 × 62.5 × 30.0
The bronze, now lost, was
exhibited at the Salon of 1872,
No. 1552
Musée Bartholdi, Colmar, Inv.
1914 no. 330
P

83
Maquette for the Monument
to General Rapp
Frédéric-Auguste Bartholdi
n.s.; 1856
Plaster
33.2 × 13.2 × 13.2
Musée Bartholdi, Colmar
(Photo: Courtauld Institute of
Art, London)
P

84
Photograph of the Maquette
for the Monument to Jeanne
d'Arc at Compiègne, No. 112
Frédéric-Auguste Bartholdi
n.s., n.d.
Albumen print
38.2 × 27.0
Musée Bartholdi, Colmar
P

85 (not illustrated)
Photograph of the Maquette
for the Monument to Jeanne
d'Arc at Compiègne
Frédéric-Auguste Bartholdi
n.s., n.d.
Albumen print
37.5 × 26.9
Musée Bartholdi, Colmar, Inv.
phot. no. 2P8
P

86
Maquette for the Monument
to Rouget de l'Isle
Frédéric-Auguste Bartholdi
n.s., n.d.
Plaster
84.5 × 47.5 × 35.0
Musée Bartholdi, Colmar, Inv.
1914 no. 295
NY, P

87
Maquette for the Monument
to Sergeant Hoff
Frédéric-Auguste Bartholdi
n.s., n.d.
Plaster
45.8 × 23.5 × 28.4
Exhibited at the Salon of
1904, No. 2645
Musée Bartholdi, Colmar, Inv.
1914 no. 176 (Photo:
Courtauld Institute of Art,
London)
NY, P

88
Le Droit Prime la Force
Frédéric-Auguste Bartholdi
Signed: A. Bartholdi;
Photograph of a watercolor
24.5 × 10.8
Inscribed in ink at bottom: Le
Droit prime la Force. A.
Bartholdi
Musée Bartholdi, Colmar
NY, P

89
Maquette for the Tombe du
Garde National
Frédéric-Auguste Bartholdi
n.s., n.d.
Terra cotta
12.8 × 21.5 × 17.5
Musée Bartholdi, Colmar, Inv.
1914 no. 139 (Photo:
Courtauld Institute of Art,
London)
NY, P

90
Le Lion de Belfort
Frédéric-Auguste Bartholdi
n.s., n.d.
Terra cotta
25.8 × 24.7 × 13.5
Musée Bartholdi, Colmar, Inv.
1914 no. 365
P

91
Le Lion de Belfort
Frédéric-Auguste Bartholdi
n.s., n.d.
Terra cotta
28.0 × 37.0 × 15.0
Musée Bartholdi, Colmar, Inv.
1914 no. 320

92
Photograph of the Lion de
Belfort in Situ
n.s., n.d.
Albumen print
37.4 × 47.7
Printed by Braun
Musée Bartholdi, Colmar, Inv.
phot. no. 2P6/2
P

93
Maquette for the Lion de
Belfort
Frédéric-Auguste Bartholdi
n.s., n.d.
Granite on wood pedestal
50.0 × 70.0 × 30.0
Former collection of Frédéric-
Auguste Bartholdi; Private
collection, Paris
NY, P

94
Lion on Which Is Seated a
Figure Representing Alsace
Frédéric-Auguste Bartholdi
n.s., n.d.
Terra cotta
26.7 × 42.0 × 12.0
Musée Bartholdi, Colmar, Inv.
1914 no. 120 (Photo:
Courtauld Institute of Art,
London)
NY, P

95
The Lion de Belfort for the
Place Denfert-Rochereau at
the Salon
n.s., n.d.
Phototype
20.2 × 25.8
Printed by Michelez
Musée Bartholdi, Colmar, Inv.
phot. no. 2P6/pl. 1
P

96
Photograph of the Maquette
for the Monument aux
défenseurs de Brisach
Frédéric-Auguste Bartholdi
n.s., n.d.
Albumen print
19.6 × 12.4
Musée Bartholdi, Colmar, Inv.
phot. no. 2P1
P

97
Frédéric-Auguste Bartholdi
Jean Benner
Signed and dated, top right:
1886 Jean Benner
Oil on canvas
93.0 × 73.0
Musée Bartholdi, Colmar, Inv.
1914 no. 15
NY, P

98
Frédéric-Auguste Bartholdi
with the Legion of Honor
Joseph Frappe
n.s., n.d.
Oil on canvas
132.0 × 99.0
Musée Bartholdi, Colmar, Inv.
1914 no. 465 (Photo:
Christian Kempf)
NY, P, T

99 (not illustrated)
Diploma of Officer of the
Legion of Honor Presented to
Frédéric-Auguste Bartholdi,
October 11, 1882; and
Diploma of Commander of the
Legion of Honor Presented to
Frédéric-Auguste Bartholdi,
January 24, 1887
Private collection, Paris
P

100
Frédéric-Auguste Bartholdi
n.s.; ca. 1900
Albumen print
15.2 × 10.2
Printed by Hoflinger ans Sohn,
Basel
Musée Bartholdi, Colmar, Inv.
phot. no. 3P1/11 (Photo:
Christian Kempf)
P

101
Maquette for a Monument to
Bartholdi
Hubert Louis Noël
n.s., n.d.
Plaster
60.0 × 29.0 × 22.6
Musée Bartholdi, Colmar
(Photo: Courtauld Institute of
Art, London)
NY, P

102
Maquette for the Project for a
Funerary Monument for the
Tomb of Frédéric-Auguste
Bartholdi
Frédéric-Auguste Bartholdi
n.s., n.d.
Plaster
56.0 × 23.0 × 31.0
Musée Bartholdi, Colmar, Inv.
1914 no. 168
P

103 (not illustrated)
Les Colosses anciens et
modernes
E. Lesbazeilles
Paris: Hachette, 1876
The New York Public Library,
Art, Prints and Photographs
Division
NY, P

104
Comparative Heights of the
Great Colossal Statues
without Their Pedestals
Frédéric-Auguste Bartholdi
n.s., n.d.
Glass positive, gelatin-silver
process
10.0 × 8.0
Inscribed on the mount:
initialed B; Proportion
comparative entre la Liberté et
autres statues colossales.
On the back: G1
Former collection of Frédéric-
Auguste Bartholdi; Private
collection, Paris
P, T

105
The Highest Monuments in
the World
ca. 1886
Engraving
(Photo: National Park Service:
Statue of Liberty National
Monument)

106
Le colosse de Rhodes
Antoine Caron
n.s., n.d.
Tapestry
476.0 × 646.0
Mobilier National, Paris, Inv.
no. GMTT 12/4
P

107
Colossal Head of the Emperor
Constantine
Late Roman Empire
Marble
Museum of the Capitol, Rome

108
The Hand of Constantine
Late Roman Empire
Marble
Museum of the Capitol, Rome

109
The Foot of Constantine
Late Roman Empire
Marble
Museum of the Capitol, Rome

110
Le Pied gauche de la statue de
Louis XIV
François Girardon
1692
Bronze
44.0 × 68.0 × 29.0
Musée du Louvre, Paris, Inv.
no. M.R. 3448

111
Photograph of L'Appenin,
Florence
Frédéric-Auguste Bartholdi
n.s., n.d.
Glass positive, gelatin-silver
process
10.0 × 8.0
Inscribed on the mount:
initialed B; L'Appenin,
Florence
Former collection of Frédéric-
Auguste Bartholdi; Private
collection, Paris

112
The Colossus of Mount Athos
Fischer von Erlach
n.s.; dated 1725
Engraving
42.0 × 58.0
École Nationale Supérieure des
Beaux-Arts, Paris
P

113
The Colossus of Rhodes
Fischer von Erlach
n.s.; dated 1725
Engraving
42.0 × 58.0
École Nationale Supérieure des
Beaux-Arts, Paris
P

114
The Pharos of Alexandria
Fischer von Erlach
n.s.; dated 1725
Engraving
42.0 × 58.0
École Nationale Supérieure des
Beaux-Arts, Paris
P

115
The Jupiter of Olympus
Fischer von Erlach
n.s.; dated 1725
Engraving
42.0 × 58.0
École Nationale Supérieure des
Beaux-Arts, Paris
P

116
Photograph of the St. Charles
Borromeo at Arona
Frédéric-Auguste Bartholdi
n.s., n.d.
Glass positive, gelatin-silver
process
10.0 × 8.0
Inscribed on the mount:
initialed B; St Charles
Borromée
Former collection of Frédéric-
Auguste Bartholdi; Private
collection, Paris
P

117
L'éléphant de la place de la
Bastille
Jean-Antoine Alavoine
n.s., n.d.
Drawing with watercolor
40.0 × 53.3
Musée Carnavalet, Paris, Inv.
no. D6186 (Photo: Musées de
la Ville de Paris–SPADEM
1986)
P

118
Photograph of the Arminius,
at Detmold, Germany
Frédéric-Auguste Bartholdi
n.s., n.d.
Glass positive, gelatin-silver
process
10.0 × 8.0
Inscribed on the mount:
initialed B; Statue d'Arminius
à Detmold en Allemagne
Former collection of Frédéric-
Auguste Bartholdi; Private
collection, Paris
P, T

119
Photograph of Bavaria,
Munich
Frédéric-Auguste Bartholdi
n.s., n.d.
Glass positive, gelatin-silver
process
10.0 × 8.0
Inscribed on the mount:
initialed B; 1841, La Bavaria,
Munich
Former collection of Frédéric-
Auguste Bartholdi; Private
collection, Paris
P

120
Projets de phares (Concours
de 2e classe à l'École des
Beaux-Arts, Paris)
From Revue Générale de
l'Architecture et des Travaux
Publics, 10 (1852), Pl. 9
Bibliothèque de l'Union des
Arts Décoratifs, Paris (Photo:
Musée des Arts Décoratifs,
Sully-Jaulmes)
P

121 (not illustrated)
Projet pour la colline de
Chaillot
Hector Horeau
Signed and dated: Horeau mai
1868
Watercolor and ink
27.0 × 45.5
Académie d'Architecture, Paris
NY, P

122 (not illustrated)
Projet de statue
Hector Horeau
n.s., n.d.
Watercolor
22.0 × 37.0
Académie d'Architecture, Paris
NY, P

123
Temple de Vénus et de Rome,
élévation restaurée de la
façade vers le Colisée
Ernest-Georges Coquart
n.s.; 1861
Drawing with watercolor
66.0 × 169.0
École Nationale Supérieure des
Beaux-Arts, Paris, Inv. no.
31494
NY, P

124
Temple de Jupiter à Olympie,
coupe transversale au 1/50°
Victor Laloux
Signed and dated: V. Laloux
1886
Watercolor and India ink
78.0 × 97.0
École Nationale Supérieure des
Beaux-Arts, Paris
P

125
Coupe transversale du
Parthénon au 1/20°
Loviot
Signed and dated: Loviot,
1880
Watercolor and India ink
125.5 × 193.0
École Nationale Supérieure des
Beaux-Arts, Paris, Inv. 90
P

126
Photograph of Daniel Chester
French's Columbia
n.s.; 1893
Glass positive, gelatin-silver
process
10.0 × 8.0
Inscribed on the mount:
initialed B; Columbia. Printed:
World's Columbian
Exposition; Chicago 1893. On
back: C. D. Arnold, Chief
Department of Photography
Former collection of Frédéric-
Auguste Bartholdi; Private
collection, Paris (Photo:
Chicago Historical Society,
ICHi-02498)
P

127
Photograph of the Monument
à la gloire du peuple américain
by Despradelles
Signed: Despradelles; n.d.
Albumen print
20.2 × 25.5
Musée Bartholdi, Colmar
P

128
Photograph of the Monument
à la gloire du peuple américain
by Despradelles
Signed Despradelles; n.d.
Albumen print
25.3 × 20.4
Musée Bartholdi, Colmar
NY, P

129
A Design for Washington
Monument
From American Architect and
Building News, 6 (November
8, 1879)
The New York Public Library,
Art, Prints and Photographs
Division (Photo: Robert D.
Rubic)
P

130
Monument à Washington
E. Chifflot
Signed and dated: E. Chifflot
1895
Watercolor and India ink
113.0 × 161.0
École Nationale Supérieure des
Beaux-Arts, Paris, Inv. no.
26381
NY, P

131
The Lincoln Memorial
Daniel Chester French
1915–22
Marble
617.7
Lincoln Memorial,
Washington, D.C. (Photo:
William Clark, National Park
Service)

132
Memorial Carving, Stone
Mountain Park, Georgia
Gutzon Borglum
1915–25
(Photo: National Park Service)

133
Mount Rushmore
Gutzon Borglum
1927–41
(Photo: The Rushmore-
Borglum Story, Keystone,
S.D.)
T

134
The Bat Column
Claes Oldenburg
1977
Flat-bar cor-ten steel
343.0
Chicago, 600 West Madison
Street (Photo: Art in
Architecture Program, General
Services Administration)
T

135 (not illustrated)
Motherland
ca. 1950
Stone
Volgograd, USSR

136 (not illustrated)
Head of Ferdinand Marcos
1985
Stone
Manila, Philippines

137 (not illustrated)
Le Génie français adopte la
Liberté et l'Égalité
1794
Allais
Aquatint
Bibliothèque Nationale, Paris,
Collection Hennin, no. 11978
NY, P

138
La Naissance de l'Amérique
libre
After S. Harding
n.d.
Engraving
Musée Nationale de la
Coopération Franco-
Américaine, Paris,
Américaine, Blérancourt,
Paris, MNB CFAC 192
NY, P

139
Libertas Americana
Gibelin
1783
Drawing
Musée Nationale de la
Coopération Franco-
Américaine, Blérancourt,
Paris, CFAC 209
NY, P

140
Libertas Americana
Dupré
n.d.
Terra cotta
ca. 10.0
Musée Nationale de la
Coopération Franco-
Américaine, Blérancourt,
Paris, 49 C²
NY, P

141
La Liberté
Dupré
n.d.
Drawing
Musée Nationale de la
Coopération Franco-
Américaine, Blérancourt,
Paris, SJ73
NY, P

142
Indépendance des États-Unis
L. Roger, after Duplessis-
Berteaux
1786
Signed and dated, bottom left:
Duplessis Berteaux dd.;
bottom right: L. Roger Sculpt.
1786
Engraving
Musée National de la
Coopération Franco-
Américaine, Blérancourt, Paris

143
The Statue of «The Freed
Slave» in Memorial Hall
Signed, bottom right: Smeeton
Tilly; 1876
Engraving
16.8 × 12.5
Union Centrale des Arts
Décoratifs, Paris
NY, P

144
Le 28 juillet 1830, la Liberté
guidant le peuple aux
barricades
Eugène Delacroix
Signed and dated: Eug.
Delacroix 1830
Oil on canvas
259.0 × 325.0
Musée du Louvre, Paris
P

145
Photograph of the Model of
the Colossal Statue Le Génie
de la Liberté for the Bastille
Column
Auguste Dumont
ca. 1836–40
Bronze
Musée du Louvre, Paris
(Photo: Giraudon)

146
La République
Honoré Daumier
n.s.; 1848
Oil on canvas
73.0 × 60.0
Musée du Louvre, Paris
P

147
La France éclairant le Monde
A.-L. Janet-Lange
n.s.; ca. 1848
Oil on canvas
72.5 × 59.0
Musée Carnavalet, Paris, Inv.
no. P 188 (Photo: Union
Centrale des Arts Décoratifs,
Paris, Sully-Jaulmes)
NY, P

148
*Étude pour une figure
allégorique de la Liberté*, from
Les Filles d'Eve, no. 454
Achille Deveria
Lithograph
Bibliothèque Nationale, Paris,
DC 178b, TX
NY, P

149
Model for the Figure for the
*Monument à la Mémoire des
héros de l'Indépendance, 1830*
Frédéric-Auguste Bartholdi
n.s., n.d.
Plaster
43.5 × 12.2 × 12.2
Musée Bartholdi, Colmar, Inv.
1914 no. 647
P

150 (not illustrated)
Maquette for the Socle of cat.
149
Frédéric-Auguste Bartholdi
n.s., n.d.
Plaster
103.5 × 58.0 × 62.0
Musée Bartholdi, Colmar
(Photo: Christian Kempf)
P

151 (not illustrated)
Photograph of the *Monument
à la Mémoire des héros de
l'Indépendance* on Its Pedestal
Frédéric-Auguste Bartholdi
n.s., n.d.
Albumen print
38.5 × 21.3
Musée Bartholdi, Colmar, Inv.
phot. no. 2P18
P

152
Photograph of the Maquette
for the *Monument aux
victimes de Callao*
Frédéric-Auguste Bartholdi
n.s., n.d.
Albumen print
26.5 × 19.4
Musée Bartholdi, Colmar, Inv.
phot. no. 2P1
P

153 (not illustrated)
Fontaine du Châtelet, 1852
n.s.; 1852
Photograph
35.0 × 25.5
Inscribed, bottom center:
Fontaine du Châtelet, 1852
Collection Guillaume Chenet,
Paris
P

154
Photograph of Elias Robert's
*La France couronnant l'Art et
l'Industrie*, atop the Palais de
l'Industrie
n.s., n.d.
Albumen matte print
22.5 × 20.3
Printed by Frères Bisson
Musée Bartholdi, Colmar, Inv.
phot. no. 3P4/16
NY, P

155
L'Oasis
Léon Belly
n.s., n.d.
Oil on canvas
50.5 × 73.0
Studio stamp, bottom right:
L. Belly
Musée des Beaux-Arts de
Tours, Inv. no. 973–6–1
P

156
*Jeune homme coiffé d'une
chéchia [Portrait de Bartholdi]*
Léon Belly
n.s., n.d.
Black ink on blue grey paper
22.6 × 19.8
Studio stamp, bottom right:
L. Belly
Musée des Beaux-Arts de
Tours, Inv. no. 925–301–3
P

157
Ruines de Karnak
Léon Belly
n.s., n.d.
Black ink highlighted with
gouache
49.0 × 32.0
Studio stamp, bottom right:
L. Belly
Musée des Beaux-Arts de
Tours, Inv. no. 925–301–10
P

158
*Vue de la plaine de Thèbes—
1857*
Jean-Léon Gérôme
1857
Signed in the middle on the
base of a column: *J-L
Gérôme*; dated underneath:
MDCCCLVII
Oil on canvas
76.0 × 131.0
Musée des Beaux-Arts, Nantes
(Photo: © Patrick Jean)
P

159a
The Colossi of Memnon
Frédéric-Auguste Bartholdi
n.s., n.d.
Salt print
25.1 × 19.4
Inscribed on the negative,
bottom left: *Sésostris*; bottom
center: *Colosses*. Inscribed on
the mount, bottom left
outside: *Egypte*; bottom right
inside: *Sésostris*; bottom
center inside: *Colosses de
Thèbes*; bottom right inside:
Memnon
Identical to photograph
1P4/66
Musée Bartholdi, Colmar, Inv.
phot. no. 1P3/61 (Photo:
Christian Kempf)
P

159b
Statues of Memnon
Frédéric-Auguste Bartholdi
n.s., n.d.
Glass positive, gelatin-silver
process
10.0 × 8.0
Inscribed on the mount:
initialed B; *Statues de
Memnon*
Former collection of Frédéric-
Auguste Bartholdi; Private
collection, Paris
P, T

160
Elephantine Island
Frédéric-Auguste Bartholdi
Signed and dated: *Aug.
Bartholdi 1856*
Albumen-salt print
8.1 × 26.0
Inscribed on the negative,
bottom left: *A. Bartholdi
1856*; bottom right: *Ile
Eléphantine*
Musée Bartholdi, Colmar, Inv.
phot. no. 1P4/32
P

161
Denderah
Frédéric-Auguste Bartholdi
n.s., n.d.
Albumen-salt print
20.1 × 25.0
Inscribed on the negative,
bottom right: *Denderah*
Musée Bartholdi, Colmar, Inv.
phot. no. 1P4/22
P

162
Ramesseum
Frédéric-Auguste Bartholdi
1856
Albumen-salt print
Bibliothèque Nationale, Paris,
BN 85B 107445
P

163
Banks of the Nile
Frédéric-Auguste Bartholdi
n.s., n.d.
Albumen-salt print
19.9 × 25.4
Inscribed on the negative,
bottom right: *[Manfahut?]*
Identical to photograph
1P3/50
Musée Bartholdi, Colmar, Inv.
phot. no. 1P4/54
P

164
Cluster of Palms
Frédéric-Auguste Bartholdi
n.s., n.d.
Salt print
18.5 × 26.4
Inscribed on the negative:
Village à Eléphantine.
Inscribed on the mount, top
right outside: *Egypte*; bottom
right inside: *Village dans l'Ile
Eléphantine*
Musée Bartholdi, Colmar, Inv.
phot. no. 1P4/30
P

165
Campground
Frédéric-Auguste Bartholdi
Signed and dated: *A. Bartholdi
1855*
Albumen-salt print
19.8 × 25.9
Inscribed on the print, bottom
right: *A. Bartholdi 1855*
Campement à Machelet
Identical to photograph
1P3/47
Musée Bartholdi, Colmar, Inv.
phot. no. 1P4/51
P

166
Bridge of the Boat
Frédéric-Auguste Bartholdi
Signed and dated: *A. Bartholdi
1855–56*
Albumen-salt print
20.0 × 26.5
Inscribed on the negative,
bottom left: *Sur la barque*;
bottom right: *A. Bartholdi
1855–56*
Musée Bartholdi, Colmar, Inv.
phot. no. 1P4/5
P

167 (not illustrated)
Café at Zebid
Signed and dated: *A. Bartholdi
1855–56*
Albumen-salt print
19.9 × 26.1
Inscribed on the negative,
bottom left: *Café à Zébid
A. Bartholdi 1855–56*
Musée Bartholdi, Colmar, Inv.
phot. no. 1P4/93
P

168 (not illustrated)
*Frédéric-Auguste Bartholdi
with Friends*
n.s., n.d.
Photograph
11.0 × 14.4
Bibliothèque Nationale, Paris
P

169
Bartholdi in Oriental Costume
n.s., n.d.
Albumen print
25.3 × 17.8
Musée Bartholdi, Colmar, Inv.
phot. no. 1P3/2 (Photo:
Christian Kempf)
NY, P

170
Project for the Suez
Lighthouse Presented to the
Khedive in 1869
Frédéric-Auguste Bartholdi
n.s., n.d.
Albumen print reproduction of
a drawing
19.1 × 12.7
Inscribed in ink: *Projet de
Phare pour Suez—Présenté au
Khédive 1869*
Musée Bartholdi, Colmar,
Ident. 2P1/1–5 (Photo:
Christian Kempf)
NY, P

171
*L'Égypte apportant la lumière
à l'Asie*
Frédéric-Auguste Bartholdi
Signed and dated, bottom
right: *B 1869*
Watercolor glued on paper
19.5 × 14.5
Musée Bartholdi, Colmar
NY, P

172
Maquette for *Suez* with Socle
Frédéric-Auguste Bartholdi
Signed and dated on the
left side: *B 1869*. On the
right, engraved scale with
dimensions
Terra cotta
37.1 × 18.1 × 20.1
Musée Bartholdi, Colmar
(Photo: Courtauld Institute of
Art, London)
NY, P, T

173
Maquette for *Suez*
Frédéric-Auguste Bartholdi
Signed and dated on the left
side: *B 1869*
Terra cotta
25.3 × 7.4 × 5.7
Musée Bartholdi, Colmar
(Photo: Courtauld Institute of
Art, London)
NY, P, T

174
Maquette for *Suez*
Frédéric-Auguste Bartholdi
Signed and dated on the left
side: *B 1869*
Terra cotta
Musée Bartholdi, Colmar
(Photo: Courtauld Institute of
Art, London)

175
Maquette for *Suez*
Frédéric-Auguste Bartholdi
Signed and dated: *B 1869*
Terra cotta
29.5 × 10.0 × 9.3
Musée Bartholdi, Colmar
(Photo: Courtauld Institute of
Art, London)
NY, P, T

176
Ferdinand de Lesseps
n.s.; ca. 1869
Photograph
18.0 × 12.0
Association pour le Souvenir
de Ferdinand de Lesseps, Paris
P

177
Detail of *La lyre chez les
Berbères*
Frédéric-Auguste Bartholdi
ca. 1856
Plaster
Musée Bartholdi, Colmar

178
L'Entrée du Canal à Port Said
Riou
Engraving
20.5 × 28.0
Association pour le Souvenir
de Ferdinand de Lesseps, Paris,
Inv. no. 14R
P

179 (not illustrated)
Port Tewfik, la sortie du Canal
Riou
Engraving
20.5 × 28.0
Association pour le Souvenir
de Ferdinand de Lesseps, Paris,
Inv. no. 16R
P

180
Project for a Mausoleum for
the Khedive in the Classical
Style
Frédéric-Auguste Bartholdi
Signed and dated, bottom
right: *B 1869*
Charcoal on paper
56.0 × 90.3
Musée Bartholdi, Colmar
(Photo: Christian Kempf)
NY, P

181
Project for a Mausoleum for
the Khedive in the Egyptian
Style
Frédéric-Auguste Bartholdi
Signed and dated, bottom
right: *B 1869*
Charcoal on paper
56.0 × 90.3
Musée Bartholdi, Colmar
(Photo: Christian Kempf)
NY, P

182
Bouddah of Kamakura
n.s., n.d.
Glass positive
10.0 × 10.0
Inscribed on the mount:
initialed B; *Bouddah*
Former collection of Frédéric-
Auguste Bartholdi; Private
collection, Paris
P

183
Maquette for *Suez*
Frédéric-Auguste Bartholdi
Signed and dated on left side:
B 1870
Terra cotta
22.7 × 7.5 × 7.5
Musée Bartholdi, Colmar
(Photo: Courtauld Institute of
Art, London)
NY, P, T

184
First Idea for the Statue of
Liberty, Similar to *Suez*
Frédéric-Auguste Bartholdi
Signed and dated on the socle:
B 1870
Terra cotta
26.2 × 8.5 × 6.5
Musée Bartholdi, Colmar
(Photo: Courtauld Institute of
Art, London)
NY, P, T

185
Study for *La Navigation*
Frédéric-Auguste Bartholdi
n.s., n.d.
Terra cotta
52.5 × 25.5 × 8.0
Musée Bartholdi, Colmar
(Photo: Christian Kempf)
NY, P

186 (not illustrated)
Study for the Allegorical
Statue of *Alsace*
Frédéric-Auguste Bartholdi
n.s.; 1873
Terra cotta
36.1 × 11.0 × 10.4
Inscribed: *A. M. Bergmann
[...]*
Musée Bartholdi, Colmar, Inv.
1914 no. 36
P

187 (not illustrated)
L'Agriculture
Frédéric-Auguste Bartholdi
n.s., n.d.
Plaster
33.0 × 12.0 × 12.0
Musée Bartholdi, Colmar
P

188
Maquette for *Liberty*
Frédéric-Auguste Bartholdi
ca. 1871
Terra cotta
56.0
Museum of the City of New
York, Gift of Estelle Cameron
Silo

189
Maquette for *Liberty*
Frédéric-Auguste Bartholdi
Signed: *Bartholdi*; n.d.
Terra cotta
48.3 × 14.0 × 14.0
Collection François de
Laboulaye, Saint-Saens
NY, P, T

190
Maquette for *Liberty*
Frédéric-Auguste Bartholdi
n.s., n.d.
Terra cotta
50.5 × 14.0 × 14.0
Inscribed on the tablet: *4 July
1776*
Musée Bartholdi, Colmar
(Photo: Courtauld Institute of
Art, London)
NY, P, T

191
Head of the Statue of Liberty
Frédéric-Auguste Bartholdi
n.s., n.d.
Bronze
18.5 × 11.0 × 12.5
Musée Bartholdi, Colmar, Inv.
1914 no. 352
NY, P, T

192
Draped Figure, after a Tanagra
Statuette
Frédéric-Auguste Bartholdi
n.s., n.d.
Plaster
39.0 × 15.5 × 11.0
Musée Bartholdi, Colmar
NY, P

193
Photograph of the *Statue
allégorique de la Douleur ou le
Génie funèbre*
Frédéric-Auguste Bartholdi
1866
Albumen print
17.6 × 12.8
Exhibited at the Salon of 1866
Musée Bartholdi, Colmar, Inv.
phot. no. 2P1
P

194
Colossal Head of Lucilla
Late Roman Empire
Marble
158.0
Musée du Louvre, Paris, Inv.
no. M.A. 1171
P

195
The Statue of Liberty
n.s., n.d.
Plaster
23.8 × 6.0 × 6.0
Musée Bartholdi, Colmar, Inv.
1914 no. 348

196
The Statue of Liberty, Variant
of the *Modèle du Comité*
Frédéric-Auguste Bartholdi
Signed and dated: *Bartholdi
1875*
Bronze
133.5 × 33.1 × 31.8
Former collection of Frédéric-
Auguste Bartholdi; Private
collection, Paris (Photo: Musée
des Arts Décoratifs, Paris,
Sully-Jaulmes)
NY, P

197
Maquette for *Liberty*
Frédéric-Auguste Bartholdi
n.s., n.d.
Plaster
55.2 × 16.8 × 17.5
Inscribed on the tablet: *4 July
1776*
Musée Bartholdi, Colmar
(Photo: Courtauld Institute of
Art, London)
NY, P, T

198
La Statue de la Liberté ...
Henri Meyer, after Pierre Petit
Unidentified periodical
illustration
Bibliothèque Nationale, Paris
NY, P, T

199
*La statue en place sur Bedloe's
Island*
Frédéric-Auguste Bartholdi
Signed and dated: *Bartholdi
1875*
Albumen print
Photograph of a lost drawing
by F. A. Bartholdi
18.5 × 25.7
Musée Bartholdi, Colmar
(Photo: Christian Kempf)
NY, P

200
*The Port of New York. Bird's
Eye View from the Battery.
Looking South*
Currier and Ives
1872
Lithograph; printed in color
58.2 × 84.3
The New York Public Library,
Art, Prints and Photographs
Division
NY, P

201
Charles Sumner
Darius Cobb
1877
Oil on canvas
127.9 × 102.1
Massachusetts Historical
Society, Boston
NY, P

202 (not illustrated)
Letter of Edouard de
Laboulaye to George Boker,
February 7, 1864
Union League of Philadelphia,
Archives
NY, P

203
Ulysses S. Grant
Thomas LeClear
ca. 1880
Oil on canvas
136.5 × 80.6
National Portrait Gallery,
Smithsonian Institution,
Washington, D.C., NPG.70.16
NY, P

204
*A. Bartholdi and Simon at
Niagara Falls, August 1, 1871*
Samuel J. Mason
Albumen print
7.4 × 9.8
Inscribed: *Niagara Falls, 12
août 1871*
Musée Bartholdi, Colmar, Inv.
phot. no. 3P1/16 (Photo:
Christian Kempf)
NY, P

205
Niagara Falls
Frédéric-Auguste Bartholdi
1871
Watercolor on paper
12.0 × 21.0
Musée Bartholdi, Colmar, AE
no. 9 (Photo: Christian
Kempf)
NY, P

206
*The Great International
Railway Suspension Bridge
over the Niagara River
Connecting the United States
& Canada, the New York
Central and Great Western
Railways*
D. L. Glover, after Ferdinand
Richardt
1859
Steel engraving
51.6 × 80.0
Printed by H. Peters, New
York. Copyrighted by
D. L. Glover, 1859
National Museum of
American History,
Smithsonian Institution,
Eugene Musial Collection

207
A Chicago Street
Frédéric-Auguste Bartholdi
n.s., n.d.
Watercolor on paper
9.2 × 13.2
Musée Bartholdi, Colmar
(Photo: Christian Kempf)
NY, P

208 (not illustrated)
A Chicago Street
Frédéric-Auguste Bartholdi
n.s., n.d.
Glass positive, gelatin-silver
process
10.0 × 8.0
Inscribed on the mount:
initialed *B; Rue à Chicago*
Former collection of Frédéric-
Auguste Bartholdi; Private
collection, Paris
NY, P

209
Chicago, Michigan Shore
Frédéric-Auguste Bartholdi
n.s., n.d.
Glass positive, gelatin-silver
process
10.0 × 8.0
Inscribed on the mount:
initialed *B; Chicago, Quai du
Michigan*
Former collection of Frédéric-
Auguste Bartholdi; Private
collection, Paris
NY, P

210
Great Plains
Frédéric-Auguste Bartholdi
n.s., n.d.
Watercolor on paper
12.0 × 21.0
Musée Bartholdi, Colmar, AE
no. 6 (Photo: Christian Kempf)
NY, P

211
Rocky Mountains
Frédéric-Auguste Bartholdi
n.s., n.d.
Watercolor on paper
12.0 × 21.0
Musée Bartholdi, Colmar, AE
no. 5 (Photo: Christian
Kempf)
NY, P

212
*Mormon Temple, Salt Lake
City*
Frédéric-Auguste Bartholdi
n.s., n.d.
Glass positive, gelatin-silver
process
10.0 × 8.0
Inscribed on the mount:
initialed *B; Temple des
Mormons à Salt Lake City*
Former collection of Frédéric-
Auguste Bartholdi; Private
collection, Paris
P

213 (not illustrated)
View of Mining
Frédéric-Auguste Bartholdi
n.s., n.d.
Glass positive, gelatin-silver
process
10.0 × 8.0
Inscribed on the mount:
initialed *B; Exploitation des
roches à minerais par l'eau*
Former collection of Frédéric-
Auguste Bartholdi; Private
collection, Paris
P

214 (not illustrated)
Wagons in California
Frédéric-Auguste Bartholdi
n.s., n.d.
Glass positive, gelatin-silver
process
10.0 × 8.0
Inscribed on the mount:
initialed *B; Diligences en
Californie*
Former collection of Frédéric-
Auguste Bartholdi; Private
collection, Paris
NY, P

215 (not illustrated)
Seal Rock
Frédéric-Auguste Bartholdi
n.s., n.d.
Glass positive, gelatin-silver
process
10.0 × 8.0
Inscribed on the mount:
initialed *B; L'Ile des phoques*
Former collection of Frédéric-
Auguste Bartholdi; Private
collection, Paris
P

216
Sketch of Republican Rally in
Circus Tent at Stockton,
California, contained in a
letter of Frédéric-Auguste
Bartholdi to Mme. Bartholdi,
September 8, 1871
Chemical Bank, New York
NY, P

217
Sequoias and Riders
Frédéric-Auguste Bartholdi
Signed, bottom left: *Bartholdi;*
1872
Watercolor on paper
24.5 × 34.5
Musée Bartholdi, Colmar, Inv.
1914 no. 230 (Vue de forêt
animée d'un cavalier) (Photo:
Christian Kempf)
NY, P

218 (not illustrated)
Redwood Forests
Frédéric-Auguste Bartholdi
n.s., n.d.
Glass positive, gelatin-silver
process
10.0 × 8.0
Inscribed on the mount:
initialed *B; Les gros arbres de
Californie*
Former collection of Frédéric-
Auguste Bartholdi; Private
collection, Paris

219 (not illustrated)
Redwoods, Yosemite Valley
Frédéric-Auguste Bartholdi
n.s., n.d.
Glass positive, gelatin-silver
process
10.0 × 8.0
inscribed on the mount:
initialed *B; Les gros arbres,
Yosumith Valley*
Former collection of Frédéric-
Auguste Bartholdi; Private
collection, Paris
P

220
Sketch of Town of Cheyenne,
Wyoming, in the Diary of
Frédéric-Auguste Bartholdi,
early September 1871
Chemical Bank, New York
NY, P

221
Photograph of Reliefs for
Brattle Street Unitarian
Church, Boston
Frédéric-Auguste Bartholdi
1871–74
13.0 × 29.5
a. Birth (not illustrated);
b. Communion (not
illustrated); c. Marriage; d.
Death (not illustrated)
Bibliothèque du Conservatoire
National des Arts et Métiers,
Paris, Musée des Techniques,
13768/8 no. 45–48
NY (c only), P (a, b, c, d)

222
Portrait of Simon
Frédéric-Auguste Bartholdi
n.s., n.d.
Albumen print
22.5 × 16.5
Musée Bartholdi, Colmar, Inv.
phot. E40₁ (Photo: Christian
Kempf)
NY, P

223
*Bartholdi, Simon, and a
Painter in Front of a Canvas
Representing the Lion de
Belfort*
Signed and dated: *Bartholdi*
1873
Albumen print
3.7 × 6.3
Musée Bartholdi, Colmar, Inv.
phot. no. 3P1/15 (Photo:
Christian Kempf)
P

224
Portrait of M. Monduit
n.d.
Albumen print
9.0 × 6.0
Printed inscription:
Th. Barenne Paris
Collection Mme. Pasquier-
Monduit, Paris
NY, P

225
La plomberie au XIXᵒ siècle
Catalogue of Gaget, Gauthier
et Cie., ca. 1880
Bibliothèque Forney, Paris
P

226
Eugène Viollet-le-Duc
Nadar
1878
Photograph
35.5 × 28.0
Collection Mme. Geneviève
Viollet-le-Duc (Photo: Jean-
Loup Charmet)
NY, P, T

227
*St. Charles Borromeo at
Arona*
From a postcard
ca. 1985
14.5 × 10.0
Artigrafiche Fotostampa
Reggiori, Laveno-M
P

228
Cross Section of the Head
(detail of cat. 289)
Bibliothèque du Conservatoire
National des Arts et Métiers,
Paris, Fonds Bartholdi no. 674
NY, P, T

229
Bust of M. Secrétan
Frédéric-Auguste Bartholdi
n.s., n.d.
Tinted plaster
67.0 × 96.0 × 33.0
Inscribed on the pedestal: *Mr.
Secretan Metallurgist Ami de
Mr. A. Bartholdi*
Musée Bartholdi, Colmar
(Photo: Christian Kempf)
P

230a–b
Fragment of the Statue of
Liberty
ca. 1875–83
Copper
2.7 × 9.2
Inscribed: *Fragment de cuivre
de la statue colossale de la
liberté exécutée par A.
Bartholdi 1875–1883.
Souvenir d'une visite aux
travaux*
a (not illustrated): Collection
Golliez, Saint Paul de Vence;
b: Musée Carnavalet, Paris
(Photo: SPADEM–1986)
NY, P, T*

231
*Taller de M. Bartholdi donde
se ejecutan las differentes
partes de la estatua*
Claverie and P. Kauffmann
From *Del Correo de
l'Ultramar*, n.d.
Bibliothèque Nationale, Paris
NY, P, T

232
La mise au point
Frédéric-Auguste Bartholdi
n.s., n.d.
Glass positive, gelatin-silver
process
10.0 × 8.0
Inscribed on the mount:
initialed *B; La mise au point;*
on the back: 67
Former collection of Frédéric-
Auguste Bartholdi; Private
collection, Paris
P

233 (not illustrated)
Charles Talansier
«La Statue de la Liberté
Éclairant le Monde»
Le Génie Civil, III, 19 (August
1, 1883), 461–471
The New York Public Library,
Science and Technology
Research Center
NY, P

234
*The Wooden Hand of the
Statue*
n.d.
Albumen print
18.6 × 25.3
Printed by P. Petit
Identical to photographs
2P14/33 to 38
Musée Bartholdi, Colmar, Inv.
phot. no. 2P14/107 (Photo:
Christian Kempf)
NY, P, T

235
*Creating a Plaster Mold from
a Wood Frame*
Fig. 4 from Charles Talansier,
«La Statue de la Liberté
Éclairant le Monde» (cat. 233)
(Photo: Bibliothèque
Nationale, Paris)

236
The Plaster Arm and Hand
n.d.
Albumen print
25.7 × 33.4
Musée Bartholdi, Colmar, Inv.
phot. no. 2P14/39 (Photo:
Christian Kempf)
NY, P, T

237
*Construction of the Drapery
and the Hand*
n.s., n.d.
Albumen print
19.4 × 23.6
Printed by P. Petit
Musée d'Unterlinden, Colmar,
Inv. phot.: M.U.C. no. 5
(Photo: Christian Kempf)
NY, P, T

238
Outline of the Wooden Laths
Fig. 5 from Charles Talansier,
«La Statue de la Liberté
Éclairant le Monde» (cat. 233)
(Photo: Robert D. Rubic)

239
Laths Laid over Drapery
n.s., n.d.
Albumen print
13.0 × 23.0
Bibliothèque du Conservatoire
National des Arts et Métiers,
Paris, Fonds Bartholdi no.
1906
NY, P

240
*Work in Progress on the
Drapery*
n.s., n.d.
Albumen print
19.3 × 25.5
Print attributed to P. Petit
Identical to photographs
2P14/19 to 23
Musée Bartholdi, Colmar, Inv.
phot. no. 2P14/104 (Photo:
Christian Kempf)
NY, P

241
Hammering: Mold Making
n.d.
Albumen print
19.6 × 25.7
Print attributed to P. Petit
Identical to photograph
2P14/16
Musée Bartholdi, Colmar, Inv.
phot. no. 2P14/103 (Photo:
Christian Kempf)
NY, P, T

242
Hammering the Drapery
n.s., n.d.
Albumen print
19.6 × 25.8
Printed by P. Petit
Musée Bartholdi, Colmar, Inv.
phot. no. 2P14/17 (Photo:
Christian Kempf)
NY, P, T

243
*Hammering a Copper Sheet
into a Mold*
n.d.
Albumen print
18.8 × 25.4
Printed by P. Petit
Musée Bartholdi, Colmar, Inv.
phot. no. 2P14/32 (Photo:
Christian Kempf)
NY, P, T

244
*Bartholdi at Gaget, Gauthier
et Cie.*
n.s., n.d.
Albumen print
19.6 × 25.7
Musée d'Unterlinden, Colmar,
Inv. phot.: M.U.C. no. 7
(Photo: Christian Kempf)
NY, P, T

245
*Assembly of the Copper
Segments*
Fig. 7 from Charles Talansier,
«La Statue de la Liberté
Éclairant le Monde» (cat. 233)
(Photo: Robert D. Rubic)

246
*Destroying One Model to
Begin Work on the Next*
n.s., n.d.
Albumen print
19.4 × 25.6
Print attributed to P. Petit
Identical to photographs
2P14/25 to 28
Musée Bartholdi, Colmar, Inv.
phot. no. 2P14/24 (Photo:
Christian Kempf)
NY, P, T

247
*La Construction de la Statue
de la Liberté*
Maurand and Claverie
From *Le Journal Illustré*, May
28, 1876
Bibliothèque du Conservatoire
National des Arts et Métiers,
Paris, No. 495–496
NY, P

248
*The Torch at Monduit, Gaget,
Gauthier et Cie.*
n.s., n.d.
Albumen print
20.2 × 14.2
Collection Liévain, Paris
(Photo: Musée des Arts
Décoratifs, Sully-Jaulmes)
NY, P

249
*The Completed Torch in Front
of a Canvas*
n.s., n.d.
Albumen print
26.3 × 20.6
Printed by E. Flamant
Musée Bartholdi, Colmar, Inv.
phot. no. 2P14/70 (Photo:
Christian Kempf)
NY, P, T

250
Finger of the Statue
ca. 1876–78
Hammered copper
Length: 180.0
Bibliothèque du Conservatoire
National des Arts et Métiers,
Paris, Musée des Techniques,
Gift of Mme. Bartholdi in
1907
T*

251
*Workshop Model with Plaster
Maquette for the Head of the
Statue*
Frédéric-Auguste Bartholdi
1879
Painted clay, plaster, wood,
metals, and thread
83.0 × 113.0
Bibliothèque du Conservatoire
National des Arts et Métiers,
Paris, Musée des Techniques
NY, P, T

252
*Workshop Model with Copper
Maquette for the Head of the
Statue*
Frédéric-Auguste Bartholdi
1879
Painted clay, plaster, wood,
metals, and thread
83.0 × 113.0
Bibliothèque du Conservatoire
National des Arts et Métiers,
Paris, Musée des Techniques
NY, P, T

253
Gustave Eiffel
Crauk
Signed and dated: *Crauk 1903*
Bronze; cast by Barbedienne
85.0 × 35.0 × 38.0
Société Nouvelle
d'Exploitation de la Tour
Eiffel, Paris (Photo: © Philippe
Pons)
NY, P, T

254
*The Gaget-Gauthier
Workshop—General View*
n.s., n.d.
Albumen print
9.7 × 36.2
Printed by P. Petit
Identical to photographs E31
and 2P14/13, 15
Musée Bartholdi, Colmar, Inv.
phot. no. 2P14/14 (Photo:
Christian Kempf)
NY, P, T

255
*Eiffel's Armature and the
Head*
n.s., n.d.
Albumen print
25.6 × 15.7
Identical to photograph E33
Musée Bartholdi, Colmar, Inv.
phot. no. 2P14/57 (Photo:
Christian Kempf)
NY, P, T

256
*Entrance to the Statue through
the Foot*
Frédéric-Auguste Bartholdi
n.s., n.d.
Glass positive, gelatin-silver
process
10.0 × 8.0
Inscribed on the mount:
initialed: *B; Entrée de la statue
par le pied.* On back: *G6*
Former collection of Frédéric-
Auguste Bartholdi; Private
collection, Paris
NY, P, T

257
The Mounting of the Statue up to the Waist
n.s., n.d.
Albumen print
41.5 × 26.3
Musée Bartholdi, Colmar, Inv. phot. no. 2P14/64 (Photo: Christian Kempf)
NY, P

258
The Mounting of the Statue
n.s., n.d.
Albumen print.
23.1 × 15.8
Collection Guillaume Chenet, Paris (Photo: Musée des Arts Décoratifs, Paris, Sully-Jaulmes)
NY, P

259
The Mounting of the Copper Pieces of the Statue
n.s., n.d.
Albumen print
Bibliothèque du Conservatoire National des Arts et Métiers, Paris, Musée des Techniques
NY, P, T

260
The Mounting of the Statue, Three-Quarters of the Body
n.s., n.d.
Albumen print
25.6 × 19.3
Printed by P. Petit
Identical to photographs 2P14/58 to 61, 63, 67, and 107
Musée Bartholdi, Colmar, Inv. phot. no. 2P14/62 (Photo: Christian Kempf)
NY, P, T

261
The Mounting of the Statue with the Head and Arm
From *Album des Travaux de Construction de la Statue Colossale de la Liberté destinée au Port de New-York*
Paris: Gontrand, Reinhard et Cie., 1883
The New York Public Library, Rare Books and Manuscripts Division (Photo: Robert D. Rubic)
NY, P, T

262
Sketch Showing Eiffel's Original Design for the Arm and Shoulder; the Arm and Shoulder as Built; the 1932 Repairs; and the 1984 Repair Scheme
1984
American Society of Civil Engineers, New York
NY, P

263
The Finished Statue, January 1884
Signed: *Bartholdi*; n.d.
Albumen print
19.5 × 12.2
Inscribed in ink on the print, top right: *La Statue de la Liberté.—Hauteur 46 m/Janvier 1884/Bartholdi*
Musée Bartholdi, Colmar, Inv. phot. no. E34 (Photo: Christian Kempf)
NY, P, T

264 (not illustrated)
Chargement de la Statue de la «Liberte,» à Bord de l'«Isère»
A. Nauger
From *L'Illustration*, June 13, 1885, p. 433
Collection Tainturier, Paris

265
Bilingual Subscription Appeal of the Franco-American Union Released to the Press on September 28, 1875
Bibliothèque du Conservatoire National des Arts et Métiers, Paris
NY, P, T

266 (not illustrated)
Edouard de Laboulaye
Nadar
ca. 1875
Albumen print, mounted on cardboard
22.7 × 18.5
Inscribed on mount, top: *Galerie contemporaine*; bottom: *126, boul. Magenta.—Paris. Phot. Goupil et Cie. Cliché NADAR*; below: *Edouard-RENÉ LABOULAYE (Né à Paris, le 18 janvier 1811)*
Collection François de Laboulaye, Saint-Saens

267
Bust of Edouard de Laboulaye
Frédéric-Auguste Bartholdi
n.s., n.d.
Plaster
70.0 × 45.0 × 33.0
Terra cotta exhibited at the Salon of 1866, No. 2627
Musée Bartholdi, Colmar (Photo: © Christian Kempf)
P, T

268 (not illustrated)
Individual Subscription Form of the Franco-American Union
ca. 1875
Bibliothèque du Conservatoire National des Arts et Métiers, Paris
P

269 (not illustrated)
Receipt for Contribution to the Franco-American Union
ca. 1875
Bibliothèque du Conservatoire National des Arts et Métiers, Paris
P

270 (not illustrated)
List of Subscribers in St. Pol (St. Fol), Pas de Calais, Contained in a Letter of Louis Lecomte to Edouard de Laboulaye, November 12, 1876
Collection François de Laboulaye, Saint-Saens
P

271 (not illustrated)
Map Showing Contributions of the Cities and Towns of France to the Subscription Drive of the Franco-American Union
Robert Second
1985
59.5 × 39.5
Musée des Arts Décoratifs, Paris
P

272
Le Banquet Franco-Américain
H. Meyer
From *Le Journal Illustré*, November 21, 1875, p. 312
Bibliothèque du Conservatoire National des Arts et Métiers, Paris, Fonds Bartholdi no. 312
P, T

273 (not illustrated)
Seating Plan for the Louvre Banquet, November 6, 1875
Bibliothèque du Conservatoire National des Arts et Métiers, Paris, Fonds Bartholdi no. 13
P

274
Plan for the Socle of the Statue of Liberty
Frédéric-Auguste Bartholdi
n.s., n.d.
Terra cotta
19.0 × 42.0 × 9.0
Musée Bartholdi, Colmar, Inv. 1914 no. 187 (Photo: Christian Kempf)
P

275
Program for the Solemnity of Music at the Opéra, April 25, 1876
Bibliothèque du Conservatoire National des Arts et Métiers, Paris, Fonds Bartholdi no. 425
NY, P

276 (not illustrated)
Musical Score of the Cantata Written by Charles Gounod for the Solemnity of Music at the Opéra, April 25, 1876
Bibliothèque Nationale, Paris
NY, P

277
Letter of Charles Gounod to Victor Hugo, March 1, 1876
Collection François de Laboulaye, Saint-Saens (Photo: Musée des Arts Décoratifs, Paris, Sully-Jaulmes)
NY, P

278 (not illustrated)
Poster for the Solemnity of Music at the Opéra, April 25, 1876
63.0 × 47.0
Bibliothèque du Conservatoire National des Arts et Métiers, Paris, Fonds Bartholdi no. 461
P

279 (not illustrated)
Will of Frédéric-Auguste Bartholdi, dated May 1, 1876
Collection François de Laboulaye, Saint-Saens
P

280 (not illustrated)
La torche à Philadelphie
n.s.; 1878
Albumen print
21.2 × 15.1
Printed by P. Petit after an original by Wilson and Adams at Philadelphia
Printed inscription, bottom center: *Souvenir du Centième Anniversaire de l'Indépendance des États-Unis. 1776–1876*
Identical to photograph M.U.C. no. 13
Musée Bartholdi, Colmar, Inv. phot. 2P14/89
P

281
Work on the Head
Signed: *Bartholdi*; n.d.
Albumen print
19.7 × 13.2
Printed by P. Petit
Printed inscription, bottom center: *Souvenir du Centième Anniversaire de l'Indépendance des États-Unis. 1776–1876*
Identical to photograph 2P14/46
Musée d'Unterlinden, Colmar, Inv. phot.: M.U.C. no. 11 (Photo: Christian Kempf)
P

282
Modèle du Comité
Frédéric-Auguste Bartholdi
ca. 1876
Terra cotta
128.0 × 43.0 × 39.0
Musée Bartholdi, Colmar
NY, P

283
a: Model of the Statue of Liberty, with Diorama in the Base
Frédéric-Auguste Bartholdi
1875–1900
Bronzed plaster and wood and bronze
365.7
b: General View of Diorama—cardboard and plaster, painted
c: Interior View of Diorama
Bibliothèque du Conservatoire National des Arts et Métiers, Paris
NY, P

284 (not illustrated)
Poster for the Diorama at the Palais de l'Industrie
Chéret
1878
Bibliothèque Nationale, Paris
P

285
Poster for the Diorama at the Tuileries
Chéret
1878
Bibliothèque Nationale, Paris, 85 B 107450
NY, P

286
The Head of the Statue at the Exposition of 1878
Frédéric-Auguste Bartholdi
1878
Montage: albumen print and drawing
34.0 × 53.5
Musée Bartholdi, Colmar, Inv. phot. no. 2P14/69 (Photo: Christian Kempf)
NY, P

287 (not illustrated)
Photograph of *La République* of Clésinger in Front of the Palais de l'Industrie
From *La Gazette des Beaux-Arts*, 62 (October 1963), 231
The New York Public Library, Art, Prints and Photographs Division
P

288
The Head at the Exposition of 1878
Frédéric-Auguste Bartholdi
1878
Albumen print
37.8 × 25.1
Musée Bartholdi, Colmar, Inv. phot. no. E35
NY, P

289
Exposition Universelle—Tête de la Statue de la Liberté
Baude
From *L'Univers Illustré*, 1878, p. 673
Bibliothèque Nationale, Paris, H56053
NY, P

290 (not illustrated)
Exposition Universelle.—La Tête de la Statue de la Liberté, de M. Bartholdi, destinée au port de New-York
After Edmond Morin
Unidentified periodical engraving
Bibliothèque Nationale, Paris, H56055
P

291
Public Notice Concerning Order and Ease of Movement in the Head of the Statue at the Paris Exposition, 1878
Bibliothèque du Conservatoire National des Arts et Métiers, Paris, Fonds Bartholdi no. 2007
NY, P

292 (not illustrated)
Public Notice Asking That Visitors Not Deface the Head of the Statue at the Paris Exposition, 1878
Bibliothèque du Conservatoire National des Arts et Métiers, Paris, Fonds Bartholdi no. 2004
P

293
Les Coulisses de l'Exposition.—Dans la Tête de la Statue de la Liberté, au Champ-de-Mars
Signed, bottom right: *Muller sc*
From *Le Monde Illustré*, September 21, 1878
Collection Debuisson, Paris (Photo: Jean-Loup Charmet)
NY, P, T

294
Souvenir Badge from the Paris Exposition, 1878
Blue satin, embroidered
25.0 × 8.0
Bibliothèque du Conservatoire National des Arts et Métiers, Paris, Fonds Bartholdi no. 660
NY, P

295
La tête de la République américaine quitte Paris avec chagrin
Cham
Signed, bottom right: *Cham*; bottom left: *Ives et Barray sc*
From *Charivari*, November 18, 1878
Collection Mme. Pasquier-Monduit, Paris
NY, P, T

296
Design Sketch for Ticket for the Lottery of the Franco-American Union
Frédéric-Auguste Bartholdi
n.s., n.d.
Drawing with watercolor and pen
30.0 × 56.0
Bibliothèque du Conservatoire National des Arts et Métiers, Paris, Inv. no. 13768/8–21
NY, P

297 (not illustrated)
Tickets and Ticket Stub for the Lottery of the Franco-American Union
Bibliothèque du Conservatoire National des Arts et Métiers, Paris, Fonds Bartholdi no. 715
NY, P

298 (not illustrated)
Poster for the Lottery of the Franco-American Union
22.0 × 30.0
Bibliothèque du Conservatoire National des Arts et Métiers, Paris, Fonds Bartholdi no. 823
P

299 (not illustrated)
Program for the Grande Cavalcade de Versailles, May 11, 1879
Bibliothèque du Conservatoire National des Arts et Métiers, Paris, Fonds Bartholdi no. 700 recto and verso
P

300
Official Notification by the Franco-American Union to the United States of the Completion of the Fund-Raising Effort for the Statue of Liberty, July 7, 1880
The New York Public Library, Rare Books and Manuscripts Division (Photo: Robert D. Rubic)
NY, P

301
Levi Parsons Morton
Léon-Joseph Florentin Bonnat
Signed and dated, bottom left: *LJ Bonnat—1883*
Oil on canvas
144.7 × 105.0
National Portrait Gallery, Smithsonian Institution, Washington, D.C., Gift of Mrs. Eustis Emmet and Mrs. David E. Finley
NY, P, T

302
Driving of the First Rivet of the Statue by Levi P. Morton, October 24, 1881
Frédéric-Auguste Bartholdi
n.s., n.d.
Glass positive, gelatin-silver process
10.0 × 8.0
Inscribed on the mount: initialed B; *Posé du premier rivet par M. Morton. 24 Octobre 1881*
Former collection of Frédéric-Auguste Bartholdi; Private collection, Paris
NY, P, T

303
Pose du Premier Rivet Devant Réunir à Son Socle la Statue de M. Bartholdi, la Liberté éclairant le monde
Signed, bottom left: *Ferat*
From *L'Illustration*, November 5, 1881
Collection Tainturier, Paris

304
Document Attesting to Driving of the First Rivet
1881
Collection Anne Eustis Emmet (Photo: Robert D. Rubic)
NY, P

305 (not illustrated)
Admission Card to See Work on the Statue at the Gaget, Gauthier Workshop
Bibliothèque du Conservatoire National des Arts et Métiers, Paris, Fonds Bartholdi no. 602
P

306 (not illustrated)
Letter of Louis-Philippe d'Orléans, Comte de Paris, to Edouard de Laboulaye, April 2, 1878
Collection François de Laboulaye, Saint-Saens
P

307 (not illustrated)
Letter of Comte Serrurier to Edouard de Laboulaye
n.d.
Collection François de Laboulaye, Saint-Saens
NY, P

308 (not illustrated)
Invitation to Visit the Gaget, Gauthier Atelier, Rue de Chazelles
Bibliothèque du Conservatoire National des Arts et Métiers, Paris, Fonds Bartholdi no. 648
P

309 (not illustrated)
Invitation for a «Visit to the Works of the Colossal Statue of Lyberty . . .»
Bibliothèque du Conservatoire National des Arts et Métiers, Paris, Fonds Bartholdi no. 602
P

310
Les travaux de la Statue colossale de la Liberté
Navellier de la Marie after Karl Fichot
From *Le Journal Illustré*, May 1883
Bibliothèque Nationale, Paris, C85149
NY, P

311 (not illustrated)
Construction de la Statue de la liberté
Karl Fichot
Signed, bottom right: *Karl Fichot*; 1885
Pencil with gray wash
34.7 × 31.2
Musée Carnavelet, Paris, Inv. PC84C
P

312
Construction de la Statue de la Liberté
Karl Fichot
1883
Drawing
Musée National de la Coopération Franco-Américaine, Blérancourt, Paris, Inv. 49C30
P

313 (not illustrated)
Preliminary Sketch for View of Statue under Construction
Karl Fichot
1883
Drawing
Bibliothèque Nationale, Paris, H87544
P

314 (not illustrated)
La Vie à Paris
Jules Claretie
Paris, 1883
Bibliothèque Nationale, Paris

315 (not illustrated)
The Statue in Paris
n.s., n.d.
Photograph
The New York Public Library

316
The Finished Statue, Rue de Chazelles
n.s., n.d.
Albumen print pasted on cardboard
14.8 × 11.5
Collection Liévain, Paris (Photo: Musée des Arts Décoratifs, Paris, Sully-Jaulmes)
NY, P

317
La Statue de la Liberté, Rue de Chazelles
Paul-Joseph-Victor Dargaud
Signed, bottom left:
Victor Dargaud; 1884
Oil on canvas
40.0 × 32.0
Exhibited at the Salon of 1884
Musée Carnavalet, Paris
(Photo: Union Centrale des Arts Décoratifs, Sully-Jaulmes)
NY, P, T

318 (not illustrated)
Liberty Enlightening the World.—Completion of M. Bartholdi's Mammoth Statue, Celebrated at Paris,
May 21, 1884
From *Weekly Register,*
May 24, 1884
Bibliothèque du Conservatoire National des Arts et Métiers, Paris, Fonds Bartholdi
no. 1785
P

319
Ferdinand de Lesseps
Léon-Joseph Florentin Bonnat
Signed and dated:
LJ Bonnat 1878
Oil on canvas
159.5 × 118.5
Musée de la Marine, Paris, Inv. 174466, Dépôt de l'Association pour le Souvenir de Ferdinand de Lesseps
NY, P, T

320 (not illustrated)
Invitation to the Official Presentation of the Statue of Liberty, July 4, 1884
Bibliothèque Nationale, Paris, B106841
P

321
Official Presentation of the Statue to the Minister of the United States in Paris, July 4, 1884
Frédéric-Auguste Bartholdi
n.s., n.d.
Glass positive, gelatin-silver process
10.0 × 8.0
Inscribed on the mount:
initialed *B; Présentation officielle de la statue au Ministre des Etats-Unis à Paris 4 juillet 1884*
Former collection of Frédéric-Auguste Bartholdi; Private collection, Paris
NY, P, T

322
Deed of Gift of the Statue of Liberty to the United States
1884
National Archives, Washington, D.C. (Photo: Musée Bartholdi, Colmar, Christian Kempf)
Facsimile: NY, P, T

323
Official Attestation of Transfer of the Statue of Liberty from France to the United States, July 4, 1884
National Archives, Washington, D.C. (Photo: Musée Bartholdi, Colmar, Christian Kempf)
NY, P, T

324 (not illustrated)
Remise à M. Morton, Ministre des États-Unis, de la Statue de la «Liberté,» par M. Bartholdi
Bellenger
July 1884
Engraving
Bibliothèque Nationale, Paris, H87553
P

325 (not illustrated)
La statue de la Liberté terminée, Rue de Chazelles
n.s.; 1884
Engraving
12.0 × 18.6
Musée Bartholdi, Colmar
NY, P

326 (not illustrated)
Choses Vues
Victor Hugo
Entry for November 30, 1884
Bibliothèque Nationale, Paris
P

327
John W. Forney
Frederick Gutekunst
Signed: *F. Gutekunst*; n.d.
Albumen-silver print
14.4 × 10.6
National Portrait Gallery, Smithsonian Institution, Washington, D.C.
NY, P

328 (not illustrated)
Rapport sur les arts décoratifs
Frédéric-Auguste Bartholdi
Paris: Imprimerie Nationale, 1877
Musée des Arts Décoratifs, Paris
P

329
The Republic of France and the Centennial Exhibition
From *The Daily Graphic,*
April 6, 1876
Bibliothèque du Conservatoire National des Arts et Métiers, Paris, Fonds Bartholdi
no. 1678
P

330
Passenger with Writing Tablet
Frédéric-Auguste Bartholdi
From *L'Album du bord*
Paris: Bartholdi, Simonin, Fouret et Cie., 1879
The New York Public Library, Rare Books and Manuscripts Division (Photo: Robert D. Rubic)

331
Le Jury Français Philadelphie
Frédéric-Auguste Bartholdi
From *L'Album du bord*
Paris: Bartholdi, Simonin, Fouret et Cie., 1879
The New York Public Library, Rare Books and Manuscripts Division (Photo: Robert D. Rubic)
NY, P

332 (not illustrated)
Photograph of the Maquette for the Washington Fountain
Frédéric-Auguste Bartholdi
n.s.; 1867
22.3 × 17.4
Inscribed in ink on the print, bottom left: *Fontaine lumineuse;* bottom right: *1867*
Musée Bartholdi, Colmar
P

333
Photograph of a Drawing of the Washington Fountain
Frédéric-Auguste Bartholdi
n.s., n.d.
Albumen print
25.8 × 16.9
Inscribed in ink on the print, bottom left: *Fontaine érigée à Washington Etats Unis;*
bottom right: *Exposition de Philadelphie 1876*
Musée Bartholdi, Colmar, Inv. phot. no. 2P8
P

334
Photograph of the Bartholdi Fountain Installed at the Centennial Exhibition, Philadelphia
1876
Free Library of Philadelphia

335
The Opéra Decor at Madison Square, New York
After E.A. Abbey
From *Harper's Weekly,*
July 22, 1876, p. 600
Cooper-Hewitt Museum Library, Smithsonian Institution, PL5413 (Photo: Scott Hyde; The Kubler Collection, Courtesy of the Cooper-Hewitt Museum, The Smithsonian Institution's National Museum of Design)
NY, P

336
Bartholdi, Striking the Pose of the Statue of Liberty
1888
Photograph, gelatin-silver process
23.2 × 28.0
Printed by Banque Paris
Musée Bartholdi, Colmar, Inv. phot. no. 2P14/99 (Photo: Christian Kempf)
P

337
View of the Installation of the Arm and Torch at the Centennial Exhibition in Philadelphia
From *L'Illustration,* October 21, 1876
Collection R. Debuisson, Paris (Photo: Jean-Loup Charmet)
P

338
F. R. Coudert
n.s., n.d.
Gelatin-silver print
19.3 × 12.8
Collection Ferdinand W. Coudert (Photo: Robert D. Rubic)
NY, P

339
Photograph of the Maquette for the *Projet du Monument au Général Lafayette*
Frédéric-Auguste Bartholdi
n.s., n.d.
Albumen print
24.2 × 20.0
Musée Bartholdi, Colmar, Inv. phot. no. 2P18/4

340 (not illustrated)
Maquette for the *Projet du monument au Général Lafayette*
Frédéric-Auguste Bartholdi
n.s.; 1872
Terra cotta
31.0 × 32.0 × 21.0
Musée Bartholdi, Colmar, Inv. 1914 no. 136
NY, P

341 (not illustrated)
Lafayette
Frédéric-Auguste Bartholdi
n.s., n.d.
Albumen print
19.4 × 11.6
Musée d'Unterlinden, Colmar, Inv. phot.: M.U.C. no. 30
NY, P

342
Maquette for *Lafayette* in Union Square
Frédéric-Auguste Bartholdi
n.d.; commissioned in 1874
Bronze
70.5 × 31.5 × 31.5
Musée Bartholdi, Colmar, Inv. 1914 no. 524
T*

343
Inauguration of the Statue of Lafayette at Union Square, September 6, 1876
n.d.
Photograph
19.0 × 23.4
Musée Bartholdi, Colmar, Inv. phot. no. 2P18/2
NY, P, T

344 (not illustrated)
Overview of Centennial Fairgrounds with Arm and Torch of Statue of Liberty
1876
Photograph
Free Library of Philadelphia, no. 2447

345
Bartholdi Standing at Torch Railing, Philadelphia Centennial Exhibition, 1876
Photograph
Free Library of Philadelphia

346
Bartholdi in New York, 1876
n.s., n.d.
Photograph
14.8 × 10.7
Inscribed in ink on the print:
À son ami E. Jacob / A. Bartholdi / 1877
Collection Douin, Paris
NY, P

347
Commerce of Nations Rendering Homage to Liberty
Edward Moran
1876
Oil on canvas
Private collection
NY, P

348
The Statue of Liberty at Night
Edward Moran
Signed, bottom left: *Ed. Moran;* dated, bottom right: *1876*
Oil on canvas
26.0 × 19.0
Musée Bartholdi, Colmar (Photo: Christian Kempf)
T*

349 (not illustrated)
Letter of Frédéric-Auguste Bartholdi to Edouard de Laboulaye, September 10, 1876
Collection François de Laboulaye, Saint-Saens
NY, P

350
The Old Union League Club, Madison Square, New York
Signed, bottom left: *E. L. Henry*
1870s
Oil on canvas
Union League Club, New York (Photo: Frick Art Reference Library, New York)
NY, P, T

351
John Jay
Jared B. Flagg
n.d.
Oil on canvas
Union League Club, New York (Photo: Frick Art Reference Library, New York)
NY, P

352
Bust of Richard Butler
Frédéric-Auguste Bartholdi
n.s., n.d.
Plaster
60.0 × 43.0 × 35.0
Inscribed on base: *RICHARD BUTLER*
Musée Bartholdi, Colmar, Inv. 1914 no. 387
T

353
Frédéric-Auguste Bartholdi and Richard Butler at Bedloe's Island
1893
Ferrotype
12.9 × 9.0
Musée Bartholdi, Colmar, Inv. phot. no. 3P1/14 (Photo: Christian Kempf)
NY, P

354
Bust of William Maxwell Evarts
Augustus Saint-Gaudens
1874
Marble
58.4 × 33.0 × 20.3
Private collection, Windsor, Vt. (Photo: Jerry L. Thompson)
NY

355 (not illustrated)
Bust of William Maxwell Evarts
Frédéric-Auguste Bartholdi
n.s.; 1881
Plaster
50.0 × 25.0 × 15.0
Terra cotta exhibited at the Salon of 1883, No. 3319
Musée Bartholdi, Colmar, Inv. 1914 no. 164
T

356
Parke Godwin
John White Alexander
1886
Oil on canvas
Century Association, New York (Photo: Robert D. Rubic)
NY, P

357
R. C. Winthrop
Daniel Huntingdon
1885
Oil on canvas
115.0 × 95.1
Courtesy Massachusetts Historical Society, Boston
NY, P

358
Nathan Appleton
ca. 1883
Engraving
Courtesy of the Bostonian Society, Old State House, Neg. No. 4351
NY, P

359 (not illustrated)
Letter of Richard Butler to Levi P. Morton, November 18, 1881
The New York Public Library, Rare Books and Manuscripts Division, American Committee Papers
NY, P

360
Bust of Joseph W. Drexel
J.Q.A. Ward
1889
Marble
The New York Public Library, Music Division
NY, P

361a–b
Medal for the Franco-American Union Commemorating the Dedication of «Liberty Enlightening the World»
Presented to Richard Butler
Louis Oscar Roty
1886
Bronze
7.0
Inscribed on obverse:
UNION FRANCO-AMERICAINE/ STATUE COLOSSALE DE LA LIBERTE ECLAIRANT LE MONDE 28 OCTOBRE M.D.CCCLXXXVI.
Inscribed on reverse:
A. BARTHOLDI/TO HIS DEAR FRIEND/RICHARD BUTLER
The Metropolitan Museum of Art, New York, Gift of the Family of Richard Butler, 1902 (93.10.21 and 02.11.2)
NY, P

362
Vase Parent
Albert Carrier-Belleuse (modeler) and Alfred Thompson Gobert (decorator)
1883–85
Sèvres porcelain
35.6
The Metropolitan Museum of Art, presented by the Family of Richard Butler, 1902
NY, P

363
Erecting, on a Temporary Site, in Madison Square, February 22d, the Hand of Bartholdi's Statue of Liberty
From *Frank Leslie's Illustrated Newspaper,* March 17, 1877, p. 29
Cooper-Hewitt Museum Library, Smithsonian Institution, PL2937 (Photo: Scott Hyde; The Kubler Collection, Courtesy of the Cooper-Hewitt Museum, The Smithsonian Institution's National Museum of Design)
NY, P

364
The Torch in Madison Square, New York
n.s., n.d.
Albumen-salt print
20.2 × 14.2
Collection Liévain, Paris (Photo: Musée des Arts Décoratifs, Paris, Sully-Jaulmes)
NY, P

365
Certificate of Subscription
1883
Musée Bartholdi, Colmar (Photo: Christian Kempf)
NY, P

366
Liberty Enlightening the World
Root & Tinker
1883
Chromolithograph
83.0 × 58.3
The New York Public Library, Rare Books and Manuscripts Division
NY, P, T

367 (not illustrated)
Liberty
Kennedy
Sheet music
The New York Public Library, Music Division
NY, P

368
Catalogue of the Pedestal Fund Art Loan Exhibition
Pedestal Fund Committee, 1883
The New York Public Library, Art, Prints and Photographs Division
NY, P

369
A Catalogue of Oil Paintings . . . in Aid of the Bartholdi Pedestal Fund
Brooklyn Art Association, January 1884
The New York Public Library, Art, Prints and Photographs Division
NY, P

370
The Tortoise and the Hare: An Old Fable Reversed
Unidentified cartoon, ca. 1885, reproduced in Jacques Betz. *Bartholdi.*
Paris: Editions Minuit, 1954, p. 178
The New York Public Library, Art, Prints and Photographs Division (Photo: Robert D. Rubic)

371
The «Statue of Liberty» One Thousand Years Later; Waiting
From *Frank Leslie's Illustrated Newspaper,* August 30, 1884
Collection John Martino, New York (Photo: Robert D. Rubic)
NY, P, T

372
Let the Advertising Agents Take Charge of the Bartholdi Business, and the Money Will Be Raised Without Delay
From *Puck,* April 8, 1885
The New York Public Library, General Research and Humanities Division (Photo: Robert D. Rubic)
NY, P, T

373
Liberty Enlightening the World
From *Harper's Magazine Advertiser,* July 1884
Collection Jeffrey and Miriam Eger
NY, P

374
The «Sons of the Revolution» Collecting Money for the Bartholdi Statue Pedestal, October 4th
After a sketch by C. Upham
From *Frank Leslie's Illustrated Newspaper,* October 24, 1884
Cooper-Hewitt Museum Library, Smithsonian Institution, PL5533 (Photo: Scott Hyde; The Kubler Collection, Courtesy of the Cooper-Hewitt Museum, The Smithsonian Institution's National Museum of Design)
NY, P

375
The Arrival of «Liberty.» Uncle Sam to Bartholdi Statue—«Here, you sit down and hold what we have of your Pedestal, while I settle the Committee dissensions. Jay Gould thinks we have too much Liberty here now.»
Unidentified newspaper cartoon, ca. November 1884, inserted into The New York Public Library copy of cat. 369
NY, P

376
*The Monument Finished—
Next. The Missing Pedestal—
The Nation Should Supply
What Niggard New York
Refuses*
Unidentified press cartoon,
December 1884
Bibliothèque du Conservatoire
National des Arts et Métiers,
Paris, Fonds Bartholdi no.
1715
NY, P

377
*The Battery Park of the
Future—A Study for the
Consideration of New Yorkers*
From *The Evening Telegram*,
July 19, 1884
Bibliothèque du Conservatoire
National des Arts et Métiers,
Paris, Fonds Bartholdi
no. 1697

378
*A Hint to the Public. The
work is being done well and
rapidly, but time flies and the
master mason must have help.*
From *The Daily Graphic*, May
22, 1885 (Photo: Simon
Taylor)

379
*The Statue of Liberty
Enlightening the World
Described by the Sculptor
Bartholdi*
Frédéric-Auguste Bartholdi
(ed. A. T. Rice)
New York: North American
Review, 1885
Collection Gregory Van
Gundy
NY, P

380
*Statue of «Liberty
Enlightening the World»*
American Committee flyer,
1885
Collection Richard Eger
NY, P

381
American Committee Model,
1885
Tin, cast figure electroplated
with copper, pedestal
electroplated with nickel with
platform base
15.2 (6")
Collection Mr. and Mrs. Set
Charles Momjian (Photo:
Christie's)
T*

382
American Committee Model,
1885
Tin, tin-alloy figure
electroplated with copper,
pedestal electroplated with
nickel
30.5 (12")
Collection Mr. and Mrs. Set
Charles Momjian (Photo:
Christie's)
T*

383
American Committee Model,
1885
Zinc, electroplated
91.4 (36")
Collection The Hill Family
(Photo: Christie's)
NY, P

384 (not illustrated)
Letter of Frédéric-Auguste
Bartholdi to Edouard de
Laboulaye, October 10, 1876
Collection François de
Laboulaye, Saint-Saens
NY, P

385
*John W. Forney. An
«Occasional» Contributor to
the Press*
Unidentified press clipping,
ca. 1875
Free Library of Philadelphia
NY, P

386
Samuel P. Avery
Raimundo de Madrazo y
Garreta
1876
Oil on wood
61.0 × 48.9
Inscribed: *à Mr. Avery/
R. Madrazo/1876*
The Metropolitan Museum of
Art, New York, Gift of the
Family of Samuel P. Avery,
1904 (04.29.1)
NY

387
*The Statue of Liberty as It
Will Appear by the Time the
Pedestal Is Finished*
From *Life*, January 17, 1884,
cover
Bibliothèque du Conservatoire
National des Arts et Métiers,
Paris, Fonds Bartholdi
no. 1739
NY, P

388 (not illustrated)
*Liberty (Bartholdi)—«Is
There No Place for the Sole
of My Foot?» Father
Knickerbocker—«Eh? What's
That? I Declare I Forgot You
Were Coming.» Telegram—«I
Reminded You Often Enough,
Old Man.»*
From *The Evening Telegram*,
December 13, 1884
Bibliothèque du Conservatoire
National des Arts et Métiers,
Paris, Fonds Bartholdi no.
1701
NY, P

389
*Sculptor Bartholdi—«Vell,
Mees Boston, If Ze Gentlemen
Vill Not Pay for Ze Pedestal
Maybe You Vould Like Ze
Statue»*
From *The Daily Graphic*,
October 6, 1882 (Photo:
Simon Taylor)

390 (not illustrated)
Letter of Frédéric-Auguste
Bartholdi to Richard Butler,
August 3, 1883
The New York Public Library,
Rare Books and Manuscripts
Division, American Committee
Papers
NY, P

391
Joseph Pulitzer
Leopold Horowitz
Signed and dated, top left:
L Horowitz 1902
Oil on canvas
72.4 × 60.3
Columbia University in the
City of New York, Gift of
Donald C. Seitz (Photo:
Robert D. Rubic)
NY, P, T

392
*The World Bartholdi Pedestal
Fund*
Flyer
Office of the *World*, April 15,
1885
Parrish Museum, Southampton,
N.Y. (Photo: Richard Hurley)
NY, P

393
*Uncle Sam Congratulates
Miss Liberty*
From New York *World*, May
16, 1885, p. 5 (Photo: New-
York Historical Society)

394
*One Hundred Thousand
Dollars! Triumphant
Completion of the World's
Fund for the Liberty Pedestal*
From New York *World*,
August 11, 1885, p. 1 (Photo:
New-York Historical Society)
NY, P

395
Testimonial Torch Presented
by the *World* to Frédéric-
Auguste Bartholdi
James Whitehouse, Tiffany
and Co., 1885
Signed: *Tiffany & Co./Sterling*
Silver and pierre dure
94.0 × 38.0 × 38.0
Musée Bartholdi, Colmar
(Photo: Christian Kempf)
NY, P

396
Sketch of Proposed Domed
Pedestal for the Statue of
Liberty, Sent to Frédéric-
Auguste Bartholdi on January
4, 1882
Richard Morris Hunt
Pencil on tracing paper
57.2 × 45.8
American Institute of
Architects Foundation,
Washington, D.C., Prints and
Drawings Collection, 82.7923
NY, P

397
*La Statue de la Liberté en
phare*
Frédéric-Auguste Bartholdi
n.s., n.d.
Watercolor on paper
12.0 × 21.0
Musée Bartholdi, Colmar
NY, P, T

398 (not illustrated)
Proposed Stepped-Pyramid
Pedestal for the Statue of
Liberty
Frédéric-Auguste Bartholdi
ca. 1880
Photograph of a drawing on
paper
53.5 × 40.8
Musée Bartholdi, Colmar
NY, P

399
Sketch for the Pedestal of the
Statue of Liberty Showing a
Pre-Columbian or Mexican
Influence
Attributed to Frédéric-Auguste
Bartholdi
ca. January 1882
Ink on paper
15.5 × 15.9
American Institute of
Architects Foundation,
Washington, D.C., Prints and
Drawings Collection, 84.8923
NY, P

400
Sketch for the Pedestal of the
Statue of Liberty Showing a
Pre-Columbian or Mexican
Influence
Attributed to Frédéric-Auguste
Bartholdi
ca. January 1882
Ink on paper
13.3 × 15.9
American Institute of
Architects Foundation,
Washington, D.C., Prints and
Drawings Collection, 84.8924
NY, P

401
Sketch for the Pedestal of the
Statue of Liberty Showing a
Tower-Like Scheme
Attributed to Frédéric-Auguste
Bartholdi
ca. January 1882
Ink on paper
35.3 × 25.7
American Institute of
Architects Foundation,
Washington, D.C., Prints and
Drawings Collection, 84.8922
NY, P

402
Early Study for the Pedestal of
the Statue of Liberty
Richard Morris Hunt
ca. 1882–83
Ink on paper
11.4 × 8.2
American Institute of
Architects Foundation,
Washington, D.C., Prints and
Drawings Collection, S79.38.1

403
Early Study for the Pedestal of
the Statue of Liberty
Richard Morris Hunt
ca. 1882–83
Ink on paper
11.4 × 8.2
American Institute of
Architects Foundation,
Washington, D.C., Prints and
Drawings Collection, S79.38.2
NY, P

404
Early Study for the Pedestal of
the Statue of Liberty
Richard Morris Hunt
ca. 1882–83
Ink on paper
11.4 × 8.2
American Institute of
Architects Foundation,
Washington, D.C., Prints and
Drawings Collection, S79.38.3
NY

405
The First Pharos Proposal
Richard Morris Hunt
August 16, 1883
Pencil on tracing paper
40.5 × 25.0
American Institute of
Architects Foundation,
Washington, D.C., Prints and
Drawings Collection, 80.5443
NY, P, T

406
Variant of the First Pharos
Scheme, Showing Two
Alternate Treatments for the
Frieze
Richard Morris Hunt
1883
Pencil on tracing paper
39.4 × 24.5
American Institute of
Architects Foundation,
Washington, D.C., Prints and
Drawings Collection, 80.5459
NY, P

407
Model of the Revised Pharos
Scheme, by Richard Morris
Hunt, 1883
Photograph
23.4 × 18.1
American Institute of
Architects Foundation,
Washington, D.C., Prints and
Drawings Collection, P79.507
NY

408
Revised Version of the Second
Pharos Scheme, Compared to
a Pier of the Brooklyn Bridge
The Office of Richard Morris
Hunt, probably drawn by
Henry Ogden Avery
1883
Pencil on tracing paper
51.6 × 65.4
American Institute of
Architects Foundation,
Washington, D.C., Prints and
Drawings Collection, 79.3635
NY, P

409
A Variation on the Rounded
Tower Theme
Richard Morris Hunt
1883
Pencil on tracing paper
57.2 × 56.2
American Institute of
Architects Foundation,
Washington, D.C., Prints and
Drawings Collection, 80.5435
NY, P

410
A Variation on the Rounded
Tower Theme
Richard Morris Hunt
1883
Pencil on tracing paper
17.2 × 14.9
American Institute of
Architects Foundation,
Washington, D.C., Prints and
Drawings Collection, 80.5466
NY, P

411
Proposal for the Pedestal
Showing a Stepped Pyramid
Similar to Bartholdi's 1880
Design (see cat. 398)
Henry Ogden Avery
1883
Pencil on tracing paper
Mounted on one sheet with
three other sketches; overall
sheet 42.0 × 61.1
Columbia University, Avery
Architectural and Fine Arts
Library
NY, P

412a–b
Sketches for the Pedestal
Demonstrating a Connection
with the Celebration of the
U.S. Centennial and American
Independence
Henry Ogden Avery
1883
Pencil on tracing paper
Mounted on one sheet; overall
sheet 47.8 × 40.6
Columbia University, Avery
Architectural and Fine Arts
Library
NY, P

413a–b
Sketches for the Pedestal
Demonstrating a Connection
with the Celebration of the
U.S. Centennial and American
Independence
Henry Ogden Avery
1883
Pencil on tracing paper
Mounted on one sheet; overall
sheet 50.4 × 42.8
Columbia University, Avery
Architectural and Fine Arts
Library
NY, P

414
Model for the Greatly
Reduced Pedestal, by Richard
Morris Hunt, 1884
Photograph
23.7 × 29.5
American Institute of
Architects Foundation,
Washington, D.C., Prints and
Drawings Collection, P79.509
NY

415
Sketch for an Unornamented
Pedestal on a Doric-Order
Socle
Richard Morris Hunt
July 1884
Pencil on tracing paper
34.0 × 20.6
American Institute of
Architects Foundation,
Washington, D.C., Prints and
Drawings Collection,
80.5430.1
NY, P

416
Sketch for the Pedestal
Resembling the First Pharos
Scheme in Rough Rustication
but Lacking Its Projecting
Stonework
Richard Morris Hunt
July 1884
Pencil on tracing paper
32.8 × 18.4
American Institute of
Architects Foundation,
Washington, D.C., Prints and
Drawings Collection,
80.5430.2
NY, P

417
Winning Design for the
Pedestal of the Statue of
Liberty
Richard Morris Hunt
July 1884
Pencil and wash on tracing
paper
47.0 × 26.7
American Institute of
Architects Foundation,
Washington, D.C., Prints and
Drawings Collection,
80.5430.3
NY, P, T

418
Sketch for the Final Pedestal
Design
Richard Morris Hunt
1884
Pencil on tracing paper
34.4 × 25.2
American Institute of
Architects Foundation,
Washington, D.C., Prints and
Drawings Collection, 84.8925
NY, P, T

419
Photograph of Brigadier-
General Charles P. Stone
Frontispiece in Pierre Crabites.
*Americans in the Egyptian
Army*
London: George Routledge
and Sons, 1938
The New York Public Library,
General Research and
Humanities Division
NY, P

420
Foundation Mass of Pedestal
ca. 1884
Photograph
20.3 × 25.4
Pinchot Family Collection,
Pinchot Institute for
Conservation Studies,
U.S.D.A. Forest Service,
Milford, Pa. (Photo: U.S.
Forest Service at Grey Towers,
Milford, Pa.)
NY, P, T

421
*View of the Foundation Mass
from the Trestle*
1884
Photograph
Pinchot Institute for
Conservation Studies,
U.S.D.A. Forest Service,
Milford, Pa. (Photo: Private
collection, Paris)
NY, P

422
*Elevation, Plans, and Sections
of Pedestal, Showing Method
of Anchoring the Statue*
From *Scientific American*, June
13, 1885, p. 375
The New York Public Library,
Science and Technology
Research Center
(Photo: Robert D. Rubic)
NY, P

423
*Platform for Cornerstone
Ceremony, August 5, 1884*
Pach Brothers
Photograph
National Park Service: Statue
of Liberty National
Monument

424
*Placing the Cornerstone,
August 5, 1884*
From *Harper's Weekly*, August
16, 1884, p. 539
Bibliothèque du Conservatoire
National des Arts et Métiers,
Paris
NY, P

425 (not illustrated)
Apron of Grand Master
Brodie
1880s
Cloth
7.6 × 45.7 × 39.8
Geneseo Lodge #214, Free
and Accepted Order of
Masons, Geneseo, N.Y.
NY, P

426
Ceremonial Trowel of Grand
Master Brodie
1884
Silver and wood
10.1 × 11.4 × 34.3
Geneseo Lodge #214, Free
and Accepted Order of
Masons, Geneseo, N.Y.
NY, P

427
*Pedestal for Bartholdi's Statue
of Liberty on Bedloe's Island,
New York Harbor*
W.P. Snyder
From *Harper's Weekly*, June 6,
1885, p. 356
Cooper-Hewitt Museum
Library, Smithsonian
Institution, PL5497 (Photo:
Scott Hyde; The Kubler
Collection, Courtesy of the
Cooper-Hewitt Museum, The
Smithsonian Institution's
National Museum of Design)
NY, P

428
*Reception of the French S.S.
Isère in New York Bay*
Edward Moran
Signed and dated, bottom left:
Edward Moran 1885
Oil on canvas
47.0 × 80.0
Collection Mr. & Mrs. Sidney
H. Kosann
NY, P

429
Arrival of the Isère Carrying the Statue into New York Harbor
1885
Photograph
Bibliothèque du Conservatoire National des Arts et Métiers, Paris
NY, P

430 (not illustrated)
L'Isère
Pierre Adam
1886
Oil on canvas
38.0 × 61.0
Musée Bartholdi, Colmar, Inv. 1914 no. 614
T*

431
Arrival of the French Transport Steamer «Isère,» with the Bartholdi Statue on Board, at the Base of the Pedestal, Bedloe's Island, Friday, June 19th—The Salute of Welcome by the Fleet
From *Frank Leslie's Illustrated Newspaper*, June 27, 1885
Collection Carole Perrault
(Photo: National Park Service: Statue of Liberty National Monument)
NY, P

432
Arrivée à New York de l'Isère, Portant à son bord la Statue de La Liberté par Bartholdi
H. A. Ogden
From *Le Monde Illustré*, June 27, 1885
Bibliothèque du Conservatoire National des Arts et Métiers, Paris, Fonds Bartholdi no. 1767
NY, P

433 (not illustrated)
Transferring the Cases Containing the Bartholdi Statue from the Hold of the «Isère» to Lighters, for Removal to Bedloe's Island
From *Frank Leslie's Illustrated Newspaper*, July 4, 1885, p. 324
Collection Jeffrey and Miriam Eger
NY, P

434
Photograph of the Projected Monument to the Memory of Lafayette and American Independence by Frédéric-Auguste Bartholdi
n.s., n.d.
Albumen print
20.7 × 26.4
Musée Bartholdi, Colmar, Inv. phot. no. 2P18
P

435
The Pedestal under Construction, March 6, 1883
Photograph
30.5 × 22.8; mount: 47.9 × 33.5
American Institute of Architects Foundation, Washington, D.C., Prints and Drawings Collection
NY, P, T

436 (not illustrated)
Steel Substructure for Fastening the Statue of Liberty to Its Pedestal
Stamped by Charles P. Stone, Engineer-in-Chief
Blueprints
67.0 × 117.0
Musée Bartholdi, Colmar
(Photo: Christian Kempf)
NY, P

437
The Great Statue
From *The Daily Graphic*, May 22, 1886, p. 697
(Photo: National Park Service: Statue of Liberty National Monument)

438
Interior Armature Completed
July 1886
Photograph
36.8 × 28.1
American Institute of Architects Foundation, Washington, D.C., Prints and Drawings Collection
NY, P, T

439
The Statue of Liberty. The Progress of the Work on the Great Statue
From *The Daily Graphic*, September 2, 1885, p. 1
The New York Public Library
(Photo: Robert D. Rubic)
NY, P

440
View of the Face of the Statue of Liberty Hung in Wooden Frame
n.s.; ca. 1885–86
Photograph
Collection Andrew J. Spano
NY, P, T

441
Interior View of the Face Hung in Wooden Frame
n.s.; ca. 1885–86
Photograph
Collection Andrew J. Spano
NY, P, T

442
Toes and Torch of the Statue near the Parapets
ca. 1885–86
Photograph
8.6 × 13.5
Library of Congress, Washington, D.C.
NY, P, T

443
View at Top of Pedestal, Showing the Shell and Bracing
From *Scientific American*, August 14, 1886, p. 100
The New York Public Library, Science and Technology Research Center (Photo: Robert D. Rubic)
NY, P

444
[*Last Stage of Mounting Copper to the Armature*]
October 1886
Unidentified German-American newspaper
Cooper-Hewitt Museum Library, Smithsonian Institution, PL5446 (Photo: Scott Hyde; The Kubler Collection, Courtesy of the Cooper-Hewitt Museum, The Smithsonian Institution's National Museum of Design)
NY, P

445
Le Flambeau électrique de la statue de «La Liberté» à New-York
From *L'Illustration*, October 29, 1887
The New York Public Library, General Research and Humanities Division (Photo: Robert D. Rubic)
NY, P

446
Now Liberty Wants to be Enlight-ened. And the Whole World Knows It.
Thomas Nast
From *Harper's Weekly*, November 20, 1886, p. 755
The New York Public Library, General Research and Humanities Division (Photo: Robert D. Rubic)
NY, P

447
Statue before Mounting of the Torch
October 1886
Photograph
25.0 × 20.2
National Park Service: Statue of Liberty National Monument, STLI 598, Accession 205
NY, P, T

448
The Great Statue.—Sketches of the Interior
From *The Daily Graphic*, October 18, 1886
(Photo: National Park Service: Statue of Liberty National Monument)

449
Completing the Bartholdi Statue of Liberty—View of the Interior of the Upper Portion of the Statue
From *Frank Leslie's Illustrated Newspaper*, October 23, 1886, p. 1
The New York Public Library, General Research and Humanities Division (Photo: Robert D. Rubic)
NY, P, T

450
Invitation to the Statue's Inauguration, October 28, 1886
Tiffany and Company
Musée Bartholdi, Colmar
(Photo: Christian Kempf)
NY, P, T

451
Stephen Grover Cleveland
Anders Zorn
Signed and dated, top left: *Zorn 1899*
Oil on canvas
122.0 × 91.5
National Portrait Gallery, Smithsonian Institution, Washington, D.C., NPG 79.229; Gift of the Reverend Thomas G. Cleveland

452
Statue Veiled before Inauguration
Frédéric-Auguste Bartholdi
1886
Photograph
17.0 × 22.0
Bibliothèque du Conservatoire National des Arts et Métiers, Paris, Musée des Techniques, 13768/8 no. 6
NY, P

453
Judge's Compliments to Bartholdi and the Monument Committee
From *Judge*, October 30, 1886
Collection Jeffrey and Miriam Eger (Photo: Visions)
NY, P, T

454
Mayor Grace Presenting the Freedom of the City to Bartholdi
From *The Daily Graphic*, October 29, 1886
(Photo: Simon Taylor)

455
Certificate of the Freedom of the City Presented to Bartholdi by the City of New York, October 28, 1886
Musée Bartholdi, Colmar
NY, P

456
Vignettes of the Inaugural Parade
From *The Daily Graphic*, October 29, 1886
(Photo: Simon Taylor)

457
The Grand Demonstration on «Liberty Day,» October 28th.—The Military and Civic Procession Passing down Lower Broadway, with the Naval Pageant in the Distance
From *Frank Leslie's Illustrated Newspaper*, November 6, 1886, p. 1
The New York Public Library (Photo: Robert D. Rubic)
NY, P

458
The Triumphal Arch Erected by The World at the Inauguration of Bartholdi's Liberty Statue
From *World Almanac*, 1887, frontispiece
The New York Public Library, General Research and Humanities Division (Photo: Robert D. Rubic)
NY, P

459
The Statue of Liberty. Its Conception, Its Construction, Its Inauguration
New York: B.W. Dinsmore & Co., 1886
The Joint Free Public Library of Morristown and Morristownship, N.J. (Photo: Jeffrey Eger)
NY, P

460
Inauguration de la Statue de la Liberté Éclairant le Monde
H. A. Ogden
Unidentified press illustration, 1886
Cooper-Hewitt Museum Library, Smithsonian Institution, PL5695 (Photo: Scott Hyde; The Kubler Collection, Courtesy of the Cooper-Hewitt Museum, The Smithsonian Institution's National Museum of Design)
NY, P

461
Inauguration of the Bartholdi Statue, Harbor of New York
Herman O'Neil
1886; copyright 1887
Photograph
Library of Congress, Washington, D.C.

462
The Dedication of the Great Statue. The Ceremonies at Bedloe's Island
From *The Daily Graphic*, October 29, 1886
Bibliothèque du Conservatoire National des Arts et Métiers, Paris, Fonds Bartholdi no. 1690
NY, P

463
Bartholdi's Statue of Liberty—The Illumination of New York Harbor
Charles Graham
From *Harper's Weekly*, November 6, 1886, pp. 716–717
The New York Public Library (Photo: Robert D. Rubic)
NY, P, T

464
Invitation to the Chamber of Commerce Banquet, October 28, 1886
Tiffany and Co.
The New York Public Library, Rare Books and Manuscripts Division (Photo: Robert D. Rubic)
NY, P

465
Menu of the Chamber of Commerce Banquet, October 28, 1886
Tiffany & Co.
The New York Public Library, Science and Technology Research Center
NY, P, T*

466
Unveiling of the Statue of Liberty, 1886
Edward Moran
Signed and dated, bottom left: *Edward Moran 1886*
Oil on canvas
Museum of the City of New York, 34.100.260

467
Statue of Liberty from the East Wharf
Office of the Chief Signal Officer, «Redbook Series»
December 1907
Photograph
24.3 × 19.0
National Archives, Washington, D.C., R.G. 111, 111-RB–3582

468
The Statue of Liberty As Now Illuminated at Night
Central News Photo Service
December 22, 1916
Photograph
23.7 × 18.4
The New York Public Library, Local History Collection

469
The Statue of Liberty
McLaughlin Air Service
ca. 1938–39
Photograph
16.0 × 24.2
The New-York Historical Society

470
View of Crown Showing Reconstruction of Spikes
Collins
August 31, 1938
Photograph
17.0 × 21.9
National Park Service: Statue of Liberty National Monument

471
Repairing Interior—Workmen Replacing Section of Band Iron Supporting Sheet Copper Cover
June 8, 1938
Photograph
17.0 × 23.9
National Park Service: Statue of Liberty National Monument

472
Pedestal Stairs—Statue of Liberty
Collins
August 8, 1939
Photograph
23.7 × 16.4
National Park Service: Statue of Liberty National Monument

473
A Donation to Build the American Museum of Immigration
October 1956
Photograph
24.0 × 19.0
National Park Service: Statue of Liberty National Monument

474
Excavation for the American Museum of Immigration
November-December 1961
Photograph
18.9 × 24.0
National Park Service: Statue of Liberty National Monument

475
Statue of Liberty—Back View (Showing American Museum of Immigration Addition)
Jett Lowe
1984
Photograph
24.0 × 17.0
Library of Congress, Washington, D.C., Historic American Engineering Record (HAER NY–138–15)

476
Drapery of the Statue
Dan Cornish
1984
Photograph
© 1986 Dan Cornish
NY, P, T

477
Scaffolding around the Statue
Dan Cornish
1985
Photograph
© 1986 Dan Cornish
NY, P, T

478
The Old Flame of the Statue
Dan Cornish
1983
Photograph
© 1986 Dan Cornish
NY, P, T

479a–b
Working Design for the Restoration of the Statue of Liberty: Torch and Flame Working Drawings
Swanke Hayden Connell and The Office of Thierry W. Despont
1984
Ink on mylar
92.0 × 108.0
© 1986 Swanke Hayden Connell and The Office of Thierry W. Despont
NY, P

480a–b
Working Design for the Restoration of the Statue of Liberty: Computer Photogrammetry
Swanke Hayden Connell and The Office of Thierry W. Despont
1984
Ink on mylar
92.0 × 108.0
© 1986 Swanke Hayden Connell and The Office of Thierry W. Despont
NY, P

481 (not illustrated)
Final Study Model of Flame at 1:12 Scale
Swanke Hayden Connell and The Office of Thierry W. Despont
1984–85
Plaster and gold leaf (identical to the gold used on the flame of the restored statue)
33.0
© 1986 Swanke Hayden Connell and The Office of Thierry W. Despont
NY, P

482
The New Flame
Dan Cornish
1985
Photograph
© 1986 Dan Cornish
NY, P, T

483
Test Lighting of a Model of the Flame
Dan Cornish
1985
Photograph
© 1986 Dan Cornish
NY, P, T

484
Model of Entrance Doors to the Monument
Swanke Hayden Connell and The Office of Thierry W. Despont
1985
Acrylic
ca. 50.0 × 40.0
© 1986 Swanke Hayden Connell and The Office of Thierry W. Despont (Photo: © 1986 Dan Cornish; Esto Photographics, Inc.)
NY, P

485
Interior View of Work on the Statue
Dan Cornish
1983
Photograph
© 1986 Dan Cornish
NY, P, T

486
Working Design for the Restoration of the Statue of Liberty: Drawing of Armature
Swanke Hayden Connell and The Office of Thierry W. Despont
1983
Ink on mylar
92.0 × 108.0
© 1986 Swanke Hayden Connell and The Office of Thierry W. Despont
NY, P

487
Working Design for the Restoration of the Statue of Liberty: Full Section of Statue Only, Showing Structure
Swanke Hayden Connell and The Office of Thierry W. Despont
1983
Pencil on mylar
92.0 × 108.0
© 1986 Swanke Hayden Connell and The Office of Thierry W. Despont
NY, P

488 (not illustrated)
Working Design for the Restoration of the Statue of Liberty: Full Section of Statue and Pedestal
Swanke Hayden Connell and The Office of Thierry W. Despont
1983
Pencil on mylar
92.0 × 108.0
© 1986 Swanke Hayden Connell and The Office of Thierry W. Despont
NY, P

489
Working Design for the Restoration of the Statue of Liberty: Head Section Showing Stair
Swanke Hayden Connell and The Office of Thierry W. Despont
1983
Pencil on mylar
92.0 × 108.0
© 1986 Swanke Hayden Connell and The Office of Thierry W. Despont
NY, P

490
Model of the Monument Showing Statue Structure and Stair System in Pedestal
Swanke Hayden Connell and The Office of Thierry W. Despont
1985
Acrylic
180.0
Swanke Hayden Connell and The Office of Thierry W. Despont (Photo: © 1986 Dan Cornish)
NY, P

491
Working Design for the Restoration of the Statue of Liberty: Section Through the Museum
Swanke Hayden Connell and The Office of Thierry W. Despont
1985
Pencil on mylar
92.0 × 108.0
© 1986 Swanke Hayden Connell and The Office of Thierry W. Despont
NY, P

492
Working Design for the Restoration of the Statue of Liberty: Section of Pedestal Only, Before Restoration
Swanke Hayden Connell and The Office of Thierry W. Despont
1983
Pencil on mylar
92.0 × 108.0
© 1986 Swanke Hayden Connell and The Office of Thierry W. Despont
NY, P

493
Working Design for the Restoration of the Statue of Liberty: Section of Pedestal Only, After Restoration
Swanke Hayden Connell and The Office of Thierry W. Despont
1984
Pencil on mylar
92.0 × 108.0
© 1986 Swanke Hayden Connell and The Office of Thierry W. Despont
NY, P

494
Study Model (cast), *Liberty* (or) *Liberty Enlightening the World*
Frédéric-Auguste Bartholdi
ca. 1875
Terra cotta, bronzed
119.4
National Museum of American Art, Smithsonian Institution, Washington, D.C., xx76, Gift of U.S. Capitol

495
Avoiron et Cie. Cast
Frédéric-Auguste Bartholdi
1878
Zinc, bronze patina
With pedestal: 11.4
Inscribed on the side: *Souvenir de l'EXPOSITION 1878 Statue de la Liberté Bartholdi.
Copyright 31 August 1876*
Collection William M. Gaines (Photo: Christie's)
NY, P

496
Avoiron et Cie. Cast, «A» Size
Frédéric-Auguste Bartholdi
ca. 1883
Zinc, electroplated with copper
132.1
Coca-Cola Bottling Company of New York (Photo: Christie's)

497
Avoiron et Cie. Cast, «C» Size
Frédéric-Auguste Bartholdi
ca. 1883
White metal
55.9; original red French marble base: 16.5
Inscribed on top of base: *Bartholdi 1875 Registered Washington 31 August 1876*; on side of base: *C17 Avoiron et Cie Paris*
Graham Gallery, New York (Photo: Christie's)
NY, P

498
Thiébaut Frères Cast
Frédéric-Auguste Bartholdi
ca. 1884–86
Bronze
55.9
Collection Stuart Pivar (Photo: Christie's)
NY, P

499
Replica of the Statue of Liberty, Pont de Grenelle
1907
Photograph
Bibliothèque Nationale, Paris, Gift of Paul Blondel
P

500 (not illustrated)
La Passerelle de Passy
Henri Rousseau
Signed, bottom left: *H. Rousseau*; ca. 1900
Oil on canvas
37.0 × 45.0
Private collection, Paris
NY, P

501
Le Pont de Grenelle en 1927
Paul Signac
Signed and dated, bottom left: *P. Signac 1927*
Watercolor
20.0 × 40.5
Musée Carnavalet, Paris, Inv. no. D 8019
NY, P

502
La Vue du Quai d'Auteuil et le Pont de Grenelle
Emile Béjot
Signed, bottom left: *E. Béjot*; n.d.
Watercolor on paper
23.1 × 30.8
Inscribed, bottom left: *Quai d'Auteuil E. Béjot*
Musée Carnavalet, Paris, Inv. no. 4978 (Photo: Union Centrale des Arts Décoratifs, Sully-Jaulmes)
NY, P, T

503
Replica of the Statue of Liberty, Pont de Grenelle
Robert Doisneau
ca. 1961
Photograph
24.0 × 18.0
Collection Bibliothèque Historique de la Ville de Paris, Inv. N.A. Album no. 71, 33
NY, P

504
Replica of the Statue of Liberty, Jardin du Luxembourg, Paris
Frédéric-Auguste Bartholdi
1900
Bronze
274.3
Sénat, Paris (Photo: André Ostier)
NY, P, T

505
Replica of the Statue of Liberty, Place Picard, Bordeaux
Postcard
Collection R. Debuisson (Photo: Jean-Loup Charmet)

506
Replica of the Statue of Liberty, Poitiers
Photograph

507
Model (cast)
Hermann Follmer
1883
Zinc, painted gold
17.8 (with pedestal: 33.0)
Collection Anne P. Griffiths (Photo: Christie's)
NY, P

508
Model, Folk Replica
ca. 1900
Carved wood
81.3
Collection The Hill Family (Photo: Christie's)
NY, P

509
Model, American Woman's League Folk Replica
ca. 1905
Copper, repoussé
139.7
Collection Mr. & Mrs. Set Charles Momjian (Photo: Christie's)
NY, P

510
The Great Bartholdi Statue
Currier & Ives
ca. 1884
Lithograph
47.6 × 26.3
Library of Congress, Washington, D.C., Prints and Photographs Division
NY, P

511
T.W. Perry Trade Card
ca. 1886
18.0 × 11.5
Collection Jeffrey and Miriam Eger (Photo: Visions)
NY, P

512
G.A. Shoudy & Son Trade Card
n.d.
26.0 × 20.3
National Museum of American History, Smithsonian Institution, Washington, D.C.
NY, P

513
Your Glass of Coca-Cola....
World War I advertisement
Courtesy of the Archives: The Coca-Cola Company

514
Spirit of Haig
Guillaume
ca. 1928
Poster
94.0 × 63.0
Collection Poster America, New York (Photo: Visions)
NY, P

515
Yankee Flame
Ben Schonzeit
1976
Poster
Collection Mobil Oil Corporation (Photo: National Museum of American Art, Smithsonian Institution, Washington, D.C., Margaret Harman)
NY, P

516
Liberté-Cola
Jean Lagarrigue
1974
Oil on canvas
43.0 × 60.0
Collection of the artist
NY, P, T

517
Over 17 Billion Served
Robert O. Blechman
1974
Pen and ink on paper
37.6 × 27.9
Library of Congress, Washington, D.C., Prints and Photographs Division
NY, P, T

518
Statue of Liberty Centennial, 1886–1986
Cosmos Sarchiapone
1976
Collage and drawing
101.6 × 76.2
Collection of the artist
NY, P

519
Selection of Stamps
Collection Jeffrey and Miriam Eger (Photo: Visions)
NY, P, T*

520
Liberty for All. Keep 'em Flying
Penna Art WPA
1932
58.4 × 45.7
Library of Congress, Washington, D.C., Prints and Photographs Division, WPA 32, bottom line, #1
NY, P

521
Alouette Helicopter Circling the Statue of Liberty
1957
Photograph
19.4 × 24.0
Fairchild Republic Co., FA-44
NY, P, T

522
[Wilbur Wright Circling the Statue of Liberty as He Makes the First American Flight Over Water]
From *Harper's Weekly*, October 9, 1909, cover
Collection Jeffrey and Miriam Eger
NY, P

523
The Moisant International Aviators
Signed, bottom right: *Guerra*;
1951
Poster
100.0 × 60.0
Musée de l'Air, Paris, Inv. 17198
NY, P

524
Tapestry Commemorating Charles A. Lindbergh's Transatlantic Flight
French; dated on obverse: *1928*
16.0 × 40.0
Collection Michael Tatich and International Aerospace Hall of Fame, San Diego, Calif.
NY, P

525a
Leave All Hope, Ye That Enter
Thomas Nast
Unidentified periodical cartoon, April 2, 1881
Collection Jeffrey and Miriam Eger (Photo: Visions)
NY, P, T

525b
Dregs of Europe
From *The Evening Telegram*, September 10, 1892
Inscribed, top left corner: *Amitiés a Monsieur & Madame Bartholdi & un cordial bonjour de nous tous. Bien a vous Rosetta Lumley*
Bibliothèque du Conservatoire National des Arts et Métiers, Paris, Fonds Bartholdi no. 1702
NY, P, T

526
Remember Your First Thrill of American Liberty
World War I Liberty Loan Poster
1917
75.6 × 50.5
Library of Congress, Washington, D.C., Prints and Photographs Division (Photo: Visions)
NY, P

527
Il Cibo Vincerà la Guerra! [Food Will Win the War!]
C.E. Chambers
1917
Poster
76.2 × 50.8
Collection George M. Dembo, Chatham, N.J.
NY, P

528
My Father Reminisces
Ida Abelman
1937
Signed, bottom right: *Ida Abelman*
Lithograph on paper
38.1 × 46.2
National Museum of American Art, Smithsonian Institution, Washington, D.C., Accession Number 1967.72.4, Transfer from D.C. Public Library
NY, P

529
Shirt Waist Maker's Strike
Signed and dated, bottom right: *Philip Reisman, 1954*
Egg tempera on gesso panel
108.0 × 171.5
Union Health Center, International Ladies' Garment Workers Union, New York
NY, P

530
Illegal Immigration
Gene Basset
1985
Drawing
28.6 × 43.8
Published originally in the Atlanta *Journal Constitution*; reprinted by permission
Collection of the artist
NY, P

531
New Immigrants (or Eurotrash)
Johanna Vogelsang
1984
Signed, bottom right: *Johanna*
Felt marker
45.7 × 33.0
Commissioned by and published in the Washington *Post*, July 22, 1984
Collection of the artist
NY, P

532
Hail, America
Joseph Pennell
1908
Mezzotint
21.5 × 38.0
Signed in pencil, bottom right: *J. Pennell*
Davison Art Center Collection, Wesleyan University, Middletown, Ct. (Photo: George E. Landis)
NY, P

533
Luncheon on the Grass
Hudson Talbott
1982
Ink and watercolor
20.3 × 27.9
Signed and dated, bottom right: *Talbott 1982*
Collection of the artist
NY, P

534
French Handkerchief
1918–19
Silk
29.0 × 28.0
Collection Jeffrey and Miriam Eger (Photo: Visions)
NY, P

535
Pour la Liberté du Monde
Sem
1914–18
Poster
118.0 × 76.0
Signed, bottom right: *SEM*
Collection Richard Eger (Photo: Bibliothèque Forney, Paris)
NY, P

536
America Calls, Enlist in the Navy
J.C. Leyendecker
1917
Poster
41.0 × 28.0
Collection George M. Dembo, Chatham, N.J. (Photo: Visions)
NY, P

537
That Liberty Shall Not Perish from the Earth
Joseph Pennell
1918
Poster
Collection Richard Eger (Photo: Visions)
NY, P

538
July Fourth, 1934
J.C. Leyendecker
1934
Signed, bottom right: *Leyendecker*
Oil on canvas
81.3 × 63.5
Published as cover of *Saturday Evening Post*, July 7, 1934
Judy Goffman Fine Art, New York, and Ft. Washington, Pa.
NY, P, T

539
Czechoslovaks, Your Allies
1945
Poster
75.6 × 55.4
Library of Congress, Washington, D.C., Prints and Photographs Division
NY, P

540
Liberation
R. Doumoulin
1944
Poster
47.0 × 31.0
Signed, top right: *R. DOUMOULIN*
The Leslie J. and Alice D. Schreyer Collections, New York (Photo: Visions)
NY, P

541
We, too, have a Job to do. Join a Boy Scout Troop
1942
Poster
68.0 × 43.0
Collection Jeffrey and Miriam Eger (Photo: Visions)
NY, P

542
Life, June 5, 1939, cover
Collection Jeffrey and Miriam Eger
NY, P

543
Saboteur
Universal
1942
Film still
23.0 × 18.0
The Museum of Modern Art, New York, Film Stills Archive
NY, P, T

544
Funny Girl
Columbia/Rastar
1968
Film still
24.0 × 18.4
The Museum of Modern Art, New York, Film Stills Archive
NY, P

545
Suffragette Margaret Wycherly Striking the Pose of the Statue of Liberty
July 1915
Photograph
8.9 × 13.5
Library of Congress, Washington, D.C., George Grantham Bain Collection, LC–B2–3541–12
NY, P, T

546
Women's Liberation Demonstration at the Statue of Liberty
Jill Krementz
August 1970
Photograph
50.8 × 40.6
Published in *Time* Magazine, 96 (August 24, 1970), 11
Life Picture Service #85175
NY, P, T

547
Two French Girls
Sheila Elias
1984
Signed and dated, outer left side of frame: *Sheila Elias 1984*
Acrylic, oil, and collage on canvas
152.4 × 251.5
Collection Mr. & Mrs. Joseph H. Merback
NY, P

548
Ms. Liberty
Mutz
1975
Acrylics
59.1 × 45.0
From *Mad* Magazine, June 1975, back cover
Courtesy E.C. Publications; © 1975 E. C. Publications, Inc. (Photo: Visions)
NY, T

549
Women and the Arts in the 1920s
Seymour Chwast
1978
Poster
71.1 × 55.9
Collection of the artist
NY, P

550
The Kin-der-kids abroad. Triumphant departure of the Kids, in the family Bathtub!!
Lyonel Feininger
Newsprint, halftone cuts, printed color
59.4 × 45.2
Published in the Chicago *Sunday Tribune*, May 6, 1906
The Museum of Modern Art, New York, Gift of the Artist
NY, P

551
Grand Completion of the Broadway Elevated Railroad System
W.A. Rogers
1887
Pen and ink drawing
39.8 × 33.0
Published in *Harper's Weekly*, May 28, 1887, p. 338
Library of Congress, Washington, D.C., Prints and Photographs Division

552
Our Statue of Liberty.—She Can Stand It
C.J. Taylor
From *Puck*, October 27, 1886
Collection Jeffrey and Miriam Eger (Photo: Visions)
NY, P, T

553
Rushing to Their Own Destruction
Louis Dalrymple
From *Puck*, November 23, 1887
Collection Jeffrey and Miriam Eger (Photo: Visions)
NY, P

554
[Untitled lithograph]
Grant Hamilton, from an idea of William Jennings Bryan
From *Judge*, January 26, 1901
Collection Jeffrey and Miriam Eger (Photo: Visions)
NY, P

555
Sacco and Vanzetti
George Grosz
1927
Signed, bottom right: *Grosz*
Brush and ink
64.9 × 47.3
Estate of George Grosz (Photo: Nathan Rabin, courtesy of Serge Sabarsky Gallery, New York)
NY, P

556
Un-American Committee
William Gropper
n.d.
Signed, bottom right: GROPPER
Ink, crayon, and whitewash
51.1 × 38.4
Collection Mr. and Mrs. Mitchell C. Shaheen, Cleveland, Ohio
NY, P

557
[Soviet Desecration of the Statue]
Kukrinisky
1968
Poster
42.0 × 27.0
The Leslie J. and Alice D. Schreyer Collections, New York (Photo: Visions)
NY, P

558
Ship of State
Saul Steinberg
1959
Signed and dated, top left: *Steinberg 1959*
Ink and colored pencil
66.0 × 57.0
Indiana University Art Museum, #77.26.2
NY, P

559
On the Right
Benny Andrews
1972
Signed, bottom right: BENNY ANDREWS—72
Oil and fabric collage on canvas
77.8 × 61.6
High Museum of Art, Atlanta, Ga., Gift of Barbara and Ronald Davis Balser and Margaret and Hank McCamish, Jr., 1982.135
NY, P

560
Food Is Not a Weapon, It Is a Human Right
Leon Klayman
1975
Linoleum cut poster
61.3 × 45.2
Library of Congress, Washington, D.C., Prints and Photographs Division
NY, P

561
Fun City
Mark Podwal
1970
Pen and ink with photograph on paper
42.7 × 30.0
Library of Congress, Washington, D.C., Prints and Photographs Division
NY, P

562
«*What Are a Couple of Nice Guys Like You Doing in a Place Like This?*»
Draper Hill
1976
Brush and ink on chemical tone board
29.8 × 38.4
Published in the Detroit *News*, October 31, 1976; © 1976 the Detroit *News*
Collection Mr. and Mrs. Draper Hill (reproduced by permission of the Detroit *News*)
NY, P

563
Liberty Inviting Artists to Take Part in an Exhibition Against Leftist Terrorists (IRA PLO FALN *Red Brigade Sandinistas Bulgarians*)
Roger Brown
1983
Oil on canvas
182.9 × 121.9
Collection Mr. and Mrs. William Kleinman, Indianapolis, Ind. (Photo: Melville McLean; courtesy Phyllis Kind Gallery)
NY, P

564
Boss Platt's Latest Outrage
Louis Dalrymple
From *Puck*, March 19, 1890
Collection Jeffrey and Miriam Eger (Photo: Visions)
NY, P

565
Dr. Haas Hog Remedy Trade Card
1884
8.0 × 13.0
Collection Jeffrey and Miriam Eger (Photo: Visions)
NY, P

566
Le Grande Grocery Calendar
1950
34.5 × 23.0
Collection Jeffrey and Miriam Eger (Photo: Visions)
NY, P

567
Her Torch Held High, the Statue of Liberty Symbolizes Peace and Security in a War-Torn World
Photograph, U.S. Army Air Corps
From *National Geographic Magazine*, June 1940, p. 759
The New York Public Library, General Research and Humanities Division (Photo: Robert D. Rubic)

568
Parisian Sauce Trade Card
ca. 1886
Collection Jeffrey and Miriam Eger (Photo: Visions)
T*

569
Human Statue of Liberty
Mole & Thomas
1918
Photograph
Chicago Historical Society, ICHi-16308

570
At the New Orleans Exposition [3. Corn Statue of Liberty]
Charles Graham after sketches by John Durkin
From *Harper's Weekly*, January 17, 1885, p. 40
Collection Jeffrey and Miriam Eger (Photo: Robert D. Rubic)
NY, P

571
...I'm Ford not Freud
Robert Grossman
Comic strip from *New York* Magazine, December 9, 1974, p. 15
The New York Public Library, General Research and Humanities Division (Photo: Robert D. Rubic)

572
The Next Morning
From *Life*, February 26, 1877, Centerfold (pp. 107–108)
The New York Public Library, General Research and Humanities Division (Photo: Robert D. Rubic)

573
War's First Casualty
Elmer
America First Committee, Chicago, 1939
Poster
73.0 × 53.3
Collection George M. Dembo, Chatham, N.J. (Photo: Visions)
NY, P

574
Untitled collage by Eric Seidman to accompany article «And, Lo!, America Was Again Pure,» by Herbert J. Gans
From the *New York Times*, September 19, 1975, p. 37
The New York Public Library, General Research and Humanities Division (Photo: Robert D. Rubic)

575
A Peep into the Future
Grant Hamilton
From *Judge*, October 30, 1886, back cover
The New York Public Library, General Research and Humanities Division (Photo: Robert D. Rubic)
NY, P

576 (not illustrated)
Make America a Better Place. Leave the Country
Public Service advertisement for the Peace Corps
ca. 1962
34.3 × 22.9
Original photograph by Carl Fischer
Collection Young & Rubicam Advertising Agency
NY, P, T

577 (not illustrated)
Liberty Welcomes the Masses
Maurice Sieven
1912
Ink on paper
18.8 × 15.5
The Jewish Museum, Gift of Esther Peterseil in memory of her husband, Joseph Peterseil
NY, P

578 (not illustrated)
President Wilson Welcomes All
Maurice Sieven
1913
Ink on paper
18.4 × 15.4
The Jewish Museum, Gift of Dorothy Tananbaum in memory of her father, Joseph Peterseil
NY, P

579 (not illustrated)
Condomania
Robert Mankoff
1984
Signed, bottom right: *Mankoff*
Ink on bond paper, watermarked
27.9 × 21.6
Published in *The New Yorker*, April 30, 1984
Collection of the artist
NY, P

580 (not illustrated)
Mixer I
Pol Bury
Signed and dated: *Pol Bury, 1972*
44.0 × 52.0
Private collection, Paris
NY, P

581 (not illustrated)
Mixer II
Pol Bury
Signed and dated: *Pol Bury, 1972*
44.0 × 52.0
Private collection, Paris
NY, P

582 (not illustrated)
Leningrad
William Gropper
n.d.
Conte crayon, ink, and whitewash
38.4 × 32.0
Signed, bottom right
Collection Mr. and Mrs. John Fazio, Dallas, Texas
NY, P

Lenders to the Exhibitions

The Board of Trustees of The New York Public Library, the Comité Officiel Franco-Américain pour la Célébration du Centenaire de la Statue de la Liberté, and the Curators wish to express their appreciation to those individuals and institutions who consented to loan important works from their collections, without which these exhibitions would not have been possible.

Particular thanks go to the City of Colmar, France, and to the Conservatoire National des Arts et Métiers, Paris, for their extensive contributions.

Individual lenders:

Gene Basset, Atlanta, Ga.
Jacques Betz, Paris
Philippe Bisson, Paris
Pol Bury, Paris
Seymour Chwast, New York
Guillaume Chenet, Paris
Ferdinand W. Coudert, Lyme, Conn.
Mme. Roxane Debuisson, Paris
George Dembo, Chatham, N.J.
Armand Doin, Saint Denis de Jouhet
Robert Doisneau and Agence Rapho, Paris
Jeffrey and Miriam Eger, Convent Station, N.J.
Richard Eger, New York
Anne Eustis Emmet
Mrs. Prescott Evarts, Windsor, Vt.
Mr. and Mrs. John Fazio, Dallas, Texas
William M. Gaines, New York
M. and Mme. Armand Golliez, Vence, France
Anne P. Griffiths, New York
The Estate of George Grosz
Katharine Hellman, New York
Draper Hill, Detroit, Mich.
The James T. Hill Family, New York
Ed Hotaling, Washington, D.C.
Mr. and Mrs. William Kleinman, Indianapolis, Ind.
Mr. and Mrs. Sidney Kosann, New York
Jill Krementz, New York
S. E. François de Laboulaye, Paris
Gerard de Laboulaye, Paris
Jean Lagarrigue, Paris
Ira Lerner, New York
Dr. Oscar Liévain, Paris
Robert Mankoff, Brooklyn, N.Y.
John Martino, New York

Mr. and Mrs. Joseph H. Merback, Bryn Mawr, Pa.
Mr. and Mrs. Set Charles Momjian, Huntington Valley, Pa.
Mme. Gabrielle Pasquier-Monduit
Carole Perrault, Boston, Mass.
Stuart Pivar, New York
Maître Maurice Rheims, Paris
Cosmos Sarchiapone, New York
Mr. and Mrs. Mitchell C. Shaheen, Cleveland, Ohio
Andrew J. Spano, Yorktown Heights, N.Y.
Hudson Talbott, New York
Gregory Van Gundy, New York
Mme. Geneviève Viollet-le-Duc, Neuilly sur Seine
Johanna Vogelsang, Takoma Park, Md.
M. Waring, Paris
and a lender who preferred to remain anonymous

Institutional lenders:

Académie d'Architecture, Paris
American Institute of Architects Foundation, Washington, D.C.
Assemblée du Sénat, Paris
Association pour le Souvenir de Ferdinand de Lesseps, Paris
Bostonian Society, Boston, Mass.
Bibliothèque de l'Heure Joyeuse, Paris
Bibliothèque de l'Union des Arts Décoratifs, Paris
Bibliothèque du Conservatoire National des Arts et Métiers, Paris
Bibliothèque Forney, Paris
Bibliothèque Historique de la Ville de Paris
Bibliothèque Nationale, Paris
Century Association, New York
Chemical Bank, New York
Columbia University, Avery Architectural and Fine Arts Library
Columbia University, School of Journalism
The Cooper-Hewitt Museum, The Smithsonian Institution's National Museum of Design, New York
Davison Art Center, Wesleyan University
E. C. Publications, New York
École Nationale Supérieure des Beaux-Arts, Paris
Fairchild Republic Company, Farmingdale, N.Y.
Free Library of Philadelphia
Geneseo Lodge No. 214, Free and Accepted Masons
Judy Goffman Fine Art, New York and Fort Washington, Pa.
Graham Gallery, New York
High Museum of Art, Atlanta, Ga.
Indiana University Art Museum, Bloomington
International Aerospace Hall of Fame, San Diego, Calif.
International Ladies' Garment Workers' Union, New York
The Jewish Museum, New York
Joint Free Public Library of Morristown and Morristownship, Morristown, N.J.

Library of Congress, Washington, D.C.
Loïs Jeans, Paris
Massachusetts Historical Society, Boston
Kevin McCarthy Associates, New York
The Metropolitan Museum of Art, New York
Musée Bartholdi, Colmar
Musée Carnavalet, Paris
Musée de la Marine, Paris
Musée des Beaux-Arts de Tours
Musée d'Unterlinden, Colmar
Musée Municipale Georges Garret, Vesoul
Musée National de la Coopération Franco-Américaine, Blérancourt
The Museum of Modern Art, New York
National Archives, Washington, D.C.
National Museum of American Art, Smithsonian Institution, Washington, D.C.
National Museum of American History, Smithsonian Institution, Washington, D.C.
National Park Service: Statue of Liberty National Monument, Liberty Island, N.Y.
National Portrait Gallery, Smithsonian Institution, Washington, D.C.
The New-York Historical Society
The Office of Thierry W. Despont, New York
Parrish Museum, Southampton, N.Y.
Pinchot Institute for Conservation Studies, U.S.D.A. Forest Service, Milford, Pa.
Société Nouvelle d'Exploitation de la Tour Eiffel, Paris
Swanke Hayden Connell Architects, New York
Union League of New York
Union League of Philadelphia
Young & Rubicam, Inc., New York

Curatorial Acknowledgments

The Curators of the exhibition wish to express their deep appreciation to the following individuals and institutions who shared information, offered professional advice and support, assisted with research and administration, and offered material and other encouragement, thus helping to make the celebration of the centenary of the Statue of Liberty the occasion for an interdisciplinary exploration of the statue's origins and implications:

Maurice Agulhon; John Albacete; Claude Arthus Bertrand; Nicolas Arthus Bertrand; Jean-François Bargot; Florence Bachelet; Aliette Baisle, Musée du Louvre, Paris; Hélène Baltrusaïtis, U.S. Embassy in Paris; Réjanne Bargiel; Laure Beaumont; Jean Becarud; Scott Bergren; Richard B. Bernstein; Sherry Birk, American Institute of Architects Foundation; Robert W. Bloch; Dominique Boisson; Anne Bonnardel; Alain Bonnefoy; Ulane Bonnel; Geneviève Bonté; Marie Louise Bossuat; Allan Boudreau, Grand Lodge, Free and Accepted Masons, New York; Jacques Boutet; Gabriel Braeuner; Pierre Broussard; Melitte Buchman; Pierre Burger, Musée Bartholdi, Colmar; Philippe Capron; Anne Carbonnet; Florence Carneiro; Eliane Carouges; Max A. Caussanel; Ernest L. Chambre; Mrs. Hubert Chanler; Jean François Chougnet; Barbara Cohen, New York Bound Books; Michele Cohen, Art Commission of New York; André Combes; Mme. Emeric Couperie; Henri-Claude Cousseau, Musée des Beaux-Arts de Nantes; Pierre Curie; Elaine Dee, Cooper-Hewitt Museum, Smithsonian Institution; George Dembo, Gallery 9; Denis Delbourg; Jean Derens; Georges Didi Hubermann; Dominique Dollé; Françoise Dolto; James Draper, Metropolitan Museum of Art; Seymour Drescher, University of Pittsburgh; Gilbert Dumas; Juliette Dupré; Tracy Edling; Jeffrey Eger; Richard Eger; Mme. Jean Eiffel; Jean Pierre Emden; Anne E. Emmet; David Epstein, W. R. Keating & Co.; Philippe Faure; Sandy Feldman; Danielle Février Ritter; Madeleine Fidell-Beaufort; Michael J. Forster; Bruno Foucart; Patricia Fride; Jean René Gaborit, Musée du Louvre, Paris; M. and Mme. André Gadaud; Thomas Gaehtgens, Kunsthistorische Institut, Berlin; Pascal Gallet; Jean-Michel Girardin; Paul Goldener, National Park Service; The Graduate Research Board of the University of Maryland; Kathryn Greenthal; André Gschaedler; Dan Hartgrove, National Archives; Phyllis Harvey, Society of Illustrators; Christian Hecq; Draper Hill; Annie Jacques, École Nationale Supérieure des Beaux-Arts; Daniel Janicot; Dora Jane Janson; Gilberte Japy Marchegay; Françoise Jestaz, Bibliothèque Nationale, Paris; Elizabeth Johns, University of Maryland; M. and Mme. Kahn Brull; Martin Karcher; Christian Kempf; Catherine Lachenal; Jean Jacques Laurent; Catherine Lawless; Anne Claude Lelieur, Bibliothèque Forney; Anne Lemistre; André Le Prat; Jean Lessay; Daniel Lesure; Alice Levi Duncan, Christie's;

Bara Levin, Chemical Bank; Oscar Liévain; Robert Looney, Free Library of Philadelphia; David Lowenherz; Wade McCann; Renée Magnanti; Marie-Claude de Maineville; Bruno Mantura; Georges Maréchal; André Marette; Nicole Marette; Bernard Marrey; Chantal Martinet; François Mathey; Caroline Mathieu; Gail Meehan, Chamber of Commerce, New York; Susan Meyer; Yutaka Mikami; Riichi Miyake; Bernard de Montgolfier, Musée Carnavalet, Paris; Phyllis Montgomery, MetaForm Incorporated; Jean-Marie Moulin; Thomas Mullarkey; Isabelle Neto; Colombe Nicholas; Laura Noesser; Maureen C. O'Brien, Parrish Art Museum, Southampton, N.Y.; Bernard O'Reilly, Library of Congress; William Pangburn; Diana Pardue, Statue of Liberty National Monument; John Peters-Campbell, University of Maryland; Anne Pingeot, Musée d'Orsay; François Pinson; François Poirel; Mme. Pouderoux; Sylvie Poujade; Jean-Louis Provoyeur; Carol Pulin, Library of Congress; Orest Ranum; Jean Yves Raude; Jane Reed, Union League Club, New York; Kym S. Rice; Michel Richard; Marthe Ridart; François Robichon; Sybille Robin-Champigneulle; Bernard Rocher; Mrs. James Rorimer; Pierre Rosenberg, Musée du Louvre, Paris; Brigitte Rozet; Robert D. Rubic; Jean-Marie Schmitt, Archives Municipales, Colmar; André Schwerzig, Musée Bartholdi, Colmar; Carol Severance, Pinchot Institute for Conservation Studies; Robert C. Singer, Deputy Grand Master, Grand Lodge, Free & Accepted Masons of New York; Serge Sirolle; Mme. Sorans de Chillaz; Claude Souviron, Musée des Beaux-Arts de Nantes; Ann Strassner; Lauren Stringer; Marvin Trachtenberg; William Truettner, National Museum of American Art, Smithsonian Institution; Odile Vaillant; Nadine Vandermarcq; Jean de Vogüé; Robert Waring, Geneseo Lodge No. 214, Free & Accepted Masons of New York; Eliane Wauquiez; Harriet Weintraub; Gabriel Weisberg; Maxwell Whiteman, Union League of Philadelphia; Denis Woronoff.

Special thanks are due to the following staff of The New York Public Library: Donald Anderle; Nicole Aron; Fred T. Catapano; David Cronin; Susan Davis; John DiRe; Moira Egan; Maryann Jordan; Gregory Long; Marilan Lund; Francis O. Mattson; Gunther Pohl; Robert Rainwater; Susan Rautenberg; Harold Snedcof; Julia Van Haaften; Roberta Waddell.

Thanks are also due to the Director and Curatorial Staff, North Atlantic Region, The National Park Service.

Exhibition Staff

Pierre Provoyeur
Conservateur des Musées de France, Conservateur en chef à l'Union des Arts Décoratifs pour la Musée des Arts de la Mode

Project Director and Curator

June Hargrove
Associate Professor of Art History, University of Maryland, College Park

Curator for the United States

Catherine Hodeir
Agrégrée d'Histoire, Institut National des Sciences Politiques

Assistant Curator

Diantha D. Schull
Manager of Exhibitions, The New York Public Library

Curatorial and Research Associates

France

Jacques Betz

Alain Daguerre de Hureaux

Thierry W. Despont

Jean-Claude Lamberti

Marielle Oberthur

Philippe Roger

United States

Ann Uhry Abrams

Barbara Bergeron

Barbara Blumberg

Pamela Hall

Janet Headley

Edward L. Kallop, Jr.

Thomas Mackey

Lawrence Parke Murphy

Anne Cannon Palumbo

Carole Perrault

Susan R. Stein

Musée des Arts Décoratifs, Paris, October 28, 1986–February 1, 1987

France

Yvonne Brunhammer
Conservateur en Chef des Musée des Arts Décoratifs

Guy Mourlon
Secrétaire Général de l'Union des Arts Décoratifs

Fabienne de Sèze-Lafont
Directrice d'Arcodif

Exhibition Design

United States

Lou Storey
Installation Specialist

Registration

France

Dominique Pallut
Chef du Service des Expositions de l'Union des Arts Décoratifs

United States

Joseph Arkins
Registrar for Exhibitions and Loan Services

Deborah Cecere
Intern, Exhibition Program Office

Conservation

United States

Myriam de Arteni
Conservator for Exhibitions

National Touring Exhibition

United States

Susan Saidenberg
Education Consultant and National Tour Coordinator

Public Relations and Press

France

Dominique Burckhardt
Attaché de Presse du Musée des Arts Décoratifs

United States

Betsy Pinover
Manager, Communications

Shellie Goldberg
Public Relations Associate

Publication

France

Gilles Plaisant
Chef du Service des Publications de l'Union des Arts Décoratifs

Sonia Edart
Chef du Service Photographique de l'Union des Arts Décoratifs

United States

Richard Newman
Assistant Manager of Exhibitions

Barbara Bergeron
Editorial Consultant

William Zeisel
Editors & Scholars

Administrative Assistance

France

Michèle Lesellier

Martine Jouhair

Delphine Dudrumet

United States

Edward Rime

Rich Rubin

Thomas Major

The Authors

Pierre Provoyeur is Director of the Musée des Arts de la Mode of the Union des Arts Décoratifs, Paris. From 1974 to 1983 he was curator of the Museum Marc Chagall in Nice; his major exhibition there was «The Temple: Representations of Sacred Architecture in Occidental Art.» He has served as guest curator for exhibitions at a number of European institutions, including the French Academy in Rome and the Georges Pompidou Centre, Paris, and has lectured on Marc Chagall throughout the United States. His publications include *Le Message biblique de Marc Chagall* (1983) and *Marc Chagall: Les Pastels du message biblique* (1985).

June Hargrove is Associate Professor of Art at the University of Maryland, College Park. She received her Ph.D. from New York University's Institute of Fine Arts. Among her publications are many that focus on the public monument, notably *The Public Monument and Its Audience*; «The Public Monument,» in *Romantics to Rodin*; and «Les Statues de Paris,» in *Les Lieux de Mémoire* (forthcoming). A monograph on the Commemorative Monuments of Paris will appear in 1988. She has written extensively on French and American nineteenth-century sculpture, ranging from the evolution of war memorials to the decorative arts. Her *The Life and Work of Albert Carrier-Belleuse* (1977) is included in Garland Publishing's series Outstanding Dissertations in the Fine Arts.

Ann Uhry Abrams teaches art history at Georgia State University. She received her Ph.D. from the Institute of Liberal Arts, Emory University, and has curated exhibitions for the High Museum of Art and Emory University. With Anne Cannon Palumbo she is cocurator of the exhibition «Goddess, Guardian and Grand Old Gal,» a hundred-year survey of the Statue of Liberty as an American symbol, sponsored by Emory University and the Georgia Endowment for the Humanities. Her publications include *The Valiant Hero: Benjamin West and Grand-Style History Painting* (1985) and articles in *Art Bulletin*, the *Journal of Popular Culture*, and *Winterthur Portfolio*.

Jacques Betz, an Alsatian born in Colmar, France, in 1912, is the author of *Bartholdi* (1954), the first book-length work on Frédéric-Auguste Bartholdi. He is a former curator of the Bibliothèque Nationale, Paris.

Barbara Blumberg teaches history at Pace University, New York. She received her Ph.D. from Columbia University and is a member of the Board of Directors of The Institute for Research in History. Her publications include *The New Deal and the Unemployed: The View from New York City* (1979) and *Celebrating the Immigrant: An Administrative History of the Statue of Liberty National Monument, 1952–1982* (1985).

Henry Steele Commager, the John Woodruff Simpson Lecturer in History at Amherst College, is the author and editor of dozens of books on American history, including *The Empire of Reason: How Europe Imagined and America Realized the Enlightenment* (1977); *Freedom, Loyalty, Dissent* (1954); *The American Mind* (1950); and, with William E. Leuchtenberg and the late Samuel Eliot Morison, *The Growth of the American Republic* (1930; 7th ed., 1980).

Thierry W. Despont is Associate Architect for the Restoration of the Statue of Liberty. A graduate of the École Nationale Supérieure des Beaux-Arts, Paris, he holds a Master's Degree in Urban Design in City Planning from Harvard University. In 1980 he opened his own practice, The Office of Thierry W. Despont, in New York. The firm's projects have included 1080 Madison Avenue; the Ballantrae showroom; and offices for Bank Audi and the Banque Privée de Gestion Financiere. With Richard Hayden he is coauthor of *Restoring the Statue of Liberty* (1986). Cited by *Engineering News Record* as one of 1985's Construction Men of the Year, Mr. Despont is a member of the French Order of Registered Architects and a charter member of the American Institute of Certified Planners.

Richard Seth Hayden is Managing Principal of Swanke Hayden Connell Architects, who are the Architects of Record for the Restoration of the Statue of Liberty. A graduate of Syracuse University's School of Architecture, Mr. Hayden has been with the firm since 1963. He has directed such outstanding architectural commissions as Trump Tower, Continental Center, and Seaport Plaza, and such interior design commissions as American Express World Headquarters and Dow Jones & Co. With Thierry W. Despont he is coauthor of *Restoring the Statue of Liberty* (1986). He is a member of the American Institute of Architects, the Architectural League of New York, and the Fifth Avenue Association.

Janet A. Headley is a doctoral candidate at the University of Maryland, College Park. Since 1979 she has served as an instructor in art history at the University of Maryland and at Notre Dame College of Maryland. Currently she is a predoctoral fellow at the National Museum of Art, Smithsonian Institution, where she is engaged in research for her dissertation, «The Influence of British Aesthetics and Literature on American Sculpture, 1825–1875.»

Catherine Hodeir received a Master's Degree in History from the Sorbonne and has taught at the Institut National des Sciences Politiques, Paris. She contributed to the 1983 exhibition «L'Expo des Expos» at the Musée des Arts Décoratifs, Paris, and has assisted with preparations for the 1989 Exposition Universelle in Paris. A regular contributor to the journal *L'Histoire*, she has written also for *Les Nouvelles Littéraires*.

Edward L. Kallop, Jr. is staff curator, North Atlantic Region, the National Park Service, with advisory responsibility for collections and curatorial management at twenty-six NPS sites throughout New England, New York, and New Jersey. He formerly served as curator for collections at the Statue of Liberty National Monument, as curator-lecturer for exhibition of American college and university museum collections in ten European university centers, and as associate curator of exhibitions at the Cooper Union (now Cooper-Hewitt) Museum. He has contributed to a number of professional journals and is author of *Images of Liberty: Models and Reductions of the Statue of Liberty, 1867–1917* (1986).

Jean-Claude Lamberti is Professor of Sociology and Intellectual History at the Sorbonne. Among his publications are *Le Notion d'individualisme chez Tocqueville* (1970) and *Tocqueville et les deux démocraties* (1983), which received a prize from the Academie Française; an English-language edition of the latter work is forthcoming from Harvard University Press.

Anne Cannon Palumbo teaches art history at George Washington University. She received her Ph.D. in American Studies from the University of Maryland, College Park, and was a Smithsonian Fellow at the National Museum of American Art. Her exhibitions include «Goddess, Guardian and Grand Old Gal,» a hundred-year survey of the Statue of Liberty as an American symbol, cocurated with Ann Uhry Abrams and sponsored by Emory University and the Georgia Endowment for the Humanities. She has written and lectured on American art and popular imagery and is completing a book on the graphic artist Joseph Pennell.

Philippe Roger is currently Chargés de Recherches at the Centre National de Recherches Scientifiques at the Sorbonne. He formerly served at New York University as Assistant Director of the Institute of French Studies, and then as Associate Professor of French Literature. His publications include *Sade. La Philosophie dans le Pressoir* (1976); *Roland Barthes, roman* (1986); and numerous articles on semiology, literary theory, and the eighteenth century.

Susan R. Stein is the curator of Thomas Jefferson's Monticello in Charlottesville, Virginia. The former director of the Octagon Museum in Washington, D.C., she was also the curator of the Richard Morris Hunt Collection of the American Institute of Architects Foundation. She has written articles on Hunt and edited *The Architecture of Richard Morris Hunt* (1986). With Morrison H. Heckscher she is curator of a major exhibition on Hunt for the Metropolitan Museum of Art, the Octagon Museum, and the Art Institute of Chicago (1986–87).

Produced by
The Stonesong Press, Inc.
and Roundtable Press, Inc.

Edited by
Barbara Bergeron
William Zeisel, Editors & Scholars

Designed by
Karen Salsgiver, Homans|Salsgiver

Production coordinated by
Nan Jernigan

Mechanical production by
Page Rhinebeck

«Liberty» was typeset in
Univers 75 and Sabon by
Trufont Typographers, Inc.
The color plates were
separated by South Seas
International Press Ltd. and
printed by Connecticut
Printers, Inc.
The balance of the book's
interior was printed by
Arcata Graphics/Halliday.
The cover was printed by
Colorcraft Lithographers, Inc.
« Liberty» was bound by A.
Horowitz & Sons.